10.50

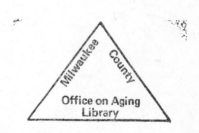

Aging in America
Readings in Social Gerontology

Aging in America

Readings in Social Gerontology

CARY S. KART
The University of Toledo

and

BARBARA B. MANARD
University of Virginia

ALFRED PUBLISHING CO., INC.

Library of Congress Cataloging in Publication Data
Main entry under title:

Aging in America.

1. Gerontology—Addresses, essays, lectures.
2. Aged—United States—Addresses, essays, lectures.
I. Kart, Cary Steven. II. Manard, Barbara Bolling.
[DNLM: 1. Geriatrics—Collected works. 2. Sociology—
Collected works. WT100 A267]
HQ1064.U5A634   301.43′5′0973   76-2051
ISBN 0-88284-035-5

ACKNOWLEDGEMENTS

The authors wish to thank the following people for permission to use their works in this book.

ROBERT C. ATCHLEY, Miami University
KURT W. BACK, Duke University
SULA BENET, Hunter College (CUNY)
VERN L. BENGTSON, University of Southern California
JAMES E. BIRREN, University of Southern California
ROBERT BLAUNER, University of California (Berkeley)
KATHLEEN BOND, Social Security Administration (Washington, D.C.)
NORMAN C. BOURESTOM, Veterans Administration (St. Cloud, Minnesota)
SANDRA E. CANDY, Wayne State University
FRANCES M. CARP, University of California (Berkeley)
ANNIE SIRANNE COPLAN, University of Chicago
ELAINE CUMMING, University of British Columbia
KENNETH J. GERGEN, Swarthmore College
LEONARD E. GOTTESMAN, Philadelphia Geriatric Center
ELIZABETH GUSTAFSON
ROBERT J. HAVIGHURST, University of Chicago
ARLIE RUSSELL HOCHSCHILD, University of California (Berkeley)
G. C. HOYT
LOLA M. IRELAN, Social Security Administration (Washington D.C.)
JERRY JACOBS, Syracuse University
RICHARD A. KALISH, Graduate Theological Union (Berkeley)
CARY S. KART, The University of Toledo
ROBERT KASTENBAUM, University of Massachusetts (Boston)
JORDAN I. KOSBERG, Case Western Reserve University
M. POWELL LAWTON, Philadelphia Geriatric Center
BRUCE W. LEMON, Los Angeles Harbor College
MORTON A. LIEBERMAN, University of Chicago
NORMAN M. LOBSENZ
BARBARA B. MANARD, University of Virginia
VICTOR W. MARSHALL, McMaster University
STEPHEN J. MILLER, Affiliated Hospitals Center, Inc. (Harvard Medical School)
BERNICE L. NEUGARTEN, University of Chicago
ERDMAN B. PALMORE, Duke University
JAMES A. PETERSON, University of Southern California
BERNARD S. PHILLIPS, Boston University
MATILDA WHITE RILEY, Bowdoin College
ARNOLD M. ROSE (deceased), University of Minnesota
CHARLES I. STANNARD, Strategies for Change and Knowledge Utilization
KEN STONE, University of California (Los Angeles)
SHELDON S. TOBIN, University of Chicago
LINDA WINIECKE, California Department of Social Welfare

CONTENTS

PREFACE

This anthology provides an introduction to the field of social gerontology. Two questions stimulated our thinking and guided our choices in compiling the articles: How can we provide students with an introduction to a field that is rapidly becoming one of the major areas of research in the biological, behavioral, and social sciences? And, how can we best disseminate the presently available knowledge about the process of aging, old people and their needs, the impact of growing numbers of old people on our institutions, and the effect of these institutions on the aged?

Although we examined hundreds of articles and papers in the process of selecting entries, we looked for and chose only articles that were issue or problem oriented and that would stimulate discussion and thus augment a classroom experience. The sections of the book are arranged so that the student will be introduced first to the theoretical foundation of the discipline ("Theoretical Approaches to Social Aging") and then to the methods used in doing research in the field ("Methodological Issues in Social Gerontology"). The articles in the next section ("Biological and Psychological Aspects of Aging") describe the aged and the ways they differ from younger people, and also attempt to account for these differences. These three sections provide the background for understanding the process sequence of the latter half of the book: the movement from "Work, Retirement, and Leisure," through a concern with "Living

Environments" among the aged, to "Institutionalization" and "Death and Dying." A brief introduction preceding each part provides the links connecting the selections within. Instructors who use the volume may see other ways to order the pieces. We invite them to do so to suit particular teaching needs.

We had three specific audiences in mind when we put together this collection. The first is the heterogeneous group of advanced undergraduates and beginning graduate students enrolled in social gerontology courses. We took into considration that many of these courses, while social or sociological in orientation, are not necessarily found in sociology departments. Rather, they are in departments of anthropology, education, health and physical education, psychology and social work. For these students the material in this volume provides a basic introduction to the field. The second audience is the group of gerontologists who will be introducing these students to the study of aging. While they too are a heterogeneous group, they all teach social gerontology in one way or another. The third audience is the general public. Social gerontology is a rapidly developing field generating increasing public attention. Greater numbers of people are surviving middle age and facing the prospect of growing old in our society. In addition, as a people, on the average we are getting older, and as the general structure of our population shifts, occupational opportunities for working with and for the aging are increasing. Thus, there may be several publics with an interest in the field of social gerontology.

Prefaces usually end with thanks to some person or persons who "made this all possible." In this case those thanks go collectively to the authors for allowing us to reprint their works. By so doing they have allowed us to share their experience and knowledge. We also wish to thank the publishers of the original papers for their permission to reprint. Professor Barry Beckham of The University of Toledo read drafts of the various section introductions and made helpful comments. Mrs. Maybelle Jones typed countless letters and provided invaluable secretarial assistance. They too deserve a thank you.

CSK
BBM

Aging in America
Readings in Social Gerontology

1

Theoretical Approaches to Social Aging

INTRODUCTION TO PART I

George Maddox (1963) has observed that "relevant geron-tological literature is not distinguished by explicit statements of theoretical orientation." Other scholars have criticized the relatively new field of social gerontology for its concern with practical issues and problems confronting the elderly. Philibert (1965) and Kastenbaum (1965) criticize the field for being a mixture of findings derived through the methods and theories of the more established disciplines. Most of these critics maintain that there is no current comprehensive theoretical frame-work within which to address the question, "What happens to human beings socially as they grow old?"

This is not to say that there have been no attempts to answer this important question. Below, we present examples of answers which may be placed into five theoretical categories: role theory, disengagement theory, subculture theory, activity theory, and age-stratification theory. These approaches show considerable overlap and often differ only in their emphasis.

The earliest attempt in social gerontology to understand the adjustment of the aged individual was placed within a role theory framework (Cottrell, 1942). Generally speaking, research done within this framework concentrates on adjustment to role change among the elderly. The changes individuals undergo in the aging process are divided into two categories: the "giving-up" of social relationships and roles typical of adulthood (e.g., retirement); and the acceptance of social relationships typical of the later years (e.g., dependency on offspring) (Cavan et al., 1949). Using the role theory framework, Phillips, in the first paper, shows the relationship between role loss and adjustment to old age, and suggests that some of this effect has to do with individual identification as old.

Disengagement theory, put forth by Cumming and Henry (1961), stands in some contrast to the role theory approach. "Disengagement" is a mutual withdrawal between the aging individual and others in the social system to which he belongs. The theory argues that gradual disengagement is functional for society (which would otherwise be faced with disruption by the sudden withdrawal of its members) and satisfying for the individual (who is socialized for dying). In the second paper, Elaine Cumming looks back at the original statement of the disengagement theory, elaborates on some basic tenets of the theory, and argues that the theory can handle a greater amount of diversity among the aged than some critics were originally willing to admit.

In the third paper, Arnold Rose argues that the elderly live increasingly within the context of an aged subculture. He observes a series of social changes in America which lend weight to this subcultural viewpoint. In essence, Rose was the first to submit that there is a growing consciousness among the aged, and as well, that they have the capacity for meeting certain of their own needs.

Activity theory has appeared implicitly in much gerontological research. The theory states that there is a positive relationship between activity and life satisfaction. To a great extent, this theory presumes a broader framework within which other theories (e.g., role theory) might be contained. Lemon, Bengtson, and Peterson, in the fourth paper, attempt a formal and explicit statement of the activity theory and then test several hypotheses. They find only social activity with friends to be related to life satisfaction.

In the final paper in this part, Matilda White Riley proposes an age-stratification theory of aging. She argues that old age is "just one ingredient in the societal macrocosm, inseparable and interdependent with the other age strata," and advises that an analytic approach similar to that used in the analysis of class stratification would be useful for shedding light on problems of old age and dying.

A ROLE
THEORY APPROACH
TO ADJUSTMENT
IN OLD AGE*

Bernard S. Phillips

Aged populations must adjust to conditions that are not generally characteristic of other stages of the life cycle, namely, the increased probability of illness and impending death. To these conditions any society imposes additional ones with which the aged must come to terms. In our own society, and in many others, the changes experienced by the aged often include (1) retirement from full-time employment by men and relinquishment of household management by women, (2) withdrawal from active community and organizational leadership, (3) breaking up of marriage through the death of one's mate, (4) loss of an independent household, (5) loss of interest in distant goals and plans, (6) acceptance of dependence upon others for support or advice and management of funds, (7) acceptance of a subordinate position to adult offspring or to social workers, (8) taking up of membership in groups made up largely of old people, and (9) acceptance of planning in terms of immediate goals.[1]

Cavan and her associates maintain that these changes may be classified under two broad headings: the relinquishment of social relationships and roles typical of adulthood, and the acceptance of social relationships and roles typical of the later

* Bernard S. Phillips, "A Role Theory Approach to Adjustment in Old Age," *American Sociological Review* 22 (1957):212-17.

years. This suggests the possible utility of a role theory framework for understanding the adjustment of the aged individual, an approach outlined by Cottrell.[2] The present study attempts to explore this possibility, giving particular attention to aspects of the relation between an individual's self-conceptions and his social roles. It is felt that adjustment may be best understood when these two categories are examined together.

Data are based on interviews with 500 respondents in the Kips Bay–Yorkville Health District of New York City and 468 respondents in Elmira, N.Y.[3] The Elmira field work was done between mid-1951 and early 1952, with respondents constituting a random sample of noninstitutionalized individuals 60 years of age or older. The Kips Bay interviewing took place during late 1952 and early 1953. As in the case of the Elmira study, a probability sample of the noninstitutionalized aged individuals 60 or over was drawn.[4]

Although the two interview schedules are not the same, a large proportion of the items are identical. The present study is based on the items common to the two studies. The purpose of utilizing samples in two areas is essentially one of replication, although the environments are not replicated. The premise is that factors affecting the adjustment of the aged in a very large city vary to some extent from those in a relatively small city. If a role theory framework provides a useful tool for predicting adjustment in cities of varying size, then it is that much more generalizable.

Before defining adjustment, it is important to point out that no value judgment is intended. Adjustment to a given sociocultural setting may or may not be a "desirable" goal for a given individual, depending largely on his own value premises.

Pollak defines adjustment as "the efforts of an individual to satisfy his personal needs as well as to live up to the expectations of others."[5] He goes on to state that "the well-adjusted person is able to satisfy his needs quickly and adequately as they arise; a poorly adjusted person is unable to satisfy certain of his needs."[6] Cavan and associates define maladjustment as "behavior which does not completely satisfy the individual and social needs of the person, even though it may reduce his drive tensions. . . . Maladjustments, because they represent partial satisfactions of the wishes and needs of the person and because certain of them become ingrained as habitual behavior, impede readjustment."[7]

The index of adjustment is, therefore, based on the degree to which there is a patterned lack of alignment between the needs of the individual and the rewards he obtains, i.e., the existence of a relatively durable state in which needs are not satisfied. This state may be indicated by the individual's degree of habitual involvement in the world of fantasy. Absentmindedness, daydreaming about the past, and thoughts of death are the three items constituting our operational definition of degree of adjustment. These items are referred to in the question, "How often do you find yourself doing the following things? Would you say often, occasionally, hardly at all?" They form a Guttman scale for both samples, and this scale may be dichotomized into "maladjusted" and "adjusted" categories.[8] This measure of adjustment was found to be related to a number of items such as expressions of unhappiness and nervousness which would be expected to be related to it if it were a valid measure. [9]

It should be noted that the data utilized were not originally collected for the purpose of testing the utility of role theory for understanding adjustment. Consequently, there are limitations to the conceptual distinctions that can be made. We will utilize Rommetveit's definition of a social role as "a system of . . . social norms directed toward one and the same individual as member of a group or representative of a psychologically distinguishable category of individuals,"[10] with social norm defined as "a pressure for a pattern of behavior existing between two or more participants in a category of recurrent situations." Our basic premise is that behavior that conforms to these pressures is generally rewarded; to the extent that the pattern of reciprocal behavior is disturbed, the rewards are neither sent nor received. Since role changes may not only result in a temporary disturbance of rewards but also in a lasting reduction, definite consequences for adjustment may be expected.

Two of the four role changes to be considered are relatively easy to delimit. It is postulated that changes in role due to the death of one's spouse or to retirement tend to involve an overall reduction in the degree of reward associated with conforming behavior in the new as opposed to the previous roles.[11]

A third role change is indicated by a "yes" answer to the question, "Do you think people treat you differently because you are older?" In this case, the role is not so circumscribed as in the previous ones but concerns the entire matrix of roles within which the individual behaves. Furthermore, it is indexed by directly examining the respondent's perception of role change.

The fourth role change is indexed by whether or not the individual has reached the age of 70. Changes in chronological age are important for their direct and indirect effects on a multitude of roles. Although it is difficult to point to definite changes in role prescriptions, role expectations, or role behavior accompanying, for example, a change from age 60 to age 70, the fact is that the combined effects of this change on various roles make it significant for the present study. It is posited for this role change, as in the case of the previous three, that the overall reward associated with conformity to the changed role prescriptions tends to be reduced.

The final aspect of the theoretical framework has to do with the "self-image," which may be regarded as a complex of self-conceptions. One of these is self-conception of age and is measured in this study by the item, "How do you think of yourself as far as age goes—middle-aged, elderly, old, or what?" The "old" and "elderly" categories may be combined to include respondents who identify themselves as old, in distinction to those who identify themselves as middle-aged or young, or who have made no clear-cut identification.[12]

Age identification is conceived as a relatively high-order generalization from various social roles as well as from relatively subtle ongoing physiological and psychological processes. Unfortunately, there are no data on these processes, and thus we are limited to considering the interrelations of the above-mentioned roles and age identification.

It is hypothesized that a self-conception as old is related to maladjustment. Because our society values youth over age, the individual who identifies as old to a degree accepts a negative cultural evaluation of himself. In so doing, he deprives himself of many of the rewards accompanying the adult status, rewards which are associated not only with specific social roles but also with behavior outside of narrow role contexts.

We may now present evidence on the interrelations among the variables of adjustment, role change, and age identification. In the general model age identification is conceived of as an intervening variable between role changes and adjustment, i.e. a variable which specifies conditions under which role changes affect adjustment. The remainder of this paper presents data on (1) the relations between each role change variable and adjustment, (2) interrelations among the various role change variables,

Table 1.

Percent Maladjusted Respondents By Role

Role	Elmira		Kips Bay	
	Percent	N†	Percent	N
Employed	22	(171)**	27	(161)**
Retired	42	(98)**	40	(200)**
Married	27	(173)**	30	(221)**
Widow or widower	40	(217)**	47	(180)**
Age 60–69	29	(277)**	31	(254)*
70 or over	52	(187)**	40	(233)*
Not treated differently	34	(366)**	32	(355)**
Treated differently	53	(87)**	48	(118)**

† In this table and in the following ones, N refers to the total number in each category. The sum of those in the employed and retired categories, as well as those who are married or widowed, is somewhat less than the total number of respondents in each sample. In the former case housekeepers are omitted from the samples, while in the latter instance respondents who never married are excluded.

* Difference is significant at the .05 level.

** Difference is significant at the .01 level.

(3) the relation between role changes and age identification, (4) the relation between age identification and adjustment, and (5) combined effects of role changes and age identification on adjustment.

Table 1 reports data indicating the relationship to maladjustment of each of the four role changes. All differences in the proportion of maladjusted respondents among those who have and have not undergone role changes are significant at the .01 level with one exception, which is significant at the .05 level.

We may now ask whether or not these relationships are maintained when control variables are introduced. With respect to the employment role, controls on marital status, age, and age identification were introduced. Thus, for example, the age control allows a comparison of employed and retired who are age 60–69 as well as employed and retired who are 70 or over. Consequently, there are six comparisons of employed and retired, two for each control variable, or a total of twelve for the Elmira

Table 2.

Percent Respondents Treated Differently By Role

	Elmira		Kips Bay	
Role	Percent	N	Percent	N
Employed	13	(170)*	24	(160)
Retired	23	(95)*	28	(187)
Married	14	(219)**	20	(169)*
Widow or widower	27	(176)**	30	(206)*
Age 60–69	13	(271)**	23	(244)
70 or over	30	(185)**	29	(230)

* Difference is significant at the .05 level.

** Difference is significant at the .01 level.

and Kips Bay samples. Of these, eleven are in the expected direction, i.e., there is a higher proportion of maladjusted respondents among the retired than among the employed, while two of the differences are significant at the .05 level.

With respect to the marital role, controls on employment, age, and age identification result in eleven of the twelve differences between married and widowed in the expected direction, of which five are significant at the .01 or .05 levels. Controls on employment status, marital status, and age identification, when introduced into the age variable, produce results similar to those obtained with respect to the marital role, except that only three differences are significant. Finally, four controls are introduced into the differential-treatment variable, resulting in sixteen comparisons in the expected direction, of which nine are significant at the .01 or .05 levels.

It may be concluded that each of the four variables in Table 1 to a degree is independently related to maladjustment. However, since a high proportion of the differences are not statistically significant after introducing the control variables, one suspects that combinations of various role changes would not greatly increase the proportion of maladjusted respondents. This does not in fact prove to be the case. For example, among those

Table 3.

Percent Respondents Who Identify As Old By Role

	Elmira		Kips Bay	
Role	Percent	N	Percent	N
Employed	12	(172)**	23	(154)**
Retired	42	(96)**	50	(195)**
Married	18	(220)**	35	(167)*
Widow or widower	35	(178)**	45	(217)*
Age 60–69	11	(273)**	27	(246)**
70 or over	47	(186)**	55	(240)**

* Difference is significant at the .05 level.

** Difference is significant at the .01 level.

respondents with all of the first three role changes in Table 1, the highest proportion of maladjusted respondents is only 52 percent for the Elmira sample and 47 percent for the Kips Bay sample, which is no greater than that for certain role changes taken individually.

The next aspects of the data to be taken up are the interrelations among the role change variables. Our approach is to view the differential-treatment variable as dependent, with the remaining three variables considered as contributing to effecting differential treatment, whether directly or indirectly. From general knowledge of how these changes occur, it would be difficult indeed to imagine feelings of differential treatment as effecting any of the other three role changes in a high proportion of instances. The differential-treatment variable is representative of a large number of dependent variables, other examples of which might be changes in various types of activities and in social participation.

Table 2 indicates a relationship between each of the three role changes and the dependent variable of differential treatment, a relationship that seems to be less pronounced in the Kips Bay sample. This perhaps is due to a greater degree of anonymity in a large city and consequently a degree of compart-

---

Table 4.

Percent Maladjusted Respondents By Age Identification

Age Identification	Elmira		Kips Bay	
	Percent	N	Percent	N
Middle-aged	31	(343)**	28	(287)**
Old	58	(118)**	49	(199)**

** Difference is significant at the .01 level.

---

mentatlization of any role change, resulting in reducing its possible influence on other role changes.

We will now consider the relation between the three relatively independent role changes and a self-conception as old, the primary data for which are presented in Table 3. This relationship is strongly indicated by five .01 level differences and one .05 level difference.

If, for each role change variable, the other two are introduced as controls, the following results are found: (1) for the employment role, all of the eight relationships between this role change and identification as old are positive, with seven being significant at the .01 level; (2) these results are identical to those obtained with the age role; and (3) with respect to the marital role, all differences are in the expected direction, and three of these are significant at the .01 or .05 levels.

These data indicate a considerable degree of independent relationship to age identification for each of the three role variables. This is substantiated upon examining the cumulative effects of the above three role changes on age identification. For the Elmira sample, the proportion of identifications as old for three role changes is 56 percent; for the Kips Bay sample, it is 65 percent. These proportions are somewhat above the analogous percentages for any one role change taken by itself.

Table 5.

Percent Maladjusted Respondents
By Age Identification And Role

Age Identification	Role	Elmira		Kips Bay	
		Percent	N	Percent	N
Middle-aged	Retired	39	(56)	31	(97)
Old	Employed	57	(21)	37	(38)
Middle-aged	Widow or widower	40	(116)	31	(119)
Old	Married	54	(41)	36	(58)
Middle-aged	Age 70 or over	44	(99)	28	(104)
Old	60-69	48	(33)	42	(66)

The fourth aspect concerns the relation between age identification and adjustment. The evidence presented in Table 4 shows that a significantly higher proportion of maladjusted respondents are found among those who identify as old as opposed to middle-aged. This is found to hold when controls on employment status, marital status, and age are introduced. All of the twelve differences are in the same direction, and eleven of them are significant at the .01 or .05 levels.

Finally, combined effects of role changes and age identification on adjustment may be considered. Table 5 compares the proportion of maladjusted respondents among those who identify as middle-aged and have undergone a given role change with the proportion among those who identify as old and have not undergone this role change. Although none of the differences

15

are significant, they are all in a direction indicating that age identification can reverse the expected relation between a given role change and adjustment. This is striking in view of the fact that the role change variables were previously shown to be significantly related to adjustment.

It is possible to carry this type of analysis one step further due to the size of the samples under consideration. For example, one might compare respondents who identify as middle-aged and have undergone any two of the three role changes with respondents who identify as old and have not experienced these role changes. There are three different combinations of two role changes for each sample. The data here indicate a turning point, for in five of these six comparisons age identification does not reverse the expected relation between the role changes and adjustment; in fact, the expected relation is statistically significant in two of the six comparisons.

This paper has outlined a theoretical framework that may be utilized in predicting the degree of adjustment of the aged In this approach, age identification is conceived of as an intervening variable between each role change and adjustment. The five aspects of the data may be summarized as follows:

1. The role changes considered are significantly related to maladjustment, although there is little tendency for multiple role changes to cumulate and result in a closer relation to the adjustment variable.

2. The differential-treatment role change, conceived of as representative of a number of variables influenced by employment, marital, and age role changes, generally is significantly related to these role changes.

3. The role changes considered are significantly related to identification as old, and there is some tendency for multiple role changes to cumulate, resulting in a closer relation to age identification.

4. Identification as old is significantly related to maladjustment.

5. Age identification can reverse the expected relation between any one of the role changes considered and adjustment. Where two role changes are combined, however, this reversal does not generally take place.

It is hoped that future studies of adjustment will further specify the relatively crude variable of role change. In addition, the significance of the age-identification variable for adjustment indicates a need for further investigation of this and other aspects of the self-image.

NOTES

1. Ruth S. Cavan, Ernest W. Burgess, Robert J. Havighurst, and Herbert Goldhamer, *Personal Adjustment in Old Age* (Chicago: Science Research Associates, 1949), pp. 6-7.

2. Leonard S. Cottrell, Jr., "The Adjustment of the Individual to his Age and Sex Roles," *American Sociological Review* 7 (October 1942): 617-20.

3. The Elmira data were collected by the Department of Sociology and Anthropology, Cornell University, under the direction of John Dean and with the assistance of Milton Barron, Bernard Kutner, Gordon Streib, and Edward Suchman. The research was supported by grants from the Rockefeller and Lilly Foundations. The Kips Bay data resulted from a cooperative venture by the Department of Health of the City of New York, the Cornell University Medical College, the Cornell University Social Science Research Center, and the Russell Sage Foundation, and were secured under the direction of Bernard Kutner, David Fanshel, Thomas Langner, and Alice Togo.

4. The sample design in the Kips Bay study involved an area sample that weighted the population in low-rental areas. City blocks were classified into three rental groups: $90 per month and over, $40-$89 per month, and $20-$39 per month. Approximately 10 percent of the sample were drawn from the high-rental group, 30 percent from the middle-rental group, and 60 percent from the low-rental group.

5. Otto Pollak, *Social Adjustment in Old Age: A Research Planning Report,* Social Science Research Council Bulletin no. 59 (New York 1948), p. 8.

6. Ibid., p. 33.

7. Cavan et al., *Personal Adjustment,* p. 15.

8. The coefficient of reproducibility is 91 percent for the Kips Bay sample and 89.5 percent for the Elmira sample. A response of "often" or "occasionally" on any of the items is scored + 1. Those who scored + 3 and and + 2 were combined to form the "maladjusted" category, with + 1 and 0 forming the "adjusted" category. It should be noted that the items scale

in different orders for the two samples. For Elmira, the order from highest to lowest marginal frequency of "maladjusted" responses is (1) absent-minded, (2) daydreaming, and (3) thoughts of death; the order for Kips Bay is (1) daydreaming, (2) thoughts of death, and (3) absent-minded. This difference in scaling order poses interesting and difficult questions about the factors in each community responsible for it but the problems will not be treated here. However, in spite of the difference, the fact that the same items scaled in both studies provides additional support for their unidimensionality.

9. Bernard S. Phillips, "A Role Theory Approach to Predicting Adjustment of the Aged in Two Communities" (Ph.D. diss., Cornell University, 1956), pp. 44–50.

10. Ragnar Rommetveit, *Social Norms and Roles* (Minneapolis: University of Minnesota Press, 1955), p. 85.

11. The statement is made in this form because there is no direct evidence for it in the data collected.

12. Twelve percent of Elmira respondents and 2 percent of Kips Bay respondents used euphemistic expressions to indicate their age rather than selecting one of the three structured categories. These individuals, who were not willing to commit themselves to a definite identification as old or elderly, were combined with the middle-aged category and other individuals who had not made a transition from a younger age identification.

FURTHER
THOUGHTS ON
THE THEORY
OF DISENGAGEMENT*

Elaine Cumming

The usefulness of a theory depends upon its ability to explain the present and predict the future. In this essay, I shall amplify and elaborate the "disengagement" theory of aging that W. E. Henry and I developed with our colleagues between 1957 and 1960.[1] I hope in this way to make that theory better able to describe and predict both the range and the limits of the aging process. In its original form, the theory was too simple; it had only enough detail to account for the main outlines of the process of growing old. By adding new elements and elaborating the basic propositions in more detail, I hope to be able to suggest a little of the complexity and diversity that we see among men and women in old age.

The General Theory of Disengagement

The disengagement theory was developed during a five-year study of a sample of aging people in an American city. The sample consisted of 275 individuals between the ages of 50 and 90 years; they were in good health and had the minimum of money needed for independence.[2] Briefly, the theory proposes

---

* Elaine Cumming, "Further Thoughts on the Theory of Disengagement," *International Social Science Journal* 15 (1963):377–393. © Unesco, 1963. Reprinted by permission of Unesco.

19

that under these conditions normal aging is a mutual withdrawal or "disengagement" between the aging person and others in the social system to which he belongs—a withdrawal initiated by the individual himself, or by others in the system. When disengagement is complete, the equilibrium that existed in middle life between the individual and society has given way to a new equilibrium characterized by greater distance, and a changed basis for solidarity.

Engagement is essentially the interpenetration of the person and the society to which he belongs. The fully engaged person acts in a large number and a wide variety of roles in a system of divided labor, and feels an obligation to meet the expectations of his role partners. There are variations, however, in the type of engagement. It is possible to be broadly engaged in a number of social systems that exert little influence over the remainder of society, and it is possible to be deeply engaged in the sense of having roles whose function is to make policies that affect others in large numbers. It is possible to be symbolically engaged by epitomizing some valued attribute—by being a famous scientist, poet, or patriot. A few men have roles that combine all three types of engagement and carry with them the extreme constraints that must accompany such a number and variety of obligations; presidents and prime ministers are among them. Roughly, the depth and breadth of a man's engagement can be measured by the degree of potential disruption that would follow his sudden death.[3] The death of someone who has an important symbolic engagement with his society, however, can result in both loss and gain because the survivors can rally around the symbols he embodied and thus reaffirm their value. For many Americans, Dag Hammarskjöld's death brought into sharp focus the need for world order.

In its original form, the disengagement theory concerned itself with the modal case which, in America, is first, departure of children from families, and then, retirement for men or widowhood for women. It did not take account of such nonmodal cases as widowhood before the marriage of the last child or of work protracted past the modal age of retirement. Most importantly, it did not, and still does not, concern itself with the effects of the great scourges of old age, poverty, and illness.[4]

20

This essay will modify and elaborate the theory somewhat and suggest some characteristics of aging people that might make an important difference to their patterns of disengagement. Like the original statement, this modification has the status of a system of hypotheses. Some of the elements are close to being operational as they stand; others are still too general for testing.

Before proceeding further, an asymmetry in the earlier discussions of the theory must be dealt with. Disengagement has been conceived as a mutual withdrawal between individual and society, and therefore the process should vary according to the characteristics of both. In earlier statements, consideration was given to the different ways in which the environment retreats—retirement, loss of kin or spouse, departure of children, and so on—but the only individual difference to be considered in any detail was that between the sexes. Eventually, if the process is to be described adequately, we must have typologies of withdrawal and retreat. I suggest that deeply rooted differences in character are a good starting point because it is reasonable to suppose that they color all of life, including the disengagement process.

Temperament and Disengagement

In its original form the disengagement theory did no more than suggest an ultimate biological basis for a reduction of interest or involvement in the environment. Variations in the process were attributed to social pressures, especially as they are differently experienced by men and women. A vital difference in style, however, can be expected between people of dissimilar temperaments, no matter what their sex. Combining biological and social variables within the framework of the disengagement theory, it might be possible to suggest a wider variety of styles of interaction in old age than would otherwise be possible.

A proposed temperamental variable, basically biological, is the style of adaptation to the environment. It seems well established that humans must maintain a minimum of exchange with the environment, or a clear anticipation of renewing exchange with it, in order to keep a firm knowledge both of it and of themselves.[5] There appear to be different modes of maintaining this relationship, which can perhaps be called the "impinging" mode and the "selecting" mode.[6] The impinger appears to try out his concept of himself in interaction with others in the environment and to use their appropriate responses to confirm the correctness of his inferences about himself, the environment, and his relationship to it. If the feedback from others suggests that he is incorrect, he will try to bring others' responses into line with his own sense of the appropriate relationship. Only if he fails repeatedly will he modify his concept of himself. In contrast, the selector tends to wait for others to affirm his assumptions about himself. From the ongoing flow of stimulation he selects these cues that confirm his relationship to the world. If they fail to come, he waits, and only reluctantly brings his own concepts into line with the feedback he receives. The selector may be able to use symbolic residues of old interactions to maintain his sense of self more efficiently than the impinger, and thus be able to wait longer for suitable cues.

We assume that temperament is a multidetermined, biologically based characteristic, and therefore that the temperamental types normally distributed in the population with few people at the extremes. We also assume that the modal person can both impinge and select as the occasion demands, although perhaps favoring one style rather than the other. A normal person will shift to the alternate pattern when it becomes necessary either for appropriate role behavior or for the prevention of "diffusion feelings."[7] If there are no complicating ego problems, a pronounced selector will probably be known as "reserved," or "self-sufficient" or "stubborn," and a pronounced impinger as "temperamental," "lively," or "brash." We would expect the impinger, as he grows older, to experience more anxiety about loss of interaction, because he needs it to maintain orientation.[8] The selector, being able to make more use of symbols, may have less difficulty with the early stages of disengagement.[9]

The disengaging impinger can be expected to be more active and apparently more youthful than his peers. His judgment may not be as good as it was, but he will provoke the comment that he is an unusual person for his age. Ultimately, as he becomes less able to control the situations he provokes, he may suffer anxiety and panic through failure both to arouse and to interpret appropriate reactions. His problem in old age will be to avoid confusion.

The selector, in contrast to the impinger, interacts in a more measured way. When he is young he may be thought too withdrawn, but as he grows older his style becomes more age-appropriate. In old age, because of his reluctance to generate interaction, he may, like a neglected infant, develop a kind of marasmus. His foe will be apathy rather than confusion.

These are not, of course, ordinary aging processes; the extreme impinger and the extreme selector are almost certain to get into trouble at some crisis point because they cannot move over to the opposite mode of interacting when it is adaptive to do so. In general, in an achievement-oriented society, the impinger may be more innately suited to middle age, the selector perhaps to childhood and old age.

To sum up, some biologically based differences among people may be expected to impose a pattern upon their manner of growing old. I shall now return to the theory, with this variable in mind, and at the same time suggest other concepts that it might profitably include.

At the Outset of Disengagement

Disengagement probably begins sometime during middle life when certain changes of perception occur, of which the most important is probably an urgent new perception of the inevitability of death. It is certain that children do not perceive the meaning of death, and it is said that "no young man believes that he will ever die." It is quite possible that a vivid apprehension of mortality—perhaps when the end of life seems closer than its start—is the beginning of the process of growing old. Paradoxically, a sense of the shortness of time may come at the height of engagement; that is, competition for time may draw attention to both its scarcity and its value. There may be a critical point beyond which further involvement with others automatically brings a sense of "there is no time for all that I must do" which, in turn, leads to evaluations of what has been done com-

23

pared to what was hoped for, and then to allocations and priorities for the future. If this process is common to many people, those who have never been very firmly engaged should feel less sense of urgency than those who are tightly enmeshed with society—all other things, including temperament, being equal.

Accompanying the need to select and allocate is a shift away from achievement. Achievement, as Parsons says,[10] demands a future; when confidence in the existence of a future is lost, achievement cannot be pursued without regard to the question, "Shall it be achievement of this rather than of that?" Such a question is the the beginning of an exploration of the meaning and value of the alternatives.[11] In American life, where achievement is perhaps the highest value, its abandonment has always been tinged with failure. We would, therefore, expect the relinquishment of achievement to be a crisis, and, indeed, general knowledge and some research tell us that in middle life competent men with a record of achievement feel sudden painful doubts about the value of what they have done.[12] Once any part of achievement is given up, some binding obligations are gone, and even if they are replaced with less demanding ties, a measure of disengagement has occurred.

Disengagement may begin in a different way, somewhat as follows: the middle-aged person who has not undergone an inner period of questioning reaches a point where losses, both personal and public, begin to outrun his ability to replace them. A friend dies, a business closes, his children move far away. For the healthy, aging impinger these losses may be replaced; for the selector they may not, and an awareness of their permanence may be a turning point. With each loss, the aging person must surrender certain potential feelings and actions and replace them with their symbolic residues in memory.[13] In a sense, this substitution of symbol for social action changes the quality of the self. Even if the role partners themselves are replaced, they cannot often substitute for the lost relationship because sentiments built up over the years cannot be copied.

The most crucial step in the disengagement process may lie in finding a new set of rewards. The esteem that achievement brings can be replaced by the affection generated in socioemotional activity. The approval that comes from meeting contracted

24

obligations can be replaced by the spontaneous responses of others to expressive acts. The inner rewards of weaving the past into a satisfactory moral fabric can partly replace the public rewards of achievement. Nevertheless, in America today there is a net loss because achievement is more highly valued than meaning or expression and because its symbols are more easily calibrated. To be rich is to be recognized a success; wisdom is often its own reward.

Finally, and perhaps most importantly, freedom from obligation replaces the constraint of being needed in an interlocking system of divided tasks. The fully engaged man is, in essence, bound; the disengaged man is free—if he has resources and health enough to allow him to exercise that freedom. The ability to enjoy old age may be the ability and the opportunity to use freedom.[14]

No matter how important the effects of the perception of time and the shift in rewards, the essential characteristic of disengagement is that once started it tends to be self-perpetuating. If the search for meaning becomes urgent, and the impulse toward seeking out others becomes less rewarding, there will be a tendency not to replace ties broken by loss.

Once withdrawal has begun, it may become more difficult to make new contacts. Not knowing quite how to behave under strange circumstances inhibits exploration, and this difficulty, in turn, can reinforce the disengaging process—many elderly people refuse to fly in aircraft, not because they are afraid but because they do not know airport etiquette! A sense of strangeness cannot, of course, in itself lead to withdrawal; any middle-aged adult feels discomfort if he finds himself in an unknown situation without a role. Prisoners of war must be helped to re-engage after long periods of isolation from their culture. For the aging, such diffusion feelings enhance a process that is already under way—a process made inevitable by man's mortality.

Thus, empirically, we see aging people interacting less and in fewer roles. Modally, ties to kindred become more salient, while more distant, impersonal, and more recent ties become less important and finally disappear. This process of reduction and simplification leaves the individual freer from the control that accompanies involvement in a larger number and greater variety of roles. Concretely, this means that the broadly engaged person receives fewer of the positive and negative sanctions that accompany and guide all interactions and control the style of everyday behavior, and, therefore, idiosyncratic personal behavior becomes possible. At the same time, ideas, removed from the scenes in which they can be tested out, become more stereotyped and general.[15]

It seems possible that those who have been deeply engaged in roles that influence considerable areas of society or those who have rare and valuable skills will remain engaged longer than those less deeply involved with the affairs of their generation. This is because the values that inform major decisions are slower to change than everyday norms, and those who have been consciously enmeshed with them may, in old age, symbolize their continuity for those who have not. Those who have been successful mathematicians, politicians, and poets can count on society remaining closer to them than those who have not influenced or represented their fellow men.

As the number of groups to which an aging person belongs is reduced, his membership in those remaining becomes more important because he must maintain a minimum of stimulation. The memberships of old age—kinship, friendship, and perhaps church—are all marked by a high level of agreement among members and many explicit common values. In such groups, it is very difficult to deviate far from the common viewpoint. Thus, the more the elderly person disengages from a variety of roles, the less likely is he to take on new ideas. The conservatism of old age is partly a security measure, related to the need to maintain harmony among the remaining companions.

As withdrawal of normative control is an essential aspect of the disengagement theory, it must be asked why old people should enter a spiral of decreasing conformity when middle-aged people, except in extreme cases, are able to endure prolonged interpersonal disruptions and quickly reconstitute contact with the norms. Moving from one city to another is an interpersonal crisis, but it does not often set in motion a process that leads to a new orientation to life. The difference seems to be that for the aging a combination of reduced biological energy, the reduction of freedom, preoccupation with the accumulated symbols of the past, and license for a new kind of self-centeredness cannot be resisted. Furthermore, all this is expected of the older person, and so the circle is further reinforced.

In contrast, if the middle-aged person feels that he is in a situation of reduced social control, he has both the energy and the opportunity to seek new constraints, and if he retreats too far from conformity he is sanctioned. In some ways, an aging person is like an adolescent; he is allowed more freedom and expressiveness than a middle-aged adult. Later, when he is very old, he is permitted the dependency and individuation of the small child.

In this view, socialization is the encouragement of children to abandon their parochialism and individuation and to accept conformity to the demands of the major institutions of society, while disengagement is a permission to return again to individuation. In all, for the old person, the circular process of disengagement results in the social tasks getting harder and the alternatives more rewarding, while for the young person, the social tasks remain rewarding and the alternatives are felt as alienation. Were it not for the value placed on achievement, the chains that the adult so willingly allows to bind him might be put off at least as readily as they are taken on.

Society's Withdrawal

The disengagement theory postulates that society withdraws from the aging person to the same extent as that person withdraws from society. This is, of course, just another way of saying that the process is normatively governed and in a sense agreed upon by all concerned. Everyone knows how much freedom from constraint is allowable and where the line between the oddness of old age and the symptoms of deviance lies. There seem to be deeply rooted reasons, in both the culture and the social structure, for this withdrawal process.

In the first place the organization of modern society requires that competition for powerful roles be based on achievement. Such competition favors the young because their knowledge is newer. Furthermore, the pressure of the young on to the highest roles cannot be met in a bureaucracy by an indefinite expansion of the powerful roles. Therefore, the older members must be discarded to make way for the younger. In America, a disproportionately large number of young adults will soon be competing for jobs that are becoming relatively fewer as industry moves toward complete automation.[16] If Americans are to remain engaged in any serious way past the seventh decade, as many observers insist they must, roles must be found for them that young people *cannot* fill.[17] Only an elaboration of available roles can accomplish this because it is impossible for a society organized around standards of achievement and efficency to assign its crucial roles to a group whose death rate is excessively high. When a middle-aged, fully engaged person dies, he leaves many broken ties, and disrupted situations. Disengagement thus frees the old to die without disrupting vital affairs.

Finally, at the end of life when one has outlived one's peers, social withdrawal consists in failure to approach. In this sense, the young withdraw from the old because the past has little reality for them. They cannot conceive of an old person in any but a peripheral role. Thus, they approach him with condescension, or do not approach at all because of embarrassment. This gulf between generations is a by-product of a future-oriented society; when it changes, America will have changed. In the meantime, it seems clear that the older person may find it more rewarding to contemplate a moment of past glory than to try to make new relationships, especially with the young. In the intimate circle, no such effort is needed; the only real social problem for the very old, given health and enough money, may be lack of such a circle.[18]

Disengagement from Roles

Whether disengagement is initiated by society or by the aging person, in the end he plays fewer roles, and his relationships have changed their quality.

Socialization ensures that everyone learns to play the two basic kinds of roles that are known as instrumental and socioemotional. In this essay, the instrumental roles in any given social system are those primarily concerned with active adaptation to the world outside the system during the pursuit of system goals. Socioemotional roles are concerned with the inner integration of the system and the maintenance of the value patterns that inform its goals.[19]

Men, for reasons at once too obvious and too complex to consider here, must perform instrumental roles on behalf of their families, and this, for most men, means working at an occupation. Although men play socioemotional roles, in business and elsewhere, they tend to assign the integrative tasks to women when they are present. In patriarchal societies, a man conceivably can live his whole adult life without playing a socioemotional role, if, in both his family and in his work, others are willing to integrate social systems around him. A married woman, on the other hand, in addition to the socioemotional role she plays in her family as a whole, must be instrumental in relationship to small children. Very few women, and those only perhaps among the wealthiest, can totally avoid instrumentality. Thus, women are in the habit of bringing either kind of role into salience with more ease than men.

Whether there is any inherent quality that makes it easier to play one role than another is obscure, although the impinging temperament may predispose toward socioemotionality. Empirically, we see a spectrum that includes goal-directed men, all of whose roles are instrumental (officers in the regular Army whose wives tremble when they shout); men who play socioemotional roles in some circumstances (comforting the baby when he falls), men who seek out socioemotional roles (in America, perhaps the personnel man); women who play instrumental roles whenever the situation allows it (club presidents), women who shift from instrumental work roles to socioemotional family roles, and women who play socioemotional roles almost all the time (the helpful maiden aunt living in a relative's household).

Most married couples with children, no matter what secondary roles they may hold, have a basic division of labor in which the husband plays a core instrumental role vis-à-vis his family by working, and the wife a core socioemotional one by maintaining their home and caring for their children. By the time

29

the children have left home and the husband has retired, the original division of labor has lost much of its basis.

A man has no clear-cut role upon retirement. He may still play an instrumental role relative to his wife, but it loses its public label; there is no special place to go to perform it, and there is no paycheck that is the obvious consequence of his daily round. He must bring his capacities for integrative acitvity into salience much of the time and perhaps even share the instrumental roles that remain available with other retired men. For these reasons, the disengagement theory proposes that it is more difficult for a man to shift to socioemotional roles and integrative activities than it is for him to assume new instrumentalities, both because it is a less familiar mode for him and because he is in danger of competing directly with his wife and possibly with his grandchildren for roles within kinship or friendship circles. Therefore, the theory predicts that retirement will bring a period of maladjustment to many American men.

A man's response to retirement may be colored by the type of work role from which he withdraws. If his role has been part of a "true" division of labor, such that he can see the contribution that he is making to the functioning of society, he is likely to have considerable ego involvement in his work—it is to him as children are to a woman, a persistent palpable achievement. If, on the other hand, the division of labor is such that the outcome of his contribution is invisible to him, he will tend to be alientated from the meaning of his work and will find his rewards in his personal relationships with his fellow workers. In the first case, his instrumental role has three facts: he can see his contribution to the larger society, to his immediate working group, and to his family; in the second case, he can see a contribution only to the primary groups, work and family. Men in these two situations may react quite differently to retirement. The first might be expected to suffer more sense of loss immediately upon retirement—as women do when children first depart—but eventually to take much satisfaction from recalling his contribution to social goals and perhaps seeing others build upon it. The second may be relieved at leaving a meaningless work role but eventually suffer from lack of the symbolic connection with his own past, especially if he is a selector and accustomed to depending upon symbols for his orientation and sense of self.

Disengagement from central life roles is basically different for women than for men. This seems to be because women's roles are essentially unchanged from girlhood to death. In the course of their lives women are asked to give up only pieces of their core socioemotional roles or to change their details. Their transitions are therefore easier[20]—the wife of a retired man can use her integrative skills to incorporate him in new groupings. She must, if she is tactful, become even more integrative through abandoning to him the more adaptive of her domestic tasks. Similarly, the problems raised by widowhood are more easily resolved than the problems raised by retirement. Moreover, the loss of status anchorage that women suffer at the time of a husband's death is less severe than the loss of status suffered at retirement because widowhood, unlike retirement, has no tinge of failure in it.[21] It is the blameless termination of a valued role. Furthermore, the differential death rate that leaves about 20 percent of American women living without a conjugal bond by the age of 60 provides a membership group for them.[22] Men, in contrast, have difficulty finding memberships to compensate for work associations.

In general we might say that a woman's lifelong training to a role that is primarily socioemotional but nevertheless includes adaptive skills leaves her more diffusely adaptable than a man's working career leaves him, because he does not automatically need integrative skills. Integrative skills are, in a sense, the *lingua franca* wherever people interact with one another. Adaptive skills, in contrast, tend to be more functionally specific and less easily transferred. The disposition toward the instrumental role can remain after retirement, but the specific skills lose relevance. Only rarely does a woman find herself with no membership group that can use her integrative contribution.

Finally, a retired man loses suitable role models—that is, role partners with whom he can try out patterns of adaptation and hence learn alternatives. He must seek out other retired men— who are themselves tinged with failure in his eyes—or learn from women. Women, again because of the differential death rate, have more models, and these are more familiar. For both men

31

and women, however, the roles of old age must be learned from others who are themselves relatively free of constraints—unlike children who are taught the roles they anticipate filling by adults who are as fully engaged and constrained as they will ever be.

Among married couples, a crucial event after retirement may be a shifting of the representative role from the man to the woman. While he works, a husband endows his family with its position in society, but after he enters the socioemotional world

---

Table 1.

Proportion of Homeless[1] Men and Women in a Time Sample of Applicants to Two Relief Agencies

Age and sex	Total	Percentage homeless
Men	*227*	*27.7*
Under 60 years	185	27.6
Age 60 and over	42	28.6
Women	*144*	*6.3*
Under 60 years	100	6.0
Age 60 and over	44	6.8

[1]Excluding migrant workers, and those temporarily stranded away from home. These data are from a study of the division of labour among the integrative agents of society financed in part by NIMH (National Institute of Mental Health) Grant M_{4735}, Principal Investigator Elaine Cumming.

---

of women and leisure, his wife tends to represent their conjugal society at kinship gatherings and social affairs—even in church activities. In this regard, also, men are more freed by retirement than women are by widowhood.

If these differences between men and women are important, there should be a visible contrast in their ability to cope with the discontinuities of the disengagement process. Two obvious examples are available, that appear related, on the one hand, to women's abilities in finding roles in social systems and, on the other, to the sudden freedom from constraint of retirement. In Table 1 we see the relative proportions of men and women in a study sample who, when seeking help from a public relief agency, were found to be homeless as well as in need of money. At no age are men who are in economic distress as able as women to maintain membership in a domestic unit. Indeed, there is no female counterpart in America to the "homeless man." In Table 2, we see that among a cohort of men and women over 60 years of age entering a mental hospital for the first time, one-third of the nonmarried men had been living in shelters and old people's homes, whereas less than one-tenth of the nonmarried women had come from such institutions. Women without husbands

Table 2.

Living Arrangements of 100 Consecutive First Admissions, Aged 60 and Over, to a Mental Hospital[1]

Sex and marital status	Number	Percentage who had been living in		
		Domestic unit	Hospital or nursing home	Shelter or home for aged
Men	*43*	—	—	—
Married	16	81.3	12.5	6.2
Non-married	27	44.4	18.5	37.1
Women	*57*	—	—	—
Married	16	87.5	12.5	0.0
Non-married	41	63.4	26.8	9.8

[1] I am grateful to Mary Lou Parlagreco and John Cumming for permission to use these data from an unpublished study.

appear able to accommodate themselves to both the households of others and the hospital environment more readily than men without wives.[23] The differences in both tables are statistically significant at better than the 1 percent level of confidence.

In Figure 1, we see the rates of suicide, by age, for men and women. At the age that disengagement is postulated to occur, 65–75, the rate of suicide among women drops and continues to drop, while among men it rises persistently.[24] The figure leads to the speculation that women go from a little too much constraint to just the right amount of freedom while men go from too much of the one to too much of the other. In spite of this dramatic difference, is is unlikely that men who survive the

33

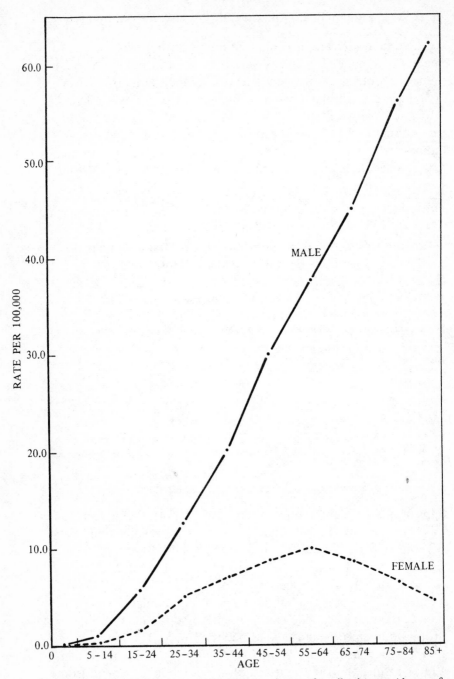

Fig. 1. Rates of suicide per 100,000 population for all white residents of continental United States, 1957. (Adapted from Table CO, *Summary of Mortality Statistics: United States, 1957,* Washington, D.C., National Office of Vital Statistics.)

transition crisis of retirement are as disadvantaged as these data make them seem; they are more likely to resemble Charles Lamb, who says of his sudden and unexpected retirement: "For the first day or two I felt stunned—overwhelmed. I could only apprehend my felicity; I was too confused to taste it sincerely. I wandered about, thinking I was happy, and knowing that I was not. I was in the condition of a prisoner in the old Bastille, suddenly let loose after a forty years' confinement. I could scarce trust myself with myself. It was like passing out of Time into Eternity—for it is a sort of Eternity for a man to have all his Time to himself. It seemed to me that I had more time on my hands than I could ever manage. From a poor man, poor in Time, I was suddenly lifted up into a vast revenue; I could see no end of my possessions; I wanted some steward, or judicious bailiff, to manage my estates in Time for me. And here let me caution persons growing old in active business, not lightly, nor without weighing their own resources, to forego their customary employment all at once, for there may be danger in it. I feel it by myself, but I know that my resources are sufficient; and now that those first giddy raptures have subsided, I have a quiet home-feeling of the blessedness of my condition."[25]

Changes in Solidarity

I have discussed disengagement as it affects temperamental types, as an inner experience, as a social imperative, and as a response to changing roles. Perhaps the most economical way of describing it is in terms of shifting solidarities that may have roots in middle life. In general, aging brings change from solidarity bonds based on differences of function and hence on mutual dependency to bonds based on similarities and common sentiments. The post-retirement part of a man's life can be considered, therefore, in terms of a two-stage shift in the nature of his relationships with his wife, his kinsmen, and the rest of the world that starts with departure of children and retirement. On the one hand, the "organic solidarity" of a divided labor that marked his conjugal life is weakened because after retirement he no longer has a clearly marked, publicly recognized, instrumental role; therefore, the "mechanical solidarity" of common belief and sentiments that must precede and accompany the division of labor becomes more salient.[26] On the other hand, the man and his wife, as a unit, are no longer functioning as a factory for making adults from children and hence are now related to other segments of society through common characteristics. Thus, both men and women abandon the mutual obligations and power problems of a divided labor among themselves as well as between themselves and society. They move into a more equalitarian relationship with each other and with the world—a relationship in which solidarity is based almost entirely upon a consensus of values and a commonality of interest. Most importantly, the new segmental solidarity is marked by an essential redundancy of the parts.[27] Loss of a member from a system of divided labor disrupts the system. Loss of a member from a group of peers diminishes the society but does not disrupt it.

The second stage of old age comes when the old person is no longer able to carry out the minimum adaptive behavior necessary to maintain health, or cleanliness or propriety. At that point, someone else must enter the conjugal society to perform adaptive functions for both man and wife, and thus they return to the asymmetrical social condition of infants—their contribution to the solidarity lies not in what they do but what they are—members by birthright of a family. A very old person with no family ties has the pathos of an orphaned child, and society deals with him accordingly. This terminal dependency excludes all other social relations. Indeed, among the extremely aged, "collective monologues" such as Piaget describes among children may replace conversation, for as Durkheim says— "society has retreated from the old person, or what amounts to the same thing, he has retreated from it."

Summarizing the shift in solidarity in more concrete terms, we may say that men at work are tied together by sentiments about the work itself and women by sentiments about children, schools,[28] and domestic matters. After work ceases, the bonds between a man and those he worked with must literally be reforged if they are to survive, because they must have new substance. After children leave home, while much must be rewrought between women, it is less than for men because they still have in common the roles of spouse and mother—although the latter may be somewhat attenuated.

Among kindred there are values and sentiments arising from many common experiences, and, therefore, it is easy for solidarity to persist after disengagement. In other words, it is the diffusely bonded solidarities that survive and the specifically bonded ties that wither. If a specific bond involves some divided labor, the attachment is stronger, but once the conditions of mutual dependency are removed, it is weakened. In diffusely bonded relationships, of which kinship is the prototype, common sentiments, values and traditions inevitably form around many activites and events. For this reason, such stable solidarities persist through role changes and become the salient relationships of old age. The energy to force such strong links as exist between siblings or very old friends because of common history, common experience, and interlocking membership, may be lost as soon as biological energy begins to fade.

It should be noted that there are certain "atemporal" roles available to men that do not become outmoded and can be the basis of a divided labor until extreme old age. The clergyman's role, for example, is concerned with persistent values, it resists obsolescence because it ties society to its timeless values. The clergyman is the instrumental leader in his family but with the larger society as the social system of reference, he performs an integrative function in an important socioemotional role. Such roles seem to perform for the whole society the function that women perform for the family—they maintain the pattern of values that inform the goals, and they reduce the tension generated by the effort of adaptation. Their content is the *lingua franca* of the general culture.

In this discursive account of the disengagement theory, I have raised more problems than I have begun to solve. The additions to the theory are untidily grafted on to the original formultaion without regard to whether or not they contradict it or shift its focus. The next task is to formalize the propositions and wherever possible cast them in terms that can be tested—but this is another undertaking for another time. Given the choice, I have taken what is for me the pleasanter alternative of thinking widely rather than rigorously, and in doing so I have drawn attention to the theory's need for greater rigor.

NOTES

1. The theory was first suggested in Elaine Cumming, Lois R. Dean, and David S. Newell, "Disengagement, a Tentative Theory of Aging," *Sociometry* 23, no. 1 (March 1960), and developed in greater detail in Elaine Cumming and William E. Henry, *Growing Old* (New York: Basic Books, 1961).

2. This means that they were able to live on their incomes from whatever source without seeking public assistance.

3. Obviously this is an oversimplification. There are many structural safeguards in any society to keep this kind of disruption to a minimum; included among them is the rational-legal system of authority.

4. The population of study was a representative sample of the Greater Kansas City metropolitan area with the lowest and the highest socioeconomic groups and all who could not fill their major roles on account of illness removed.

5. Philip Solomon et al., *Sensory Deprivation* (Cambridge, Mass.: Harvard University Press, 1961).

6. For a discussion of the implications of this typology of temperament for psychopathology see John Cumming and Elaine Cumming, *Ego and Milieu* (New York: Atherton Press, 1962).

7. I use this phrase in the way that Erikson does in *Childhood and Society* (New York: W. W. Norton, 1950). Roughly, it refers to the anxiety that attends the doubt that others will confirm in the future either the relationship presently established or the identity currently implied by the interaction.

8. It is fairly obvious that these proposed temperaments are related to the psychological dimension, introversion-extroversion.

9. This raises a problem of the difference between the *appearance* of engagement and the *experience* of it. This problem is enhanced by a tendency to contrast disengagement with activity (see Robert Havighurst, "Successful Aging," *Gerontologist* 1 (1961):8-13. In fact, activity and engagement are not in the same dimension. A disengaged person often maintains a high level of activity in a small number and narrow variety of roles, although it is doubtful if it is possible to be at once firmly engaged and inactive. In any event, the opposite of disengagement is engagement, a concept different from, though related to, the concept of activity. The result of confusing these two variables is that *active* people are judged to

be *engaged*. They may, however, be *relatively disengaged impingers*. They may also, depending upon the type of activity, be exceptionally healthy or restless. There is no real way to judge, because the issue has not been put to the test. Unfortunately, many of the populations used for gerontological studies are volunteers and thus can be expected to include a disproportionately large number of impingers. For example, Marc Zborowski (in "Aging and Recreation," *Journal of Gerontology* 17, no. 3 [July 1962]) reports that a group of volunteers reported little change over time of their recreational activites and preferences. The author concludes from this that the subjects are not disengaging, using the concept in Havighurst's sense as the opposite of active. His finding is only unexpected inasmuch as the disengagement theory would predict a *rise* in recreational activities after retirement among a population that might include numerous disengaging impingers. In contrast to this report is a careful study of a *general population* of older people in New Zealand (see "Older People of Dunedin City: A Survey," J. R. McCreary and H. C. A. Somerset [Wellington: Dept. of Health, 1955]) among whom only 10 percent belonged to, or wanted to belong to, recreational groups, and only 9 percent of those not working would seek work if the restrictions on their pensions would allow them.

10. Talcott Parsons, "Toward a Healthy Maturity," *Journal of Health and Human Behavior* 1, no. 3 (1960).

11. Of course, at all times in the life span, priorities must be set up, because it is impossible to do more than one thing in one space of time. But as long as there is the possibility of postponement until a later date, the problem of allocation has little poignancy.

12. William E. Henry, "Conflict, Age, and the Executive," *Business Topics* (Michigan State University, n.d.).

13. No concept of "economy of libido" is implied here. The inference is quite simply that a person with a store of memories is less likely to give full attention to the world around him than the person who has fewer symbolic residues to capture his attention. Of course, there are obvious limits on preoccupation with the past including some minimum level of interaction that seems almost mandatory for life itself.

14. See Emile Durkheim, *Suicide* (Glencoe, Ill.: Free Press, 1951), pp. 157-59.

15. When the Kansas City respondents were asked the question, "What do you think of the younger generation?" the middle-aged people gave concrete examples of youthful behavior that they found compelling or unattractive while the older people answered in large generalizations, usually negative.

16. The whole problem of retraining for automation is complex. On the surface, retraining an older person seems wasteful, but if the rate of technical change remains the same, retraining may be necessary so

frequently that older workers may economically be included in the program. Retraining may not be necessary if Parsons is right in suggesting that as American society becomes more sophisticated there will be more variety of roles for old people just as there are more available to women past the childbearing age. If this is true, there would be demonstrable differences in the attitude toward older people between groups with different levels of sophistication and between countries with different kinds of cultural elaborations.

17. For a full discussion of this possibility, see Parsons, "Healthy Maturity."

18. It is interesting that American ideology holds that it is not good for an old person to live in his adult child's household. Nevertheless a very large number do so, and apparently successfully. In these cases there seems to be a tendency to define the situation as in some way extraordinary so as to keep honoring the shibboleth in the breach. See Seymour Bellin, "Family and Kinship in Later Years," (Ph. D. diss., Columbia University,).

19. In this general statement, the word "system" means any social system. In any particular case the system must be specified because the same acts can be part of an instrumental role viewed from one system and a socioemotional role viewed from another. The clergyman plays an integrative role in society in general, but an instrumental role vis-à-vis his family—and all his professional acts can thus be categorized differently according to the system of reference.

20. This point is strikingly made by Peter Townsend who has described (*The Family Life of Old People* [Glencoe, Ill.: Free Press, 1957]) how working-class women in London pass smoothly through the roles of daughter, mother, and grandmother. The pattern in America may be somewhat less straightforward, but the disjunction for women still seems far less acute than for men.

21. When the data from which the disengagement theory was induced were gathered, the responsibility of women to feed their husbands in such a way as to avoid coronary heart disease had not appeared in the mass media. There may be a tendency since then for widowhood under some circumstances to be construed as role failure.

22. This does not mean that women go out and "join" a group of widows. My impression is that they reestablish old bonds, or move closer to other women who have lost their husbands or never married. They probably tighten their ties to their children at this time also.

23. In the area of study, a shelter, which is really a "poorhouse," and even an old people's home, is considered much less desirable than a nursing home or hospital.

24. This may be an exaggerated phenomenon in America. In England, for example, the rates for men and women are more nearly parallel.

25. Charles Lamb, "The superannuated man," in *Aging in Today's Society,* ed. Clark Tibbitts and Wilma Donahue (New York: Prentice-Hall, 1960), pp. 99-100.

26. It is, of course, impossible to imagine a division of labor between people who are not bound by any common sentiments.

27. This is not so for the conjugal society toward the end of life. Immediately after retirement, husbands seem redundant to many women who have developed lives of their own since the termination of child raising. However, extremely old people, with no division of labor at all, become dependent upon one another to such an extent that if one dies the other is likely to follow quickly. This special case of a very binding mechanical solidarity is probably the result of these extremely old people being almost merged into one identity like twin infants.

28. American society strongly encourages women to belong to school-related organizations and thus to meet the mothers of other children.

THE SUBCULTURE OF THE AGING: A FRAMEWORK FOR RESEARCH IN SOCIAL GERONTOLOGY*

Arnold M. Rose

This paper presents a theoretical framework for research in social gerontology which would parallel, but not necessarily be in opposition to, researches which are centered around the concepts of loss of social roles, social adjustment and maladjustment, and disengagement.

The Developing American Subculture of the Aging

A subculture may be expected to develop within any category of the population of a society when its members interact with each other significantly more than they interact with persons in other categories. This occurs under two possible sets of circumstances: (1) The members have a positive affinity for each other on some basis (e.g., gains to be had from each other, long-standing friendships, common background and interests, common problems and concerns). (2) The members are excluded from interaction with other groups in the population to some significant extent. In American society, both sets of circumstances occur for a large and perhaps growing proportion of older people, although for some (who thereby become isolates)

* Arnold M. Rose, "The Subculture of the Aging: A Framework for Research in Social Gerontology," in *Older People and Their Social Worlds*, ed. A. M. Rose and W. Peterson (Phila., Pa.: F. A. Davis Company, 1965), pp. 3-16.

only the second develops with age, and these individuals never come to express an affinity with other older people. In other words, the aging subculture is developing and is, at the present moment, far from comprehensive in content or in coverage of older people.

The positive affinity which many older people feel for each other is based in some measure on their physical limitations, and hence common interests in a physically easy and calm existence, partly on their common role changes, and partly on having had common generational experiences in a rapidly changing society. The rejection by younger age groups is based to some extent on the same factors, but also on the low value given to inefficacy in our general culture. Retired people—who can no longer earn a living, whose physical abilities to "get around" and engage in sports are limited, and whose prospects for new achievements and success in competition are slim—experience a sharply diminished status. This is abetted by the absence of special marks of prestige attached to aging which are found in other societies— such as the attribution of special wisdom, the automatic accession to a higher political position, or the use of titles of respect (such as the title "U" in Burma, applied to all persons over 40 years of age). Thus for both sets of reasons, the elderly tend to interact with each other increasingly as they grow older, and with younger persons decreasingly, and hence develop a subculture. The greater the separation of older people from other age categories, both as individuals and as a social group, the greater the extent and depth of subcultural development. In other words, older Americans are now historically in the process of changing from a category into a group, although the extent of this change varies from individual to individual. Every group has a subculture—a set of meanings and values which is distinctive to that group—although not every group is necessarily conscious of its distinctiveness or of the fact that it is a group. This chapter will consider some of the respects in which older people in the United States are developing a subculture, and will pose the question as to whether or not they are becoming conscious of themselves as a distinctive group.

There are certain trends occurring in our society which are tending to create some of the conditions necessary for the development of a subculture. These trends are of three types—demographic, ecological, and social organizational—and will merely be listed here with a minimum of discussion. First, there is the growing number and proportion of persons who live beyond the age of 65, from 4.1 percent in 1900 to over 9 percent in 1960. This is relevant only in that there are more people eligible for creating an aging subculture, that is, there is more opportunity now than formerly for older people to interact with each other. Second, because of the advances in preventive medicine and in acute, communicable disease control, and because of general progress in sanitation and increased use of birth control (reducing the age at which most women stop bearing children), there has been a tendency for a much larger proportion of the population to reach the age of 65 in physical vigor and health, and hence capable of creating a subculture. Third, the same causes have resulted in a larger proportion of older people attaining an advanced age when they are likely to develop chronic illnesses[1] which cost a great deal more to treat than acute illnesses because of the long period of treatment. This is a new major common grievance to older people. It was a major source of the political battle in the Congress, beginning in 1957, over the Forand Bill and its successors in dealing with medical care for the aging, which has given many older people a sense of common lot and common interest.

Fourth, there have been some self-segregating trends among older people. "Retirement communities" in Florida and in other areas of good climate *to* which older people migrate are well-known examples of this self-segregation. Now there are studies showing that older people often do not follow general patterns of migration *out* of a rural county and so are left behind to form the dominant element in the population of the area.[2] This trend also seems to be operating *within* a metropolitan area: apparently it is the young adults, mainly, who move to the suburbs and the outlying sections of the city, leaving the older people concentrated in the inner section of the city.[3] Further, older suburbanites now show some tendency to move back to the central city. This ecological accessibility of older people to each other helps to create the conditions necessary for the development of a subculture.

44

Fifth, there has been an increase in compulsory and voluntary retirement, and a corresponding decline in self-employed occupations (at which a healthy older person could work as long as he wished past the age of 65). The decline in employment of older people, independent of its other effects and values, has meant a loss of integration into the general society because an occupation necessarily obliges one to interact with others of various ages. Sixth, because of the long-run improvement in the standard of living and in educational level, an increasing proportion of people reach the age of 65 with the means (in terms of funds, knowledge, and leisure) to do something they consider constructive, and what they do often becomes part of their subculture. Seventh, the development of social welfare services for the elderly (particularly group work activities that bring older people together) serves to enhance their opportunities for identifying with each other and for developing a subculture. The increasing number of retirement homes, nursing homes, housing projects, specialized recreational facilities, and meeting places for the elderly—sponsored by churches, fraternal associations, and other private associations as well as by government—tend to separate older people from the rest of the society. Eighth, for various reasons associated with increasing migration and apartment dwelling, there has been less of a tendency for adult children to live in the homes of their parents who retain their positions as heads of the household, and more of a tendency for older people to live by themselves, or for intergenerational dwelling-together to take the form of the elderly parents living as dependents in the homes of their adult offspring.[4] This separation of vigorous older people from constant[5] contact with their adult offspring helps to create the conditions for the development of a subculture.

Not all of the distinctive behavior of the elderly can be attributed to the aging subculture; the following may also be involved: (1) biological changes and personal idiosyncrasies associated with physical aging; (2) general cultural norms for the behavior of the elderly held by all in the society (for example, conservative styles of clothing which are favored for the elderly by all age levels); (3) generational changes which cause older people to act out a "general culture" appropriate for an earlier

45

period but which has become "old-fashioned" for contemporaries. This last-mentioned point brings out the fact that American society, like most others, is to some extent age-graded throughout. People tend to associate to a large extent with those of their own age level at every age. However, we shall be asserting throughout this paper that there are certain cultural trends which are making the elderly more segregated from other age categories than is true for the rest of the society.[6]

Since a person only gradually becomes old, and must continue to play some role in the general society, the elderly retain a good deal of the general culture and some even carry on roles typical of younger age groups. The extent of isolation from the larger society—for example, through congregate living or through differential migration—varies from one older person to the next. Thus, different old people have different degrees of involvement in the aging subculture. An age-graded subculture must necessarily be limited as compared to a subculture which has members who live most or all of their lives in it (e.g., that of an ethnic group, a class, a region). In an age-graded subculture, the time it takes to be socialized into it and out of it and the limited period for which it is expected to be followed by an individual are factors which prevent the subculture from becoming highly elaborate or enveloping most of its followers completely. This is true of the teen-age subculture and of the young marrieds' subculture, as it is of the subculture of the past-65.

There may even be categorical differences in involvement of older people in the aging subculture, for example, the possible tendency for the wealthy and educated elderly to retain more contact with the larger society than do the poorer and ill-educated, and hence to acquire less of a distinctive aging subculture. Perhaps one of the most important bases of differentiation among older people in regard to the extent to which they participate in an aging subculture is the type of community they live in. Those in retirement communities, in rural communities from which younger people are rapidly emigrating, and in the central parts of big cities are most age-separated and hence are most likely to develop a subculture. Those, on the other hand, who live in typical small cities, villages, and rural areas, and in suburbs and the outlying parts of large cities are probably least age-separated. In the former settings, the elderly may so dominate the community that the culture of the entire community may be characterized by what we are calling the aging subculture: the commercial establishments, the recreational facilities, the newspapers, and many other local institutions may be marked by the domination of the elderly. This is more likely to be apparent in a small town than in a large city, even when the proportion of older people happens to be equally great in the latter. When there is a large proportion of the elderly in a large city, and the latter have developed a subculture, it is more likely to be segregated from the rest of the city. In a small town, the aging subculture could more readily become dominant. If this differential does in fact exist, it could be a function of the class composition of the elderly as well as a function of the size of the community. In the large city, it seems likely that the segregated elderly would include more lower-class persons, while in the small town, they would include more middle-class persons who could more readily dominate the town.

The aging subculture is a general one that cuts across other subcultures—those based on occupation, religion, sex, and possibly even ethnic identification—which are characteristic of the middle-aged population.[7] Insofar as older people are somewhat more likely to unite on the basis of age than on the basis of these other divisions, relatively speaking, they are likely to weaken the other subcultures as they substitute a new one for them. On the other hand, for some of the elderly, perhaps for those who have been socially mobile, there may be regression to earlier ethnic and class characteristics of their childhood which had been temporarily superseded in middle age.

Influences which keep the elderly in contact with the larger society, and thus tend to minimize the development of an aging subculture, include: (1) The contacts with the family, which are not reduced by the parents getting older and in some respects may increase as the adult children settle down after marriage and as the older man after retirement has more time for association with his family. Declining health may also force closer dependence on, and hence more frequent contact with, adult children. (2) The mass media, which seem to play an increasing role in contemporary society and which have a tendency to cut across all subcultural variations. (3) Continued employment, even on a part-time basis, which keeps the older person in contact with a work group, an occupational association, and the economic standards of the general society. (4) The increasing number of contacts with social welfare agencies, both public and private, which "do" things for the elderly. The social workers themselves are generally not elderly, although they often put the older people into closer contact with each other and tend to separate them from the rest of the society. (5) An attitude of active resistance toward aging and toward participation in the aging subculture. This might result from unusually good physical and mental health so that the person is biologically younger than his chronological years would indicate, from an opportunity to have a special identification with some younger group in the society, or from a rejection of the aging and the aging subculture. The latter alone, if not associated with some opportunity to have contacts with the general society beyond those afforded to most older people, will often result in isolation and group self-hatred.[8]

Characteristics of the Subculture of the Aging

Let us turn from a consideration of the general factors creating and influencing an aging subculture in our society to a consideration of some of the specific contents of that subculture. The areas of life chosen for analysis represent some of the variation in the facets of the aging subculture; they do not present a comprehensive picture. In one respect, a subculture may be said to mold the entire lives of those who participate in it, so that in singling out a few aspects of a subculture we are selecting only its more salient and distinctive ones. On the other hand, a subculture exists within a general culture, and the elderly whose subculture we are examining must also be understood to be Americans whose lives are dominated by a general American culture.

Just as the reasons for the formation of the aging subculture are both positive and negative, so the content of the subculture is both positive and negative. The positive things are those which older people enjoy doing together, or which the whole society encourages them to do together, or which they interpret as being a special opportunity for those with their status. The negative things are those which the elderly do together because they find themselves rejected or otherwise in opposition to the rest of the society. While it may not always be possible to specify that a given behavior pattern or way of thinking of older people is positive or negative, it should be recognized that to some extent the aging subculture is a contraculture—in opposition to the rest of the society. In some ways the contraculture of the aging is similar to that of other discriminated-against groups in the society, certain ethnic minorities, for example. But the aging are not distinguished from the rest of the society solely by discrimination and segregation, so that their subculture has a positive aspect even though distinctive from the general culture.

First, the status system of the elderly is only partially a carryover of that of the general society.[9] Two kinds of status must be recognized for the retired elderly—one accorded them by the general society (which is generally markedly lower than that for a younger person of like wealth, education, achievement, and so forth), and one developed out of the distinctive values of the aging subculture. Certainly wealth carries over from the general culture as an important factor in status, with some significant exceptions: (1) With income from occupation gone, the variation in incomes from investments, pensions, and Social Security tend to be significantly less for most persons than were previous incomes from occupations, and the reduced variation probably tends to diminish the use of wealth for invidious distinctions of status. (2) Some of the attitudes toward wealth must develop of the type "you can't take it with you," and yet expenditures for night life, travel, and other expensive amusements must be curtailed for reasons of health, so that wealth must have somewhat less importance than it did at any earlier age. Possibly occupational prestige also carries over into old age, but its effect is probably less when the occupation is no longer practiced by the individual and the occupation itself is changing. The same is true of the prestige arising from the former holding of power. As previous holding of power and earlier achievement fade into the past, they are of diminishing influence in conferring prestige.

General education probably carries over more since it is of current utility to the aging, but it, too, must have something of a dated quality. In preceding generations, youngsters were much less likely to be kept in school to the levels they are now likely to be, and the education they received is, in some respects at least, regarded as old-fashioned today.

These sources of status which carry over from the earlier years are probably of maximum influence for the elderly when they continue to live in the same community. If they have changed communities, occupational prestige after retirement must go down markedly, and the other factors be of reduced importance. If the aged individual is socially isolated, as sometimes happens, these factors in former status carry current prestige only as a sort of legend.

Two related factors may be hypothesized as having special value in conferring status within the subculture of the elderly. One is physical and mental health. This is not a highly significant value for most younger people (except for the relatively small percentage who do not have it, and they react as individuals, not as members of a group with a subculture).[10] But good health is sufficiently rare, and becomes rarer with advancing age, so that old people make much of it and exhibit a special admiration for those who remain healthy. A sickly old man who cannot take care of himself has little status among the elderly (or among any others in the society, except perhaps his family) even if he is wealthy, whereas a vigorous old man with keen senses will be accorded high status among his compeers even though he lives exclusively on a modest pension.

The second distinctive factor in the status system of the aging is social activity. This is, of course, partly based on physical and mental health, but it includes much more. Especially in recent years, many of the aging accord high status to those of their number who are willing and able to assume leadership in various associations of a social influence or expressive character composed primarily of the aging. We shall give more extended consideration to this in our later discussion of aging group consciousness. Here it may simply be noted that, because social activity among some of the elderly is based partly on physical and mental health, some of those who rise to prominence among the aging are persons of little previous eminence or skill and experience in group leadership.

There may be other distinctive factors in the status system in the aging subculture which deeper observation would reveal. One approach would be through an examination of the social participations and communications of the elderly. Little is known about this among social gerontologists, but there must be quantities of data in the commercial studies of audiences for the mass media and in other types of public opinion polls. A content analysis of the many magazines for the elderly, which have appeared during the last decade or so, should reveal much about the specific values of the aging subculture and suggest some of the processes through which that subculture is emerging.

Another important social value toward which the attitudes of the aging must differ markedly from those of the rest of the population is sex. While recent studies[11] suggest that older people are more capable of having sex relations and actually do have them than was formerly supposed, it seems likely that interest in sex declines with the years. Many older people in the United States today were raised in an era of sexual puritanism and the "double-standard," in which it was assumed to be natural that men had strong sex drives until they grew impotent in old age, while women naturally did not have significant sexual drives and they lost what they did have when they became older. This generational factor helps to keep interest in sex low. There are, of course, a few sexual radicals among older people, who keep up a high level of sexual interest and acitivity.

It was estimated for 1959 that about 2.4 percent of all marriages taking place in the United States were those involving a bride or groom, or both, over the age of 65. Of these marriages, about one-third joined brides and grooms who were both over 65. Of the approximately 16,000,000 older people in the United States, about one-third of 7 percent got married during the typical recent year of 1959. Of course, the majority of older people were already married, and hence not currently eligible for marriage. About 93 percent of the older brides and grooms had been married at least once before.[12]

After retirement, when men spend as much time around the house as do housewives, and there is much less of a clear-cut difference in economic roles, the social and sexual distinctions between men and women are diminished. Many older men and women, particularly in the lower income groups, seem to seek sex differentiation by means of their social life. The unbalanced sex ratio among older people (121 women past 65 for every 100 men) must have some effect on their attitudes toward sex and sex differentiation. Perhaps it is simply that men are pampered and fussed over by their female associates; perhaps it is a woman-dominated social relationship in which men's wishes and interests are ignored because they are so greatly outnumbered.

There are many other areas of the aging subculture that could be analyzed and speculated about. Their self-conceptions, their attitudes toward death, marriage,[13] their interpersonal relationships and leisure activities,[14] their argot, their distinctive rituals,[15] their hobbies,[16] and scores of other important factors in their behavior and outlook must be significantly affected by the particular social settings in which they interact. There is perhaps less basis for speculation about these topics, in the almost complete absence of empirical data, than about the topics we have already considered. There is one topic, however, for which there is some empirical evidence available, one which is of growing significance for the aging. This is what I call "aging group consciousness," and to define it effectively I must first talk about the "aging self-conception." These concepts, as aspects of the aging subculture, will take up the remainder of this paper.

The Aging Self-Conception

The age of 65 has more or less come to be considered as the age of entering "old age" in American society. It seems likely that the Social Security Act of 1935 did more to define this limit than any other single event. Most private pension schemes adopted or proposed since that date have taken the age of 65 as the date of retirement. Compulsory retirement requirements have become much more frequent since 1935, and they have often adopted 65 years as the age of effectuation. The double exemption on the income tax for those past the age of 65 did not become highly significant until the great increase of tax rates during the Second World War, but then it served to accentuate the importance of turning 65. Thus a legal definition helped to differentiate more sharply a social category. But even today not all persons past the age of 65 are considered elderly. The exceptions among men are mainly those who are not retired, which is mainly among the self-employed, and generally in the upper-status occupations. Among nongainfully employed women, for whom there is no definite age of retirement or who in effect retired much earlier when their youngest child left home, entrance into the social category of "the elderly" is not so clear-cut.

Regardless of precisely at what age they begin to think of themselves as elderly, for most Americans there tends to be a marked change in self-conception. This includes a shift in thinking of oneself: as progressively physically and mentally handicapped, from independent to dependent, and from aspiring to declining.[17] Because most of the changes associated with the assumption of the role and self-conception of being elderly are negatively evaluated in American culture, and because there is no compensatory attribution of prestige, as in other societies, the first reaction of many older people is some kind of disengagement and depression. The disengagement is by no means completely voluntary. The older person is *pushed* out of his occupations, out of the formal and informal associations connected with occupation, and even out of leadership roles in many kinds of nonoccupational associations. It is a matter mainly of social fact, not so much of natural inevitability, that many Americans reaching the age of 65 shift into a social role of disengagement.[18] The actual physical and mental decline is not generally very great under today's conditions of advanced medical science and social welfare, and in any case usually develops gradually rather than suddenly. But the culture defines the past-65 person as elderly, and this definition is applied in a variety of ways. Some, of course, resist the shift to the new role and the negative self-conception; they try, whether successful or not, to hold onto the pre-65 role and self-concpetion. When senility, feebleness, chronic illness, or mental illness sets in, of course disengagement from the society is the only possible condition for all but the most unusual older person.

Aging Group Consciousness

During the past decade in the United States, we have been witnessing the growth of a new phenomenon which is greatly expanding the scope of the aging subculture. This is what may be called "aging group consciousness"or "aging group identification." Some older people have begun to think of themselves as members of an aging group. In their eyes the elderly are being transformed from a category into a group. Probably only a minority of the elderly have so far taken this social psychological step, but their number is growing. One of the early manifestations of this attitude is for them to join some kind of recreational or other expressive association in which they can interact almost exclusively with persons of similar age. Then they begin to take some pride in the association, as evidenced, for example, by the titles of such organizations—"Golden Age Club," "Senior Citizens Club," or "Live Long and Like It" club. A social worker may have helped to get the club started, but the elderly sometimes take it over and the social psychological transformation toward group pride is theirs. This group identification of the elderly may take place within organizations that are not age-graded—that is, the elderly members simply interact more with each other than with the other members because of their physical limitations or their common attitudes and interests. But they are more likely to develop group identification in organizations that are set up exclusively for the elderly. There their distinctive characteristics and interests are clearly made evident to them, and they can develop their distinctiveness unhindered by obligations to a non-age-graded group.

The next phase occurs when they begin to talk over their common problems in a constructive way. Probably elderly people have been complaining for some time about their reduced income, their inadequate housing, the difficulty of paying for medical care if they should be struck with a chronic illness, their reduced prestige and general social neglect. But recently some have come to talk about such problems not only with reference to themselves as individuals, but with an awareness that these things occur to them as a social group. Furthermore, they have begun to talk in terms of taking social action, not merely individual action, to correct the situation. Thus far, this advanced minority has supported certain government actions, both legislative and executive. Their current support of Congressional bills for financing health care is to be seen in this context. It is all the more significant that they are radical supporters of this legislation for the benefit of the elderly when the majority of them are political conservatives on most other issues.[19] The elderly seem to be on their way to becoming a voting bloc with a leadership that acts as a political pressure group. Even the elderly who are organized into recreational groups sometimes shift naturally into political pressure groups. For example, in San Francisco and Los Angeles social clubs for the elderly formed a pressure group to get reduced bus fares for those past 65, ostensibly so that their low-income members could afford to get to the meetings. It remains to be seen whether the future political activities of the aging become integrated into the existing political parties, or whether they become segregated as in the McLain movement in California.[20]

The trends listed on an earlier page as contributing to the development of an aging subculture are also specifically contributory to an aging group self-consciousness. All of these trends have combined to create new problems for the older population at the same time as it has given them a new, distinctive position in the society, set apart from those under the age of 65. These are the conditions which enhance the likelihood that the elderly will develop a sense of group consciousness.

For the growing minority that has reacted against the negative self-conception characteristic of the aging in our society and has seen the problems of aging in a group context, there are all the signs of group identification. There is a desire to associate with fellow-agers, especially in formal associations, and to exclude younger adults from these associations. There are expressions of group pride and corollary expressions of dismay concerning the evidence of "moral deterioration" in the outgroup, the younger generations. With this group pride has come self-acceptance as a member of an esteemed group, and the showing off of prowess as an elderly person (for example, in "life begins at eighty" types of activities). There are manifestations of a feeling of resentment at "the way elderly people are being mistreated," and indications of their taking social action to remove the sources of their resentment. These are the signs of group identification that previous sociological studies have found in ethnic minority groups.[21] I do not mean to exaggerate this parallel, or to state that most older people today show most of these signs. But the evidence of the growing group-identification among older people in the United States today is available to even the casual observer.

Future Research on the Subculture of the Aging

Sociologists now need to go beyond casual observation and engage in systematic studies of this formation of group identification, of this transformation of a social category into a social group. The whole area of the subculture of the aging needs objective investigation, in the same manner in which sociologists have already studied ethnic, regional, and occupational subcultures. The opportunity to study these things in birth and in development should not be missed. One reason they have been neglected by sociological researchers thus far is that the aging have been a low-prestige segment of the population, and only those interested in social reform have been willing to study them. But the objective trends seem to point to a higher status for the aging in the future, so we can anticipate that even the sociologists will find it respectable to conduct research in this field.

In conducting this research, it is to be recalled that by no means all persons past the age of 65 participate in the subculture. There are those who retain the identifications and the cultural behavior patterns of middle-aged persons. It may be that, as the social movement of aging group consciousness gains more prestige for the elderly, the number of the past-65 who are not forcibly disengaged from the general society but are allowed to continue their prestige roles in that society will increase. If this happens, the self-segregating aspects of the aging group-consciousness movement will decline and ultimately disappear, and the movement itself thus become automatically self-liquidating. Secondly, there are those elderly persons who "disengage" and become relatively isolated from all cultural patterns and all associations except those of the family, either by their own volition or as a consequence of rejection by the larger society, or because of physical and mental decline which forces disengagement. Thirdly, there are some who combine both of these sets of characteristics because they *never* were "engaged" in most of the institutional and associational structures of the society, and remain so after they reach the age of 65. Those elderly persons who develop and participate in an aging subculture, such as we have described in these pages, are different from the individuals in these other three categories. We need to know something about the *characteristics* of these people and the *conditions* under which they form or participate in the subculture. We should also remember that individuals participate in the subculture to different degrees, and the factors associated with this *extent* and *form* of participation can be studied at the same time. Insofar as we approach the study of the aging subculture with these questions, the observations of this paper may be considered as hypotheses for testing in order to develop nomothetic generalizations, rather than as statements of empirical fact which contribute to a historical description of a single society at a given time.

The extent of participation in an aging subculture varies with types of communities—e.g., declining rural areas, central cities, retirement towns—and a delineation of characteristics of their residents and conditions under which they participate in an aging subculture will further add to our knowledge. We have hypothesized, too, that several significant trends now affecting American society will favor the conditions under which elderly people engage in a subculture. These trends need to be studied for their effect and for their relationship to the aforementioned conditions under which the aging are found currently to engage in subcultural behavior.

NOTES

1. Whereas in 1901 only 46.0 percent of deaths were caused by chronic illnesses, the proportion had risen to 81.4 percent by 1955. Source: Metropolitan Life Insurance Company, Statistical Bulletin no. 39 (August 1958), p. 9.

2. Jon A. Doerflinger and D. G. Marshall, *The Story of Price County, Wisconsin,* Agricultural Experiment Station, University of Wisconsin Research Bulletin no. 220 (1960).

3. This does not apply to certain minority groups who are prevented from moving freely to the suburbs.

4. This is here suggested to be a long-run trend, not necessarily as yet a dominant factor nor always a short-run trend. A study by Shanas suggests that most intergenerational dwelling together still takes the form of adult children living in the homes of their aging parents. See Ethel Shanas, *Family Relationships of Older People* (New York: Health Information Foundation, 1961), especially p. 12.

5. Many recent studies, by Marvin Sussman, Eugene Litwak, and others, show that there is a great deal of intergenerational *visiting.* As we have suggested elsewhere ("Reactions to the mass society." *The Sociological Quarterly* 3 (1962):316-30) this is probably on the increase after a period (roughly 1880-1940) in which intergenerational visiting reached a low point.

6. Obviously the degree of age-group separation is a function of such mechanical factors as the number of age groups and the number of persons in each age group, as well as of cultural and demographic factors. In this paper, only the latter are considered.

7. For case evidence of this, see Gordon J. Aldridge, "Informal Social Relationships in a Retirement Community," *Marriage and Family Living* 21 (1959):70-73.

8. By "group self-hatred" I mean a strongly negative attitude toward the self because one has a negative attitude toward the group or category which nature and society combine to place one in. The concept grew up in dealing with certain social and psychological phenomena in minority groups. See, for example, Arnold M. Rose, *The Negro's Morale* (Minneapolis: University of Minnesota Press, 1949), pp. 85-95.

9. For case evidence of this, see Aldridge, *op. cit.,* and G. C. Hoyt, "The Life of the Retired in a Trailer Park," *American Journal of Sociology* 59 (1954):361-70.

10. Cultural values have at least one characteristic in common with economic values: to have high value they must be relatively scarce. Thus, younger people do not gain much status merely by being healthy (because most of them are) unless they are prize specimens of good health.

11. Mainly the Kinsey studies: A. C. Kinsey, W. B. Pomeroy, and C. E. Martin, *Sexual Behavior in the Human Male* (Philadelphia: W. B. Saunders, 1948); A. C. Kinsey, W. B. Pomeroy, C. E. Martin, and P. H. Gebhard, *Sexual Behavior in the Human Female* (Philadelphia: W. B. Saunders, 1953).

12. These statistics are derived from "Cupid Comes to Older People," *Aging,* no. 93 (July 1962), pp. 8-9.

13. Robert W. Kleemeier, "Moosehaven: Congregate Living in a Community of the Retired," *American Journal of Sociology* 59 (1954):347-51.

14. Hoyt, *op. cit.;* L. C. Michelen, "The New Leisure Class," *American Journal of Sociology* 59 (1954):371-78; R. W. Kleemeier, ed. *Aging and Leisure* (New York: Oxford University Press, 1961).

15. Wayne Wheeler is undertaking a study of rituals among the aging.

16. Edwin Christ's study of hobbies among the aging is partially reported in Chapter 6 of A. M. Rose and W. Peterson, eds., *Older People and Their Social Worlds* (Philadelphia: F. A. Davis Co., 1965).

17. These changes in social role and self-conception have been discussed more fully in my paper, "The Mental Health of Normal Older Persons," *Geriatrics* 16 (1961):459-64. Also see Irving Rosow, "Retirement Housing and Social Integration," *Gerontologist* 1 (1961):85-91.

18. Compare Elaine Cumming et al., "Disengagement: A Tentative Theory of Aging," *Sociometry* 23 (1960):23-35; Elaine Cumming and William E. Henry, *Growing Old* (New York: Basic Books, 1961). Cumming's theory of disengagement applies to those elderly persons who are in good physical and mental health. Those in poor health are necessarily disengaged, of course, and thus their disengagement is not a matter of sociological theory but of biological fact. Cumming's theory also excludes family contacts from the definition of disengagement. With these qualifications, Cumming hypothesizes disengagement of the elderly to be a matter of "natural inevitability"—which places her theory in opposition to that presented in this paper.

19. Angus Campbell, "Psychological and Social Determinants of Voting Behavior" (paper presented at Fourteenth Annual Conference on Aging, University of Michigan, Ann Arbor, June 19, 1961).

20. F. A. Pinner, P. Jacobs, and P. Selznick, *Old Age and Political Behavior* (Berkeley: University of California Press, 1959).

21. Probably the first to note the minority group aspects of the aging was Milton L. Barron in "Minority Group Characteristics of the Aged in American Society," *Journal of Gerontology* 8 (1953):477-82. See also: Milton L. Barron, "Attacking Prejudices Against the Aged," in *Growing with the Years,* New York State Legislative Committee on Problems of Aging. Legislative Document no. 32, pp. 56-58, 1954; Leonard Z. Breen,

"The Aging Individual," in *Handbook of Social Gerontology*, ed. Clark Tibbitts (Chicago: University of Chicago Press, 1960), especially p. 157; Samuel M. Strong, "Types of Adjustment to Aging," Proceedings of the Minnesota Academy of Science, 35-36, 398-405 (1957-58), especially p. 399; James H. Woods, *Helping Older People Enjoy Life* (New York: Harper & Row, 1953), pp. 1-2.

AN EXPLORATION OF THE ACTIVITY THEORY OF AGING: ACTIVITY TYPES AND LIFE SATISFACTION AMONG IN-MOVERS TO A RETIREMENT COMMUNITY*[1]

Bruce W. Lemon, Vern L. Bengtson,
and James A. Peterson

This research examines the relationship between types of social activity and life satisfaction among a sample of individuals in a retirement community. The principal intent in the paper is the statement, formal and explicit, of a theory which has long been implicit in gerontological literature, the so-called activity theory of aging. The essence of this theory is that there is a positive relationship between activity and life satisfaction and that the greater the role loss, the lower the life satisfaction. A second goal of the paper is to empirically test hypotheses derived from the theory thus constructed, using secondary data, as a means of illustrating theory development applied to a common proposition in gerontology.

The Problem

Many researchers in gerontology have been concerned with the association between social activity and life satisfaction. Over two decades ago, Havighurst and Albrecht (1953) made the first explicit statement concerning the importance of social role participation in positive adjustment to old age. Since that time,

* Bruce W. Lemon, Vern L. Bengtson, and James A. Peterson, "An Exploration of the Activity Theory of Aging: Activity Types and Life Satisfaction Among In-Movers to a Retirement Community," *Journal of Gerontology* 27 (1972):511-23.

several investigators have affirmed the general validity of this statement in varied contexts (Burgess, 1954; Kutner, 1956; Lebo, 1953; Reichard, Livson, & Peterson, 1962; Tallmer & Kutner, 1970; Tobin & Neugarten, 1961). A few have challenged the position (for example, Cumming & Henry, 1961; Neugarten & Havighurst, 1969). Maddox (1963) observes that most previous research supports the importance of social role participation in adjustment to old age and that implied in the theoretical orientation of most of the research is the assumption that

> . . . the social self emerges and is sustained in a most basic way through interaction with others . . . (conversely) structural constraints which limit or deny contacts with the environment tend to be demoralizing and alienating.

It seems clear, however, that adequate theoretical formulation built upon these and related concepts is still lacking. The deficiency of adequately formalized, let alone articulated, theory has been noted by several scholars in the field. Maddox (1963), for example, observes wryly that "relevant gerontological literature is not distinguished by explicit statements of theoretical orientation."

It is the purpose of the present research to partly fill this void by presenting a formal axiomatic statement of activity theory and to test a small subset of hypotheses derived from the theory using secondary data.

Previous Research

On the basis of past investigation, one is led to the conclusion that activity in general, and interpersonal activity in particular, seem to be consistently important for predicting an individual's sense of well-being in later years. Burgess (1954) and Lebo (1953) reported a greater amount of time in social and voluntary organizations to be characteristic of subjects with high personal adjustment. Kutner et al. (1956), as well as Reichard et al. (1962), have presented data to indicate a direct relationship between high levels of activity and high degrees of morale. Other studies published during the 1960s continued to give empirical support to this general relationship. For example, Tobin and Neugarten (1961) found that, with advancing age, activity becomes increasingly important for predicting life satisfaction. Tallmer and Kutner (1970) find no confirmation for Cumming and Henry's prediction that high morale is found among the highly disengaged (i.e., withdrawn from social participation).

A longitudinal investigation by Maddox (1963) revealed that both interpersonal activity and noninterpersonal activity were significantly related to morale. Lowenthal and Haven (1968) found relationships with a close confidant to be positively associated with mental health and morale. That is, the maintenance of a stable, intimate relationship appeared to be more important for predicting high morale than was sheer frequent social interaction or the maintenance of present social roles. In a cross-cultural study, Havighurst, Neugarten, Munnichs, and Thomae (1969) report a substantial positive correlation between total activity in twelve social roles and general life satisfaction. Data from subjects of six different nation-cultures were analyzed. The relationship holds up in retirees from two very different occupational styles (Bengtson, Chiriboga, & Keller, 1969).

Certain demographic variables and social conditions have been specified by a number of researchers as factors which increase or decrease the general relationship between activity and life satisfaction. These conditions are usually referred to as role losses or role changes; they include phenomena such as widowhood, retirement, and failing health. Rosow (1967) found high morale to characterize 72 percent of the subjects who had lost no major role; only 30 percent of those with three or four major role losses had high morale. Phillips (1957) found all differences in the proportion of maladjusted respondents among those who have and have not undergone role changes to be statistically significant.

An issue related to the amount and type of interpersonal activity is the extent of change in activity. In general, the literature suggests that the presence of a role change is inversely related to morale, and usually serves to decrease the strength of the relationship between activity and life satisfaction (see Cavan 1962; Phillips 1957). It appears that a change in roles may involve a disturbance of interaction patterns and social rewards.

In contrast to the activity theory framework implied in much gerontological research, Cumming and Henry (1961) claimed that the degree of consistency between the simultaneous expectations of the individual and the society for disengagement (i.e., decreased interaction or activity) is the strategic correlate of successful aging. Cumming and Henry made a commendable attempt to formalize their theory, something no one with the implicit activity theory orientation had ever attempted. Although Cumming and Henry report some empirical evidence supporting their Disengagement Theory, these findings conflict with those reported by many other investigators (Burgess, 1954; Kutner, 1956; Lebo, 1953; Maddox, 1965; Reichard et al., 1962; Tobin & Neugarten, 1961, to name just a few).

Disengagement theory has led to considerable discussion concerning the application and validity of disengagement as it relates to life satisfaction (Bengtson, 1969; Maddox, 1964; Neugarten & Havighurst, 1969; Rose, 1964; Youmans, 1969). Perhaps the most general conclusion is that

> In the balance, disengagement theory has been found wanting empirically and its original formulation is rarely defended by anyone (Maddox, 1969).

Axiomatic Statement of Activity Theory

Of the many priorities for research effort in the field of aging, perhaps few are as crucial as the development of formalized, explicit theory. The reasons for this are summarized in the conclusion section of this paper. We can define theory as

> a set of interrelated constructs (concepts) definitions, and propositions that present a systematic view of phenomena by specifying relations among variables, with the purpose of explaining and predicting phenomena (Kerlinger, 1964).

There are many types, strategies, and purposes of theory in social research. Each has its advantages and limitations. The specific form of theory construction that will be utilized here, axiomatic, has been elaborated by Zetterberg (1965). The axiomatic theory presented below is in part constructed on the basis of findings reported in previous research and in part based on what might be called the activity model implicit in many studies used to explain these findings.

In addition to choosing the method of theory construction, it is necessary to define the substantive frame of reference that is appropriate to the constructs and concepts under investigation. This allows the research to be placed within the context of a much broader frame of discourse in the discipline. Concepts and issues from the general theoretical orientation are applied to the specific phenomena under investigation. Often researchers do not make explicit the substantive theory within which they are working. In this research, an interactionist framework is utilized, drawing primarily from the statement of the theory found in McCall and Simmons (1966) and in Rose (1962). This is, perhaps, more of a frame of reference or a model of social reality than a theory in the formal sense of the word. Concepts derived from this frame of reference are quite difficult to operationalize successfully.

Definition of Concepts

The first step in formal theory presentation is a nominal definition of terms. The central concepts to be utilized in this theory—activity, role supports, self-concept, role change, and life satisfaction—are defined below.

Activity is defined as any regularized or patterned action or pursuit which is regarded as beyond routine physical or personal maintenance. The present study involves three separate types of activity: (1) informal activity includes social interaction with relatives, friends, and neighbors; (2) formal activity includes social participation in formal voluntary organizations; and (3) solitary activity includes such pursuits as watching television, reading, and hobbies of a solitary nature. Note that there is an ordering in terms of interpersonal intimacy or intensity; this should be kept in mind throughout the discussion to follow. Note also that there is an implied gradient of frequency of activity in each type. Thus, some activities are more intimate than others; some activities occur more frequently than others.

65

Role support is defined as "the expressed support accorded to an individual by his audience for his claims concerning his role identity" (McCall & Simmons, 1966). Role identity, the central concept of the interactionist framework, may be considered as the character and the role that an individual devises for himself as an occupant of a particular social position. Put differently, it is his imaginative view of himself, as he thinks of being and acting as an occupant of a social position (McCall & Simmons, 1966).

Self-concept is defined as "that organization of qualities (i.e., role identities) that the individual attributes to himself" (Kinch, 1963).

Role loss is defined as an alteration in the set of behavior patterns expected of an individual by virtue of the loss of some status position within a given social structure. For example, a major role loss occurs when a male has his status of worker changed to the status of retiree.

Life satisfaction is defined as the degree to which one is presently content or pleased with his general life situation.

Interrelation of Concepts

Once concepts are defined, there should be a statement of the relationship among concepts. Then narrative justification should be made for these statements.

The justification should be as general as possible, relating to the substantive theoretical frame of reference employed. In this case justification is presented using concepts from interactionist theory.

The self-concept and role support. One's self-concept can be viewed as a variety of role identities acquired during one's lifetime. When we interact with strangers, only general social roles are taken into account; but as we come to know others more intimately we "act toward them not merely in terms of their social roles but also in terms of their role identities" (McCall & Simmons, 1966). The more personal in nature the activity, the more specific and effective the responses of others are for reaffirming one's role identities and thus one's general self-concept.

66

Individuals form their self-concepts or social selves through interpreting the reactions of others toward them. Throughout the course of the life cycle, interaction with others is what sustains one's social self (Maddox, 1963; McCall & Simmons, 1966). Although self-conceptions are relatively stable by adulthood, they must still be "reaffirmed from time to time by the confirming responses of other people" (Shibutani 1961). Thus, the more one interacts with others or is exposed to the responses of others, even in adulthood, the greater the opportunity for reaffirming specific role identities.

Types of activity as sources of role supports. Activity in general, and interpersonal activity in particular, offer channels for acquiring role supports or reinforcements which sustain one's self-concept. The more intimate the nature of the activity, the more role supports one receives because specific role identities are being taken into account by the audience. Both types of interpersonal activity (formal and informal) offer greater potential for developing role supports than does activity of a solitary nature. Solitary activity cannot offer as much role support since it can involve only symbolic or mentally constructed audiences. In solitary activity the confirming responses of others are not actually present; this serves to make this type of activity less important as a source of role supports.

Informal activity is frequently on a personal or intimate level and is thus the most important type of activity for reinforcing the self-concept. The greater intimacy of informal activity usually involves more primary group relationships and spontaneity, which, in effect, makes the role supports more specific for confirming one's role identities. In formal activity, role supports are usually geared toward more generalized social roles.

In sum, activity of an interpersonal nature holds the greatest potential for offering role supports, with informal activity being more effective than formal activity (i.e., participation in voluntary organizations). Solitary activity is the least effective of the three activity types for offering role supports; however, a minimum of role support is possible because the actor is imagining the confirming responses of others.

In addition to the intimacy of activity, the frequence of activity is also obviously related to potential role supports. The greater the frequency of activity, the greater the opportunity and probability that role supports will result from the interaction. Both the intimacy or nature of the activity and the frequency of activity relate to differential role supports.

Role supports and life satisfaction. In complex societies such as the United States of America, many sets of differential norms exist and are imposed upon a given individual simultaneously. Hence, each individual has a variety of role supports for sustaining the self-concept. One's general satisfaction with life is contingent upon adequately satisfying a number of different role identities.

The more intimate and the most frequent one's total array of activities, the more likely it is that one will receive sufficient role supports for reaffirming all of one's various role identities. This in turn results in a more positive self-conception (unless, perhaps, one's role is defined as deviant).

An individual's degree of contentment and pleasure with his life situation is dependent upon a positive self-concept. In order for the self-concept to be sufficiently reinforced, organization of role identities must be validated by the audiences which react to the claims one has concerning specific role identities. The more a person's specific role identities (and thus his self-concept) are validated, the greater the probability of having high life satisfaction. On the other hand, a low degree of life satisfaction is encouraged by an individual's role identities not being validated by his audiences.

Role loss, role supports, and life satisfaction. So far only role supports provided via various types of activity have been taken into consideration in relation to differential life satisfaction. We move next to a consideration of how these mechanisms relate to life satisfaction under the condition of a major role change. Phillips (1957) contends that

> role changes may not only result in a temporary disturbance of rewards, but also in a lasting reduction; definite consequences for adjustment may be expected.

In other words, specific role supports or reinforcements which previously reaffirmed one's self-concept and role identities are severed due to the loss of the previous role. Logically, the general relationship between activity and life satisfaction is decreased as a result of this loss in role supports.

A role change causes a disruption in the equilibrium of role supports. When an individual is separated from his customary roles, either temporarily or permanently, he is likely to experience "an acute sense of hollowness and of being adrift" (McCall & Simmons, 1966).

The individual with a high frequency of intimate activity has a larger variety of mechanisms or channels for reestablishing an equilibrium in his role supports when a major role change occurs. From this reasoning, it follows that the person with high activity will not have as much of a decrease in life satisfaction as the person with low activity because his greater amount of role support acts as a cushioning mechanism or a source for shock absorption during the period of actual role change. The individual with high activity also has a larger repertoire of interactions and greater social life space which likewise facilitates the readjustment process; at the same time new role supports must be acquired. High activity may decrease frustration, anxiety, and the sense of hollowness likely to occur under such conditions.

It can be logically deduced from the foregoing that the frequency and intimacy of one's activity is directly associated with how one adapts to major role changes. If role changes were held constant, the individual with high activity would maintain greater life satisfaction than his counterpart with low activity.

Summary of the theory. Activity provides various role supports necessary for reaffirming one's self-concept. The more intimate and the more frequent the activity, the more reinforcing and the more specific will be the role supports. Role supports are necessary for the maintenance of a positive self-concept which in turn is associated with high life satisfaction.

In order to explain more fully the relationship between activity and life satisfaction, the concept of role change is utilized for analyzing conditions that further specify increases and decreases in this relationship. The presence of a role loss should diminish the magnitude of the relationship, but the direction of the relationship should remain positive.

Statement of Postulates and Theorems

Following definition of concepts and a narrative discussion of relationships among concepts, the next step in theory building involves the statement of relations in formal terms (often symbolic). This is done to clarify the logical relations among all concepts, considered two at a time, and to enable the next step, deriving hypotheses based on those relations.

On the basis of the foregoing interrelation of concepts, the following postulates and theorems relating activity to life satisfaction can be stated:

P 1. The greater the role loss, the less activity one is likely to engage in.

P 2. The greater the activity, the more role support one is likely to receive.

P 3. The more role support one receives, the more positive one's self-concept is likely to be.

P 4. The more positive one's self-concept, the greater one's life satisfaction is likely to be.

There are three first-order theorems that can be deduced from these postulates:

T 1. The greater the role loss, the less role support one is likely to receive.

T 2. The greater the activity, the more positive one's self-concept is likely to be.

T 3. The greater the role support, the greater one's life satisfaction is likely to be.

Two second-order theorems can then be deduced from combining the above:

T 4. The greater the role loss, the lesser the positive self-concept.

T 5. The greater the activity, the greater one's life satisfaction.

Finally, one third-order theorem can be deduced:

T 6. The greater the role loss, the lower the life satisfaction.

Hypotheses Tested In This Study

Because of the necessity of using a secondary data source in the present study, a complete testing of propositions resulting from the foregoing theory is impossible. It was decided therefore to concentrate on Theorem 5, since this is the most central part of the theory as it has been applied to problems of aging. The following hypotheses, then, are based on the proposition that the greater the frequency of activity, the greater one's life satisfaction is likely to be. Various specifications of this proposition, deriving from the differentiation of activity in terms of frequency and intimacy as discussed earlier, will be considered.

First, let us examine the case where activity is specified according to frequency within various categories. Since the types of activity are qualitatively distinguished in terms of intimacy (informal activity, formal activity, solitary activity), the frequency of activity cannot be summarized in additive fashion. Thus, specified hypotheses must be constructed for each type:

Ho 1: Informal activity (with friends, relatives, and neighbors) is directly associated with life satisfaction.

Ho 2: Formal activity (participation in voluntary organizations) is directly associated with life satisfaction.

Ho 3: Solitary activity (leisure pursuits, maintenance of household) is directly associated with life satisfaction.

Second, in addition to the frequency of activity, the nature or type of activity is also hypothesized to be differentially related to life satisfaction. That is, the more intimate the type of activity (i.e., the degree to which one has close personal interaction with others) the higher one's life satisfaction is expected to be. The following hypotheses are based upon further specification of concepts in Theorem 5.

Ho 4: Informal activity (with friends, relatives, and neighbors) is more highly associated with life satisfaction than formal activity.

Ho 5: Formal activity is more highly associated with life satisfaction than is informal activity.

71

Finally, additional specification of the foregoing relationships is made by analyzing the conditions of role change. Role changes are hypothesized to decrease the magnitude of the relationships between various types of activity and life satisfaction. The role change involving retirement for the male, and widowhood for the female, are considered to be the two most salient role changes. The following hypotheses are based upon Theorems 5 and 6:

Ho 6: The direct association between acitivity types and life satisfaction among females is less pronounced among widows and more pronounced among married women.

Ho 7: The direct association between activity types and life satisfaction among males is less pronounced among retirees and more pronounced among employed males.

In summary, it has been demonstrated that a formal axiomatic statement of activity theory can be constructed and various hypotheses can be derived from the central theorem of the theory to be tested empirically.

Sample Description And Data Collection

The sample used in this study was drawn from a larger population of persons who were potential in-movers to Laguna Hills Leisure World, a retirement community located in Southern California. Other publications (Hamovitch, Peterson, & Larson, 1969; Peterson, Hadiven, & Larson, 1968) have described in detail the methods and procedures of this research; only a brief summary will be made here. A systematic sample was defined, consisting of every third dwelling unit (after purchase but before the construction was completed). A sample N of 411 subjects (182 males and 229 females) were interviewed for the present study prior to their anticipated move to Leisure World.

Subjects were highly homogeneous concerning variables such as social class, marital status, religion, and race. Approximately 81 percent of the sample were married, 83 percent were middle and upper middle-class, 84 percent were Protestant, and 100 percent were Caucasian. The age distribution of the sample was as follows: 39 percent between 52 and 64 years of age, 46 percent between 65 and 75, and approximately 15 percent over 75 years. Seventy of the 182 males were fully retired; 52 of the 229 women were widowed.

Trained interviewers were employed to conduct structured interviews with respondents in their homes. Over 200 items were included in the interview schedule, which took an average of 1½ hours to complete.

The major dependent variable of this study, life satisfaction, was operationalized by using the 13-item Life Satisfaction Scale B (LSR–B) devised by Neugarten, Havighurst, and Tobin (1961). The major independent variables of this study (informal, formal, and solitary activity types) were measured by computing the frequency of interaction with close friends, ("About how many friends do you have that you would call really close, people you can confide in and talk over personal matters with? How often do you get together with your close friends?"), neighbors, relatives; number of memberships and degree of participation in formal organizations; and frequency of involvement with solitary activities (for the exact items see Peterson et al. 1968).

Goodman and Kruskal's (1954) coefficient or ordinal association (G or "gamma") was judged to be the most appropriate statistical test of significance. Calculations for level of significance of gamma were computed by transforming gamma values to Z scores (Sommers 1962). Levels of measurement for independent variables as well as the dependent variable are ordinal in nature.

Results

Tests of Hypotheses concerning Frequency of Activity and Life Satisfaction

Hypotheses 1 through 3 state that the greater the frequency of the various activity types (informal activity, formal activity, and solitary activity), the greater one's life satisfaction is likely to be. Table 1 shows gamma values and significance levels for these five relationships using the entire sample. Three tests are made of Hypothesis 1 in this table, keeping activity level with friends, relatives, and neighbors separate.

Only the relationship between informal activity with friends and life satisfaction was statistically beyond the .05 level (G=.21). This is, it will be noted, a very low relationship in terms of substantive significance. Informal activity with relatives or neighbors, formal activity, or solitary activity were not significantly associated with life satisfaction in the present sample.

Table 1.

Activity Types Related to Life Satisfaction: Gamma Values and Significance Levels for the Total Sample (N=411)

	Gamma Values	Significance Level
Informal activity with friends	.21	.05
Informal activity with relatives	.04	NS [a]
Informal activity with neighbors	.01	NS
Formal activity	.08	NS
Solitary activity	.01	NS

[a] Gamma is statistically nonsignificant at the .05 level or greater.

Because of the low levels of association considering the total sample, it was decided to specify conditions under which these relationships are more or less pronounced. Thus, three variables were used as control measures: sex, age, and perceived health status. When analyzing data for males and females separately, only the relationship between informal activity with friends and life satisfaction among females was statistically significant (G=.23).

Age was controlled by dichotomizing subjects into two categories, 64 and under and 65 and over. Only relationship between informal activity with friends and life satisfaction among persons over 65 (G=.22) was statistically significant beyond the .05 level.

Subjects were divided into good health and fair health categories to control for perceived health status. Again, only the association between informal activity with friends and life satisfaction was significant beyond the .05 level, and this only for subjects with fair health (G=.26) [this relationship between informal activity and life satisfaction was not statistically significant for subjects reporting good health (G=.18)].

In summary, none of the hypotheses relating frequency of activity to life satisfaction received consistent empirical support. Only informal activity with friends was associated with life satisfaction, regardless of specification variables, and this was at a substantively insignificant level.

Tests of Hypotheses concerning Type of Activity and Life Satisfaction

The degree of intimacy of activity is hypothesized to be positively associated with life satisfaction in Hypotheses 4 through 6. The three indexes of informal activity are hypothesized to be more highly associated with life satisfaction than is formal activity. Activity of a formal nature is likewise hypothesized to have a stronger association with the dependent variable than is solitary activity.

When considering the total sample (Table 1) the most well supported suggestion is that informal activity with friends is more highly associated with life satisfaction than is formal activity. Because of the low magnitudes of gamma values for many of the relationships, apparent trends may be a function of chance variations and thus do not warrant emphasis. Thus, the findings for this set of hypotheses lend little or no substantive support to the theoretical propositions.

Tests of Hypotheses concerning Role Loss Specifications

Role loss is hypothesized to decrease the magnitude of relationships between various types of activity and life satisfaction. The major role loss for males (i.e., retirement) and the major role loss for females (i.e., widowhood) are both analyzed for purposes of specifying either increases or decreases in the magnitude of association between activity and satisfaction.

Table 2 indicates gamma values for specifying relationships between various activity types and life satisfaction under the condition of widowhood among females. Theoretically, relationships are hypothesized to be more pronounced among married subjects and less pronounced among widowed subjects

Table 2.

Activity Types Related to Life Satisfaction: Gamma Values and Significance Levels for Widowed Females and Married Females Compared with the Total Female Sample

Activity Type	Widowed Females (N=52)		Total Female Sample (N=229)		Married Females (N=177)	
	Gamma Value	Signif- icance Level	Gamma Value	Signif- icance Level	Gamma Value	Signif- icance Level
Informal activity with friends	.06	NS	.23	.05	.33	.05
Informal activity with relatives	-.12	NS	-.02	NS	.01	NS
Informal activity with neighbors	-.14	NS	-.02	NS	.01	NS
Formal activity	.10	NS	.09	NS	.07	NS
Solitary activity	-.09	NS	-.06	NS	-.03	NS

(Hypothesis 6). Data indicate very minor support concerning four of the five activity types, with the one exception of formal activity. The magnitude of increases and decreases comparing the gammas of widows (N=52) with the total female sample are extremely small and thus have little theoretical relevance. The only statistically significant relationship involves activity with friends and life satisfaction among married subjects, which is expected from previous findings.

Specification of relationships involving retirement among males in relation to the total male sample (Hypothesis 7) is presented in Table 3. The magnitudes of relationships between the various activity types and life satisfaction are hypothesized to decrease for male subjects who have undergone the role change from employee to retiree. Males who are still employed are expected to exhibit more pronounced associations between activity types and life satisfaction. Data do not support this hypothesis, and again the magnitudes for gamma values are extremely small. Four of the five activity types have slightly greater

Table 3.

Activity Types Related to Life Satisfaction: Gamma Values and Significance Levels for Retired Males and Employed Males Compared with the Total Male Sample

	Retired Males		Total Male Sample		Employed Males	
	(N=70)		(N=182)		(N=112)	
Activity Type	Gamma Value	Signif-icance Level	Gamma Value	Signif-icance Level	Gamma Value	Signif-icance Level
Informal activity with friends	.20	NS	.19	NS	.14	NS
Informal activity with relatives	-.05	NS	-.07	NS	-.10	NS
Informal activity with neighbors	.09	NS	.07	NS	.01	NS
Formal activity	.03	NS	.07	NS	.11	NS
Solitary activity	.08	NS	.06	NS	.00	NS

rather than reduced, levels of association with life satisfaction among retired males (N=111). This finding may, in part, be explained by the fact that subjects have mostly white collar or professional occupations which represent the most successful persons in terms of adjustment to retirement.

In general, the magnitude of the differences in increases and decreases is so small in most cases that chance variation may account for many of the changes.

Summary of Results

Of seven hypotheses tested in this study, only Hypothesis 1: informal activity is directly associated with life satisfaction, and Hypothesis 4: informal activity is more highly associated with life satisfaction than is formal activity, received support of any kind. Hypothesis 6 received some, but not highly significant support.

The overall trends in these data suggest no support for the general set of propositions relating activity to life satisfaction. Only one type of activity (informal activity with friends) is significantly correlated with life satisfaction. The consistently non-significant relationships concerning informal activity with relatives and neighbors, formal activity, and solitary activity may indicate these types of activity are not important sources of role support for subjects in this sample.

Many of the gamma values are of such low magnitudes that any attempt to infer trends would be tenuous speculation. Specification of major control variables does not alter the basic findings for the total sample to any meaningful degree.

The specification of major role changes follows the general pattern of other findings; only informal activity with friends among married females reaches statistical significance, and the level of the relationship is substantively insignificant.

Discussion And Conclusions

Implications for Activity Theory from These Data

While some of the relationships found in the data supported the theory being tested, most did not. There are two sets of implications for activity theory that seem warranted from these results: the first implications specific, and the second general.

In the first place, the most specific suggestion from these data is that participation in an informal friendship group appears to be an important correlate of life satisfaction—but not, contrary to what may be deduced from a formal activity theory, frequency of activity in general.

78

Friendship is perhaps the type of relationship most likely to involve specific role supports. Friendships are not only more voluntary than the other informal activities with relatives and neighbors, but are more intimate in nature, i.e., characterized by primary relationships. Rather than reacting to only general social roles, as might characterize neighboring or formal activities, friends react toward one another in terms of their specific, idiosyncratic role identities. The whole person, or in the somewhat more precise terminology of interactionist theory, the totality of one's role identities, is thus taken into account to a greater extent. The friendship may also provide a sense of continuity and depth for one's role identities; this is especially important for the high life satisfaction in a rapidly changing, complex society.

The findings of this study, although intended to measure frequency of activity rather than intimacy or depth of a single relationship, may be considered alongside the data reported by Lowenthal and Haven (1968). They suggest that the presence of a stable, intimate relationship with a single "confidante" is the strategic correlate of high morale. The quality or type of interaction, not the quantity, is to them the more important predictor of life satisfaction. The present data concerning intensity of interpersonal activity provide some corroboration of this line of thinking. Future research should add the "confidante" concept to specify aspects of this theory.

In the second place, the more general conclusion from this study is that the data provide surprisingly little support for the implicit activity theory of aging which has served as the theoretical base for practice as well as research in gerontology for decades. The propositions that the greater the frequency of activity, the greater one's life satisfaction and that the greater the role loss, the lower the life satisfaction were in the main not substantiated by this research. There are several reasons which may be advanced to explain this.

The first place to look when data do not substantiate a carefully constructed theory is probably at the nature and quality of the data. Perhaps activity theory is correct and the operations used in this particular research are inadequate to test it. The use of secondary data—material collected for one purpose and used

79

later by a researcher to test another set of ideas—has, in this research, placed substantial strictures on what we would have liked to do in testing fully the theory. For example, the information on activity came from items, not scales; obviously one is more confident in the reliability and validity of a scale than of a single item measuring a construct. Moreover, the data relied on the respondents' own reports of various types of activity; perhaps interpersonal activity is better measured using other methods such as observation (which, unfortunately, gerontological research has utilized very little) rather than self-report in surveys. Or, finally, perhaps the definitions of activity were much too global to differentiate the complex interplay among activity types; perhaps the measurement of the dependent variable, life satisfaction, is inadequate. However, in considering these explanations, it is important to remember that other researchers have used these concepts and these operationalizations to their own satisfaction, although they have not as rigorously tested their relationship within a formal theoretical model. For the moment, then, we feel it is necessary to look further for an explanation of these findings.

Second, the theory may be correct but the sample inadequate or inappropriate to obtain substantiation of the theory. The present sample was composed of primarily upper-middle-class subjects; moreover, they had chosen to move to a retirement community for reasons that may indicate seeking an "active" social environment. Past research indicates that activity or social interaction is not as important for predicting morale or life satisfaction among persons with high SES as it is for persons with low SES (Kutner 1956). Persons of higher SES are perhaps less dependent upon activity, per se, as a source of role supports since they have more success experiences in terms of educational and career pursuits. All too many studies in social gerontology have focused on upper-middle class respondents. In other socioeconomic groups the relationships predicted by the theory may in fact obtain. If this is so (and we invite other researchers to test this) the theory should be modified to introduce socioeconomic class as an important specification of the theory. However, this seems to us a relatively unsatisfactory conclusion: for reasons given below, we look still further to other implications of activity theory.

Third, perhaps there are other concepts, unmeasured in this investigation, which affect in crucial ways the relationship predicted by the theory. The extremely low gamma values indicate that perhaps other types of variables such as personality and psychological factors, are important for determining differential life satisfaction among aged individuals. We are reminded of the conclusion of Neugarten, Havighurst, and Tobin (1968) that patterns of aging can be discerned in accordance with long-term styles of personal adaptation and interaction. Thus, personality factors may determine whether an individual is comfortable in a disengaged pattern of aging, where low social interaction is associated with high life satisfaction; or in a reorganized pattern characterized by high role activity and high life satisfaction. This perspective points to an important limitation of activity theory as systematized in this paper: the exclusion of concepts relating to previous life style and to personality attributes of the individual. In our view, this is perhaps the most persuasive reason for the lack of positive results in our data. This implies again the modification of the theory so as to include these concepts.

A fourth explanation is that the theory as implied in gerontological practice and research, and as formally presented here, is totally inadequate in representing reality. The frequency of interpersonal activity may have no direct, linear relation to life satisfaction in contemporary cohorts of normal, advantaged elderly individuals; moreover, no useful purpose is served in attempting to create global, linear characterizations of the sort we have made explicit here in an attempt to predict life satisfaction in older people.

It is this conclusion which we feel is most important to consider at the end of this investigation. The linear model upon which this and most other investigations of the social psychology of aging is based appear simply insufficient to capture the complex interplay between the individual and his changing social system. As suggested in another paper (Kuypers & Bengtson, 1972) a model employing the features of systems theory seems more realistic. It makes more sense to focus on the process involved in adaptation to aging, rather than the static relations among elements; to construct a paradigm reflective of the cyclical qualities implied in feedback loops, rather than linear combinations of terms. Finally, one should attempt to examine the multiple interdependent contingencies among variables rather than two-by-two relationships. This the common-sense, simplistic statement of activity theory is incapable of doing.

The process of growing old involves a complex interchange between the individual, who carries with him a set of experiences and expectations, and his social world; the interplay may best be seen as a system implying a trajectory of ever-changing elements, some common to most members of his cohort, some idiosyncratic. To assert that activity in general is predictive of life satisfaction in general is to obscure the nature of this complex system.

Implications for Theory Building in Social Gerontology

The primary goal of this paper has been the formal and explicit statement of theory that has long been implicit in the literature of social gerontology: that activity is directly related to life satisfaction in old age. In stating and testing a portion of the theory, we have illustrated some of the advantages and disadvantages of an attempt to build explicit theory in life-cycle sociology.

Obvious advantages accrue when one is careful to define the concepts used, to create postulates stating the linkages of concepts, to deduce theorems and then test hypotheses resulting from the theory. Among these advantages are, first, the greater clarity and parsimony of the theoretical statement, to say nothing of the higher probability of logical closure. Second, even more important is the greater likelihood of replication and reformulation by other researchers. Science is useful only insofar as it is cumulative; and the stating of propositions in formal and general terms enhances the prospect of critical replication. We hope that the formalization of activity theory in this paper will lead other researchers to revise and retest propositions relating activity to life satisfaction; or, even better, to construct alternative types of theories examining these phenomena.

Third, and perhaps the greatest advantage: if more attention is given theory building, there is a greater possibility of linkage to more general propositions in the social sciences. There has been a deplorable tendency in social gerontology to perpetuate numerous ad hoc descriptive studies without ever advancing to the scientifically higher level of theory building and theory testing. Researchers in this field must, with greater frequency, orient themselves to this higher level of conceptualizing, else they run the risk of forfeiting generalization and confirmation of the relationships they find. For example, there are important propositions in the sociology of stratification that have never been tested in gerontology but which have direct applications to problems of growing old (see Cutler, 1972 a, b; Riley, 1971).

But this paper has also demonstrated the problems associated with the effort of explicit and formal theory testing. In the first place, it is simply more work to move to this higher level of abstraction in research than it is to stay at a descriptive level of investigation. Many gerontologists have not been trained in the rites of theory construction. Many more would argue that our knowledge of social aspects of aging is so limited that it is useless to attempt theory building until descriptive classification is more advanced. (We do not agree with this position, especially in the light of the codification of research by Riley & Foner, 1968). Second, the theory often is more elaborate or more powerful than the data available to test it; the theory must therefore be carved up, or the operationalization of the concepts must be carried out apologetically. Rigorously defined concepts and highly abstract relationships are difficult to operationalize adequately in the social sciences, and the present research is no exception. Third, and related to the above, once the researcher states his theory clearly and explicitly enough, the deficiencies become glaringly apparent. Vagueness can be comfortable; the rigors of axiomatic statement, and even more the disappointment of nonconfirming data once the research is carried out, make the limitations of one's theory painfully apparent. Finally, theory development is by nature a long-term, continuously ongoing process: theory once stated and tested must inevitably be revised. It is difficult to marshal the resources or the patience to continuously refine one's theory. For these reasons, most of which deal with the cost to the researcher, it is not difficult to see why in a relatively young discipline such as gerontology there has not been much effort given to the articulation of formal theory.

Yet, it is our conclusion that theory development *must* be given a high priority in social gerontology in the next decade. The statement and testing of activity theory in this paper illustrates the need for revision of the general proposition, so often implied in the literature, that activity is directly related to life satisfaction in old age. The substantive findings of this study lend weight to the views of Bengtson (1969), Neugarten, Havighurst, and Tobin (1968), Rosow (1967), and Youmans (1969) that neither activity theory nor disengagement theory by themselves can adequately account for optimal aging. Perhaps it is good to be reminded again of the *variability* of aged individuals in terms of their value systems, personalities, physical and social situations, and the danger of stereotyping or of building theory that is overgeneralized. This does not mean, of course, that explaining something so complex as optimal aging is so difficult that one should give up trying to test formally stated theory. Rather, the implication is that one must continually broaden and specify one's theory, using formal and explicit concepts and defensible logic, in order to more adequately account for variations in the population of aging individuals under investigation.

Summary

This paper has presented a formal axiomatic theory in an attempt to articulate more precisely the so-called activity theory of aging. This theory suggests a positive relationship between social activity and life satisfaction in old age and further specifies that salient role loss is inversely related to life satisfaction. Various hypotheses derived from the theory were tested with data from a study of in-movers to a retirement community. Because the data are secondary (not orignally designed to test the theory advanced here), only a portion of the postulates could be directly tested.

We can conclude from the results that, for this sample at least, only social activity with friends was in any way related to life satisfaction. No significant relationship was found between activity with neighbors, relatives, formal organizations, or solitary activity. The use of various specification variables (i.e., age, sex, marital status, and employment status) did not change the initial findings of the total sample. The data lend only limited support to some of the propositions of the theory. Overall it points out the need to both revise or enlarge the theory, including as concepts personality configurations and availability of intimates (confidants), and second to test it on a broader spectrum of the aged population than the present sample of in-movers to a retirement community.

Finally, this paper has pointed to the advantages and problems of attempting to develop and test formal, explicit theory in social gerontology. The advantages include clarity, parsimony, logical closure, greater likelihood of replication and reformulation, and linkage to more general perspectives in the social sciences. Problems are the greater difficulty of this type of research, compared to sheer description; lack of isomorphism between theoretical concepts and data available; the discouraging probability of nonconfirmation of the theory; and the requirement of continual revision as elements in the theory are revised, reformulated, or discarded. In sum, each problem represents an advantage from the view of better science.

It is our conclusion that explicit theory development must be given higher priority by researchers. If social gerontology is to advance beyond the perpetuation of ad hoc descriptive analyses, to the higher level of science involving logically related and empirically verified propositions of a truly general nature, we must attend more to theory development.

Notes

1. This is a revision of a paper presented at the 8th International Congress of Gerontology, Washington, 1969. The data are from a larger study of in-movers to retirement communities conducted by Dr. James A. Peterson and supported by grant MH 1520 from the National Institute of Mental Health. Acknowledgement is made to Dr. William Larson and Mrs. Aili Larson for their assistance in the research. We wish to thank Dr. LaMar Empey, Dr. Steven Lubeck, and Dr. James Carroll for suggestions in revising this paper.

The first author would like to acknowledge and express his appreciation to the Gerontology Center, University of Southern California, Los Angeles, and the National Institute of Child Health and Development (training grant HD 00157) for support during his graduate training.

SOCIAL GERONTOLOGY AND THE AGE STRATIFICATION OF SOCIETY*[1]

Matilda White Riley

One decade after "the" White House Conference, and on the eve of another, the Gerontological Society and all of us involved in research in this field can survey with satisfaction the amount of information accumulated in these ten years and the impact of this information upon professional practice, public policy, and popular attitudes. That much remains to be done is patent to all gerontologists, but that the title of this symposium is "Research Goals and Priorities in Gerontology" suggests that we have reached a point where we can pick and choose among alternative strategies.

What we propose as a high priority for the future is a sociology of age stratification. Gerontologists working in the social science fields have amassed a remarkable body of facts on two main topics: being old and growing old.[2] Our immediate aim is not so much to add to these facts and ideas as to look at them from a fresh perspective. This perspective emphasizes not just old age, but all the age strata in the society as a whole; it emphasizes not just aging, but also the societal processes and changes that affect aging and the state of being old.

What do we mean by age *stratification*, which is only now emerging as a new field of sociology? A comparison with the

* Matilda White Riley, "Social Gerontology and the Age Stratification of Society," *Gerontologist* 11 (1971):79-87.

well-established sociology of class stratification is provocative. In that field, two concepts, heuristically stimulating as analogous to our concepts of age strata and aging, have demonstrated their power in explaining diverse social phenomena. These concepts are *social class* (variously defined in terms of inequality of income, prestige, or power) and *social mobility* (consisting of upward or downward movement between lower and higher classes). These concepts of social class and social mobility, which any one of us can grasp intuitively from firsthand experience, have proved scientifically useful in defining and suggesting answers to many important questions. We shall list four sets of these questions briefly, as they may stimulate us to find answers to similar questions in relation to age and aging.

> *First,* how does an individual's location in the class structure channel his attitudes and the way he behaves? Here there is much evidence that, for example, a person's health, his desire to achieve, his sense of mastery over his own fate, or the way he relates to his family and to his job depend to a considerable extent upon his social class.

> *Second,* how do individuals relate to one another within, and between, classes? Within class lines, many friendships are formed, marriages often take place, and feelings of solidarity tend to be widespread. Between classes, relationships, even if not solidary, are often symbiotic, as people of unlike status live harmoniously in the same society. However, there seems to be greater opportunity between, than within, classes, for cleavage or conflict, as in struggles over economic advantages or clashes in political loyalties.

> *Third,* what difficulties beset the upwardly (or downwardly) mobile individual, and what strains does his mobility impose upon the group (such as his parents of one class) whom he leaves behind and upon the new group (such as his wife's parents of a different class) who must now absorb him?

> *Fourth,* to the extent that answers can be found to these three sets of questions, what is the impact of the observed findings upon the society as a whole? If there are inequalities between classes, for example, what do these portend for the prosperity, the morality, or the stability of the

overall structure of classes? What pressures for societal change are generated by differences, conflicts, or mobility between classes?

The literature on these four aspects of class stratification is impressive, pregnant with insights that might be extended to analyses of kindred phenomena. Our concern is to test the utility of the questions it evokes for understanding old age as just one stratum in a society stratified or differentiated, not by class, but by age. Thus we shall start by thinking of society as divided into strata according to the age of its members. *People* at varying ages differ in their capacity and willingness to perform social roles (of student, spouse, worker, or retiree, for example). Moreover, the age strata differ in the social *roles* members are expected to play and in the rights and privileges accorded to them by society. At any given period of time, old people must live as members of such a society, finding their place in relation to the other members who are younger than they, and making choices among whatever opportunities are available to them. Over time, not only old people but people of different ages are *all* growing older, moving concurrently through a society which itself is undergoing change.

Age Stratification And The Individual

To ask our first question, then: how does an individual's location within the changing age structure of a given society influence his behavior and attitudes? (Mannheim 1952). In the sociological literature generally it has been well established that individuals are conditioned by society. As Robert Merton puts it, "Structure constrains individuals variously situated within it to develop cultural emphases, social behavior patterns, and psychological bents" (Merton, 1957). Similarly, it has been well established in the literature of social gerontology that the state of old age reflects the structural context, showing wide variations (as well as some similarities) when primitive and modern societies are contrasted (Simmons, 1960), or even when modern Western nations are compared with one another (Burgess, 1960;

Havighurst, Munnichs, Neugarten, & Thomae, 1969; Shanas & associates, 1968). But how does it come about that, *within* a given society at any given time, individuals located in *different age strata* differ from one another? How are older individuals set off from the middle-aged and from the young?

The answer to such a question as this involves two distinct dimensions of time: a life course dimension and an historical dimension. These two dimensions can be thought of as coordinates for locating the individual in the age structure of society. On the first dimension, individuals at the *same* stage of the *life* course have much in common. They tend to be alike in biological development, in the kinds of roles they have experienced (such as worker, spouse, parent of dependent child), and in the sheer number of years behind and potential years ahead. People at *different* life course stages tend to differ in these very respects. The rough index of this life course dimension is years of chronological age—we say that a person is aged 20, or in the age category 45 to 60. But chronological age is of interest to us, not intrinsically, but only because it can serve as an approximate indicant of personal (that is biological, psychological, and social) experience—and this experience carries with it varying probabilities of behavior and attitudes. This life course dimension is the familiar one that includes the age-related organic changes affecting physical and mental functioning and that links the biological and the social sciences.

But there is a second time dimension for locating an individual in the age strata that also affects his probability of behaving or thinking in particular ways. This dimension refers to the *period of history* in which he lives. People who were born at the *same* time (referred to as a cohort) share a common historical and environmental past, present, and future. For example, when Americans born in 1910 had reached the age of 30, they had all (in one way or another) experienced World War I and the Great Depression, they were all currently exposed to World War II, and they all confronted the future of the 1940s through the 1970s. People who were born at *different* times (that is different cohorts) have lived through different intervals of history; and even when they encounter the same historical situation, they may, because they differ in age, experience it differently. Thus any one of us—just as we might be ethnocentric—is almost certainly (to add a needed term to our vocabulary) *"cohort-centric."* That is, we view old age, or any other stage of life, from the unique point of historical time at which we ourselves are standing. The rough index of this historical (or environmental) dimension is the date, or the calendar year. Here again our concern is not with dates themselves, but with the particular sociocultural and environmental events, conditions, and changes to which the individual is exposed at particular periods.

It comes as no surprise, then, that each of the age strata has its own *distinctive subculture.* By age differences in subculture we mean that a cross-section view of society shows, for myriad characteristics, patterns that are closely related to age. In our own society today, familiar instances of the differing subcultures among young, middle-aged, and old include such varied aspects of life as labor force participation, consumer behavior, leisure-time activities, marital status, religious behavior, education, nativity, fertility and childrearing practices, or political attitudes—to name only a few. Such age-related patterns differ from time to time and from place to place, as all the age strata in a society—not the old alone—display differences (or similarities) in behavior and attitudes on the two dimensions of life course and history.

If we want to go beyond a mere description of these age-related subcultures, however, we must examine them further, which leads to our next topic.

Age Stratification And Social Relationships

The second set of questions suggested by the analogy between class stratification and age stratification points to the utility of exploring *relationships* both *between* and *within* age strata. For not only the behavior and attitudes of discrete individuals, but also social relationships—people's positive or negative feelings and actions toward each other—are channeled through the age structure of the particular society. Thus a sociology of age stratification, by investigating these relationships, should help to illuminate the nature of old age.

Many aspects of the cleavages or the bonds *between* old and young, dramatized by philosophers and poets of the ancient past, are still widely discussed today. Is there an inevitable gap between generations? Do the elderly constitute a disadvantaged minority group, regarded with prejudice by the majority? Or do they control important centers of power, refusing to yield to the young? Are old people likely to form political blocs, seeking to solve their own problems with little regard for the rest of society? And, if many conditions foster intergenerational conflict or exploitation, what other conditions foster relationships of harmony or reciprocity?

As a preliminary to addressing such momentous issues, one small illustration of the *sequential relations* among generations within the family will point out the interconnectedness of the age strata. If we start with the elderly generation of parents and their adult offspring, a well-known finding from the gerontological literature reports widespread exchanges of material support. This support varies in amount and kind, ranging from financial contributions and care in illness to baby-sitting and help with housework and home repairs. Contrary to previous notions of an upward flow of contributions *to* older people, the flow of support between aged parents and their adult offspring appears to be two-directional, either from parent to child or from child to parent as need and opportunity dictate (Riley et al. 1968). Indeed (in the United States, at least), the proportions of older people who *give* help to their offspring appear to exceed the proportions who *receive* help from their offspring (Shanas, 1966; Streib, 1965; Streib & Thompson, 1960).

Let us now, however, include in the example still a third generation of the family, for it is our contention that many a commonplace observation about old people can take on new significance through extension to other age strata. Let us move from the flow of material assistance between aged parents and their middle-aged children to the flow between this middle generation and *their* young children. The principle can be illustrated by one small study (Foner 1969) in which parents of high school students were asked what they would do with money unexpectedly received. Only 2 percent said they would use it to help their aged parents. But this was not because they would spend it on themselves or save it for their retirement; it was rather because, in the main, they would reserve it to help their children get started in life. Furthermore, the aged generation concurs; they do not expect repayment. The middle generation, then, does not neglect the old because of preoccupation with their own needs (in fact, they are far readier to offer help than are their aged parents to want or to accept it), but because of their preoccupation with the needs of their young children. In short, the flow of material support tends to be, not reciprocal, but sequential—with each generation (regardless of its means) attempting to aid the next younger generation.

As such a finding intimates, many middle-aged parents, by investing their resources in the future of their young children, are not only restricting any potential help they might give to the older generation; they are also restricting the accumulation of assets for their own later life. In this example, then, extension of the analysis from the oldest to the youngest generation in the family helps to clarify one aspect of the meaning of old age. Any lack of family support for aged parents now appears, not as willful indifference or neglect, but as an expression of normative agreement among all the generations about the direction in which aid should flow.

Many other conditions of the aged might similarly be better understood against the backdrop of the other strata with whom old people live and relate. Consider the work force data on older men as this might be compared with the differing circumstances of employment of younger people at various periods of history. In the early days of the Industrial Revolution in England, the father (or grandfather), as a skilled workman in his own right, could take his children with him into the factory, himself training the adult sons and supervising the little children throughout the long workday (Smelser, 1968). Thus his authority within the family could penetrate into the workplace, preserving traditional ties among the generations. If such an arrangement encouraged between-strata solidarity, then the subsequent changes in conditions of work may have undermined this basis. More recently, in the United States, quite another set of changes have marked the relative positions of older men and boys in the work force. Between 1900 and 1930, while the majority of older men remained economically active, the proportion of boys aged 10 to 15 who were fully employed declined from 25 percent to only 6 percent. Since World Ware II, as older men have been winnowed from the labor force, boys too are being extruded; the Census no longer counts children under 14 in compiling labor force statistics, and the participation rates of boys from 16 through 19 show slight but consistent declines. Thus older men today live in a society where the situation of both the old and the young must be interpreted in relation to the productivity and economic prestige of men in their middle years (Kalish 1969).

Such examples suggest a general principle: important increments to gerontological knowledge are obtainable by studying the entire age-differentiated society, not merely the old. The same principle hold when the research focus is on relationships *within* rather than *between* age strata. Here we shall simply allude to the concern of gerontologists with questions of age similarity as a basis for friendship, or age homogeneity as a feature of residential settings for older people (Madge 1969; Riley et al. 1968). It has been shown that, outside of family groups, older people tend (although by no means exclusively) to have friends who are similar to themselves in status characteristics—notably age—that signal mutuality of experiences, tastes, or values. However, as the sociological literature shows (Hess, 1971), such choice of age mates is only a special case of the widespread phenomenon of homophily (or similarity among friends in status or in values) (Lazersfeld & Merton, 1954).

Age homophily, not only among the old but also at younger age levels, may be especially pronounced in the United States today as a number of factors converge to produce solidarity within age lines. Simply the rapidity of social change, for example, can sharpen the differences among strata and can thereby contribute to a sense of uniqueness among members of each single stratum. The expansion of education has extended the social (and often the physical) segregation of age-similars from children in the lower schools to older adolescents and even to young adults in colleges and universities (Parsons & Platt, 1971). Today's middle-aged people, too, many of whom have left the city to rear their children in the suburbs, have experienced long

94

years of age-homogeneous neighborhood settings (Starr, 1971). And old people because of increasing longevity retain larger numbers of their age peers as associates (Spengler, 1969). In many respects, then, we live in an *age-graded* society, with a high potential for strong ties to develop within each age stratum.

However, the possible long-term consequences of such heightened conditions of within-stratum solidarity may be double-edged. On the one hand, homophily may be beneficial to the individuals involved. Age peers have long been recognized as easing the transition from childhood to adulthood (Eisenstadt, 1956); and they may perhaps aid adjustment in old age and at other points of transition in the life course as well. On the other hand, if age peers increasingly turn to each other for aid and comfort, detriments to relationships between strata may ensue as ties between generations may become attenuated or the potential for cleavage or conflict may be increased.

Aging And Cohort Flow

It is the third set of questions—those relating to the processes of *mobility* of individuals from one stratum to another—that brings into bold relief certain similarities, but also the essential differences, between class stratification and age stratification.

At points of similarity between the two processes, much can be learned about aging from the rich literature on class mobility. We tend to take aging for granted (much as before the development of physiology as a science, laymen took their bodily functioning for granted). Yet, when aging (social, psychological, and biological) is viewed as mobility through the age strata, it is revealed as a process that entails many of the same tensions and strains as class mobility. Aging individuals must pass through key transition points in the society—from infancy to childhood, for example, from one school grade to the next, from adolescence to adulthood, or from work life to retirement (Clausen, 1971). And the degree of strain engendered by such transitions depends upon diverse social conditions—upon the continuity or discontinuity in the role sequences (Benedict 1938); upon how fully institutionalized a particular role may be (Donahue, Orbach, &

95

Pollak, 1960); upon the internal consistency of role expectations, facilities, and sanctions;[3] or upon how effectively people are trained or socialized at every stage of life (Brim 1968; Brim & Wheeler, 1966). For example, consider the stress entailed in our society because we crowd formal education almost exclusively into the younger stages of life rather than spreading it over the life course as individuals require it. Since we do not regard students as full-fledged adults, what tensions must be endured by the young person who stays in the role of student beyond adolescence well into adulthood (tensions that are all too evident in universities today)? What difficulties beset the older person if, in order to obtain the further education he needs or desires, he must sacrifice his job? Like social mobility, too, aging places strains not only upon individuals but also upon the groups through which the aging individual passes. Thus a family must regroup itself after the marriage of its youngest child, or a community after the death of an elder statesman. Similarly, group adjustments are necessitated by the advent of new members like the birth of a child into a family, the entry of a new class of children into a school grade, or the move of a widowed old person into the household of her married daughter.

Despite such similarities, however, aging differs from class mobility in certain fundamental respects. Exactly because the analogy breaks down in these respects is age stratification revealed in its full uniqueness and in its intrinsicality to social change. In the first place, mobility across social classes affects only selected individuals, who can move either upward or downward, and who can reverse direction at different stages of life. But mobility through the age strata is, of course, universal, unidirectional, and irreversible. Everybody ages. Everybody changes over his life course as personality develops, experience accumulates, and adjustments are made to new roles. Nobody can ever go back, although individuals may age in different ways and at different rates.

In the second place, knowledgeable as we are about the inevitability of aging, we take much less cognizance of the inexorability of birth and death, and of the endless succession of cohorts (or generations of individuals born at the same time)—for which there is no precise parallel in class mobility. Yet the sociology of age stratification requires examination of the fact that, within a given society, different cohorts can age in different ways. Each cohort is tied through its date of birth to societal history. Thus the aging of each new cohort is affected by the special situation of that cohort's particular era in history—by the changing cultural, social, and material conditions in the society and by events in the external environment. While all the members of one particular cohort move together over their life course through the same period of time, the various cohorts in the society can differ because they start at distinct times. Cohorts can also differ markedly in size and in composition (in the proportions of males and females, for example, or of blacks and whites, or of natives and foreign-born).

Consider a few examples of intercohort differences in the way people have aged in our own society in the *past*. Epidemiologists tell us that, in comparison with women born a century ago, today's women have experienced menarche at earlier ages and menopause at later ages (National Center for Health Statistics, 1966; Susser, 1969; Tanner, 1962). That is, the period of potential fertility has appreciably lengthened. In practice, however, *recent* cohorts spend fewer years of their lives in childbearing. Women have telescoped the phase of actual reproduction, having fewer and more closely spaced offspring nowadays than did their mothers or grandmothers (Glick & Parke, 1965). Moreover, the trauma of reproduction have been drastically reduced, as fewer women die in childbirth and fewer of their infants die.

Most striking of all the cohort differences, perhaps, are those in longevity—in the proportions of cohort members who outlive the ills of infancy, who escape maternal deaths and the other mortality risks of young adulthood, and who thus survive into the higher ages of the life span. The average lifetime (estimated at only two to three decades among cohorts born in ancient Rome or in medieval Europe) has risen in the United States from four decades among cohorts born in the mid-nineteenth century to an estimated seven decades among those born in the mid-twentieth—a situation apparently unparalleled in human history.[4] The profound implications of such cohort differences in longevity can be intimated by just one of the many associated changes, the one called the "revolution in family structure"

(Glick & Parke, 1965; Shanas, 1969).[5] The single nuclear household of a century ago (parents and their children, sometimes including a grandparent) has been replaced, because of increased joint survival, by several generations of related nuclear households: the young couple with their dependent children, the middle-aged parents, the aged generation of grandparents, and the great-grandparent who also often survives.

What do such differences between earlier and later cohorts presage for the people who will become old in the *future?* Speculation about many of these differences can prove fruitful of hypotheses. We might speculate, for example, about the extended period of husband-wife relationships in the middle years: the more recent couples have had more time to accumulate assets, or to learn independence from their offspring, or to prepare themselves for retirement. But not all predictions about future implications of cohort differences are entirely speculative, since everybody who will reach 65 during this century or during the early decades of the twenty-first century is already alive. Much information is already in hand about the size of existing cohorts, for example, or about their place of birth or their educational level. Thus, apart from unforeseeable changes (as through wars, depressions, or major shifts in migration or in values), fair estimates can be made about numerous characteristics of old people at particular dates in the future. The *size* of the aged stratum at the turn of the century will reflect the small numbers of babies in the Depression cohorts; but the size of the aged stratum will predictably increase again in the early decades of the coming century with the influx of the "baby boom" cohorts born after World War II (Spengler, 1969). In respect to *nativity,* the much-studied cohort who had passed age 65 or more by 1960 had contained a sizable proportion of early immigrants who were largely illiterate and unskilled, whereas the more recent cohorts who will reach old age in subsequent decades contain fewer and better-educated immigrants. Or in respect to formal *education,* we know that over 70 percent of the cohort aged 75 or more in 1960 had had less than nine years of school, contrasted with only 17 percent of the cohort aged 25 to 29, who will not reach age 75 before the year 2005 (Riley et al. 1968). We are aware, also, of many changing societal or environmental conditions, not all of them salutary, that may influence in special ways the future life course of existing cohorts—as, for example, the spread of pollution might have the greatest effect on young cohorts subject to a full lifetime of exposure, or as the increase of smoking among women might bring female death rates more nearly into line with the currently higher male rates. We cannot overestimate the importance of charting such cohort differences for an understanding of old age.

Age And Social Change

We have been discussing the dual processes affecting individuals (or cohorts of individuals) in a society: aging as a social, psychological, and biological process; and the succession of cohorts which do not all age in exactly the same ways. We shall now ask how these processes relate to the macrocosm of the changing society (Ryder, 1965) of which the old people who concern us are one integral part.

Mannheim (1952) once proposed a tantalizing mental experiment. Imagine, he said, a society in which one generation lived on forever, and none followed to replace it. Let us, as social scientists, policymakers, and professional groups, make such an experiment! If everybody grows old together, what distinctions might remain between old and young? A few moments' thought are enough to suggest the ineluctable connections among the succession of cohorts, aging, and age stratification. For, in contrast to Mannheim's imaginary society, our own consists of successive cohorts, each with its own unique life-course pattern. It is clear that these cohorts fit together at any given time to form the age structure of young, middle-aged, and aged strata. And over time, as the particular individuals composing the particular strata are continually moving on and being replaced, the society itself is changing.

Certain connections now become apparent between the flow of cohorts and the age-related societal patterns and changes in individual behaviors, attitudes, and relationships (noted in the first sections of the paper). In the simplest case, because successive cohorts often age in different ways, some of these societal

99

patterns and changes can be viewed as direct reflections of the differing cohorts that comprise the age strata at particular periods. Education is a noteworthy example of the significance of cohort flow for cross-sectional differences among age strata (Riley et al., 1968). The rapid pace of educational advance over the century, leaving its mark on successive cohorts of young people, now sets the age strata clearly apart from one another. And these strata differences in education have incalculable importance for many aspects of behavior and attitude—for prejudice, feelings of powerlessness, narrow ranges of interest and friendships, and the like. Of course, such strata differences do not remain fixed. Not only do new cohorts come along, but society itself can change in its related institutions and practices. The age pattern of education today is a reversal of that in earlier societies where the old were honored for their greater knowledge. If one looks ahead from today's knowledge explosion, the information gap between the very young and even the not-so-young is deepening, creating pressures to change the entire structure of education if people beyond the earliest years are to maintain competitive equality.[6]

In another example, the cross-section age patterns for drinking or smoking have shown a general decline from younger to older strata; and these differences among strata are in part reflections of the past tendency for each new cohort to espouse these practices to an increasing degree (Riley et al., 1968). Today's younger cohorts, however, may be introducing new habits that could, over the next decades, drastically change the cross-section age pattern. A recent campus interview elicited the student comment, for example, that

> . . . upperclassmen still prefer beer, but a large majority of underclassmen prefer pot. Pot is big in the high schools, and it is very popular with freshmen who just came out of that environment. The trend is definitely away from beer (Cicetti, 1970).

Are these newcomers to the college likely to set the pace for the cohorts that follow?

In such instances, changes in societal age strata can be interpreted as the shifting composite of cohorts who, themselves

100

affected by differing historical backgrounds, have aged in differing ways. In other instances, life-course differences among cohorts in one social sphere appear to stimulate further changes in other spheres. For example, far-reaching shifts in the relations between men and women at various ages—the decreasing differentiation between the sexes or the greater freedom of sexual behavior—might be traced in part to a reversal in cohort patterns of female participation in the labor force (Riley et al., 1968, 1971). Many cohorts of women born during the late nineteenth century showed steadily declining rates of participation over the life course. Following World War II, a new pattern began to emerge, as many married women entered the labor force during their middle years, although work force participation of young women in the child rearing ages remained low. The conjunction of these cohort trends meant that, for a considerable period, it was only the young mothers with little children whose labor force participation was low. This situation may have prompted a classic observation (foreshadowing the full force of the Women's Liberation Movement) that "for the first time in the history of any known society, motherhood has become a full-time occupation for adult women" (Rossi, 1964). Women at other times and places shared motherhood with demanding labor in the fields, the factory, or the household.

Can we expect that full-time motherhood is now institutionalized and will persist into the future? If so, we may be victims of our own "cohort-centrism"—one more proof that our understandings of society are influenced by our particular historical background. For this full-time preoccupation of American mothers with their young children seems already to be eroding as recent cohorts have developed a rather different pattern. Not only have the proportions of married women in the labor force during their middle years more than doubled, but there have been pronounced increases also among young married women, even those with little children (Manpower Report of the President, 1970). Thus it may appear to historians of the future that full-time motherhood was a peculiar phenomenon, existing in American society only for a few decades of the twentieth century. Whatever the future may actually hold, the example begins to suggest how the confluence of cohorts with differing life-course patterns in one respect (economic activity of women) can change society in other respects as well. Think, for example, of the mature women who no longer "retire" from major social roles many years before their husbands retire from work. Or think of the young husbands and wives who now share the work of homemaking and infant care. May such changing work habits result in entirely new modes of relationship in the family and—if only because of the widespread unavailability of working wives for daytime activities at home or in the community—in other social institutions?

In addition to the impress of cohort succession upon the history of society, it can sometimes happen that innovations emanating from a single cohort ramify rather quickly through the other age strata, without awaiting the lag over a long series of cohorts. Thus the excessive size of the "baby boom" cohort born after World War II has required drastic adjustments throughout a society unprepared to absorb it—from the initial requirements for obstetrical facilities through the successive pressures on housing, schools, the job market, the marriage market, and so on into the future. Among the many other widely discussed instances are the increased financial burden borne (through transfer payments) by the remainder of society because so many retired old people have inadequate incomes (Bernstein 1969; McConnell 1960); or the potential changes in the ethos surrounding work and leisure as large numbers of old and young no longer participate in the work force (Donahue et al. 1960; Riley, Foner, Hess, & Toby, 1969). It has even been suggested that a completely revolutionary "consciousness," now informing the values and behaviors of many young people, may affect the entire society (Reich, 1970).

To return to the immediate topic of this essay, we offer a special challenge to the oncoming cohorts of social gerontologists—not merely to continue looking for new materials, but also to reexamine and fit together the existing materials in a new way. We suggest a review of old age as one ingredient in the societal macrocosm, inseparable from, and interdependent with, the other age strata. We suggest a review of aging and of the succession of births and deaths as integral parts of societal process and change that follow their own rhythm and that in themselves constitute immanent strains and pressures toward innovation. Such a sociological review can, we submit, help to explain old age and aging and can at the same time suggest potential solutions to some of the problems of great immediate concern.

In sum, the forces of social change, whether through deliberate intervention[7] or as an indirect consequence of existing trends, are not only constantly affecting the aging process, but are also bringing new influences to bear on the situation, on the characteristics of persons who are old, and on the younger age strata with whom old people are interdependent. Discovery and evaluation of the implications for old age of these forces for change constitutes a whole new field of opportunity for social scientists, professional groups, and policymakers in gerontology.

Notes

1. Paper presented at a Symposium on Research Goals and Priorities in Gerontology, 23rd Annual Scientific Meeting of Gerontological Society, Toronto, Oct. 23, 1970. A more extensive treatment of this topic is contained in Riley, Johnson, and Foner, *A Sociology of Age Stratification* (1971). This is the third volume of a series on *Aging and society,* published by Russell Sage Foundation, under a grant from The Ford Foundation. In addition to the authors of this third volume, the following persons have read earlier versions of this manuscript and made valuable criticisms and suggestions: Beth Hess, Robert K. Merton, Mary E. Moore, M.D. and John W. Riley, Jr.

2. A team of us at Rutgers required several years to gather, abstract, and organize this impressive body of knowledge before we were able to produce an inventory of research findings, roughly 600 pages of *selected* social science results, in Riley, Foner, and Associates, 1968.

3. Back (1969) claims ambiguity of retirement which, although socially defined as a right of the individual, offers low rewards and is socially undervalued.

4. To be sure, infant deaths weigh heavily in these averages. Moreover, the data are based on hypothetical, rather than true, cohorts. See Riley et al., 1968.

5. Among couples born a century ago, the last child in the family was married, on the average, at about the same time as the death of one of the parents. But among recent cohorts, husbands and wives typically survive together as two-person families for a good many years after the last child has married and left home. Changes in family structure are associated with changes, not only in longevity, but also in child-bearing and in household living arrangements; see Riley et al., 1968.

6. If such a change is not effected, we may expect increasing convergence of age and class stratification as education achieves preeminence among the distinguishing criteria of social class.

7. Many possibilities for intervention in the several professional fields are discussed in the series of essays in Riley, Riley, and Johnson, 1969, in which experts discuss the implications of social science knowledge for public policy and professional practice affecting older people.

2

Methodological
Issues in
Social Gerontology

INTRODUCTION TO PART II

Broadly speaking, as James Birren (1959) asserts, the purpose of research on aging is to characterize the nature of the older organism and to explain how the organism changes over time. The procedures available for developing knowledge in the field of social gerontology are innumerable and to a great extent overlap with general research procedures. Still, there are several methodological issues which are of special importance to the study of older people. Papers in this part address three of these issues: heterogeneity of the elderly; measurement; and research design.

Until recently, America's elderly were often treated as if they were of one population, with more or less common features. Much research has accumulated revealing in detailed form the characterisitcs of the elderly, and we have learned that this population is not as homogeneous as once was thought. We have learned that many of the factors which distinguish different segments of the total U.S. population are good "distinguishers" among the elderly: age, sex, race, ethnic origin, education, income, and so forth. However, a major dimension of the elderly has been commonly overlooked in almost all descriptive studies of the elderly: their distribution over space. Just as it has become conventionally understood that the general population and its style of living varies from region to region, and state to state, so too it may be that the elderly and their "style of aging" varies in a like manner. Kart and Manard, in the first paper, examine the assumption of spatial homogeneity of the elderly. Using the state as the unit of analysis, and employing factor analytic techniques, these researchers questioned the assumption of homogeneity based on traditional regional designations. Put more simply, they asked, Are the elderly populations of contiguous states in traditional regional areas similar? The answer was Yes and No. They found "aging regions" which fit traditional regional designations and "aging regions" made up of noncontiguous states showing "sociocultural homogeneity" on a series of demographic variables.

The next two papers in this part are concerned with problems of measurement. The first of these, by Neugarten, Havighurst, and Tobin, reports on the difficulties of attempting to devise an instrument for accurately measuring an important concept in social gerontology: life satisfaction. The paper by Gergen and Back reflects on respondent error. These authors ask, How does the personal orientation of aged respondents affect survey results?

The final paper in this part concerns the issue of research design. Using data on the institutionalization of the elderly, Kastenbaum and Candy show how a cross-sectional research design (research conducted in a short time with inferences as to the effect of aging per se made by comparing people of different ages at the time the research is conducted; Atchley, 1972) may seriously underestimate the probability of an elderly person going to an extended care facility. The alternative, a longitudinal study, is designed to permit observations over an extended period of time. Thus, inferences as to the effect of aging per se may be drawn by observing individuals at different phases of the aging process. The advantages of longitudinal research, despite the report of Kastenbaum and Candy, often come with a heavy investment of time and money.

AGING REGIONS OF THE UNITED STATES: 1970[1]

Cary S. Kart and Barbara B. Manard

Chevan and O'Rourke (1972), using 1960 Census data, tested a conventional assumption about the elderly population of the United States: it is a homogeneous group. Their analysis demonstrated that this population is not distributed across the U.S. in a homogeneous fashion. Using multivariate techniques, they distinguished six distinct groups of states, or aging regions, whose elderly populations exhibited high degrees of consistency on a combination of social, economic, and demographic characteristics. These aging regions of "sociocultural homogeneity" were not, in all cases, congruent with the traditional state groupings or geographical regions.

This paper reports the findings of a study in which these same multivariate techniques were applied to 1970 Census data in an attempt to determine the stability of the aging regions distinguished by Chevan and O'Rourke. Such a determination may have practical import. Between 1960 and 1970, federal, state, and local programs for the elderly increased at a rapid pace. These programs were in some measure a response to a segment of the U.S. population which on the one hand was growing rapidly, and which, on the other hand, was contributing a disproportionate number of new members to what some have come to call the "vulnerables" in our society. The major public welfare program for the elderly has been Old Age Assistance (OAA). This program, paid for by a combination of federal,

109

state, and local funds, was administered until 1974 by the separate states; eligibility requirements and benefit levels varied considerably. Two supplements to OAA were introduced in the 1960s: food stamps and the surplus commodity program. There has been considerable interstate variation in the amount of free food eligible elderly individuals receive from these programs each month. In 1974, OAA was replaced by Supplementary Security Income (SSI), a federally administered program which has attempted to standardize eligibility requirements and benefit levels. States that were paying higher benefit levels before the new program have been required to continue that level by supplementing federal payments. Medicaid and Medicare are two other large-scale programs servicing the elderly which were generated during the 1960s and which are currently facing pressures for standardization across the states. Such standardization of programs across states would seem to presume homogeneity among the target populations, in this case, state elderly populations. Below we present the results of a test of this presumption. We sought to determine if the 1970 elderly population is more or less homogeneous than the 1960 population.

The Data

Following Chevan and O'Rourke, data for twenty variables were abstracted from the 1970 Census of the Population (U.S. Bureau of the Census, 1970). The focus was upon characteristics of the population aged 65 and over living in the 48 contiguous states. Table 1 presents the high and low state values for these twenty variables; 27 states are represented in these extreme values. Several of the variables require further comment. Data on "in-migrants" and "out-migrants" were taken from a special subject report on mobility among the states (U.S. Bureau of the Census, 1973a). The "percentage of elderly-headed households living in owned homes" was derived from a Census report on the housing of senior citizens (U.S. Bureau of the Census, 1973b). In following Chevan and O'Rourke, we were unable to determine how the variable "median years of education completed by 65+" was calculated. Instead of attempting to generate a

Table 1

High and Low State Values of Selected Characteristics of the Older Population, U.S., 1970

Population Characteristic	High Value	Low Value
1. % of state population aged 65+	14.8 (Fla)	6.4 (Nev)
2. % of elderly living in urban areas	90.5 (RI)	35.4 (Vt)
3. % of elderly living in rural farm areas	16.8 (ND)	0.3 (RI)
4. % of elderly living alone or with non-relatives ("Primary Individuals")	31.1 (Ark)	21.4 (NC)
5. % of elderly married and living with spouse	61.0 (Fla)	33.3 (Ala)
6. % of elderly living dependently in child's household	18.1 (NY)	3.9 (Ore)
7. % of elderly in institutions of all types	8.0 (ND)	2.3 (Fla, WVa)
8. % of elderly who are native to state	82.7 (Ky)	9.1 (Ariz)
9. % of elderly who are foreign born	35.2 (NY)	0.7 (Miss)
10. % of elderly who are non-white	35.9 (Miss)	0.3 (Vt, NH)
11. % of elderly who moved to state between 1965 and 1970 (in-migrants)	20.8 (Ariz)	1.2 (NY)
12. % of elderly who left state between 1965 and 1970 (out-migrants)	10.9 (Nev)	1.9 (Ark, Tex)
13. % of elderly who received any income in 1969	98.8 (Kan)	86.1 (Wash)
14. % of elderly receiving income with income below $3,000	85.8 (Miss)	45.1 (Conn)
15. % of elderly males in labor force	36.4 (Wis)	17.6 (Conn)
16. % of elderly employed males in white-collar occupations	51.8 (NY, NJ)	26.2 (SD)
17. % of elderly-headed households living in owned homes	81.0 (Kan)	45.9 (NY)
18. Median years of school completed by women aged 70–74	10.5 (Ariz, Nev)	7.6 (La)
19. Number of elderly males per 100 elderly females (sex ratio)	100.1 (Mo)	64.3 (Mass)
20. Average number of children ever born to elderly women who ever married	3.6 (Utah, ND)	1.5 (Wyo)

comparable value from grouped data, we substituted a similar measure using a cohort of women aged 70–74. While we acknowledge that members of this cohort may have completed more years of schooling than the 1970 elderly population generally, there is little reason to believe that the distribution of values among the states on this variable is different than the distribution of such values among the state elderly populations-at-large. In addition, we chose to employ a more accurate measure of fertility, and thus divided "children ever born" by the number of women aged 65 and over who ever married (the variable employed in the 1960 study was "children ever born per female 65+).

Finally, we substituted "percent in institutions" for the variable used in 1960, "percent in group quarters." With the introduction of Medicare and Medicaid in the mid-sixties, the number of old-age institutions has more than tripled, while "group quarters"—boardinghouses and the like—are rapidly disappearing. We have elsewhere shown (Caplow et al., 1974) that the elderly population of nursing and rest homes has swelled with people who in earlier times would have lived in "group quarters." Hence, in 1970, the measure of congregate living comparable to the 1960 "percent in group quarters" is "percent in institutions."

As Table 1 shows, there is a wide range of differences among the states on these variables. For example, 61.0 percent of Florida's elderly are married and living with a spouse, while only 33.3 percent of Alabama's elderly population have such living arrangements. Eighty-three (82.7) percent of Kentucky's elderly are native to that state; only 9.1 percent of Arizona's aged are.

The Analysis

A two-part factor analytic treatment was applied to the data described above. In part one, the twenty variables for the 48 states were subjected to a "Q analysis" in which the data were transposed; such an analysis acts to turn the basic correlation matrix "on its side"; thus the states become the variables and

Table 2

Q Analysis of the 48 States by Selected Characteristics of the Older Population Varimax Solution: 1960, 1970*

1960

| | I | | II | | III | | IV | | V | | VI |
State	Factor Loading	State	Factor Loading	State	Factor Loading	State	Factor Loading	State	Factor Loading	State	Factor Loading
Neb	93	Conn	94	Ga	96	NM	92	Colo	75	Fla	-87
Iowa	93	NJ	93	Ala	96	Wyo	69	Wash	68	Ariz	-67
Kan	93	RI	92	SC	91	Nev	62	Okla	63		
SD	86	Mass	90	NC	88	Utah	62				
Ind	80	NY	90	Tenn	83						
Mo	75	Ill	89	La	83						
Wis	75	Pa	88	Miss	81						
Minn	73	Del	73	KY	72						
Idaho	68	Ohio	73	Va	70						
Vt	67	NH	70	Ark	66						
Ore	66	Cal	66	Tex	64						
Mont	63	Mich	66	WVa	63						
ND	61										

1970

| | I | | II | | III | | IV | | V | | VI | | VII |
State	Factor Loading	State	Factor Loading	State	Factor Loading	State	Factor Loading	State	Factor Loading	State	Factor Loading	State	Factor Loading
SC	94	Neb	93	NY	84	Wash	76	Fla	84	Del	69	NM	76
Ala	94	SD	88	Conn	84	Cal	68	Ariz	79	Va	60	Nev	68
Ga	91	Kan	86	NJ	83	Colo	62						
Miss	90	Iowa	84	Ill	83								
La	89	Wisc	75	Mass	79								
Tenn	86	Ind	74	RI	77								
NC	83	Minn	73	Pa	74								
Ark	80	Idaho	71	Ohio	61								
WVa	78	ND	69										
Ky	74	Mont	68										
Tex	65												
Va	60												

* The 1960 Q analysis results are taken from Chevan and O'Rourke (1972).

the variables become readings (Rummel, 1970). In this transposition, the state with the low value on a variable was given the lower or zero boundary score while the state with the high value was given the upper or one boundary score. All other states fell proportionately between zero and one. The transposed data were submitted to a principal components analysis, and the resulting factor loadings were subjected to a varimax orthogonal rotation (Chevan & O'Rourke, 1972). The result was seven groupings of states which showed similar configurations of values among the variables. Together, these Q groups, defined by Census characteristics, form a typology of elderly populations.

In part two, the data were subjected to a conventional factor analysis. A varimax orthogonal rotation was employed, using the untransposed data, to produce factors, or dimensions, along which the groups might differ. Four such factors were generated, accounting for 80.2 percent of all the variance among the states.

The Q Groups

Table 2 presents the results of the Q analysis for 1960 and 1970. In each case, a factor loading of ±.60 was used as the criterion for including a state in a particular Q Group. Figure 1 shows the 1970 Q Groups in the United States.

There are three obvious differences between the 1960 and 1970 findings. First, although 46 states were included in some Q Group in 1960, only 39 are so found in 1970. Second, in both years three large groups of states are distinguishable; however, in the 1970 analysis, four additional smaller clusters of states are evident, compared with only three in 1960. Both of these changes indicate increasing differentiation among the states. Third, we find a much stronger geographical base to the 1970 Q Groups.

A Southern aggregation of states is easily identifiable in Q Group I (1970). This is precisely the 1960 Q Group III, though the rank order of the individual state factor loadings is somewhat different. Two other Southern states, Delaware and Florida, appear in other Q groups, while Maryland and Oklahoma did not achieve factor loadings of ±.60 or above in any of the Q groups.

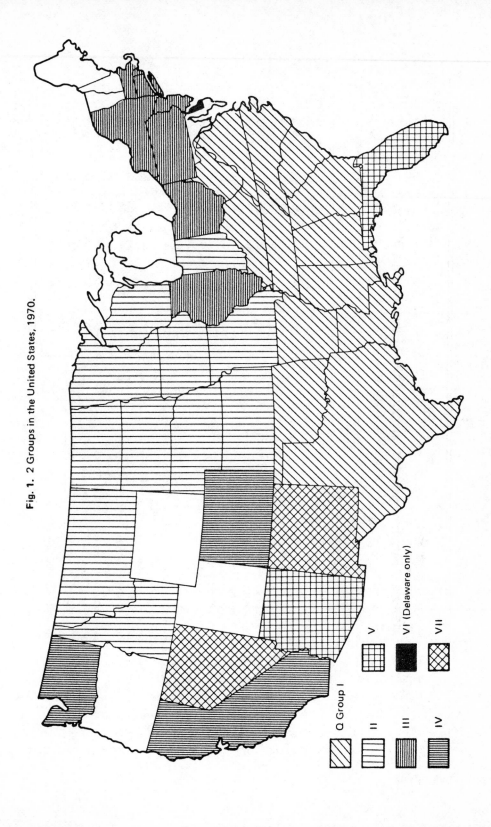

Fig. 1. 2 Groups in the United States, 1970.

Q Group I

II

III

IV

V

VI (Delaware only)

VII

Table 3

Factor Analysis of Selected Characteristics of the Older Population, Varimax Solution: U.S., 1970

Population Characteristic	Factor				Communality
	I	II	III	IV	
1. % of state population aged 65+	08	-02	08	00	.813
2. % of elderly living in urban areas	-91	11	-14	00	.920
3. % of elderly living in rural farm areas	83	-04	05	18	.845
4. % of elderly living alone or with non-relatives ("Primary Individuals")	00	15	-10	18	.898
5. % of elderly married and living with spouse	15	41	-05	-19	.564
6. % of elderly living dependently in child's household	-48	-12	07	-03	.899
7. % of elderly in institutions of all types	03	-15	-15	68	.783
8. % of elderly who are native to state	37	-64	18	10	.923
9. % of elderly who are foreign born	-73	13	-05	20	.944
10. % of elderly who are non-white	21	-39	16	-46	.871
11. % of elderly who moved to state between 1965 and 1970 (in-migrants)	-16	88	-05	-31	.965
12. % of elderly who left state between 1965 and 1970 (out-migrants)	-12	81	-01	19	.760
13. % of elderly who received any income in 1969	00	02	89	05	.827
14. % of elderly receiving income with income below $3,000	28	-16	88	-13	.938
15. % of elderly males in labor force	08	-05	03	-75	.601
16. % of elderly employed males in white-collar occupations	-72	00	-11	-20	.628
17. % of elderly-headed households living in owned homes	65	04	06	-07	.878
18. Median years of school completed by women aged 70-74	-22	58	-20	02	.885
19. Number of elderly males per 100 elderly females (sex ratio)	30	55	06	-14	.707
20. Average number of children ever born to elderly women who ever married	68	-29	03	-18	.654
PERCENT OF VARIANCE ACCOUNTED FOR	32.1	24.6	14.1	9.4	

Q Group II (1970) has an unmistakable Midwest–North Central mark; only Indiana is not contiguous with the other states in the group. In the case of Q Group III (1970), the states have ties to the Eastern industrial complex. Illinois, highly urbanized and industrialized, is the only state not bordering on the others in this grouping.

The 1960 Q analysis also showed state groupings with clear attachments to the Midwest–North Central region (Q Group I) and the Eastern region (Q Group II). Yet, these groupings included states located on the opposite coasts of the nation; for example, Oregon and Vermont in Q Group I, California and Delaware in Q Group II. It is interesting to observe that, with the exceptions noted above, those areal units that are not physically contiguous with the core states in these 1960 Q groups "fell out" of the respective Q groups by 1970. In each case as well, one geographically contiguous state did not achieve a factor loading of ±.60 in the 1970 Q groups, Missouri (1960 Q Group I) and New Hampshire (1960 Q Group II). Thus, Q Group I "lost" Vermont, Oregon, and Missouri, while 1960 Q Group II "lost" Delaware, New Hampshire, California, and Michigan.

Washington, California, and Colorado, all located in the Western region, make up Q Group IV (1970). Three other Q groups were yielded in this analysis, with only Q Group V showing no geographical rationale for its existence. Virginia, included in Q Group I, appears again in Q Group VI. We placed Virginia in both groups because of its contiguity with the Southern region represented in Q Group I, and because the two-state grouping represented as Q Group VI differs from the other Q groups along several key dimensions to be discussed.

The Factor Analysis

Table 3 presents the results of the factor analysis of selected characteristics of the aged population. Using eigenvalues of 1.0 or greater, a four-factor solution is reported. As in the Q analysis, only items with factor loadings of ±.60 and above are examined. The communalities are presented in this table as well. In the common factor analysis model, the communality may also be

117

looked at as a measure of the common variance of a variable. It indicates the extent to which a variable is related to the others, that is, the degree to which the variance of a variable can be derived from the common factors. The percent of elderly who are married and living with spouse has the lowest communality, .564. Thus, it is least related to the other variables.

Factor I, which accounts for 32.1 percent of the variance among these variables, consists of a population with a low proportion of urbanites, a high proportion living in rural farm areas, a low proportion of foreign born, a low proportion of elderly males employed in white-collar occupations, a high proportion living in owner-occupied households, and a high proportion of children ever born. Many of these characteristics are associated with a farm-based population. In fact, this factor drew variables which were spread over four of the factors produced in the analysis of the 1960 data, indicating, as will shortly be seen, the increasing similarities in the elderly populations of the Southern and Midwest–North Central Q Groups which load high on this factor.

Factor II is reflective of a highly mobile population: high inmigration and out-migration with a low proportion of the elderly being native to the state. The sex-ratio characteristic as well as the "median years of schooling completed by women aged 70–74" miss inclusion in this factor by slim margins.

Factor III is an income factor and contains the two variables dealing with income characteristics of the elderly population: percent of elderly who received any income in 1969, and proportion of the elderly with income below $3,000.

The fourth factor, on which only two items achieve factor loadings of ±.60 or above, characterizes a population in which a high proportion of the elderly males are in the labor force and a high proportion of the elderly are in institutions. Previous research (Caplow et al. 1974) has indicated that institutionalization rates are a fairly good indirect indicator of the level of social disaffiliation in a particular elderly population. We expect a high rate of elderly male labor force participation to be associated with the factor for the following reason: Men work longest in agricultural areas. We have found that the isolation of the elderly (and eventual institutionalization) is greatest in areas

118

where the younger population, but not the elderly, are highly mobile. Generally speaking, such areas are economically depressed, rural, and non-Southern. Hence, Factor IV makes conceptual sense and may be thought of as a "social disaffiliation" factor.

Both parts of the analysis presented in this paper, the Q and conventional factor analysis, operate on the same data. It remains to establish and display the relationships between the two outcomes. Table 4 serves this purpose. Mean factor scores and factor score standard deviations for the seven Q groups are shown in this table. The table indicates the relative contribution of the factors to the Q groups thus revealing the factors of greatest importance in the respective Q groups and the essential bases for distinguishing one Q group from another. This table underscores the utility of a factor analytic strategy whereby the multivariate basis of differentiation among the Q groups is revealed. It enables us to see readily the manner in which the various Q groups are based on differing combinations of factors.

A Q group's mean factor score was obtained through a four-step procedure: (1) computing a z-score distribution of states for each item which loaded ±.60 or above on a factor; (2) weighting the z-scores by the item loading on each factor; (3) summing the weighted z-scores (factor scores) for the states within each Q group; and (4) dividing the sum by the number of states in a Q group. Arbitrarily, mean factor scores of ±.40 or greater are designated as important for our purposes.

Q Groups I and II are similar in their relatively high positive Factor I mean scores. In both regions, in the past and present, elderly populations have been located in the rural farm areas and have been described in terms relevant to the dimension appearing in our analysis: low-percentage foreign born, low-percentage in white-collar occupations, high proportion living in owned homes, and high fertility. Nevertheless, these groups do differ greatly on two other dimensions. Q Group I achieves a mean factor score of −.59 on Factor II, the mobility factor. The Southern states all have out-migration rates which are quite low. Looking back to Table 1, Arkansas and Texas are found with the low value on this variable. Kentucky has the highest percentage of elderly citizens native to the state, with the other

119

Table 4

Mean Factor Scores and Factor Score Standard Deviations for Q Groups

Factor		I	II	III	IV	V	VI	VII
					Q Group			
I	Mean	.45	.54	-.69	-.62	-.66	.06	-.17
	S.D.	.30	.35	.40	.33	.20	.08	.24
II	Mean	-.59	-.02	-.13	.28	2.08	.04	1.54
	S.D.	.23	.18	.16	.06	.16	.05	.84
III	Mean	.23	.14	-.29	-.65	.10	.68	-.15
	S.D.	.23	.44	.43	.83	.14	.04	.20
IV	Mean	-.42	.66	.18	-.17	-1.33	-.08	-.22
	S.D.	.29	.55	.23	.08	.13	.06	.19

states in this region not far behind. Q Group II achieves an insignificant mean score on the mobility factor. A further important difference between these two groups of rural states is that the Southern states score negatively on the institutionalization/disaffiliation factor, in distinct contrast with Q Group II.

Q Groups III, IV, and V are quite similar in their high negative mean scores on Factor I. The elderly populations of these state groups are essentially urban with a large proportion of males still employed in white-collar occupations. Still, these populations may be distinguished by their mean factor scores on the other dimensions. For example, Q Group V, consisting of Arizona and Florida, has the highest mean factor score on Factor II, reflecting the extreme mobility of residents of these two retirement states. In this respect, another retirement group, Q Group VII, also has a population which is characterized by high mobility.

Q Group V shows the highest loading on Factor IV. It is interesting to note that with respect to this institutionalization/disaffiliation factor, the retirement states of Arizona and Florida are quite similar to the traditional deep Southern states; both Q Groups I and V show high negative mean scores on Factor IV. Institutionalization rates are low in these states, and as well, true despite the mobility of the retirement states' elderly popul-true despite the mobility of the elderly retirement states' population and suggests that new forms of social affiliation may be emerging to replace traditional familial ties.

Q Group VI is different from all other groups in that it loads positively (and beyond +.40) on Factor III, income. So, while a high proportion of the elderly population of this Q group receives income of some kind, a high proportion of those doing so receive income of less than $3,000. It will be noted that on Factors I and IV, Q Group VI (Delaware and Virginia) scores somewhere between Q Group I (the Southern states) and Q Group III (the Eastern states). In a sense, between 1960 and 1970, Delaware and Virginia "dropped out" of their respective geographical groups and became a distinctive, separate population type midway between the other two.

Summary And Conclusions

The 1960 Q analysis gave us reason to believe that the traditional criterion of geographic regionality was not the most efficient technique for conceptualizing the elderly population of the United States. Only 1960 Q Groups III and IV were "pure" regional types. In two other Groups, I and II, the presence of extraregional areas had to be explained, despite dominant regional identities. In Q Groups V and VI, no geographic basis for the state groups could be discerned. On the basis of this analysis, Chevan and O'Rourke (1972, p. 125) suggested that the concept of regionality be redefined in social rather than geographical terms, and they substituted a notion of social and economic congruence among states for the regionality explanation.

The results of our analysis of the 1970 data offer mixed support for this substitute explanation. This not unexpected result is itself a product of social processes that in the last decade have acted to make the elderly population both more homogeneous and more heterogeneous. On the one hand, it would seem from the Q Groups yielded in this analysis, states that border do have elderly populations that are quite similarly constituted. And at least for the core states in the South, Midwest–North Central, and Eastern regions, these populations may be more similarly constituted in 1970 than they were in 1960. On the other hand, nine states did not fall into any of the Q groupings; an increase from two in 1960. In terms of the twenty social and economic indicators employed in this study, these states had aged populations that were quite different from one another and from those of all other states. This evidence of greater heterogeneity among state elderly populations between 1960 and 1970 is reason enough to maintain that under certain conditions, characterization of a particular elderly population can be made only in terms specific to that population. This evidence also suggests that the assumption of homogeneity across state elderly populations which seems to be present in attempts to federally standardize programs for these populations may have unfortunate consequences.

We have seen that state elderly populations are not alike. Thus, a program which is effective in one state or region of the country may be unsuccessful in other locations simply because the target populations differ.

Notes

1. The research reported in this paper was conducted at the Center for Program Effectiveness Studies, University of Virginia, as part of the Old Age Institutions Project, directed by Theodore Caplow and Howard Bahr and supported by a grant from the Administration on Aging, U.S. Department of Health, Education and Welfare (#93 - P - 57620-01).

THE
MEASUREMENT OF
LIFE SATISFACTION*[1]

Bernice L. Neugarten,
Robert J. Havighurst,
and Sheldon S. Tobin

There have been various attempts to define and to measure the psychological well-being of older people, usually with the goal of using such a measure as an operational definition of "successful" aging. Different terms have been used in approaching this problem (terms such as adjustment, competence, morale, or happiness); and different criteria, as well as different techniques of measurement, have been employed. A number of cogent criticisms have been made of these attempts at definition and measurement, largely because they are inextricably involved with value judgments (e.g., Rosow).

In many researches on aging, however, it becomes necessary to establish some measure of success or well-being in relation to which other social and psychological variables can be studied. In such research undertakings, therefore, rather than forego a measure of psychological well-being, it becomes the goal instead to construct as refined and as valid a measure as possible. Once the investigator makes his value judgments explicit by the choice of his terms and his criteria, furthermore, the actual construction and validation of such a measure can go forward in relatively straightforward and value-free manner.

In earlier approaches to this problem, there have been two general points of view. One focuses upon the overt behavior of

* Bernice L. Neugarten, Robert J. Havighurst, and Sheldon S. Tobin, "The Measurement of Life Satisfaction," *Journal of Gerontology* 16 (1961):134–143.

the individual and utilizes social criteria of success or competence. Studies that fall within this category tend to be ones in which level and range of activities and extent of social participation are the variables to be measured; and in which the assumption is made, implicitly or explicitly, that the greater the extent of social participation, and the less the individual varies from the pattern of activity that characterized him in middle age, the greater is his well-being.

The other point of view focuses upon the individual's internal frame of reference, with only secondary attention given to his level of social participation. Here the variables to be measured have been the individual's own evaluations of his present or past life, his satisfaction, or his happiness. The assumptions are, whether or not explicitly stated, that the individual himself is the only proper judge of his well-being; that the value judgments of the investigator can thus be minimized; and, perhaps most important, that it is not appropriate to measure well-being in old age by the same standards that apply to middle age, namely, standards based upon activity or social involvement.

As an example of the first point of view, Havighurst and Albrecht (1953), using public opinion as the criterion, developed a scale for measuring the social acceptability of the older person's behavior. Another example is the activity score on the schedule "Your Activities and Attitudes" (Cavan, Burgess, Havighurst, & Goldhamer, 1949; Havighurst & Albrecht, 1953), a score which sums up a person's participation in a number of different activities.

Most of the measuring instruments used in previous studies do, in fact, combine elements from both general approaches. For instance, in the Chicago Attitude Inventory (Cavan et al., 1949; Havighurst & Albrecht, 1953; Havighurst, 1957), a person is asked about his economic situation, work, family, friends, health, and so on, and about his happiness and feelings of usefulness. While the emphasis is upon feelings of satisfaction, a high score depends indirectly upon a high level of activity.

A second such measure is the Cavan Adjustment Rating Scale (Cavan et al., 1949; Havighurst, 1957). This is a rating based on interview data which takes into account not only the person's associations with family, friends, and formal and informal groups, but also his feelings of importance and satisfaction and his emotional stability.

Another measure that combines elements of both approaches is the social role performance measure used by Havighurst (1957). Here competence in the social roles of worker, parent, spouse, homemaker, citizen, friend, association member, and church member is rated from interview data; with the ratings based not only upon extent of reported activity, but also upon the individual's investment in and satisfaction with his performance in each role.

As part of a larger study of psychological and social factors involved in aging, the Kansas City Study of Adult Life,[2] the present investigators sought to develop a measure of the second general type—one that would use the individual's own evaluations as the point of reference; and one that would be relatively independent of level of activity or social participation. There have been other attempts to devise a measure with these general characteristics. For example, a few investigators (Kuhlen, 1956; Lebo, 1953; Rose, 1955; Pollak, 1948) have used direct self-reports of happiness. Although they are extremely vulnerable to conscious and unconscious psychological defenses, such self-reports have not usually been checked for validity against a more objective criterion.

Another example is Kutner's Morale Scale (Kutner, 1956), which is based upon responses to seven items such as, "On the whole, how satisfied would you say you are with your way of life today?" This instrument was not regarded as satisfactory for our purposes for several reasons: (1) It has not been validated against an outside criterion; (2) it is based upon the assumption that psychological well-being is a unidimensional phenomenon, for the scale has been constructed to form a scale of the Guttman type; (3) there have been scaling difficulties when the items have been used with populations other than the one originally studied. Thus, one of the seven items had to be scored differently for a New York City population than for an Elmira population (Kutner, 1956, p. 303); and an even greater effect of this type was seen when the scale was adapted for use with rural residents of South Dakota (Morrison & Kristjanson, 1958). In short, the items which are successful in producing a Guttman scale for one population are not altogether the same for another population.

Most recently, a Morale Index was developed by our collaborators on the Kansas City Study of Adult Life (Cumming, Dean, & Newell, 1958) consisting of four questions of which one was, "Do you wish you could see more of your relatives than you do now? Less? Your neighbors? Your friends?" (R is scored positively if he answers "Things are all right as they are.").

At the time the present investigators began work on this problem, that Index seemed unsatisfactory for several reasons.[3] It was based on so few items that scores might prove highly unreliable; the Index had been validated against only a small sample of cases; and, most important, it appeared to be a unidimensional measure reflecting, for the most part, resignation or conformity to the status quo. The Index seemed, therefore, not to reflect our own concepts of psychological well-being.

The research reported here had two purposes, each requiring a somewhat different set of procedures. The first, as already indicated, was to devise a measure of successful aging for use in the Kansas City Studies, a measure that would be derived relatively independently from various other psychological and social variables. The second purpose was to devise a short, easily administered instrument that could be used in other studies and to validate that instrument against Kansas City data.

After a description of the study population, the report that follows deals with the derivation and validation of the Life Satisfaction Ratings (LSR) and the scales upon which the ratings are based; then with the derivation and validation of two short self-administered instruments, the Life Satisfaction Index A (LSIA) and the Life Satisfaction Index B (LSIB).

The Study Population

Table 1 shows the distribution of the study population by age, sex, and social class. In brief, the upper-middle class represents business and professional levels; lower-middle, white-collar occupational levels; and the upper-lower represents blue-collar levels.

127

Table 1

The Study Population:
By Age at First Interview, Sex, and Social Class

Social class	Age group					Total
	50–56	57–63	64–70	71–79	80–89	
Upper-middle						
Men.	6	7	5	2	2	22
Women	7	6	6	6	3	28
Lower-middle						
Men.	4	4	7	7	6	28
Women	6	3	5	7	6	27
Upper-lower						
Men.	8	7	4	17	5	41
Women	5	7	6	10	3	31
Total. . . .	36	34	33	49	25	177

Note: Social class placements for panel members (the first three age groups in the table) were based upon an Index of Social Characteristics in which occupation (or former occupation), level of education, and area of residence were the three main factors. For the quasi-panel (the last two age groups in the table) this Index is less useful, since, with advancing age of R, neither educational level nor former occupation can be assumed to have the same social-class values as for the group who are presently middle-aged. (For example, the semiskilled worker today generally occupies a lower position in the social system than 40 years ago). We are indebted to Dr. Wayne Wheeler, present Field Director of the Kansas City Study, for his assistance in analyzing the social data available on these older persons and in arriving at their class placements. Because this whole problem of social-class placements for aged persons remains a difficult one, however, we may still have placed a disproportionate number into the upper-lower class.

This population was composed of members of two groups. The first, referred to as the panel group, were persons aged 50 to 70 at the time of the first interview in 1956. The panel represents a stratified probability sample of middle and working-class white persons of this age range residing in the metropolitan area of Kansas City. Excluded were the chronically ill and the physically impaired. The method by which the panel was selected resulted in a group that is biased toward middle class—in other words, that is better educated, wealthier, and of higher occupational and residential prestige than the universe of 50- to 70-year-olds.

The second group, referred to as the quasi-panel, were persons aged 70–90 who joined the Kansas City Study two years after field work had begun. This older group was built up on the basis of quota sampling rather than probability sampling. The group consists of middle- and working-class persons, none of them financially deprived and none of them bedridden or senile.

While the panel probably has a greater middle-class bias than the quasi-panel, it is likely that the older members of the study population are less representative of their universe than is true of the panel members. Not only are these older persons better off financially, but they are in better health than most 70- to 90-year-olds, and thus represent an advantaged rather than a typical group.

Of the original panel, 74 percent remained as cooperating respondents by the end of the fourth round of interviews, at which time the Life Satisfaction Ratings described below were made. Of the original quasi-panel, 83 percent remained at the same point in time, after two rounds of interviews. Thus, in addition to the various biases operating in the original selection of the two groups (for instance, 16 percent of those contacted refused to join the panel), there is an unmeasurable effect on the present study due to sample attrition. Of the attrition, 15 percent was due to deaths; 10 percent, to geographical moves; and the rest, to refusals to be interviewed the second, third, or fourth time. There is evidence also that persons who were relatively socially isolated constituted a disproportionate number of the dropouts.

All these factors should be kept in mind in considering the

range of Life Satisfaction Ratings obtained for this study population and in considering the generalizations that emerged regarding age differences.

The data. The data consisted of lengthy and repeated interviews covering many aspects of the respondent's life pattern, his attitudes, and his values. Included was information on the daily round and the usual weekend round of activity; other household members; relatives, friends, and neighbors; income and work; religion; voluntary organizations; estimates of the amount of social interaction as compared with the amount at age 45; attitudes toward old age, illness, death, and immortality; questions about loneliness, boredom, anger; and questions regarding the respondent's role models and his self-image. The first interview for the quasi-panel was a special schedule combining questions from the first three panel interviews. Both groups had the same fourth-round interview.

The Life Satisfaction Ratings

The first problem was to analyze our concept of psychological well-being into a sufficient number of components to represent its complexity, and then to find ways of measuring these components from interview data. Working with a group of graduate students in a research seminar, the investigators began by examining the measures of adjustment and morale that had been used in previous studies, and by defining distinguishable components. Definitions were tried out against case material; independent judgments of the cases were compared; the concepts were redefined; and so on.[4] Finally, operational definitions of the following components were obtained: Zest (vs. apathy); Resolution and fortitude; Congruence between desired and achieved goals; Positive self-concept; and Mood tone. More detailed definitions appear in the scales reproduced below, but in brief, an individual was regarded as being at the positive end of the continuum of psychological well-being to the extent that he: (A) takes pleasure from the round of activities that constitutes his everyday life; (B) regards his life as meaningful and accepts resolutely that which life has been; (C) feels he has succeeded in achieving his major goals; (D) holds a positive image of self; and (E) maintains happy and optimistic attitudes and mood.

Each of these five components was rated on a five-point scale (with 5, high); and the ratings were summed to obtain an overall rating with a possible range from 5 to 25.

We then sought a suitable term by which to refer to this overall rating; or, in other words, the best name for the five scales. The term "adjustment" is unsuitable because it carries the implication that conformity is the most desirable pattern of behavior. "Psychological well-being" is, if nothing else, an awkward phrase. "Morale," in many ways, captures best the qualities here being described, but there was the practical problem that there are already in use in gerontological research two different scales entitled Morale. The term Life Satisfaction was finally adopted on grounds that although it is not altogether adequate, it comes close to representing the five components.

In making the Life Satisfaction Ratings, all the interview data on each respondent were utilized. Thus the ratings are based not on R's direct self-report of satisfaction (although some questions of this type were included in the interview), but on the inferences drawn by the raters from all the information available on R, including his interpersonal relationships and how others reacted toward him.

The four rounds of interviewing had been spaced over approximately two and one-half years. In those few cases where marked changes had occurred in R's life situation within that interval of time, and where psychological well-being seemed to have changed accordingly, the rating represented the situation at the most recent point in time, at Interview 4.

Life Satisfaction Rating Scales[5]

A. *Zest vs. apathy.* To be rated here are enthusiasm of response and degree of ego-involvement—in any of various activities; persons, or ideas, whether or not these are activities which involve R with other people, are "good" or "socially approved" or "status-giving." Thus, R who "just loves to sit home and knit" rates as high as R who "loves to get out and meet people." Although a low rating is given for listlessness and apathy, physical energy per se is not to be involved in this rating. Low ratings are given for being "bored with most things"; for "I have to force myself to do things"; and also for meaningless (and unenjoyed) hyperactivity.

5 ... Speaks of several activities and relationships with enthusiasm. Feels that "now" is the best time of life. Loves to do things, even sitting at home. Takes up new activities; makes new friends readily, seeks self-improvement. Shows zest in several areas of life.

4 ... Shows zest, but it is limited to one or two special interests, or limited to certain periods of time. May show disappointment or anger when things go wrong, if they keep him from active enjoyment of life. Plans ahead, even though in small time units.

3 ... Has a bland approach to life. Does not seem to get much pleasure out of the things he does. Seeks relaxation and a limited degree of involvement. May be quite detached (aloof) from many activities, things, or people.

2 ... Thinks life is monotonous for the most part. May complain of fatigue. Feels bored with many things. If active, finds little meaning or enjoyment in the activity.

1 ... Lives on the basis of routine. Doesn't think anything worth doing.

B. *Resolution and fortitude.* The extent to which R accepts personal responsibility for his life; the opposite of feeling resigned, or of merely condoning or passively accepting that which life has brought him. The extent to which R accepts his life as meaningful and inevitable, and is relatively unafraid of death. Erikson's "integrity." Not to be confused with "autonomy" or the extent to which R's life has been self-propelled or characterized by initiative. R may not have been a person of high initiative, but yet he may accept resolutely and relatively positively that which life has been for him. R may feel life was a series of hard knocks, but that he has stood up under them (this would be a high rating).

There are two types of low ratings; the highly intropunitive, where R blames himself overly much; and the extrapunitive, where R blames others or the world in general for whatever failures or disappointments he has experienced.

5 ... Try and try again attitude. Bloody but unbowed. Fights back; withstanding, not giving up. Active personal responsibility—take the bad and the good and make the most of it. Wouldn't change the past.

4 ... Can take life as it comes. "I have no complaint on the way life has treated me." Assumes responsibility readily. "If you look for the good side of life, you'll find it." Does not mind talking about difficulties in life, but does not dwell on them either. "You have to give up some things."

3 ... Says, "I've had my ups and downs; sometimes on top, sometimes on the bottom." Shows a trace of extrapunitiveness or intropunitiveness concerning his difficulties in life.

2 ... Feels he hasn't done better because he hasn't gotten the breaks. Feels great difference in life now as compared to age 45; the change has been for the worse. "I've worked hard but never got anywhere."

1 ... Talks of hard knocks which he has not mastered (extrapunitive). Feels helpless. Blames self a great deal (intropunitive). Overwhelmed by life.

C. *Congruence between desired and achieved goals.* The extent to which R feels he has achieved his goals in life, whatever those goals might be; feels he has succeeded in accomplishing what he regards as important. High ratings go, for instance, to R who says, "I've managed to keep out of jail" just as to R who says, "I managed to send all my kids through college." Low ratings go to R who feels he's missed most of his opportunities, or who ways, "I've never been suited to my work," or "I always wanted to be a doctor, but never could get there." Also to R who wants most to be "loved," but instead feels merely "approved." (Expressions of regret for lack of education are not counted because they are stereotyped responses among all but the group of highest social status.)

5 ... Feels he has accomplished what he wanted to do. He has achieved or is achieving his own personal goals.

4 . . . Regrets somewhat the chances missed during life. "Maybe I could have made more of certain opportunities." Nevertheless, feels that he has been fairly successful in accomplishing what he wanted to do in life.

3 . . . Has a fifty-fifty record of opportunities taken and opportunities missed. Would have done some things differently, if he had his life to live over. Might have gotten more education.

2 . . . Has regrets about major opportunities missed but feels good about accomplishment in one area (may be his avocation).

1 . . . Feels he has missed most opportunities in life.

D. *Self-concept.* R's concept of self—physical as well as psychological and social attributes. High ratings go to R who is concerned with grooming and appearance; who thinks of himself as wise, mellow (and thus is comfortable in giving advice to others); who feels proud of his accomplishments; who feels he deserves whatever good breaks he has had; who feels he is important to someone else. Low ratings are given to R who feels "old," weak, sick, incompetent; who feels himself a burden to others; who speaks disparagingly of self or of old people.

5 . . . Feels at his best. "I do better work now than ever before." "There was never any better time." Thinks of self as wise, mellow; physically able or attractive; feels important to others. Feels he has the right to indulge himself.

4 . . . Feels more fortunate than the average. Is sure that he can meet the exigencies of life. "When I retire, I'll just substitute other activities." Compensates well for any difficulty of health. Feels worthy of being indulged. "Things I want to do, I can do, but I'll not overexert myself." Feels in control of self in relation to the situation.

3 . . . Sees self as competent in at least one area, e.g., work; but has doubts about self in other areas. Acknowledges loss of youthful vigor, but accepts it in a realistic way. Feels relatively unimportant, but doesn't mind. Feels he takes, but also gives. Senses a general,

but not extreme, loss of status as he grows older. Reports health better than average.

2 ... Feels that other people look down on him. Tends to speak disparagingly of older people. Is defensive about what the years are doing to him.

1 ... Feels old. Feels in the way, or worthless. Makes self-disparaging remarks. "I'm endured by others."

E. *Mood tone.* High ratings for R who expresses happy, optimistic attitudes and mood; who uses spontaneous, positively toned affective terms for people and things; who takes pleasure from life and expresses it. Low ratings for depression, "feel blue and lonely"; for feelings of bitterness; for frequent irritability and anger. (Here we consider not only R's verbalized attitudes in the interview; but make inferences from all we know of his interpersonal relationships, how others react toward him.)

5 ... "This is the best time of my life." Is nearly always cheerful, optimistic. Cheerfulness may seem unrealistic to an observer, but R shows no sign of "putting up a bold front."

4 ... Gets pleasure out of life, knows it and shows it. There is enough restraint to seem appropriate to a younger person. Usually feels positive affect. Optimistic

3 ... Seems to move along on an even temperamental keel. Any depressions are neutralized by positive mood swings. Generally neutral-to-positive affect. May show some irritability.

2 ... Wants things quiet and peaceful. General neutral-to-negative affect. Some depression.

1 ... Pessimistic, complaining, bitter. Complains of being lonely. Feels "blue" a good deal of the time. May get angry when in contact with people.

Reliability of ratings. Ratings were made on every case by two judges working independently. The judges were members of a student-faculty research seminar. A system was followed by which judges and groups of cases were systematically varied. In all, fourteen judges rated the 177 cases, and all but one judge maintained a high level of agreement with the others with whom he was paired. The coefficient of correlation between two LSR ratings for the 177 cases was .78. (Since, in all subsequent steps, the average of the two ratings was used, the Spearman-Brown coefficient of attenuation can be employed to raise the coefficient to .87.) Of 885 paired judgments, 94 percent showed exact agreement or agreement within one step on the 5-step scale. (On the same basis, interjudge agreement varied only

---

Table 2

Intercorrelations of the Components of Life Satisfaction (N = 177).

	Resolution	Congruence	Self-concept	Mood Tone
Zest.	.67	.56	.70	.84
Resolution		.70	.83	.48
Congruence			.73	.57
Self-concept				.82

---

slightly from one component to the next. It was 97 percent for Zest, 96 percent for Resolution; 92 percent for Congruence; 96 percent for Self-concept; and 92 percent for Mood tone.)

For the 177 cases, LSR scores ranged from 8 to 25, with the mean, 17.8, and the standard deviation, 4.6.

Intercorrelations between components. Table 2 shows the intercorrelations between the five components of Life Satisfaction. While positively interrelated, they nevertheless show a fair degree of independence, supporting the assumption that more than one dimension are involved in the scales. Without submitting these coefficients to a factor analysis, it appears that Zest, Mood tone, and possibly Self-concept involve one factor, with the probability of one or two other factors operating in the matrix.

Characteristics of the LSR. For this sample of 177 cases there was no correlation between Life Satisfaction and age (r was -.07). (It is likely that, with a less advantaged group of people, there will be a negative relationship between the two variables.)

Using an Index of Social Characteristics (LSC) based on three factors, level of education, area of residence, and occupation (or former occupation), the correlation between LSR and LSC was .39. Thus, there is a positive, but not marked, relationship between Life Satisfaction and socioeconomic status.

There was no significant sex difference on LSR scores. The mean for the women was 17.9 (S. D., 3.58); and for the men, 17.5 (S. D., 4.04).

With regard to marital status, the nonmarried (the single, divorced, separated, and widowed) had significantly lower LSR scores. This relationship held true for both sexes, and for both younger and older subgroups in the study population.

Validity of the ratings. The LSR depended on scoring by judges who had read all the recorded interview material, but who had not themselves interviewed the respondent. In seeking to establish an outside criterion by which these ratings could be validated, the investigators thought it desirable to have an experienced clinical psychologist interview the respondents and then make his own ratings of Life Satisfaction.

For various practical reasons, it was not until some 18 to 22 months had elapsed after Interview 4 that these clinical interviews were begun.[6] By this time, a fifth and sixth wave of interviewing had intervened, and there had been further attrition of the study population due not only to deaths and geographic moves, but also to refusals. Nevertheless, over a three-month period, 80 respondents were interviewed at length by the clinical psychologist; and it is his ratings (LSR–Cl) that constitute a validity check on the LSR. These interviews and ratings were made by the clinician without any prior knowledge of the respondent—that is, without reading any of the earlier interviews and without discussion of the case with other members of the research staff.

The 80 cases were representative of the 177 as regards sex, age, and social class. They had, however, a slightly higher mean score on the LSR. (Mean LSR for the 177 cases was 17.8; for the 80 cases seen by the clinician, it was 18.9. Twenty-five percent of the total 177, but only 15 percent of the 80 cases, were persons with LSR scores of 14.5 or less.) In other words, a disproportionate number of dropouts in the 18- to 24-month interval were persons who were low on Life Satisfaction.

Using the average of the two judges' ratings for the LSR score, the correlation between LSR and LSR-C1 for the 80 cases was .64. Of 400 paired judgments, 76 percent represented exact agreement or agreement within one step on the 5-step scale. (On the same basis, agreement between LSR and LSR-C1 varied somewhat from one component to the next. It was 86 percent for Zest; 76 percent for Resolution; 73 percent for Congruence; 78 percent for Self-concept; and 69 percnet for Mood tone.)

Further study was made of several cases for whom there was marked disagreement between the LSR and the LSR-C1. As anticipated, these cases were of two types: (1) There were a few who had been rated higher on LSR, and where it seemed a reasonable explanation that the clinical psychologist had succeeded in probing beneath the respondent's defenses and had obtained a truer picture of his feelings.

> Mrs. B, for instance, was a woman whose facade was successful throughout the first four interviews in convincing the judges reading the interviews that she was a person who had achieved all her major goals; that she was resolute, competent, happy, even in the face of repeated physical illness. In the more intensive interview, however, she broke down and wept, and said she felt life had been unjust and that she had been an unlucky person. It was the clinician's interpretation that she had long been depressed, and that the somatic illnesses had been a defense against the depression. She was a woman with a strong moral code and with tremendous pride; who went through life feeling that at no time must she reveal her disappointments.

(2) There were a few cases where the respondent's life situation had changed drastically in the interval of time between the LSR and the LSR-C1 ratings. The respondent had suffered severe illness, or had been widowed, and the crisis had brought on a depression. In a few instances, however, the change had been for the better, as reflected in a higher LSR-C1 rating.

> One man, at the time of Interview 4, had just been widowed. A year earlier he had been retired from his job as a

salesman. He was worried about money as well as being depressed over the death of his wife. When seen by the clinical psychologist, however, he freely discussed the fact that two years earlier he had experienced a depression, but that now he was recovered. He had found a new job selling, door to door, and he enjoyed what he called his "contacts with the public." He was living in a small apartment near his daughter's family, and he described with enthusiasm his grandchildren and the outings he had with them on weekends.

In general, the correlation of .64 between LSR and LSR-C1 was interpreted by the investigators as providing a satisfactory degree of validation for the LSR, given the various factors already mentioned: (1) the lapse of time between the two ratings; (2) the fact that a number of persons low on Life Satisfaction had dropped out of the study, thus narrowing the range of LSR scores for the 80 cases—a fact that, in turn, tended to lower the coefficient of correlation; (3) the fact that the LSR was based only on recorded interview data; the LSR-C1, on face-to-face interaction; (4) the greater depth of the clinical psychologist's interviews.

It is of some interest in this connection that the correlation between LSR and LSR-C1 was higher for the older members of the sample. For 30 cases aged 70 and over, r was .70; for the 50 cases aged 69 and below, r was .53. It may be that the aged individual has less of a tendency to give conforming or "normative" responses in the regular interview situation than does the younger individual; thus providing fewer instances in which the clinical psychologist's depth questions revealed a different level of functioning than shown by replies to the more structured interviews. It might be, on the other hand, that in some manner of which the investigators were unaware, they devised interview questions and rating scales for Life Satisfaction that are more appropriate for the very old respondent than for the somewhat younger respondent and that, as a result, different judges were more likely to agree in their evaluations of persons over 70.[7] Whatever the explanation, age differences such as these should be explored further in future studies.

The Life Satisfaction Indexes

While the LSR is likely to prove useful in other studies where the amount of information about a respondent is less extensive than in the Kansas City Study, the LSR will require at least one long interview with the respondent. It may therefore be too cumbersome to be used on a large scale. Consequently, using the LSR as the validating criterion, the investigators attempted to devise a self-report instrument which would take only a few minutes to administer. Two such instruments were devised, to be used separately or together.

The derivation of the Indexes. From the larger group on whom LSR scores were available, a sample of 60 cases were selected that represented the full range of age, sex, and social class. Of these 60 cases, the high scorers and the low scorers on LSR were used as criterion groups. A long list of items and open-ended questions from Interviews 1 through 4 were then studied to select those that differentiated these two groups. (Some of these items had originally been taken from Kutner's Morale Scale.) In addition to this item analysis, certain new items were written which reflected each of the five components of Life Satisfaction.

Two preliminary instruments then emerged. The first, called the Life Satisfaction Index A (LSIA) consisted of 25 attitude items for which only an "agree" or "disagree" response is required. The second, the Life Satisfaction Index B (LSIB) consisted of 17 open-ended questions and check-list items, to be scored on a three-point scale.

These two instruments were then administered to 92 respondents along with Interview 6. (A number of respondents had already been interviewed in this sixth wave of field work by the time these instruments were ready. Because 92 seemed a large enough *N* for our purposes, no attempt was made to return and administer these instruments to those who had already been interviewed.)

When 60 of the 92 cases were in, preliminary computations were made. Scores on LSIA correlated .52 with LSR; scores on LSIB correlated .59 with LSR. These results seemed to warrant further efforts at refining and trimming the instruments. When all 92 cases were in, therefore, an item analysis was undertaken whereby each item of the Indexes was studied for the extent to which it differentiated the high and low LSR groups among the 92. (Top and bottom quartiles on LSR were used as criterion groups.)

As a result of this analysis, five items of LSIA and seven items of LSIB were discarded. In their final form, these Indexes are given below, together with their scoring keys.[8]

Life Satisfaction Index A

Here are some statements about life in general that people feel differently about. Would you read each statement on the list, and if you agree with it, put a check mark in the space under "AGREE." If you do not agree with a statement, put a check mark in the space under "DIS-AGREE." If you are not sure one way or the other, put a check mark in the space under "?." PLEASE BE SURE TO ANSWER EVERY QUESTION ON THE LIST.

(Key: score 1 point for each response marked X.)

	AGREE	DIS-AGREE	?
1. As I grow older, things seem better than I thought they would be.	...X..	....	....
2. I have gotten more of the breaks in life than most of the people I know.	...X..	....	....
3. This is the dreariest time of my life.	....	...X..	....
4. I am just as happy as when I was younger.	...X..	....	....
5. My life could be happier than it is now.	....	...X..	....
6. These are the best years of my life.	...X..	....	....
7. Most of the things I do are boring or monotonous.	....	...X..	....
8. I expect some interesting and pleasant things to happen to me in the future.	...X..	....	....
9. The things I do are as interesting to me as they ever were.	...X..	....	....
10. I feel old and somewhat tired.	....	...X..	....

141

11. I feel my age, but it does not bother me. ....X.. ....

12. As I look back on my life, I am fairly well satisfied. ....X.. ....

13. I would not change my past life even if I could. ....X.. ....

14. Compared to other people my age, I've made a lot of foolish decisions in my life. ....X.. ....

15. Compared to other people my age, I make a good appearance. ....X.. ....

16. I have made plans for things I'll be doing a month or a year from now. ....X.. ....

17. When I think back over my life, I didn't get most of the important things I wanted. ....X.. ....

18. Compared to other people, I get down in the dumps too often. ....X.. ....

19. I've gotten pretty much what I expected out of life. ....X.. ....

20. In spite of what people say, the lot of the average man is getting worse, not better. ....X.. ....

Life Satisfaction Index B
(with scoring key)

Would you please comment freely in answer to the following questions?

1. Whate are the best things about being the age you are now?
   1........a positive answer
   0........nothing good about it
2. What do you think you will be doing five years from now? How do you expect things will be different from the way they are now, in your life?
   2........better, or no change
   1........contingent—"It depends"
   0........worse
3. What is the most important thing in your life right now?
   2........anything outside of self, or pleasant interpretation of future

    1........"Hanging on"; keeping health, or job

    0........getting out of present difficulty, or "nothing now," or reference to the past

4. How happy would you say you are right now, compared with the earlier periods in your life?

    2........this is the happiest time; all have been happy; or, hard to make a choice

    1........some decrease in recent years

    0........earlier periods were better, this is a bad time

5. Do you ever worry about your ability to do what people expect of you—to meet demands that people make on you?

    2........no

    1........qualified yes or no

    0........yes

6. If you could do anything you pleased, in what part of——would you most like to live?

    2........present location

    0........any other location

7. How often do you find yourself feeling lonely?

    2........never; hardly ever

    1........sometimes

    0........fairly often; very often

8. How often do you feel there is no point in living?

    2........never; hardly ever

    1........sometimes

    0........fairly often; very often

9. Do you wish you could see more of your close friends than you do, or would you like more time to yourself?

    2........O. K. as is

    0........wish could see more of friends

    0........wish more time to self

10. How much unhappiness would you say you find in your life today?

    2........almost none

    1........some

    0........a great deal

11. As you get older, would you say things seem to be better or worse than you thought they would be?

    2........better

    1........about as expected

    0........worse

12. How satisfied would you say you are with your way of life?

    2........very satisfied

    1........fairly satisfied

    0........not very satisfied

As shown in Table 3, the coefficient of correlation between the final form of LSIA and LSR was .55. (The mean score on LSIA was 12.4, and the standard deviation, 4.4). The correlation between the final form of LSIB and LSR was .58. (The mean score for LSIB was 15.1, the standard deviation, 4.7). For combined scores on the two Indexes, the correlation with LSR was .61. (The mean for the combined scores was 27.6; the standard deviation, 6.7).

Table 3

Coefficients of Correlation for Various Measures of Life Satisfaction

	1	2	3	4	5	6
1) LSR.	——	.64 (80)	.55 (89)	.58 (89)	.39 (177)	-.07 (177)
2) LSR-C1.		——	.39 (51)	.47 (52)	.21 (80)	.09 (80)
3) LSIA			——	.73 (91)	.36 (79)	-.10 (86)
4) LSIB				——	.41 (80)	-.07 (86)
5) Socioeconomic status.					——	——a
6) Age						——

Note: The number of cases on which the correlation is based is shown in parentheses.

a This relationship is zero by definition, since the sample was deliberately selected to control for age and socioeconomic status.

Validity of the Indexes. As just described the derivation and validation of the Indexes proceeded as a single set of operations; and the LSR cannot be regarded as an outside criterion. It is noteworthy, despite this fact, that the correlations between Index scores and LSR are only moderate in size.

It is true that the sixth wave of interviewing began about 14 months after the fourth wave, so that the interval of time between LSR and the two Index scores for the same respondent was, in some instances, as much as 18 to 20 months. This lapse of time probably operated to lower somewhat the congruence between the measures.

144

Nevertheless, the more important point is undoubtedly that direct self-reports, even though carefully measured, can be expected to agree only partially with the evaluations of life satisfaction made by an outside observer (in this case, the judges who made the LSR ratings.)

Certain additional steps were carried out in respect to validation. Scores on the two Indexes, for instance, were compared with LSR-C1 (the ratings made by the clinical psychologist). Of the 80 cases on whom LSR-C1 scores were available, only 51 had LSIA scores; 52 LSIB. For this relatively small number of cases, the correlations with LSR-C1 were .39 and .47 respectively. These correlations were probably lowered by the fact already mentioned, that the respondents interviewed by the clinical psychologist constituted a superior group with regard to Life Satisfaction, thus providing a narrow range of scores on which to assess these correlations.

The question was also raised regarding the extent to which LSIA and LSIB were more reflective of Mood Tone alone than of the other components of LSR. Scores on each of the two Indexes correlated no higher, however, with ratings on Mood tone alone than with LSR ratings.

Age differences. We have already commented on the fact that, in rating Life Satisfaction (LSR and LSR-C1), agreement between the clinical psychologist and the other raters was greater for the older respondents than for the younger. A parallel pheonomenon was true with regard to scores on the two Indexes. For persons under 65, LSR-C1 correlated .05 with LISA, and .32 with LSIB. For persons over 65, the correlations were .55 and .59 respectively. While the *N*s on which these correlations are based are small, the finding parallels the earlier one with regard to greater consistency between measures for respondents of advanced age.

The question once more arises as to whether this greater consistency is an artifact of the measures themselves, or whether it reflects an increasing consistency in psychological behavior in aged persons.

Whatever the explanation, a review of all the relationships here reported between LSR, LSR-C1, LSIA and LSIB seems to warrant the conclusion that the Indexes are more successful instruments for persons over 65 than for younger persons.

Summary

This paper reports the derivation of a set of scales for rating Life Satisfaction, using data on 177 men and women aged 50 to 90. The ratings were based on lengthy interview material, and were validated against the judgments of a clinical psychologist who re-interviewed and rated 80 cases. The scales appear to be relatively satisfactory and may prove useful to other investigators interested in a measure of the psychological well-being of older people.

In addition, two short self-report Indexes of Life Satisfaction were devised and validated against the Life Satisfaction Ratings. While considerable effort was expended in refining these instruments, the effort was only moderately successful. If used with caution, the Indexes will perhaps be useful for certain group measurements of persons over 65.

The rating scales and the two Indexes are reproduced here.

Notes

1. A partial report of this research was included in a paper by R. J. Havighurst, Successful aging: definition and measurement, presented at the International Research Seminar on the Social and Psychological Aspects of Aging, August 1960. The seminar papers will be published in a volume edited by Richard H. Williams, James E. Birren, Wilma Donahue, and Clark Tibbitts, *Psychological and social processes of aging: An international seminar.*

2. The Kansas City Study of Adult Life is financed by Grant 3M9082 from the National Institute of Mental Health to the Committee on Human Devlopment of the University of Chicago. It is under the supervision of William F. Henry (Principal Investigator), Robert J. Havighurst, and Bernice L. Neugarten. The Study Director has been Elaine Cumming, and the Field Director, Lois R. Dean. The present Field Director is Wayne Wheeler.

3. The Morale Index, in its most recent form, is described by Cumming and Henry (in press).

4. The investigators were aided by Dr. Lois Dean, who was then Field Director of the Kansas City Study. Dr. Dean had interviewed certain of the respondents at great length, and had made an analysis of morale in the aged. Several of the components later incorporated into the LSR stemmed from her analysis.

5. Other investigators may use the Scales and Indexes reproduced in this report without permission from either the present investigators or the *Journal of Gerontology*.

6. We are indebted to Mr. William Crotty for obtaining these 80 interviews and making the LSR-C1 ratings.

7. In this connection, it is not uncommon for psychiatrists to remark that a half-hour interview is sufficient to evaluate the adjustment or mental health of an old person; but that it takes considerably more time to make a similar evaluation for a younger person.

8. See Footnote 5

COMMUNICATION
IN THE INTERVIEW
AND THE
DISENGAGED RESPONDENT*[1]

Kenneth J. Gergen and Kurt W. Back

Responses to questions in a survey interview may be viewed as resulting from both the specific item content of the various questions and the stylistic orientation of the respondent to the interview situation. In the former case, the response is generally considered an expression of an attitude or opinion. For present purposes, such responses can be considered a *direct* form of communication. However, in the *indirect* mode, responses may not be affected so much by specific item content as by more personal factors. For example, the way in which conditions of the interview situation are seen by the respondent may affect his responses in various pervasive ways. In this regard, such factors as respondent anonymity, interviewer rapport, and differential group membership of interviewer and respondent have been studied.[2] Indirect communication may also reflect certain features of the respondent's personality. This indirect component of communication is normally considered response error in a survey interview, and the attempt is typically made to reduce and control it.

On the other hand, for many purposes indirect communication may be an extremely important source of information. In fact, experimentation in social psychology often uses relatively

---

* Kenneth J. Gergen and Kurt W. Back, "Communication in the Interview and the Disengaged Respondent," *Public Opinion Quarterly* 30 (1966): 385-98.

unimportant question content in order to maximize the effects of various interpersonal factors. In the area of personality assessment, projective tests are largely based on the notion that highly unstructured test items will yield considerable information about the personality of the respondent.

Perhaps the two most important factors influencing indirect communication are the personal orientation of the respondent and the structure of the social interview. The respondent's personal orientation may affect his communication in many ways. Recently, there has been widespread interest in what has been termed "response bias," or the tendency of a person to respond in a consistent pattern to a variety of questions regardless of specific question content. "Yea saying," socially desirable responding, and deviant response sets have all received attention in this regard.[3] With the possible exception of socially desirable responding, the exact significance of these stylistic modes of response is not yet well understood. However, the underlying assumption is that there are deep-seated personality differences among people that give rise to specific response patterns regardless of item content.

A second important factor influencing indirect communication may be derived from what has been called the "ecology of the interview."[4] Here it is assumed that the survey interview is similar to other types of social situations with respect to the presence of built-in social demands, and that these demands may influence the information disclosed by the respondent. This approach would be exemplified by Lenski and Leggett, who have demonstrated the effects of interviewer and respondent class differences on acquiescent responding, and Taietz, who found that the presence of a third person in the interview had a significant effect on the respondent's answers.[5]

Although survey interviews are generally designed to elicit information on specific questions and to minimize indirect expressions of personality, such expressions may enter into responses on even the best designed and executed survey interview. One method of exploring these expressions is to focus on a large number of conceptually similar questions answered by sizable populations of persons whose personality characteristics differ in systematic ways. Such an approach should facilitate

149

both further understanding of the personality dimension and an evaluation of the meaning of responses in a survey interview.

Disengagement and the Aged in the Interview

The effects of aging on personality have received much attention within the past decade. Perhaps one of the most significant contributions in this area within recent years has been Cumming and Henry's theory of aging and disengagement.[6] These authors characterize the transition from middle age to senescence as a progressive disengagement of the person from the other members of his society. Broadly speaking, this might be called a constriction in the social life space and, as the authors indicate, includes a diminution in the variety, density, and number of social interactions. As social disengagement occurs, there is also less contact with the norms of society. One result is that the aged person is increasingly freed from many of the norms governing everyday behavior. This is evidenced in less conformity to the dominant values of the culture and more idiosyncratic responses in a variety of situations. From the present point of view, the disengaged person may not hold different opinions from others, but the mode of expressing his opinions may differ considerably. In his broad pattern of responding, the disengaged person can provide much information about the general structure of his world view.

How might the personality of the disengaged or aged person manifest itself in the survey interview and, more specifically, with regard to the two sources of indirect communication discussed above? In terms of the personality of the aged person, it has been suggested that he has been forced into a position somewhat peripheral to the society at large. As a result, he may become less attuned to the issues that are of central importance in the society. According to disengagement theory, this lack of interest should manifest itself across a wide range of topics, and thus, in terms of response bias, should operate with litte regard to specific item content.

As far as the social situation of the interview is concerned, it has been noted that the disengaged person becomes less constrained by the bonds of normative social interaction. The social demands placed on the respondent by the inquisitive interviewer are, of course, considerable; however, the interviewer may have less power to motivate and direct the aged respondent toward the "proper" manner of responding. The disengaged person should be no less disengaged in the survey interview than in the remainder of his social spheres.

This lack of interest and unresponsiveness to social pressure should lead the disengaged person to express fewer opinions in a quantitative sense. He should respond with more "no opinion" answers, and even if he gives an opinion, his decreased attention to both the question and the interviewer should manifest itself in the tendency to avoid finger gradations and intermediate response categories.[7] Because of the inability of the interviewer to motivate him to give attention to detail, the disengaged person should prefer either nondifferentiating or extreme answers regardless of the content of the question. The applicability of this rationale to a number of response patterns found in survey results can now be more closely examined.

Degree of Opinionation

As stated, one might expect aging to be negatively related to the degree of general opinionation. This was measured in several national surveys in terms of the percentage of persons who were designated as having "no opinion." From four Gallup surveys all items that allowed the "no opinion" response were analyzed as they related to increasing age. Using three age groups (young: 20–39, middle: 40–59, and old: 60 years and over) the percentage of "no opinion" responses was computed for each item. As the level of "no opinion" response is generally quite low, which is understandable in surveys in which interviewers are trained to obtain definite answers, the absolute value of the differences between age groups in any given item is small. Thus, to investigate the consistency of the data on opinionation the following method was first used.

For each item it was noted whether the percentage of "no opinion" responses was greater in the middle-aged group than in the young, and greater in the old group than in the middle. The number of items on each survey for which the direction of these differences supported the hypothesis (i.e. middle greater than young and old greater than middle)[8] was then summed. As can be seen in Table 1, for each of the four surveys the middle-aged group exceeded the young in terms of the number of items for which the percentage of "no opinion" responses was greater. A sign test reveals that this difference is significant at beyond the

Table 1

Age and Frequency of Greater Percentage of No Opinion Responses

Survey	Number of Items	Number of Items in which Percent of "No Opinion" Responses was Larger for Older Group	
		Middle > Young	Old > Middle
AIPO 456	9	5	7
AIPO 457	9	5	8
AIPO 549	13	11	9
AIPO 580	15	12	14
Total	46	33	38

.05 probability level in two of the four surveys. As one might expect from disengagement theory, the difference between the old group and the middle-aged group is even more striking. A sign test again reveals significant differences in two of the four surveys and probability levels that are just shy of significance in the two remaining surveys. Collapsing across surveys, significant differences emerge between each age group.

Several arguments can be raised against the present interpretation of these findings. First of all, it might be argued that since the Gallup surveys have traditionally contained a large percentage of political questions, these results essentially reflect political opinionation. An analysis of the content of the forty-six items used revealed that only eleven of the items were political in nature. Thus, whereas these results may be slightly weighted toward political issues, and there are most certainly some issues about which the aged are more opinionated, the lack of opinionation seems to be broadly pervasive.

Second, it might be argued that on a statistical basis the findings for any given survey may only be reflecting the lack of opinionation of a few individuals responding consistently. Such a criticism would also, of course, raise doubts about the use of a sign test in the above analyses. Although the reliability of the

---

Table 2

Age and Opinionation as Measured by the Opinionation Index, Gallup Survey 580
(in percent)

Opinionation	20-39 Years (637)	40-59 Years (625)	60 Years and Over (275)
High	77.1	73.4	67.6
Low	6.9	9.4	11.6

---

findings throughout all four surveys vies aginst such an argument, a more rigorous assessment of the relationship between aging and opinionation may be based on an "opinionation index" involving all items from a given survey. With ten items, for example, a score of "zero" might be given to an individual who responded with an opinion on each item, and a score 10 to one who failed to respond to all items. The data from the Gallup survey 580 were subjected to such an analysis. Those who failed to render an opinion five or more times were termed the "low opinionation" group. Those who have opinions on all items, or all but one, were termed the "high opinionation" group.[9] The results of this analysis are featured in Table 2. In support of the hypothesis, the percentage of respondents who were highly opinionated decreases with age, while the percentage of those who were low in opinionation increases with age.

153

A chi-square test indicates that this difference is significant at beyond the .05 level.

It could also be maintained that since auditory or visual impairments increase sharply with the onset of senescence, the above results are reflecting nothing more than the physical state of the respondents. Although there was a general decrease in opinionation between the young and middle-aged groups, neither of which should be particularly beset by physical difficulties, an additional survey allowed a more intensive analysis of the differences between these two groups. On this survey there were only two groups of respondents: 18–25 years and 40–55 years of age. The number of respondents used in this survey was also practically twice that of any other survey. Twenty-three items offered "don't know" as one response alternative. The results indicated that the frequency of larger percentages of "don't know" responses was overwhelmingly in the direction predicted. In the entire group of twenty-three items, only two reversals occurred.

One final criticism of the data in this section concerns the fact that the aged population is generally less well educated. Since education may be related to the amount of information a person has available, differences in education may be accounting for these differences in opinionation. To assess the legitimacy of this argument, it was first determined with the data from Gallup 580 that age and education were, for this sample, actually negatively related. Using the opinionation index discussed above, it was also found that degree of opinionation was positively related with amount of education. Thus, the crucial question was whether holding education constant, there remained a decrease in opinionation with increasing age. The results of the analysis, depicted in Table 3, show that the relationship between age and opinionation becomes somewhat more complicated when education is taken into account. Among those with at least a high school education, increased age is related to opinionation in the hypothesized manner. However, among those with less than a high school education, degree of opinionation *increases* with advancing age.

Two alternative explanations for these findings suggest themselves. On the one hand, it could well be that measuring

"education" by number of formal years of schooling is misleading for those whose education is minimal. Quite often a person
with little formal education acquires much more knowledge in
later years in other than formal channels. Thus, for the lower
education groups these results may well be reflecting the accumulation of informal learning experiences. On the other hand,
it is conceivable that the less educated respondent, advanced in
years, becomes more highly sensitized to the interviewing situation. Feeling that he may be judged negatively by the inquisitor,
he overreacts in order to *appear* informed. In this manner he

Table 3

Age, Education, and Degree of Opinionation, Gallup Survey 580
(in percent)

	20-39 Years		40-59 Years		60 Years and Over	
Opinionation	Grammar and Less (105)	High and More (532)	Grammar and Less (239)	High and More (385)	Grammar and Less (159)	High and More (116)
High	60.9	80.8	63.3	79.7	64.1	72.4
Low	16.2	5.1	12.5	6.8	13.8	8.6

would be able to overcome publicly the deficit of having little
formal training. Although the former of these interpretations
would seem to have the greatest intuitive appeal, data related to
the alternative hypothesis will be discussed in the final section
of this paper.

The Nondiscriminating Response

Extremism. The authors have elsewhere demonstrated how
a constricted time perspective, also characteristic of the aged
person, can lead to certain kinds of extreme responses.[10] Such
extremism was largely related to decision-making situations in

which persons were allowed to choose among long-, short-, or intermediate-range solutions to problems. However, it was reasoned above that when given a wide variety of possible alternatives lying along a single dimension, the elderly person will feel himself under less pressure to make fine discriminations among alternatives than the younger respondent. He can, as discussed above, choose not to answer the question or, as will be explored here, choose to answer it in an extreme fashion. In effect, the extreme choice would indicate disregard for the intermediate scale points.

This notion was supported by results from two separate surveys. In the first (Gallup Survey 456), a series of six questions dealt with the degree to which the respondent worried about certain topics, such as another war, making ends meet, etc. For each of the items the respondent could choose among four alternatives: worry a lot, some, little, or none. Although the question of age and amount of worry is an interesting one in its own right,[11] the present interest was in the effect of age on choosing either of the extreme responses, i.e. "a lot" or "none." Combining all six items, it was possible to determine how many times out of the six items an individual chose either one of the extremes or one of the middle-range alternatives. The results indicate that the percentage of respondents who chose no extremes out of the six items decreased with age, while those who chose six extreme responses increased with age. Whereas 6.0 percent of the middle-aged group chose no extremes and 13.4 percent chose all extremes, of the old-aged group only 2.7 percent chose no extremes and 24.7 percent chose all extremes (x^2 probability $<$ .05). The middle vs. young comparison showed no difference.

On a second survey, respondents were asked to rate their like or dislike of a number of political figures or nations on a ten-point scale ranging from +5 for extreme like to −5 for extreme dislike. Here the interest was in the tendency for respondents to choose either the extreme like or dislike responses. Dropping from each age group those respondents who avoided the question by failing to respond, the percentage of respondents endorsing extremes was computed. As can be seen in Table 4, there is a marked tendency, regardless of nation or

Table 4

Age and Choice of Extreme Reactions, Gallup Survey 538
(in percent)

	20–39 Years	40-59 Years	60 Years and Over
England			
Extreme like	12.9	11.0	16.1
Extreme dislike	5.5	8.5	11.9
Total	18.4	19.5	28.0
(N)	(565)	(447)	(168)
France			
Extreme like	9.1	7.6	9.1
Extreme dislike	4.6	6.7	9.1
Total	13.7	14.3	18.2
(N)	(541)	(432)	(164)
West Germany			
Extreme like	9.7	10.9	16.9
Extreme dislike	7.0	8.7	6.9
Total	16.7	19.6	23.8
(N)	(527)	(414)	(160)
Senator McCarthy			
Extreme like	13.9	13.9	19.8
Extreme dislike	26.0	31.9	33.5
Total	39.9	45.8	53.3
(N)	(531)	(417)	(167)
Winston Churchill			
Extreme like	14.7	23.0	26.9
Extreme dislike	5.3	7.4	7.0
Total	20.0	30.4	33.9
(N)	(617)	(447)	(186)
Anthony Eden			
Extreme like	9.8	13.1	15.7
Extreme dislike	5.1	8.1	10.7
Total	14.9	21.2	26.4
(N)	(429)	(360)	(140)
Pierre Mendès-France			
Extreme like	9.2	10.8	9.6
Extreme dislike	6.1	9.5	10.6
Total	15.3	20.3	20.2
(N)	(359)	(231)	(104)
Konrad Adenauer			
Extreme like	11.2	16.1	15.2
Extreme dislike	5.5	6.0	7.1
Total	16.7	22.1	22.3
(N)	(329)	(267)	(112)

individual, for endorsement of the extreme responses to increase with advancing age. As will be noted, the only reversal in total percentage of extreme responses took place when respondents were asked about Mendès-France. However, this item also elicited the greatest percentage of "no opinion" responses. In the elderly group, almost 50 percent of the sample was unable to give any opinion at all. If the present contention is correct, that giving an extreme response is similar to giving no opinion, then the failure to find the hypothesized result on this item is quite understandable.

The "no difference" response. A second form of response that fails to make precise discriminations is found when respondents are asked to make comparisons. If a situation is demanding enough, and the issue is an evaluative one, a person can generally come to a decision about wheter A is "better" than B, "more" than B, etc. However, given sufficient detachment from the situation, the path of least resistance is merely to respond neutrally, i.e. A and B are "the same." Generally, a large number of questions allowing such responses do not appear on a single survey. However, on one survey there were ten items that offered one of the following alternatives: "no difference," "same," or "neither." Since these were all conceptually similar from the present standpoint, an index of "differentiation" was derived from counting the number of times a given person responded with one of these alternatives. Those who gave such responses six or more times were called "low differentiators," whereas those who gave them either once or not all, out of the ten possibilities, were termed "high differentiators."[12] The results, depicted in Table 5, show that with increased age the tendency to choose the nondifferentiating response increases $(x^2 = 18.18; p < .001)$.

Similar evidence was provided from single items appearing in Gallup surveys 128, 356, 399, and 456. Of the seven items available, the percentage of nondifferentiating responses for the elderly group was greater than for the middle-aged group in six instances (with the seventh even). The greatest percentage difference was 9.4. In comparing the middle-aged with the young group it was possible to add two additional items from a Roper Fortune Survey (71). For all nine items thus considered, the middle-aged group was less differentiating than the young. Percentage differences ranged from 1 to 6.

Discussion

The present investigation consisted primarily of an application of the disengagement theory of aging to a certain type of respondent behavior in the survey interview. In general, the results of the investigation were consistent with the theory.

Table 5

Age and Degree of Differentiation, Gallup Survey 596
(in percent)

Differentiation	20-39 Years (646)	40-59 Years (612)	60 Years and Over (315)
High	53.9	51.0	47.6
Low	4.8	8.2	12.7

However, it should be noted that the present findings are similar to most findings of a correlational nature in being subject to alternative explanations. One could argue, for example, that the above results simply reflect generational differences, that the aged person was exposed to different influences during the formative years. However, the fact that the results of the present study were taken from surveys conducted over a fifteen-year time span would seem to lessen the force of this argument. On the other hand, it is also possible that the aged respondent may have more complex opinions than the younger, and thus be less capable of providing responses that fit readily into the forced-choice categories found on most interviewing schedules. He may also be less impulsive or less willing to provide responses on topics about which he is unfamiliar. In addition, the relative age of the interviewer in comparison to the respondent may be an important factor; greater age differentials may cause the respondent to lose interest in the interview. Although none of these factors forms an integral part of any one theoretical system, future work in this area might fruitfully concentrate on assessing the independent contribution of such factors. In this connection, Maddox has shown that the disengagement of the aged respondent in the interviewing situation corresponds to his reaction to laboratory experiments.[13] In both cases it is also possible that behavioral differences attributed to aging fail to appear if the interviewer or experimenter can engage the aged respondent during the interaction.

However, present findings do shed light on communication problems often arising when studying the aged person. For example, if an interview is designed to elicit direct communication, these findings would suggest that the interviewer employ more forceful tactics of rapport building when dealing with the aged person. This suggestion gains empirical support when one reconsiders the "opinionation" index data presented above. Interviewers differ considerably in the degree to which they can elicit opinions; this can be caused by differences in contact or rapport building, the degree to which opinions are forced, the amount of editing done by the interviewer, etc. However, the interviewers who participated in this survey were divided into four groups depending on the degree to which they were able to elicit opinions. For all these groups except the one that elicited fewest opinions, the results coincided with those depicted in Table 3. However, for this final group, rather dramatic differences emerged. As can be seen in Table 6, the hypothesized decrease in opinionation with age is magnified considerably in the high education group. For the low education group, a reversal of the previous result is found; opinionation now decreases with age in the anticipated direction.

It is, of course, difficult to ascertain all the factors that contribute to an interviewer's effectiveness in eliciting opinions. There is some support, however, for the idea that the interviewers on whom the above analysis was based were those who devoted the least amount of time, and thus contributed least to the course of events in each interview. Looking at the mean number of respondents contacted by each interviewer, there is a monotonic increase in means, from the interviewer group eliciting most to the one eliciting least number of opinions. The members of the interviewer group obtaining the greatest number of opinions interviewed an average of twenty-five persons, whereas those obtaining fewest averaged thirty respondents each. It thus seems that the aged respondent who has had little education, in distinction to his educated counterpart, is differentially responsive to the interviewer depending on the interviewer's concern with eliciting opinions. When the interviewer presses for opinions, the aged respondent with little education

Table 6

Degree of Opinionation as Assessed by Interviewers Eliciting Fewest Opinions, Gallup Survey 580
(in percent)

Opinionation	20-39 Years		40-59 Years		60 Years and Over	
	Grammar and Less (42)	High and More (132)	Grammar and Less (76)	High and More (101)	Grammar and Less (44)	High and More (20)
High	59.5	70.5	50.0	75.2	56.8	70.0
Low	19.1	12.1	23.7	13.9	29.5	25.0

reacts to a greater extent than the younger. With increased education, the aged respondent is less reactive regardless of the behavior of the interviewer.

The question now arises as to who is the better interviewer and who gets better information. In general, interviewers are instructed to get answers to every question. This instruction is based on the assumption that persons should have opinions on all issues presented in the interview. If respondents have never considered a given question, the poll taker is interested in the opinions they would have if pressed on the issue at the present time. In this sense, the interviewer who obtains the greatest number of opinions is the better interviewer. If, however, differences in the degree of opinionation between respondents are relevant, the interviewer who accepts "no opinion" responses

161

will obtain regular differences according to age. The value of accepting or rejecting "no opinion" responses depends, therefore, on the interpretation and the purpose of the survey.

More important, perhaps, is the question of how the investigator can determine when a given response can be considered direct rather than indirect communication or bias.[14] Here it is important to point out that both the so-called "content" and "personality style" approaches proceed from the assumption that the person has a basic unitary structure, either of opinion or personality, and that this structure will manifest itself on all occasions provided proper measuring devices are used. This assumption has elsewhere been called the "organism error" or the "error of thinking of behavioral traits as fixed attributes of an *organism,* as stable and unchanging as a fingerprint or a birth mark."[15] The opposite approach would be to assume that there are no true opinions, but only self-representations tailored by the respondent for optimum return in each situation. However, here one is committing what has been called the "situation error," or the "error of assuming that all behavior is determined solely by the specific situation."

In the long run, the most valid approach would seem to fall somewhere between these two poles.[16] Here one might begin with the assumption that the individual usually has more than one feeling or opinion about events in his environment. On various occasions, under certain stimulus conditions, certain of these opinions or feelings will become more salient than others. More precisely, one might consider that each of these feelings has been learned in rather specific situations, and when these conditions reappear, the likelihood of evoking the appropriate feeling is increased. Following the principle of stimulus generalization, it might be deduced that opinions learned in situation A will appear most frequently in situation A, and also in all situations resembling A. The more potent the basic learning experience, the more situations to which the opinion will generalize. On the other hand, in some instances the person may have very salient feelings about a given topic but realize that the stimulus conditions are inappropriate or inimical to their expression. Here, "situationally appropriate" behavior would occur.

Cast in this framework, the standard response in the survey interview takes on a specific kind of significance. The investigator need not be overly concerned with whether a given response is a direct form of communication or is more indirectly prompted. Rather, the question might be asked: Given the type of situation represented by the survey interview, and given the type of question asked, in what other situations is it likely that this same response will occur? Applying this reasoning to the data presented above, it might be anticipated that, given the social nature of the interview, the elderly person can be expected not to respond or differentiate in numerous other superficial social situations. In situations where more is at stake for the aged person, his behavior may differ very little from his younger counterpart. In any event, the present study does suggest that closer attention be paid to the psychological underpinnings of demographic characteristics in attempting to understand respondent behavior in the survey interview.

Notes

1. This research was supported jointly by the Office of Naval Research (Nonr 1181-11), the Ford Foundation, the National Institute of Mental Health (MF-14, 799), and the Duke University Research Council . The data were made available through the cooperation of the Roper Public Opinion Center, Williamstown, Massachusetts. Computations were carried out in the Duke University Computing Laboratory, supported in part by the National Science Foundation. We are indebted to Raymond A. Bauer and Thomas F. Pettigrew for their useful appraisals at various stages of the research and to Emily Sherwood for her careful assistance.

2. Herbert H. Hyman's *Interviewing in Social Research* (Chicago, University of Chicago Press, 1954) remains the classic presentation of these factors and of the methods of reduction and control.

3. Cf. Arthur Couch and Kenneth Keniston, "Yeasayers and Naysayers: Agreeing Response Set as a Personality Variable," *Journal of Abnormal and Social Psychology* 60 (March 1960): 151-74; Douglas Crowne and David Marlowe, *The Approval Motive* (New York: Wiley, 1964); Irwin A. Berg, "The Unimportance of Test Item Content," in *Objective Approaches to Personality Assessment,* ed. B. M. Bass and I. A. Berg (New York: Van Nostrand, 1959). pp. 83-99.

163

4. David Riesman and Mark Benney, "The Sociology of the Interview," *Midwestern Sociologist* 18 (Winter 1956): 3-15.

5. Gerhard E. Lenski and John C. Leggett, "Caste, Class and Deference in the Research Interview," *American Journal of Sociology* 65 (March 1960): 463-67; Philip Taietz, "Conflicting Group Norms and the 'Third' Person in the Interview," *American Journal of Sociology* 68 (July 1962): 97-104.

6. Elaine Cumming and William E. Henry, *Growing Old* (New York: Basic Books, 1961).

7. The "no opinion" response has long been of interest to social science methodologists (cf. H. H. Anderson and G. L. Anderson, *An Introduction in Projective Techniques* [New York: Prentice-Hall, 1951]; and J. P. Guilford, *Psychometric Methods* [New York: McGraw-Hill, 1954]). Degree of opinionation has been used as an indicator of respondent interest in the interview in Alex Inkeles and Raymond Bauers, *The Soviet Citizen* (Cambridge, Mass.: Harvard University Press, 1959). See also Sidney Jourard's finding that certain decreases in amount of self-disclosure accompanied advancing age, in "Age Trends in Self-disclosure," *Merrill-Palmer Quarterly* 7, no. 3 (1961): 191-97.

8. Although the Cumming and Henry theory is primarily relevant to the comparison between the old and the middle-aged groups, there is good reason to suspect that some manifestations of disengagement should take place before the age of 60. The departure of offspring from the family would be one primary determinant here, as would the decrease in mobility caused by physical deterioration. The female should be affected in her loss of function as mother. The comparison between the middle and young groups thus takes on a particular significance.

9. This particular breakdown of opinionation was dictated solely by considerations of the adequacy of sample sizes in the various comparison groups.

10. Kurt W. Back and Kenneth J. Gergen, "Apocalyptic and Serial Time Orientations and the Structure of Public Opinions," *Public Opinion Quarterly* 27 (1963): 427-42.

11. Kurt W. Back and Kenneth J. Gergen, "Personal Orientation and Morale of the Aged," in *Social Aspects of Aging,* ed. Ida H. Simpson and John C. McKinney (Durham, N.C.: Duke University Press, 1966).

12. This particular split of the data was made in order to obtain sufficient cell frequencies for reliable comparisons.

13. George L. Maddox, "Disengagement Theory, A Critical Evaluation," *Gerontologist* 4, no. 2, pt. 1 (June 1964): 80-83.

14. A concrete example of this type of problem appears in Kurt W. Back and J. Mayone Stycos, *The Survey under Unusual Conditions* (Ithaca, N.Y.: Society for Applied Anthropology, 1959), Monograph No. 1.

15. Donald W. MacKinnon, "The Structure of Personality," in *Personality and the Behavior Disorders,* ed. J. McV. Hunt (New York: Ronald), 1:3-48.

16. An outline for a theoretical model attempting to deal with these factors may be found in Kurt W. Back and Kenneth J. Gergen, "Idea Orientation and Ingratiation in the Interview: A Dynamic Model of Response Bias," presented at the 1963 Proceedings of the Social Statistics Section, American Statistical Association, pp. 284-88.

THE 4% FALLACY:
A METHODOLOGICAL AND
EMPIRICAL CRITIQUE OF
EXTENDED CARE FACILITY
POPULATION STATISTICS*

Robert Kastenbaum and Sandra E. Candy

It is often said that only 4 percent or, at the most, 5 percent of the elderly in the United States are to be found in nursing homes and other extended care facilities. Evidence to support this statement is not lacking. Riley and Foner used the United States census data for 1960 to show that only 2.4 percent of Americans over the age of 65 were residing in homes for the aged and dependent. The percentage of institutionalized could be increased to 3.7 percent if other kinds of group quarters and extended care facilities are included in the total. It could be increased again to 4.8 percent if those in mental hospitals are also included. Population data for 1965, also summarized by Riley and Foner, yielded a similar picture. Slightly less than 4 percent of Americans over the age of 65 were residing in group facilities or institutions. This information is adequate for the purposes of the present paper, although more recent population statistics are becoming available.

Most gerontologists appear to be familiar with the figures that have been cited here. References to the 4 percent figure are encountered frequently in journals, books, classes, conferences, and governmental deliberations. This statistic has many implications. Perhaps the most common usage has been to emphasize

* Robert Kastenbaum and Sandra E. Candy, "The 4% Fallacy: A Methodological and Empirical Critique of Extended Care Facility Population Statistics," *International Journal of Aging and Human Development* 4 (1973): 15–21. © Baywood Publishing Company, Inc. 1973.

166

the overwhelming percentage of elders who are *not* institutionalized. This, in turn, spins off other implications, for example,
"Conditions may be deplorable in many extended care facilities,
but it is more practical to concentrate our attention elsewhere
because so few elders are institutionalized."

It seems to us that a very elementary kind of error is being
perpetuated here, the sort we teach our students to avoid. Our
utilization of these population statistics is often fallacious because we fail to recognize that *the data are cross-sectional.*
Knowing how many elders are institutionalized at this moment,
no matter how accurate a statement, does not tell us how many
people will have resided in extended care facilities at some time
in their lives. It does not give us the probabilities for an individual; only a series of longitudinal studies could answer that question satisfactorily.

Assume for sake of simplicity that the percentage of institutionalized elders at a particular point in time remains constant.
Are we in a position to conclude that only 1 person in 25 who
reaches old age will become institutionalized? We can conclude
nothing of the sort. Common sense urges that the probabilities
must be higher. How *much* higher is an empirical question.

Perhaps it is sufficient just to have called attention to a
popular fallacy in generalizing from population data in gerontology. However, we felt that a small exercise in the gathering
of corrective data might be appropriate. A pair of small studies
were conducted to satisfy our own curiosity and encourage
others to carry out more extensive and sophisticated work on
this problem. For those who are cost-conscious, it might be
mentioned that the total budget was 25 ¢ (not supported by
a grant).

STUDY I

The first study was based upon the premise that if a person
died in a nursing home or other extended care facility, then it is
reasonable to conclude that he had indeed *been* there. The
method was to read all the obituaries reported in the *Detroit
News* ("Detroit Area Obituaries" rubric) for a one-year period

(January 3, 1971–January 2, 1972). Place of death was the critical item noted, although other information was abstracted as well.

This method resulted in the identification of 1,184 deaths. Slightly more than half of this sample (52.7 percent) died in hospitals, according to the obituary notices. Interestingly, place of death was not specified in more than 20 percent (21.79 percent) of the entries. Approximately 13 percent were reported to have died in private homes, and a little over 10 percent in nursing homes. About 2 percent died in other locations, for example, in automobile accidents.

If we eliminate obituaries that did not specify place of death, we then have 926 cases remaining. Of these, 13.3 percent died in nursing homes. Deaths in private homes remained slightly more common (16.4 percent), and hospital deaths proved even more dominant, rising to 67 percent.

This reduced sample thus consists of all deaths of persons over the age of 65 reported in the daily newspaper of a large metropolitan area with place of death specified. We see that more than three times as many elders died in nursing homes than are reported as existing in same by cross-sectional population counts. The discrepancy becomes even more pronounced if we compare deaths with the figures for elders said to reside only in homes for the aged and dependent. Our method of data classification seems to justify this comparison. We now find that 13.3 percent died where only 2.4 percent lived—a discrepancy ratio that approaches 6 to 1.

One of the obvious difficulties with this study was the high percentage of deaths in which place was not specified. Another difficulty was the question of possible missing cases, i.e., elders whose death may not have been reported in the form of a newspaper obituary. For these and other reasons we moved on to the second study.

STUDY II

Our premise remained the same—use the fact of death to establish place of residence. The difference was in source of information. This time we went directly to the death certificate.[1] Access was obtained to the microfilm records of all death certificates filed in the metropolitan Detroit area during the 1971 calendar year. These mortality records included 28,755 entries for persons aged 50 and over. This report is limited to those 65 and over, a population that numbered 20,234.

One could ask how many of these people died in a nursing home; this would not be identical with those who died in institutions of every type. We will report separately upon deaths in

Table 1

Place of Death for All Persons Aged 65 and Over in Metropolitan Detroit Area, 1971
N = 20,234

Place of Death	Number	Percent of Total
All extended care facilities	4,796	23.70
Nursing homes only	4,099	20.02
Hospitals	12,631	62.43
Other	36	.18

nursing homes, in extended care facilities of all types, and in hospitals. The focus is upon the first two categories. The first is limited strictly to those who died in a place that could be positively identified as a nursing home. The second includes nursing home deaths and adds those which occurred in other types of extended care facilities as well. If there was doubt concerning the nature of the facility, the death was not included in either of these categories. Typically, this meant recording a death in the hospital category, although the medical facility in question could perhaps be described more accurately as a nursing home with delusions of grandeur. Any errors in classification therefore should have resulted in an *under*estimation of deaths occurring in nursing homes and other extended care facilities.

169

Results

We find that approximately 20 percent of all deaths in the 65+ age range occurred in nursing homes, and approximately 24 percent occurred in the larger category that included all identifiable extended care facilities. The basic data are presented in Table 1.

Make a point-by-point comparison now with the usual cross-sectional population data. More than eight times as many elders died in nursing homes than were assumed to be living there. Six times as many people died in extended care facilities (the larger category) as the population data would have led us to believe.

Look at the same data from the perspective of the individual. When population data are used carelessly we assume that the odds of a person entering an extended care facility of some type are only 1 in 25. If we at least reasoned fallaciously with the appropriate figures, we would set the odds at about 1 in 40 for a person taking up residence in a home specifically designated for the aged and dependent. The present data offer a radically different set of odds: 1 chance in 4 of being in an extended care facility; 1 chance in 5 for a nursing home.

We should immediately acknowledge another factor that influences the data. Any person who resided in a nursing home but did not die there would not be counted among those deceased in institutions. This is an additional source of underestimation: more people have lived in nursing homes than have died there. The opposite is not true. Everybody who did expire in a nursing home was a resident, whether long- or short-term.

Discovery was made of 72 documented instances in which an elderly person sustained an injury in a nursing home, was transferred to a hospital, and died soon thereafter of pneumonia, pulmonary emboli, myocardial infarction, or some other form of heart disease. These individuals obviously had been in a nursing home although they died elsewhere. How many other old men and women were transferred from nursing homes for other medical reasons, and subsequently died in the hospital? No information was available on this point, although moving out a terminally ill resident to die elsewhere is a well-known practice.

All the circumstances that affect the way in which death certificates are completed and in which this study was conducted, veer in the direction of underestimating the number of people who spend some time as a resident of a nursing home or other extended care facility.

Table 2

Place of Death by Sex and Race for Persons Aged 65 and Over in Metropolitan Detroit Area, 1971

Group	Total	Extended care facility	Hospital	Private home	Other
Women	9,541	2,789	5,350	1,305	7
Black	1,197	325	709	161	2
White	8,245	2,463	4,634	1,143	5
Other	9	1	7	1	0
Men	10,761	2,004	7,272	1,456	29
Black	1,398	277	943	170	8
White	9,363	1,727	6.329	1,286	21
Other	22	3	9	10	0
Black	2,595	602	1,652	331	10
White	17,608	4,190	10,963	2,429	26

Sex and Race

Are there differences in place of death between men and women, and between blacks and whites? Whites comprised 87 percent of the total sample, blacks 13 percent. There was a slight predominance of males over females: 53 percent/47 percent. The ratio of men to women was approximately the same for blacks and whites; there were about seven male deaths for every six female deaths in both samples. Data on sex and race are presented in Table 2.

It is clear that place of death was not equally distributed by sex. Males were underrepresented in nursing home and extended care facilities, and overrepresented in deaths recorded in hospitals and private homes. More women (58 percent) than men

171

(42 percent) died in nursing homes, a difference of 23 percent from statistical expectations. This finding will not surprise those who are familiar with geriatric institutions. We would like to emphasize, however, that the present data do not include information on length of residence. We cannot say that the observed differences are related entirely to the predominance of female admissions to nursing homes. It could be that more men than women are removed from nursing homes to die elsewhere.

There is another finding that is worth pausing over. Of more than 20,000 deaths, only 36 were listed as occurring in some place other than an extended care facility, hospital, or private home. It is striking that 29 of these fatalities (about 80 percent) involved males. We have the impression that most of these deaths were sudden or traumatic, but our information is not complete.

The picture is quite different for race. The percentage of blacks in each of the major place-of-death categories was close to the total percentage of blacks in the study population. Remembering that 13 percent of all deaths in this sample involved black elders, we find 12.6 percent in nursing homes, 13 percent in hospitals, and 12 percent in private homes. There was a difference, however, in the fractional category of "other" deaths: here 10 of the 36 fatalities, about 28 percent, were black.

It remains to examine sex-by-race combinations. The tendency for a higher percentage of the women to die in nursing homes was approximately equal for both blacks and whites. There were no instances in which the relative proportion of deaths by sex was reversed for blacks and whites. On the basis of the death certificate information, then, sex appears to be a more differentiating variable than race.

Discussion

If we are concerned about "death with dignity," to use the now-popular phrase, then perhaps the hospital should be our primary concern. Almost two out of every three deceased elders (62.4 percent) in the metropolitan Detroit area died in a hospital. (In all, 86 percent died in some kind of institution.) However, there is also much reason to be concerned about the nursing home as a final environment. We have seen that approximately one elder in four dies in an extended care facility, the odds being slightly higher for women. How many of these facilities are equipped to provide physical, social, and emotional comfort to the terminally ill old man or woman? Whether we choose to emphasize quality or duration of life for the terminally ill person, it is highly doubtful that nursing homes are providing adequate services for either goal.

Many old people die in nursing homes and other extended care facilities. In the Detroit metropolitan area alone, no fewer than 336 and as many as 476 men and women died *every month* during 1971. Yet relatively little attention is given, even by nursing home activists, to improving the quality of terminal care. Federal and local governments have also been remiss.[2] Governmental policies and practices have done little to encourage minimally acceptable care within institutions. This failing is all the more unfortunate in view of a similar lack of attention to the development of realistic alternatives to the nursing home as a final environment.

The reluctance to become involved in terminal care and the 4 percent fallacy, tend to fuel each other. Dying is so unimportant or unworthy that a person should not really be counted as "living" in an extended care facility if he is in a process of terminal decline. Similarly, the misleading usage of extended care facility population statistics tends to draw attention away from the fact that many of our elders end their lives among strangers in an environment that offers little true "nursing" and scarcely resembles a "home." Perhaps abandonment of the 4 percent fallacy will also contribute to the abandonment of destructive attitudes and practices.

The most general implication of this study is its reinforcement of every problem that gerontologists have already identified in the nursing home. All the painful shortcomings of the inadequate extended care facility must be regarded as of even greater consequence than previously noted. This statement perhaps should be amended to: of greater *social* consequence. Despair and indignity are as real if only one person is affected. We have known that many thousands are affected. And now we must face the fact that the true extent of the institutional care problem is of greater magnitude than usually assumed. To look at the same facts from a brighter perspective, every action that is taken to improve the quality of life in extended care facilities will be a blessing to a very considerable number of our fellow citizens.

We hope that the 4 percent fallacy will now be retired—gracefully or otherwise—and give rise to renewed determination to understand and overcome the problems of institutional care for our elders.

Notes

1. We are grateful to the Michigan Cancer Foundation for use of their microfilm records.

2. A notable exception is the recent inquiry into "Death with Dignity" conducted by the U.S. Senate Special Committee on Aging, chaired by Sen. Frank Church (August 7-9, 1972).

3

Biological and Psychological Aspects of Aging

INTRODUCTION TO PART III

The central irony of aging is that, as English author Jonathan Swift put it, "Every man desires to live long, but no man would be old." While in some cultures the aged are more respected than in others, most of us associate growing older with declining physical and mental vitality. Investigators concerned with the biological and psychological aspects of aging attempt to answer two major questions: (1) In what ways do the elderly actually differ from younger people? (2) How do we account for these differences?

The first paper in this part is a brief summary of the physical changes typically observed in the elderly. Because man is both a biological and a social creature, an organism with an ancient genetic ancestry continuously interacting with the physical and social environment he lives in, understanding the "causes" of these changes is an extraordinarily complex matter. One prominent theory in the biology of aging today holds that there is a genetically programmed life span for various cell groups. Although environmental factors such as diet, stress, or disease may speed up the aging process, there is strong evidence that longevity has predetermined maximum limits. With the exception of a few groups, the life expectancy of human beings at age eighty is remarkably similar in all countries—developed and undeveloped, rich and poor.

Research concerned with the psychological aspects of aging

includes studies on memory, reasoning, language facility, intelligence, response speed, concept formation, psychological rigidity, personal adjustment, and a wide variety of other matters. In general, cross-sectional studies (which compare people of different ages at a single point in time) report peak performance among those in the twenties and early thirties, with steep declines afterwards. Longitudinal studies (which test the same group of people over a period of time) show much later peaking of mental functioning and a far more gradual decline. Hence, many of the psychological and mental differences we observe between older and younger people at one point in time reflect their different social and educational experiences, in addition to aging.

James Birren, reporting on a longitudinal study of elderly men, adds an important additional insight. The "mental decline" of the elderly is not something that "occurs in everyone a little bit," as it would appear when test results for a large sample are averaged. Birren's data indicate that "some individuals may show stability of mental functioning in the later years where other persons show rather precipitous decline."

Robert Havighurst's article also emphasizes psychological differences among aged people. His data indicate that personality differences are a pivotal factor in the relationship between an elderly person's life satisfaction and level of social "engagement."

The final two articles in this part illustrate the relationship between an individual's cultural environment and his biological and psychological functioning. Numerous studies—including those by Kinsey, Masters and Johnson, and Duke University's Gerontological Center—have indicated that the physical ability to function sexually persists into old age. Norman Lobsenz discusses the attitudes and cultural factors in American society which are said to restrict sexual activity among the elderly. This is seen as a social problem.

In contrast, Sula Benet reports that the Abkhasians attribute their longevity to sexual restraint. An important difference between the two cultures is that the Abkhasians have a unified value system and demand public modesty and sexual restraint for persons of all ages.

SOME
BIOLOGICAL
ASPECTS
OF AGING
Cary S. Kart

The physician Alexander Leaf (1973) quotes Frederic Verzar, the Swiss gerontologist, as saying the following: "Old age is not an illness. It is a continuation of life with decreasing capacities for adaptation." Some students of aging would disagree. Some have argued, and it is a popular current view, that if old age is not an illness in and of itself, there is at least a strong relationship between biological aging and pathology. This view simply posits that biological deteriorations create a state of susceptibility to disease, and susceptibility to particular disease leads to mortality.

One way out of this disagreement may be to distinguish between biological and pathological aging (Blumenthal, 1968). While it is difficult to say at what point in life a person is old, it is clear enough that everyone becomes so. Everyone ages. Genetic and other prenatal influences set the stage for the aging sequence, and postnatal environmental factors (demographic, economic, psychological, and social) act to modify this sequence (Sobel, 1966; Wilson, 1974). The changes that accompany aging occur in people at different chronological ages and progress at different rates. Changes in physical appearance are the most easily recognized. That physical capabilities diminish is also well known. These changes may be placed in the category of biological aging.

Disease is another matter. As individuals grow older, they are more likely to become afflicted with certain diseases—many of which prove fatal. Changes that occur as a result of disease processes may be categorized as relating to pathological aging.

In the remainder of this paper we will look briefly at the various systems of the human body in an attempt to understand how they are affected by the aging process. In this regard we will be concerned explicitly with biological aging.

Senescence

Senescence is the term used by biologists, gerontologists, and others to describe biological aging. Comfort (1964) describes the study of senescence as the study of those processes which lead to a decline in the viability of the human organism and an increase in its vulnerability. Senescence may be distinguished from other biological processes in four ways (Atchley, 1972; Strehler, 1962): (1) its characteristics must be universal; (2) the changes which constitute it come from within the individual; (3) the processes associated with senescence occur gradually; and (4) the changes which appear in senescence have a deleterious effect on the individual.

Gerontologists use the term senescence to describe not one process, but rather many. In some measure, this accounts for the numerous existing theories of biological aging. "Programmed" theory, "mutation" theory, and the "autoimmune" theory of aging are just a few of those receiving attention from catalogers of the theories of senescence (Atchley, 1972; Curtis, 1966; Rockstein, 1974).

We will not discuss the merits of these theories of senescence here. Such a discussion would have a low yield, and we could not definitively determine precisely why the body ages—that is a task for others with competence in this area. What we can and will do here is simply discuss the results of senescence—those important bodily changes that occur as age increases. As Atchley (1972, p. 47) so aptly points out, understanding these changes is salient for the social gerontologist "because they represent the concrete physiological limits around which social arrangements are built."

Skin

* With age, skin tends to become wrinkled and rough, and pigment plaques are not unusual. The skin is more vulnerable and while easily broken, heals slowly. Sweating is considerably less in older people than in young, and hair loss may occur.

Skeletal–Muscular System

Stiffening of joints, particularly at the hip and knee, is evidenced with age. There is a reduction in height, and typically, a stooped posture in older individuals. The total mass of muscle tissue is reduced progressively with age. Muscular strength and coordination decline; muscular efficiency does not.

Senses and Reflexes

The sensations of touch and pain are reduced. Statistically, there is a decline in the visual acuity of older people. There is a progressive change in the tension of the muscle that operates the pupil and the lens; less light reaches the retina, and the curvature of the lens changes. Cataracts are found increasingly with age. The older person has less ability to distinguish pitch and intensity of sound. Taste and smell apparently become less sensitive also. Reflexes decline. Reaction time is slowed. Short-term memory is reduced, although long term memory appears to be retained.

Nervous System

There is loss in the total bulk of brain substance. Brain weight diminishes to about 92 percent of age-30 value by age 75 (Leaf, 1973). Hardening or occluding of blood vessels creates

181

circulatory problems in the brain, thereby reducing the speed of nerve impulses to nerve tissue. This is often reflected in strokes, senility, and/or other psychological impairments.

Circulatory System

By age 75, the cardiac output (at rest) of the average individual is about 70 percent of the age-30 value (Leaf, 1973). This reduced cardiac output, itself a function of reduced elasticity or "hardening" of the arteries, may result in heart disease or an interrupted flow of blood to the brain. Circulatory-system failure and related illnesses are a common cause of death in the middle and later adult years.

Respiratory System

As a result of weakening muscles involved in lifting the rib cage, and a reduction in the expandibility of the lungs, the total capacity of the lungs decrease with age. The vital capacity, or maximum one-breath capacity, is reduced as well. Leaf (1973) reports maximum breathing capacity at age 75 to be 43 percent of the age-30 value.

Digestive System

Digestive-tract difficulties are common to the elderly. There is a reduction in peristalsis of the intestines, and motility of the stomach, yet much digestive difficulty relates in one way or another to diet, poor or no teeth, and/or ill-fitting dentures.

Other Systems

The reproductive, temperature control, and kidney filtration systems all show decline with age. The kidney filtration rate of a person aged 75 is about two-thirds (60 percent) the

182

rate of a 30-year-old (Leaf, 1973). Rarely does the decline in other systems cause serious problems in older people.

Conclusions

Two concluding notes are in order:

1. Everyone ages, but it is important to recall that biological aging occurs in people at different chronological ages and progresses at different rates.

2. Biological aging does not take place in a social vacuum. Demographic, economic, psychological, and social factors appear to operate alongside biological ones to produce the results of senescence.

PSYCHOLOGICAL ASPECTS OF AGING: INTELLECTUAL FUNCTIONING*

James E. Birren

Man ages in three ways: biologically, psychologically, and socially. One can view an individual as having three ages in accord with the three main processes of aging. His *biological age* can be defined by the years of remaining life or the extent to which he had "used up" his biological potential for length of life. His *psychological age* can be defined by level of his adaptive capacities. His ability to adapt to his environment depends upon his accuracy and speed of perception, memory and learning and reasoning, to mention a few. Man's *social age* can be defined by the differentiated social roles he leads in society. These ages are mutually dependent upon one another and yet one knows from commonplace experiences that individuals may vary somewhat in their relative youth and age in their major dimensions of existence. Behind each of the three "ages" there are processes of aging. These have to be studied developmentally, that is, observed in detail over the whole life span. In this paper only one component of one of the ages of man is considered, his mental ability.

Why ask a question about the increments and decrements in mental abilities over the adult years? There are at least three reasons for raising questions. The first of these reasons is cultural,

---

* James E. Birren, "Psychological Aspects of Aging: Intellectual Functioning," *Gerontologist* 8 (1968): 16-19.

the second is a scientific reason, and the third is a matter of practical concern. The cultural reason for raising a question about increments and decrements in intellectual function in the aged is that such knowledge influences our expectations of ourselves and others. There is a normative base in our society as well as in others which governs what we expect of the mental performance of persons of different ages. These expectations are realistic to the degree that they correspond to the best available research information about how intellectual abilities transform themselves over the life-span. Professional judgment is also involved. A psychiatrist, a physician, a social worker, a psychologist, a lawyer, dealing with the elderly implicitly have some yardstick in mind governing their relationships with and expectations of the aged.

There are several scientific reasons to raise questions about increments and decrements in mental ability with age. The most important of these is to establish the species trend of cognitive development and aging. This is part of the content of developmental psychology, although most child psychologists and behavioral scientists who are interested in the development of mental ability in children rarely consider the course of abilities through the entire adult age range. We need much more evidence of the adult trends in the components of mental ability to complement the data on childhood.

A secondary scientific question concerns the nature of the organized and idiosyncratic departures from the general species trend. There are parallel questions to those frequently studied in childhood. What is the pattern of mental abilities in identical twins in late life? To what extent does this suggest a genetic pacing of changes in mental ability in late life? Other questions come to mind. Is the factor structure of mental ability so well studied in childhood stable in the adult years, or are there systematic trends in the structure? Are there the same number of factors or are fewer factors needed to account for the variance in mental abilities of the aged? What are the consequences of long years of use of particular abilities as in occupational specialization? Are there fewer changes and delayed decline in the components of the abilities of those initially more capable? Is there any evidence of a general ability factor in late life? These

185

questions can be translated into quantitative studies involving age at which peaks are found in mental components and of the relative changes with age, in definable subpopulations.

These scientific questions soon lead to practical questions not unlike those surrounding the mental measurements of children. One practical implication of measurement of mental abilities in the older adult is the relevance of assessment to employability. Industries change; new production methods require retraining of adults. For this reason, adults 40, 50, and 60 can be evaluated in relation to their trainability for new positions or an enlargement of old responsibilities.

Some aspects of mental ability and employability relate to the presence or absence of disease. That is, a portion of all persons aged 50 may be experiencing degradative mental changes due to the presence of chronic disease. The president of a corporation, a military officer, or a professor is not excepted from the probabilities of deteriorative changes should cerebral arteriosclerosis develop. Professional services will have to be developed if we are to examine pilots, car drivers, and others with regard to their likelihood for continued responsibility. These services must attend to the measurement of the component mental abilities. Behavior is the final pathway through which the individual expresses his well-being and his adequacy to function. Detection of subclinical illness or illness that is likely to emerge into severe problems of concern to the individual, his job, and family can involve mental measurement to a considerable extent.

There are also matters of differential diagnosis of hospitalized patients in which one wants to sort out consequences of disease from the relatively normal physiology of aging. One may also need to make judgments about the relative reversibility or irreversibility of the level of mental functioning shown in an individual. For example, one may note the limitations of cognitive function accompanying significant losses of brain tissue as in senile dementia, cerebral arteriosclerosis, and other diseases. The relationships between behavior and hypertension are just beginning to be explored and it would appear that hypertension is related to patterns of cognitive functioning. It is reasonable to expect that a well-controlled and objective assessment of mental abilities will be increasingly useful in the evaluation and diagnostic efforts of the adult. We should not be surprised that if under many circumstances the output of the nervous system proves to be a more sensitive indicator of the well-being of the individual and integrity of the nervous system than attempts to study biochemical segments.

Validity of Intellectual Decline Indices

In considering the mental performance of an aged individual one would like to know the previous level of performance. One looks for signs, therefore, of recent deterioration. In addition, one might look for changes that would suggest focal brain damage. Some years ago, a study was undertaken to examine the usefulness of our measures of mental deterioration (Botwinick & Birren, 1951). The issues are pertinent despite the fact that the data are somewhat old. While it is too much to ask of a single measure that it not only yield an estimate of present level of intellectual functioning but also yield an estimate of the amount of decline from a previous level, it is important to make such an inference. Judgments are often needed about the prognosis of elderly individuals and accompanying guidance for managing their lives, if not for matters of therapy. Since it was found in an earlier study (Fox & Birren, 1950) that there was no correlation between indices of intellectual deterioration in the elderly, a direct approach to estimating the validity of these measures was undertaken. The three measures were: the efficiency index of the revised examination for the efficiency of mental functioning by Babcock and Levy (1940), the deterioration quotient of the Wechsler–Bellevue Scale, and the Senescent Decline Formula of Copple (1948) based upon the Wechsler–Bellevue Scale.

The study proceeded by selecting a sample of 31 institutionalized patients who had been diagnosed as psychotic with cerebral arteriosclerosis or senile psychosis. The patients were compared in performance with a group of 50 control Ss of similar age and background. The general selection criteria of both groups were that individuals were 60 to 70 years with not less than four years of formal schooling and were born in England or the United States. All individuals had hearing adequate to follow

187

directions and were able to read typewritten material with corrected vision.

The results showed that only two of the three indices significantly differentiated between the senile patients and the control Ss. The deterioration quotient of the Wechsler–Bellevue was not effective. It is interesting to point out that the Senescent Decline Formula of Copple (1948) based upon the Wechsler–Bellevue test did significantly differentiate the patients from the control groups. Thus, differentially weighing the same tests on which the noneffective deterioration quotient was based, one can derive a valid index of deterioration.

Before becoming too impressed with the fact that two of the measures did show significant differences between the patients and control group, a caution is required because the correlation between the *Efficiency Index* and the *Senescent Decline Formula* was only 0.39. Either these measures are insufficiently reliable or else, what is more likely, they are measuring different aspects of intellectual decline and thus are not interchangeable in evaluating the mental status of an elderly individual. It should be noted that there is a relatively higher correlation between the I.Q. and the Senescent Decline Formula, 0.54. Perhaps this is not too surprising because the same sub-test scores enter into both computations. It does suggest, however, that one might better estimate decline from a measure of present mental performance compared with knowledge about the individual's previous educational level rather than trying to infer both change and previous level from the same set of measurements.

The distributions of the measurements on the two groups can be compared. Some aspects of mental deterioration are being tapped by at least two of the indices, although it is obvious that the scores leading to the I.Q. itself gave the most marked difference between the two groups of individuals. The purpose of the study was to estimate the efficiency of measures of intellectual decline from a previous level rather than a valid estimate of current level.

It is interesting to note that the Digit Symbol Sub-Test, which has been commonly found to decrease most with age, showed a smaller difference between the patient and control groups than did the information subtest which characteristically declines minimally with age. If deterioration in the senile psychosis were a process of accelerated aging, the subtests such as the Digit Symbol, which show the largest difference with age, might also be expected to show the largest differences between the patient and control groups. This leads to the suspicion that the process of normal aging and of senile decline are rather different. There may be, of course, a technical qualification in that the digit symbol performance can be so slow in the aged that one may be getting a "floor effect" in which it is not possible to detect further change even if due to manifest organic brain deterioration.

The larger difference between the two groups on the verbal tests like information and vocabulary should be kept in mind. A healthy group of male Ss over the age of 65 was found to have higher verbal scores than young controlled Ss, which leads to the proposition that, with advancing age, one tends to accumulate stored information particularly of a verbal character (Birren, Botwinick, Weiss, & Morrison, 1963). Of the total group of 47 Ss, 27 were regarded as being of optimal health and 20 Ss were regarded as having subclinical disease. The question posed of the latter group, since they had scores in the verbal test area about equal to young Ss, is whether they had a failure to gain information earlier in life or they had undergone a loss of stored information in years just prior to testing. The latter point can best be evaluated in a longitudinal study.

Longitudinal Study of Mental Abilities in Aged Men

A follow-up study was made five years after the original testing of the 47 elderly men. Of the original group, 13 failed to survive over the nearly five years between the original and follow-up studies. By dividing the Ss in terms of survivors and nonsurvivors, one can examine some of the initial differences in mental performance. It is most important to note that the original measurements that most distinguished between the subsequent nonsurvivors and the survivors were those tests containing verbal information. It may be recalled that these were the tests that differentiated the Ss according to level of health in the initial

189

study. Surprisingly, the measurements involving speed of response known to be intimately associated with age did not show significant differences between the nonsurvivors and the survivors. This is not to suggest that the widespread slowness of behavior with advancing age is an indifferent matter for individuals. Rather, the implication is that slowness of behavior with advancing age appears independently of disease and perhaps of a wide range of environmental conditions. In contrast, the relative intactness of the brain, in particular the cerebral cortex, likely closely reflects vascular disease and influences the amount of stored information.

One can also examine the retest data with regard to the differences in the Wechsler Adult Intelligence Test scores between the initial and five-year retests. It can be noted from the tables in the study that some Ss showed no change in the five-year interval despite the fact that they were of advanced age, whereas others showed considerable change. It would thus seem that stability of mental functioning can be found in individuals as well as a dramatic decline over the age of 70. Thus mental decline in the later years is not something that occurs in everyone a little bit, but it is irregularly distributed in the population such that a subset of individuals suffering from organic brain disease shows dramatic changes. If the tests of such individuals are averaged in with the population at large, as one does in a cross-sectional study, then one might misleadingly derive a rather smooth age curve. In fact, what occurs in individuals may be sudden changes after a substantially protracted plateau.

Similar results were seen in an earlier unpublished study by Kleemeier and associates (Birren, 1964a, b). Their data illustrated the fact that some individuals may show marked stability of mental functioning in the later years where other persons show rather precipitous decline. Precipitous decline in mental functioning in the aged is likely indicative of a short survival.

The present data have implications at several levels of significance. They suggest that the average person growing older in our society need not expect to show a typical deterioration of mental functioning in the later years. Rather, limitation of mental functioning occurs precipitously in individuals over the age of 65 or 70 and is closely related to health status. For this reason, the expectations of mental performance must be based upon the elderly individual's characteristics rather than on assumption about the averages in the population at large. The expectation is, therefore, given good health and freedom from cerebral vascular disease and senile dementia, individuals can expect high-level mental competence beyond the age of 80. How many individuals fit such a pattern can only be determined by sophisticated epidemiological studies. Studies giving detailed information about the distribution of mental competence of the elderly in the general population have not been conducted.

One gathers from existing evidence that there is no gradual decline with age in general mental ability. The only aspect of mental performance that seems to change in most persons is that of slowing speed of response. Age changes in speed of response do not seem to bear as intimate a relationship to survival as does stored verbal information.

Using increasingly sophisticated methods of measurement, the psychologist and psychophysiologist in the future may expect to collaborate with the internist and the psychiatrist not only to measure change accurately within individuals but to explore the determinants of change. In addition, one can expect collaboration between psychologists and the sociologists to assay some of the long-term consequences of occupational specialization and socioeconomic class on the patterning of mental abilities. One suspects that 40 years in an occupation and in a social class will impress a pattern of mental functioning in the individual that is potentially measurable. At still another level, one may look forward to an era of psychological epidemiology when one may know more accurately the distribution of mental capacity in the aging population. At the present time, we know little about the distribution of deficit states in the population.

PERSONALITY
AND PATTERNS
OF AGING*[1]

Robert J. Havighurst

Happiness and satisfaction in the latter part of life are within reach of the great majority of people. The external conditions of life are better for people over 65 than they have been at any time in this century. Social Security benefits and company pensions are at record high levels. Medicare has underwritten much of the major medical expense. Almost no one is forced to work after the age of 65 if he prefers not to. Most of the states have programs, supported under the Older Americans Act, to improve the social adjustment of older people. In other words, society has done just about as much as anyone could ask it to do on behalf of older people. At least this is the conclusion one would draw from a superficial look at social statistics.

Yet we know that many people are unhappy and dissatisfied in their later years. Some of them suffer from poor health, but this is only a minority. The average person at age 65 will live 4 more years. According to research, the person who is in good health suffers very little impairment in his ability to learn, to initiate actions, to be effective in the ordinary relations of life until he is 85 years old or more.

Since a great many people after 65 have good enough health and enough income to support a life of happiness and satisfaction, we must turn to the psychologist to ask why some of these

* Robert J. Havighurst, "Personality and Patterns of Aging," *Gerontologist* 8 (1968): 20-23.

people are unhappy and dissatisfied. Have they been unhappy all their lives? Are they unhappy due to remediable present situations? Are there forms of psychotherapy or of environmental improvement that would substantially increase the numbers of happy and satisfied older people?

Theories of Successful Aging. There are at present two contrasting theories of successful aging. Both are unsatisfactory because they obviously do not explain all the phenomena of successful aging. Yet both have some facts to support them. The first, one that might be called the *activity theory,* implies that, except for the inevitable changes in biology and in health, older people are the same as middle-aged with essentially the same psychological and social needs. In this view, the decreased social interaction that characterizes old age results from the withdrawal by society from the aging person; and the decrease in interaction proceeds against the desires of most aging men and women. The older person who ages optimally is the person who stays active and who manages to resist the shrinkage of his social world. He maintains the activities of middle age as long as possible, and then finds substitutes for work when he is forced to retire and substitutes for friends and loved ones whom he loses by death.

In the *disengagement theory* (Cumming & Henry, 1961), on the other hand, the decreased social interaction is interpreted as a process characterized by mutuality; one in which both society and the aging person withdraw, with the aging individual acceptant, perhaps even desirous, of the decreased interaction. It is suggested that the individual's withdrawal has intrinsic or developmental qualities as well as responsive ones; that social withdrawal is accompanied by, or preceded by, increased preoccupation with the self and decreased emotional investment in persons and objects in the environment; and that, in this sense, disengagement is a natural rather than an imposed process. In this view, the older person who has a sense of psychological well-being will usually be the person who has reached a new equilibrium characterized by a greater psychological distance, altered types of relationships, and decreased social interaction with persons around him.

In order to test these two theories empirically, the data of

the Kansas City Study of Adult Life were used, consisting of repeated interviews with 159 men and women aged 50–90, taken
over the period from 1956 through 1962. The sample at the end
of the study consisted of 55 percent of the people who were
originally in the study. Of the attrition in the sample, 27 percent had been due to deaths; 12 percent to geographical moves;
and the rest to refusals to be interviewed at some time during
the series of interviews, usually because of reported poor health.
There is evidence also that persons who were relatively socially
isolated constituted a disproportionate number of the dropouts.
The original sample excluded people living in institutions and
those who were so ill that they could not be interviewed. The
original sample also excluded people at the very bottom of the
socioeconomic scale and a few people who would have been
diagnosed as neurotic by a psychiatrist, as well as people who
were chronically ill if the illness was one that confined a person
to bed. Some of the sample became quite ill, physically or mentally, during the period of the study, but they were continued
in the study if they could be interviewed.

The results of this study indicated that neither the activity
theory nor the disengagement theory was adequate to account
for the observed facts. While there was a decrease of engagement
in the common social roles related to increasing age, some of
the people who remained active and engaged showed a high degree of satisfaction. On the whole, those who were most active
at the older ages were happier, but there were many exceptions
to this rule.

Need for a Personality Dimension. Since it is an empirical
fact that some people are satisfied with disengagement while
others are satisfied with a high degree of social engagement, it is
clear that something more is needed to give us a useful theory
of successful aging. Possibly that something is a theory of the
relationship of personality to successful aging (Havighurst, Neugarten, & Tobin, 1964; Neugarten, 1965).

A substantial beginning on such a theory was made by Else
Frenkel-Brunswik and her colleagues Reichard, Livson, and
Petersen (1962) in their study of 87 elderly working men in the
San Francisco area, 42 of them retired and 45 not retired. After
interviewing these men intensively and rating them on 115

personality variables, the researchers rated them on "adjustment to aging" using a 5-point rating scale. Sixty men were rated either high (4 or 5) or low (1 or 2). Their personality ratings were subjected to a "cluster analysis" to identify men highly similar to one another. The high group produced three clusters and the low group produced two clusters, leaving 23 of the 60 not in any cluster. The five clusters or "types" of men were given the following names:

High on Adjustment	N	Low on Adjustment	N
Mature	14	Angry	16
Rocking-chair	6	Self-haters	4
Armored	7		

Among those judged successful in aging, the "mature" group took a constructive rather than an impulsive or a defensive approach to life. The "rocking-chair" group tended to take life easy and to depend on others. The "armored" men were active in defending themselves from becoming dependent. They avoided retirement if possible, and one of them who was ill complained of his enforced idleness, something the rocking-chair type would have been glad to accept. Even the oldest of this group, an 83-year old, still worked a half-day every day.

Among those judged unsuccessful in aging, the "angry" men were generally hostile toward the world and blamed others when anything went wrong. They were poorly adjusted to work and several had been downwardly mobile socially. They tended to resent their wives. This group was especially fearful of death.

The "self-haters" differed primarily from the "angry" men by openly rejecting themselves and blaming themselves for their failures. They were depressed. Death for them was a longed-for release from an intolerable existence.

These types of men were making quite different behavioral adjustments to aging. Thus the armored and the rocking-chair were judged to be equally successful in adjustment to aging, but their adjustments were diametrically opposed. One group was active while the other was disengaged.

The Kansas City Study of Adult Life

The Kansas City Study of Adult Life carried on this search for a personality dimension by studying women as well as men, over a social class range from upper-middle class through upper-working class. The 159 persons were rated on 45 personality variables reflecting both the cognitive and affective aspects of personality. Types of personality were extracted from the data by means of factor analysis. There were four major types, which we have called the integrated, armored-defended, passive-dependent, and unintegrated personalities.

Patterns of behavior were defined on the basis of a rating of *activity* in eleven common social roles: worker, parent, grandparent, kin-group member, spouse, homemaker, citizen, friend, neighbor, club and association member, church member. Ratings were made by judges on each of the eleven roles, based on a reading of the seven interviews with each person. The sum of the role-activity scores was used to divide the respondents into activity levels—high, medium, and low.

A third component of the patterns of aging was a measure of *life satisfaction* or psychological well-being, which was a composite rating based on five scales recording the extent to which a person (a) finds gratification in the activities of his everyday life; (b) regards his life as meaningful and accepts both the good and the bad in it; (c) feels that he has succeeded in achieving his major goals; (d) has a positive image of himself; and (e) maintains happy and optimistic moods and attitudes. Scores on life satisfaction were grouped into high, medium, and low categories.

The analysis based on these three dimensions (personality, role activity, and life satisfaction) was applied to the 59 men and women in the study who were 70 to 79. This is the group in which the transition from middle age to old age has presumably been accomplished. Fifty of these people were clearly one or another of eight patterns of aging, which are presented in Table 1.

Group A, called the *reorganizers,* are competent people engaged in a wide variety of activity. They are the optimal agers in terms of the American ideal of "keeping active, staying young." They reorganize their lives to substitute new activities for lost ones.

Group B are called the *focused*. They are well-integrated personalities with medium levels of activity. They tend to be selective about their activities, devoting their time and energy to gaining satisfaction in one or two role areas.

Group C we call the *successful disengaged*. They have low activity levels with high life satisfaction. They have voluntarily moved away from role commitments as they have grown older.

Table 1

Personality Patterns in Aging

Personality Type	Role Activity	Life Satisfaction	N
A. Integrated (reorganizers)	High	High	9
B. Integrated (focused)	Medium	High	5
C. Integrated (disengaged)	Low	High	3
D. Armored-defended (holding on)	High or medium	High	11
E. Armored-defended (constricted)	Low or medium	High or medium	4
F. Passive-dependent (succorance-seeking)	High or medium	High or medium	6
G. Passive-dependent (apathetic)	Low	Medium or low	5
H. Unintegrated (disorganized)	Low	Medium or low	7

They have high feelings of self-regard, with a contented "rocking-chair" position in life.

Group D exhibits the *holding-on* pattern. They hold as long as possible to the activities of middle age. As long as they are successful in this, they have high life satisfaction.

Group E are *constricted*. They have reduced their role activity presumably as a defense against aging. They constrict their social interactions and maintain a medium to high level of satisfaction. They differ from the *focused* group in having less integrated personalities.

Group F are *succorance-seeking*. They are successful in getting emotional support from others and thus maintain a medium level of role activity and of life satisfaction.

Group G are *apathetic*. They have low role activity combined with medium or low life satisfaction. Presumably, they are people who have never given much to life and never expected much.

Group H are *disorganized*. They have deteriorated thought processes and poor control over their emotions. They barely maintain themselves in the community and have low or, at the most, medium life satisfaction.

These eight patterns of aging probably are established and predictable by middle age, although we do not have longitudinal studies to prove this proposition. It seems reasonable to suppose that a person's underlying personality needs become consonant with his overt behavior patterns in a social environment that permits wide variation.

Conclusions

In some ways the Kansas City Study and other studies of behavior and life satisfaction support the activity theory of optimal aging; as level of activity decreases, so also do the individual's feelings of contentment regarding his present activity. The usual relationships are high activity with positive affect; and low activity with negative affect. This relationship does not decrease after age 70.

At the same time, the data in some ways support the disengagement theory of optimal aging: there are persons who are relatively high in role activity who would prefer to become more disengaged from their obligations; there are also persons who enjoy relatively inactive lives.

Neither the activity theory nor the disengagment theory of optimal aging is itself sufficient to account for what we regard as the more inclusive description of these findings: that as men and women move beyond age 70 in a modern, industrialized community, they regret the drop in role activity that occurs in their lives; at the same time, most older persons accept this drop as an inevitable accompaniment of growing old; and they succeed in maintaining a sense of self-worth and a sense of satisfaction with past and present life as a whole. Other older persons are less successful in resolving these conflicting elements—not only do they have strong negative affect regarding losses in

198

activity but the present losses weigh heavily and are accompanied by a dissatisfaction with past and present life.

The relationships between levels of activity and life satisfaction are influenced also by personality type, particularly by the extent to which the individual remains able to integrate emotional and rational elements of the personality. Of the three dimension on which we have data—activity, satisfaction, and personality—personality seems to be the pivotal dimension in describing patterns of aging and in predicting relationships between level of activity and life satisfaction. It is for this reason, also, that neither the activity nor the disengagement theory is satisfactory, since neither deals, except peripherally, with the issue of personality differences.

Notes

1. This paper is a result of cooperation among the following three people: Bernice L. Neugarten, Sheldon S. Tobin, and Robert J. Havighurst. A description of the central research has been published by Dr. Neugarten under the same title in *Gawein J. of Psychol. Univ. Nijmegen* 13 (1965): 249-56.

SEX
AND THE
SENIOR CITIZEN*
Norman M. Lobsenz

A writer looking for a funny ending to his interview with
Bob Hope asked the comedian recently if he thought there was
still sex after 65. "You bet," said Hope, "and awfully good, too
[*Pause for a beat of exquisite timing.*] Especially the one in
the fall."

The image of geriatric lovemaking seems always good for a
laugh. A few years ago, Dr. Mary Calderone, executive director
of SIECUS, the Sex Information and Education Council of the
U.S., and one of the nation's leading authorities on sex education, was answering questions from an audience of Chicago
high-schoolers. When one daring teenager asked, "How old are
you, are you married, and are you still doing it?" the students
broke into giggles. Dr. Calderone was characteristically forth-
right. When the laughter died down, she said, "The answer to
the first part of that question is 64, and the answer to the other
two is yes." Then she added, "Young people do not have a
monopoly on sexuality. It is with you all your life."

Indeed, every medical study conducted during recent years
indicates that there is no physiological reason why older men
and women in reasonably good health should not have—and be
able to have—an active and satisfying sex life. Yet, despite increasing scientific evidence to the contrary, our culture continues

* Norman M. Lobsenz, "Sex and the Senior Citizen," *New York Times Magazine,*
20 January 1974. Copyright © by Norman M. Lobsenz.

to foster the belief that by the time one is in his or her 60s, sex is neither necessary nor possible. Or if it *does* occur, it is somehow not quite normal. Or that it certainly isn't nice for the old folks to be indulging in it.

In a time of ever more tolerant attitudes toward sexual self-determination for everyone else, why this puritanical approach to "senior citizens"? Some of the reasons may stem from long-dormant Oedipal fears and incest taboos associated with the idea of sexual expression on the part of parental figures, from remnants of childhood's disbelief that one's mother and father—and by extension any older person—actually ever make love. Manhattan psychotherapist Dr. Leah Schaefer reports, for example, that none of the women she interviewed for a book on sex could accept with any equanimity the idea of their own parents engaging in intercourse.

Another source of sexual puritanism toward the aged is the clichés of a youth-fixated society. Given the movie-television-advertising stereotype that sexuality exists only in and for beautiful people with firm flesh and agile bodies, the notion of older persons enjoying it—wrinkles, flabbiness and all—seems at first ludicrous and then repugnant.

For the 20 million Americans over 65, these attitudes present formidable problems. Having been conditioned to believe erroneously that sexual performance declines to the vanishing point with age, or that sexual exertion is dangerous to their health, many older persons tend to give up sex more or less completely.

Others shut off sexual feelings out of shame and embarrassment about having them. Doctors and counselors report that when older people *do* admit to having sexual desires, they often apologize for having such "undignified" or even "depraved" sensations. Dr. Joseph T. Freeman, a Pennsylvania gerontologist who has written for medical textbooks on the sexual aspects of aging, cites the case of an 84-year-old man who complained to his physician about the frequent demands for intercourse made by his 79-year-old wife. The husband was able to meet them, Freeman writes, but felt that this activity was "not natural for such an old man and woman." Another couple in their early 70s had continued to make love at least once a day; yet both believed,

201

says Freeman, "that they were doing something unnatural . . . an expression of some abnormal inclination."

Some older people fear the ridicule or censure of younger persons if they show signs of still being interested in sex. Children and even grandchildren disapprove, make them feel guilty. I was told of a recently remarried 78-year-old man whose daughter greets him every morning with a derisive "How did it go last night?" A Florida psychiatrist reported two instances where children tried to commit their parents to a mental institution because they had moved in with friends of the opposite sex. It's not just coincidence that we never refer to even the most profligate youth as a "dirty young man," but are quick to label any older person who shows some interest in sex as a "dirty old man." (One California septuagenarian struck back with a bumper sticker on his sports car: "I'm not a dirty old man, I'm a sexy senior citizen.")

The D.O.M. label is applied with even greater vehemence if the aging man or woman is involved with a much younger person, although there's no reason why love or sex should be age-segregated. May–December relationships can and do flourish. It is true that in many such cases the attraction is not necessarily romantic: Younger woman often marry older men—and younger men often marry older women—for their money, fame, power, wisdom, or out of neurotic needs.

Yet if this general climate of deprecation hampers sexual expression for married older persons, it creates far greater obstacles for two-thirds of those men and women over 65 who never wed or are widowed or divorced. And because of a combination of demographics and cultural standards, women are affected more seriously.

To begin with—thanks to a longer life expectancy, plus the fact that women are usually younger than their husbands—older women outnumber older men. According to the latest available statistics from the Department of Health, Education and Welfare, for every 100 people in the over-65 age bracket, 57 are women. Moreover, two-thirds of them are widows, and there are three times as many widows as widowers. In terms of sheer availability of partners, therefore, older men have a far better statistical opportunity for sex.

Social custom offers men a similar advantage. It's much easier for an older man to find a wife than for an older woman to find a husband (in a typical year, 35,000 such men and only 16,000 such women will wed) largely because he retains the male prerogatives. He's more likely to take the sexual initiative. Age is not deemed to make as much difference to his looks. It is more acceptable for him to wed a young wife than for an older woman to wed a young man.

Moreover, *non*marital sex is more available to men than to women. Since one tends to follow in old age the cultural patterns of one's youth, today's over-65s—who grew up when "illicit" sex was a serious transgression—cannot easily accept the idea of such relationships. Even so, men are still freer to pursue them. Dr. Eric Pfeiffer, head of Duke University's Center for the Study of Aging and Human Development, reports that close to 90 percent of the women interviewed for its long-term study of geriatric sex behavior had stopped having intercourse when their husbands became ill, impotent or died. "By contrast," reports Dr. Pfeiffer, "marital status had little or no effect on the incidence of sexual activity among elderly men."

The "double standard" he grew up with—permitting greater sexual freedom to men—enables the older man to purchase sex without the guilt or social disapproval that it would create for the older woman. (And from a purely practical viewpoint, there are far more women who will sleep for money with an older man than there are men who will do the same for an older woman.) Similarly, it is morally easier for an older man to accept the idea of an affair, or some other variety of an "illicit" relationship.

However, this attitude may be changing. Dr. Paul Glick, senior demographer with the population division of the U.S. Census Bureau, has reported that more than 18,000 couples over 65 listed themselves in the last census as unmarried and living together. This is surely a vast underestimate of the actual number. Those who deal with older persons—gerontologists, counselors, retirement-community administrators—say that the aged are increasingly pairing off in long-term affairs. For some, it is a purely practical matter, a way to preserve maximum Social Security income and to keep the "widow's benefits" from company or union pensions—payments that are usually cut off if a woman remarries. (It also cuts down interference from children worried about the possibility of losing their inheritance if a parent remarries.) For others, it may be an "unmarriage of convenience," a way of sharing chores, alleviating loneliness. But for a growing number of older couples, living together is seen as a logical solution to their desire for emotional closeness and sexual expression.

They do not take the step easily. Struggling with guilt, many seek guidance from ministers who themselves must struggle to sort out the conflict among legalities, religious principles, and compassion. For example, the Rev. Dr. Benton Gaskell, minister of the Pilgrim United Church in Pomona, Calif., whose congregation of more than 2,000 people includes a high percentage of over-65s, told of a couple, both widowed, who came to him for help.

"They were in their 70s," he said, "and living together clandestinely because they couldn't afford to marry since they would lose pension income. They said they felt 'faithless' to their late spouses, never knew what to tell their children or friends, and were in spiritual distress over their predicament. They asked me to ease their guilt by solemnizing their union in the sight of God."

For Dr. Gaskell, the plea presented a quandary. A minister may not conduct a marriage ceremony if there is no marriage license. Nor could he compromise the church. Yet he could not turn away the couple's plea. After consultation with his staff, Dr. Gaskell fashioned a ritual which enabled him formally to bless the couple's "union." With this emotional support, the couple were able to live together openly. "I don't know what they told friends or family," says Dr. Gaskell, "and I don't care. I know what they told me. 'We feel better about ourselves now,' they said. 'It makes us feel our relationship is all right.' "

Are our sexual drives and capacities really so persistent and long-lasting? From time to time a scientist returns from such Shangri-Las as Hunza, Soviet Georgia, or an Andean village in Ecuador with reports of virile octogenarians. Dr. Alexander Leaf of the Harvard Medical School, who has been to all three of those centers of longevity, recently reported that he was convinced that "a vigorous life—sexual activity included—was possible for at least 100 years. . . ." Occasionally, too, a charismatic elder offers similar evidence: a Chaplin, a Picasso, a Senator Thurmond fathering children late in life; or Somerset Maugham complaining, in his 80s, that "one loses one's looks and desirability yet the desire itself remains."

But is that also true for the typical older man or woman? To echo Dr. Calderone, the answer is yes—and much of the sexual indignity the aged suffer could be eased if the biological facts were better known. The three most significant studies of geriatric sexual behavior have been made by Kinsey, Duke's Center for the Study of Aging, and Masters and Johnson. In each, the findings clearly show that men and women in a state of general good health are physiologically able to have a satisfying sex life well into their 70s, 80s and beyond. The studies also indicate that those who were most active sexually during youth and middle age usually retain their vigor and interest longer into old age.

Though Kinsey interviewed only a small number of older persons, his was the pioneering survey. It showed for the first time that four out of five men over the age of 60 were capable of intercourse, and that there was no evidence of sexual decline in women until much later in life. The Duke studies, which have been conducted on a continuing basis for twenty years, are unique in that researchers have been able to follow the trend of sexuality in aging individuals over a sustained time period. One fascinating result was evidence that 15 percent of men and women studied showed a steady *rising* rate of sexual interest and activity as they got older.

While such a complex survey as Duke's cannot be simplistically summarized, the main findings indicate that two out of three men are sexually active past 65, and one out of five is still active in his 80s. And though activity may decline, interest remains: About half of the 80- and 89-year-olds reported a moderate degree of interest. The story is somewhat different for women. "In their 60s," writes Duke's Dr. Eric Pfeiffer, "about one in three reports sexual interest while only one in five is actually having sex. However, their rates of interest and activity don't seem to fall off with increasing age." There are several obvious explanations for the lower activity rate for women: the lack of available men, a greater reluctance to accept nonmarital sex, more anxiety over physical appearance, and a willingness to believe that sex is, or should be, ended after menopause.

Dr. William Masters and Virginia Johnson not only interviewed the aged, but also clinically monitored their sexual performance. For one thing, this helped to discount faulty memory, wishful thinking, bragging or its converse, embarrassed understatement. For another, it provided the first detailed picture of the older body's physiological sexual reactions. Masters and Johnson found that a man's capacity for erection and climax, and a woman's capacity for orgasm, were slowed but not terminated by the aging process. "Inevitably," they say, "all physical responses are slowed. . . . A man can't run around the block as fast as he could 20 or 30 years previously. Yet the simple fact that his sexual functioning is but one more element of his total physiologic functioning may never occur to him."

Thus, it takes the older man longer to achieve a full erection and to reach a climax. He experiences fewer genital spasms, and there is a reduction in both the force and amount of his ejaculation. It takes him longer before he can have another erection. None of this, however, detracts from the pleasure an older man experiences in intercourse.

Yet many men, Masters and Johnson point out, interpret such slowing-down as the sign of inevitable sexual bankruptcy. The fear of impotency itself then further inhibits their sexual functioning. Some men react to this threat to their masculinity by rationalizing that it is time to "give up" sex, that it should not be that "important" any more. (Similarly, women who have never been quite emotionally comfortable with their sexuality find aging an excuse to avoid it—"We're too old for that sort of thing now.") Still, an older man's sexual performance can be particularly satisfying to both himself and his partner just *because* he can maintain an erection for a longer period of time before climaxing. Indeed, if they do not talk themselves out of it, say Masters and Johnson, older couples "can and should continue unencumbered sexual functioning indefinitely."

A similar set of physiological changes occurs in the older woman. There is less lubrication and elasticity of the vagina. The tissues lining it become thin and more easily irritated. The uterine contractions that accompany orgasm may become spasmic and painful. Fortunately, all these symptoms can be eased or counteracted by hormonal treatment. The older woman, write Masters and Johnson, "is fully capable of sexual performance at orgasmic response levels." Medical literature offers numerous case histories of women who not only are orgasmic in their 60s and 70s, but of women who *became* orgasmic for the first time during those years.

In addition to the three major studies, a number of limited surveys confirm this continued sexuality of the aged. Some show, for example, that men past 65 can average four climaxes a month for many years; others show that many men and women without a sexual partner, or whose spouse is unable or unwilling to have a physical relationship, masturbate regularly. One of the more intriguing experiments was conducted by psychiatrist Dr. Charles Fisher at the Sleep Laboratory of New York's Mount Sinai Hospital. He developed techniques to detect and measure penile erection during REM sleep—when the characteristic "rapid eye movement" signals that the sleeper is dreaming. Twenty-one men, aged 71 to 96, spent several nights connected to an EEG recorder and a penile "strain gauge." During REM sleep, three-quarters of them (including the 96-year-old) developed erections. The dreams they later described all revolved around sexual themes.

Every day, 4,000 more Americans reach the age of 65, and they can expect an average of fifteen more years of life. What is truly distressing is that those who deal with the rapidly growing number of older persons—family and friends, doctors and social workers, staffs of old-age homes—are either unaware of the data proving the sexual interest and capability of the aged or cannot psychologically accept it. Just as Freud's findings about childhood sexuality met enormous emotional resistance at first, so are the discoveries about sexuality in the aged. Some authorities manage to reject them altogether. For example, a current book, *How to Deal with Aging and the Elderly,* states: "Most persons lose interest somewhere along the line. . . . A normal development is a displacement of passionate physical sexual relations for a deeper marital relationship that revolves more about . . . philosophical thought about the hereafter."

This sort of attitude cuts older persons off from reassuring information, deprives them of helpful guidance, and reinforces their own sense of shame for still having sexual feelings. Dr. Laura Singer-Magdoff, a New York therapist and former president of the American Association of Marriage and Family Counselors, recently included the topic of sexuality in a talk she gave to a group of older persons. "A gray-haired womam about 70 came up to me with tears in her eyes," the counselor recalled. "She said it was the first time anyone had discussed sex in old age as if it were a normal thing."

The men and women in nursing and old-age homes are probably the most deprived on this score. Their environment is almost totally desexualized: It is considered progress when dining or recreation halls and residential wings are not sex-segregated. Privacy is virtually nonexistent: the administrator of one Delaware convalescent home told me that her staff respected patients' privacy, but added that "we run a bed-check every two hours to make sure they are all right." Only a minority of institutions make an effort to provide areas where a couple can be alone together even to talk, much less to court. Dr. Calderone cites an instance in which one home forbade any unmarried man and woman to watch television together late in the evening. Even married couples may be separated; some state institutions segregate them, or permit the sexes to mix only under "supervision." If only one spouse is in a home, the other seldom has the right to privacy during a visit. A vigorous woman of 71 recently complained to the director of a convalescent home because there was neither the opportunity nor the facility for her to have a sexual relationship with her husband, who was a patient there. "He entered the home to be cared for during his recovery from a serious eye operation," the woman said. "I can't take care of him properly at home. But there is nothing else wrong with him, no reason why we cannot make love. Yet when I come to visit him we must meet only in 'public' areas. Even if we *could* be alone in his room, there's only a narrow hospital bed there. When I suggested to the home's director that he put at least a three-quarter bed in my husband's room, the man looked at me as if I were some sort of sexual monster."

"Society tends to say," observes Dr. Calderone, " 'You should be finished with sex—especially since trying to meet your sexual needs adds to the bother of looking after you.' " Thus staff members, from administrators to attendants, for the most part avoid any reference to the idea that their residents may have sexual needs or even feelings. An older person who evidences them in any way is often reproved, or considered sick or depraved—the "dirty old man" label again.

In its fifteen years of existence, the American Nursing Home Association, which includes 7,000 public and private facilities, has never scheduled a discussion of sexuality at any of its meetings. A spokeswoman said the American Association of Homes for the Aging was "concerned" about residents' sexual rights—the A.A.H.A. is in the process of drawing up a "Patient's Bill of Rights" which includes privacy—but added that the topic was "sort of taboo, people don't like to think about it, and since it isn't a front-line issue, we don't concentrate on it." (In fairness, some distinctions should be drawn. Many homes care for the chronically ill, for whom sex is not an issue. Publicly supported homes operate under legislative restrictions. Some privately supported ones have large budgets and trained staffs, while others are short of money, facilities, and trained personnel. Some reflect conservative community mores, or the conventional attitudes of their administrators. And all believe they have to deal with problems far more important than geriatric sexuality.)

Nevertheless, some small progress is being made. According to Hannah Weiner, a sociologist and head of a counseling group called SOMA (Services to Ongoing Mature Aging), this can range from establishing beauty parlors in old-age homes to scheduling talks on sex by gynecologists and urologists. A few homes now set aside small lounges where one or two couples can talk or have tea. Too, SOMA has had an encouraging response from institutions to the "sexuality and aging" seminars it conducts.

But no amount of frills or lectures can substitute for privacy, and certainly not for a more understanding approach. "Those are needed most," says Jacob Reingold, executive director of the modern, 600-guest Hebrew Home for the Aged on the banks of the Hudson in New York City. An energetic and empathic man, Mr. Reingold once shocked a nurse who came running to him to report that an elderly couple were making love in the woman's room. "What should I do?" the nurse asked frantically. Answered Mr. Reingold: "Tiptoe gently out so you don't disturb them."

Recently a Canadian doctor suggested that all old-age homes should set aside "petting rooms." But privacy is important, Mr. Reingold points out, not so much to isolate affection or intimacy as to give it legitimacy. "Because of their cultural background," he says, "older people tend to separate what's 'right' in public from what's 'right' in private. So a woman rebuffs a man's overtures, or a man turns a blind eye to a little flirting—but I think they would act differently if there weren't so many witnesses. They are caught in a bind. Either they behave 'acceptably' and miss out on emotional satisfactions, or feel they must run the risk of disapproval and embarrassment."

We may be slowly acclimating ourselves to the idea that there is sexuality after 65, but we are still a long way from actively helping older people to express it fully, or to deal with their feelings about it. That is the opinion of Dr. Robert N. Butler, a Washington, D.C., psychiatrist and an expert in the mental health of the aging. *Aging & Mental Health,* which he has written with Myrna I. Lewis, a mental-health specialist, calls for "positive psychosocial approaches" to the question. "What we need," the authors say, "is a campaign of sex education for the aged. For example, techniques of intercourse especially pertinent to the needs of older people should be clarified. Thus, sex in the morning may be preferable for those who fatigue easily at night. Certain coital positions may make intercourse more feasible for those who are crippled by arthritis."

Butler feels doctors have a responsibility to be more specific about the sexual effects of medical problems. A man or woman with a heart condition, for instance, ought to know that a coronary attack during sex occurs much less often than the patient may fear is the case. "If a person is taking nitroglycerine pills as medication," says Butler, "there's no reason he can't take one *before* beginning intercourse, as a precautionary measure to ease his concern. A woman who experiences vaginal discomfort should be encouraged to have hormonal replacement therapy, even in her older years. A man facing a prostatectomy should be reassured that the likelihood of impotence resulting is comparatively small. And if a doctor has a choice among the varying techniques for that surgery, he should consider the sexual effects in making his decision."

Butler also inveighs against the indiscriminate dosing of old people with tranquilizers and antidepressants, often just to make them "easier to handle." One of the pills' side effects is to cut sexual drive and inhibit ejaculation. "The average doctor," says Butler, "does not really think sex matters in old age." For example, a 72-year-old man recently asked his physician's help just before he planned to remarry. During the past two or three years, the man had experienced lessened potency. Occasionally he could not achieve an erection at all. He wondered if he could be given hormone pills or an injection that would help him. "The woman I'm going to marry is a wonderful person, and I don't want to embarrass or disappoint her," the man said. Instead of examining the man to see if anything could be done medically to aid him, the doctor dismissed the idea as not worth bothering about. "If she's a wonderful woman," he pontificated, "she'll understand."

But sexual activity can actually be therapeutic for an older person. "There is some evidence," says Butler, "that it helps arthritics by increasing adrenal-gland output of cortisone. The sex act also helps to reduce psychological tension."

But though Butler and other experts believe that much can be done to improve the physical aspects of sex for the aged, they emphasize that, in the best sense, older persons should be encouraged to explore the broader emotional limits of sexuality. Researchers focus on quantitative questions—outlet, frequency, response. They seldom seek answers to qualitative questions— needs, desires, hopes.

"Perhaps I am romanticizing," Butler says, "but old age may be the time to make sex a work of art. It would be tragic if older persons seek merely to recapture the physical sensations of their younger days. Age offers the opportunity to view sex as intimate communication in its best sense."

Clearly, there is more to sexuality after 65 than just the act of sex. For a man, there is the satisfaction of feeling still masculine; for a woman, still feminine; for both, still being wanted and needed. There is the comforting warmth of physical nearness, the pleasure of companionship. There is the rewarding emotional intimacy of shared joys. All we need, the song says, is love, love, love. Do not those who are older need it as much as any of us?

WHY THEY LIVE
TO BE 100,
OR EVEN OLDER,
IN ABKHASIA*
Sula Benet

Not long ago, in the village of Tamish in the Soviet Republic of Abkhasia, I raised my glass of wine to toast a man who looked no more than 70. "May you live as long as Moses (120 years)," I said. He was not pleased. He was 119.

For centuries, the Abkhasians and other Caucasian peasants have been mentioned in the chronicles of travelers amazed at their longevity and good health. Even now, on occasion, newspaper reports in the United States and elsewhere (never quite concealing bemusement and skepticism) will tell of an Abkhasian who claims to be 120, sometimes 130. When I returned from Abkhasia to New York displaying photographs and statistics, insisting that the tales are true and preoccupied with the question of why, my American friends invariably responded with the mocking question that contained its own answer: "Yogurt?" As a matter of fact, no, not yogurt; but the Abkhasians *do* drink a lot of buttermilk.

Abkhasia is a hard land—the Abkhasians, expressing more pride than resentment, say it was one of God's afterthoughts—but it is a beautiful one; if the Abkhasians are right about its mythical origin, God had a good second thought. It is subtropical on its coast along the Black Sea, alpine if one travels straight

* Sula Benet, "Why They Live to Be 100, or Even Older, in Abkhasia," *New York Times Magazine,* 26 December 1971. Copyright © 1971 by The New York Times Company. Reprinted by permission.

213

back from the sea, through the populated lowlands and valleys, to the main range of the Caucasus Mountains.

The Abkhasians have been there for at least 1,000 years. For centuries they were herdsmen in the infertile land, but now the valleys and foothills are planted with tea and tobacco, and they draw their living largely from agriculture. There are 100,000 Abkhasians, not quite a fifth of the total population of the autonomous Abkhasian Republic, which is, administratively, part of Georgia, Joseph Stalin's birthplace; the rest are Russians, Greeks, and Georgians. However, most of the people in government are Abkhasian, and both the official language and the style of life throughout the region are Abkhasian. The single city, Sukhumi, is the seat of government and a port of call for ships carrying foreign tourists. They are often visible in the streets of the city, whose population includes relatively few Abkhasians. Even those who live and work there tend to consider the villages of their families their own real homes. It is in the villages—575 of them between the mountains and the sea, ranging in population from a few hundred to a few thousand— that most Abkhasians live and work on collective farms.

I first went there in the summer of 1970 at the invitation of the Academy of Sciences of the USSR. The Abkhasians were fascinating; I returned last summer and will go again next year. It was while interviewing people who had participated in the early efforts at collectivization that I became aware of the unusually large number of people, ranging in age from 80 to 119, who are still very much a part of the collective life they helped organize.

After spending months with them, I still find it impossible to judge the age of older Abkhasians. Their general appearance does not provide a clue: You know they are old because of their gray hair and the lines on their faces, but are they 70 or 107? I would have guessed "70" for all of the old people that I encountered in Abkhasia, and most of the time I would have been wrong.

It is as if the physical and psychological changes which to us signify the aging process had, in the Abkhasians, simply stopped at a certain point. Most work regularly. They are still blessed with good eyesight, and most have their own teeth. Their posture

214

is unusually erect, even into advanced age; many take walks of more than two miles a day and swim in the mountain streams. They look healthy, and they are a handsome people. Men show a fondness for enormous mustaches, and are slim but not frail. There is an old saying that when a man lies on his side, his waist should be so small that a dog can pass beneath it. The woman are darkhaired and also slender, with fair complexions and shy smiles.

There are no current figures for the total number of aged in Abkhasia, though in the village of Dzhgerda, which I visited last summer, there were 71 men and 110 women between 81 and 90, and 19 people over 91—15 percent of the village population of 1,200. And it is worth noting that this extraordinary percentage is not the result of a migration by the young: Abkhasians, young and old, understandably prefer to stay where they are, and rarely travel, let alone migrate. In 1954, the last year for which overall figures are available, 2.58 percent of the Abkhasians were over 90. The roughly comparable figures for the entire Soviet Union and the United States were 0.1 percent and 0.4 percent, respectively.

Since 1932, the longevity of the Abkhasians has been systematically studied on several occasions by Soviet and Abkhasian investigators, and I was given full access to their findings by the Ethnographic Institute in Sukhumi. These studies have shown that, in general, signs of arteriosclerosis, when they occurred at all, were found only in extreme old age. One researcher who examined a group of Abkhasians over 90 found that close to 40 percent of the men and 30 percent of the women had vision good enough to read or thread a needle without glasses, and that over 40 percent had reasonably good hearing. There were no reported cases of either mental illness or cancer in a nine-year study of 123 people over 100.

In that study, begun in 1960 by Dr. G. N. Sichinava of the Institute of Gerontology in Sukhumi, the aged showed extraordinary psychological and neurological stability. Most of them had clear recollection of the distant past, but partially bad recollection for more recent events. Some reversed this pattern, but quite a large number retained a good memory of both the recent and distant past. All correctly oriented themselves in

215

time and place. All showed clear and logical thinking, and most correctly estimated their physical and mental capacities. They showed a lively interest in their families' affairs, in their collective, and in social events. All were agile, neat, and clean.

Abkhasians are hospitalized only rarely, except for stomach disorders and childbirth. According to doctors who have inspected their work, they are expert at setting broken arms and legs themselves—their centuries of horsemanship have given them both the need and the practice.

The Abkhasian view of the aging process is clear from their vocabulary. They do not have a phrase for "old people"; those over 100 are called "long living people." Death, in the Abkhasian view, is not the logical end of life but something irrational. The aged seem to lose strength gradually, wither in size and finally die; when that happens, Abkhasians show their grief fully, even violently.

For the rest of the world, disbelief is the response not to Abkhasians' deaths but to how long they have lived. There really should no longer be any question about their longevity. All of the Soviet medical investigators took great care to cross-check the information they received in interviews. Some of the men studied had served in the army, and military records invariably supported their own accounts. Extensive documentation is lacking only because the Abkhasians had no functioning written language until after the Russian Revolution.

But why do they live so long? The absence of a written history, and the relatively recent period in which medical and anthrophological studies have taken place, preclude a clear answer. Genetic selectivity is an obvious possibility. Constant hand-to-hand combat during many centuries of Abkhasian existence may have eliminated those with poor eyesight, obesity and other physical shortcomings, producing healthier Abkhasians in each succeeding generation. But documentation for such an evolutionary process is lacking.

When I asked the Abkhasians themselves about their longevity, they told me they live as long as they do because of their practices in sex, work, and diet.

The Abkhasians, because they expect to live long and healthy lives, feel it is necessary self-discipline to conserve their energies, including their sexual energy, instead of grasping what sweetness is available to them at the moment. They say it is the norm that regular sexual relations do not begin before the age of 30 for men, the traditional age of marriage; it was once even considered unmanly for a new husband to exercise his sexual rights on his wedding night. (If they are asked what is done to provide substitute gratifications of normal sexual needs before marriage, Abkhasians smile and say, "Nothing," but it is not unreasonable to speculate that they, like everyone else, find substitutes for the satisfaction of healthy, heterosexual sex. Today, some young people marry in their mid-20s instead of waiting for the "proper" age of 30, to the consternation of their elders.)

Postponement of satisfaction may be smiled at, but so is the expectation of prolonged, future enjoyment, perhaps with more reason. One medical team investigating the sex life of the Abkhasians concluded that many men retain their sexual potency long after the age of 70, and 13.6 percent of the women continue to menstruate after the age of 55.

Tarba Sit, 102, confided to me that he had waited until he was 60 to marry because while he was in the army "I had a good time right and left." One of his relatives had nine children; the youngest born when he was 100. Doctors obtained sperm from him when he was 119, in 1963, and he still retained his libido and potency. The only occasions on which medical investigators found discrepancies in the claimed ages of Abkhasians was when men insisted they were younger than they actually were. One said he was 95, but his daughter had a birth certificate proving she was 81, and other information indicated he was really 108. When he was confronted with the conflict he became angry and refused to discuss it, since he was about to get married. Makhti Tarkil, 104, with whom I spoke in the village of Duripsh, said the explanation was obvious in view of the impending marriage: "A man is a man until he is 100, you know what I mean. After that, well, he's getting old."

Abkhasian culture provides a dependent and secondary role for women; when they are young, their appearance is stressed, and when they are married, their service in the household is their major role. (As with other aspects of Abkhasian life, the period since the revolution has brought changes, and some

217

women now work in the professions; but in the main, the traditions are still in force.) In the upbringing of a young woman, great care is taken to make her as beautiful as possible according to Abkhasian standards. In order to narrow her waist and keep her breasts small, she wears a leather corset around her chest and waist; the corset is permanently removed on her wedding night. Her complexion should be fair, her eyebrows thin; because a high forehead is also desirable, the hair over the brow is shaved and further growth is prevented through the application of bleaches and herbs. She should also be a good dancer.

Virginity is an absolute requirement for marriage. If a woman proves to have been previously deflowered, the groom has a perfect right to take her back to her family and have his marriage gifts returned. He always exercises that right, returning the bride and announcing to the family, "Take your dead one." And to him, as well as all other eligible men, she is dead: in Abkhasian society, she has been so dishonored by his rejection that it would be next to impossible to find a man to marry her. (Later on, however, she may be married off to an elderly widower or some other less desirable male from a distant village. When she is discovered, she is expected to name the guilty party. She usually picks the name of a man who has recently died, in order to prevent her family from taking revenge and beginning a blood feud.)

For both married and unmarried Abkhasians, extreme modesty is required at all times. There is an overwhelming feeling of uneasiness and shame over any public manifestation of sex, or even affection. A man may not touch his wife, sit down next to her or even talk to her in the presence of strangers. A woman's armpits are considered an erogenous zone and are never exposed, except to her husband.

A woman is a stranger, although a fully accepted one, in her husband's household. Her presence always carries the threat that her husband's loyalty to his family may be eroded by his passion for her. In the Abkhasian tradition, a woman may never change her dress nor bathe in the presence of her mother-in-law, and when an Abkhasian couple are alone in a room, they keep their voices low so that the husband's mother will not overhear them.

218

Despite the elaborate rules—perhaps, in part, because they are universally accepted—sex in Abkhasia is considered a good and pleasurable thing when it is strictly private. And, as difficult as it may be for the American mind to grasp, it is guiltless. It is not repressed or sublimated into work, art or religious-mystical passion. It is not an evil to be driven from one's thoughts. It is a pleasure to be regulated for the sake of one's health—like a good wine.

An Abkhasian is never "retired," a status unknown in Abkhasian thinking. From the beginning of life until its end, he does what he is capable of doing because both he and those around him consider work vital to life. He makes the demands on himself that he can meet, and as those demands diminish with age, his status in the community nevertheless increases.

In his nine-year study of aged Abkhasians, Dr. Sichinava made a detailed examination of their work habits. One group included 82 men, most of whom had been working as peasants from the age of 11, and 45 women who, from the time of adolescence, had worked in the home and helped care for farm animals. Sichinava found that the work load had decreased considerably between the ages of 80 and 90 for 48 men, and between 90 and 100 for the rest. Among the women, 27 started doing less work between 80 and 90, and the others slowed down after 90. The few men who had been shepherds stopped following the herds up to the mountain meadows in spring, and instead began tending farm animals, after the age of 90. The farmers began to work less land; many stopped plowing and lifting heavy loads, but continued weeding (despite the bending involved) and doing other tasks. Most of the women stopped helping in the fields and some began to do less housework. Instead of serving the entire family—an Abkhasian family extended through marriage, may include 50 or more people—they served only themselves and their children. But they also fed the chickens and knitted.

Dr. Sichinava also observed 21 men and 7 women over 100 years old and found that, on the average, they worked a four-hour day on the collective farm—the men weeding and helping with the corn crop, the women stringing tobacco leaves. Under the collective system, members of the community are free to work in their own gardens, but they get paid in what are, in effect, piecework rates for the work they do for the collective. Dr. Sichinava's group of villagers over 100, when they worked for the collective, maintained an hourly output that was not quite a fifth that of the norm for younger workers. But in maintaining their own pace, they worked more evenly and without waste motion, stopping on occasion to rest. By contrast, the younger men worked rapidly, but competitively and tensely. Competitiveness in work is not indigenous to Abkhasian culture but it is encouraged by the Soviet Government for the sake of increased production; pictures of the best workers are posted in the offices of the village collectives. It is too soon to predict whether this seemingly fundamental change in work habits will affect Abkhasian longevity.

The persistent Abkhasians have their own workers' heroes: Kelkiliana Khesa, a woman of 109 in the village of Otapi, was paid for 49 workdays (a collective's workday is eight hours) during one summer; Bozba Pash, a man of 94 on the same collective, worked 155 days one year; Minosyan Grigorii of Aragich, often held up as an example to the young, worked 230 days in a year at the age of 90. (Most Americans, with a two-week vacation and several holidays, work between 240 and 250 days, some of them less than eight hours, in a year.)

Both the Soviet medical profession and the Abkhasians agree that their work habits have a great deal to do with their longevity. The doctors say that the way Abkhasians work helps the vital organs function optimally. The Abkhasians say, "Without rest, a man cannot work; without work, the rest does not give you any benefit."

That attitude, though it is not susceptible to medical measurements, may be as important as the work itself. It is part of a consistent life pattern: When they are children, they do what they are capable of doing, progressing from the easiest to the most strenuous tasks, and when they age, the curve descends, but it is unbroken. The aged are never seen sitting in chairs for long periods, passive, like vegetables. They do what they can, and while some consider the piecework system of the collectives a form of exploitation, it does permit them to function at their own pace.

Overeating is considered dangerous in Abkhasia, and fat people are regarded as ill. When the aged see a younger Abkhasian who is even a little overweight, they inquire about his health. "An Abkhasian cannot get fat," they say. "Can you imagine the ridiculous figure one would cut on horseback?" But to the dismay of the elders, the young eat much more than their fathers and grandfathers do; light, muscular and agile horsemen are no longer needed as a first line of defense.

The Abkhasian diet, like the rest of life, is stable: investigators have found that people 100 years and older eat the same foods throughout their lives. They show few idiosyncratic preferences, and they do not significantly change their diet when their economic status improves. Their caloric intake is 23 percent lower than that of the industrial workers in Abkhasia, though they consume twice as much vitamin C; the industrial workers have a much higher rate of coronary insufficiency and a higher level of cholesterol in the blood.

The Abkhasians eat without haste and with decorum. When guests are present, each person in turn is toasted with praise of his real or imaginary virtues. Such meals may last several hours, but nobody minds, since they prefer their food served lukewarm in any case. The food is cut into small pieces, served on platters, and eaten with the fingers. No matter what the occasion, Abkhasians take only small bites of food and chew those very slowly—a habit that stimulates the flow of ptyalin and maltase, insuring proper digestion of the carbohydrates which form the bulk of the diet. And, traditionally, there are no leftovers in Abkhasia; even the poor dispose of uneaten food by giving it to the animals, and no one would think of serving warmed-over food to a guest—even if it had been cooked only two hours earlier. Though some young people, perhaps influenced by Western ideas, consider the practice wasteful, most Abkhasians shun day-old food as unhealthful.

The Abkhasians eat relatively little meat—perhaps once or twice a week—and prefer chicken, beef, young goat and, in the winter, pork. They do not like fish and, despite its availability, rarely eat it. The meat is always freshly slaughtered and either broiled to the absolute minimum—until the blood stops running freely or, in the case of chicken, until the meat turns white. It

221

is, not surprisingly, tough in the mouth of a non-Abkhasian, but they have no trouble with it.

At all three meals, the Abkhasians eat *abista,* a corn meal mash cooked in water without salt, which takes the place of bread. *Abista* is eaten warm with pieces of homemade goat cheese tucked into it. They eat cheese daily, and also consume about two glasses of buttermilk a day. When eggs are eaten, which is not very often, they are boiled or fried with pieces of cheese.

The other staples in the Abkhasian diet—staple in Abkhasia means daily or almost so—include fresh fruits, especially grapes; fresh vegetables, including green onions, tomatoes, cucumbers, and cabbage; a wide variety of pickled vegetables, and baby lima beans, cooked slowly for hours, mashed and served flavored with a sauce of onions, peppers, garlic, pomegranate juice, and pepper. That hot sauce, or a variant of it, is set on the table in a separate dish for anyone who wants it. Large quantities of garlic are also always at hand.

Although they are the main suppliers of tobacco for the Soviet Union few Abkhasians smoke. (I did meet one, a woman over 100, who smoked constantly.) They drink neither coffee nor tea. But they do consume a locally produced, dry, red wine of low alcoholic content. Everyone drinks it, almost always in small quantities, at lunch and supper, and the Abkhasians call it "life giving." Absent from their diet is sugar, though honey, a local product, is used. Toothaches are rare.

Soviet medical authorities who have examined the Abkhasians and their diet feel it may well add years to their lives: the buttermilk and pickled vegetables, and probably the wine, help destroy certain bacteria and, indirectly, prevent the development of arteriosclerosis, the doctors think. In 1970, a team of Soviet doctors and Dr. Samuel Rosen of New York, a prominent ear surgeon, compared the hearing of Muscovites and Abkhasians, and concluded that the Abkhasians' diet—very little saturated fat, a great deal of fruit and vegetables—also accounted for their markedly better hearing. The hot sauce is the only item most doctors would probably say "no" to, and apparently some Abkhasians feel the same way.

Although the Abkhasians themselves attribute their longevity to their work, sex and dietary habits, there is another, broader aspect of their culture that impresses an outsider in their midst: the high degree of integration in their lives, the sense of group identity that gives each individual an unshaken feeling of persoanl security and continuity, and permits the Abkhasians as a people to adapt themselves—yet preserve themselves—to the changing conditions imposed by the larger society in which they live. That sense of continuity in both their personal and national lives is what anthropologists would call their spatial and temporal integration.

Their spatial integration is in their kinship structure. It is, literally, the Abkhasians' all-encompassing design for living: It regulates relationships between families, determines where they live, defines the position of women and marriage rules. Through centuries of nonexistent or ineffective centralized authority, kinship was life's frame of reference, and it still is.

Kinship in Abkhasia is an elaborate, complex set of relationships based on patrilineage. At its center is the family, extended through marriage by the sons; it also includes all those families which can be traced to a single progenitor; and, finally, to all persons with the same surname, whether the progenitor can be traced or not. As a result, an Abkhasian may be "kin" to several thousand people, many of whom he does not know. I first discovered the pervasiveness of kinship rules when my friend Omar, an Abkhasian who had accompanied me from Sukhumi to the village of Duripsh, introduced me to a number of people he called his brothers and sisters. When I had met more than 20 "siblings" I asked, "How many brothers and sisters do you have?"

"In this village, 30," he said. "Abkhasian reckoning is different from Russian. These people all carry my father's name."

I took his explanation less seriously than I should have. Later, when I expressed admiration for a recording of Abkhasian epic poetry I had heard in the home of one of Omar's "brothers," Omar, without a word, gave the record to me as a gift.

"Omar, it isn't yours," I said.

"Oh yes it is. This is the home of my brother," he said. When I appealed to the "brother," he said, "Of course he can give it to you. He is my brother."

The consanguineal and affinal relationships that make up

the foundation of the kinship structure are supplemented by a variety of ritual relationships that involve lifetime obligations—and serve to broaden the human environment from which Abkhasians derive their extraordinary sense of security. Although there are no alternative life styles towards which the rebellious may flee, the Abkhasians are ready to absorb others into their own culture. During my visit, for instance, a Christian man was asked to be the godfather of a Moslem child; both prospective godfather and child were Abkhasians. When I expressed surprise, I was told, "It doesn't matter. We want to enlarge our circle of relatives."

The temporal integration of Abkhasian life is expressed in its general continuity, in the absence of limiting, defining conditions of existence like "unemployed," "adolescent," "alienated." Abkhasians are a life-loving, optimistic people, and unlike so many very old "dependent" people in the United States—who feel they are a burden to themselves and their families—they enjoy the prospect of continued life. One 99-year-old Abkhasian, Akhba Suleiman of the village of Achandara, told his doctor, "It isn't time to die yet. I am needed by my children and grandchildren, and it isn't bad in this world—except that I can't turn the earth over and it has become difficult to climb trees."

The old are always active. "It is better to move without purpose than to sit still," they say. Before breakfast, they walk through the homestead's courtyard and orchard, taking care of small tasks that come to their attention. They look for fences and equipment in need of repair and check on the family's animals. At breakfast, their early morning survey completed, they report what has to be done.

Until evening, the old spend their time alternating work and rest. A man may pick up wind-fallen apples, then sit down on a bench, telling stories or making toys for his grandchildren or great-grandchildren. Another chore which is largely attended to by the old is weeding the courtyard, a large green belonging to the homestead, which serves as a center of activity for the kin group. Keeping it in shape requires considerable labor, yet I never saw a courtyard that was not tidy and well-trimmed.

During the summer, many old men spend two or three months high in the mountains, living in shepherds' huts, helping to herd or hunting for themselves and the shepherds (with their arrested aging process, many are excellent marksmen despite their age). They obviously are not fearful of losing their authority during their absence; their time in the mountains is useful and pleasurable.

The extraordinary attitude of the Abkhasians—to feel needed at 99 or 110—is not an artificial, self-protective one; it is the natural expression, in old age, of a consistent outlook that begins in childhood. The stoic upbringing of an Abkhasian child, in which parents and senior relatives participate, instills respect, obedience, and endurance. At an early age, children participate in household tasks; when they are not at school, they work in the fields or at home.

There are no separate "facts of life" for children and adults: The values given children are the ones adults live by, and there is no hypocritical disparity (as in so many other societies) between adult words and deeds. Since what they are taught is considered important, and the work they are given is considered necessary, children are neither restless nor rebellious. As they mature, there are easy transitions from one status in life to another: a bride, for instance, will stay for a time with her husband's relatives, gradually becoming part of a new clan, before moving into his home.

From the beginning, there is no gap between expectation and experience. Abkhasians expect a long and useful life and look forward to old age with good reason: in a culture which so highly values continuity in its traditions, the old are indispensable in their transmission. The elders preside at important ceremonial occasions, they mediate disputes and their knowledge of farming is sought. They feel needed because, in their own minds and everyone else's, they are. They are the opposite of burdens; they are highly valued resources.

The Abkhasians themselves are obviously right in citing their diet and their work habits as contributing factors in their longevity; in my opinion, their postponed, and later prolonged, sex life probably has nothing to do with it. Their climate is exemplary, the air (especially to a New Yorker) refreshing, but it is not significantly different from many other areas of the world, where life spans are shorter. And while some kind of genetic selectivity may well have been at work, there simply is not enough information to evaluate the genetic factor in Abkhasian longevity.

My own view is that Abkhasians live as long as they do primarily because of the extraordinary cultural factors that structure their existence: the uniformity and certainty of both individual and group behavior, the unbroken continuum of life's activities—the same games, the same work, the same food, the same self-imposed and socially perceived needs. And the increasing prestige that comes with increasing age.

There is no better way to comprehend the importance of these cultural factors than to consider for a moment some of the prevalent characteristics of American society. Children are sometimes given chores to keep them occupied, but they and their parents know there is no *need* for the work they do; even as adults, only a small percentage of Americans have the privilege of feeling that their work is essential and important. The old, when they do not simply vegetate, out of view and out of mind, keep themselves "busy" with bingo and shuffleboard. Americans are mobile, sometimes frantically so, searching for signs of permanence that will indicate their lives are meaningful.

Can Americans learn something from the Abkhasian view of "long living" people? I think so.

4

Work,
Retirement,
and Leisure

INTRODUCTION TO PART IV

As many have pointed out, the transition from work to post-work is rapidly becoming a normal part of the life process. Retirement which occurs when a person leaves the job held during the working years is a recent innovation in history. Never before have so many lived to be able to retire, and to be retired for so long. As more people live to become "old" (i.e., as the life expectancy of the population increases), the proportion of people's lives spent in the labor force declines. Such is the case in America, where both the number of persons in retirement and the number of years between end of work and end of life are increasing. Social gerontologists have been attempting to determine the impact of retirement on individuals leaving the labor force and to determine how people use the time retirement from work gives to them.

One such research effort is the Social Security Administration's Longitudinal Retirement History Study. This national study, which began in 1969, is designed to examine withdrawal from work life. The paper by Irelan and Bond describes this project and presents some important findings about individuals (aged 58–63) in their last years of work before retirement. The life satisfaction and retirement expectations of the national sample are discussed and related to socioeconomic status, health, and social relations. Generally speaking, those approaching retirement believed it would be a pleasant time of life, with, however, some constraints and problems related to income, health, and mobility.

In the next paper Palmore focuses on the effects of aging on activities and attitudes. Principally, he asks, "Is there a persistence of life style among the aged?" The answer, contrary to some commonly held assumptions, is yes—there was no significant overall change in activities or attitudes among men in the sample and only small overall changes among women. This was interpreted as supportive of an "activity" approach to aging.

The paper by Miller discusses leisure and retirement. One problem the elderly face, he argues, is that they must find meaningful rationales for the leisure activities in which they are involved. As well, the process of engaging in new activities involves taking on new roles the person may or may not be able to fulfill. Social embarrassment or anticipation of it (for the older person and others with whom he interacts) can result in the aging person excluding himself from such activities.

Stone and Kalish, in their provocative paper, make some observations on a leisure-time pursuit of some California "oldsters" which appears to be quite meaningful: gambling. They suggest the possibility of winning, the social interaction involved, the unplanned nature of the activities, and the fact that the elderly gambler is an active agent in his or her own fate as reasons for the importance of gambling for these old people.

In the final paper in this part, Atchley presents the outlines of a "continuity theory" for explaining the relationship between retirement and leisure participation. He suggests, in some opposition to the paper by Miller, that "it may be more profitable to consider leisure participation in retirement as a source of satisfaction to be freely utilized rather than as a trauma to be avoided."

RETIREES
OF
THE 1970s*

Lola M. Irelan and Kathleen Bond

Our information about the background and salient characteristics of the people who will be the American retirees of the
1970s comes from the first wave of interviews in the Social
Security Administration's Longitudinal Retirement History
Study, a national sample longitudinal study concentrated on the
retirement process.

In the spring of 1969 baseline data were collected from
11,153 members of the 1905–11 birth cohort. Three subsamples
represented 4,117,000 married men with spouses present in the
household, 729,000 men with no spouses present, and 1,954,000
women living with no spouses present. At the first interview, all
were between 58 and 63 years old. These respondents were re-
interviewed in 1971 and 1973 and will be questioned at least
three more times—in 1975, 1977, and 1979. Over this ten-year
period, the respondents will have aged from 58–63 to 68–73
years and will have passed through the typical ages at which
most Americans retire from a full-time working life. In 1969
most were workers or would-be workers; by 1979 we expect
that the large majority of them will have retired.

Our sample of the 1905–11 birth cohort (minus the married
women) represents an interesting generation whose members'

* Lola M. Irelan and Kathleen Bond, "Retirees of the 1970s," in *Migration, Mobility,
and Aging,* ed. C. Osterbind (Gainesville: University of Florida Press, 1974), pp.
42–63. © 1974 Board of Regents of the State of Florida.

backgrounds may herald the beginning of a change in the characteristics of the American aged population (see Cain, 1967). Most of these characteristics are related to the nation's advancing industrialization. The majority of the members of this cohort were better educated, had fewer children, and worked a shorter work week than previous generations. Too, the women of this group were more likely to work for pay than the women born before them and thus the married couples were more likely to bring home two paychecks. The Retirement History Study will enable us to look at the effects of these characteristics on retirement behavior.

Such research as exists on societal characteristics and social handling of aging makes clear that there is no one-to-one relation between stages of social evolution and the status of the aged—or even the existence of an "aged" status (Simmons, 1960). Rather, the options available to older people, the roles they may claim, and the esteem they can expect seem to result from interaction among other entities more basically affected by change. The most noticeable overall change, as the society becomes industrially advanced, is in the degree of social complexity. Institutions multiply. Family and the kinship network lose functions to other social units—to school systems, religious organizations, political and judicial systems, wage-paying organizations, and impersonal systems of social insurance. The family itself becomes a less substantial unit. Individual and nuclear family living arrangements come to be typical. Labor specialization sets in. Values shift.

Too, important demographic changes occur. At the same time as the United States has been experiencing the social changes attending advanced industrialization, a more readily measurable change—one which makes even more timely the study of retirement—has been going on. Today, as you well know, there are more people over the age of 65 than ever before in our history. In 1900, there were 3 million people 65 years old and over; by 1970 their numbers increased to 20 million. Projections made by the Bureau of the Census show that there will be close to 29 million old people by the year 2000 and 40 million in 2020 (U.S. Census, P-23, no. 40).[1]

As well as being here in larger numbers, older people composed a larger proportion of the population in 1969 than they did at the beginning of the century. Those aged 65 and over made up 4.1 percent of the population in 1900 compared with 9.8 percent in 1970. The proportion is predicted to be between 8.9 and 10.6 percent by the year 2000 (depending on future fertility).

Along with the increasing numbers and proportion of old-sters in the population, genuine retirement has become more widespread. In 1900, the labor force participation rate of men 65 and over was 68.3; in 1960 only 30.5 percent of aged men were employed; and by 1970 the proportion was down to 25 percent (Jaffe, 1972). Work filled almost the entirety of men's adult lives at the beginning of the century, but by midcentury, retirement characterized most men's lives after age 65. Now, in fact, the age at retirement is edging downward toward 60. In 1955, approximately 83 percent of men between 60 and 64 were employed; by 1970 the proportion had declined to 75 percent.

The Social Security Administration's reasons for studying retirement are probably obvious. We want to learn the details of the role of social security coverage and benefits in this phase of American life. This information is necessary not only to assess effectiveness of the Social Security program as it is but as input for the legislators and planners who consider the program's amendment and improvement.

The Retirement History Study's sample is one tailored to the study of withdrawal from work life. Keeping in mind the standard American retirement age of 65, plus the inclination of that life point to edge downward to even younger ages, we elected to sample initially 58–63-year-olds, hoping thereby to net people mostly in their last years of work before retirement. Concerned specifically with retirement and not with aging, we did not sample women in that age range who had husbands living in the same household. Pretesting in several different cities had persuaded us that most wives thought of retirement in terms of their husbands' retirement. So—constrained as all researchers are by problems of money, personnel, and time—we chose to spend our resources in finding and studying a national sample of 11,153 men (of all marital statuses) and women without husbands in their homes at the time of sample selection. So far, analysis has been possible only of the first year, the 1969 data, and simple descriptive reporting is all that can be done. Most of it will sound familiar, some will be news, and some of it might be provocative.

In the broadest sense, we are studying influences on the quality of life of those approaching retirement. Major parts of each year's interview center on such items as income and financial resources, expenditures, health, social contacts, and work history. Subjective measures of morale and respondents' own assessments of their life situations are also included.

Now, what were they like in 1969—and what does the answer to that augur for their future? One measure of the quality of an older persons's life is that of life satisfaction. Since life satisfaction appears to be most strongly associated with socioeconomic status, health, and social relations (Edwards & Klemmack, 1973), let us use those rubrics to organize a summary of most of our findings before touching on the sample's retirement expectations.

Socioeconomic Status

The operational relationship among the factors related to life satisfaction is one of undoubted circularity. In the course of a life span, one's occupation, his income, his physical condition, his own evaluation of his health, activity, contact with other people, all interact and react to elevate or depress each other. It is socioeconomic status, however, which weighs most heavily in swaying individual statements of satisfaction. Several studies provide evidence of the persistent relation of one's socioeconomic condition to his outlook on life and its circumstances. Happiness rises and worrying lessens with educational level (Gurin et al., 1960). The Cornell Longitudinal Study found that satisfaction with life decreased over a two-year period among older men who felt economically deprived. Older people in nonmanual occupations are more disposed to view their own health positively than those in manual occupations (Riley & Foner,

1968). And, as we shall see, health and life satisfaction are related. Mental illness is less likely to occur with higher economic status (Riley & Foner, 1968), and the positive relationship between income and happiness has been documented in some 30 surveys in 19 different countries (Easterlin, 1973).

Of the three standard ingredients of socioeconomic status (occupation, education, income), incomes may be most important in accounting for the objective quality of retirees' lives. Mollie Orshansky, who devised the Social Security Administration's poverty index, is fond of noting that while money may not be everything, it's way ahead of whatever is in second place. For retirees, education will still be a source of some prestige, and former occupations will contribute to prestige and will in large measure have determined retirement income. Education and occupation, with other social influences, will have shaped a retiree's values and preferences. But income by itself will be the primary determinant of whether or not those preferences and values can be realized. One's financial status directs the type of leisure activities he or she can undertake, the amount of diagnostic and preventive medical care he or she can seek, the amount of traveling he or she can do, the quality of housing, the quality of diet, and so on.

The respondents of the Retirement History Study (RHS) were nearing the end of work life in 1969. Their occupational histories were almost complete. Despite pleas for continuing education throughout adulthood so that one's education is not outmoded in times of rapid social change, the vast majority of Americans, when they reach the ages of 58 to 63, have long since completed formal education. For the most part, our sample members' earnings had peaked and their assets were at the highest levels of their careers. Any personal saving for retirement was almost complete.

What did the pre-retirees of 1969 look like in terms of the three dimensions of socioeconomic status? As a generation, they appeared to be a bit more educated than their predecessors. Most had completed at least some high school. The nonmarried women as a group had 10.5 years of education, the married men had 10.2 years, and the nonmarried men had an average of only 8.9 years. Less than a tenth of each subsample had completed a

235

college education. The married men were most likely to have finished college; they were followed by the women and then the unmarried men. Median education for the sample as a whole is 10.2 years.

Comparison of RHS respondents with other age groups shows the historical gain in formal education by successive generations. The two age groups older than our cohort, those 65–74 and those 75 and older, averaged 7.8 and 7.5 years, respectively. The younger age groups (those 45–54, 35–44 and 25–34) have a little more than 11 years as median years of formal education (U.S. Bureau of the Census, 1970a).

Occupationally, this has been a relatively stable group of workers. Recall that they were born between 1905 and 1911 and were probably beginning their working careers in the twenties and early thirties. Their work careers may have been diverted by the Depression. On the other hand, their peak working years correspond to the post-World War II period of general and rising prosperity. In 1969, many were still working on their longest-held jobs. This was so for 55 percent of the married men and 38 percent of the nonmarried men and women.

Although sample members were typically pre-retirees in 1969, some proportion of each of the three subgroups was neither working nor looking for work when the first wave of data was collected. We expect that most of those out of the labor force in 1969 will not return to full-time employment. In effect they are the "early retirees" of the study.[2] Married men were most likely to be in the labor force in 1969 with 84 percent employed or actively seeking employment; only two-thirds of the nonmarried men were labor force participants and a comparable 65 percent of the nonmarried women in the sample were working or looking for jobs at the time of the interview.

The most common occupational categories for the married men still in the labor force were craftsmen and foremen, followed by managers-officials-proprietors and then operatives. Operatives were most common among the unmarried men in the sample; craftsmen and foremen and managers-officials-proprietors were the next most common occupational classifications. The unmarried women were most likely to be clerical workers, service workers, or professional and technical workers, in that order.

The men in this age group (58–63), then, were most likely to be blue-collar workers, with the single men in less prestigious manual occupations than the married men. The largest number of women were white-collar clerical workers. The same occupational distribution describes the last job of those respondents who were not in the labor force in 1969.

The most common occupational categories listed above for our sample of pre-retirees correspond to the predominant categories among married men aged 45–54 in 1970 so that occupationally the retirees, following our sample of married men, will probably be much like this one (U.S. Bureau of the Census, 1970b):

A very close tie between occupation and retirement operates through the existence and quality of work-related pension plans. The country's private pension systems are not uniform in quality of coverage, sufficiency of benefits, or predictability for workers. (This picture may change if proposed legislation for pension reform is passed by Congress.) Less than half of the employed within each subsample of respondents reported pension coverage on their current jobs—47 percent of the married men, 40 percent of the nonmarried men, and only 35 percent of the working women. Of those reporting pension coverage, a small proportion (around 5 percent) within each subgroup reported noneligibility for full pension benefits upon retirement. However, close to 7 percent did not know whether they would ever be eligible for benefits.

The three subsamples reported markedly different financial statuses. The married men and their wives were most well off with an annual median income of $8,122 together. The nonmarried men's median income was $4,183 and that for the nonmarried women a meager $2,788. This distinction illustrates the general pattern for almost all aspects of financial status—the married men and their wives were clearly better off than the nonmarried men and women.

Labor force participants reported on their annual salaries from their current jobs. Working married men made a median annual salary of $7,125, nonmarried men earned about $4,780, and employed nonmarried women earned $3,948.

Simply reporting median incomes does not convey a picture of the total income distribution, so let us tell you the proportions

237

of respondents at the extreme ends of the distribution. Only 6 percent of the married men and their wives had annual incomes in 1968 of less than $2,000. This proportion compares to 30 percent of the nonmarried men and 40 percent of the nonmarried women. Considering those with annual incomes equal to or surpassing $15,000, 13 percent of the married men and their wives fell into that category compared to only 4 percent of the nonmarried men and less than 1 percent of the nonmarried women.

Financial assets are a potential retirement resource to be taken into account. A pattern similar to that which held for income applies to the comparison of the three subsamples in terms of assets (for a detailed analysis of assets, see Sherman, 1973). Again the married men and their wives were better off than the nonmarried persons—they were most likely to hold some kind of asset, and the values of their holdings were higher than those of the nonmarried. The only difference here is that the nonmarried men did not fare as well as the nonmarried women, the majority of whom (64 percent) were widows.

Homeownership was a widespread form of investment for these pre-retirees—a full 80 percent of the married men had an investment in a nonfarm home in 1969. A considerably smaller proportion of homeowners appeared in the other two groups—41 percent of the nonmarried men and 47 percent of the nonmarried women. Median home equity for the three groups ran $14,115 for the married men, $12,796 for the nonmarried woman, and $11,413 for the nonmarried men. Ownership of other property such as a farm home, business, or professional practice or other real estate was less common.

In addition to investment in property, most Retirement History Study respondents held some amount of financial assets, the most common being checking and savings accounts. Stocks, bonds, and mutual funds were the most common nonliquid assets. The value of the assets was frequently very small. Considering only those who reported some financial assets, median values were $3,660 for married men, $2,589 for nonmarried men, and $2,296 for the nonmarried women.

Financial assets do not offset the lack of investment in a home. Nonhomeowners were two to three times as likely as

238

owners to report zero financial assets and among those with some assets, the median for nonhomeowners was lower than that of homeowners in each of the three subsamples. There is also an association between size of income and value of assets— those with high incomes were most likely to have large holdings of assets.

Sample members' views of their own financial adequacy correspond with objective financial status; that is, the married men saw their situations more favorably than the unmarried men and women. Fourteen percent of the married men said that they could not make ends meet compared to 21 percent of the unmarried men and 26 percent of the currently unmarried women. Similarly, on the other end of the satisfaction measure, the unmarried women were the least likely to say that they always had money left over and the married men were most likely.

Health

At any level of socioeconomic status, health can decisively affect both activity and morale. It is always related to the continuity of work life, and poor health can bring about retirement. In retirement, health can either enable or prevent the activities which are essential to many people's contentment. It is also, for many older people, a deciding factor in the extent of their contact and interaction with other people.

Comparing the actual health of the upcoming generation of older people with that of any of their forebears would be a difficult task. More people now live longer but—perhaps because they *do* live longer—the incidence of disease and disability among the elderly is the same as or higher than for previous generations. A good prediction of the probable prevalence of good or bad health, or of particular health problems, among the retirees of the 1970s would be quite a feat.

We do know that, for some workers, poor health had already brought their working lives to a halt. Seventeen percent of the men represented by our sample, and 41 percent of the women, had already stopped working and were not looking for another job. Of these nonworkers, 65 percent of the men and 38 percent of the women gave the condition of their health as the primary reason for leaving their last jobs. These people are not, as one might be tempted to think, the vanguard of people retiring because of the encroaching advance of old age and its ills. Rather, most had been nonworkers for several years. Only 10 percent of the nonworking men had stopped work in the year before the survey; 58 percent had not worked for three or more years. The effects of physical work limitations are intensified by occupational status and by race: manual workers and blacks with limitations were more likely to have stopped work on account of health (Schwab, 1974).

Retrospective accounting for retirement was not the only indicator that workers themselves knew the power of health to influence their work careers. Of those who were still in the labor force but regularly worked less than full-time (35 hours a week), 14 percent said the reason for part-time status was related to health. Among those, both workers and nonworkers, who had turned down job offers in the preceding two years, 21 percent said poor health was the reason. Workers were posed a hypothetical question on their probable reactions to job loss in the near future. Some said they would retire; about one in five of these explained it by reference to health or a physical limitation. Workers who definitely expected to retire gave various reasons; 14 percent expected that deteriorating health would bring it about.

Despite the relationship between work and health, most respondents in this 58–63-year-old age range were approaching standard retirement age in the conviction that they were as healthy as or healthier than others their own age. When asked, "Is your health better, worse, or the same as that of other people your age?" about 41 percent considered their health to be the same as others of that age, and 34 percent evaluated their own health as better. A sex-related difference did appear. Men living with their wives and women with no husbands in the same household had a similar pattern of responses: 35 percent of each described their health as comparatively better than that of others, and about 20 percent described it as worse. Men without or away from their wives produced 28 percent who felt themselves healthier and 27 percent who said they were less healthy than age peers.

240

Self-reporting like this is a widely used, useful, and, for most purposes, sufficiently valid health measurement. It is particularly important, even more than objectively recorded physical health, as an influence on life satisfaction (Riley & Foner, 1968; Edwards & Klemmack, 1973). However, for people dealing with older persons, both as individuals and as consumers of community services, a more practical matter is that of actual physical capacity. Retirees who are overly optimistic or pessimistic about their health and/or limitations are occasionally a problem—indeed a real one. But the matter of genuine mobility limitations is a larger and more practical concern.

In 1969, most of the 58–63-year-olds represented by the Retirement History Study sample described themselves as having no limitations or handicaps affecting either their ability to get around or their capacity for work. Four percent had mobility limitations which did not impinge on work. Thirty-five percent reported work limitations. Disability (both work limitation and mobility limitation) was more frequent among the 62- and 63-year-olds in all three basic analytic categories.

Most of the disabled had nevertheless continued working. There was a noticeable difference, however, between the proportions of disabled married men who considered themselves still able to work—68 percent—and their counterparts among the unmarried disabled—54 percent of the men without wives, 56 percent of the women. This incidence of work-limiting physical disabilities overlaps the occurrence of early "retirement" among Retirement History Study respondents. It is not a recent phenomenon. A little over half the disabled said disability had begun five or more years before 1969—when they were between 53 and 58 years old. Only 11 percent had become disabled in the year before the interview.

The dental health of older people has been a long-time object of at least a small amount of concern—on the part of dentists and some geriatric specialists. By 1969 only 5 percent of the 58–63-year-olds being studied had managed to keep a full set of teeth; 34 percent had lost all their teeth, and 61 percent had lost some. Most of those with no natural teeth did have complete dentures. Only a little more than half of those with a partial loss of teeth had partial dentures. Older women, and

241

older married men, had more teeth replaced by partial dentures than their younger counterparts. For men without wives, the difference was in the opposite direction: a higher proportion of the 58–59-year-olds had partial dentures than was true of the 62–63-year-olds.

It appears that less than half of all the people represented by the sample get the recommended semi-annual dental checkup. Only 40 percent had visited dentists in 1968, the year before the interview.

For whatever purpose, one or more incidents of some health care were reported by about 90 percent of the sample. This includes physician care (reported by 67 percent), prescription drugs (67 percent), hospital care (14 percent), dental care (40 percent), other miscellaneous services and supplies (39 percent), and free care or services (18 percent). One cannot construe these figures as an accurate reflection of the sample's level of health or illness. The intervention of social factors such as income and education between the existence of a health condition and the receipt of care is too pervasive to allow that. Here again, however, the distinctly different rate for single men was noticeable and provocative. Eighty-two percent reported getting one or more health services, compared with 90 percent for men with wives and women without husbands.

They were not, however, the category which most frequently reported postponing needed health care. All respondents were asked, "Is there some kind of care or treatment you have put off, even though you may still need it?" By a slight margin, the single women—with the sample's lowest average income—were the most frequent postponers of needed care. Reasonably enough, of the reasons given for postponement, financial ones were given by these women more often than by either category of male respondents. It was the most frequent reason given by all types of respondent. Postponements were also attributed to the inconvenience of getting care, to emotional causes (fear), and sometimes were not explained by any specific reason.

Dental treatment was the type of care most often being put off (by 39 percent of the sample). Second in frequency were diseases of the nervous system and sense organs (22 percent).

In summary, about three-fourths of the sample considered

themselves at least as healthy as others of their age. Three-fifths were free of disabling health conditions. Ninety percent brushed the medical world in some way in 1968—for examination, treatment, prescriptions, and so forth. About a fourth were postponing some medical care they felt to be needed (Motley, 1972).

Social Relations

Turning now to social relations, the Retirement History Study concentrated on pre-retirees' contact and support relations with their families.

The nature of the family's role in the lives of older persons and its relation to satisfaction has received a fair amount of attention. High morale appears to be associated with independence from children (Kerckhoff, 1964; Kutner, 1956). Both elderly parents and their children express a preference for living in separate dwellings. Shanas (1961) reports that very few people say they would most like to live in the home of a child or relative.[3] The trend in living arrangements corresponds to expressed preference. Between 1952 and 1967 the proportion of the elderly population living with relatives declined 40 percent, from a third to a fifth, among married couples; 20 percent, from about a half to two-fifths, among nonmarried men; and 33 percent, from three-fifths to two-fifths, among nonmarried women (Murray, 1971).

On the other hand, during the past decade or so, sociologists have rediscovered a high degree of interaction among family members maintaining separate households. Studies show that the exchange of services, gifts, advice and counsel, and information about family members among the members of an extended family are common (Sussman & Burchinal, 1962; Sussman & Slater, 1963; Hill, 1970).

We have noted that as societies advance industrially some of the economic, educational, and protective activities of the family are taken over by specialized institutions in the society. In the United States today, common living arrangements with family members beyond the individual or nuclear unit are not usual; the family has lost many of its economic functions as far

243

as its elderly members are concerned, yet extended family contact seems to prevail. Does this mean the family is not important in the lives of older people?

To give an idea of the family relations of Retirement History Study respondents, the availability of family members will be described by detailing the specific marital statuses of sample members and the number of living children, parents, and siblings of each respondent. Then a short account will be given of living arrangements, support patterns, and contact with absent family members.

Most men—85 percent—surveyed were married. And the great majority of the nonmarried had been married in the past. Among the nonmarried men (15 percent of the total sample), 29 percent were widowed, 20 percent divorced, 12 percent separated, and 32 percent never married. The majority of the nonmarried women were widows—64 percent. Thirteen percent were divorced, 6 percent separated, and 16 percent never married.

A surprising finding is that close to a fifth of each of the subsamples of respondents had at least one living parent, though the percentage decreases as the age of the respondent increases. When the married men and their wives are considered together as units, over 40 percent had at least one parent still living. Since life expectancy is longer for women than for men, most often the living parent was a mother. These parents may become a financial burden after respondents withdraw from the labor force.

Most of the ever married members of each subsample had at least one living child—87 percent of the married men, 53 percent of the currently nonmarried men, and 68 percent of the currently nonmarried women. For those with living children, the median number hovers around two for the three subgroups, although the married men and their wives were likely to have more children than the currently nonmarried respondents.

Living brothers and sisters are the only other relatives sample members were questioned about. Almost all the pre-retirees had brothers or sisters. The median number is close to three for each group.

Though most of our 58–63-year-olds had some close relatives—either parents, children, or siblings—the majority (around 60 percent) of each of the subsamples lived alone (the married

244

men with their wives). Those couples and nonmarried women who did not live alone were most likely to have children living with them. The older respondents among the two groups were less likely than young respondents to have children in their households, however. This difference with age suggests that the children living with sample members were dependents most of whom will eventually move away from their parents. Those non-married men who did not live alone most often lived with relatives, though not with children.

Very few of the pre-retirees' households included a parent. Of the married men and their wives who reported having at least one living parent, only 4 percent reported a parent in the household. Larger proportions of the nonmarried respondents with a living parent reported sharing a household with the parent—35 percent of the nonmarried men and 31 percent of the nonmarried women.

Most Retirement History Study respondents had several living close relatives but they did not typically live with them. What about patterns of financial support among relatives? By and large, Retirement History Study data show that "relatives are neither a major financial resource nor, for the most part, a financial burden" (Murray, 1973).

There is *some* financial support of parents by pre-retirees. The men in the sample were more likely to contribute to their parents than the women. Less than 1 percent of those making contributions to parents supported them completely, however—most reported regular partial support or simply occasional contributions.

Support of children was more common than support of aged parents for the married men among our respondents—nearly a third of them supported children. A quarter of the nonmarried men with children contributed some support to them while only 10 percent of the nonmarried women did so.

The nonmarried women who had children were least likely to contribute any support to them and the most likely to receive financial aid from their children. A fifth of the women reported receiving assistance from their children. This compares to only 6 percent of the nonmarried men and 3 percent of the married men and their wives. This pattern may occur because the non-

245

married women in the sample were typically older than the wives of the married men and therefore more likely to have adult children able to contribute to their parents and/or because these women were the least well off financially of the sample groups. Only 2 percent of the women reported the presence of minor children in the household, compared to 15 percent for the currently married men.

Almost none of our pre-retirees contributed support to brothers or sisters or received support from them.

While common living arrangements and widespread intergenerational support patterns were not the norm for most Retirement History Study respondents, contact with family members not living in the household was frequent. Around 70 percent of each of the subsamples reported seeing or telephoning an absent parent at least once a month. A little over half of each subsample reported such contact with an absent parent as often as once a week.

Contact with absent children was even more widespread than contact with parents—87 percent of the married men and their wives with children away from home saw or talked to at least one of their absent children once a month or once a week. The corresponding figure for the nonmarried men is 74 percent and that for the nonmarried women is 82 percent.

The majority of each subgroup also maintained frequent contact with brothers and sisters. Two-thirds of the married men (and their spouses) and the nonmarried women saw or spoke to siblings once a month or once a week, and three-fifths of the nonmarried men did so.

To sum it up, perhaps the phrase "intimacy at a distance" best describes the family relations of Retirement History Study respondents (Murray, 1973).

Retirement Expectations

What will retirement be like for them? The possibilities—in terms of work/leisure combinations, family relations, and the like—are flexible. As a society we have not prescribed a structured role for aged persons. We have not seen life, as have some peoples, as a series of discrete stages. The closest we have come is in assigning different privileges and responsibilities to children and adults. We do think of "retirement" as a possible subpattern— available to older adults, but not required of them and not limited to them.

Our overt national attitude toward retirement has been one of some ambivalence, suggested by the word itself. Retirement is pleasant, but is a withdrawing from something, not the achievement of something. It is a withdrawing from work—historically claimed as a basic American value. We have assigned prestige to the worker, and assumed that he received gratification from work. We have lamented forced retirements and assumed reluctance on the part of retirees.

Whatever the social impact of widely available retirement, we are beginning to learn, from studies of older people themselves, that a leisure existence is not all that unpalatable to individual Americans. The strongest determining element affecting older people's choices between work or retirement appears to be the level of available income other than earnings from work (Barfield & Morgan, 1969; Reno, 1971). It appears, indeed, that the source of current income is a defining element in retirement status. It is more likely, other things being equal, that a nonworking man will call himself "retired" if he is receiving some sort of pension income than if he is not (Irelan & Bell, 1972).

The 58–63-year-olds interviewed in 1969 were of an age to be thinking realistically about a possible future withdrawal from work life. Their intentions were probably being influenced by the same factors which sway older persons' actual decisions about retirement (U.S. Department of Labor, 1970). When their intentions change—and we will observe and analyze those changes—it will probably be part of a pattern which also includes changes in conditions eventually to be associated with retirement.

We are concerned with the actual variety among patterns of work or retirement people expect to achieve for themselves in their later years. For our first look at retirement intentions, we sorted the workers of the sample into only two categories: the intended retirees, a group which included those who said they did expect to "retire" and replied in some definite way to the question "At what age do you expect to stop working at a regular

job?"; and the nonretirees, the workers who either did not expect to "retire," or did not give an age for stopping regular work
even though they expected to retire. A considerable number of
the working 58–63-year-olds appeared to be inclined against
definite withdrawal from work. Forty-five percent of the men
and 59 percent of the women either said they would not retire
or gave no age at which they expected to stop working for a living.

Prospective retirees and those not planning to retire differed
from each other primarily in their economic situations. Intending retirees were, in 1969, consistently a bit better off than non-
intenders. Their annual salaries were likely to be higher. Reasonably enough, with higher salaries, they were more likely to have
accumulated more financial assets and are probably more likely
to be covered by private pensions. Proportionately more prospective retirees described themselves as able to get along on their
current incomes than did the nonretirees. There were smaller
differences, but consistent ones, in responses to a couple of
purely attitudinal items. People who intended to retire appeared
to be slightly more apt to be content with their current levels
of living.

The other facets of socioeconomic status do not—at least at
this early stage of analysis—seem to be uniformly useful indicators of retirement intentions. Kind of occupation made no noticeable difference, although self-employment, not really a
status item, did for men. Those who intended to retire were less
likely to be self-employed than those who did not. Married men
who did not plan to retire were more likely to have completed
some education beyond high school than those with retirement
intentions. Prospective retirees among the women, on the other
hand, were likely to be better educated than those not intending to retire.

Our preliminary analyses do not show married men's retirement intentions to be associated with some of the first variables
one might think important. Prospective retirees were not much
different from those not planning retirement in the extent to
which their wives worked, the size of working wives' salaries,
the numbers of children being supported, or the numbers of
children still in school.

The intersection of health status with retirement is more a

question than a datum for us at this point in the study. Poor health and work-limiting physical conditions had already in 1969 terminated the work lives of some 58–63-year-olds. Some workers expected that poor health would eventually lead to their retirement. Subjectively evaluated current health was likely to be better among those who intended to keep on working than among aspiring retirees. But the more objective and, one would think, influential fact of presence or absence of work limitations did not seem at all associated with those intentions.

What will retirement be like for these people? In 1969 their own expectations were, for the most part, that it would be a pleasant time of life with, nevertheless, some constraints and problems. Their estimates of needed retirement income were relatively modest. Married men thought they would need more than did others, but close to 50 percent of all respondents placed their yearly financial needs in the $2,000–$5,000 category. Around a fifth said they did not know what would be needed.

A large part of the workers who intended to retire told us they expected no retirement income other than social security benefits. This amounted to 58 percent of the married men, 57 percent of the men without wives, and 74 percent of the women. These are probably realistic expectations. In aggregate proportions, they are similar to findings from Social Security Administration studies of the finances of retirees and other older people (Lauriat & Rabin, 1970; Bixby, 1970). It is not likely that many people will have large amounts of money coming in from other sources. Only 6 percent of the married men and 3 percent of the men and women without spouses expected more than $5,000 annually from sources other than social security.

If their own expectations are realized, many will be working to some extent after their regular work lives have stopped. Men were a little more likely than women to expect post-retirement work. For some it will probably be a necessity. About two-fifths of the married men and the single women, and a little over one-fifth of the single men, expected to have financial problems as retirees. Work was the most favored response to that difficulty. A few expected some help from relatives and/or public assistance and a few had no idea how they would cope with money problems.

249

Not many workers planned to move, after retirement, very far from their 1969 homes. Less than 50 percent expected to move at all. Less than 5 percent contemplated an out-of-state move. If trends observed in Florida and other states attractive to retirees continue, more of them will move than now expect to.

Wherever they are living, the retirees of the seventies will be in most ways very much like contemporary old people. The descriptive data presented indicate that the retirees of this decade will be somewhat better off financially than their predecessors, although most will live in modest circumstances. The increase in resources from institutional programs such as social security, private pensions, and Supplemental Security Income will help keep an income floor under most of them. Although some number of Retirement History Study respondents have already left the labor force on account of declining health, most sample members considered themselves at least as healthy as other people of the same age. Whatever their health status is now, they will undoubtedly demand health services in the future. Our data support findings from other studies which show that although the family does not provide such intergenerational economic support to its members, it does play a role in patterns of interaction and can still be a barrier against social isolation in old age.

We must wait for the analyses of the longitudinal data to give any firm generalizations concerning the quality of the retirement lives of Retirement History Study respondents. Sample members are certainly not all alike now, nor will they all change in similar patterns. As the Retirement History Study progresses we will be able to trace patterns of change and continuity in the quality of life of this decade's retirees.

Notes

1. Barrring catastrophe and given current medical technology, these projections should be quite accurate—the people who will be 65 and over in 2000 and 2020 are living now. Should there be a breakthrough in one of several directions of investigation on degenerative diseases, these figures may represent lower limits.

2. Karen Schwab (1974) has written a detailed analysis of the correlates of early withdrawal from the labor force among the men in the Retirement History Study sample.

3. If the older person already lives with relatives he is more likely to advocate shared living arrangements. The same is true if his health is poor.

THE EFFECTS
OF AGING
ON ACTIVITIES
AND ATTITUDES*[1]

Erdman B. Palmore

Does aging reduce activities and attitudes? Most cross-sectional surveys agree that it does, but recent longitudinal evidence tends to question the extent of this reduction. Are decreases in activities related to decreases in satisfaction? Disengagement theory maintains that high satisfaction in aging results from acceptance of the "inevitable" reduction in interaction, while "activity theory" maintains that reduction in activity results in reduction of satisfaction. Is there a persistence of life style among the aged? There is evidence that, regardless of the average effects of aging, individual persons tend to maintain relatively high or relatively low levels of activity and satisfaction during their later years. Does aging increase homogeneity or differentiation? Again, theories have been advanced supporting both positions.

Such questions and theories have fascinated social gerontologists for at least the two decades since the Chicago group developed their Activity and Attitude Inventory (Cavan, Burgess, Havighurst, & Goldhamer, 1949). A major reason for the uncertain answers and conflicting theories is that usually cross-sectional data were used even though these questions deal with change over time. It was not until 1963 that longitudinal data were first

---

* Erdman B. Palmore, "The Effects of Aging on Activities and Attitudes," *Gerontologist* 8 (1968): 259–63.

presented in an attempt to clarify these uncertainties (Maddox, 1963). The present paper discusses new longitudinal findings relevant to these questions from data that now cover a ten-year period of tests and retests.

Methods

One hundred twenty-seven (out of 256) volunteer participants in a longitudinal, interdisciplinary study of aging were examined and interviewed the first time during 1955–1959 and were reinterviewed at approximately three-year intervals so that they had completed four waves of interviews by 1966–1967.[2] When interviewed the fourth time, they ranged in age from 70 to 93 with a mean age of 78. Fifty-one were men and 76 were women. There was less than one year's difference between the mean age for men and the mean age for women. All were ambulatory, noninstitutionalized residents of the central North Carolina area. The initial panel of 256 persons did not constitute a random sample of Durham residents, but were chosen from a larger number of volunteers so that their sex, racial, and occupational distribution approximated that of the area. Nevertheless, analysis of selection and attrition factors indicates that the panelists were a social, psychological, and physical elite among the aged and became more so through time (Maddox, 1962). However, since longitudinal analysis uses each S as his own control and examines changes over time rather than comparing younger with older Ss, the degree to which the sample of an age category represents the universe of an age category is a less critical issue than in cross-sectional studies.

We need not discuss here the various advantages of longitudinal analysis for studying aging, such as its greater sensitivity and its ability to measure change directly rather than inferentially (Goldfarb, 1960; Maddox, 1965), but we might point out one advantage of repeated measurements that has not been widely recognized. This is the ability to use consistency as a test of reliable and significant change when one has three or more repeated measurements on the same sample. When a change is observed between two points in time, there is always the possibility that this change might be due to temporary or chance fluctuations. But when the same change is observed between the second and third points in time, our confidence in the reliability and significance of this change can be greatly increased because the probability of two such changes occurring by chance is much smaller. Thus, in the present discussion we shall focus on consistent changes (or lack of consistency) as well as on the statistically significant changes.

The Inventory of Activity and Attitudes questions were read to the Ss by a social worker as part of a longer social history. The Activity Inventory consists of twenty questions dealing with five areas of activities (about four questions for each area): health (physical capacity to act); family and friends (frequency of contacts); leisure (ways of spending time, hobbies, reading, organizations); economic (amount of work or housework and lack of economic restrictions on activity); and religious activity (attendance at religious services, listening to them on radio or TV, reading religious literature).[3] Each subscore could range from zero to ten with the higher scores indicating more activity. The total activity score is the sum of the subscores in these five areas (total range: 0–50).

The Attitude Inventory consists of 56 agree-disagree items about the Ss satisfaction with eight areas of his life (seven items in each area): health, friends, work, economic security, religion, usefulness, family, and general happiness.[4] The score in each area could range from zero to six (one item of the seven is neutral in the scoring) with the higher scores indicating more satisfaction. The total attitude score is the sum of the scores in these eight areas (total range: 0–48). Further discussion of the development, purpose, scoring, reliability, and validity of these inventories may be found in Cavan et al. (1949) and Havighurst (1951). These inventories have been used in more than twenty different studies, and the results show a relatively high degree of reliability and validity.

As a check on the Inventory of Activity and Attitudes, the social worker interviewing the Ss used the Cavan Adjustment Rating Scale to give her estimation of the Ss activities and attitudes (Havighurst & Albrecht, 1953). In general, the results

254

from these scales were similar to those from the Activity and Attitude Inventory.

Some may question the appropriateness of comparing mean scores and correlations on the grounds that such analysis assumes equal intervals in the scales even though we are not sure this assumption is justified. However, several statisticians have recently pointed out that treating ordinal scales as equal-interval scales (1) involves assumptions that may be no more misleading than

Table 1

Mean Activity Scores at Four Points in Time

Activities	Time 1	Time 2	Time 3	Time 4
Men				
Health	2.4	3.9[a]	3.1	2.6
Family and friends	6.8	7.5	6.8	6.9
Leisure	6.9	5.8[a]	5.7[a]	5.6[a]
Economic	4.8	4.9	5.3	6.0
Religious	6.3	6.1	5.5	6.0
Total	27.2	28.4	26.1	27.3
Women				
Health	2.5	3.2	2.6	2.5
Family and friends	5.9	6.1	5.5	5.3[a]
Leisure	7.7	7.2	6.6[a]	6.3[a]
Economic	7.4	7.5	8.1	8.4[a]
Religious	6.7	7.1	6.4	6.7
Total	30.1	31.1	29.4[a]	28.8[a]

[a] Difference between this score and score at Time 1 is significant at .01 level according to the *t*-test for paired observations.

the use of arbitrary cutpoints that obscure differences in amount of variation (Blalock, 1961); (2) has been useful in developing more accurate measurements and theory in most sciences (Burke, 1963); (3) usually involves relatively little error (Labovitz, 1967); and in general allows much more powerful and sensitive analysis. Since we are interested primarily in direction of change and relative changes rather than absolute amounts of change, this type of analysis seems worth the risk of assuming equal intervals.

Results

Small reductions. The men had almost no overall reduction over the ten years in either activities or attitudes (Tables 1 and

Table 2

Mean Attitude Scores at Four Points in Time

Attitudes	Time 1	Time 2	Time 3	Time 4
Men				
Health	3.8	3.7	4.1	3.5
Friends	4.6	4.4	4.3	4.2
Work	3.7	3.6	3.8	3.4
Economic security	3.3	3.6	4.0[a]	3.7
Religion	5.2	5.3	5.3	5.5[a]
Usefulness	4.3	4.3	4.3	4.0
Family	4.9	4.6	4.9	5.0
Happiness	4.3	4.4	3.6[a]	4.1
Total	34.0	33.8	34.2	33.3
Women				
Health	4.0	3.8	3.7	3.6[a]
Friends	4.5	4.4	4.5	4.3
Work	3.9	3.8	3.7	3.5[a]
Economic security	3.8	3.9	4.0[a]	4.0[a]
Religion	5.5	5.6	5.7[a]	5.6
Usefulness	4.6	4.3	4.4	4.1[a]
Family	4.7	4.8	4.9	4.8
Happiness	4.2	4.1	3.6[a]	3.6[a]
Total	35.3	34.6	34.2[a]	33.3[a]

[a] Difference between this score and score at Time 1 is significant at .01 level according to the *t*-test for paired observations.

2). The women had significant but quite small (less than 7 percent) reductions in both activities and attitudes. This lack of substantial reduction in activities is contrary to disengagement theory which asserts that marked withdrawal from activities is the modal pattern in aging (Cumming & Henry, 1961). It is also contrary to the findings of most cross-sectional surveys (for example, Havighurst & Albrecht, 1953) and contrary to the commonly held assumption that most people become less active as they age. On the other hand, it is consistent with previous longitudinal findings from this panel (Maddox, 1963) (Table 3).

Table 3

Correlations (r) of Changes in Activities with Changes in Total Attitudes (Time 1 to Time 4)

Activity	Men	Women
Health	.07	.09
Family and friends	.12	.27[a]
Leisure	.22	.10
Economic	.36[a]	.30[a]
Religious	.26	.13
Total Activity	.42[a]	.40[a]

[a] The probability of this correlation occuring by chance is less than .01.

There are two plausible explanations for this apparent contradiction. While the aged may disengage or reduce activities in *some* areas such as belonging to organizations and attending meetings (as shown by the declining leisure activities scores) or retiring from work (most of our panel was already retired), they may compensate by increasing activities in other areas such as contacts with family and friends or reading religious literature. Or a temporary decrease may be compensated for by a subsequent increase. Or some may reduce while others increase. The net effect would then be little or no change in the average total activities score. Second, this panel represents those relatively healthy aged who were community residents and who survived for over ten years from the first wave to their fourth wave, "ripe old age," of 70 to 93. It may be that the relatively healthy aged do maintain a fairly stable plateau of activity up until just before

257

death and that it is only the ill or disabled aged who pull the average activity level down in cross-sectional studies. The cross-sectional association of poor health and low activity is well established (Jeffers & Nichols, 1961; Havighurst & Albrecht, 1953). The same explanations would apply to the mixed changes in attitudes which show some increases, some decreases, and no significant net decrease in total attitudes among men.

It is unlikely that this pattern of small or insignificant decreases could be attributed to unreliability in the tests, because

Table 4

Correlations (r) of Earlier Score with Later Score for Total Activities and Total Attitudes

Variable	Time 1 with Time 2	Time 2 with Time 3	Time 3 with Time 4	Time 1 with Time 4
Men				
Total activities	.57	.57	.46	.27
Total attitudes	.74	.73	.71	.65
Women				
Total activities	.75	.65	.74	.60
Total attitudes	.67	.66	.79	.56

the reliability of these tests has been demonstrated elsewhere and is confirmed in this study by the moderately high correlations of earlier scores with later scores (Table 4).

The fact that women had larger and more consistent decreases in both activities and attitudes seems to indicate that aging produces greater net changes for women than men, at least in this age range. This may be related to the fact that most of the men had already retired before the beginning of this study and thus did not have to adjust to that change in status during the course of the study. Indeed, their increasing economic activity scores indicate that many men went back to work or increased their work during the study.

The small but significant increases of interest in religion, despite no increase in religious activities, confirm the findings of the cross-sectional studies (Moberg, 1965). This has been related to approaching death and increasing concern with after-life. However, Havighurst (1951) found that religious attitudes had practically no correlations with the total scores nor with the other subscores. He suggested that, since the religious items seemed to be measuring a different kind of dimension from the rest of the attitude scale, they should not be included in the total score. We also found that the religious attitude scores had almost no correlation with the total attitude score at any point in time (most of the correlations were less than .15) and that many of the correlations with the other subscores were even negative. We agree with Havighurst that the religion items should be dropped or considered separately from the rest of the attitude scale.

Activity correlates with attitudes. Changes in total activities were significantly and positively correlated with changes in total attitudes (Table 3). This means that those who reduced their activities as they aged tended to suffer reduction in overall satisfaction, and, conversely, those who increased activities tended to enjoy an increase in satisfaction. This finding is contrary to what might be predicted from disengagement theory which asserts that disengagement is associated with the maintenance of high morale (Cumming & Henry, 1961). Even though disengagement is more than reduced activity, and morale is not exactly equivalent to our measure of satisfaction, it is fair to say that disengagement theory would probably predict no association or a negative association between changes in activity and changes in attitudes. That is, when activities decrease, attitudes should remain high or even increase, rather than decline as in our study.

This positive correlation of activity with attitudes supports rather the activity theory of aging which has been stated as the "American formula for happiness in old age . . . keep active" (Havighurst & Albrecht, 1953). This theory is favored by most of the practical workers in the field of gerontology:

> They believe that people should maintain the activities and attitudes of middle age as long as possible and then find substitutes for the activities which they must give up—substitutes for work when they are forced to retire; substitutes

259

for clubs and associations which they must give up; substitutes for friends and loved ones whom they lose by death (Havighurst, 1961).

It may well be that disengagement theory is applicable to some and the activity theory is applicable to others; that some find most satisfaction in disengaging and others find most satisfaction in remaining active. But apparently in our panel the activity theory was most applicable to most of the participants.

Among the specific activities related to attitudes, changes in economic activities were the most closely related to changes in total attitudes. This is congruent with Kutner's (1956) finding that having a job is more closely associated with high morale than is keeping busy with recreational activities. However, because the economic activities subscale contains an item on the restrictions on activities resulting from lower income we cannot be sure at this point whether it is the change in job status or change in income or both that account for the association with attitudes.

Changes in health had almost no association with changes in total attitudes. This is surprising in view of the substantial associations between health and activity on the one hand and between activity and attitudes on the other. Perhaps this indicates that unless health changes activity, there is little effect on attitudes.

Persistence of life style. There is a clear tendency for aged people to persist with the same relative levels of activities and attitudes as they grow older. Most of the correlations of earlier scores with scores three years later were .57 or higher; half were over .70 (Table 4). This means that over half of the variance in later scores can be accounted for by the earlier scores in the majority of comparisons. Correlations between scores at Time 1 with scores at Time 4 (ten years later) were much lower because of the greater time lapse which made possible a greater number of events that could change the relative levels of activity and attitudes.

This persistence in scores over three-year periods, and even over the entire ten years, indicates both that the inventories are fairly reliable and that patterns of behavior and attitudes among

260

the aged tend to be fairly stable over long periods of time. This also supports the results of a different type of persistence analysis (Maddox, 1966).

However, the correlations do not show consistent trends toward increasing persistence in the later intervals. The men's correlations actually decline somewhat in the third interval. Thus, the idea that the aged become increasingly rigid and "set in their ways" is not supported by this data.

Table 5

Standard Deviations for Activity and Attitude Scores at Four Points in Time

Variables	Time 1	Time 2	Time 3	Time 4
Men				
Total activities S.D.	6.2	6.5	6.1	5.4
Total attitudes S.D.	4.9	5.3	5.3	5.7
Women				
Total activities S.D.	5.8	6.3	6.6	5.7
Total attitudes S.D.	5.5	5.5	5.5	5.8

Increasing homogeneity. The standard deviations show no consistent trend toward either increasing homogeneity or differentiation (Table 5). The women's standard deviations remained about the same while the men's decreased in activities but increased in attitudes. However, there was a generally consistent decrease in differences between the mean scores for men and women (Tables 1 and 2). There is practically no difference left between men and women in their total attitude scores by Time 3 and 4.

Thus, these data do not support the ideas that the aged become more differentiated in their behavior or attitudes (Havighurst, 1957) or that the "sexes become increasingly divergent with age" (Neugarten, 1964). On the contrary, the decrease in differences between men and women is consistent with

Cameron's (1968) recent finding of converging interests between aged men and women.

Summary

Changes in activities and attitudes over a ten-year period among 127 panelists in a longitudinal study of aging were assessed by use of the Chicago Inventory of Activity and Attitudes. There was no significant overall decrease in activities or attitudes among men and only small overall decreases among women. This was interpreted as evidence contrary to the findings of most cross-sectional surveys and the commonly held assumption that most people become less active as they age. It was suggested that normal aging persons tend to compensate for reductions in some activities or attitudes by increases in others, or to compensate reductions at one point in time with increases at other times. The greater decreases among women seem to indicate that at this stage in life aging causes more overall changes among women than men.

Changes in activities were positively correlated with changes in attitudes so that reductions in activity were associated with decreases in satisfaction. This was interpreted as contrary to disengagement theory but supportive of activity theory: the "American formula for happiness in old age . . . keep active."

There was a strong tendency for the panelists to persist with the same overall level of activites and attitudes over time, but there was no evidence that patterns of behavior or attitudes became increasingly rigid or differentiated. In fact, mean differences between men and women tended to disappear.

Notes

1. The research on which this paper is based was supported in part by Grant HD-00668, National Institute of Child Health and Human Development, USPHS. The computations involved were carried out in the Duke University Computing Laboratory, which is supported in part by the National Science Foundation. Programming for the computations was done by Mrs. Nancy Watson.

2. A few *S*s missed the second or third wave of interviews but all 127 returned for the fourth wave.

3. Typical questions: How many days did you spend in bed last year? How often do you see some of your family or close relatives? How many club meetings do you usually attend each month? Are you working now (full-time, part-time, or not working)? How often do you attend religious services?

4. Typical items: I feel just miserable most of the time. I have all the good friends anyone could wish. I am satisfied with the work I now do. I am just able to make ends meet. Religion is a great comfort to me. My life is meaningless now. I am perfectly satisfied with the way my family treats me. My life is full of worry.

THE SOCIAL DILEMMA OF THE AGING LEISURE PARTICIPANT*[1]

Stephen J. Miller

The contemporary concern with aging as a social problem emphasizes the material implications of growing old—for example, the economic circumstances, housing arrangements and health needs of the aged. However, a material concern with the problem, based on the assumption that the problems of aging are basically economic, neglects the social-psychological implications of growing old. In recent years, an increasing number of students of social phenomena have approached the subject of aging in terms of its more subtle aspects, that is, the effects of growing old on the social-psychological life and future of the person.[2] The object of the latter approach is to place the role of the aging in Western culture in its appropriate historical and cultural context and to explore the implications of the contemporary social scheme for the older person.

The aspect of aging which readily lends itself to social-psychological considerations is that of occupational retirement, possibly the most crucial life change requiring a major adjustment on the part of the older person. The urban-industrial society of today has developed a policy for old age which provides pensions, housing, and medical care when the worker, due to his advanced years, is no longer required to trade the major part of

* Stephen J. Miller, "The Social Dilemma of the Aging Leisure Participant," in *Older People and Their Social Worlds,* ed. A. M. Rose and W. Peterson (Philadelphia, Pa.: F. A. Davis Company, 1965), pp. 77-92.

his time spent in labor for the necessities of subsistence. The implication of such a policy is that the worker, by his lengthy labor, has earned the right to rewards which will make his remaining years comfortable. However, it is tacitly understood, the worker is allowed to retire and receive the accompanying benefits in order to facilitate his removal from a role which he is arbitrarily considered no longer capable of playing.[3] In these terms, retirement is not so much a system of rewards as it is the instrumentality by which the removal of those persons perceived as useless is accomplished. The older persons who are so removed suffer a debilitating social loss—the loss of occupational identity and a functional role in society.

Though the occupational identity and role of each person, as well as the succession of other conventional roles, are taken very much for granted and are a matter of little conscious concern, they are the crucial elements which facilitated the varying social role performances demanded of each person. Work not only provides the individual with a meaningful group and a social situation in which to develop a culturally approved and personally acceptable self-concept, it also provides an identity with an accompanying rationale for his performance in other social situations as well. The occupational identity of the individual establishes his position in the social system at large, allowing others to evaluate his status and role and providing a context within which his social activity can be interpreted. For example, the occupational identity of a male places him in appropriate relationship to other members of his family and supports his roles in that social system. Before retirement, the role of "husband" as mediated by his occupational identity results in high prestige and supports the various roles that the person is expected to assume in the family system. It would be extremely difficult to maintain the role as "head of the family" if an occupational identity were lacking. The occupational identity is that which provides the social substance by which other identities are maintained, various roles are coordinated, and the appropriateness of social activity is substantiated. In other words, the retired person finds himself without a functional role which would justify his social future, and without an identity which would provide a concept of self which is tolerable to him and acceptable to others.[4]

In anticipation of the day when the worker retires, the day he will lose his occupational identity and functional role, he is encouraged by his family, friends, and even employer, to adjust by spending his leisure time in some activity which holds meaning for him. It is assumed that the problem of retirement adjustment will be solved if the individual will engage in some sort of activity which will fill his leisure time. Such an attitude to the value of leisure for adjustment during old age takes little note of the associational aspects and social needs of life. For example, solitary leisure will not provide a person with the opportunity for interpersonal contacts and might well only increase withdrawal from social participation.[5] Even those activities which provide interpersonal contacts may not provide a social group which will replace former coworkers. A recreational group may facilitate the development of an identity, but, as Cavan notes, the identity may well be limited and may not be expressible in any group except the recreational group itself.[6]

If leisure activities are to provide a new role, the retired person must engage in some meaningful activity, appropriate in terms of cultural values, which will afford him a rationale for a social identity and a concept of self. In the case of the retired person participating in leisure activity, this poses a dilemma—that is, he must justify an identity in terms of his leisure activity which is by definition "superfluous in character, extraordinary . . . and stands apart from work."[7] "While [leisure] has a definite value," writes Cavan, "to make a career of recreation, hobbies, and the like, goes against deeply instilled values."[8]

The present chapter outlines the dimensions of such a dilemma and the manner in which it is dealt with, as observed by the writer and expressed by elderly participants in systematized leisure groups. The focus will be on the following points: (1) the nature of leisure in contemporary culture; (2) the rationale for leisure, i.e., the manner in which the older person may justify his career of recreation; (3) the portent of embarrassment, the effects of age on actual participation in the systematized leisure group.

Data for this study were gathered from a number of sources:

(1) interviews and correspondence with involuntarily retired leisure participants; (2) local and national newspapers, specific interest pbulications, etc., which were searched for information regarding the participation of elderly persons in systematized leisure groups; and (3) the literature concerned with aging, work, and leisure. In addition, the writer entered the social worlds of leisure participants, posing as, and being accepted as, a young man interested in learning the intricacies of various activities. The fact that the writer was conducting field work was disclosed to only a few people. The field observation differed from systematic observation in that it was neither constant nor total—that is, field work was restricted to a level of activity which approximated the normal career of a novice participant.

The Tradition of Leisure and the Aging

Work and leisure are complementary components of human activity. The style and pattern of both are reflections of the culture of the time and subject to the societal ideology, development, and organization which are characteristic of that culture. "The problems faced in studying leisure," writes Gross, "are both consequence and cause of the problems faced in studying work, for one is usually defined as the absence of or preparation for the other."[9] In the light of the complementary nature of work and leisure, a consideration of the leisure activity of the aging must also be concerned with the social developments which affect work and the cultural values which dominate the social circumstances. Historically, three work-leisure traditions are discernible: (1) preindustrial: traditional work alleviated by related customs, practices, and rites; (2) industrial: the polar opposition of work and leisure, and (3) postindustrial, or contemporary: the integration of work and leisure.[10]

The preindustrial culture, based on an agricultural economy and rural in character, lacked (with few exceptions) any commercial recreation or organized leisure which would draw the person away from his work and family. Clement Greenberg notes that most work during this period was "work on the land . . . adulterated more or less by irrational practices—customs, rites,

267

observances—that, conceived of originally as means of helping work . . . actually furnished occasions *inside* work for relief from the strain of its purposefulness."[11] The cultural tradition did not separate work and leisure, nor did the demands of labor segment the life of the person into a world of work and another of the family.[12] The place of work was the home and the economic and social roles of the person were functional, useful, and significant in terms of the family. The problem of finding some activity which would amuse or occupy the old was nonexistent, for the old remained functional until failing health forced withdrawal from most, if not all, activity.

The rise of industrialization and the accompanying urbanization not only affected the economy of Western culture but had a decided impact, one still felt on the social life of the person. Work, which required organization and structure to assure efficiency and production, became the central life interest, regulating economic, social, and family life. Unlike the preindustrial period, the place of work was no longer the home but a place removed from home and family. The extended family was becoming a thing of the past and its social life, which the aged had previously enjoyed, was rapidly curtailed.[13] "To the exact end of greater productivity," writes Greenberg, "capitalism, Protestantism, and industrialism have brought about a separation of work from all that is not work which is infinitely sharper and more exclusive than ever in the past."[14] The time not occupied by work, that is, leisure, became diametrically opposed to productive labor, and the Puritanical tradition emphasizing work as the major cultural value was established. In this period, a man's work as the basis of his social identity has its roots, and his functional role, in terms of cultural values, emerges. In accordance with the structured nature of work, labels were attached to various types of work placing men in categories and locating them in the patterned activities of society. The functional role and occupational identity of the person were readily available for evaluation by his social audience. A man's conception of himself, developed and reinforced by his recurrent social relationships, was directly influenced by his work.[15]

A society which emphasizes efficiency and production will define the value of the person in terms of his ability to play a functional role in the industrial system. When, as in the case of growing old, an individual is subject to limitations which presumably reduce his ability to play such a role, he must be removed and replaced—hence, the development of an industrial policy toward old age requiring occupational retirement at some point in the life cycle. The industrial changes not only established the occupational role as the basis for social identity but also developed the manner in which that identity could be subverted.[16] The constituent elements of work—a work group and a work situation—are the basis of a culturally approved and personally acceptable self-concept. These are lost to the older person when he is retired from the vocational world to which he has belonged. In place of work, the retired worker is offered leisure which is the opposite of work and of doubtful, if not negative, cultural value. In such cultural circumstances, leisure participation cannot reduce the problem of finding a new identity and role. The lack of an occupational identity is culturally characterisitic of the old, and leisure activity only supports the position of the old as nonmeaningful, nonfunctional or, at best, superannuated.

In postindustrial society, or, for the purposes of this study, in the "American" pattern of work and leisure, work remains as the basis of social identity. However, the nature of work has changed. The boredom of routine and the performance of repetitive tasks has been noted and acknowledged—in fact, work no longer requires the degree of routine and structuralization that was necessary during the early phases of industrialization. The nature of contemporary work has led to attempts to make work meaningful and reduce fatigue and boredom, though, as Riesman notes, "by and large [they] succeeded only in making it more time-consuming and gregarious but not more challenging."[17] Whatever the reasons, though apparently they are functional, a characteristic of the twentieth century is the reintroduction of leisure into work. Gross explains the situation in terms of the concept of adaptation as follows: "Work results, inevitably, in fatigue and often in boredom, and one of the forms of leisure—recreation—is essential here insofar as it restores, though, it is recognized, it may not always do so."[18] The nature of work has come a full cycle and is marked by related customs, practices, and rites, furnishing occasions of leisure inside work to alleviate fatigue and boredom.[19] Outside work, Rose indicates that "the opportunity to engage in something creative, even if only in a hobby association, provides a compensation for the deadening effect of working on a simple repetitive task . . ."[20]

In addition to the reduction of opposition between work and leisure, a cultural value which affects the American pattern of life is the contemporary emphasis on action. In much the same manner as work and leisure were earlier opposed, activity of any sort is valued over nonactivity. "People who are not active," writes Buhler, "are made to feel useless, indeed, even worthless."[21] Hence, in terms of the contemporary scheme of work and leisure, in which leisure has become a value, the older person showing an interest in some activity, no matter what, is less subject to social labeling as "nonfunctional," "ineffectual," and so on, than one who disengages himself from activity. It would appear, therefore, that leisure has the potentiality to reduce the social loss to which the aged are subject and facilitate adjustment. (It is not the contention of the writer that participation in leisure activities is the only way in which the aging may establish a new identity and achieve social adjustment. The cultural trend which sets the old apart from the young may well result in the formation of a social group of the aging which will provide them with a meaningful social audience, a frame of reference, and a range of participation which will help them to develop a new identiy, role, and self-concept). This new social situation of the aging is a way open to those of the aging who wish to remain socially active but resist the cultural trends which are making the elderly more segregated from other age categories. They may employ their leisure as an opportunity to establish an identification with other groups in society. That is, they may reduce their social loss by participating in activities which are respected in general by others as well as by those of their own social category or group.

The Rationale for Leisure

The problem of social adjustment faced by the leisure participant is apparently rooted in the lack of social substance (meaning) or cultural value of the majority of ways in which he might occupy his leisure time. In the light of the values which are characteristic of the American pattern of life, the person who is now free of work should be socially able to overcome the problem by spending his leisure in some activity which holds meaning for him and is generally respected by others. If this were the sole dimension of the problem (as is the contention of this writer and that of Christ), then participation in systematized leisure groups would not only fulfill the social needs of the older person, but facilitate the development of a new social identity as well. However, the work which the person is ultimately free of is exactly that which has allowed him to justify leisure or, as Mead has put it, work is not only necessary to obtain the means but the right to leisure.[22]

An employed person, prior to his retirement with its loss of occupational identity, is free to use his leisure time any way he chooses. No matter how far removed from work, so long as the leisure activity is not otherwise culturally defined as deviant, a rationale is readily available to justify its legitimacy. The interrelationship of work and leisure as a necessary condition for adjustment to and performance of work plus the value placed on activity are the constituent elements of that rationale. Those who are engaged in work are not required to justify their leisure since socially supportive factors, occupational identity, and the halo effects of labor operate on the social circumstances to do just that. On the other hand, the older person operates without such support. For example, the employed person occupied in leisure activity of some sort will, more often than not, be perceived by others as engaged in "recreation" whereas the retired person engaged in the same activity will be perceived as occupying his "free" time. In other words, the numerous activities in which the older person may participate, thereby reducing the degree of his social loss, may have no further cultural value than that they are "activity."

A career of leisure (play) is characteristic of the socially immature (children) or the socially superannuated. For the aging individual, it can only serve to add to his social loss, negating any social benefits that might be derived from remaining active by serving to reinforce a definition of him as superannuated.

271

There are other leisure interests—for example, genealogy, the writing of an ethnic cook book, family history or autobiography, to mention a few encountered by the writer—which are often considered to be interests peculiar to people nearing the end of life, the assumption being that such interests are reflections of a concern with perpetuating life in some manner or with death itself. It is also likely that participation in groups created for, and composed of, older people only which offer an old-age identity—for example, the Golden Age Club or Senior Citizens— only aggravate the social situation of the aged by reinforcing the stereotype of the older person as one set apart from those who are not old. This is one of the factors in the development of an aging subculture. The older person, in order to establish a new identity and acceptable self-concept on the basis of leisure must first establish a rationale for the activity on which he bases that new or altered identity. He must legitimatize it in some manner other than in those terms which sanction leisure for the very young and the old. The leisure activity of the retired and elderly must, therefore, be in some way appropriate in terms of traditional and contemporary values which do not apply specifically to the aging but to the population in general.

The retired leisure participant is in the unique position not only of having to find an activity in which to participate but, once having found such an activity, if he wishes to reduce his social loss, also of establishing a meaningful rationale for participating in that activity.[23] The current compatibility of work and leisure offers the older person an opportunity to change his social situation—that is, to establish the cultural value of his leisure which will act as the basis for a social identity. He may do so by introducing, in much the same fashion as leisure has been introduced into work, aspects of work into his leisure.[24] The person may choose among the alternative avocations available to him those which offer the possibility of establishing a rationale, in keeping with the cultural and social circumstances, which will serve to legitimitize a social future. The problems posed by aging and retirement have been well documented, but the manner in which the aging introduce aspects of work into leisure and establish an appropriate rationale for this has, to the writer's knowledge, been explored only incidentally.

272

The attitude regarding meaningful leisure participation and the elements of a rationale are expressed in the following comments of the wife of an aging leisure participant: "Hobbies are eccentric when you never make anything [useful] out of them or get anything [monetary] out of them." It is not simply participation in *some activity* which is desirable but participation in activity with culturally acceptable manifest goals, or at least with latent implications of being useful and/or gainful in some way.

A notable example of the way in which such a rationale for useful and gainful activity may be established is the case of the aging American collector of coins, stamps, books, antiques, and what have you. The gainful rationale for a leisure activity is similar to the major perspective of these modern collectors which parallels and reflects the current and growing interest of the general population in the stock market, investment programs, etc., and is focused on the monetary and investment aspects of collecting. The following comments by a collector with some thrity years' experience bring this out:

> It [leisure] can be commercial. When I started [collecting] people took the time and trouble of assembling a collection. The real interest was research and the arrangement of your collection . . . the originality of showing, too. Only a little attention, if any, was paid the expense of collecting. Now, thousands and thousands of people, because of the publicity that has been given to the value of coins and stamps, have gone into collecting. They [collectors] go to banks and to the mints and buy coins and put them away for the future or sell them. In other words, they are *investors* and *speculators.*

A search of the literature pertaining specifically to numismatic, philatelic and similar leisure activities offers further evidence of this contemporary view of such activity. The literature is heavily laden with advertisements urging the hobbyist to invest in coins, to invest profitably in stamps, or to "cash in on your hobby," as well as others which offer investment lists of money-making items, investment bulletins, market reports, and labor guides—all of which purport to be *necessary* for the leisure participant. There also exist the usual people and organizations

273

that one expects when dealing in a marketable commodity. For example, besides the dealers who buy and trade in the commodity, there are others who will accept the collected objects or products of leisure as security for money-lending transactions.

In addition to the collector who may also be an investor and speculator, there are, for example: (1) persons who buy, restore or otherwise improve, and sell antiques, household goods, appliances, etc.; (2) the handicraftsman, who may find a market, or at least a demand, for what he makes; and (3) the do-it-yourself person who manages to supplement the neighborhood or community demand for the skilled labor which is becoming increasingly expensive and difficult to find. These examples certainly do not exhaust the variety of activities which lend themselves to a gainful rationale; they are illustrative of the way in which personally meaningful activity can be infused with the aspects of work which are culturally understood and accepted. It is interesting that many of the retired individuals who are so engaged deny that their activity is work in the traditional sense. The activity is enjoyable, interesting, or challenging, only incidentally profitable, and rarely, if ever, demanding. If what is labeled leisure were to be defined as work, the person would be expending himself entirely in work without leisure and operating in a manner contrary to the American pattern of work and leisure.

Other types of activity, though in no way economically productive, are contributory to the general good and may be exploited by the person as a basis for a new social identity. Those who offer their leisure service to others—the retired cabinet maker who supplements the efforts of the high school manual arts teacher, or the older woman who becomes an integral part of the community hospital as a volunteer—enjoy high public esteem by acting in a subordinate auxiliary role to more essential work roles. These activities and the roles which the aged may assume in them are part of larger work systems which lend them vicarious status, authority, and other meaningful satisfactions which operate to the social advantage of the participants, allowing them to establish a useful rationale for their leisure. Though slightly more difficult for the participant to legitimitize, activity which is educational or develops a skill or talent also provides a

274

social future since there exists the potentiality for its future productive application.

The economic perspective on leisure reflects a contemporary cultural value, an economic ethic, so to speak, while the supplemental nature of other useful activities meets certain societal needs. Activity in these spheres will be defined as acceptable if presented in the appropriate terms. It will not be perceived as far removed from work since, like work, it offers a reward for labor or is contributory to work in some way, factors which can be employed in evaluating the worth of the individual. Any activity presented in these terms has recognizable goals which lend it meaning and, therefore, is considered as an understandable activity in which to engage. Though the writer is concerned with the social life of the aging, the analysis is relevant for other types of persons in the social system as well. As a case in point, the person who engages in avocational pursuits without thought of work or profit is considered at best a dilettante. It is probable that the person who manages to develop an avocational interest into a profitable business represents more of the American dream than is imagined. In the latter instance, the individual, by introducing aspects of work into his avocation, has established a rationale which enables him to meet the societal expectations that he be productive and his role meaningful. It is when this rationale is absent that the activity of the individual is defined as superfluous and lacking in meaning, and when the individual is subject to the stigma and embarrassment of being considered an idler which makes the support of an acceptable identity difficult, if not impossible.

Though the gainful and useful rationales are discussed as if they were distinct activity themes, they are not mutually exclusive, but rather variations of the same mechanism. For example, any collecting activity which is characterized by a gainful rationale also requires the classification, description and, in some cases, the authentication of that which is collected, procedures providing an opportunity to employ a useful rationale for such activity. The rationale for leisure is similar to the mechanism which Becker and Carper refer to as the *acquisition of ideology* in their discussion of the development of identification with an occupation.[25] In much the same manner as the person preparing for an occupation attempts to determine the worth of the activity on which his identity will be based, the aging retired person establishes the worth of his avocational activity to legitimitize a base for a new social identity—that is, to justify a career of leisure.

The Portent of Embarrassment

The rationale for leisure, once established, provides a background for the social participation of the involuntarily retired person which allows the projection of a meaningful and acceptable social future on which may be based a new identity. However, the person is not entirely free of the social implications of his retirement and advanced age. He has not left his occupational role in a way which reflects favorably upon his ability to perform a work role, in particular, and other social roles, in general—that is, he is still, though somewhat less, vulnerable to the stigma attached to retirement.[26] In addition, he must continue to operate in an age-graded social system which defines the aging as people who are most likely to fail. Once the person has selected a leisure activity which offers him a social future and identity, that social future remains subject, within the leisure group, to the implications of retirement and aging.

If a rationale is to be maintained and an identity developed, the person, once he participates in some activity, must be capable of supporting a role in the group throughout the social interactions and performances required of a participant. Identity, writes Gross and Stone, "must be continually reaffirmed, must be maintained, and provision made for repair in case of breakdown."[27] The result of identity breakdown—a social occurrence which belies what the person has announced he is, and what he is capable of, by assuming the role of participant—is embarrassment. In turn, embarrassment makes continued role performance difficult and undermines the foundation of the new identity.

The results of embarrassment are most often treated in terms of their implications for the continued social participation of the person. That is, once an embarrassing encounter or performance has taken place the question is, what are the social implications for the person.[28] The implications of embarrassment may also be considered in a related though somewhat extended manner: A person who is aware of some socially restrictive factors to which he is subject may anticipate the embarrassing encounter and subsequent identity breakdown, and choose either to curtail or end participation entirely. That is to say, embarrassment not only has implications for continued but also for initial social participation as well. In any analysis of the leisure careers of the aging the factor of social embarrassment, including both actual and anticipated embarrassing encounters, is particularly important. The implications of actual embarrassment for social performance have been treated elsewhere by others and apply equally to the situation of the aging leisure participant; the writer will concern himself with anticipatory embarrassment, that is, the portent of embarrassment, as a correlate of social participation and its implications for social performance.

The obvious implication of the portent of embarrassment is that it may result in the aging person excluding himself from social interaction with others not of his social category. The frequency of possibly embarrassing encounters would be higher for the person participating in the social system at large than for the person limiting his participation to groups which are composed of members who share his circumstances, problems, and concerns—that is, a group of older people. The portent of embarrassment operates, in addition to the circumstances noted by Rose to facilitate the development of a subculture of the aging. It is sufficient for the purposes of this essay, since Rose discusses the subculture of the aging at length, to note that the positive affinity many other people have for each other may well be the result of negative expectations of social participation with persons not of their social category or group. A similar argument may be offered in explanation of the apparent decline in social participation of people as they grow older—that is, they become increasingly aware of the possibility of social embarrassment and make preparations accordingly.

In the work conducted by the writer, those of the aged who were only somewhat active offered the obvious reasons, such as health, expense, transportation, as explanations of their limited participation. These recurrent themes, however, seemed to be but reflections of a more socially based reason for nonparticipation. In general, nonparticipation or limited participation was a matter of choice resulting from a feeling of inability to meet the demands of participating. The person who embarks on a leisure career is announcing who he is and what he is capable of; he is committing himself to a role which requires he meet the expectations of others. If he feels or finds that he is unable to meet these expectations, or expects to encounter difficulty which would subvert his identity, role, and self-concept, he is likely to choose not to make such a commitment or limit his participation to those aspects of an activity which reduce the possibility of identity subversion and embarrassment.[29]

As observed by, or told to, the writer, the instances of embarrassment which caused the aging leisure participant particular concern, and were usually accompanied by decreased commitment or participation, were one or more of the following types: (1) an inability to reciprocate due to family, economic, or health circumstances which could be attributed to aging; (2) requests for the performance of a task which the person was assumed prepared for, or capable of, because of his age and experience but for which he was not—that is, the peculiar position of the older person as a novice and subordinate to other younger participants; and (3) faux pas which announced to other participants that the person and his knowledge were superannuated ("How would you like some young wise-guy to tell you things aren't done that way anymore?").[30] The portent of embarrassment, anticipation of the occurrence of such social incidents, has, for at least a minority of the aging, a decided effect on the pattern of their participation. It influences a number of variables usually employed to measure social participation—for example, number and type of voluntary associations, frequency of attendance at meetings, number of contacts with others engaged in the activity, and the social category of those who are contacted.

It is possible that the portent of embarrassment may assume such proportions that it inhibits entirely participation in any specific activity. If a person, under these circumstances, withdraws from the activity but replaces it with another which reduces the portent of embarrassment (assuming a rationale to which he may subscribe is available), he continues to minimize his social loss and retains a base for an identity.[31] On the other hand, the person who withdraws and has no suitable replacement places himself in a situation in which he is subject to the additional stigma of nonactivity. The attempt to erase the stigma of nonparticipation ususally results in solitary activity of some sort, for example, reading. A number of aging leisure participants who were interviewed had done this and employed health, expense, and transportation, as an understandable rationale for nonparticipation in systematized or group leisure.

The aging are not operating alone to avoid embarrassing encounters and reduce the portent of embarrassment. The aging participant is perceived as the person most likely to fail and "becomes defined as someone who must not fail, while at the same time arrangements are made to decrease the chances of his failing."[32] The arrangements made by other participants to assure that embarrassment will not occur is not the result of an altruistic or patronizing concern with the problems faced by the aging. Embarrassment not only incapacitates the embarrassed person but others with whom he is interacting as well. When the identity of the aged participant is subverted, it is difficult for others to continue interacting and inhibits the social performances of all participants. "Embarrassment," writes Gross and Stone, "exaggerates the core dimensions of social transactions, bringing them to the eye of the observer in an almost naked state, for embarrassment occurs whenever some central prop in the transaction has unexpectedly given way so that the whole encounter collapses."[33] The occurrence of embarrassment incapacitates *all* the performers for the continued and possibly future performances of their roles by disrupting identity and destroying the assumptions the performers have made about each other—assumptions on which they operate socially.

In the specific social system in which the older person is active, the portent of embarrassment may, and often does, result in his being excluded from interaction with other participants not of his social category. The result is increased interaction between the aging who share a common situation and the development of a group identification of the aging within the system.

However, in systems which are not specifically for one social category, it is necessary for purposes of structure and cohesion that the roles played by the various participants be integrated into the role-scheme of the system. The need for such integration does not prohibit the development of a group of the aging who share a common social life *outside* the system and identity with each other within the system. In fact, such a group of the aging would reduce further the portent of embarrassment by permitting social life outside the system to be conducted on the basis of common interests, concerns, and shared problems. This is a situation which, since those involved are subject to similar embarrassments, reduces the chance of failure outside the system disrupting performance and subverting identity within the system.

The anticipation of social difficulty for and with the aging by other participants encourages them to make available to the older person a role which he is capable of assuming, or at least less likely to fail at playing. The problem of embarrassment and its ramifications are avoided by providing the aging participant with a social role within the system which he can maintain—that is, an identity system of interactions and performances of which he is capable. The older person is induced to assume this role identity by others who ascribe the necessary attributes to him and interact with him as if he did possess these attributes. There is only a subtle difference between such action and the exclusion of the aging from social roles which would form in a public identity that might be discredited or subverted.

There are numerous cases which illustrate the action taken to avoid embarrassment for and with the aging. The family in need of home improvements, which the aging handyman who services the neighborhood is not capable of carrying out, may call him in for consultation before hiring an outside firm or tradesman to do the work. If the handyman had not been involved in some manner, by implication his identity would have been subverted and future interaction with him impossible. On the other hand, if he had been expected or allowed to do the work, the anticipated unfavorable outcome would have been equally embarrassing and ended the relationship. The solution was the ascription of certain qualifications as an expert to the handyman, attributes inducing him him to assume a role which he was capable of performing and allowing him to maintain his identity.

To be a member of a subordinate auxiliary group is also defined in a way which allows for a supportable identity for the older person. The main organization which the auxiliary group serves has a staff with occupational and professional roles which operate to delimit the activity of the older person. For example, the hospital volunteer is prohibited by their operational codes to assume the role of doctor, nurse, or of any other ancillary hospital personnel—only those activities which may be and are delegated to the volunteer are undertaken. The tasks delegated— for example, personal contact with the patient or with the family of the patient—comprise a role, status, or relationship, and are never such as to make great demands on the person.[34] In more formal recreation, i.e., systematized leisure, possibly the most important roles the older person may play are that of "recruiter" and "socializer." By recruiting and socializing new members the aging participant not only facilitates the entrance of the novice into the activity group, but also contributes to group structure and the efforts of the group to perpetuate itself. Other roles for which the aging are considered suited and likely not to fail at are "learned elder," "keeper of the tradition," and, for those who have specialized and are recognized as proficient, "expert" or "resource person."

Though participants in social and leisure groups attempt to induce the aging participant to assume roles which lessen the portent of embarrassment, as noted earlier, the reasons are not patronizing. In addition to the services mentioned, such roles for the aging act to reduce the demands made on the time and energy of other participants. The roles have intrinsic value and are not artificially created to meet the needs of the aging. In these terms, the "most challenging problem of solving the present roleless role of the aging" is not so much *inventing* new leisure patterns and functional roles for the aging—which will only become culturally defined as "for the old"—as determining what roles presently exist in the social system, related to a specific subsystem and offering vicarious satisfaction, that can reduce the socially debilitating loss accompanying occupational retirement.[35]

Notes

1. The writer is indebted to Community Studies, Inc., for the assistance which allowed him to explore the social situation of the aging leisure participant and write this paper. He is grateful to Edwin A. Christ, Howard S. Becker, Francis G. Caro, Arnold M. Rose, Warren A. Peterson, and Gregory P. Stone for their conversations, comments, and criticism.

2. A statement of the social-psychological problems, in terms of interactionist concepts, is presented by Ruth Shonle Cavan, "Self and Role in Adjustment during Old Age," in *Human Behavior and Social Processes,* ed. Arnold M. Rose (Boston: Houghton Mifflin, 1962), pp. 526-35. Clifford Kirkpatrick also offers a brief but adequate example of a social-psychological approach to the problems of aging, "Sociological Implications of Retirement," *Geriatrics* 10 (1959):312-17. Cf., for example, the writings of Ernest W. Burgess, Irwin Deutscher, Robert J. Havighurst, and Arnold M. Rose.

3. A number of socially based factors—for example, the impact of continued employment of the aged on a labor force becoming increasingly more concerned with unemployment—operate to maintain a retirement policy, though the original reasons for doing so, such as failing health, are fast disappearing.

4. Ernest W. Burgess, in *Aging in Western Societies,* ed. Ernest W. Burgess (Chicago: University of Chicago Press, 1960), pp. 20-21, refers to the loss of occupational identity and a functional role as a state of being "imprisoned in a roleless role."

5. Kutner, and others, in a study of older people, found morale and personal satisfaction related to participation in activities which provided achievement, status, and recognition, in addition to simply filling leisure time. Cf. *Five Hundred Over Sixty* (New York: Russell Sage Foundation), 1956.

6. Cavan, *op. cit.,* pp. 529-30.

7. Gregory P. Stone and Marvin J. Taves. "Camping in the Wilderness," in *Mass Leisure,* ed. Eric Larrabee and Rolf Meyersohn (Glencoe, Ill.: Free Press, 1960), p. 296.

8. Cavan, *op. cit.,* p. 529.

9. Edward Gross, "A Functional Approach to Leisure Analysis," *Social Problems* 9 (Summer 1961):2.

10. Cf., *Mass Leisure,* pp. 38-43, 54-64, 85-95, and 253-63; also David Riesman, *The Lonely Crowd: A Study of the Changing American Character* (New Haven: Yale University Press, 1950).

11. Clement Greenberg, Work and Leisure under Industrialism," *Commentary* 16 (July 1953):58.

12. Foster Rhea Dulles presents a picture of rural life in Chapter 26 of *America Learns to Play* (New York: Appleton-Century, 1950).

13. A number of studies indicate that the decline of the extended family may have been exaggerated. See, for example, E. Litwak, "The Use of Extended Family Groups in the Achievement of Social Goals," *Social Problems* 7 (1959-60):179; Scott Greer, "Urbanism Reconsidered," *American Sociological Review* 21 (1956):22; Marvin B. Sussman, "The Help Pattern in the Middle-Class Family," *American Sociological Review* 18 (1953):27. The writer favors the opinion expressed by Rose in "Reactions against the Mass Society," *Sociological Quarterly* 3 (October 1962), p. 323: "The authors of all this research implicitly assume that their findings prove that extended family relationships have not declined as much as earlier sociologists thought. However, in the absence of earlier or longitudinal studies, the alternative hypothesis can reasonably be entertained that the extended family did deteriorate badly in Western cities toward the end of the nineteenth century and has been reviving somewhat within the last few decades."

14. Greenberg, *op. cit.*

15. Cf. Everett C. Hughes for a discussion of the influence of work on the conception of the self, in *Social Psychology at the Crossroads* (New York: Harper & Row, 1951), pp. 313-23.

16. Cf. Chapter 15 in this volume, where such identity subversion is referred to by Coe as "devaluation" or "depersonalization."

17. David Riesman, "Leisure and Work in Post-Industrial Society," in *Mass Leisure*, p. 367.

18. Gross, *op. cit.*, p. 5.

19. The image of the congenial group at the office water-cooler, the coffee break, and even the office Christmas party, which is fast disappearing, are examples. Of course, all such customs and practices are not occasions of leisure but may as well be worker rebellion, "goofing off," etc. Cf. Riesman, *op. cit.*, p. 372.

20. Arnold M. Rose, *Sociology* (New York: Knopf, 1956), p. 330.

21. Charlotte Buhler, "Meaningful Living in Mature Years," in *Aging and Leisure*, ed. Robert W. Kleemeier (New York: Oxford University Press, 1961), p. 35.

22. Cf. Margaret Mead, "The Pattern of Leisure in Contemporary Culture," *Annals of the American Academy of Political and Social Science* 313 (1957):11-15.

23. The writer has excluded from the analysis those who have voluntarily retired, those who are subject to failing health, and the social isolate, a number of whom were met and interviewed during field work but wanted nothing more than "to be left alone."

24. For the writer, the fact that many retired individuals remain partly active in the world of work, or embark on a new work career, strengthens the argument for the need of a rationale by the aging. What could be a more appropriate work-oriented rationale for activity with which to support an identity and role than work itself?

25. Howard S. Becker and James W. Carper, "The Development of Identification with an Occupation," *American Journal of Sociology* 4 (January 1956):297.

26. Cf., for a discussion of social loss, Erving Goffman, "On Cooling the Mark Out: Some Aspects of Adaptation to Failure," *Psychiatry* 15 (1952):451-63; also, Goffman, "On Face-Work," *Psychiatry* 18 (1955): 213-31.

27. Edward Gross and Gregory P. Stone, "Embarrassment and the Analysis of Role Requirements" (Paper read at the meetings of the Midwest Sociology Society, Milwaukee, Wisconsin).

28. Cf. Gross and Stone, *op. cit.*, pp. 2-4; Goffman, *op. cit.*, and "Embarrassment and Social Organization," *American Journal of Sociology* 62 (1956):264-71.

29. The writer, in an analysis of the client-practioner relationship as a social transaction, has hypothesized that a person will increase or decrease his commitment and participation in terms of the degree to which the activity offers a favorable social-psychological outcome. Cf. Stephen J. Miller, "The New Car Salesman and the Sales Transaction" (Paper presented at the meetings of the Midwest Sociological Society, Milwaukee, Wisconsin, 1963).

30. A general type of embarrassment, which applies equally to persons of the social categories as well as the aging, occurs when the motive for participation becomes obvious as peculiar to the aging, e.g., "having something to do," and contrary to the generally accepted motivation for participating. Cf., for a discussion of such embarrassment, Goffman, "Embarrassment and Social Organizations."

31. The portent of embarrassment offers an interesting scheme for the analysis of the acceptance of some and the rejection of other activities by the aging.

32. Goffman, "On Cooling the Mark Out," p. 499.

33. Gross and Stone, *op. cit.*, p. 2.

34. The observation of the aging volunteer was the result of a number of research projects the writer has conducted in general hospitals.

35. Burgess, *op. cit.*, p. 21, has stated that the most challenging problem calls for a solution to the "roleless role of the aging" by *inventing* new leisure activities and functional roles for the aged. The writer takes little issue with Burgess but does object to what, by implication, appears to be the attempts to establish a social system for the aging apart from the rest of society—it is his contention that social adjustment for the aging can only be achieved when they are integrated into the social system at large and that there are processes and mechanisms by which many of the aging do just that.

OF POKER, ROLES, AND AGING: DESCRIPTION, DISCUSSION, AND DATA*

Ken Stone and Richard A. Kalish

"Goals based only on power or acquisitiveness, which were compelling in an earlier phase of life, are no longer appropriate. New ways must be found to use time and to enhance satisfaction and self-realization."[1] The White House Conference on Aging background paper on retirement roles and activities was expressing a frequently held assumption. They overlooked, albeit understandably, a role for the elderly that does lead to a goal based in large part upon power and acquisitiveness, an old—indeed ancient—way of enhancing satisfaction: gambling.

McLuhan[2] makes an interesting pronouncement in contrasting gambling and the use of alcohol. He states that alcohol leads to "festive involvement" in the Western world of highly individualistic and fragmented relationships. On the other hand, "In tribal societies, gambling . . . is a welcome avenue of entrepreneurial effort and individual initiative to the point of mocking the individualist social structure. The tribal virtue is the capitalist vice"[2] (p. 249). And a little later, ". . . When we, too, are prepared to legalize gambling, we shall, like the English, announce to the world the end of individualist society and the trek back to tribal ways"[2] (p. 249). The authors are not quite ready to join the McLuhan trek back to tribal ways, but we have

*Ken Stone and Richard A. Kalish, "Of Poker, Roles, and Aging: Description, Discussion, and Data," *International Journal of Aging and Human Development* 4 (1973): 1-13. © Baywood Publishing Company, Inc. 1973.

observed considerable movement toward the legalization of gambling in this country.

Our presentation is divided into four sections. First, we will briefly discuss gambling itself. Second, we will describe in some detail a specific setting where gambling proceeds with full legal sanction and where older and retired persons constitute up to half the clientele. Third, we will present some new research findings, and fourth, we will attempt an analysis of role satisfactions for the older gambler, a highly speculative venture at best.

Gambling: A Few Comments

"Gambling has existed in every known society from the most primitive to the most complex."[3] Gambling has been noted in Stone Age cultures, among the South African Bushmen and Australian aborigines, and the pre-Columbus American Indians. Dice have been found in an Egyptian tomb; a gaming board was located at the Acropolis; additional evidence of gambling was found in the Roman Empire. Casting lots is mentioned in Joshua, 18:10.[3] And *Newsweek* (4-10-72) estimates that gambling is a $50 billion annual business in the United States and growing steadily. In 1968, *Life Magazine* referred to 47 million Americans wagering $45 billion each year on poker alone (8-16-68).

Regardless of laws or community pressures, gambling occurs. Our own nation is an excellent example of the confusion of laws and mores, with some states permitting some kinds of gambling under some kinds of conditions on certain days at certain places . . . but outlawing everything else. Nevada, of course, has extensive legal gambling. State-run lotteries have come into being in New Hampshire, New York, New Jersey, Pennsylvania, and Massachusetts; California and Virginia are studying off-track betting while Connecticut and Pennsylvania have already made the decision to proceed; casinos have been proposed in New Jersey and New York legislatures and already exist in California. All told, 34 states permit some form of gambling.

Academic writing about gambling is sparse. A collection of articles appeared a few years ago, drawing from the literature of the previous 25 years, but most were descriptive and none presented any sort of research data (other than financial).[4] Two recent volumes suggest more sophistication,[5] and the same author has also developed a bibliography for distribution.[6] But academic researchers still appear reluctant to become involved with the topic. One hopeful sign: a 1971 article on card hustlers in *Trans-Action* mentioned that the senior author had been a professional gambler prior to the academic career that was leading to a doctorate in communications.[7] An earlier article in the same journal, a rather convincing analysis of why people play poker, was also co-authored by a person with experience working in gambling establishments.[8]

To our knowledge, there is no meaningful epidemiology of age of gamblers available. However, we can make a crude estimate from statistics for arrests provided in 1966 by the FBI.[9] The overwhelming preponderance of persons over 65 who are arrested are charged with drunkenness (61.5 percent). Of the remaining causes for arrest in this age group only disorderly conduct (8.4 percent) accounted for more arrests than gambling, with 4.5 percent of all arrests of persons over age 65 being for gambling. Comparable percentages at 25–34 and 45–54 are 1.0 percent and 3.2 percent, respectively.

Many elderly persons in the United States and Canada have continued the kinds of gambling that prevailed in their country of origin. Thus, older Italian men are found playing dominoes, elderly Filipinos and Puerto Ricans often find ways to put on cockfights, in spite of their illegality; mah jong is still popular among elderly Chinese; and all ethnic groups seem to have a high proportion of poker players.

Lest the reader assume that geriatric gambling is restricted to the low-income and foreign-born, we suggest that a trip to an accessible stockbroker's office will change their thinking. One Los Angeles brokerage office is well-known locally for its "standing room only, wall-to-wall old men's gallery, and that after recent expansion." Some of the men observing the tape and the changing numbers on the wall have substantial investments, while others may have only a few hundred shares altogether; some probably have no money invested at all, but come to partake of the company and of the feeling that they are part of some meaningful activity. These elderly observers according

288

to the brokers themselves are no more likely to make a sale or purchase than are their counterparts sitting at home. However, they will sit and watch the board for hours at a time, frequently with little discussion. Some readers may reject the assumption that playing the market is like playing the horses, but it is difficult to deny the element of gambling.

Gambling, in company with drinking, drugs, and sex is a victimless crime that seems to be here to stay, in spite of efforts to make it go away. Yet, it is not unknown for a back-porch poker game to be raided through the efforts of a district attorney on the rise. For example, several years ago, police in a major west coast city cracked down on a pinochle game that had been going on openly in a park for several months. Six or seven elderly men had gathered that day for camaraderie and fresh air to participate in the low-stake game, and one died immediately of a heart attack. Nonetheless, on a recent Sunday the senior author visited several parks and found some forty to fifty older men playing and kibbitzing, as they do every Sunday. They are careful not to exchange money openly. One of them quipped that "90 percent of us here are under doctor's orders not to play cards."

Ignoring the cost in physical and emotional health, there is serious question as to whether the financial cost of breaking up such kinds of gambling is a useful public investment. In New York City it cost $3,500 in police expenses to bust one "bank" (the numbers or policy racket in the ghettoes), which consisted of two people. In 1970, 356 arrests occurred, with an average fine of $117 per person. During a ten-year period, one individual was imprisoned for one day. (Based upon Mary Minone, Ph.D., Research Director, Policy Sciences Center, New York City, on National Educational Television broadcast, *The Advocates,* 12-22-71.) No data regarding age were provided, but we suspect the proportion of elderly was not negligible.

Today's elderly were reared in an era when gambling was probably more discussed and less professionalized than it is in 1972. Slot machines, pinball games, punchboards, bingo games, pinochle and casino, all these were part of the scene 50 and 60 years ago. Gambling was often seen as a sign of sin and debauchery, but with an aura of romance. The autobiographical novel, *The Gambler,* by Dostoevski, the short stories by Bret Harte,

289

Mark Twain, O. Henry, Stephen Crane, and so many others, the characters of Damon Runyon, the man who broke the bank at Monte Carlo—all became part of the cultural folklore. Gambling is still big business, bigger than ever, but it seems less romantic. Whatever romance exists in Las Vegas must compete with the big business image of the entrepreneurs and corporations that ostensibly run the city.

Obviously a great many gamblers are persons in their 60s and beyond, yet—except for bridge and bingo, plus an occasional "Gambler's Night" with scrip—programs for the elderly have taken little heed. Certainly this is not because the elderly are antagonistic or uninterested, but perhaps because the program planners are concerned that these older persons not lose the little money they have in gaming—and perhaps because of a lingering feeling that gambling is immoral. While the planners hesitate, the California senior citizen clubs charter buses for Nevada gambling centers and make their way to the California poker casinos in large numbers (see Fig. 1).

The Setting

Gardena (population 50,000) is contained within a few square miles of the flatlands of Greater Los Angeles, undifferentiated from the surrounding communities except for the existence of six poker palaces clustered within a few blocks of each other. These six clubs—bright, well-lit, heavily neoned, garish, comfortable, an almost inaudible level of hum and bustle broken primarily by the soft clatter of chips—provide tables, cards, chips, services, supervision and some protection against being cheated for a charge, collected twice an hour, ranging from $0.75 to $4.00 per player—all for the privilege of sitting there and playing poker.

Draw poker has been legal in Gardena since 1936, in spite of six attempts to vote the law out. At one time, 40 percent of the city's revenue was generated by the clubs, but this has slowly diminished to 13 percent in 1970. Gardena is the only community in Los Angeles County with legalized poker, although some 175 other California communities permit this through local option.[10] The clubs are in business for the long haul, and their management is careful not to violate the numerous city restrictions or to anger either local citizens or customers. Licenses for three of the clubs are held by veterans organizations, which receive around $25,000 for this formality.[10]

Wed. Apr. 5th. $30. Twin (3 days, 2 nights)	**FANCY HOTEL** This fabulous new hotel invites our Senior Citizen members to enjoy a 3 day holiday. Your cost includes transportation, twin bedroom, one buffet breakfast, one buffet dinner, $3.00 in nickels, one free cocktail and lounge show. Also included is a trip to the Xyzabs with cocktail, a trip to Hahaha-Hohoho with free nickels and booklet, and one breakfast at Le Sucker with fun book. One suitcase per person. Twin accommodations only. No deposits.

Fig. 1. An almost uncensored, verbatim excerpt from a mimeographed mailing by the Blank Tours for Senior Citizens in Southern California

By regulations, each club has 35 tables, seating 8 persons each. They are open from 9:00 a.m. in the morning until 5:00 a.m. the next morning, with somewhat shorter hours on Sunday; each club closes down one day a week, with the days rotating so that at least four clubs are functioning at any given time, and six on Friday, Saturday, and Sunday. During the evening, 100 percent occupancy is standard for the game tables, and each club probably has an additional 100 or so persons on the premises—waiting for a table, lounging, watching television, talking, or eating in the very reasonably priced dining rooms. From opening to closing, there are seldom fewer than 200 people playing in each club.

It works very simply. The prospective player enters, leaves his initials with the "board man" as he tells him the game he wants to play (five-card draw or low-ball) and the stakes (fifty cents to twenty dollars); he is called when the right opening appears. Greetings are given, if at all, perfunctorily, whether an old and familiar face or a new participant. He is as anonymous as he cares to be—nicknames seem even more common than other identifications. As soon as he sits down the play continues, with the deal rotating as in most private games at home. A woman, usually youngish, and probably sporting a complicated wig or bouffant hairdo, comes around every 30 minutes to collect the rent—in cash. No one at the table represents the house. The house cut is strictly from the table charges.

A quarter-million patrons come annually from all over southern California, but mostly from the Greater Los Angeles area.[10] And they leave behind—a little in the restaurant, but primarily in table charges—over $15 million a year to support their pleasure. An indication of the profitability is that a 1 percent interest in one club reportedly sold in 1970 for $65,000, as against an initial 1949 investment of $5,000.

The Study

Actual studies of the gambling behavior of any population are rare. To our knowledge, no one has attempted to study the participants of the Gardena poker clubs since 1953[11] (cited also in L. A. Herald Express, 6-1-53), nor has anyone had much luck in surveying the feelings, beliefs, and attitudes of any group of gamblers. Neither did we.

Questionnaire

Based largely upon the experience of the senior author, a 52-item questionnaire was devised. The information requested included demographic data, involvement in Gardena and other gambling opportunities, experiences with gambling, and relevant attitudes. It was pilot tested on a handful of players, and changes were made accordingly.

Procedures and Sample

Initial attempts to distribute the questionnaire in the clubs were firmly rebuffed, although our explanations were sufficient—and our attitudes appropriate—so that we were not "hassled" when giving the forms out to people as they left the clubs. Some 250 forms were distributed. An attempt was made to avoid including respondents below age 50.

Place, hour, and day were randomized, and every eligible person leaving the selected club was given a questionnaire. It was explained that the project was under the supervision of the School of Public Health, UCLA, and that all responses would be anonymous. A stamped, addressed envelope was attached to each questionnaire, returning it to the university. About half the persons approached refused to take one.

The first indication of our probable rate of return came the day following the distribution of our initial 100 questionnaires. Three envelopes had arrived within less than 24 hours after distribution; they were all apparently mailed from the same postal station and were assumed to belong to three elderly women who engaged the research assistants in pleasant conversation. All three were blank. Eventually, the total return was 44 questionnaires (18 percent) of which 29 were usable (12 percent); 10 women and 19 men returned these forms. Of the 15 returned manuscripts that we did not include, 9 were dropped because of too many omitted items.

Results and Discussion

That the elderly of the area make substantial use of the clubs is apparent. Although their proportion of the total assemblage varies as a function of the time of day, with many more being around during daylight hours, they are never absent. The senior author made a careful estimate of the percentage of players he perceived as being 65 or older. These estimates were conducted at all of the clubs and were made at various times and days. During each three-hour period the clubs were open, one count was made, with the checks rotating among the clubs and among the days of the week. These counts were carefully done, but subject to the obvious bias of lack of external validation. During the daylight hours 40 percent of the players were over the age of 65; this dropped slightly in the late afternoon; by early evening, the percentage was closer to 20 percent, where it remained until closing time. A *Los Angeles Times* article estimated that 60–70 percent of the regular players—those who play three or four times a week or more—are over 65;[10] our own estimates would be similar.

One club is even referred to as "the old folks home" because they have done so much to encourage older people to attend.[10] This club probably also has the largest number of group cab arrangements (see below). A recent advertisement in the *Los Angeles Times* announced their Tuesday special: Chicken in the pot, along with carrots, potato noodle, matzo ball chicken broth, vegetable, roll, low-calorie cheese cake, and coffee, for $2.00. Nowhere on the five-inch, two-column advertisement was there any mention of poker.

The elderly were not equally distributed among tables, but clustered at the less expensive ones where the stakes and the table costs were both lower. For this, they would pay $1.50 to $2.00 per hour, and they could buy in for $5.00 or $10.00. A rough guess of the proportion of the $15 million plus take of the clubs contributed by older persons would be $3.5 to $4 million. The ratio of the cost of playing to the stakes was highest for these less expensive tables meaning—as usual—that the elderly pay relatively more money for what they receive.

Of equal interest, we found that between 50 percent and 90 percent of the nonplayers were estimated to be in the 65+ age group. Thus, the restaurant, bar, and informal meeting places were more likely to be inhabited by the older customers, suggesting either less endurance (both physical and financial) or greater needs to socialize.

To look at our data: Our 29 respondents had a mean age of 62, ranging from 47 to 75. Ten were 65 or over; 5 were between 60 and 64; 13 were under 60 (one did not state). Over 80 percent were native-born; roughly two-thirds were Jewish; political views tended to the middle-of-the-road Democrats. Twenty-one had living children; 18 had living grandchildren; 1 was a great-grandparent. Sixteen saw their children and/or grandchildren at least once a month. Eleven were retired; 11 were employed (3 of them part time); and 4 were housewives. The median annual income from all sources, of the 12 who responded to that item, was about $6,000.

These are not casual players—over 60 percent of our respondents visited Gardena for poker at least two of three times a week, with half of those coming at least four times a week, and one person playing almost every day. Since we did not include "Daily" as an alternative (the respondent pencilled it in), we probably underestimated the number of daily patrons.

When asked how long they usually stayed, the mean response was 5.7 hours, with a range of between 3 and 12 hours; the respondents over age 65 did not differ from the younger persons. Most drive to Gardena either by themselves (14) or with a friend (10), while a few (3) make use of a group cab arrangement that many customers—especially the elderly—use; only one arrives by bus.

A very little bit of arithmetic quickly establishes a minimum cost per person. With an average of about 2.5 visits per week, for an average of 5.7 hours per visit, each individual spends 14 hours each week at the clubs. Assuming as much as one hour per visit for eating and socializing, since two-thirds of our sample eat one meal per visit on the average (this is much longer than most persons spend away from the tables, as anyone familiar with Gardena will attest), we still end up with better than 11 playing hours a week. Based upon the stakes they say they play for, i.e., an average of about $1.25 per *half*-hour (less for the older), average table costs amount to about $28 per week per individual, somewhat lower for the 65+ group (and we have been erring on the side of caution). Add to this a median round-trip of about 30 miles, with expenses not usually shared, and our respondents begin their gambling stint well over $30 behind. It is doubtful that the older gamblers average much less than this. Undoubtedly the observation that attendance of the elderly shrinks during the later part of the month reflects the wait until the next social security check.

The obvious explanation for the willingness of these older persons to continue to play against such high odds would be that they expect to win. Strangely, this is not the case. Of the 10 persons over 65 who responded, 7 expected to lose at Gardena, 2 anticipated breaking even, and only 1 expected to win; of the 15 under 65, 10 thought they would win, 3 believed they were breaking even, and only 2 assumed they would lose. When asked about all gambling efforts, the results were comparable—none of the oldsters believed they came out ahead, 5 were losing, and 2 were breaking even (the others did not respond); among the younger gamblers, 8 thought they ended up ahead, 2 broke even, and 1 lost. Even back in 1954, psychologist William McGlothlin concluded that most of the 31 women gamblers he interviewed expected to lose.

Therefore, in addition to transportation costs of several dollars a week and table costs of $25 a week or so, our geriatric gambler does not expect to win. The implications are quite clear; his gambling will cost him a substantial portion of his income from all sources, perhaps as much as 20–25 percent in many instances—perhaps more.

And still he makes the trip two or three times a week. Why? Nearly 75 percent state they just like to gamble. Slightly over half think that "Gardena is a good gamble." A similar number like the people and almost as many like the atmosphere. One-third admit to having nothing better to do, and one-third feel they need to get away from where they live. Fewer still—and almost none of the elderly—figure they can win some money. Only 2 feel compelled to come. Not only do they like to gamble, but they prefer poker to all other kinds (18), although they also enjoy pinochle (9), blackjack (9), horseracing (8), bridge (5), pan (5), craps (5), keno or bingo (3), and the slots (2). But the enjoyment of gambling is the most important reason they give for coming and the most important reason they assume others will give for coming. Only one person gives winning money as his most important reason for playing.

These poker players are not new to gambling, even though two-thirds admitted to playing cards more often for money now than 20 years earlier. Nonetheless, the mean age of initial interest in gambling was 31. And they have supportive spouses. Of the 16 married respondents, only 5 have spouses who never play, and only 2 show any disapproval—and only 1 admits to having a child showing any disapproval.

Personal observations during the period of the study, plus at other occasions, suggest that the regular "oldsters" comprise something of a clique, where they are well-known and sympathetic to each other, in contrast to the clubs' usual atmosphere of anonymity and every man for himself.

The older players will frequently allow each other to save money and will extend otherwise rare courtesies in game situations. For example, one oldster may indicate to another that he is beat and should not call. Informal arrangements are made to avoid bluffing each other; this is known as "soft-playing" and is often costly to the participants, because other players "pick up on it" and utilize the information. Other methods of mutual support include defending each other in disputes, protecting each other's hands from being "fouled," i.e., rendered unplayable, usually by having other cards touch it, keeping the pots from being short-changed, loaning money, returning a few chips for luck or giving the ante, providing a rundown on opponents' styles, advising of minor cheating going on. (Although the older players are normally oblivious to the more expert cheater, the saving grace is that even "sharps" could hardly afford the size of the collection at the small games where most elderly play.)

The gambling losses of colleagues—as they come to see each other—are frequent topics of conversation, as is the illness or death of a playing companion. Although the casual observer would not notice anything that passes for conviviality among the players, even the older players, a sense of camaraderie apparently does develop and may occasionally sustain itself beyond the club parking lot.

An Attempt at Analysis

We had no hypotheses to test in a formal sense—only a wish to explore a matter of personal interest. However, we feel that the implications of Gardena's success in drawing the elderly of Los Angeles to its poker tables should not remain unnoticed. Given the physical difficulties of getting to Gardena, the immense (relative to the average income of the elderly) table costs, and the generally "bad name" that gambling has, something is taking place that is worthy of attention. What is the intrigue of gambling and how does this relate particularly to older persons in the United States?

Bergler[12] attributes gambling to unconscious motivation. For him, gambling unconsciously revives childhood fantasies of grandeur and activates rebellion against the reality principle, in favor of the pleasure principle. According to Bergler, the gambler has a great deal of unconscious aggression which is acted out through self-punishment. Many gamblers have read Bergler—few if any see themselves in his analysis, although his descriptions of behavior often elicit a positive response. This, obviously, is not an ultimate criterion for the validity of Bergler's insights. For what it is worth, the authors are in strong agreement with the gamblers.

We are trying to explain the behavior of only a few individuals. However, we firmly believe that, given the opportunity, they would be joined by many, many more. That is, were it not for limitations of money, for the lack of transportation facilities, and for the moderately high skill level of the present players against whom they would need to compete, vast numbers of elderly would join the parade to Gardena.

Some of the reasons are obvious. First, there is always the chance of winning, with the possibility of riding a streak of luck and skill into substantial financial reward. Even though the elderly realize that they lose overall, the chance for a big win is possible. Second, they enjoy the social life of the poker palaces more than that of its alternatives, e.g., senior citizen recreation centers (which are much more accessible to most of the players), the Santa Monica shuffleboard games, walking and sitting on benches, observing the passing parade of hippies and tourists on the beach at Venice. Third, the mere fact that he is participating in a program that is *not* planned for senior citizens is motivation enough for some of the elderly.

Martinez and LaFranchi[8] describe the "loser," i.e., the gambler who ends up fairly consistently behind at the end of a month or of six months or a year, as being social isolates. "Neither job, nor friends, nor leisure activities and hobbies are as

298

meaningful to the loser as is poker"[8] (p. 35). ". . . for losers, poker is sought as a form of compensation or escape from anoic social relations"[8] (p. 35). Martinez and LaFranchi may well be correct—we suspect that they are. Unfortunately their analysis only skims lightly on the surface, the major query being: Why poker? If they are social isolates, why come to a crowded club when they might arrange a game at home without having to give a cut to the house? Their article is among the best available, but it helps only a little in understanding the older "loser."

We sense another element that is too readily overlooked. Older people are losing their decision-making options and their ability to rely upon their own instrumentality. Their income is from a source that, although stable and assured (ignoring, for the moment, the importance of inflation), has little or nothing to do with their own capabilities and is beyond their power to influence. Increasingly, others—their children, their physicians, various social planners, and others—are making decisions for them. Long-range payoffs are impractical and short-range payoffs are unavailable. Not only has disengagement taken place in the social sense, i.e., reduced numbers of contacts, but the available challenges are much less engaging on a psychological basis, i.e., ego involvement. The excitement of facing success or failure on a job, in a sexual or affective encounter, with a variety of athletic activities—all these are now either greatly diminished or absent.

Gambling changes this. First, the payoff in gambling is real— it matters, it affects what the gambler eats or drinks or wears. And the game is part of the real world and not of planned programs.

Second, the gambler is pitting his skill and his good fortune against that of others without being patronized or planned for because he is old; the poker table is a total leveler of age. One wins or loses because of skill (John Scarne, the noted gambling expert, considers poker to have the greatest element of skill of all card games, bridge included), not because of age-related factors. The older player, even though he expects to lose, can decide himself whether or not to play, how to play, when to play. The locus of control does not reside in outside forces, but within himself. The gambler is an active agent in his own fate, even

299

in games of pure chance, because he must still decide whether to take the chance. We are suggesting, then, that it is not the winning that counts so much as the possiblity of winning on one's own decisions, whether through skill or chance.

Third, gambling is engaging, in the sense that it provides the opposite of disengagement. For the most part the elderly person can anticipate a predictable income, with minor fluctuations from the erosion of inflation or the politics of election year. At the poker table, each draw, each bet, each grimace or grin has meaning. Not only is the player socially engaged, in that he is interacting in meaningful fashion with many individuals, but he is immensely psychologically engaged—he is absorbed, involved, caught up in the action of the moment. (In *A Poker Game,* Stephen Crane says of poker, "Here is one of the most exciting and absorbing occupations known to intelligent American manhood; here a year's reflection is compressed into a moment of thought; . . .".) No artificial barriers of age limit, no reminders of lack of power because of age status, no helpful middle-aged person trying to shelter him against the real pains of a real situation.

To add a bit of icing to the cake, all this is conducted in an atmosphere where—at nearby tables—thousands of dollars are changing hands, where a touch of sin is suggested, where a bit of the tawdry quality of the gambling den rubs off.

And, finally, the payoff is now, today, this minute, not in building for some potential future that, for the elderly, may never come to pass. Although these elderly assume they will lose during the course of a year, there are days when they go home winners. How many nongambling friends can say the same?

Conclusion

The authors are not program planners, and yet cannot help but feel that one conclusion stands out over all others: Here is a role for the elderly based—for better *and* for worse—on power and acquisitiveness. Isn't there something that can be learned by this?

300

Notes

1. Streib, G. F. 1971. *Retirement roles and activities.* Background paper for the White House Conference on Aging. Washington, D.C.: Government Printing Office, p. 1.

2. McLuhan, H. M. 1964. *Understanding media.* New York: McGraw-Hill.

3. Morehead, A. H., Gambling. In *Encyclopedia Britannica,* vol. 9 (1968), pp. 1115 ff.

4. Herman, R. D. 1967. *Gambling.* New York: Harper & Row.

5. Kusyszyn, I. 1972. Psychology of gambling, risk-taking, and subjective probability: A bibliography. *Journal Supplement Abstract Service Catalog of Selected Documents in Psychology* 2: 7.

6. Kusyszyn, I., ed. 1972. *Studies in the psychology of gambling.* Toronto: Author.

7. Mahigel, E. L., and Stone, G. P. How card hustlers make the game. *Trans-action* 8, no. 3 (1971): 40-45.

8. Martinez, Thomas M., and LaFranchi, Robert. Why people play poker. *Trans-action* 6, no. 9 (1969): 30-35, 52.

9. Riley, M. W.; Foner, A.; and Associates. 1968. *Aging and society,* vol. 1, An inventory of research findings. New York: Russell Sage Foundation.

10. Shaw, D. Gardena. Poker draws young and old to the tables. *Los Angeles Times,* 28 March, 1971, Section B, pp. 1-3.

11. McGlothlin, W. 1954. A psychometric study of gambling. *Journal of Consulting Psychology* 18: 145-49.

12. Bergler, E. 1957. *The psychology of gambling.* New York: Hill and Wang.

RETIREMENT AND LEISURE PARTICIPATION: CONTINUITY OR CRISIS?*

Robert C. Atchley

Recreation and leisure are institutions that are different yet closely related. *Recreation* refers to activities such as sports, games, the vacation, hobbies, and the like that aim to renew mind and body by either relieving them of tension or delivering them from boredom. Recreation is thus primarily a reaction to some state of body or mind. *Leisure* activities, on the other hand, are pursued as ends in themselves. They are unplanned and unrequired. Leisure is primarily *action,* directed generally toward self-development.

Leisure and recreation share one prime characteristic: both are reserved for time periods not already set aside for working at a job, sleeping, performing domestic tasks, or meeting family obligations.

Recreation and leisure aim primarily at relaxation, entertainment, and personal development. As such, they are institutions that are oriented around the needs of individuals, particularly the needs for tension management, enhancement of self-esteem, and identity (Atchley, 1970).

For simplicity we will lump recreation and leisure together under the general label of leisure.

Information about patterns of leisure among older people is essential in examining the nature of growing old. People gradually

* Robert C. Atchley, "Retirement and Leisure Participation: Continuity or Crisis?" *Gerontologist* 11 (1971): 13-17.

expand the time they spend in leisure roles as age increases (Riley & Foner, 1968). Upon retirement, leisure pursuits occupy a great deal of the individual's time, and there is a question as to whether leisure roles can fill the void left by work. There is little doubt that leisure can fill the *time* formerly occupied by work, but the problem is whether leisure is capable of giving the individual the kind of *self-respect* and identity that he got from the job.

The Identity Crisis Theory

Perhaps the most articulate and repeatedly quoted spokesman on the negative side is Miller (1965) who has taken the following position:

1. Retirement is basically degrading because although there is an implication that retirement is a right that is earned through lifelong labor, there is also a tacit understanding that this reward is being given primarily to coax the individual from a role he is no longer able to play.

2. Occupational identity invades all of the other areas of the person's life. Accordingly, the father and head of household roles, the friend role, and even leisure roles are mediated by the individual's occupational identity.

3. The identity that comes from work is related to deeply ingrained values as to which roles can give a legitimate identity.

4. Leisure roles cannot replace work as a source of self-respect and identity because it is not supported by norms that would make this legitimate. That is, the retired person does not *feel justified* in deriving self-respect from leisure. Leisure is simply not defined as a legitimate source of self-respect by the general population.

5. Beyond the simple need to be doing something there is a need to be engaged in something that is defined by most people as utilitarian or gainful in some way. Thus, the stamp collector must emphasize the financial rewards, paintings are offered for sale, or woodworking is confined to immediately "useful" objectives. In short, the only kinds of leisure that can provide identity are work substitutes.

303

6. There is a stigma of "implied inability to perform" that is associated with retirement and carried over into all of the individual's remaining roles and that results in an identity breakdown.

7. Identity breakdown involves a process whereby the individual's former claims to prestige or status are invalidated by the implied inability to perform, and this proves embarrassing for the stigmatized person. Miller calls this result "the portent of embarrassment."

8. Embarrassment leads to the individual's withdrawal from the situation or prevents him from participating to begin with.

9. The answer lies not in inventing new roles for the aging, but rather in "determining what roles presently exist in the social system . . . offering vicarious satisfactions, that can reduce the socially debilitating loss accompanying occupational retirement."

10. Miller implies that creating an ethic which would make full-time leisure an acceptable activity for a worthwhile person is a possible way to resolve the dilemma of the retired leisure participant.

Miller's analysis of the situation is an insightful one. Nevertheless, it rests on the assumption that prior to retirement the individual derived his identity primarily from his jobs. Also implied in Miller's identity crisis theory is the assumption that most people want to stay on the job, since this is their main identity, and that therefore most retirement is involuntary. This is no doubt related to the fact Miller leaves out of his discussion those who retired voluntarily. Miller also implies that he subscribes to the activity theory of adjustment to aging since he assumes that lost roles need to be replaced (Havighurst, 1963).

Evidence Concerning Identity Crisis

There are several sets of questions which thus emerge from an examination of the identity crisis theory presented by Miller. First, is his portrayal of the relationship between involuntary retirement and leisure an accurate one? Second, is the pattern, even if accurate, typical of most older leisure participants?

Third, what is the pattern among those who are voluntarily retired? Data from recent studies of retired people can shed some light on these questions.

Some of these data will be drawn from the Scripps Foundation Studies in Retirement, a series that has produced several published reports (Atchley, 1967, 1969; Cottrell, 1970; Cottrell & Atchley, 1969) and which is still continuing.[1]

1. Retirement has been found to result in a loss of a sense of involvement, but this was unrelated to other self-concept variables of optimism and autonomy (Back & Guptill, 1966).

Disengagement theory tells us to expect some withdrawal from involvement, and it is noteworthy that this loss of involvement does not appear to have adverse results for other aspects of the self-concept. This leads to skepticism concerning Miller's "portent of embarrassment."

2. Strong work-orientation *is* frequently found among retired people, but this is *not* accompanied by anxiety, depression, dislike of retirement, or withdrawal from activity (Cottrell & Atchley, 1969).

Our findings indicate that a strong positive orientation toward work "*exists* apart from the job itself but . . . has no *import for the individual* apart from the job itself." In terms of adjustment, there was apparently *no* negative result from carrying a positive orientation toward work into retirement.

3. When men retired from upper-white-collar, middle-status, and semi-skilled jobs were compared, it was found that the upper-white-collar people had internalized occupationally oriented norms. Middle-status workers were oriented toward specific tasks and situations often resulting in the acquisition of skills that were transferable to leisure situations. Semi-skilled workers were engaged mainly in activities oriented about things (Simpson, Back, & McKinney, 1966).

Of these occupational strata, the upper-white-collar stratum comes closest to Miller's model of the retired person. These are work-oriented people. However, neither of the other two strata fill the work-oriented model. Middle-status people develop skills on the job that carry over into other roles. Thus, the salesman may carry his smooth-talking style over into his leisure roles.

Semi-skilled people are oriented around the job, but not necessarily because they have any deep abiding commitment to the job. For them it may be purely a matter of not having been trained for anything other than a job.

4. The style of work activities tends to remain dominant in retirement.

Simpson et al. (1966) found that upper-white-collar jobs were oriented about symbols, middle-status jobs were oriented around people, and semi-skilled jobs were oriented around things. The middle-status people showed the greatest continuity in style from pre- to post-retirement. This suggests that retirement, and leisure roles in particular, offers greater opportunities for practicing interpersonal skills than for practicing skills oriented around symbols or things.

The implication of this finding is that it is not so much the ethic learned on the job that interferes with successful pursuit of leisure in retirement but rather the skills. Those who learn job skills that cannot be readily used in leisure pursuits have a hard time adjusting to an increase in leisure unless they have had the opportunity to learn these skills elsewhere. This concept is reinforced by the finding that in terms of retirement activities, middle-status people who had thing-oriented jobs resembled the semi-skilled more than they did their middle-status peers.

5. In addition, data from retired railroaders indicate that there are continuities in the situations people face that minimize the impact of retirement (Cottrell, 1970). Family, friends, church, and other roles continue despite retirement. Cottrell's data suggest that the portent of embarrassment and loss of identity is minimized by the tendency to select friends on the job from among those of one's own age. The end result of this process is to create retirement cohorts of people who have known each other on the job and who retire together. In the Scripps Foundation studies of retirement, this phenomenon has been observed among those retired from occupations as diverse as teacher, railroader, and telephone operator (Atchley, 1967; Cottrell, 1970; Cottrell & Atchley, 1969). It results in a group of retired friends who have known each other for years and whose concepts of each other involve a great deal more than the mere playing of an occupational role. Nevertheless, this group

is also capable of sustaining the prestige gained on the job because they know all about how this prestige was generated.

To the extent that older people are geographically mobile, they might tend to lose these continuities, but most retired people, particularly the semi- or unskilled, do not move away from their place of long-term residence (Riley & Foner, 1968).

6. Cottrell's data (1970) also indicate that as the concept of retirement is incorporated into the culture, the tendency to look upon work as a temporary part of life increases.

The implication here is that if work is not a permanent part of life, then one puts greater emphasis on other parts of life that are more permanent. For example, if a man knows the day he begins working that he will work 25 years and then quit, he is very likely to avoid letting work become an all-consuming part of his life.

7. In terms of ethic, it is not at all clear whether most people regard work as a necessary prerequisite for making leisure legitimate or simply as a necessary economic function which interferes with the pursuit of leisure. It *is* quite clear that our heritage has always included those who did not work because they could afford not to. Accordingly, legitimacy of leisure may rest not so much on work as on the idea that the money used to sustain leisure came from a legitimate source, that is, it was either earned by working or inherited. In the Scripps Foundation studies of retirement many middle-income retired people have shown not the slightest reluctance to embrace leisure roles, given the fact that their income was secure (Atchley, 1967; Cottrell & Atchley, 1969). Perhaps if most retired people were not pauperized by retirement the "portent of embarrassment" mentioned by Miller would fade away.

8. Nearly two-thirds of retired men retired as a result of their own decision. Less than 1 in 5 was retired involuntarily as a result of reaching retirement age (Cottrell & Atchley, 1969; Riley & Foner, 1968).

By leaving out those in poor health and those who voluntarily retired, Miller (1965) effectively limited the group he was talking about to less than a third of the retired men and an even smaller proportion of the retired women.

307

Identity Continuity Theory

It may seem that we have dwelt too long and too deeply with the relation between leisure and retirement. Nevertheless, if we are to understand the nature of leisure among older people, it must be put in its proper context. Miller's position is a very common one and is constantly being used as a basis for decisions that influence older people's lives. Our detailed examination of this approach has shown it to be at least questionable and very possibly false.

To begin with, there is evidence in the Scripps Foundation studies and elsewhere that the adjustment problems sometimes associated with retirement are not the result of the loss of work and the identity it provides. In fact, a highly positive orientation toward work had little influence on retirement adjustment. There is no indication that highly work-oriented people are unable to take up leisure roles; in fact, just the opposite. We could find no concrete evidence that retirement in and of itself negatively influences the quality of one's family life, friendships, or associations.

Accordingly, an alternative to Miller's identity crisis theory of the relationship between retirement and leisure might contain the following points:

Many people are never highly work-oriented and thus they may very well provide a model for others concerning what it would be like to derive self-satisfaction from leisure. In addition, the ethic of the system allows this as long as the money used to lead a life of leisure is legitimately earned.

Self-respect can be gained from leisure pursuits in retirement if (a) the individual has enough money, and (b) he has a cohort of retired friends who will accept his full-time leisure as legitimate and help him to negate the stigma of implied inability to perform, if such a stigma exists. As retirement becomes more and more an expected part of the life-cycle, this orientation should spread beyond the cohort of friends. In any event, the retired individual will continue to see himself as a railroader, teacher, etc. even though he no longer plays the role. Thus, the crux of this alternative theory is identity continuity.

Wide occupational differences exist in the concept of the

usefulness of an activity. There are many people for whom interpersonal interaction was their occupational skill and it is this activity that is useful rather than some abstract goal. In this sense, then, leisure can act as a work substitute where it needs to and provide identity continuity.

Very few people rest their entire identity on a single role. If they did, there would surely be far more suicides than there are now. The only thing that makes failure bearable is that we seldom fail in all our roles at once.

Each person generally has several roles that he stakes his identity on. Work may be at or near the top, but not necessarily so. There simply is not the kind of homogeneous consensus on the value of work that would keep it at the top for everyone. In fact, the many systems of competing values in a complex society insure that there will be a wide variety of self-values. Thus, the probability that retirement will lead to a complete identity breakdown is slight, and there may be just as many people who rely on leisure pursuits for self-respect as there are who rely on work, particularly among those with unsatisfying jobs.

Some decline of involvement may be natural as the individual adjusts to declining energy, but most people expand their leisure involvement when they retire. Nevertheless, this change is not regarded negatively by most retired people. In fact, most people voluntarily retire, and many of these volunteers cite a preference for leisure as their reason for retiring.

Conclusion

There is no doubt that there are some people for whom Miller's identity crisis pattern is a grim reality, but it does not appear to be a typical pattern, even among the minority of older people who are forced to retire. Among voluntary retirees, a third retired to devote more time to leisure. The ethical issue may be difficult for some to resolve, but not for the majority, even among the highly work-oriented.

The identity continuity theory and the data which give rise to it suggest that leisure can have a great deal of positive value

INTRODUCTION TO PART V

Elderly Americans, like those of all ages, live in a variety of settings from Skid Row flophouses to Palm Beach condominiums, urban apartments, and isolated rural farmhouses. Public discussion of housing and the elderly focuses largely on the special problems they may have, relative to younger people, in securing physically adequate housing at a reasonable cost. The relative merits of rent-supplement programs, public housing, special property-tax reductions, and construction incentives for private developers are all important issues. However, the interests of social gerontologists have centered increasingly on fundamental questions about the relationship between behavior and living environments.

How and to what extent is the physical, social, and psychological functioning of an elderly individual influenced by the kind of environment in which he lives? M. Powell Lawton, author of the first selection, suggests that some of the apparent "effects of aging" may result from elderly people having to cope with environments designed for younger people. Moreover, he hypothesizes that aging increases the importance of environmental influences: "the less competent the individual in terms of personal disability or deprived status, the more susceptible is his behavior to the immediate environmental situations."

In the second article, Frances Carp reports impressive improvements in morale, social activity, and even sleeping patterns for a group of people who moved into an attractive apartment complex for the elderly. While the residents' changed attitudes

313

are clearly related to an environmental change, we may not infer a relationship between any particular feature of Victoria Plaza and the morale or activity of the aged in general. Victoria Plaza is, among other things, an "age-segregated" environment. Many researchers have found higher morale and social activity among elderly persons in this type of environment. However, as Linda Winiecke demonstrates in the third article, people select age-segregated housing in large part because they are lonely and bored. It is difficult to determine whether people are more satisfied because they have altered some personally distressing situation in moving, or whether age-segregated housing per se offers some advantages for elderly people in general.

The last three papers in this part take a close look at a particular type of age-segregated housing situation. The environments described range from a fraternally operated trailer community studied over twenty years ago, to a California apartment house. The elderly inhabitants include upper-middle class professionals, retired farmers, and persons with blue-collar urban backgrounds. Despite this variety, a number of common factors may be seen.

In each setting, there is a range of people from those who are active social participants to those who are socially isolated. This is true both in the poorly integrated community of Fun City and at Merrill Court where there are strong social pressures to join in. Environment has a facilitating rather than a determining effect on the social integration of particular aged individuals.

Each author notes that physical features of the environment influence social patterns. At Merrill Court, the addition of a coffee machine to the recreation room spurred the beginning of group activities. The common laundry room and physical proximity of units enhance social interaction at Bradenton Trailer Park, while the absence of such things is reported to promote social distance among Fun City residents.

Each author reports a status hierarchy based on values such as being a good sport, "pitching in," maintaining one's health, and having attentive relatives. Education, income, property, and former occupation seem to have diminished importance. It seems likely that this phenomenon is enhanced by an age-segregated environment.

314

SOCIAL ECOLOGY
AND
THE HEALTH
OF OLDER PEOPLE*

M. Powell Lawton

Introduction

I should like to present today the basically simple-minded idea that the context in which older people behave is a significant determinant of how they perform. I shall suggest that some apparent "effects of aging" are in fact the result of the environments our society creates for the elderly segment of our population. On the one hand, performance levels are lowered by the necessity of dealing with environments built for younger people. On the other, there is a major potential for the massive use of "environmental therapy," with good prospect of payoff. Attention to the design of health-engendering environments may either significantly raise the functional competence of the individual ("therapy") or elevate his functioning without altering his basic competence ("prosthesis").

It is not difficult to document the differential richness of the environment for young and old. The young and middle-aged receive far more stimuli of all kinds requiring the exercise of learning capacities. Social demands for the everyday performance of student, worker, family, and community roles drop radically as official retirement nears. Even more importantly, reinforcement for the successful performance of these roles decreases.

*M. Powell Lawton, "Social Ecology and the Health of Older People," *American Journal of Public Health* 64 (1974): 257–60.

One ceases to advance on his job, to be sought after for advice, to be reacted to as if sexually attractive, to be considered worthy of sharing the news with. The negative reinforcement of portraying senility as the normal course of aging is deeply embedded into our culture, as is the dirty old man syndrome, and the cluster of negative personality traits attributed to old age. Baltes[1] has pointed out that the larger social environment of today is far less stable than it was in earlier historical periods. In earlier times the learning accomplished in early life remained relevant for a lifetime of coping with the same environment, whereas today much of a person's physical, social, and resource environment is totally replaced in less than a generation. Yet, society has headed the opposite direction in allowing opportunities for learning new coping styles relevant to this pace of environmental change. People retire earlier, three-generation households are out, we build new communities that are learnable only with the use of a car, and old communities are psychologically walled by the fear of crime.

Attenuated Performance

Thus, the older person may well have many abilities that never reach full performance potential because of the way we deprive our environments and program their rewards and punishments for the otherwise competent older person. However, there are some real deficits that become more frequent during old age. Health as measured by any index does become poorer with age. If one controls properly for health, as has been done in several landmark studies,[2,3] it becomes clear that much of the decline that has been wrongly attributed to age is, in fact, associated with chronic disease. The incidence of alcoholism, suicide, and several varieties of chronic brain disease does increase during old age. Thus, while we can say confidently that old age alone does not inevitably result in negative psychological changes, there is a statistically greater incidence of many such changes. These changes lead to an increased state of dependency of some older people on resources other than their own.

I have described two sources of lowered performance: environmental deprivation and decline in biological efficiency, both of which appear to leave the older person in a state of vulnerability. That is, the person deprived of the clearly stated environmental contingencies of youth, and the person with a health-related incapacity to learn new tasks are both less capable of finding adaptive ways of responding to new environmental situations. I have stated this in "the environmental docility hypothesis": the less competent the individual in terms of personal disability or deprived status, the more susceptible is his behavior to the influence of immediate environmental situations. Evidence supporting this hypothesis came from research done at the Philadelphia Geriatric Center on friendships among older people in age-segregated housing[4] and in research reported by Rosow.[5] In our research, older people who were in poor health and those who were foreign-born were more closely bound to proximate neighbors in choosing friends than were those born in this country and in better health. Rosow found that working-class elderly were more dependent on local friends than were middle-class elderly. Thus, the deprived groups' social behavior was more constrained by the environmental variable, physical distance between neighbors. Many other examples come to mind. Economically independent younger people have the option of moving to the suburbs; the older person in poverty remains in the high crime area. The person in good health adapts to the nuisance of climbing steps; the person in poor health fails to continue earlier tasks, such as shopping or organization membership.

The environmental docility hypothesis thus first cautions us regarding the assumption that the adaptations of earlier life will be appropriate in later life. An aspect of the environment may be neutral, or even a facilitator of self-fulfillment in earlier life, but may constitute a veto over some kinds of satisfaction in later life.

Ecological Change Model

Conversely, an implication of the hypothesis is that desirable behavior may be elicited, or elevated in quality, by the provision of a favorable environment. Finally, the hypothesis suggests that methods which directly increase the competence of the individual will give him greater control over his environment. My co-worker Lucille Nahemow and I have developed an ecological change model which looks at treatment in terms of whether the measures are applied to the individual or to the environment, and whether the individual initiates the treatment or responds to the external application of a treatment. Thus, the four possible treatments are:

1. The individual initiates; the point of appliation is the individual. This is the normal way that individuals grow, where they actively seek stimulation, strive toward self-determined goals, and are alert to the need for change in themselves. Where personal competence is high and the social milieu friendly, the older person continues to behave uninterruptedly in this mode.

2. The individual initiates; the point of application is the environment. Another positive change mechanism is the attempt to redesign one's own environment in such a way as to maximize the congruity between one's own needs and the offerings of the environment. It is easy to be pessimistic about the possibility of such active creation in a society that appears to be thrusting the individual further and further into anonymity and powerlessness. However, migration to a pleasanter climate or to a community where health care is more readily available are ways of producing a new environment. The strongly activist Gray Panther organization is determinedly seeking ways to change the behavioral environment of older people: more accessible transportation, better designed banking facilities, and so on. For every level of competence there are appropriate ways of controlling one's environment. Some tenants of our housing sites for the elderly whose behavioral range was greatly restricted leave their apartment doors open during the day; not at all by chance they are the people who are most often chosen as friendly in a sociometric survey.

3. The individual responds to a treatment that is applied individually. This is the change model to which the helping professionals are most accustomed, best exemplified by individual therapy. While some may object that good psychotherapy involves the patient's being a true co-therapist, the essential factor distinguishing this type of change from growth is the activity of

318

a professional in the change system. Over much of the half-century where individual therapy was the change method of choice, the environment has been assumed to be a constant, and consequently unfortunately ignored as an agent for change. However, during the heyday of psychotherapy the older person was totally excluded from the company of those thought to be suitable for individual therapy, and things are no better today. The NIMH, for example, has reported that only 2 percent of all patients treated in outpatient clinics are 65 and over. Now that there does seem to be some hope of mobilizing interest among therapists in treating the elderly, one can hope that the possibilities inherent in the creative use of environmental intervention will be recognized as well. This, of course, is the fourth change type.

4. *The individual responds to a change applied to the environment.* Planners, designers, and architects have long had some control over behavior by virtue of their determination of the shapes of the physical environment, but have only recently begun consciously to give equal time to human needs along with esthetic values. Social designers similarly have tried, with varying success, to construct need-fulfilling environments. Prospects for change are theoretically greatest in this quadrant, since designing one environment may direct the behavior of a large number of people. However, we all are aware of how resourceful people are in doing as they wish (or as they are forced to) in spite of "ideal" environments, and this easy intervention scheme has not been as effective as might have been hoped—urban renewal, for example.

I suggest that disillusionment with the environmental design approach to behavior change should be reserved for its inappropriate application, but that encouragement be taken for its judicious use. Any instance of reduced status or competence, such as those that are more frequent in old age, is potentially changeable through environmental intervention. In psychological jargon, a change in environment will be most effective in changing behavior when the individual is at a threshold level of competence.

319

Examples of Change

Let us look very briefly at a few examples of change instituted through environmental design. Lindsley[6] has referred to the "prosthetic environment," meaning a treatment environment programmed so that behavior-elevating responses are reinforced. Our Philadelphia Geriatric Center conducted a pilot study involving the redesign of two large rooms for mentally impaired aged into a suite consisting of six small private rooms opening onto a small social space, which in turn was separated from the main hallway by a half-wall.[7] Our hypothesis was that behavioral range would be increased by opening up the area visually and that social interaction would be enhanced by providing an area designated as social space and containing the environmental props consistent with this purpose. The first hypothesis was confirmed strongly. (Postalteration observations showed a 7.1 percent increase in the number of residents in the hallway or beyond, as compared with the prealteration occasion). The second hypothesis was not borne out, although the number of patient-patient interactions remained the same despite the fact that on about 20 percent of the occasions, residents exercised their newly available option to remain in their private rooms. Findings such as these have been incorporated into the design of a treatment institution for mentally impaired aged patients now under construction at the Philadelphia Geriatric Center.

Perhaps the best documented change broadly related to mental health is found in the case of age-segregated housing for the elderly. Several impact studies by Carp,[8] Lipman,[9] and our center[10] show that to varying degrees a favorable change is experienced by elderly people during the year following such a move, particularly in the areas of organizational activity, social interaction, and perceived change in life satisfaction. Finer detailed examination of some of the processes involved in such an increase in well-being seems to indicate that the physical proximity of age peers and the establishment of a normative system appropriate to the level of competence of the average elderly tenant are major factors in the beneficial effect.

320

Involuntary Relocation and Stress Tolerance

On the negative effect side of the ledger, evidence is rapidly accumulating to indicate that the involuntary relocation of physically and mentally vulnerable older people may have a catastrophic effect. At least half a dozen studies, done with appropriate controls, on naturally occurring closings of institutions, requiring the mass transfer of residents to new institutions, indicate higher than expected mortality and morbidity in the relocated populations.

The contrast between the findings of the planned housing and the institutional types of relocation may be examined in light of the environmental docility hypothesis. Both conditions involve a major environmental change. There is a major difference in degree of competence of the two relocated groups, however. The rehoused are quite independent, while the institutionalized have no choice. In both cases, the environmental change is major, but in the case of the housing group, the change generally means growth, while for the institutionalized it means decline. Thus, the concept of stress-tolerance level became necessary to make this differential prediction: the amount of change demanded of an individual by an environmental intervention has an upper limit determined by the individual's level of competence beyond which the change exceeds his ability to handle in an adaptive manner. In our model of adaptation, *either* a drop in competence or an increase in environmental pressure may elicit nonadaptive behavior or negative affect. As discussed in greater detail elsewhere,[11] environmental pressure may be reduced through the application of supportive services. An essential element in making medical and other services available under conditions of low environmental pressure is transportation. Functional equivalents of adequate transportation might be the easement of barriers through an ombudsman, a move to a location more proximate to medical services, or if competence is very low, institutionalization.

Adaptation Level

In any case, our model suggests that when environmental demands are slightly above the individual's accustomed level of responsiveness ("adaptation level"[12]) his maximum performance may be elicited. When demands are slightly below his adaptation level, he tends to become complacent—the "zone of maximum comfort." Raising environmental demands too far beyond adaptation level (overloading) or too far below (deprivation) both risk maladaptive responses. Our model also suggests that the range of tolerable response is far smaller for the less competent person. A corollary of this assertion is that *small* changes in environment may produce substantial changes in the adaptiveness of behavior. This is another way of saying that the payoff for effective environmental intervention is very high for older people in poor mental or physical health.

Thus, there seems to me to be good reason to encourage the joint participation of social planners, health professionals, behavior scientists, and designers in the task of producing health-engendering environments for older people. Such effort may be effective on any scale, from prosthetic furniture to household design to health facility to areawide service program.

Notes

1. Baltes, P. 1973. Adult development of intellectual performance: Description, explanation and modification. In *The Psychology of Adult Development and Aging,* ed. C. Eisdorfer and M. P. Lawton. American Psychological Association, Washington, D.C.

2. Birren, J. E., et al. 1963. *Human Aging.* Bethesda, Md.: National Institute of Mental Health.

3. Granick, S. (ed.). 1971. Human Aging II. Washington, D.C.: Health Services and Mental Health Administration.

4. Lawton, M. P., and Simon, B. 1968. The ecology of social relationships in housing for the elderly. *Gerontologist* 8:108–15.

5. Rosow, I. 1967. Social Integration of the Aged. New York: Free Press.

6. Lindsley, O. R. 1964. Geriatric behavioral prosethetics. In *New Thoughts on Old Age*, ed. R. Kastenbaum. New York: Springer.

7. Lawton, M. P.; Liebowitz, B.; and Charon, H. 1970. Physical structure and the behavior of senile patients following ward remodeling. *Aging Hum. Dev.* 1:231-39.

8. Carp, F. M. 1966. *A future for the aged.* Austin: University of Texas Press.

9. Lipman, A. 1968. Public housing and attitudinal adjustment in old age: A comparative study. *J. Geriatr. Psychiatry* 2:88-101.

10. Lawton, M. P., and Cohen, J. The generality of housing impact on the well-being of older people. *J. Gerontol.,* in press.

11. Lawton, M. P., and Nahemow, L. 1973. Ecology and the aging process. In *The Psychology of Adult Development and Aging*, ed. C. Eisdorfer and M. P. Lawton. Washington, D.C.: American Psychological Association.

12. Helson, H. 1964. Adaptation Level Theory. New York: Harper & Row.

THE IMPACT
OF
ENVIRONMENT
ON OLD PEOPLE*[1]
Frances M. Carp

Problem

Can old people be changed by altering the environments in which they live, or have responses become rigid with time? Are their dissatisfactions responsive to present reality or have they become intrinsic to individuals and therefore impervious to situational change? As one specific: do improved housing and social opportunities really matter?

Procedure

In 1960 data were collected on demographic, biographic, attitudinal, and other psychological variables on 352 applicants for a new public housing facility (Victoria Plaza) designed for older people. Eight of its stories are made up of apartments. The Senior Center for the county is on its ground floor. Applicants lived in physically substandard housing and/or social isolation or stress. Decisions regarding admission were made by Housing Authority staff. There were no significant differences between inmovers and others on variables relevant to this research.

Twelve to fifteen months after the new residence was occupied, follow-up materials were obtained. One data analysis dealt

* Frances M. Carp, "The Impact of Environment on Old People." *Gerontologist* 7 (1967): 106-8, 135.

with changes over time which were different for the 204 applicants who moved into Victoria Plaza from those for the 148 who did not. This analysis used standard covariance design. A regression model was selected because it involves a minimum of assumptions regarding the nature of the variables and because it seems particularly well suited to the investigation (Bottenberg & Ward, 1963).

Data processing output is in terms of the regression line(s) which relate the initial to the final score. Effects of residence and sex are represented by the number of regression lines. Extent and direction of change, and their relationships to the size of initial score, are represented by slopes and intercepts.

This use of the regression line(s) relating baseline to follow-up information seems preferable to analysis using means. Compensating changes in different individuals are not reflected in the latter, which may cause outcomes to be masked. For example, improvement during the interval by persons at one end of an original score distribution and reduction in score by those at the other end might produce a mean change of zero although the conclusion of no change would be erroneous.

Here the major purpose is to compare residential status groups in order to determine the effect of changed environment on various indicators. Each residence group is further divided into men and women, to test differential effect of residence by sex. For any indicator, the question is whether individuals' scores tended to shift during the period of observation, the direction of shift that occurred, and the consistency of score stability of change from subgroup to subgroup. The regression model seems ideally suited to answer these questions.

Results of Changed Setting

Evidence of the dramatic effect of improved life-setting on this group of older people was overwhelming and was similar for men and women (Table 1). Consistently, scores of residents improved, those of nonresidents showed no change or slight decrement. On some variables improvement was consistent among residents. On others it was related to the score at first contact,

325

in some cases the "haves getting" and in others the originally most deprived showing greatest change. The influence of improved physical and social environment appeared not only in increased satisfaction of residents with their living situation but also in more favorable attitudes about themselves and toward others, in signs of improved physical and mental health, and in more active and sociable patterns of life.

Table 1

Changes Associated with Residence in Victoria Plaza.

Index	F	x^2
Attitude: Happiness	24.79**	
Feel About Accomplishments in Life	5.79*	
Number of Leisure Activities	9.41**	
Activities Compared to Those of Age 55	30.67**	
Percent Social Activities	12.83**	
Number of Close Friends	13.88**	
Attitude: Friends	42.76**	
Attitude: Family	10.37**	
Rating of Health	6.41*	
Attitude: Health	5.93*	
Major Problem: Health	5.90*	
Neurotic Problems	5.98*	
Time on Health Care	5.53*	
Time Sleeping	7.86**	
"Lost" Time	23.02**	

  * Significant at the .05 level.
 ** Significant at the .01 level.

Most people increased all kinds of activity subsequent to moving into the Plaza. Social activities increased most markedly and gave the greatest satisfaction. Groups formed quickly about hobbies or other pastimes and they were maintained. Friendships flourished. There were a few romances, one leading to marriage within the first year.

The quality of relationships with family members improved following the move, regardless of whether there was more or less contact. Social isolation and interpersonal friction had been major sources of applicants' dissatisfaction and they continued to be for nonresidents. However, most of these people wanted to maintain their own households as long as possible and to feel free to make decisions for themselves. Above all, they dreaded becoming burdens, financially, or emotionally, upon members of their families. They did not want to strain the highly valued bonds of kinship by constant contact in crowded housing. They did not want to make demands for separate housing which would curtail the budgets of younger households.

Too, love for their children and grandchildren did not preclude interest in other people. Many applicants perceived as particularly hazardous to sound family relationships their own lack of social life and consequent emotional dependence on the kinship group. This occurred among those who lived alone as well as those in family residences. These people had applied for apartments in which they could live "independently" among others in their age group, not to sever family relationships and not because they felt unloved or unloving, but to nourish family relationships and provide for others. The data support their wisdom.

The environmental change was deeply and almost unanimously satisfying to people who lived in Victoria Plaza. They had wanted to make the move, they were delighted to be selected as residents, and after living in the Plaza for a year or more they continued to revel in its physical comfort and convenience and social opportunities.

They had fewer health complaints and, among those they had, fewer were neurotic in type. They spent less time in bed on account of illness and less time in health-care activities. Napping and sleeping took up fewer hours, and "lost time" was drastically diminished.

The consistent alterations in outlook and lifestyle among the resident group are more clearly attributable to housing because it was possible to view them in relation to changes among applicants who had not made the move. Unsuccessful applicants, initially similar to successful ones, exhibited little difference in behavior or attitude from 1960 to 1961.

The relative consistency of nonresident records supports attribution of resident change to environment. Also it lends confidence to the initial research material as realistic report of conditions and reactions. Had there been a successful attempt on the part of applicants to manipulate response to maximize likelihood of acceptance, significant shifts should have appeared in the 1961 material of nonresidents.

Implications of the Results

The change among Plaza residents contra-indicates rigidity as an integral component of the aging personality. The behavior of these people calls into question the difficulty, with increasing age as distinct from decreasing opportunities, of forming new social relationships. The results suggest strongly that old people's dissatisfactions with the circumstances of their lives are realistic reaction to difficult physical or social situations and that expressions of discontent cease when the causes are alleviated.

The findings suggest that more attention should be paid to the role of the setting in determining the experience and behavior of people within it, even of people who are old. (The median age of this group was over 72 at first contact). Results point also to the necessity for more careful scrutiny of traits considered to be age-related. Some environmental alterations may so regularly accompany chronological age that their effects are mistaken for those of aging itself.

The new facility was not a panacea. It did not, for example, cure alcoholism, exhibitionism, or filthy personal habits. Nor did all residents consider it ideal. Had such choices been open to them, most would have preferred to live in a different part of town, many would have chosen a small house with a yard, some would rather have lived among people varying more widely in age, or with fewer people of any sort. However, Victoria Plaza was the best situation obtainable, and they were grateful for it because the alternatives were much less attractive.

Residents were only reacting like people who toured Victoria Plaza when they commented on the beauty of its design, the imaginative and pleasing use of building materials, the comfort and convenience of the apartments, and the welcoming atmosphere of the recreation area. Certainly a major portion of the

328

satisfaction expressed with Victoria Plaza stems simply from the fact that it was a desirable residence. In comparison with other living situations available to these old people, it was extremely so.

The overwhelming nature of its success probably results partly, also, from characteristics of the people who were residents. They had expressed interest in such housing and had taken active steps to secure it; they were generally capable of caring for themselves and their apartments; and they were strongly motivated by the need for independence. (As it is used here, "independence" is not the opposite of interdependence with other persons. Quite the contrary, most members of this group of people recognized their need for others and were eager to fill it.)

Perhaps it is important, in determining the success of the first group of residents in the Plaza that they had not spent all of their lives either in substandard homes or in social isolation. Such adjustment would not be expected among old people who had never had good housing or who did not value it sufficiently at present to make some effort to obtain it or among confirmed recluses. Predictions would be different for the physically or emotionally disabled.

However, the rather comprehensive background information on this group suggests that they are much like most old people in this country today. Probably also the fact that the changes came about in a group of individuals who were simply getting along as well as they could as normal members of a community, rather than achieving visibility either through acknowledgment of physical or economic helplessness, or identification with some privileged group, supports the prospect of more widespread improvement of the later years of life through changes in the environmental settings in which they are lived.

Limitations

There must be several reservations concerning the consistent and extreme changes among inmovers. They were the first occupants of the building. First occupants may be a special group. The resulting prestige and "in-group" feeling may even be detrimental to the adjustment of replacements. Expressions of satisfaction and other indexes of change were based on only a year to fifteen months of experience in the situation. Satisfaction may moderate with time. Increased activity, sociability, interest in personal appearance, and pride in home may be temporary. The basic process of disengagement may have been only briefly interrupted.

Did changes which differentiated residents from nonresidents reflect a "honeymoon period" or a "Hawthorne effect" or were they, on the other hand, enduring results of changes in the life situation? How did the original inmovers relate to people who replaced members of the first group who died or moved away? Data are being collected on surviving members of the original group in order to test the persistence of satisfaction, activity, sociability, etc. and on second-generation residents in Victoria Plaza.

Were changes specific to the sample or do they occur in other groups of elderly people who move into other residential facilities? To test the generality of these results, data are being collected from applicants to another public-housing facility now under construction, and both successful and unsuccessful applicants will be followed.

Notes

1. This research was supported by grants from The Hogg Foundation for Mental Health and The Social Security Administration. Details of research design, selection of subjects, data analysis, and numerical results of statistical procedures are reported in *A Future for the Aged*. (Austin: The University of Texas Press, 1966).

THE APPEAL
OF AGE SEGREGATED
HOUSING
TO THE ELDERLY POOR*[1]

Linda Winiecke

Public housing for the aged is designed to provide the elderly poor with safe, attractive dwelling units at rents they can afford. Besides providing improved living conditions, the housing centers also offer older persons opportunities for increased contact with age peers. Close proximity to elderly neighbors will facilitate the formation of new friendships. In short, the housing project is to become a home in which an older person can live out his remaining years in comfort, security, and safety.

Previous research has focused on the physical and social features of aged persons' housing. Emphasis has been placed on objective analysis of structure (size, plumbing, recreational rooms, etc.) or on social analysis of the people who get in. Considerably less is known about the situational factors and personal characteristics which lead tenants to apply in the first place. It is the intent of this paper (1) to identify the correlates of interest in public housing for the aged among a sample of older, poor persons who presently live in independent arrangements, and (2) to shed some light on the aspects of public housing which seem to have the strongest potential appeal to the aged poor.

* Linda Winiecke, "The Appeal of Age Segregated Housing to the Elderly Poor," *International Journal of Aging and Human Development* 4 (1973): 293-306. © Baywood Publishing Company, Inc. 1973.

Background

Recent concern expressed by city planning agencies with the dearth of adequate low-cost housing for the aged poor has stimulated public interest in building additional projects specially for the aged. The new housing will provide more than just additional housing units:

> (The) intention is to channel public funds into quality housing that will enrich the environment of the city—rather than merely warehouse the poor . . . to build on the principle that human spirit is inspired at the sight of excellence (Teitelbaum, 1972).

Carp (1966, p. 93) is even more emphatic in her praise of Victoria Plaza, an age segregated senior's housing project in San Antonio:

> They (new residents) had moved from substandard housing to a freshly completed, totally modern apartment building, and they appreciated and enjoyed the convenience, cleanliness, and beauty. From social isolation or resentment producing interpersonal situations they had been transported into the midst of a bountiful supply of people yet with control over privacy and choice of associates.

Three salient advantages to aged housing projects are stressed: improved living conditions, increased social contacts, and reduced rents. The new housing is to be cheaper than housing available in the open market. One quarter of the aged Americans over 65 years have an annual income below the poverty level (Bureau of Census, 1971b) and are restricted in their ability to compete in the open housing market (Cantor et al, 1970). For many, low-cost public housing is the only way they will ever be able to afford modern, attractive accommodations. Applicants to Victoria Plaza included lowered rents and better housing among their reasons for applying (Carp, 1966).

The housing is also intended to be safe and convenient. Planning agencies are designed aged housing projects with built-in safety features especially for older persons. Indoor features include corridors with handrails, elevators, grab bars in the apartments, as well as an emergency alarm system throughout (Sacramento Housing Authority, 1971). Nash and Nash (1968) report that new tenants in high-rise aged projects express a great deal of satisfaction with the safety features and modern fixtures in their new apartments. The convenience and safety of neighborhoods also comes under consideration when choosing housing. Cantor et al (1970) suggest that in rapidly changing neighborhoods, accessibility to needed facilities and perceptions of safety may be more important to older persons than structural fitness.

The third advantage to public housing for the aged is the opportunity for increased social contact. Age segregated housing concentrates rather than diffuses the field of potential acquaintances. Age concentrated environments have been observed to provide greater interactional opportunities for those residents inclined to take advantage of them (Messer, 1967). Elderly persons who choose to live in a retirement park consider sociability to be the chief advantage (Hoyt, 1954).

Rosow (1961) views environment as a stage on which social forces play themselves out. He considers four factors to be important to the maintenance of social integration in neighborhoods:

1. Long term residency,
2. Neighborhood stability,
3. Social homogeneity, and
4. Intact primary groups.

However, normal neighborhoods often alienate the elderly. In changing, mobile areas the opportunities for maintaining friendships become scarce (Rossi, 1955). Isolation of the elderly is common. Rosenberg (1970) suggests that social composition is central to interaction and the lack of it.

Schooler (1970) is of the opinion that environment is more than just a stage. Introducing environment as an interactive variable, he observed that it modifies the relationship between social factors and morale. He pointed out that "environment is not simply the screen against which the dynamics of life are interacted, but rather a matrix not only from which but within which the quality of certain life processes is determined (p. 28)."

Commenting on the improved life satisfaction of Victoria Plaza residents a year after entry, Carp (1967, p. 108) suggests that dissatisfaction with life circumstances are "realistic reactions to difficult physical or social situations, and the expressions of discontentment cease when the causes are alleviated."

To the older person interested in moving to aged housing, the positive factors (be they rent, modern conveniences, or sociability) would seem to outweigh any negative aspects associated with relocation. And yet the disadvantages must be taken into consideration when contemplating an abrupt change in one's sociophysical environment.

Relocation from a familiar to a strange environment induces numerous stresses (Briggs, 1968). There is attachment to the familiar elements of current living arrangements. Although present arrangements may leave something to be desired, at least they are predictable. Moving induces ecological shock in all people; however, older persons may find readjustment somewhat harder. Then too, some older persons are just not interested in living in an age dense environment. The very factors that serve to attract some people might repel others. Elderly persons do not have the same social needs to be fulfilled. Many elderly persons are quite satisfied with their present housing and see little reason to change.

Nevertheless, the appeal of aged housing remains broadly based, and many older persons are willing to accept the initial discomfort of a new environment for the advantages in store. What then can be said about the older person opting for such housing and his reasons for this choice? One might best check by looking at the aged welfare recipients who are, in theory, the natural clientele for low-cost public housing.

Based on data gathered from a sample of aged welfare recipients, the present study explores the background, current activity and morale of elderly persons who would consider living in age dense housing as opposed to those who would not. In spite of similar financial limitations, what is it about their circumstances that makes some individuals favor the idea of special housing for the aged and others reject the idea? Can such information be used as a predictor of actual applications to aged public housing?

334

Sample

The data are drawn from an ongoing study of Old Age Assistance recipients in Sacramento County, California. The original sample consisted of 256 noninstitutionalized recipients
recently approved for cash grant assistance and selected from a
complete roster of cases approved in July–October 1969. The
only exclusions were those in which extremely poor health, language difficulty, or simple refusal made interviewing impossible.

The data reported here were gathered from the 235 members of the initial cohort who were reinterviewed in the summer
of 1970. Of the original sample 7 died, 4 became too ill to re-
interview, 3 refused, and 7 had moved out of the state.

At the time of the second interview most of the respondents
continued to live in independent arrangements, although 6 had
been institutionalized. Some renters were living in county sub-
sidized accommodations, but none were living in the new age
specific public housing units that Sacramento County was building at the time.

Most respondents were aware that aged public housing was
soon to be available in Sacramento. At the time the second interview was being conducted, the Sacramento Housing Authority
was beginning construction of 800 new housing units for the
elderly, many of which were scheduled for completion within
the following year. Local news coverage featured the Housing
Authority and heavily publicized the proposed units, as well as
the 2,000 existing units available through the leased housing
program.

Interest in age segregated housing was determined by the
recipients response to a two-item set of questions:

1. How do you feel about special housing centers or apartment buildings for old people? Do you think they are a
   good idea or not?
2. Would you ever like to try living in a place like that?

A "yes" to the second question was considered a favorable response. Our sample contained 107 respondents interested in age
segregated housing, 126 not interested, and 2 who were undecided. The latter are excluded from further analysis.

Findings

Respondents interested in public housing for the aged did not differ appreciably from uninterested respondents with respect to their sex, race, or adult social class (Hollingshead and Redlich, 1958). They were however, more likely to be the younger members of the sample; those under 70 years of age (Table 1). Interestingly enough, the latter finding does not cor-

Table 1

General Characteristics

	Interested (N = 107) %	Not interested (N = 126) %	p by X^2
Sex			
Women	57	59	>.10
Ethnic Label			
White	85	79	>.10
Actual Age			
Under 70 years	62	46	.02
Adult Social Class			
Middle (I-III)	52	48	>.10
Working (IV-V)	48	52	

respond with available data on residents in elderly public housing apartments: many more women than men apply and are accepted, and their average age is over 70 (Carp, 1966; Nash and Nash, 1968; Sacramento Housing Authority, 1971). The disparity may be an artifact of the present sample, however, Because it was drawn at intake to the Old Age Assistance program, the sample is skewed in favor of younger recipients.

A look at the current housing arrangement reveals sharp differences between respondents who would consider living in age segregated apartment buildings and those who would not (Table 2). The basic distinction lies in the type of housing in which respondents currently live. Renters, whether they occupy apartments, houses or hotels, are more likely to opt for aged housing than are home and trailer owners, persons in institutions, or

336

those currently living in someone else's home. Elderly persons living alone express a greater preference for senior housing.

In discussing current housing, one speculates about the reasons some elderly would choose to leave their present dwelling in favor of age dense housing. There are two approaches which can be aken. The first is that present conditions are so bad that anything else represents improvement. Under these circumstances, the elderly are not drawn by the positive features

Table 2

Living Arrangement

	Interested (N = 107) %	Not interested (N = 126) %	p by X^2
Type of Housing			
Renters	65	46	.01
Living Arrangement			
Lives Alone	60	43	.01
Sacramento Location			
Suburban	62	71	$>$.10

of age concentrated public housing but are, instead escaping from the negative conditions imposed by their current situation. The second approach is that the present situation is satisfactory, but age dense housing sounds even better. In this case, the desired housing is the motivating force for change.

Admittedly, this is a fine line to draw. The concept of being "forced out" of housing is easier to discuss in terms of neighborhood dissatisfaction, structural difficulties or money problems than in terms of unsatisfactory social conditions. On the other hand, the possibility of increased sociability seems to be one of the attractive features of age concentrated housing.

Negative reaction to current living conditions would constitute a "push" from current housing. Respondents do not seem particularly distressed by the physical conditions of their housing or the neighborhood in which they live (Table 3). Although five-sixths of the sample live in neighborhoods in which rent or

337

home value is below the median price range in Sacramento County (Bureau of the Census, 1971a), only a few of the respondents describe their neighborhoods as other than "good." Even persons expressing dissatisfaction with their present neighborhoods are no more likely to prefer aged housing. Aged housing interest does not seem to be contingent on a desire for improved housing. Respondents were asked to describe features of their housing and then give their places an overall rating.

Table 3

Neighborhood, Housing, and Transportation

	Interested (N = 107) %	Not interested (N = 126) %	p by X^2
Neighborhood rating			
Fair, poor	30	38	$>$.10
Overall house rating			
Fair, poor	51	46	$>$.10
House description			
Comfort (fair, poor)	40	40	$>$.10
Attractiveness (fair, poor)	60	62	$>$.10
Safety (fair, poor)	20	28	$>$.10
Convenience (fair, poor)	37	26	.10
Transportation			
Takes buses	56	34	.001
Walks	39	29	$>$.10
Drives automobile	23	27	$>$.10
Others drive	59	62	$>$.10

Persons interested in aged housing did not differ significantly from uninterested persons in their ratings of the comfort, attractiveness, safety, and overall condition of their housing. They were more likely to think of their housing as being inconvenient (p = .10).

Inconvenience is a function of one's source of transportation. Aged housing appeals to respondents who are dependent on local buses for transportation. The reason seems fairly obvious. The public transportation system in Sacramento does not provide extensive service, but the buslines that do exist all pass through the central city. Consequently the best bus service is available around many of the sites where new highrise public housing units will be constructed. For persons dependent on buses for mobility, living directly on a busline is an added advantage when choosing a place to live. Other modes of transportation do not significantly relate to interest to age dense housing.

Another, related factor to consider is housing cost. Currently the Old Age Assistance budget allots only $65 for housing. If the recipient's housing costs are more, he must make up the

Table 4

Current Problems

	Interested (N = 107) %	Not interested (N = 126) %	p by X^2
Need money	63	68	>.10
Needs more than $25	50	48	>.10
Wants to move	28	19	>.10
Is lonely	36	23	.05
Is bored	43	31	.10

difference with money marked for his other personal needs. Age segregated public housing has rent that is less than the housing allotment; however, the desire for low rent apparently has limited appeal in attracting elderly welfare recipients to such units. Presumably reduced rents would free money for other uses, and yet neither the perception of financial problems nor the desire for additional money to get by on stand out as important factors which distinguish respondents interested in age segregated housing.

Although specific housing problems do not seem to be forcing respondents out of current living arrangements, still some elderly persons want to live somewhere else. However, the wish to move does not mean the respondent is considering public housing for the aged.

Except for transportation difficulties, negative responses to the current housing situation do not relate to age dense housing interest. On the other hand, more personal, subjective problems do (Table 4). Interested respondents report feeling lonely and bored. For persons with empty hours, age concentrated housing offers a variety of people and activities to fill up the day. Besides close proximity to elderly neighbors, the buildings also provide recreational rooms in which tenants can get together for a variety of social functions, including games, crafts, and classes.

An examination of the social contacts maintained with other people shows that the concept of social homogeneity is important to age segregated housing interest (Table 5). The degree

Table 5

Social Contacts

	Interested (N = 107) %	Not interested (N = 126) %	p by X^2
Two or more friends	65	52	.05
Weekly contact with friends	74	60	.05
Less than weekly contact with children N = 162	57	77	.01
Sees neighbors as friends	46	48	>.10
Wants to live around people like self	56	37	.01
Wants to be around same age group	36	26	>.10

to which contact is maintained with family and friends relates to respondents' interest in age dense housing. The respondents who express interest in age segregated housing have more friends whom they see with greater frequency. At the same time, many have lost contact with their children and see them less than weekly. Previous research by Bultena and Wood (1969) revealed that older persons who migrated to Southwestern retirement communities saw their children less frequently prior to and after settlement than did elderly peers who remained in their midwestern hometowns.

Whether or not neighbors are seen as friends is apparently unimportant to one's choice of housing. What is important is

Table 6

Factors Associated with Living Arrangement

	Renters (N = 130)		Other Housing (N = 103)	
Overall Housing Rating	Good	Fair—Poor	Good	Fair—Poor
Aged housing interest	53%	56%	33%	37%
	(N = 58)	(N - 72)	(N = 62)	(N = 41)
	p > .10		p > .10	
Perceived Money Problems	Money a problem	Not a problem	Money a problem	Not a problem
Aged housing interest	52%	58%	34%	37%
	(N = 85)	(N = 45)	(N = 68)	(N = 35)
	p > .10		p > .10	
Transportation	Uses bus	Doesn't	Uses bus	Doesn't
Aged housing interest	65%	42%	44%	33%
	(N = 71)	(N = 59)	(N = 32)	(N = 71)
	p = .02		p > .10	
Perceived Loneliness	Loneliness a problem	Not a problem	Loneliness a problem	Not a problem
Aged housing interest	68%	49%	32%	32%
	(N = 40)	(N = 89)	(N = 28)	(N = 73)
	p = .05		p > .10	
Perceived Boredom	Boredom a problem	Not a problem	Boredom a problem	Not a problem
Aged housing interest	67%	47%	35%	33%
	(N = 51)	(N = 79)	(N = 34)	(N = 69)
	p = .05		p > .10	
Contact with Friends	Sees weekly	Sees less	Sees weekly	Sees less
Aged housing interest	55%	54%	46%	19%
	(N = 93)	(N = 37)	(N = 61)	(N = 42)
	p > .10		p = .01	
Kind of People Liked	Like self	Different types	Like self	Different types
Aged housing interest	69%	44%	44%	26%
	(N = 52)	(N = 76)	(N = 53)	(N = 50)
	p = .01		p = .05	

the type of people with whom one prefers to associate. Age segregated housing appeals to respondents who "would rather live in a place where everyone is pretty much like themselves rather than live among different types of people" (terminology directly from item on the questionnaire). Surprisingly, response to a similar item regarding the age group preferred (same age or other age groups) was in the desired direction but failed to reach the .05 level of significance. Evidently the concept of aged housing encompasses more than chronological age. Although age grouping plays a part in the patterning of social relationships, other factors such as marital status, social class, beliefs, and life styles must also be taken into account in discussing status and value homophily as bases for friendship.

Clearly several items relate to interest in aged housing. To clarify more specifically the relationship between living arrangements, social contacts and affective response, several factors were examined simultaneously. The results of this procedure are shown in Table 6.

Even when living arrangement is controlled, response to current housing and perceived money problems remain unrelated to aged housing interest. Dependency on buses continues to relate to housing interest, but only for renters. Bored and lonely renters express the greatest interest in age segregated housing. That age dense housing appeals to two-thirds of bored and lonely renters supports Rosow's (1967) contention that loneliness and social isolation in one's neighborhood intensify existing housing dissatisfaction. Nonrenters who see their friends weekly are more interested in aged housing than are those who maintain infrequent contact with friends. The relationship does not hold for renters.

Both renters and nonrenters interested in age specific housing would prefer living in a socially homogeneous neighborhood rather than with different types of people. The concept of social homogeneity is the only factor which cuts across living arrangement. Age dense housing attracts certain elderly persons who desire to get close to people whose values and status are similar to their own.

To this point, the discussion has examined the indices which relate to interest in age segregated housing. The remaining

342

question relates to the respondents' application to the County Housing Authority. Can expressed interest in aged housing be used as a prediction of actual application for elderly housing projects?

Encouragingly, expressed interest is a predictor of eventual application. A quarter of the respondents who voiced a favorable opinion for aged housing in the second-year interview have since applied to the Sacramento Housing Authority, and thirteen currently reside in aged public housing. Only 5 percent of the

Table 7

Respondents Who Applied for Aged Public Housing

	Renters		Other Housing	
	Applied	Did not	Applied	Did not
Aged housing interest	85%	44%	*	*
	N = 33	N = 97	N = 2	N = 101
	p .001			

* Distribution such that tests not indicated.

noninterested respondents have since changed their minds and applied. All but two of the applicants were renters (Table 7).

Given the size of the sample, an attempt to predict application for elderly public housing on the basis of expressed interest must remain highly speculative. Nevertheless, it seems obvious that only the renters follow through and actually apply for elderly public housing. As such, the social factors which correlate with expressed interest in aged housing must be considered in relationship to living arrangement. Even though nonrenters preferred neighborhood homogeneity, our data indicate that nonrenters seldom apply for elderly public housing. Home ownership, living in another's home, and institutionalization bind an individual to a definite location, and it is much more difficult to pick up and move when the whim strikes.

Discussion and Summary

The data reveal sharp and consistent differences between older persons who are interested in aged housing and those who are not interested. The groups differ in terms of age, living arrangement, social contact, and affective response to the perceived problems of loneliness and boredom.

The majority of respondents interested in age dense housing are renters who live in apartments, separate houses, and hotel rooms. They are younger and live alone. By and large, they depend on local buses for transportation and find their present living arrangement inconvenient. They do not see their children often, but they do have a number of friends whom they see weekly. Many are bored and lonely and would prefer to live in a place where people are similar to themselves.

Noninterested respondents are basically nonrenters, owning a home or a trailer, living in another's home (usually with one of their children), or living in an institution. They are older, in their seventies, and live with other people (usually family). They are infrequent users of the local transit system. Present neighborhood convenience is thought to be good. Although they see few friends regularly, they see their children at least weekly. Less likely to be lonely or bored with present circumstances, they accept living around a variety of people.

Aged housing interest is not related to the respondents' sex, race, or adult social class. Present neighborhood and housing characteristics do not identify an interest in age specific housing. Respondents' rating of their neighborhoods and homes, including such features as safety, comfort and attractiveness, and the desire to move are not related to aged housing interest. Respondents with money problems are no more likely to express interest in age dense housing than are those persons who don't think money is a problem or think they would need only a few more dollars to live comfortably. There is no relationship between aged housing interest and neighborhood friendship or age group preference.

The second issue under investigation was the identification of the public housing factors which have the strongest potential appeal to the aged poor. Three factors—rent, modern accommodations, and social contacts—were examined and tested against aged housing interest. Social correlates alone were significantly related to housing interest.

It remains unclear why respondents interested in aged housing wish to live around people like themselves but not specifically of the same age. Perhaps the former present the image of an age category, whereas the latter is too limiting. Or perhaps aged housing per se connotes more than just older people living together but draws to mind sociability with people of similar social class and interests.

Living arrangement is more than incidentally related to aged housing. The elderly are not being offered cheap age dense housing but cheap, age dense *apartment* housing. As our data indicate, almost all the elderly who apply for aged public housing are currently living in rental units. It becomes almost irrelevant to focus on the nonrenter's expressed interest in public housing, because in most cases, he simply will not leave his current dwelling.

For the class of renters without strong ties to family or property, their eagerness to relocate in aged housing is related to friendship patterns and affective response to their relationship (or perceived lack of relationship) with other people. In our sample, self-selection for aged public housing correlates best with Rosow's age density hypothesis. The desire for low-cost modern accommodations may be an important consideration for applicants to aged public housing, but does not seem to be the primary reason for applying. Rosow however, focuses too narrowly on age composition as primary to social integration. Certainly age plays an important role, but as our data suggest, age grouping alone does not relate to interest in age concentrated housing. Yet the fact remains that age segregation in association with social homogeneity rather than poor housing is the impetus which triggers age segregated housing interest.

The permanency of residency and the degree of security it offers figure strongly in an elderly person's decision to move to age segregated housing. The poor, aged homeowner has little desire to give up his home. For many, the home is all that is left of the past. It is filled with memories of friends, family, job,

345

and better times. For many widows, her house symbolizes her husband's hard work and effort, and she does not feel it is proper to sell his belongings and move out. Especially for the elderly person who finds he has to turn to the government for assistance, a home offers a familiar base on which to reestablish stability.

In a similar vein, living with one's children provides many older persons more security than does living alone. They have the privacy and additional living space that a house affords, plus they can maintain daily contact with their children. Aged housing cannot compete with family ties.

Unfortunately a house can isolate and trap some elderly owners. The lonely widow who remains in her house may desire aged housing but cannot muster the resources necessary to make the move. The neighborhood may change, her social contacts may dwindle, but she stays, tied to her house. Her social needs may be unfulfilled, but aged housing is not the solution she seeks. As Carp (1966, p. 170) so aptly noted, "from the individual's point of view it is no kindness in the long run to move him into a situation which makes demands he cannot or doesn't want to meet."

Lest it be misunderstood, it has not been the author's intent to dictate who should be accepted for aged housing projects, but merely an attempt to describe those individuals who have expressed interest in such housing. In reference to application of older persons for voluntary institutionalization, Brody and Gummer (1967, p. 243) have suggested, "Either decision to apply or not apply may be healthy and constructive, or may represent an inability to mobilize psychological and social resources to move toward an appropriate solution." Perhaps further research can further focus and refine such study as to better describe the circumstances under which an individual's interest becomes his motivation for application for age concentrated housing.

Notes

1. This investigation was supported by Research Grant No. 93-P-75040/9-02 from the Title IV Research and Development Grants Program Administration on Aging, Social and Rehabilitation Service, Department of Health, Education, and Welfare, Washington, D.C. 20201.

THE LIFE
OF
THE RETIRED
IN A TRAILER PARK*
G. C. Hoyt

Older persons have characteristically been the least mobile group in our population. Recently, however, two studies have focused attention on their increasing mobility. Hitt finds a substantial increase in the migration of older persons in the decade 1940-50 over the 1930-40 period[1] and states that in 1950 over one-fourth of Florida's old people were immigrants to the state. Smith, in a similar analysis of the problem, reports that the areas to which the largest numbers of older persons migrate are southern California, peninsular Florida, and the eastern part of Texas.[2] Aged persons, he finds, like to move to more desirable parts of the country upon retirement, and they may be expected to do so to an even greater extent in the future.

Why do these persons leave relatives, friends, and other associations in the home community? Several explanations have been offered.[3]

1. The transition from a rural to an urban-industrial society. The changing nature of the productive processes means that the worker is, characteristically, either fully employed or not employed at all. The growth of retirement systems frequently imposes an upper age limit on employment.

---

*G. C. Hoyt, "The Life of the Retired in a Trailer Park," *American Journal of Sociology* 59 (1954): 361-70. Reprinted by permission of The University of Chicago Press © University of Chicago.

2. The replacement (in the rural-urban transition) of extended family and kinship ties by the family consisting only of parents and their dependent children.

3. Loss of status and role of the older person in modern urban society.

4. The transition from the economic dependence of aged parents upon children to economic independence, brought about by the Social Security program and the growth of industrial pension systems.

Parsons sums up some aspects of the situation in the following terms:

> In view of the very great significance of occupational status and its psychological correlates, retirement leaves the older man in a peculiarly functionless situation, cut off from participation in the most important interests and activities of the society. . . . Not only status in the community but actual place of residence is to a very high degree a function of the specific job held. Retirement not only cuts the ties to the job but also greatly loosens those to the community of residence. Perhaps in no other society is there observable a phenomenon corresponding to the accumulation of retired elderly people in such areas as Florida and Southern California in the winter. It may be surmised that this structural isolation from kinship, occupational and community ties is the fundamental basis of the recent political agitation for help to the old. It is suggested that it is far less the financial hardship of the position of elderly people than their social isolation which makes old age a problem.[4]

In what way, then, can the older person with a small assured income expect to find a solution to these problems? One answer would be the development of communities composed entirely or mainly of retired persons, preferably located in a suitable climate, such as trailer parks. These mobile-home communities are now well established in peninsular Florida and enjoy a certain popularity among older, retired persons in that area. An outstanding example is the Bradenton Trailer Park, founded by the Bradenton Kiwanis Club in 1936 and now the oldest and largest trailer park in Florida.

348

The general question to be raised is: "To what extent, and in what sense, does this type of community meet the needs and interests of older, retired persons?" Specifically, this paper will deal with (1) the park and its residents; (2) the program of social activities and the extent of participation in it; (3) the values reported to have most significance; (4) the degree of preference for a retired community and the reasons given in support of the preference; and, finally, (5) the advantages and disadvantages of mobile-home living as reported by the residents.

The Park and Its Residents

At the time of its inception, the community consisted of 100 trailer spaces and has grown somewhat gradually, with the exception of the addition of large tracts in 1946 and 1947, to the present 1,093 spaces, all of which are rented each year. Rental charges for parking facilities vary from $3.00 per week in the newest section, through $3.50 in the main section, to $4.50 for front lots (which are nearest to recreation and shopping facilities). These rates are among the lowest to be found, especially among parks which provide recreational facilities. The rental also entitles each occupant family to full participation in the recreation program at no further cost, a basic amount of electrical service, water, laundry, and ironing facilities, which are located in the nine utility buildings dispersed throughout the community. All these provide lavatory and shower and toilet facilities, and four have laundry and ironing rooms.

Membership in the sponsoring organization is not a condition of residence in the park. Other than payment of the rental charge, the sole condition of residence is that no resident may be employed in Manatee County and the adjacent counties. This restriction, initially imposed to prevent the residents from competing on the local labor market, was lifted during the housing emergency of World War II. Reinforcement of it after the war came about as a consequence of pressure from the residents, not from the park management or city officials.

From the community of 1,093 dwelling units a simple areal sample was selected, and this is defined as having a male head of household who is not too ill to participate and who is in residence at some time during the period of the study. (The study was conducted from the latter part of November, 1952, to February, 1953.) A total of 194 interviews provides the basis for the tabulations which are reported in part in this paper.[5] The interviews with residents were supplemented by observation,

Table 1

Occupational Distribution

Occupation	No.	Percent
Self-employed		
Farm	48	24.7
Retail business, insurance, etc.	43	22.2
Professional	2	1.0
Non-self-employed		
Industrial and transportation workers	60	30.9
Executives, managers, and officials		
including army officers	16	8.2
Services, business, finance, civil service.	22	11.3
Teachers	2	1.0
No reply	1	0.5
Total	194	99.8

available data in the records of the park management, and informal interviews with leaders and other persons in the community.

The age range of males in the sample was from 41 to 90, with a median[6] age of 69 years. Current occupational status was found to be as follows: 73.7 percent are fully retired, 19.1 percent are quasi-retired (i.e., working only in reduced or seasonal capacity in life's work [11.4 percent] or different work [7.7 percent]), and 7.2 percent are not retired.

In view of the restriction on local employment, the proportion of quasi-retired and nonretired may seem surprisingly high, at least in view of the 6.7-month median annual residence. However, the lifetime occupational groupings show a large representation of those occupations in which gradual retirement is facilitated, such as farming. The occupational distribution is shown in Table 1.

Almost 12 percent of the group is in residence 10 months or more each year, with a median annual residence of 6.7 months. The number of years of continuous residence yields a median of 6.1 years, with 2.6 percent of the sample having been in residence each year since the inception of the park in 1936. A further indication of the stability of the population is the fact that 31 percent of the trailers have had some sort of permanent structure added which precludes moving them. Sometimes, a trailer coach has a cabana added which serves as a living room, a permanent roof to give protection against sun and rain, and a carport for the automobile. Many lots have, in the place of the above-mentioned structures, concrete patios and awnings. All these permanent installations are at the expense of the resident and, if he leaves, become the property of the park. Some residents state that they prefer to have no inclosed cabana; "it cuts down your association with your neighbors."

At present, 58.8 percent own the same home they owned during their working years, 10.3 percent have a different home, 24.7 percent have sold their homes, and 6.2 percent did not own their homes at retirement. Of the latter two groups, the house trailer is the only home at present.

The East North Central group of states was the place of residence at retirement of 73.7 percent, 17 percent coming from New England and the Middle Atlantic States, the remainder coming from widely distributed areas. Over 38 percent come from rural areas and towns up to 10,000 population, 34.5 percent from cities of from 10,000 to 100,000 population, and 27.3 percent from cities of over 100,000 population.

Median monthly income is $172.22 for individuals and families. The range of incomes is considerable, varying from less than $50 per month to over $10,000 per year. In 90.7 percent of the cases the family unit consists of two persons, 4.1 percent have three persons, and 5.2 percent are males living alone.

Activities and Participation

At and around the main entrance of the park is found the focal point of activity. Here is located the park office, shuffleboard and horseshoe courts, post office, and the recreation hall, in which a regular calendar of events is held. The calendar of events in the recreation hall is shown below.

Although each of the activities is technically sponsored and operated by the management of the park, the conduct of it is relatively autonomous. In the first place, leadership in all cases comes from the residents of the community. Second, each activity has been carried on among essentially the same group of participants long enough for it to have become a part of the informal way of life of the community and thus to require a minimum of organization and direction.

Sunday:	Church Service
	Family Hour
Monday:	Bingo
Tuesday:	Square dance lessons and practice
	Rebekahs
	Star Club
	Dance (orchestra)
Wednesday.	Men's Bible Class
	Ladies' Bible Class
	Movie
Thursday:	Hobby Club
	Card Party
	Square Dance (recordings)
Friday:	Choir practice
	Dance (orchestra)
Saturday:	Family Hour practice
	Bingo

Finally, most, if not all, of these activities have become traditional, and the roles of the participants have become an integral part of the individual's expectations. Some practices have grown up in a genuinely spontaneous fashion, having originated among the residents, the management of the park playing no role whatever in the early stages. The best illustration is to be found in the history of the "Family Hour," a Sunday-evening institution which began with a small group of neighbors gathered under the trailer awning of Mrs. L., the widow of a minister.

The group sang a few of the old-fashioned hymns and "had such a good time we decided to do it again the next week." It grew steadily more popular; people brought camp chairs from other parts of the park, until it overflowed to the street and several adjoining lots. The use of the recreation hall on Sunday evenings was readily permitted. This became a regular event, with other elements added from time to time, such as storytelling, playing musical instruments, vocal solos, travelogues, concerts by outside groups, skits, etc. At the time of the study, Family Hour was about seven years old. Nonetheless, it has never lost its quasi-religious character, as is illustrated by the objections raised following the program at which a guest performed a tap dance.

Mrs. L., the leader of the program, says that "we try to keep it just like a large family entertaining itself on a Sunday evening. The mistakes [in the performance of an individual] don't matter. A poor performance is still a beginning." This refers to the attempt to bring out those who have no experience in entertaining. "It gives them a feeling of importance, and everyone, regardless of age, wants to feel needed." A conscious attempt is made to keep out elements of theatricalism or professionalism, in part to prevent inhibiting those who have no prior experience.

Mrs. L. also tries to interest persons, especially those who have been recently widowed, in creative work. Approximately fifty women from the park engage in ceramics or oil painting each week at a hobby workshop in the town.[7]

Several aspects of the Family Hour suggest a rural background. This may be attributable primarily to the high representation of former rural occupations and residence and to a lesser extent to the age distribution. The importance of the Family Hour in the lives of the residents is attested in part by the large attendance. The not infrequent statement, "This is just like one family here [in the park]," may derive in part from the name and nature of the Family Hour.

In addition, there is a men's and ladies' card room in the same building, and these are open from 8:00 A.M. until 10:00 P.M. daily. Outdoor activities are provided for by eight horseshoe pits and nineteen shuffleboard courts. Shuffleboard, which is popular at virtually every trailer park in Florida, is perhaps the main focus of recreation and social contact. Small grandstands surrounding the courts provide a gathering place for nonplaying as well as playing residents of the community from 8:00 A.M. until 10:00 P.M. (artificial lighting is used after dark), and usually there are two tournaments per week. Often there are one "pot-luck" elimination, in which one's partner is chosen by chance, and one team competition, ususally against a visiting team from another trailer park in the vicinity.

Neighborhood "pot-luck" dinners are frequent affairs, especially in celebration of holidays, birthdays, and wedding anniversaries. At these the main dish is either financed out of contributions by all or provided by the host, other dishes being contributed and prepared by other participants. The dinner is held out of doors on the host's patio, with tables, chairs, tablecloths, and utensils contributed by the group.

Table 2 shows the degree of participation in the recreational activities available in the park, with the number of mentions received by each activity and the percentage of respondents mentioning it in reply to the question, "Which of the recreational activities here in the park do you take part in?" Probing was used rather than a check list.

In all, 61 percent of the men and 52 percent of the women take part in at least one activity that calls for active participation, such as dancing, shuffleboard, etc. Only 17 percent of the men and 33 percent of the women participate in roles that are no more than passive (bingo, cards, etc.), and 16 percent of the men and 10 percent of the women play roles of spectator only. The median number of activities participated in by families is four. Since these are sometimes daily events, or at least weekly, the association of these retired persons is higher than would be true in the usual work-oriented community.

However, participation in more formal voluntary associations is a little different. In the former home community 72 percent of the respondents attended meetings of voluntary associations. The mean monthly attendance for this group was 3.3 meetings. After immigration, however, only 8 percent attended such meetings, and the mean monthly attendance for this 8 percent is only 1.6. The above results refer to all voluntary associations of a social, business, or fraternal nature except church. In the original home community 69 percent of the respondents reported an average church attendance of 3.4 times per month; after immigration only 59 percent attended an average of 3.6 times per month. Protestant church services are held in the recreation hall, with ministers from various denominations in the city rotating in the services. The very real decrease in participation in voluntary associations outside the trailer park suggests that (*a*) the trailer park is not well integrated with the larger community or city, and/or (*b*) the trailer park is socially self-contained. Of course, one expects a certain decrease in partici-

Table 2

Activities Participated in by Resident Families by Number of Activities Mentioned and by Percentage of 186* Men Mentioning Each Activity

Activity	No. of Mentions	Percent of Persons Mentioning
Family Hour.	123	66.1
Shuffleboard.	111	59.7
Cards	103	55.4
Movies	91	48.9
Dancing	82	44.1
Bingo.	54	29.0
Bible Class	28	15.0
Women's Hobby Club	27	14.5
Informal visiting.	14	7.5
Neighborhood "pot-lucks".	13	7.0
Horseshoes.	10	5.4
Star Club (women)	9	4.8
Rebekahs (women)	1	0.5
Park Band	1	0.5
None	3	1.6
Total activites mentioned	667	. . . .

* Eight men did not reply to questions.

pation in work- and business-oriented groups such as unions or the Rotary Club after retirement.

Over 82 percent of the residents interviewed reported that they got all or most of their recreation within the park. Among those who do go outside the most frequent activities are fishing, pot-luck picnics, and trips to the beach, and these are commonly done in groups composed of park residents.

The Significant Values of Park Living

Each respondent was asked, "What part of the life here appeals to you the most?" The question was left unstructured; "here" was never specified by the interviewer as referring to either Florida or the trailer park. The replies to this question are classified in Table 3.

A definite majority relate to social aspects of the way of life *within* the trailer park rather than to the climate or other conditions usually thought of as primary factors in the immigration

---

Table 3

Part of Life With Most Appeal to Men in the Park
by Number and Percentage of Men Giving Each Answer

Category	Number	Percent
Sociability; association	102	55.4
Free, carefree life	10	5.4
People have lot in common	3	1.6
Park activities	28	15.2
Outside activities (fishing)	10	5.4
Climate	27	14.8
Other and don't know	4	2.2
Total	184*	100.0

* Ten persons did not reply to question.

---

of older people. Each respondent had been asked (in a section on factors affecting immigration, to be reported in a separate paper) the importance of climate. Climate was reported as being of first importance in immigration by 49.5 percent, of second importance by 37.6 percent, a factor by 5.7 percent, and not a factor by only 6.7 percent. Thus climate shows quite a discrepancy from its apparent role *after* migration.[8] This comparison illustrates in another way the comment of one man who said, "Well, I came here for the climate, but I stay for the sociability. The sociability is the big thing here." The term "sociability" is frequently employed by residents in conversation in describing the park to others. Cases are often cited, when a resident describes the advantages of the park to an outsider, of persons who "came down here to this park and liked Florida so well that they decided to build a home here. They got moved in and before long they are hanging around down at the shuffleboard. Before you know it they sell their house and come right back in the park. They miss the sociability. Once you get used to it here, it gets pretty lonesome in town." At least six couples are reported as examples.

Preference for Retired Community Living

A total of 155 (87.6 percent) persons stated that they preferred to "live in a community such as this where everyone is retired" rather than in another in which most people are working. Seven persons (3.9 percent) preferred a working community, and 15 (8.5 percent) were undecided of a total of 177 persons who answered the question. Table 4 shows all reasons cited and the chief reason cited by those who prefer the retired community.

The category of "Less disturbance" refers both to the absence of children and also to persons going to work. Categories referring to the mutuality of residents are more commonly mentioned than was true in Table 3. "We are all in the same boat here. A retired person just doesn't fit in a working community, but here everybody cooperates to have a good time," is a statement which typifies this category.

Local neighborhood groups respond quickly to the illness of another resident, helping with the care of the sick person if necessary and, particularly, taking over the household and cooking chores of a sick woman. The wife of one of the persons in the sample was ill and during the interview, which lasted about an hour and a quarter, five women from the neighborhood stopped in to assist; one took care of the laundry, one did the day's shopping, one cleaned the trailer, and two brought cooked dishes. The residents often tell of an incident of a few years ago as an illustration of mutual aid. A couple on a limited income had spent their cash reserves to purchase a new trailer and construct a cabana. It was destroyed by fire. Other residents contributed

357

Table 4

All Reasons and Chief Reason for Preference for Retired Community by Number of Times Mentioned and by Percentage Mentioned

All Reasons	No.	Percent	Chief Reason	No.	Percent
Sociability or association.	72	46.4	Association	74	48.4
More or better activities	44	28.4			
Not so lonesome	23	14.8			
Don't feel out of place	23	14.8			
All same age	12	7.7	Mutuality	65	42.5
Same status and interests.	66	42.6			
Mutual aid	10	6.4			
Less disturbance.	29	18.7	Less disturbance.	14	9.2
Other	1	0.6			
No reason given	2	1.3			
Total	155	. . . .	Total	153	100.1

cash or their labor and rebuilt the entire unit and turned over a cash balance so that the couple could replace their clothing.

Of the seven who preferred a working community, two said that they would rather work themselves, four like young people around, and one found that "the high number of deaths and illnesses are depressing here."

Advantages of Mobile-Home Living

Table 5 shows the advantages of mobile-home living for retired people as reported by 186 persons, with the category into which the chief advantage fell.

The frequent mention of sociability and activities, although these are not necessary concomitants of mobile-home living in general, suggests that to most residents "living in Florida," "living in a trailer," and "living in this community" are so closely associated that distinctions are difficult to make. Thus, when asked about the advantages of mobile-home living for retired persons, "We are all in the same boat here," was a not uncommon reply.

Only 49 persons reported any disadvantages, and 6 of these replies—that trailers were unsatisfactory when raising children—do not apply to their use by retired couples. Size was the most frequent disadvantage (to 12 persons), while others referred to the lack of toilet and bath facilities in many trailers and their high rate of depreciation. Eleven persons stated that "a trailer is no place to be sick," which is interesting in that in cases where residents were actually ill it was contended that caring for one's needs was far easier owing to the convenience and compactness of the trailer. Several persons stated that, while there were no specific disadvantages in trailer living, they would not want it the year round or as a permanent home.

In the analysis of these data cross-tabulations were made to determine the extent and nature of any association between several variables and the stated preferences and advantages. Table 6 shows the frequencies when preference for a retired community is tabulated according to present retirement status.

Table 5

All Advantages and Chief Advantage of Mobile-Home Living Named by 186 Respondents*
by Number Mentioned and by Percentage Mentioned

All Advantages	No.	Percent	Chief Advantage	No.	Percent
Economy.	105	56.4	Economy.	46	24.7
Sociability and mutuality	112	60.2	Sociability and activities	97	52.2
Activities.	43	23.1	Less work	25	13.4
Less-work convenience	96	51.6			
Mobility	29	15.6	Mobility and less worry	18	9.7
Free, independent, no worries.	18	9.7			
Good climate	17	9.1			
Separate from children	1	0.5			
Total	421	. . . .	Total	186	100.0

* Seven persons did not reply, and one had just moved in to "try it out."

While the association obtained would not meet the arbitrary .05 level of confidence if the data in the table were corrected for the small numbers involved, the association is nonetheless observable and in the expected direction. Analysis of the preference for a community of the retired by former occupation shows no association.

Table 6 *

Preference for a Retired Community by Present Retirement Status of 177 Men

Preference	Retirement Status		Total
	Not Retired and Quasiretired	Retired	
Retired community.	28	127	155
Undecided and other community	8	14	22
Total	36	141	177

* $X^2 = 3.84$; $n = 1$; $p = .05$; $T = .15$. The formula used in computing T (Tschuprow's coefficient) is:

$$T^2 = \frac{X^2}{N \sqrt{(s-1)(t-1)}}$$

(See G. U. Yule and M. G. Kendall, *An Introduction to the Theory of Statistics* [London: Charles Griffin & Co., 1947], pp. 70–76.)

A tendency is shown for the fully retired to give the mutuality of residents and the lack of disturbance, rather than sociability, as their reason for preferring a community of the retired; the converse being true, of course, for the nonretired and quasiretired. The difference, however, is not statistically significant in this case. However, in a similar analysis of the chief reason for preference by a major occupational group a significant association is found to exist (Table 7).

The data in Table 7 show a very pronounced tendency for persons who were formerly self-employed to give sociability as their reason for preferring a retired community, while those who were not self-employed prefer to live in a community of

361

retired persons because of the mutuality and the lack of disturbance. This relationship also holds when present retirement status is held constant. Such a relationship may be thought to indicate a feeling of different status following upon retirement of the urban-industrial employee, in contrast to the self-employed person (since we know that the self-employed group consists largely of farmers and small businessmen). However, no similar association is found when the chief reasons for the preference are tabulated according to rural-urban residence at retirement or when the tabulation is made according to income.

Table 7*

Reason for Preference of a Retired Community
by Major Occupational Group of 152 Men

Occupational Group	Reason for Preference			Total
	Sociability	Mutuality	Less Disturbance	
Self-employed	47	25	1	73
Non-self-employed	27	39	13	79
Total	74	64	14	152

* X^2 = 18.494; n = 2; p = .001; T = .25.

Both lower-income groups and those who are fully retired manifest some tendency to give economy as an advantage of mobile-home living, but in neither case does the tendency approach the significant level. Contrary to expectations, there is no tendency for lower-income groups to spend more months each year in residence in the park, when the tabulation is made for the fully retired group only.

In summary, then, the community manifests, first of all, a well-developed and diversified activity program in which residents take part to a relatively high degree. When they assess this way of life and the most important values which it holds for them (Table 3), a high proportion refer to "sociability" and association. The overwhelming proportion who prefer to live in a community composed exclusively of retired and quasi-retired persons and their reasons for such a preference also point to the value which status feelings and association have for them. With respect to mobile-home living itself, a strong tendency was noticeable for people to give such values as sociability as an advantage, and certainly for this group the advantages outweighed the disadvantages.

To a certain extent, an increase in association may be expected because of certain physical aspects of trailer-coach living and trailer parks in general. In a favorable climate especially, the limited size of the dwelling unit may lead to increased time being spent out of doors, and this fact, when taken in conjunction with the close physical proximity of the dwelling units and the use of central laundry and lavatory facilities, gives rise to increased social contact and, in time, to informal associations of a more intimate nature.

For the most part our interest in this community stems more from the fact that at least partial retirement is a condition of residence than from the incidental fact that it is a trailer park. Since all residents are greatly interested in recreation and leisure pursuits, these activities tend to be more highly sanctioned than would be likely to be the case in a community in which the predominant interests centered around economic activity. To a certain extent, however, preoccupation with leisure activities such as bingo and dancing may be regarded by outsiders as adolescent and unbecoming to persons in this age group. It reflects the different code of conduct which develops in such a self-contained community the needs and interests of whose residents are not fully shared outside the community.

Status differences based upon occupational roles or upon the competence with which these roles were performed are not prominent. There is, of course, a certain degree of carryover of status from former life,[9] but status within this social group is at least equally dependent upon one's "being a good sport," or an exceptionally good dancer or shuffleboard player, or perhaps from just being very friendly. Perhaps the important thing is that there are no sharp feelings of status—the residents are likely to assert that there are no status differences, even with respect to income differences. Of course, this is partly true, since the rental entitles each resident to full participation in the recreation program, and relatively few persons seek recreation other than fishing outside the community.[10]

It is particularly interesting to note that, with respect to housing for the aged, a community of this type, although mobile with single residences privately owned, has certain elements in common with institutions. These are the similarity of age and employment status, the central facilities including the organized recreation, the interest in leisure pursuits, and, to a lesser extent, if not similar financial status among the residents, at least similar patterns of spending.

Personal adjustment in retirement and old age is facilitated by the attitudes and institutional practices of mobile-home communities. Social roles which are congruent with the needs and interests of the retired person are sanctioned. The primary interests center around leisure and recreation. Therefore a further impetus may be provided to the migration and ultimate relocation of older persons. Since the advantage of mobility is seldom actually utilized by the occupants of these mobile homes, the future growth of such retired communities in warm er climates might not be confined to the growth of new mobile home communities. The implementation of a central recreation program is, of course, greatly facilitated by the nature of the trailer park, but further research is needed to determine the extent to which such facilities are practicable in a small cottage community. However, the potential mobility of the trailer home provides a sense of freedom, important to many persons, which cannot be provided in the cottage community.

Notes

1. H. L. Hitt, "The Role of Migration in Population Change among the Aged." Paper presented at the meeting of the American Sociological Society, Atlantic City, September 1952.

2. T. Lynn Smith, "The Migration of the Aged," in *Problems of America's Aging Population,* ed. T. Lynn Smith ("Southern Conference on Gerontology," Vol. I [Gainesville: University of Florida Press, 1951]), pp. 15-28.

3. See, e.g., W. E. Moore, "The Aged in Industrial Societies," in Derber (ed.), *The Aged and Society* (Champaign, Ill.: Industrial Relations Research Association, 1950), pp. 24–39; T. Lynn Smith, "The Aged in Rural Society," *ibid.*, pp. 40–53; and E. W. Burgess, "Personal and Social Adjustment in Old Age," *ibid.*, pp. 138–56.

4. Talcott Parsons, *Essays in Sociological Theory, Pure and Applied* (Glencoe, Ill.: Free Press, 1949), p. 231.

5. From an initial selection of 256 dwelling units which presumably are occupied by a family unit having a male head of household, 7 yielded information which was too scant for tabulation, 13 were refusals; in 16 cases the respondent could not be contacted, 4 dwelling units were not occupied during the period of the study, 10 male heads were too ill to participate, and 12 dwelling units were occupied by single women or widows who were not registered as such in the park records. There are approximately 250 such dwelling units which are occupied by women only (either singly or in pairs). These women have either continued to live in the trailer after the death of their husbands or, in some cases, have adopted this way of life after becoming widowed. Unfortunately, time did not permit of a systematic investigation of this decidedly significant group.

6. The medians given throughout this study are based upon grouped data.

7. It may be that the relative importance of cultural and creative activities as a part of the recreation program will increase in the future. The three activities in the park which are of this basic nature, the Family Hour, the Hobby Club, and the group referred to above all originated from among the residents rather than from the park management. The Hobby Club may be of more significance than Table 2 indicates; handicrafts and other articles produced as hobbies are offered for sale by the makers at two yearly sales held in the recreation hall in the fall and in the spring. In March 1953, 125 persons entered such articles. In some cases the return is a welcome supplement to the retirement income, but articles are also sold primarily as testimony to their worth and the skill of the maker.

8. A negative association is found to exist between climate as a factor in migration and climate as the most appealing factor at present. However, since the expected frequency in some cells of the cross tabulation is so low, X^2 may not be computed. A negative association is also found between health as a factor in migration and the mention of climate at present. In this case the association is not significant, however.

9. This is especially noticeable in the case of professional persons who are, even though retired, still referred to as "Doctor," "Professor," or "Reverend," and as such are held up as proof of "the nice class of people that we have here in this park." The retired industrial executive or banker

is, by contrast, simply "Mr.," and his past position and prestige in the occupational hierarchy are, accordingly, less readily communicable.

10. For a report on other mobile groups and their community organization and the importance of status, see W. F. Whyte, Jr., "The Transients," nos. I-IV, *Fortune,* Vol. XLVII, nos. 5 (May 1953) and 6 (June 1953), and Vol. XLVIII, nos. 1 (July 1953) and 2 (August 1953).

COMMUNAL
LIFE STYLES
FOR THE OLD*
Arlie Russell Hochschild

The 43 residents of Merrill Court (a small apartment building
near the shore of San Francisco Bay), 37 of them women, mainly conservative, fundamentalist widows from the Midwest and
Southwest, don't seem likely candidates for "communal living"
and "alternatives to the nuclear family." Nonetheless, their
community has numerous communal aspects. Without their
"old-agers commune" these 60-, 70-, and 80-year-olds would
more than likely be experiencing the disengagement from life
that most students of aging have considered biologically based
and therefore inevitable.

The aged individual often has fewer and fewer ties to the
outside world, and those which he or she does retain are characterized by less emotional investment than in younger years. This
case study, however, presents evidence that disengagement may
be situational—that how an individual ages depends largely on
his social milieu, and that socially isolated older people may disengage but that older people supported by a community of appropriate peers do not.

Rural Ways in Urban Settings

Merrill Court is a strange mixture of old and new, of a vanishing Oakie culture and a new blue-collar life style, of rural

* Arlie Russell Hochschild, "Communal Life-Styles for the Old." Published by permission of Transaction, Inc., from *Society* 10, no. 5 (July/August 1973). Copyright
© 1973, by Transaction, Inc.

ways in urban settings, of small-town community in mass society, of people oriented toward the young in an age-separated subculture. These internal immigrants to the working-class neighborhoods of West Coast cities and suburbs perceive their new environment through rural and small-town eyes. One woman who had gone shopping at a department store observed "all those lovely dresses, all stacked like cordwood." A favorite saying when one was about to retire was, "Guess I'll go to bed with the chickens tonight." They would give directions to the new hamburger joint or hobby shop by describing its relationship to a small stream or big tree. What remained of the old custom of a funeral wake took place at a new funeral parlor with neon signs and printed notices.

The communal life which developed in Merrill Court may have had nothing to do with rural ways in an urban setting. Had the widows stayed on the farms and in the small towns they came from, they might have been active in community life there. Those who had been involved in community life before remained active and, with the exception of a few, those who previously had not, became active.

For whatever reason, the widows built themselves an order out of ambiguity, a set of obligations to the outside and to one another where few had existed before. It is possible to relax in old age, to consider one's social debts paid, and to feel that constraints that do not weigh on the far side of the grave should not weigh on the near side either. But in Merrill Court, the watchfulness of social life, the Protestant stress on industry, thrift, and activity added up to an ethos of keeping one's "boots on," not simply as individuals but as a community.

Forming the Community

"There wasn't nothin' before we got the coffee machine. I mean we didn't share nothin' before Mrs. Bitford's daughter brought over the machine and we sort of had our first occasion, you might say."

There were about six people at the first gathering around the coffee machine in the recreation room. As people came downstairs from their apartments to fetch their mail, they looked into the recreation room, found a cluster of people sitting down drinking coffee, and some joined in. A few weeks later the recreation director "joined in" for the morning coffee and, as she tells it, the community had its start at this point.

Half a year later Merrill Court was a beehive of activity: meetings of a service club; bowling; morning workshop; Bible study classes twice a week; other classes with frequently changing subjects; monthly birthday parties; holiday parties; and visits to four nearby nursing homes. Members donated cakes, pies, and soft drinks to bring to the nursing home, and a five-piece band, including a washtub bass, played for the "old folks" there. The band also entertained at a nearby recreation center for a group of Vietnam veterans. During afternoon band practice, the women sewed and embroidered pillow cases, aprons, and yarn dolls. They made wastebaskets out of discarded paper towel rolls, wove rugs from strips of old Wonder Bread wrappers, and Easter hats out of old Clorox bottles, all to be sold at the annual bazaar. They made placemats to be used at the nursing home, totebags to be donated to "our boys in Vietnam," Christmas cards to be cut out for the Hillcrest Junior Women's Club, rag dolls to be sent to the orphanage, place cards to be written out for the bowling league banquet, recipes to be written out for the recipe book that was to go on sale next month, and thank you and condolence cards.

Social Patterns

The social arrangements that took root early in the history of Merrill Court later assumed a life of their own. They were designed, as if on purpose, to assure an "on-going" community. If we were to visually diagram one community, it would look like a social circle on which there are centripedal and centrifugal pressures. The formal role system, centered in the circle, pulled people toward it by giving them work and rewards, and this process went on mainly "downstairs," in the recreation room. At the same time, informal loyalty networks fluctuated toward and away from the circle. They became clear mainly "upstairs," where the apartments were located. Relatives and outsiders pulled the individual away from the circle downstairs and network upstairs although they were occasionally pulled inside both.

Downstairs

Both work and play were somebody's responsibility to organize. The Merrill Court Service Club, to which most of the residents and a half-dozen nonresidents belonged, set up committees and chairmanships that split the jobs many ways. There was a group of permanent elected officials: the president, vice-president, treasurer, secretary and birthday chairman, in addition to the recreation director. Each activity also had a chairman, and each chairman was in charge of a group of volunteers. Some officers were rotated during the year. Only four club members did not chair some activity between 1965 and 1968; and at any time about a third were in charge of something.

Friendship Networks

Shadowing the formal circle was an informal network of friendships that formed over a cup of coffee in the upstairs apartments. The physical appearance of the apartments told something about the network. Inside, each apartment had a living room, kitchen, bedroom, and porch. The apartments were unfurnished when the women moved in and as one remarked, "We fixed 'em up just the way we wanted. I got this new lamp over to Sears, and my daughter and I bought these new scatter rugs. Felt just like a new bride."

For the most part, the apartments were furnished in a remarkably similar way. Many had American flag stickers outside their doors. Inside, each had a large couch with a floral design, which sometimes doubled as a hide-a-bed where a grandchild might sleep for a weekend. Often a chair, a clock, or picture came from the old home and provided a material link to the past. Most had large stuffed chairs, bowls of homemade artificial flowers, a Bible, and porcelain knickknacks neatly arranged on

370

a table. (When the group was invited to my own apartment for tea, one woman suggested sympathetically that we "had not quite moved in yet" because the apartment seemed bare by comparison.) By the window were potted plants, often grown from a neighbor's slip. A plant might be identified as "Abbie's ivy" or "Ernestine's African violet."

Photographs, usually out of date, of pink-cheeked children and grandchildren decorated the walls. Less frequently there was a photo of a deceased husband and less frequently still, a photo of a parent. On the livingroom table or nearby there was usually a photograph album containing pictures of relatives and pictures of the woman herself on a recent visit "back east." Many of the photographs in the album were arranged in the same way. Pictures of children came first and, of those, children with the most children appeared first; and childless children at the end.

The refrigerator almost always told a social story. One contained homemade butter made by the cousin of a woman on the second floor; berry jam made by the woman three doors down; corn bought downstairs in the recreation room, brought in by someone's son who worked in a corn-canning factory; homemade Swedish rolls to be given to a daughter when she came to visit; two dozen eggs to be used in cooking, most of which would be given away; as well as bread and fruit, more than enough for one person. Most of the women had once cooked for large families, and Emma, who raised eight children back in Oklahoma, habitually baked about eight times as much corn bread as she could eat. She made the rounds of apartments on her floor distributing the extra bread. The others who also cooked in quantities reciprocated, also gratuitously, with other kinds of food. It was an informal division of labor although no one thought of it that way.

Most neighbors were also friends, and friendships, as well as information about them, were mainly confined to each floor. All but four had their *best* friends on the same floor and only a few had a next-best friend on another floor. The more one had friends outside the building, the more one had friends on other floors within the building. The wider one's social radius outside the building, the wider it was inside the building as well.

371

Neighboring

Apart from the gratification of friendship, neighboring did a number of things for the community. It was a way of relaying information or misinformation about others. Often the information relayed upstairs influenced social arrangements downstairs. For example, according to one widow,

> The Bitfords had a tiff with Irma upstairs here, and a lot of tales went around. They weren't true, not a one, about Irma, but then people didn't come downstairs as much. Mattie used to come down, and Marie and Mr. Ball and they don't so much now, only once and again, because of Irma being there. All on account of that tiff.

Often people seated themselves downstairs as they were situated upstairs, neighbor and friend next to neighbor and friend, and a disagreement upstairs filtered downstairs. For example, when opinion was divided and feelings ran high on the issue of whether to store the club's $900 in a cigar box under the treasurer's bed or in the bank, the gossip, formerly confined to upstairs, invaded the public arena downstairs.

Relaying information this way meant that without directly asking, people knew a lot about one another. It was safe to assume that what you did was known about by at least one network of neighbors and their friends. Even the one social isolate on the third floor, Velma, was known about, and her comings and goings were talked about and judged. Talk about other people was a means of social control and it operated, as it does elsewhere, through parables; what was told of another was a message to one's self.

Not all social control was verbal. Since all apartment livingrooms faced out on a common walkway that led to a central elevator, each tenant could be seen coming and going; and by how he or she was dressed, one could accurately guess his or her activities. Since each resident knew the visiting habits of her neighbors, anything unusual was immediately spotted. One day when I was knocking on the door of a resident, her neighbor came out:

372

I don't know where she is, it couldn't be the doctor's, she goes to the doctor's on Tuesdays; it couldn't be shopping, she shopped yesterday with her daughter. I don't think she's downstairs, she says she's worked enough today. Maybe she's visiting Abbie. They neighbor a lot. Try the second floor.

Neighboring is also a way to detect sickness or death. As Ernestine related, "This morning I look to see if Judson's curtains were open. That's how we do on this floor, when we get up we open our curtains just a bit, so others walking by outside know that everything's all right. And if the curtains aren't drawn by mid-morning, we knock to see." Mattie perpetually refused to open her curtains in the morning and kept them close to the wall by placing potted plants against them so that "a man won't get in." This excluded her from the checking-up system and disconcerted the other residents.

The widows in good health took it upon themselves to care for one or two in poor health. Delia saw after Grandma Goodman who was not well enough to go down and get her mail and shop, and Ernestine helped Little Floyd and Mrs. Blackwell who could not see well enough to cook their own meals. Irma took care of Mr. Cooper and she called his son when Mr. Cooper "took sick." Even those who had not adopted someone to help often looked after a neighbor's potted plants while they were visiting kin, lent kitchen utensils and took phone messages. One woman wrote letters for those who "wrote a poor hand."

Some of the caretaking was reciprocal, but most was not. Three people helped take care of Little Floyd, but since he was blind he could do little in return. Delia fixed his meals, Ernestine laundered his clothes, and Irma shopped for his food. When Little Floyd died fairly suddenly, he was missed perhaps more than others who died during those three years, especially by his caretakers. Ernestine remarked sadly, "I liked helping out the poor old fella. He would appreciate the tiniest thing. And never a complaint."

Sometimes people paid one another for favors. For example, Freda took in sewing for a small sum. When she was paid for lining a coat, she normally mentioned the purpose for which the money would be spent (for example, bus fare for a visit to relatives in Montana), perhaps to reduce the commercial aspect of the exchange. Delia was paid by the Housing Authority for cleaning and cooking for Grandma Goodman, a disabled woman on her floor; and as she repeatedly mentioned to Grandma Goodman, she spent the money on high school class rings for her three grandchildren. In one case, the Housing Authority paid a granddaughter for helping her grandmother with housework. In another case, a disabled woman paid for domestic help from her social security checks.

The "Poor Dear" Hierarchy

Within the formal social circle there was a status hierarchy based on the distribution of honor, particularly through holding offices in the service club. Additionally, there was a parallel informal status hierarchy based on the distribution of luck. "Luck" as the residents defined it is not entirely luck. Health and life expectancy, for example, are often considered "luck," but an upper-class person can expect to live ten years longer than a lower-class person. The widows of Merrill Court, however, were drawn from the same social class and they saw the differences among themselves as matters of luck.

She who had good health won honor. She who lost the fewest loved ones through death won honor, and she who was close to her children won honor. Those who fell short of any of these criteria were often referred to as "poor dears."

The "poor dear" system operated like a set of valves through which a sense of superiority ran in only one direction. Someone who was a "poor dear" in the eyes of another seldom called that other person a "poor dear" in return. Rather, the "poor dear" would turn to someone less fortunate, perhaps to buttress a sense of her own achieved or ascribed superiority. Thus, the hierarchy honored residents at the top and pitied "poor dears" at the bottom, creating a number of informally recognized status distinctions among those who, in the eyes of the outside society, were social equals.

The distinctions made by residents of Merrill Court are only part of a larger old-age status hierarchy based on things other than luck. At the monthly meetings of the countywide Senior Citizens Forum, to which Merrill Court sent two representatives, the term "poor dear" often arose with reference to old people. It was "we senior citizens who are politically involved versus those 'poor dears' who are active in recreation." Those active in recreation, however, did not accept a subordinate position relative to the politically active. On the other hand, they did not refer to the political activists as "poor dears." Within the politically active group there were those who espoused general causes, related only to old age, such as raising social security benefits or improving medical benefits. Those in politics and recreation referred to the passive card players and newspaper readers as "poor dears." Uninvolved old people in good health referred to those in poor health as "poor dears," and those in poor health but living in independent housing referred to those in nursing homes as "poor dears." Within the nursing home there was a distinction between those who were ambulatory and those who were not. Among those who were not ambulatory there was a distinction between those who could enjoy food and those who could not. Almost everyone, it seemed, had a "poor dear."

At Merrill Court, the main distinction was between people like themselves and people in nursing homes. Returning from one of the monthly trips to a nearby nursing home, one resident commented:

> There was an old woman in a wheelchair there with a dolly in her arms. I leaned over to look at the dolly. I didn't touch it, well, maybe I just brushed it. She snatched it away, and said "Don't take my dolly." They're pathetic, some of them, the poor dears.

Even within the building those who were in poor health, were alienated from their children, or were aging rapidly were considered "poor dears." It was lucky to be young and unlucky to be old. There was more than a 20-year age span between the youngest and oldest in the community. When one of the younger women, Delia, age 69, was drinking coffee with Grandma Goodman, age 79, they compared ages. Grandma Goodman dwelt on the subject and finished the conversation by citing the case of Mrs. Blackwell, who was 89 and still in reasonably good health. Another remarked about her 70th birthday:

> I just couldn't imagine myself being 70. Seventy is old! That's what Daisy said too. She's 80 you know. It was her 70th that got her. No one likes to be put aside, you know. Laid away. Put on the shelf you might say. No sir.

She had an ailment that prevented her from bowling or lifting her flower pots, but she compared her health to that of Daisy, and found her own health a source of luck.

Old people compare themselves not to the young but to other old people. Often the residents referred to the aged back in Oklahoma, Texas, and Arkansas with pity in their voices:

> Back in Oklahoma, why they toss the old people away like old shoes. My old friends was all livin' together in one part of town and they hardly budged the whole day. Just sat out on their porch and chewed the fat. Sometimes they didn't even do that. Mostly they didn't have no nice housing, and nothin' social was goin' on. People here don't know what luck they've fallen into.

They also compared their lot to that of other older people in the area. As one resident said:

> Some of my friends live in La Casa [another housing project]. I suppose because they have to, you know. And I tried to get them to come bowling with me, but they wouldn't have a thing to do with it. "Those senior citizens, that's old folks stuff." Wouldn't have a thing to do with it. I tried to tell them we was pretty spry, but they wouldn't listen. They just go their own way. They don't think we have fun.

On the whole, the widows disassociated themselves from the status of "old person," and accepted its "minority" characteristics. The "poor dears" in the nursing home were often referred to as childlike: "They are easily hurt, you know. They get upset at the slightest thing and they like things to be the way they've always been. Just like kids." Occasionally, a widow would talk

about Merrill Court itself in this vein, presumably excluding herself: "We're just like a bunch of kids here sometimes. All the
sparring that goes on, even with church folk. And people get so
hurt, so touchy. You'd think we were babies sometimes."

If the widows accepted the stereotypes of old age, they did
not add the "poor dear" when referring to themselves. But
younger outsiders did. To the junior employees in the Recreation and Parks Department, the young doctors who treated
them at the county hospital, the middle-aged welfare workers
and the young bank tellers, the residents of Merrill Court, and
old people like them, were "poor dears."

Perhaps in old age there is a premium on finishing life off
with the feeling of being a "have." But during old age, one also
occupies a low social position. The way the old look for luck
differences among themselves reflects the pattern found at the
bottom of other social, racial, and gender hierarchies. To find
oneself lucky within an ill-fated category is to gain the semblance
of high status when society withholds it from others in the category. The way old people feel above and condescend to other
old people may be linked to the fact that the young feel above
and condescend to them. The luck hierarchy does not stop with
the old.

The Sibling Bond

There were rivalries and differences in Merrill Court, but
neither alienation nor isolation. A club member who stayed up
in her apartment during club meetings more often did it out of
spite than indifference. More obvious were the many small,
quiet favors, keeping an eye out for a friend and sharing a good
laugh.

There was something special about this community, not so
much because it was an old-age subculture, but because the subculture was founded on a particular kind of relationship—the
sibling bond. Most residents of Merrill Court are social siblings.
The custom of exchanging cups of coffee, lunches, potted
plants, and curtain checking suggest reciprocity. Upstairs, one
widow usually visited as much as she was visited. In deciding

who visits whom, they often remarked, "Well, I came over last time. You come over this time." They traded, in even measure, slips from house plants, kitchen utensils, and food of all sorts. They watched one another's apartments when someone was away on a visit, and they called and took calls for one another.

There are hints of the parent-child bond in this system, but protectors picked their dependents voluntarily and resented taking care of people they did not volunteer to help. For example, one protector of "Little Floyd" complained about a crippled club member, a nonresident:

> It wasn't considerate of Rose to expect us to take care of her. She can't climb in and out of the bus very well and she walks so slow. The rest of us wanted to see the museum. It's not nice to say, but I didn't want to miss the museum waiting for her to walk with us. Why doesn't her son take her on trips?

The widows were not only equals among themselves; they also were remarkably similar. They all wanted more or less the same things and could give more or less the same things. They all wanted to *receive* Mother's Day cards. No one in the building *sent* Mother's Day cards. And what they did was to compare Mother's Day cards. Although there was some division of labor, there was little difference in labor performed. All knew how to bake bread and can peaches, but no one knew how to fix faucets. They all knew about "the old days" but few among them could explain what was going on with youth these days. They all had ailments but no one there could cure them. They all needed rides to the shopping center, but no one among them needed riders.

Their similar functions meant that when they did exchange services, it was usually the same kinds of services they themselves could perform. For example, two neighbors might exchange corn bread for jam, but both knew how to make both corn bread and jam. If one neighbor made corn bread for five people in one day, one of the recipients would also make corn bread for the same people two weeks later. Each specialized within a specialization, and over the long run the widows made and exchanged the same goods.

Hence the "side by sideness," the "in the same boat" quality of their relations. They noticed the same things about the world and their eyes caught the same items in a department store. They noticed the same features in the urban landscape—the pastor's home, the Baptist church, the nursing homes, the funeral parlors, the places that used to be. They did not notice, as an adolscent might, the gas stations and hamburger joints.

As a result, they were good listeners for each other. It was common for someone to walk into the recreation room and launch into the details of the latest episode of a mid-afternoon television drama ("It seems that the baby is not by artificial insemination but really Frank's child, and the doctor is trying to convince her to tell . . ."). The speaker could safely assume that her listeners also knew the details. Since they shared many experiences, a physical ailment, a death, a description of the past, an "old-age joke" could be explained, understood, and enjoyed. They talked together about their children much as their children, together, talked about them. Each shared with social siblings one side of the prototypical parent-child bond.

This similarity opened up the possibility of comparison and rivalry, as the "poor dear" hierarchy suggests. Whether the widows cooperated in collecting money for flowers, or competed for prestigious offices in the service club, bowling trophies or front seats in the bus, their functions were similar, their status roughly equal, and their relations in the best and worst sense, "profane."

Not all groups of old people form this sibling bond. Although we might expect subcultures to arise in nursing homes, certain hospital wards or convalescent hospitals, the likes of Merrill Court is rare. It is not enough to put fairly healthy, socially similar old people together. There is clearly something different between institutions and public housing apartments. Perhaps what counts is the kind of relationships that institutions foster. The resident of an institution is "a patient." Like a child, he has his meals served to him, his water glass filled, his bed made, his blinds adjusted by the "mother-nurse." He cannot return the service. Although he often shares a room or a floor with "brother" patients, both siblings have a nonreciprocal relationship to attendants or nurses. Even the research on the institutionalized

379

focuses on the relation between patient and attendant, not between patient and patient. If there is a strong parent-child bond, it may overwhelm any potential sibling solidarity. If the old in institutions meet as equals, it is not as independent equals. The patient's relation to other patients is like the relation between *real,* young siblings, which may exaggerate rather than forestall narcissistic withdrawal.

The widows of Merrill Court took care of themselves, fixed their own meals, paid their own rent, shopped for their own food, and made their own beds; and they did these things for others. Their sisterhood rests on adult autonomy. This is what people at Merrill Court have and people in institutions do not.

The Sibling Bond and Age-Stratification

The sibling bond is delicate and emerges only when conditions are ripe. Rapid currents of social change lead to age-stratification, which, in turn, ripens conditions for the sibling bond. Tied to his fellows by sibling bonds, an individual is cemented side by side into an age stratum with which he shares the same rewards, wants, abilities and failings.

French sociologist Émile Durkheim, in his book *The Division of Labor,* describes two forms of social solidarity. In organic solidarity there is a division of labor, complementary dependence and differences among people. In mechanical solidarity there is no division of labor, self-sufficiency and similarity among people. Modern American society as a whole is based on organic solidarity, not only in the economic but in the social, emotional and intellectual spheres.

Different age strata within the general society however, are more bound by mechanical solidarity. This is important both for the individual and the society. Although division of labor, complementary dependence and differences among people describe society's network of relations as a whole, they do not adequately describe relations among particular individuals. An individual's complementary dependence may be with people he does not know or meet—such as the person who grows and cans the food he eats, or lays the bricks for his house. And in his most intimate relations, an individual may also have complementary relations (either equal or unequal) with his spouse and children. But in between the most and least intimate bonds is a range in which there are many sibling relationships which form the basis of mechanical solidarity.

In fact, many everyday relations are with people similar and equal to oneself. Relations between colleague and colleague, student and student, friend and friend, relations within a wives' group or "the guys at the bar," the teenage gang or army buddies are often forms of the sibling bond. These ties are often backup relations, social insurance policies for the times when the complementary bonds of parent and child, husband and wife, student and teacher, boy friend and girl friend fail, falter or normally change.

From an individual's viewpoint, some periods of life, such as adolescence and old age, are better for forming sibling bonds than are other periods. Both just before starting a family and after raising one, before entering the economy and after leaving it, an individual is open to, and needs, these backup relationships. It is these stages that are problematic, and it is these stages that, with longer education and earlier retirement, now last longer.

From society's point of view, the sibling bond allows more flexibility in relations between generations by forging solidarity within generations and divisions between them. This divides society into age layers that are relatively independent of one another, so that changes in one age layer need not be retarded by conditions in another. The institution that has bound the generations together—the family—is in this respect on the decline. As it declines, the sibling bond emerges, filling in and enhancing social flexibility, especially in those social strata where social change is most pronounced. The resulting social flexibility does not guarantee "good" changes, and continuity is partly sacrificed to fads and a cult of newness. But whether desirable or not, this flexibility is partly due to and partly causes the growing importance of the sibling bond.

The times are ripe for the sibling bond, and for old-age communities such as Merrill Court. In the social life of old people the problem is not the sibling bond versus the parent-child bond.

381

Rather, the question is how the one bond complements the other. The sisterhood at Merrill Court is no substitute for love of children and contact with them; but it offers a full, meaningful life independent of them.

The Minority Group Almost Everyone Joins

Isolation is not randomly distributed across the class hierarchy; there is more of it at the bottom. It is commonly said that old age is a leveler, that it affects the rich in the same way it affects the poor. It doesn't. The rich fare better in old age even as they fared better in youth. The poorer you are, the shorter your life expectancy, the poorer your health and health care, the lower your morale generally, the more likely you are to "feel" old regardless of your actual age, the less likely you are to join clubs or associations, the less active you are and the more isolated, even from children. Irving Rosow's study of 1,200 people over 62 living in Cleveland found that roughly 40 percent of the working class but only 16 percent of the middle class had fewer than four good friends. Another study of 6,000 white working-class men and women showed that of those over 65 with incomes under $3,000, a full third did not visit with or speak to a friend or neighbor during the preceding week. The rock bottom poor are isolated, but they are not the only ones.

The isolation of old people is linked to other problems. The old are poor and poverty itself is a problem. The old are unemployed and unemployment, in this society, is itself a problem. The old lack community and the lack of community is itself a problem. There is some connection between these three elements. Removed from the economy, the old have been cast out of the social networks that revolve around work. Lacking work, they are pushed down the social ladder. Being poor, they have fewer social ties. Poverty reinforces isolation. To eliminate enforced isolation, we have to eliminate poverty, for the two go together. The social life of Merrill Court residents, who had modest but not desperately low incomes, is an exception to the general link between social class and isolation.

Even if every old person were in a Merrill Court, the problem of old age would not be solved. But, allowing every old person the possibility of such an arrangement could be part of the solution. The basic problem far exceeds the limits of tinkering with housing arrangements. It is not enough to try to foster friendships among the old. Even to do that, it is not enough to set up bingo tables in the lobbies of decrepit hotels or to hand out name cards to the sitters on park benches. This would simply put a better face on poverty, a cheerful face on old age as it is, at not much social cost.

Merrill Court is not set in any island of ideal social conditions; it is essentially an adjustment to bad social conditions. For the lives of old people to change fundamentally, those *conditions* must change. In the meantime, Merrill Court is a start. It is a good example of what can be done to reduce isolation. I do not know if similar communities would have emerged in larger apartment houses or housing tracts rather than in a small apartment house, with the married rather than the widowed, with rich rather than poor residents, with people having a little in common rather than a lot, with the very old person rather than the younger old person. Only trying will tell.

Merrill Court may be a forecast of what is to come. A survey of 105 University of California students in 1968 suggested that few parents of these students and few of the students themselves expect to be living with their families when they are old. Nearly seven out of ten (69 percent) reported that "under no circumstances" would they want their aged parents to live with them, and only 3 percent expected to be living with their own children when they are old. A full 28 percent expected to be living with *other* old people, and an additional 12 percent expected to be "living alone or with other old people."

Future communities of old people may be more middle class and more oriented toward leisure. Less than 10 percent of the students expected to be working when they passed 65. A great many expected to be "enjoying life," by which they meant studying, meditating, practicing hobbies, playing at sports and traveling.

But some things about future communities may be the same. As I have suggested throughout this book, communal

383

solidarity can renew the social contact the old have with life. For old roles that are gone, new ones are available. If the world watches them less for being old, they watch one another more. Lacking responsibilities to the young, the old take on responsibilities toward one another. Moreover, in a society that raises an eyebrow at those who do not "act their age," the subculture encourages the old to dance, to sing, to flirt and to joke. They talk frankly about death in a way less common between the old and young. They show one another how to be, and trade solutions to problems they have not faced before.

Old age is the minority group almost everyone joins. But it is a forgotten minority group from which many old people dissociate themselves. A community such as Merrill Court counters this disaffiliation. In the wake of the declining family, it fosters a "we" feeling, and a nascent "old age consciousness." In the long run, this may be the most important contribution an old age community makes.

AN
ETHNOGRAPHIC
STUDY OF
A RETIREMENT SETTING*

Jerry Jacobs

Description of the Town

Fun City is a planned retirement setting located in a warm, relatively smog-free valley, approximately 90 miles southeast of a large western metropolitan area. It is situated adjacent to a major state artery and is comprised of approximately 6,000 white middle- to upper-class residents over the age of 50. Nearly all residents are owners of single level ranch-style tract homes varying in price from $19,000 to $50,000.

The streets, while organized in an ordinary grid pattern, are remarkable in several regards: (1) they are all about the width of a 4-lane highway, (2) there are very few cars parked or driven on them, (3) they are well kept and immaculately clean, and (4) they are lined on both sides with wide well-kept sidewalks that no one walks on. The above state of eerie desolation can be observed at any time, barring the occurrence of some special function.

The houses, like the streets, are clean and orderly. If the streets receive little use, the houses look unlived in. In fact, from a distance, the lack of activity, the orderliness, and well-kept look of Fun City gives it the appearance of a middle-class tract community being readied for habitation. The sameness of

* Jerry Jacobs, "An Ethnographic Study of a Retirement Community," *Gerontologist* 14 (1974): 483–87.

most tract home communities is highlighted in Fun City by its gray-on-gray architecture. This is further accentuated by its "low maintenance yards," characterized by crushed rock "lawns," frequently stained green, and sometimes set off by one or more live or plastic bushes to enhance the landscaping decor.

The interior of the homes are in keeping with the rest of the town's "cleanliness is Godliness" motif. Home furnishings are frequently done in "Mediterranean-modern." Most homes have either a carport or double garage in which one invariably finds a large, late-model American car.

The shopping center, activity center, golf club, and town hall area (the hub of the community) are all prominently displayed off the main entrance to the town (an exit from the major state highway noted above), while the ambulance service, rest home, and mortuary complex, situated in that order, are located across the highway and out of sight.

To round out the living arrangements available to the potential resident is a set of "garden apartments," now nearing completion, which will provide intermediate facilities for those who are neither totally able to care for themselves and live in their own homes nor sufficiently disabled to be confined to the nursing home. The garden apartments provide maid service, a common dining hall, and total maintenance service for those who are only marginally able to care for themselves. This intermediate living accommodation provides the missing link for the care and feeding of older persons with different levels of competence— from early retirement to death.

The Residents

Fun City is a planned retirement community designed to overcome the culture shock one is likely to encounter, not only upon going from a work to a leisure ethic, but upon moving abruptly and totally into an unnatural environment, unnatural in that most residents formerly resided in the large adjacent metropolitan area where they were obliged, in the course of their everyday lives, to encounter and associate with all kinds of individuals. This is no longer true in Fun City.

386

The homeowner's guide in outlining features of Fun City to the prospective resident notes that living in Fun City are ". . . retired carpenters, plumbers, salesmen, sergeants, generals, janitors, corporation executives, inventors, teachers, doctors, lawyers, union officials, . . . a complete cross-section of Americana, and representatives from all of the 50 states," not to mention those from 14 foreign countries. However, this entry is deceiving.

Ethnicity

Notwithstanding this chamber-of-commerce presentation, an analysis of the place of origin and former occupation of residents living in Fun City, taken from the homeowner's guide, in conjunction with census data information on the ethnicity of Fun City residents, reveals that conspicuously absent from this "cross-section of Americana" are blacks, Chicanos, Chinese, Japanese, and other ethnic groups, all of whom are found in abundance in the adjacent metropolitan area from which the majority of Fun City residents were recruited. More specifically we find: total population, 5,519; white, 5,516; Negro, 0; Indian, 0; other specified races, 2; reported other races, 1.

Former Occupation

If ethnic groups are not in evidence, what of occupational groupings? Here the guide lists people from a wide range of occupations. The question arises, how many janitors and how many professionals live in Fun City? Using the owner's guide as a source of data and coding unambiguous listings of former occupations into occupational categories that emerge naturally from the data, we find that the claim that residents come from all walks of life is also deceiving. The number of janitors can be counted on one hand. In fact, the sum total of those from the ranks of "unskilled" labor comprises less than 4 percent of Fun City residents. On the other hand, professionals, businessmen, skilled labor, civil servants, salesmen, i.e., white-collar middle- and upper-class persons comprise over 80 percent of all Fun City

residents. In addition to the civilian personnel, there is a substantial number of higher-echelon retired military men among
Fun City residents.

Former Place of Origin

What of the claim that residents come from the 50 states of
the USA and 14 foreign countries? The homeowner's guide
notes residents from 8 foreign countries, 12 from Canada, and
1 each from 7 other countries, for a total of 19 foreigners out
of a total population of approximately 6,000. Looking at the
distribution of persons by state of origin, there are more residents
from within state than the sum total of all residents recruited
from all other states combined. It is clear that the notation in
the guide regarding the place of origin of Fun City residents is
also deceiving.

Summary

In fact, a fair description of Fun City residents is that they
are a homogeneous group of conservative, professional, white
middle- to upper-class persons whose average annual fixed income is $8,000. Add to this that there are no children in Fun
City, no industry, no city government or Civil Service (it is an
unincorporated town), little employment opportunity and few
gainfully employed persons, its geographical isolation, and lack
of inpatient (and outpatient) medical facilities, and the absence
of a police force, and we have a very atypical social setting
which one resident aptly referred to as "a false paradise."

Planned Activities

In order to overcome culture shock, the developers initiated
a number of planned activities designed to (a) engage the residents in activities and (b) take their mind off the problems of
retirement and, more specifically, problems of retiring in Fun

City. Most of these formal activities center about the Town Hall, Golf Club, Activity Center Area, and Shopping Center Complex. In all there are some 92 clubs and formal organizations available to Fun City residents. For a population of 6,000 persons, this would seem to provide something for everyone. Who participates in these activites? How many participate? What do the nonparticipants do? An analysis of the membership of these organizations reveals a large paper membership, i.e., a large number of residents claiming membership in one or more clubs. However, observations of these activities and the number of persons attending them reveal a low rate of participation. In short, while there is a big paper membership, there is very little active participation, and primarily by the same persons over time.

Fun City is billed as a retirement setting devoted to promoting "an active way of life." However, looking at these activities and the lack of involvement in them, we see "a passive way of life" to be by far the dominant life style. Not more than 500 of the 6,000 residents participate in the planned formal activities of Fun City. On a good day, perhaps another 300 or 400 may be found in the informal interaction network centering about the Shopping Center Complex. These represent the "active minority." What of the other 5,000 residents, the "invisible and passive majority?" Where are they and what are they doing? One resident sums up a typical day as follows:

Mr. N: Well, for me a typical day is—I get up at 6:00 a.m. in the morning, generally, get the newspaper. I look at the financial statement and see what my stocks have done. I generally fix my own breakfast because my wife has, can eat different than I do. So I have my own breakfast—maybe some cornflakes with soy milk in it—milk made out of soybeans that they sell in the health food store. And uh, then at 8:00 a.m. my wife gets up. The dog sleeps with her all night. And uh, she feeds the dog. Then the dog wants me to go out and sit on the patio—get the sun and watch the birds and stuff in our backyard and have quite a few rabbits back in there. And I finish my paper there. And then she sits and she looks at me. She'll bark a little bit. And uh, then she'll go to my wife, stand by my wife and bark at her. She wants me to go back to bed. So I have to go back to bed with her. So about 8:30 a.m. I go back to bed again with my dog for about an hour. And then I get up and I read.

And then I walk up around here and I go over to oh, the supermarket and sit there and talk to people. We go over to the bank. They have a stockroom over there, for people that own stock. We discuss stocks and events of the day. And then I come home and maybe have lunch if I want to or not—it doesn't make any difference. **In fact, down here it doesn't make any difference when you eat or when you sleep because you're not going any place. You're not doing anything. And uh, if I'm up all night reading and sleep all day, what's the difference.** (Emphasis added.) But then, I'll sit around and read and maybe a neighbor will come over or I'll go over to a neighbor's and sit down and talk about something. And then, lots of times, we go over to a neighbor's and we play cards 'til about 5:00 p.m. and then we come home and have our dinner. And the evening is . . . we are generally glued to the television until bedtime comes. And that's our day.

Dr. Jacobs: Is that more or less what your friends and neighbors do?

Mr. N: Some of them do. Some of them don't do that much.

Space does not permit an elaborate description of club activities. However, the following are some large membership clubs that promote "an active way of life"—Golf, Lawn Bowls, Shuffle Board, Square Dancing, and Bicycle Club. Card Clubs, Arts & Crafts, and the Camera Club exemplify large membership clubs promoting "a passive way of life." Within the above groupings the Sport Clubs have the largest number of active members, while the card clubs have the largest number of members participating in a passive way of life. If we consider the sum total of the number of nonparticipating residents (those holding only paper memberships or no membership in clubs and planned activities, day and night TV watchers, those physically disabled or more generally the "shut-ins") there is probably not more than 10 percent of all Fun City residents who are routinely involved in an active way of life.

Notwithstanding the developers' good intentions or efforts to overcome the novice's culture shock upon retiring to Fun

City, by involving him in, or at least providing for his involvement in, planned social and physical activities, very few residents participated in these planned activities and by far the greatest number experienced serious culture shock, not only upon initial contact but over time.

A Theory of Aging. A Test of "Goodness of Fit"

One theory of aging that probably has most often been cited and generated the greatest degree of controversy is the Disengagement Theory, as presented by Cumming and Henry (1961).

Rose (1964) summarizes the disengagement position as follows:

> It is not an hypothesis which states that, as people get older, they are gradually separated from their associations and their social functions. . . . Nor does the theory of disengagement state that, as people become physically feebler or chronically ill, they are thereby forced to abandon their associations and social functions. . . . Finally, the theory of disengagement does **not** say that because older people tend to have reduced income in our society, they can no longer afford to participate in many things. . . . (The) theory of disengagement is that the society and the individual prepare **in advance** for the ultimate "disengagment" of incurable, incapacitating disease and death by an **inevitable, gradual and mutually satisfying process of disengagement from society.**

How well did the life style of Fun City residents fit this model? Where did they fall along the engagement-disengagement continuum? The answer to this question will be considered with respect to the following four groups of Fun City residents.

(1) *Engaged in Pre- and Post-Retirement Period*

First, there are the 500 or 600 active club members who comprise about 10 percent of Fun City's population. These residents are clearly engaged. In fact, engagement during the pre- and post-retirement period characterizes the life style of this group. They represent a clear counter-instance to the position

391

that disengagement is a general phenomenon among the aged. This group represents those residents who were actively engaged in one or more of Fun City's 92 planned social or fraternal clubs.

(2) *Disengaged in the Pre- and Post-Retirement Period*

A second group of residents also runs contrary to the expectations of disengagement theory. While it is true that this group may be generally characterized as currently disengaged, and happy to be so, it is not a situation that they accomplished or tended toward in old age. Disengagement was for them as much a pre- as a post-retirement way of life. The residents in this group are not active members of Fun City's many formal organizations and prefer to keep to themselves or interact only on a very limited scale with a few close friends. It is impossible to say precisely how many residents fall into this category. However, judging from informant's self-evaluation of their own life style and their assessment of their neighbor's life style in the before and after retirement period, upwards of 15 percent of all Fun City residents are now and had previously been disengaged as a way of life. This would bring to 25 percent those who do not fit the disengagement model.

(3) *Formerly Engaged "Dropouts"*

There is yet another group of residents who were happily engaged in the pre- and early post-retirement periods but because of a recent deterioration in their health, or their spouses' health, had to drop out. Those who suffered a forced disengagement of this kind do not fit the expectations of the disengagement model either, in that it assumes that members choose to disengage in later life. While the above persons were disengaged, it was not a mode of adaptation that they either anticipated or intended nor was it gradual or welcome. I believe a substantial number of persons fit this category of Fun City residents, perhaps 25 percent. This group then, does not fit the conditions of the disengagement model either.

(4) *The Disengaged*

This leaves what is probably the largest category of residents, those who do seem to fit the disengagement model, i.e., those

392

who are now disengaged, choose to be disengaged, and were not formally disengaged as a way of life. These do not exceed half of Fun City's total population. This group came to Fun City to retire. They meant to withdraw from the society for the most part and watch television, read, play an occasional game of cards, and walk the dog. The residents comprising this group participate little, if at all, in Fun City's social life and are characterized by more active residents as loners or shut-ins. While this group considers the above activities (or lack of them) to be "taking it easy," something they look forward to, Fun City's more active residents and "outsiders" refer to the above life style as "vegetating." The latter look upon the former with a combination of pity and disdain.

In brief, judging from the activity and inactivity of Fun City residents in the pre- and post-retirement periods, something we would need to assess in order to see whether or not Fun City residents were subject to ". . . an inevitable, gradual, and mutually satisfying process of disengagement from society," one can only conclude that the process of disengagement, as that term is currently employed in disengagement theory, is neither inevitable, universal, nor unchanging.

Finally, it is clear that even for the 50 percent of the Fun City residents comprising the fourth category, i.e., who do seem to be "disengaged," there is no prooof for or against the contention that their disengagement is beneficial, either for them or society. The reasons for this have been dealt with in greater detail in a prior work (Jacobs, 1974) as well as the critiques of others (Kuhlen, 1968; Rose, 1964).

Conclusions

This paper is based upon a year-long study of the life styles of residents in a retirement community and is based upon formal and informal interviews, field observations, an analysis of written records, and the transcribed verbatim accounts of residents. The findings reveal that the older person's search for heaven on earth in the form of a retirement setting of his choosing, frequently leads him to a "false paradise."

In choosing a retirement setting it was felt by the retirees one would do well to retire "among his own kind," in a healthy climate, where it was uncongested and "safe in the streets," and there was "plenty to do." However, these great expectations frequently miscarried. The search for such a Shangri-La often led to many untoward consequences.

Among these were the fact that Fun City had no inter- or intracity public transportation, police department, adequate health care facilities, and was geographically isolated. These and many other features were contrary to the needs and expectations of the retirement aged, ailing, white middle-class homeowner, who characterized the typical Fun City resident. Residents had to contend with these unforeseen and undesirable features notwithstanding their efforts and those of the developer to screen out "undesirables," or if they infiltrated, to get them to leave. Life in Fun City exhibited, then, most of the negative aspects residents associated with everyday life "outside" and few of its more beneficial effects. While these negative features need not characterize all retirement settings (Hochschild, 1973), they were features of Fun City living.

Prior knowledge of these shortcomings (as perceived by the residents) might have led many of them to retire in the familiar environment from which they came, one that was neither "unnatural" nor required "some getting used to." What was missing was recognition on the part of residents that people live in Fun City and that people, no matter how well they were screened, exhibit many differences, and work for, with, and against one another. An understanding of this basic truth would have led many to realize that any effort on their part at finding a heaven on earth could only lead to their discovery of "a false paradise."

6

Institutionalization

INTRODUCTION TO PART VI

In 1970, nearly half the people in American custodial institutions—prisons, hospitals, nursing homes, and the like—were over sixty-five years old. Thus, the problems of institutionalization are of special interest to the social gerontologist. The articles in this section deal with a variety of issues including the rising rate of institutionalization, the quality of nursing-home care, and patient-staff relations. A common theme, however, is found in each of the papers: "socially advantaged" elderly persons— those with money, family, and friends; those who are white; those who are in relatively better health—fare better in every respect. They are less likely than others to be institutionalized in the first place. If institutionalized, they are more likely to be found in private nursing homes than in public mental hospitals and other institutions. Among those in private nursing homes, the socially advantaged elderly are in homes with better resources. And within individual nursing homes, persons with money, family, and friends appear to get the most attention.

The first paper in this section examines issues in institutionalization on a national scale and includes an historical perspective. Manard and Kart ask why rates of institutionalization vary from state to state and over time. They explicate the relationship between these variations and important social factors including the age structure of different populations, social cohesion and disaffiliation, and the impact of public welfare programs.

The next two selections illustrate different approaches to the difficult task of assessing nursing-home quality. Jordan Kosberg discusses a number of studies relating nursing-home quality to the affluence of residents, including his own investigation of 214 Chicago-area facilities. In that study, the availability of "treatment resources" (professional staff, equipment, and the like) was used as an indirect measure of quality. Kosberg found fewer resources in facilities with more blacks and more publicly supported residents.

Are such differences simply a matter of differences among facilities in the amount of money each has to spend on residents? Gottesman and Bourestom, reporting on a study of Detroit-area nursing homes, suggest that "accountability" is a key issue in quality of care. They recorded the activities of 1,144 residents and their interaction with staff members in forty nursing homes.

Quality was assessed in terms of what actually happened in the sample nursing homes. Among the important correlates of high-quality care were that the resident had personal possessions, visitors, and was in a home where most of the people were private-paying. The authors suggest that the implicit meaning of these attributes is that such residents have "someone out there who cares about them and is able to act in their behalf." In other words, they suggest that good care depends in large part on the degree to which the staff is held accountable for quality of care. Gottesman, Bourestom, and their colleague Jane Barney have urged that patient-advocacy programs be expanded as a means of increasing accountability and improving nursing-home care.

The two concluding articles in this section provide a more subjective and intimate look at life in an old-age institution. Each article is based on the author's lengthy involvement with a single nursing home. Charles Stannard's detailed description of the staff attitudes, interpersonal relations, and organizational factors which facilitate opportunities for patient abuse greatly amplifies our understanding of the importance of accountability. In the nursing home Stannard observed, staff members "emphasized the hopeless condition of their patients, their enfeebled mental states, and the necessity of controlling them with drugs and cloth restraints." From the staff point of view, patient

complaints, rule breaking, and unconventional behavior were ir-
ritating and frustrating disruptions of the daily work routine.

Elizabeth Gustafson, author of the final selection, presents
provocative speculations about the "career" of nursing-home
patients as they move through a series of stages toward death.
Her intriguing theory suggests a new way of understanding aspects of patient behavior described by Bourestom, Gottesman,
and Stannard.

SOCIAL FACTORS AND INSTITUTIONALIZATION OF THE ELDERLY*

Barbara B. Manard and Cary S. Kart

Between 1960 and 1970, the number of people over age 65 in old-age institutions (nursing homes, rest homes, homes for the aged) increased 105 percent. Among the factors thought to have influenced this change are the impact of federal welfare programs, the growth in numbers of the elderly population, and "changes in family living arrangements."[1] The relative importance of each factor is still undetermined.

In addition to changes over time, we observe variations from state to state in the proportion of the elderly in old-age institutions (OAI). In 1970, the range was from 7.5 percent in North Dakota to 1.2 percent in New Mexico. Most of those states with a relatively large proportion of their elderly in OAI are in the West and Midwest; those with a relatively small proportion in OAI are in the East and South.

In order to assess the pattern of interstate variation, we calculated the rate of institutionalization (in OAI) of the elderly populations in each of the forty-eight contiguous states, and correlated these rates with thirty-five social, demographic, and economic measures. The results are summarized in Table 1, where precise definitions and sources are also given. In this paper, using the results of that study and historical material, we discuss the interrelationships among the various factors that

---

* Abridged from Barbara B. Manard, Cary S. Kart, and Dirk W. L. van Gils, *Old Age Institutions* (Lexington, Mass.: D. C. Heath, Lexington Books, 1975), pp. 107-31.

seem to influence both the rate of institutionalization of the elderly and the types of institutions that accommodate them.

I
Social, Economic, and Demographic Characteristics

Compared to the general elderly population, those in OAI are disproportionately unmarried, over 75, and poor.[2] Furthermore, those admitted to these institutions are disproportionately drawn from the elderly population living "extrafamilially"— that is, those living alone or with nonrelatives. We can thus characterize the pool from which the OAI population is drawn as unmarried, aged, poor, and "extrafamilial." We asked to what extent differences among the states in the proportion of old people in OAI were associated with variations in the size of this "at risk" population.

We found that states with relatively large numbers of very aged elderly, and extrafamilial elderly, had relatively large institutionalized populations. However, these states did not also tend to have relatively large numbers of unmarried or poor elderly. A closer look at these findings suggests that the underlying factor in institutionalization is the level of social isolation and disaffiliation of the elderly; measures that tap this characteristic are quite useful in "explaining why" institutionalization rates are higher in some states than in others.

Age of the Elderly Populations

For each state, we calculated the proportion of the elderly who were 75 years of age and older. The range among the states was from a low of 32 percent in Nevada to a high of 44 percent in Montana. We found that states with a high proportion of "senior" elderly had a high proportion of institutionalized elderly (Pearson $r = .79$). Of all the social and economic population characteristics we considered, the age of the elderly best accounted for variation among the states in the proportion of the elderly in OAI.

402

Table 1

The Association between 35 State Characteristics and the Proportion of the Elderly in OAI: 48 States, 1970[a]

Variable[b]	r	High Value	Low Value
1. % of state population aged 65+	.34	14.8 (Florida)	6.4 (Nevada)
2. % of elderly living in urban areas	−.09	90.5 (Rhode Island)	35.4 (Vermont)
3. % of elderly living in rural farm areas	.38	16.8 (North Dakota)	0.3 (Rhode Island)
4. % of elderly living alone or with non-relatives ("primary individuals")	.50	31.1 (Arkansas)	21.4 (North Carolina)
5. % of elderly married and living with spouse	−.09	61.0 (Florida)	33.3 (Alabama)
6. % of elderly living in group quarters	.37	1.5 (New Hampshire)	0.3 (Alabama, Utah, Arkansas, Wyoming)
7. % of elderly who are foreign born	.09	35.2 (New York)	0.7 (Mississippi)
8. % of elderly who are nonwhite	−.47	35.9 (Mississippi)	0.3 (Vermont, New Hampshire)
9. % of elderly who moved to state between 1965 and 1970 (inmigrants)[c]	−.31	20.8 (Arizona)	1.2 (New York)
10. % of elderly who left state between 1965 and 1970 (outmigrants)[c]	−.05	10.9 (Nevada)	1.9 (Arkansas, Texas)
11. % of elderly who received any income in 1969	−.10	98.8 (Kansas)	86.1 (Washington)
12. % of elderly males in labor force	.37	36.4 (Wisconsin)	17.6 (Connecticut)
13. % of elderly employed males in white-collar occupations	−.30	51.8 (New York, New Jersey)	26.2 (South Dakota)
14. % of elderly-headed households living in owned homes[d]	.23	81.0 (Kansas)	45.9 (New York)
15. Median years of school completed by women aged 70–74	.10	10.5 (Arizona, Nevada)	7.6 (Louisiana)
16. Number of elderly males per 100 elderly females (sex ratio)	.00	100.1 (Missouri)	64.3 (Massachusetts)
17. Average number of children ever born to elderly women who ever married	−.08	3.6 (Utah, North Dakota)	1.5 (Wyoming)
18. % of elderly in institutions of all types	.90	8.0 (North Dakota)	2.3 (Florida, West Virginia)
19 % of elderly living dependently in child's household	−.58	18.1 (New York)	3.9 (Oregon)
20. % of elderly who are native to state	−.10	82.7 (Kentucky)	9.1 (Arizona)

Table 1 (Cont'd)

The Association between 35 State Characteristics and the Proportion of the Elderly in OAI: 48 States, 1970[a]

Variable[b]	r	High Value	Low Value
21. % of elderly receiving income with income below $3,000	−.22	85.8 (Mississippi)	45.1 (Connecticut)
22. $\frac{\text{Number of OAI residents}^e}{\text{Number of elderly persons}} \times 100$	.93	8.0 (Massachusetts)	1.2 (West Virginia)
23. "Availability of Beds" $\frac{\text{Number of OAI beds}^f}{\text{Number of elderly persons}} \times 100$	.92	85.9 (North Dakota)	13.1 (West Virginia)
24. "Average amount of public money spent on OAI residents"[g] $\frac{\text{Total public money paid to OAI's in 1969}}{\text{Number of OAI residents (all ages) in 1969}}$	−.14	$5,638 (Nevada)	$233 (N. Carolina)
25. Mean hospital expense per patient day, 1969[h]	−.06	$93.68 (Massachusetts)	$46.50 (Wyoming)
26. "Skilled-care bed ratio"[i] (percent of all OAI beds that are certified for Medicare ECF program)	−.39	89.0 (California)	7.0 (Oklahoma)
27. Number of elderly persons in state	−.09	1,960,752 (New York)	30,204 (Wyoming)
28. Percent of elderly persons who are aged 75+	.79	43.5 (Montana)	31.9 (Nevada)
29. Percent of elderly who never married	.01	15.0 (Kansas)	4.4 (Florida)
30. "Childless women" (percent of elderly women who never married, or married but had no children)	.22	45.6 (Massachusetts)	11.0 (Utah)
31. "Extrafamilial elderly" (percent of noninstitutionalized elderly who live alone, with nonrelatives, or in group quarters)	.68	47.8 (Illinois)	18.7 (Maine)
32. Percent of the elderly who are extra-familial and poor	.27	24.4 (Oklahoma)	8.8 (Virginia)
33. Annual mean per-capita income in state (persons of all ages)[j]	.21	$4,432 (Connecticut)	$2,140 (Mississippi)
34. Average monthly per person OAA grant[k]	.18	$167 (New Hampshire)	$49 (S. Carolina)
35. Median monthly rent paid by house-holds with elderly heads[l]	.05	$110 (New Jersey)	$47 (Mississippi)

[a] The "proportion of the elderly in OAI" refers to the proportion of the elderly reported in the 1970 Census to be living in homes for the aged. The Census describes its category "homes for the aged" as "a somewhat heterogeneous group of places in which the great majority of the inmates are older persons."

[b] Unless otherwise noted, data on the characterisitcs of the states' populations are from: U.S. Department of Commerce, Bureau of the Census, *1970 Census of Population* pts. 1–51.

404

Table 1 (Cont'd)

The Association between 35 State Characteristics and the Proportion of the Elderly in OAI: 48 States, 1970[a]

c   U.S Department of Commerce, Bureau of the Census, *1970 Census of Population, Subject Report: Mobility for States and the Nation.*

d   U.S Department of Commerce, Bureau of the Census, *Subject Report: Housing of Senior Citizens, 1970.*

e   "Number of elderly persons" refers to the number of people 65+ reported in the 1970 Census. ' Number of OAI residents" refers to the number of residents (of all ages) counted in "nursing and personal care homes," 1969 National Center for Health Statistics Master Facility Census. Data derived from: U.S. Department of Health, Education and Welfare, National Center for Health Statistics, *Nursing Homes: A County and Metropolitan Area Data Book,* table 1.

f   See footnote e above. "Number of OAI beds" refers to the number of beds in "nursing and personal care homes." U.S. Department of Health, Education and Welfare, National Center for Health Statistics, *Nursing Homes: A County and Metropolitan Area Data Book,* table 1.

g   "Public money paid to OAI's" refers to total local, state, and federal money spent on "nursing home care" (no definition of nursing home is given in source) in fiscal 1969. Barbara S. Cooper and Nancy L. Washington, *Personal Health Care Expenditures by State, vol. I., Public Funds 1966 and 1969* (U.S. Department of Health, Education and Welfare, October 1972), table 23. For definition of "OAI residents," see footnote e above.

h   Barbara S. Cooper and Nancy L. Washington, table A, p. 4.

i   *Ibid.,* table I, p. 11.

j   *Ibid.,* table A, p. 4.

k   As of July 1972. Social Security Bulletin 35 (1972):63.

l   U.S. Department of Commerce, Bureau of the Census, *Subject Report: Housing of Senior Citizens, 1970.*

Two important factors contribute to the relationship between age and institutionalization: the chances both of developing major health problems and of losing one's living companion (spouse, friend, sibling) increase with age. Thus, states with a large proportion of "senior" elderly tend to have a relatively large proportion of elderly living alone ($r = .55$). Although these two characteristics are related, each is also independently associated with rates of institutionalization among the states. When we controlled for the proportions of the elderly living alone, the relation between the age of the elderly populations and the proportions in OAI remained quite strong ($r = .68$).

Living Arrangements, Marital Status, Mobility

Among the states, there are strong relationships between the proportion of the elderly in OAI and the living arrangements of the noninstitutionalized elderly. We found that states in which a high proportion of the elderly are in OAI tend to have a high proportion of the noninstitutionalized elderly living alone ($r = .50$) and in group quarters ($r = .37$). Among the states, the strongest association is between the proportion of extrafamilial elderly (the total number living alone, with nonrelatives, or in group quarters) and the proportion in OAI ($r = .68$).

It is logical to assume a direct relationship between extrafamiliality and institutionalization. Generally speaking, people who grow old and sick will be less able to cope with that situation if they live alone. We found that the size of this "at risk" pool was related to the proportion of the population institutionalized.

The fact that high rates of institutionalization and extrafamiliality occur together suggests that both factors reflect a third and linking characteristic of the state populations. It is probable that in considering living arrangements we have indirectly measured levels of affiliation and independence and that therein lie the important relationships. This can be seen by examining the relationship between institutionalization rates and other types of living arrangements.

In 1970, approximately 10 percent of the elderly lived dependently with their children.[3] Variation among the states ranged from a low of 4 percent in Oregon to a high of 18 percent in New York. We found that states where a relatively large proportion of the elderly lived in this sort of arrangement had relatively few elderly in institutions ($r = -.58$).

The states in which a high proportion of the elderly live dependently with their children line the eastern seaboard from Connecticut to Georgia.[4] One factor contributing to this pattern is the relative stability of the younger population in these states. The median outmigration between 1965 and 1970 was 9.7 percent.

Probably because of higher outmigration rates of the young, Maine and the deep southern states of Mississippi, Tennessee,

406

Alabama, Kentucky, and Louisiana have fewer elderly people living dependently with their children than is found in the eastern seaboard states.[5] Nevertheless, the general level of extrafamiliality is quite low; old people in these states live with cousins, brothers, sisters, and other relatives in greater proportion than in any other section of the country. The quite low rates of institutionalization in Maine and the deep South seem to result from a traditional social cohesion which is maintained despite a moderate outmigration of young people.

By contrast, many of the northwest and central states are characterized by high rates of institutionalization, large proportions of the elderly living extrafamilially, and few living dependently with their children. In addition, these states have had quite mobile younger populations, a fact which has obvious implications for social cohesion and, by extension, the rate at which the elderly are institutionalized. North Dakota, for example, had the highest rate of institutionalization of the elderly in 1970, and also had a five-year outmigration rate (19.3 percent) which was nearly twice the national average.

In 1970, nearly half of the elderly population was married and living with a spouse.[6] As we have mentioned, people living in this type of arrangement are less likely than others to be institutionalized. However, among the states, there is virtually no association between the size of this low-risk population and the size of the institutionalized population ($r = -.09$). This is because both the states with the greatest number of elderly—the "retirement states"—and those with the fewest—the deep South—have quite low rates of institutionalization.

The "retirement states" are an interesting group because their pattern differs so markedly from that found elsewhere. In 1970, 18 percent of Nevada's elderly, 25 percent of Arizona's elderly, and 28 percent of Florida's elderly had moved to these retirement states in the preceding five years. Almost by definition, mobility means the breaking of ties, the loss of affiliation. Although there are quite large proportions of married elderly in the retirement states, there are also quite large proportions living alone. The proportions living with relatives are almost negligible. Nevertheless, very few elderly are institutionalized in the retirement states. Nevada, Arizona, and Florida rank forty-third, forty-sixth, and forty-fifth, respectively, in the proportion of the elderly in OAI.

It should be remembered that in all states only a small number of the elderly are institutionalized. Those who are not manage by coping alone, purchasing help, or getting along with the assistance of friends and family. The special conditions of the retirement states, including relatively high incomes and concentrations of age peers, seem to afford the same sort of "protection" against institutionalization found in areas where familial ties are stronger.

Fertility, Living Arrangements, and Institutionalization

We looked at two indicators of the number of children produced by the elderly women in each of the forty-eight contiguous states: the average number of children born to elderly women who ever married ("completed family size") and the proportion of all elderly women who had either remained single or had married but been childless ("childless women"). The range in the completed family size of elderly ever-married women was from an average of 3.6 children (in Utah and North Dakota) to 1.5 (Wyoming). There was considerable variation in the proportion of childless women: from a high of 27 percent in Wyoming to a low of 11 percent in Utah.

Among the states:

1. There is virtually no association between the completed family size of elderly women and the proportion of the elderly in OAI ($r = -.08$).
2. There is a slight association between the proportion of childless elderly women and the proportion of the elderly in OAI ($r = .23$).
3. There is a slight association between the completed family size of elderly women and the proportion of the elderly living extrafamilially ($r = -.34$).
4. There is a slight association between the proportion of childless women and the proportion of the elderly living extrafamilially ($r = .29$).

5. The associations between the proportion of the elderly living dependently with their children and both completed family size ($r = -.09$) and childless women ($r = .15$) are negligible.

Given the small amount of variation among the states in the completed family size of elderly women, it would be inappropriate to deduce a great deal from the observed associations with that variable alone. Looking, however, at both measures of childbearing, we see a pattern that makes sense.

In the first place, it might be expected that states in which a relatively large proportion of the elderly women never had children would also be those in which a relatively large proportion live extrafamilially. But it is also not surprising that the statistical associations found among fertility, living arrangements, and institutionalization are rather weak. The historical record indicates a similar weak relationship. Between 1940 and 1970 the proportion of elderly women (nationally) with no living children changed very little—from 27 percent to 29 percent.[7] This is because declining fertility has been largely offset by an increase in marriage and a decline in infant mortality. During the same period, however, the proportion of the elderly living extrafamilially has substantially increased and the proportion living dependently with their children has decreased by half (Table 4, discussed below).

Although fertility and living arrangements (and, by extension, institutionalization) are clearly related—in order to live with a child an elderly person must first have a child—it appears that the living arrangements of the elderly are more directly influenced by economic factors.

Income, Living Arrangements, and Institutionalization

We have noted that elderly people in OAI are disproportionately drawn from the aged poor. However, we found that states with a relatively large proportion of very poor elderly people tend to have fewer institutionalized elderly: the greater the percentage of the elderly who had less than $3,000 in income, the smaller the percentage in OAI ($r = -.22$).

That apparent anomaly appears to result from the fact that where the elderly are very poor, they can not afford to live alone. States in which the elderly are relatively poor tend to have a small extrafamilial population ($r = -.56$). Apparently, it is the poorest of those who had just enough money to live extra-familially who constitute a large portion of the OAI population. States with a relatively large proportion of extrafamilial elderly *with incomes below poverty* tend to have a large institutionalized population ($r = .27$).

There is a considerable amount of additional evidence of the relationship between income and living arrangements (and, by extension, patterns of institutionalization). In 1970, elderly persons living with relatives had lower median incomes than elderly persons who were living alone. The median income of elderly men living with relatives was $1,707. The median income of elderly women living in families not headed by their spouses was $1,194. However, the median income of persons aged 65 to 74 living alone was $2,300 for men and $1,990 for women. The median income of persons aged 75 and over living alone was $1,900 for men and $1,600 for women.[8]

An earlier study comparing the incomes of elderly persons in various living arrangements in 1951 and 1959 reported similarly that higher income was associated with extrafamiliality.[9] In 1959, the median income for aged married couples living by themselves was $2,670, aged married couples with other relatives in the household had a median income of $2,400, independent of the contribution of the other relatives. Among these elderly who were single, widowed, divorced, or separated, median income was highest for those who lived alone or with non-relatives. Sixty percent of the unmarried elderly with incomes over $1,000 were living alone; while only forty percent of those with lower incomes were living alone. Parallel differences were reported for 1951.

Taking these facts together, we speculate that marginal increases in income for the elderly may put a significant proportion of them in the extrafamilial population, and that this may increase their eventual susceptibility to institutionalization.

410

II

The Impact of Public Money

We have shown that some of the interstate variation in rates of institutionalization is related to differences among states in the social and economic characteristics of their elderly populations. However, among the states, the factor most strongly associated with institutionalization of the elderly is the "availability of OAI beds."[10] Those states with the highest proportion of elderly in OAI are those in which proportionately more OAI beds are available ($r = .92$).

How do we account for interstate variations in the availability of OAI beds? Nearly all OAI are run for profit; their existence depends on the willi ,ness and ability of people to pay for the services these institutions offer. Between 1960 and 1970, the number of nursing-home beds tripled nationally.[11] This growth cannot be accounted for by the increase in the number of elderly persons. Moreover, the sorts of social changes we have discussed and believe to be related to the "demand" for OAI—changes in living arrangements and the like—simply do not occur fast enough to account for such rapid change.

Clearly an important factor in the rapid development of nursing homes during the 1960s was the introduction of federal programs which pumped public money into the industry: Medical Assistance for the Aged (Kerr-Mills) in 1964, followed by Medicare and Medicaid. The initial lack of controls on the Medicare program assured windfall profits for the nursing-home industry. The impact of public money on the availability of nursing-home beds over time has been obvious. Moreover, it has also been reported that, at least between 1961 and 1964, differences between states in the number of available beds were associated with differing levels of public assistance for medical care. We asked to what extent differences among the states in the relative availability of beds observed in 1970 were also related to levels of public assistance.

Definitions of the Variables

OAI and "public monies"

"Old-age institutions" is a term we use to include all types of nursing and rest homes. Old-age institutions are classified by state and federal agencies according to the "level of care" (roughly equivalent to the amount of professional services available) they provide. Unfortunately, there is a tremendous amount of variation from agency to agency in these classification schemes. It is almost impossible to tell from a particular publication what sorts of facilities have been included under the rubric *nursing home*. Hence, some of the data we use in this section may not be strictly comparable.

Our figures on the total amount of public money—federal, state, and local—paid to OAI in 1969 are derived from a publication which reports the amount of money paid to "nursing homes," but does not define the term. However, in that publication, "public assistance" (i.e., welfare) is included as a source of state and local funds to "nursing homes." Such funds commonly support indigent people in OAI where only the barest "personal care" services are rendered, usually by persons with no special training. Thus, the types of facility to which public monies go, as indicated in the data available to us, probably include both nursing and rest homes.

Our figures on the number of OAI beds and residents are derived from the 1969 HEW Master Facilities Inventory. That inventory included all OAI except those in which only room and board were provided.

For a measure of the *average amount of public money spent on OAI residents* we divided the total public monies paid to OAI in fiscal 1969 by the total number of OAI residents counted in the 1969 HEW Master Facilities Inventory.

The number of OAI beds per 1,000 persons aged 65 and over was calculated with data from the 1969 HEW Health Facilities Inventory. We speak of this figure as the "availability of beds."

Types of OAI beds and relative cost of care among the states

Comparisons among the states with respect to the average

amount of public monies spent on OAI residents could not be made without introducing controls for the relative costs of care among the states. Differences among the states in the cost of care in OAI are related both to the general cost of medical care (higher, for example, in the northeast) and to the proportion of OAI beds in expensive, highly staffed "skilled-care" nursing homes, rather than in low-cost "intermediate-care" nursing homes, or in rest homes.

We used the average expense per patient day in general hospitals as a yardstick of health-care costs. For an estimate of the proportion of skilled-care beds to "lower-level" beds in each state, we divided the number of Medicare certified beds in each state by the total number of OAI beds to obtain the *skilled-care-bed ratio.*

Findings

1. Among the states there is an appreciable correlation between the skilled-care-bed ratio and the average amount of public money spent on OAI residents ($r = .36$). This association is not affected by the relative costs of care.

2. Among the states, the correlation between the average amount of public money spent on nursing home residents and the availability of beds is negligible ($r = -.19$). Controlling for the relative costs of care, this association virtually disappears ($r = .01$).

Discussion

The first finding reported above seems simply to say that states with a greater proportion of their beds certified for Medicare got more public money on the average. This makes sense in view of the facts that in 1969 most public support of nursing homes was still coming from Medicare and that these skilled-care beds are more expensive than lower-level ones.

However, the association can be read in another way. In most states, facility development has tended to follow the public

413

money.[13] That is, the types of facility most readily developed are those which qualify for the most profitable public reimbursement programs. We therefore suspect that in states where relatively greater amounts of public monies were being spent on OAI residents in 1969, a larger proportion of the facilities sought certification for the then highly profitable Medicare program. Although the formal requirements for Medicare participation are standardized, the manner in which that and other programs are administered allows for regional and interstate variations in the profitability of particular public reimbursement programs.

The second finding reported above indicates that to the extent that we have devised an adequate measure of the comparative amount of public monies being pumped into the nursing-home industries of the various states, in 1970 that factor apparently accounted for virtually none of the interstate variation in OAI bed availability. The factors that were strongly associated with the availability of beds are those social and economic characteristics discussed above. The states in which OAI beds were relatively plentiful in 1970 tended to be those with relatively large "at risk" elderly populations: they tended to have relatively large proportions living extrafamilially ($r = .61$), small proportions living dependently with their children ($r = -.56$), and relatively large proportions of the elderly over 75 ($r = .70$).

The data presented so far indicate that—considering interstate variations—public monies have a more direct effect on the types of OAI available, while other social and economic factors are more closely associated with the general "demand" for OAI and with the rate of institutionalization of the elderly.

III

The Historical Pattern

We turn now to consider the historical development of OAI in the United States. The changes that have occurred over time mirror the relationships we have found at one point in time.

Tables 2 and 3 show the percent of elderly persons in institutions and group quarters of all types from 1904 to 1970. The

414

Table 2

Percentage Distribution of Institutionalized Elderly Population by Type of Institution, 1904–1970[a]

Type of Institution	1904	1910	1940	1950	1960	1970
OAI			33.7	35.2	49.7	72.4
Prison, reformatory	(2,851)		.8	.5	.4	.2
Local jail or workhouse			.5	.4	.3	.2
Mental institutions	(20,374)	(34,610)	23.6	22.9	23.2	10.3
Tuberculosis hospitals				1.1	1.8	.5
Other chronic disease hospitals				1.4	2.9	3.2
Homes and schools for the mentally handicapped	(34)					1.0
Almshouses	(52,795)	(46,032)		.7	.6	
Other institutions			.9		2.8	
Group quarters			40.5	37.8	21.2	12.3
Total population 65+ in institutions and group quarters	76,054	80,642	373,000	617,000	780,000	1,100,000
			100.0	100.0	102.9	100.1

[a] For detailed explanatory notes on this table, see Manard et al., *Old-Age Institutions.*

Table 3

Distribution of Elderly Population by Type of Residence, 1904–1970[a]

Total Population 65+	1904	1910	1940	1950	1960	1970
(in thousands)	100%	100%	100%	100%	100%	100%
	(5,621)	(3,949)	(9,019)	(12,269)	(16,560)	(20,097)
In institutions	1.4	2.0	2.3	3.1	3.7	4.8
In group quarters	(unknown)	(unknown)	1.7	1.9	1.0	.7
In private households	98.6	98.0	96.0	95.0	96.3	94.5

[a] For explanatory notes on this table, see Manard et al., *Old-Age Institutions*.

most dramatic changes have occurred in the distribution of the institutionalized elderly among different types of institutions. Increases in the proportion of the elderly in all institutions and group quarters have been more gradual. For the most part, the latter changes have occurred at rates consistent with the slower rates at which broad social-structural changes occur.

From Table 2, it can be seen that between 1940 and 1960, those elderly persons not living in private households were shifting from boarding and rooming houses (group quarters) into OAI. In large part, boardinghouses were being transformed into "homes for the aged."

Between 1960 and 1970, this trend was accelerated. In that decade, the proportion of the institutionalized elderly in group quarters declined 42 percent; the proportion in OAI increased 46 percent. In addition, the proportion of the institutionalized elderly who were confined to mental hospitals declined by half. Viewing the historical pattern, we clearly see the impact of Medicare and Medicaid on the distribution of the institutionalized elderly. The total proportion of the elderly in all types of institutions and group quarters has changed relatively less.

If it is true, as it appears to be, that the OAI population is now swelled by elderly persons who in past years might have been in jails, lodging houses, and mental hospitals, then we may expect this redistribution itself to increase the rate of institutionalization of the elderly. The support provided for the elderly in "licensed," "inspected," and otherwise socially certified nursing homes should eliminate much of the stigma associated in the past with institutionalization of the elderly.

We turn now to consider changes over time in the proportion of the elderly in institutions. Between 1910 and 1970, this percentage increased 140 percent, an average of 2.3 percent a year. During the same period, the living arrangements of the noninstitutionalized elderly have changed considerably.

From Table 4 it can be seen that between 1940 and 1970, the porportion of the elderly living dependently with their children has been halved. No information is available on the numbers of old people living alone in 1940, but between 1960 and 1970 the proportion of the elderly living extrafamilially increased 23 percent. During the same period, the percentage of

417

the elderly in institutions increased 29 percent. Whether the living arrangements of the elderly directly contribute to the "risk of institutionalization," or whether by describing living arrangements we measure a dimension of social affiliation, it is clear that institutionalization and living arrangements are closely and perhaps causally linked.

We have argued that as a general rule, public welfare programs for the elderly have had a greater direct effect on the

Table 4

Household Situations of Elderly Persons, 1940, 1960, 1970[a]

	1940	1960	1970
Old-age institutions	2.3	3.7	3.8
Other institutions			1.0
Group quarters	1.7	1.0	.7
Lodgers, partners, resident servants	4.6	2.5	1.8
Primary heads of households (alone or with nonrelatives)		19.7	25.6
Family heads (in 1940, includes those alone)	53.6	37.7	35.4
Wife of head	15.2	18.4	19.1
Parent or parent-in-law of head	16.4	11.8	8.6
Other relative of head	5.4	5.1	4.0
	99.3%	100.1%	100.1%
Total persons 65+	(9,019,314)	(16,197,834)	(20,065,502)

[a] For detailed explanatory notes on this table, see Manard et al., *Old-Age Institutions.*

types of institution that accommodate the elderly than on the rate of institutionalization of the elderly. However, there is also evidence of more complex relationships Looking more carefully at the increasing institutionalization of the elderly (Table 3), between 1910 and 1940 the percentage increased by 15 percent; between 1940 and 1970, by 108 percent. That difference seems clearly linked to the beginnings of social welfare programs for the elderly: the establishment of Social Security and Old Age Assistance in the 1930s; and the subsequent expansion of these

418

programs, in addition to the development of Medicare and Medicaid in the 1960s. It can be seen from Table 4 that the greatest changes have occurred between 1940 and 1950 and between 1960 and 1970.

Public welfare for the elderly appears to increase the institutionalization of the elderly in two ways. First, there is the direct effect of more cash to pay for relatively acceptable institutional care. More subtly, there is the effect of allowing economically marginal widows and single people to establish independent households. Such people—the aged, unmarried, extrafamilial poor—constitute the pool of high risk for institutionalization.

If the patterns we have discerned continue to hold, we may predict an unanticipated consequence of the new federally administered program (Supplementary Security Income) which guarantees a minimum income for the elderly. We expect that this program will be accompanied by an increase in the proportion of institutionalized elderly in most states, because more economically marginal persons will have just enough money to live alone. Moreover, the current provisions of the program specifically state that benefits to elderly individuals or couples are reduced by one-third if they live in the household of a relative, even if the elderly share in household expenses. Economically marginal persons living extrafamilially, as we have emphasized, are at a high risk for future institutionalization.

Notes

1. U. S. Department of Health, Education and Welfare, *Medical Care Expenditures, Prices, and Costs: Background Book,* DHEW publication no. (SSA) 74-11909, 1973, p. 68.

2. Barbara Manard, Cary Kart, and Dirk van Gils, *Old-Age Institutions* (Lexington, Massachusetts: D. C. Heath, 1975), pp. 44–49.

3. Those living "dependently with their children" refers to those elderly designated in the Census as "Parents of Head of Household." This category does not include all the elderly who live with their children. If a 75-year-old grandfather has retired to the home of his 50-year old son, the grandfather may still be designated by the family to the Census taker as the "Head of Household."

4. States in which more than 10 percent of the elderly live dependently with their children are: Connecticut, New York, New Jersey, Delaware, Maryland, Virginia, North Carolina, South Carolina, and Georgia.

5. These states all have fewer than 4 percent in OAI, fewer than 30 percent living extrafamilially, and fewer than 10 percent living dependently with children.

6. Manard, Kart, and van Gils, p. 21.

7. Ibid., p. 118.

8. Ibid., p. 120.

9. Lenore A. Epstein, "Living arrangements and income of the aged," *Social Security Bulletin* 26 (1963):3-8.

10. "Availability of beds" $= \dfrac{\text{Number of OAI beds in State}}{\text{Number of elderly in State}}$ x 1,000.
Although people of all ages use nursing-home beds, in every state nearly all the residents are over 65. Hence it is more accurate to measure the relative availability of beds using the number of persons 65 and over as a base.

11. Marjorie Bloomberg Twin, *Older Americans* (National Council on the Aging, 1971), p. 47.

12. The total number of people who enter nursing homes during any year (and hence contribute to the annual total expenditures) is greater than the number of residents at any one time. However, since the mean length of stay for nursing-home residents is about a year, we do not expect that the actual average amount of public money spent per resident would be much different from the number we calculated; and that, in any event, errors should not be systematically different among the states.

13. This practice is demonstrated in detail for Massachusetts, Utah, and Virginia in Manard, Kart, and van Gils, *Old-Age Institutions* (Lexington, Massachusetts: D. C. Heath, 1975).

DIFFERENCES IN PROPRIETARY INSTITUTIONS CARING FOR AFFLUENT AND NONAFFLUENT ELDERLY*

Jordan I. Kosberg

Most people would agree that the poor are second-class citizens in the United States. This class transcends racial, ethnic, and religious considerations and becomes most indiscriminate in old age. To be old as well as poor exacerbates the problem and magnifies the discrepancy in opportunities and benefits of life found to exist at younger ages between the rich and the poor. The dearth of resources for the aged poor who are in declining health is striking. They are often financially unable to maintain independent living in the community as a result of deteriorating health which, in part, may result from nutritional deficiencies and inadequate medical attention caused by their poverty. In addition, they are unable to afford private nurses, special services, or escape to environments with more desirable climates. Too often, institutionalization is society's answer to the question of how to care for the nonaffluent elderly.

To be sure, the rich as well as the poor are institutionalized. There are marked differences, however, in the characteristics of institutions caring for affluent and nonaffluent elderly. It is the purpose of this paper to discuss several areas of differences between proprietary institutions caring for welfare recipients and institutions caring for private residents, as well as explore the

---

* Jordan I. Kosberg, "Differences in Proprietary Institutions Caring for Affluent and Nonaffluent Elderly," *Gerontologist* 13 (1973): 299-304.

421

reasons for the differences which exist. The dissimilarities to be discussed include: (1) quality of care, (2) quantity of resources, (3) physical factors, and (4) staff treatment and attitudes. Nursing homes will be most often used as examples, and it is believed that these types of institutions may be representative of other types of proprietary institutions caring for the aged.

Quality of Care

Studies have consistently and statistically indicated that institutions caring for welfare recipients are inferior to those institutions caring for nonwelfare recipients. Townsend (1964) surveyed homes for the aged in England and Wales and concluded that public assistance facilities, which cared for the poorest elderly, provided an inferior form of care more so than homes caring for the more affluent elderly. The quality of care was determined by the physical facilities, staffing and services, freedom for residents in daily life, and by social provisons.

Penchansky and Taubenhaus (1965), in their study of nursing homes, defined quality as being related to the provisions of services and performance of employed personnel. It was their contention that the quality of care in nursing homes was affected by the method of reimbursement. They argued that welfare departments generally place welfare recipients in the most inexpensive institutions. The low and fixed reimbursement system does not provide a financial incentive for quality care; therefore, a lower quality of care is provided to welfare recipients.

From a study of 26 nursing homes, Greenwald and Linn (1971) also concluded that more expensive homes were superior along several dimensions. They utilized a Nursing Home Rating Scale which combined factual data with impressionistic evaluations. It was found that higher average-cost homes were significantly correlated with a pleasant atmosphere, patient communication, satisfaction, and cleanliness, physical facilities available and the proper provision of meals. These higher-cost homes, of course, served a more affluent aged group.

In a study of 118 nursing homes in Minnesota, Anderson, Holmberg, Schneider, and Stone (1969) attempted to ascertain

422

organizational factors related to care. Their definition of quality consisted of 9 indicators pertaining to physical features of facilities (i.e., space, bathrooms, etc.), staffing characteristics, patient participation in social and psychological programs, and administrators' attitudes toward rehabilitation. Nursing-home characteristics were then correlated to the quality scores and heading the list of the 12 characteristics, correlated to quality, was the percentage of welfare patients—in an inverse relationship. As the authors state: "The higher the percent of patients receiving welfare in a home, the lower the quality of the home."

Even from the findings of these few studies, it becomes apparent that homes caring for the nonaffluent (that is, homes with inexpensive rates for care) are different from homes caring for affluent individuals. Although the definitions of quality were different, these studies all disclose the fact that institutional settings for the elderly poor (specifically, nursing homes) are qualitatively inferior.

Quantity of Resources

While the above-mentioned studies referred to the quality of institutions or care provided therein, this writer attempted to ascertain the organizational correlates to treatment resources existing within 214 nursing homes in the Chicago area (Kosberg, 1971). It was stipulated that quality was beyond the scope of the study but that there should be a relationship between the existence of treatment resources and the quality of care. Implicit was the assumption that for treatment resources (e.g., professional personnel, equipment, facilities) to be effectively utilized, the resources must first exist within an institution.

Depending upon the existence and adequacy of treatment resources, each institution received a Resource Score. Organizational characteristics were correlated to the scores. Of interest were the findings of inverse relationships between Resource Scores and percentage of black residents (-.27), percentage of public aid payments (-.57), and percentage of residents referred by public aid (-.48). The independent variables were intercorrelated and it was further found that institutions located in

423

urban areas serve populations who are on welfare and who are likely to be black (Kosberg & Tobin, 1972). Homes serving these populations were measured to have low scores.

State licensing and Medicare standards necessitate long-term care facilities meeting minimum requirements. These requirements include various quantitative features which attempt to ensure—among other things—a minimum level of resources. While, in principle, such standards do provide minimum requirements which each institution must meet or be denied licensure or certification, unfortunately, this is not the case in actuality. For example:

> Of the Springfield [Illinois] nursing homes with over half of their patients on public aid, most cannot meet 1970 state standards for nursing homes, according to state officials (Katz, 1970).

Given low welfare reimbursement rates, the limited number of institutions willing to care for welfare aid recipients, and the great demand for such facilities, often minimum requirements are not enforced. Witness the conclusions reached by Project FIND, conducted by the National Council on the Aging:

> Though nursing homes were available in every community, it was clear that in many cases beds for elderly poor were in short supply. Often even Old Age Assistance clients were placed in nursing homes with low standards (in one community the use of unlicensed facilities was reported) because of the low rate payment allowed by the Department of Public Welfare (National Council on Aging, 1970).

Closing institutions which cannot meet standards would seriously limit the supply of institutions caring for elderly poor. To preclude this occurrence, it can be argued that even an inferior facility is better than none.

Nursing homes certified by Medicare as extended-care facilities (ECF) are believed to be quantitatively better than homes which cannot meet Medicare requirements, in terms of the existence of professional staff and provisions for intensive nursing care. The study by this writer, referred to above, did find a positive association between the extent of resources and Medicare certification. While we can conclude that ECF facilities are quantitatively superior, we cannot assume that the aged poor take advantage of the Medicare program and, thus, would get into Medicare facilities.

> . . . Medicare seems to have reached the Negro to a much smaller degree than it has reached whites. Although the proportion of FIND aged poor who said they were not signed up for Medicare (. . .) was 15%, about twice the proportion of the aged in general, a larger proportion of Negroes, about 22%, reported that they had not signed up. This is over three times the national average (National Council on Aging, 1970).

A report by the Senate Special Committee on Aging concluded that although aged blacks had urgent medical needs which would warrant placement into Medicare facilities, they could not afford the deductible, and so were excluded from Medicare benefits (Special Committee on Aging, 1971).

Although the aged poor have been discussed as a group, without racial differentiation, it is apparent that being old, poor, and black compounds the probability of placement into an inferior institution, or preclusion of placement into an ECF or expensive facility which can meet higher standards. This group of elderly are often on welfare and would be placed in institutions caring for welfare aid recipients. In one study, Weeks and Darsky (1968) found that one-third of the blacks over 75 years of age were receiving Old Age Assistance, while only 1 out of 20 of the whites were. A Cook County (Illinois) Dept. of Public Aid report (1966) indicated that of all blacks in nursing homes, 82 percent were on Old Age Assistance. Project FIND confirmed the association between race and Public Assistance.

Physical Factors

The aged poor generally are found in urban, rather than suburban, areas. For the aged and poor minority group member, economic and racial discrimination results in their being limited to geographically condensed areas (called barrios, inner cities, ghettoes, etc.). It is institutions located in such urban areas to which these elderly poor are referred. Such institutions, located in old and run-down areas are often converted homes and are smaller than suburban facilities or those facilities built more recently (Kosberg, 1971). Often these converted facilities have no elevators, and there are steep staircases to upper floors, making it extremely difficult and painful (if not impossible) for the elderly to go, for example, from one's living quarters on the second floor down to the TV room or lobby on the ground floor.

Many of the owners of these small, old, and converted nursing homes, claiming that welfare reimbursements are too low, cannot afford to upgrade their facilities to meet minimum standards. Instead, they seek licensure as Sheltered Care Facilities (which require lower standards). Yet, the characteristics and needs of the residents cared for remains basically unchanged.

In a study of the relationships between the sources of referral and payment and spatial distribution of institutional placements for aged in Chicago, Gold (1971) found differences between the aged who were placed in institutions by welfare and those who were self-referred. She found that the aged who were self-referred were, on the average, 2.5 miles closer to relatives than the public aid referrals. In addition, it was found that private referrals are about 1.5 miles closer to their last noninstitutional address than were the aged referred by public aid.

Supplementing Gold's findings is information obtained from interviews with administrators of nursing homes caring for welfare recipients (Kosberg, 1972). The administrators believed that the major criterion used by the welfare departments for the referral of an elderly person (on welfare) to a nursing home was the existence of a vacant bed in a facility accepting welfare aid recipients. They did not believe that the convenience for the family or proximity to former place of residence was considered in the placement made.

Staff Treatment and Attitudes

It has often been shown that the poor and powerless of any age are generally considered to have less moral worth than those with more money or those with access to the ear of those with money (Markson, 1971).

Granting such a view, which certainly extends to the elderly poor, it is believed that there is differential treatment given by professional and nonprofessional staff within institutional settings. While such a conclusion may be—at this point in time—more impressionistic than empirical, such a relationship may very well exist between socioeconomic status of residents and treatment by staff.

Hollingshead and Redlich, in their book *Social Class and Mental Illness* (1958), do not address the matter of differential personal treatment by staff directly (to be distinguished from different types of treatment), but do allude to it when discussing the care given to the wealthy in expensive private mental hospitals.

> The comfort, welfare, and treatment of patients . . . is the acknowledged function of the institution. The administrators and staff know the patients pay for these surroundings, and are aware of the manifest and latent values in this setting.

Conversely, where the patients are poor and on welfare, we might expect that there are no ulterior motives to provide warm and humane treatment—such as fear that the resident will go to another institution if he, or his family, are dissatisfied. This fact might be compounded by the custodial orientation of institutions caring for the poor. By and large, owners and staff of facilities caring for welfare recipients will not even verbalize the fact that they are providing therapeutic care and treatment. They realize that they do not have the professional staff or equipment necessary to implement such a program for the aged (Kosberg, 1972).

Custodial care is, thus, provided to residents on welfare. This results in not only different treatment but different attitudes toward the institutionalized population.

> Patients are conceived of in stereotyped terms as categorically different from "normal" people, as totally irrational,

> insensitive to others, unpredictable, and dangerous . . . Custodialism is saturated with pessimism, impersonalness, and watchful mistrust (Gilbert & Levinson, 1957).

Whether or not institutions caring for affluent residents actually provide therapeutic care may be rhetorical; the fact that those working in such settings think they do may result in a more humane orientation. The facilities caring for welfare recipients provide custodial care in theory as well as in practice.

Most administrators of institutions caring for the affluent elderly realize that their staffs receive gifts from the families of residents for good care provided to a parent or for the promise to "take good care of mama." The fact that such gratuities (i.e., money, food, alcohol, etc.) can influence treatment, again, is of benefit for the affluent resident but does not operate for the nonaffluent resident—whose family cannot afford gifts for staff. Indeed, it has been found that friends and relatives of elderly poor do not visit as often as their affluent counterparts (Kosberg, 1972).

Most staff caring for residents within institutional settings are non- or subprofessional aides, orderlies, custodians, etc. The socioeconomic backgrounds of these individuals employed in institutions can be quite similar to the backgrounds of the nonaffluent elderly for whom they cared. This is especially true in those facilities located in urban ghettoes, where both the majority staff and aged residents are black and from lower socioeconomic levels.

At present, we have insufficient knowledge regarding the treatment of poor elderly persons by those with similar socioeconomic backgrounds. Are these employees sympathetic and kind? Or do they tend to look down upon these elderly for any one of many possible social or psychological reasons? Further, do black professional and nonprofessional staff differentially care for blacks and whites? To be sure, the care given by an employee in an institutional setting will be determined by the individual personality, yet, there is a need for research to answer many questions.

Economic Interpretation

It may appear logical to assume that the elderly poor go into inferior facilities because welfare reimbursement to these facilities is low. Indeed, such a conclusion may be reached by administrators of institutions, public officials, department bureaucrats, as well as the general public. "You get what you pay for," goes the popular saying.

> Economically speaking, the nursing home usually is a small business enterprise, unable to afford an extensive rehabilitation team or its services; this may often be related to the method of reimbursement for the care of welfare patients. These fixed and rather low welfare rates, coupled with the characteristically slow reimbursement, make regular efficient rehabilitation programs an impossibility for many homes (Hefferin, 1968).

Money does seem to be at the root of the problem. Administrators put blame for their inability to upgrade care upon the welfare departments' low reimbursement rates and believe that if institutional standards are raised by public agencies, such bodies have a responsibility to provide grants and loans for such improvements. Welfare departments, in turn, feel their hands are tied by legislative requirements and fiscal allocations. Welfare workers are overworked, undertrained, and cannot ensure the adequacy of each institution in which welfare recipients are placed. State departments claim they need economic assistance to hire and train inspectors, whose functions would center around ensuring that institutions continue to conform to licensing standards.

It is reasonable to expect that proprietary institutions, which receive high rates for care, owe an amount to put back into the institution, after expenses and profit, in way of services, equipment, professional staff, etc. Indeed, representatives of expensive nursing homes justified the high rates for care charged by indicating that the rates allowed them to purchase services and staff for the residents (Kosberg, 1972). Proprietary institutions receiving lower rates for care (such as from public welfare) would have a smaller cash inflow and, thus, would be operating within

429

a smaller margin. These homes caring for nonaffluent aged populations would be less able to afford needed equipment and personnel. This is true for proprietary facilities, but perhaps equally true for nonprofit facilities as well.

From this author's study of 214 nursing homes referred to earlier (Kosberg, 1971), some of the facilities were measured to be rich in treatment resources, yet, with sizable proportions of public aid recipients. Administrators from two such homes were interviewed at length, in the effort of learning how these homes were able to afford the resources they had with such a large proportion of residents being reimbursed by public welfare. It was found that while public aid rates were below costs, the rates for private residents were raised proportionally. This latter private revenue compensated for low welfare rates, allowing for both profit to the owners and resources for the residents. Clearly, such a financial arrangement would be impossible for facilities caring almost exclusively for welfare aid recipients.

Thus, there is validity in economic interpretations for the inability to upgrade facilities caring for nonaffluent residents. Caution must be maintained, however, for it cannot be proven that an additional dollar to an institution will result, *ipso facto,* in an additional dollar's worth of care for the institutionalized population.

Issues for the Future

The purpose of this paper was to indicate areas of differences between the characteristics of proprietary facilities caring for the nonaffluent and affluent elderly. Different social scientists have attempted to measure the quality of institutions and while their measures have varied, their conclusions regarding the relationships between quality of an institution and socioeconomic composition of the residents are similar.

The existence of resources within institutions has also been found to be related to the characteristics of the institutionalized population. While ECF institutions must meet higher resource requirements, the poor often cannot take advantage of the

Medicare program and are—thus—precluded from placement within these facilities.

The elderly poor—especially members of minority groups—are often institutionalized in small, old, and substandard nursing homes; most converted from private dwellings. The elderly poor are further inconvenienced by being placed in facilities which are located further from their families and previous dwellings than is true for the affluent elderly.

Finally, the attitude toward and treatment of the elderly poor by both professional and nonprofessional staff is perhaps different. The need for research in this area is prodigious, and findings will be of great importance in the further assessment of facilities caring for the elderly poor.

Let us assume that the characteristics of proprietary institutions caring for the elderly poor are less desirable (if not detrimental to the institutionalized population). Should we seek to close these facilities caring for welfare aid recipients? Where would these elderly go? What alternatives exist? Markson (1971) asks similar questions regarding where the elderly poor will go who are denied an unnecessary admission at a mental hospital. The answers to such questions have planning and policy implications. As each community has its own system for the care of the elderly poor, it is important to determine whether institutional placements have become community panaceas and the major method by which to care for the elderly who are poor and in declining health.

The characteristics of nursing homes, and other similar types of institutions, caring for the elderly poor are reflections of the more pervasisve attitudes of society toward both the aged and the poor. These facilities exist because they serve a societal function in providing a setting for the elderly who cannot or will not be cared for in other noninstitutional settings. And such institutional settings are, in the main, inferior to those caring for affluent elderly. The conditions found within these institutions could not exist wihtout public apathy and disinterest. What is needed, in addition to further research, are policy revisions which will attempt to alleviate the disparities which exist in facilities for the aged of different socioeconomic status. That these conditions and disparities exist in American society—and continue to—is at once damning and challenging.

WHY
NURSING HOMES
DO WHAT THEY DO[*][1]

Leonard E. Gottesman
and Norman C. Bourestom

Of all the criteria which one might wish to consider in de
scribing what nursing homes do, actual observation is preferable.
Such observation need not rely on staffing patterns, equipment
lists, or staff attitudes as secondary indicators of performance.
Instead, observation can discover exactly what happens, when,
where, and to whom.

The Study

The Nursing Home Research Project at the University of
Michigan, and later at the Philadelphia Geriatric Center, under-
took in 1971–1972 to develop observation-based outcome measures which would reflect the care given in all of Greater Detroit's
nursing homes. Briefly, the measures conceptualize nursing-home
services into three observable categories of activities (Bourestom
& Gottesman, 1973). First, basic services, which include support
of personal care and activities of daily living; second, medical
and rehabilitative services which include medications, language
or range of motion training and other activities which are intended to undo a malfunction or improve level of function; and
third. psychosocial services given either individually or in groups

* Leonard E. Gottesman and Norman C. Bourestom, "Why Nursing Homes Do What
They Do," *Gerontologist* 14 (1974): 501-06.

432

including occupational and recreational therapies, social services, religious services and diversional activities. These categories included all times when staff helped residents and whenever residents helped each other or themselves. The measure also had two indicators of less desirable nursing-home care. The first, passive activity, included instances when the resident was in a very limited degree of interaction with the physical or social world around him, as, for example, when sitting and mechanically smoking or rocking or when standing about but not interacting with another person. The final level of behavior, null activity, included all those instances when the person observed appeared to be out of contact with his world, either sleeping, sitting, or standing while blankly staring into space. Using this conceptualization of behavior, it was possible to record virtually every activity which occurred in nursing homes.

The procedure used for recording behavior employed two trained assistants who observed residents during 24 1-hour segments between 6:30 a.m. and 7:30 p.m. on 2 days. In each hour the resident was observed for one full minute in a predetermined sequence. Each time a record was made of the services given or the activity of the patient and of his location, position, and involvement with other people.

These observations were planned to sample nursing-home activity during the peak daylight hours. In each home prior to beginning their observations, the assistants were introduced by the home's director of nursing, explained the study, and obtained residents' agreement to be included in the study. In essence, the procedure was to locate the resident, observe his behavior, and move on to the next resident. Occasionally judgments of the nature of behavior observed were difficult as, for example, in differentiating between active TV watching and sitting out of contact in front of a TV set. Also when residents were behind closed doors, their behavior was either not recorded or judged from the context. These problems were rare, and three sorts of evidence support the accuracy of the observations as measures of nursing-home performance. First, the observers felt they were getting an accurate picture; second, the nursing-home staff believed the observers were seeing a real picture of the nursing home and that their records were congruent with that reality.

433

Finally interobserver agreement, i.e., two observers viewing the same events measured on several occasions, was between 70 and 100 percent (average 85 percent).

Five samples were selected for study with the assistance of the sampling branch of the University of Michigan Institute for Social Research: (1) nursing homes, (2) residents of the selected homes, (3) their administrators, (4) directors of nursing, and (5) nurses aides. The population for the study included all of Detroit's licensed nursing homes which were not operated by a hospital and not exclusively homes for the aged, rehabilitation hospitals, mental hospitals, or TB Sanataria. All 169 homes which met this definition were stratified according to size, ownership, and proportion of public-aid recipients. Probability sampling then selected 40 homes which would together yield valid estimates of the total group. By design these 40 homes oversampled nonprofit church-related nursing homes by including all 10 which existed in Detroit.

In each selected home the administrator and the director of nursing within the selected homes were selected for study. On the basis of probability sampling 1,144 residents and 200 nurses aides were selected in proportion to the actual distribution of residents and aides in all 169 nursing homes. Several characteristics of the homes, residents, and staff selected suggest that this sample is similar to nursing homes throughout the country (Bourestom & Gottesman, 1973).

In addition to observation of residents described above, each home was rated by our staff with regard to a number of physical and social characteristics, and each staff member selected was interviewed about his training and experience and his knowledge and attitudes about residents. Using the Katz ADL Scale, each resident's level of self-care ability was determined. Direct administration of the Kahn-Goldfarb Mental Status Questionnaire examination determined the mental status of each sample resident.

The results will be reported in four sections: residents' traits, what was observed, the relationship of the residents' physical and mental conditions to the observed behaviors, and the relationship of other characteristics of the residents, the staff, and the homes to the observations.

434

1a. *Residents' functional abilities.* The Katz ADL scale asks a knowledgeable staff member to rate each resident as needing no help (score 1), some help (score 2), or much help (score 3) with each of six activities of daily living (bathing, dressing, toileting, transfer, continence, eating). These ratings showed that 60 percent of residents needed considerable help in bathing, and 26 percent needed some help; 56 percent needed considerable help dressing, and 9 percent some help. Persons requiring considerable help toileting totaled 16 percent, while 30 percent needed some help. Only 2 percent of the residents needed considerable help getting around, and 39 percent needed some help. One-quarter of those sampled were incontinent, and 19 percent more needed occasional help. Eating required much assistance for 14 percent of those studied, and 22 percent required some help.

Those persons requiring considerable help in one activity generally required help with other activities. Based on the total scores for the six activities, 6 to 9 points were considered indicators of relatively little need for assistance, 10 to 14 as need for some assistance, and over 14 as need for considerable help. By this definition of the 1,144 persons rated, 47 percent needed little assistance over-all, 34.1 percent some assistance, and 22.2 percent were dependent on much staff assistance.

An additional indicator of the functioning of the residents is that 20 percent of them were never observed in bed, and 60 percent were out of bed during at least 19 of the 24 observations.

1b. *Residents' mental status.* The modified Kahn-Goldfarb Mental Status Questionnaire asked residents to identify the current date, their age and date of birth, their current location, and the last two presidents of the USA (total 6 points). Forty-seven percent of subjects got all six of the elements correct and were judged alert; 28 percent more were moderately alert (4–5 points); and 25 percent were confused (0–3 points). There was a strong tendency for those who were most physically dependent to also be the most confused ($r = .43$).

2. *Residents' activities and social interactions.* Of 27,456 observations made, 39 percent were of the residents in null activity. Another 17 percent of the time the residents were engaged in passive activity—sat, rocked, or just stood. Thus, 56 percent

435

of the residents' time during the day, from morning to evening, was spent doing nothing.

Nearly 23 percent of observations were residents' bathing, dressing, or in other personal care, 4½ percent of this was with a staff member. Another 20 percent was spent watching TV or socializing, 3 percent with a staff member. In other words, 43 percent of the time was spent in personal care or social activity. Of this time 7.6 percent was with staff.

During the entire 27,456 observations only 2 percent of the time were residents observed receiving a nursing service from a professional or nonprofessional staff member.

Residents were in contact with any other person in 17 percent of the observations.

Residents' contact with nonstaff persons totaled 7.5 percent of all observation time. Psychosocial activity was 6.1 percent of the total, and personal care 1.4 percent of the time.

The study measured not only the number of times an activity occurred but also if it happened at all. Based on that measure during the observations, 23 percent of all residents were observed receiving at least one nursing contact, 98 percent in some personal care activity, and 80 percent in at least one psychosocial activity.

3. *Correlates of observed activities.* The data documenting the number of times a person was observed in basic, social, or nursing activity were grouped as measures of quality of nursing home care. Since staff contact occurred so seldom, all activity whether with staff members or not were combined.

As expected, residents who were physically and mentally dependent were observed doing less of their own basic physical care than more able residents, but even the disabled did many things for themselves (r = .15). On the other hand, when aides were observed helping residents, those helped were the most physically disabled (r = .42). People who were frequently observed in bed were the ones most likely to be observed receiving staff attention. As one might expect, the most socially active residents were the least disabled physically (r = .37) and the most alert (r = .45). So little nursing care was observed that meaningful statistical tests were not possible.

436

4. *Observed activities and characteristics of homes, management, and staff.* From a variety of instruments used in the larger study, 26 characteristics of residents, staff, and management were found to have appropriate distributions for analysis (e.g., not seriously skewed) and to be of conceptual interest for examining their relationship to observed basic, psychosocial, and nursing behavior. These variables were examined using the statistic *gamma* (γ).[2] Because of the large number of subjects all relationships at or above $\gamma = .04$ were significant at the $p < .05$ level. Eighteen of the relationships with basic care, 16 with psychosocial care, and 24 with nursing care reached this level of significance within each set of comparisons, all γ values were then ranked to find the strongest relationships. The five strongest relationships to basic care, psychosocial care and nursing care ranged respectively from $\gamma = .24$ to .14; $\gamma = .49$ to .17; and $\gamma = .43$ to 27.

In order of magnitude, residents observed receiving the largest amount of *basic care* were in a home (1) where residents had possessions, (2) where new aides were expected by management to have prior experience working with residents, and (3) which is either nonprofit or proprietary and with 2/3 or more private patients. Two other high correlates were that the (4) resident was white and (5) had visitors at least once a month.

Residents receiving or engaging in the most psychosocial activity were (1) judged by staff as easy to motivate, (2) had visitors at least once a month, (3) were in a home where residents have personal possessions, (4) were younger than residents of homes with less psychosocial activity, and (5) were in a home where the director of nursing was observed in contact with residents.

The four characteristics most strongly related to amount of nursing care observed were that: (1) the residents' care was privately supported, (2) the resident was white, (3) he had visitors at least once a month, and (4) management valued aide training. Two characteristics tied for fifth place were that: (5) (6) the home was nonprofit or proprietary with 2/3 or more private residents and the resident was recently admitted.

The three types of care, while having somewhat different correlates, had sufficient commonality so that a combined ranking of the three was made. Based on this combination the top five correlates of overall quality of nursing home care were that: (1) the resident had had a recent visitor, (2) the resident had personal possessions, (3) most of the residents in the homes were white, (4) the home was either nonprofit or proprietary with 2/3 or more private residents, and (5) residents had jobs they could do around the nursing home.

These data contain good news and bad. It is good that the people receiving the most care are the most impaired and needful. This means that nursing homes do what they are intended to do. It is also good that most residents were observed in some personal care and social activities. For many people life in nursing homes is better than we had feared. On the other hand, since for the most part we were observing residents of skilled nursing homes, it seems bad that only 2 percent of resident contact observed was skilled nursing.

We have no comparative data which describe people in their own homes. For that reason we can only raise as a point for discussion that 56 percent of people's time was spent doing so little. To us this amount seems excessive, even assuming that people are disabled and have no compelling demands on their time. In fact, lack of demand seems part of the problem. We think that people would feel very isolated if they are in a group setting but spend no more than 17 percent of their time in contact with any other person. They must also feel abandoned if they are in a care setting and their contact with a staff member for all reasons fills only 10 percent of their time.

The two kinds of settings which appear to give the most care are those which have a clear-cut nursing mission and mobilize staff skills for short periods of treatment time and those which provide a place for social and personal activities for longer periods. It is too bad that the best of both of these are provided disproportionately to the white family member with private resources to pay for his care.

These homes are described elsewhere (Gottesman, 1974). They are the nonprofit and elite private homes that cater to a very limited clientele—a clientele which is better off in a number of ways than most people who use nursing homes. By far the most common type of nursing home serves publicly paid-for residents who do not have families. However, what works for the elite can realistically be mobilized for others. I would like to make three recommendations:

The first is that nursing homes be made more accountable. Our colleague, Barney (1974), has discussed the failure of ordinary regulatory mechanisms in dealing with a service which has disabled, powerless people as its clientele. In seeking maximum efficiency and productivity, the usual organizational goals, nursing homes may take advantage of clients who cannot stand up for their own wishes. There is nothing in these data which suggests that this danger results from a profit motive in nursing-home care. Some of both types of homes give good care. But, what seems to mark the best of them is their accountability. The implicit meaning of white, private pay, family members as residents is that someone out there cares about them and is able to act on their behalf. To the extent that public payment is unlimited and without careful accountability, the system of care is not likely to be responsive to the needs of either the payor or the client. Barney (1974) describes a role for a community presence—anyone going into and out of a nursing home—as exerting a subtle influence on care. She calls for more volunteers, more suppliers, more inspectors, more relatives and friends visiting, more community sponsorship of nursing homes. Three models she discusses are administrators inviting relatives' participation in nursing-home activities, involvement of community groups in providing supplementary programs, and the Federal Ombudsman Program, which is training senior citizens to hear and solve residents' problems. She suggests that nursing homes might function with a kind of elected citizen board similar to a school board.

Our data support the strong relationship of visitors to good care. This finding is amplified by Glaser and Strauss' (1968) discovery that in the acute-care hospital, patients who have relatives get more care. Since most nursing-home residents do not have relatives, the Federal Ombudsman program may be an important resource. To be most effective, the ombudsman should not simply be an inspector. Being a friend of a resident is a stronger base from which to influence care. Also, the role of friend is likely to be acceptable to resident, nursing home administrator,

439

and the ombudsman, while the role of inspector is likely to foster a great deal of counterproductive hostility.

Implicitly, the ombudsman as a visitor would also help to alleviate problems caused by isolation of the home and its residents. If each of the 1,100 people we observed had frequent visitors their lives would be richer and more closely resemble a normal tempo.

The second recommendation is that nursing-home life in general be modeled more on normal life roles. Already most of the life in nursing homes is invested in personal care, and a great deal of it is independent of direct staff involvement. A good reason for the nursing home's existence is that it provides a structured opportunity for as much independence as the resident can manage. This means that, properly operated, the home would place more power in its residents. The most active homes in our study already allow for resident roles and possessions, both of which are symbols of power. It would not be too hard to build these and more into nursing-home life. To begin with, one must recognize that for many residents the nursing home is their home. The average nursing-home stay is 2 years, and the average resident does not expect to leave. She sees the place as her only home. In one's home, one ought to have her own space, her own things, and her thing to do.

Several programs developed in institutions have suggested how nursing homes might offer these amenities. The role of the staff in these programs becomes less one of doing things for residents and more one of staging opportunities for resident independence. This can be accomplished first by identifying areas of life where levels of behavior acceptable to the resident can be maintained without staff help. In these areas, staff must carefully keep uninvolved. Second, the staff must try to structure opportunities for independent behavior in other ways desired by the resident. For example, independence can be fostered by such environmental aids as good lighting and marked pathways on the floor. Both of these interventions are inexpensive and easily provided. In addition, planned opportunities for engagement in moderately demanding and meaningful activities can be developed by trained staff members. Examples include sheltered workshops, social groups, and resident government. In all of

440

these programs the central characteristic is that meaningful activities become a planned and valued focus of the entire day. The extent to which such a program meets that criterion is the priority it is given in the daily schedule.

Our data also suggest that a third way to improve nursing homes is to consolidate their care. Most residents spent most of their time without interaction. Most residents also did most things for themselves. These facts do not mean that the residents had no need for a supportive environment, but they do suggest that many of them would do well if they lived in a home providing bed and board and could go out several days a week for an engaging activity. A day-care program would provide such an opportunity. Besides providing planned activities, a day-care program would also need to include planned arrangements for occasional intensive nursing care and for home-care service to help the person to manage in his home. For this approach, the combination of residence, engagement and other service is essential. Based on the history of prior reforms, I am reluctant even to suggest this plan, for fear that to many it would suggest a string of boarding homes or a simple downgrading of all (or most) skilled nursing home care. This would be devastating; it would damage people we care about and create a horror of substandard living much worse than the scandals that appall us today.

There is nothing in our data which suggests less care. Our data only suggest a different focus of care. Whether this care would cost less is still open to study, but there is reason to suppose that, rather than wasting staff and physical plant resources by spreading them over 24-hour, 7-day care, we can organize them to provide at once a more efficient use of resources and a more humane kind of care.

Notes

1. NIMH Grant 7 RO 1 MH22083.

2. A statistic closely related to *tau*, which reflects differences in order of variables. The difference between *gamma* and *tau* is that *gamma* is specifically appropriate for data arranged in order class.

OLD FOLKS
AND DIRTY WORK:
THE SOCIAL CONDITIONS
FOR PATIENT ABUSE
IN A NURSING HOME*
Charles I. Stannard

This report will try to show how patient abuse can occur in a small, proprietary nursing home without the nurses who work there being aware that it is a recurring problem. I will try to show how the everyday conditions of work in the nursing home and people's reactions to them not only prevent the nurses from seeing much of the abuse that goes on, but also, by impeding the development of trust and communication among the groups who work and reside there and coloring the relations that obtain among these people with distrust, hostility, and cynicism, these conditions keep the nurses from hearing about abuse. These same conditions, finally, also provide the nurses with a variety of reasonable denials of the occurrence of abuse when infrequent allegations of its use by orderlies and aides are made. These denials and differentials in the awareness of abuse reduce its visibility to the nurses, making it appear random and infrequent, thereby masking the fact that it appears to be a patterned response of the aides and orderlies to their recurring problems of controlling the patients. In so doing, they serve to perpetuate the abuse (Coser, 1969; Moore and Tumin, 1949).

The data on which this analysis is based were gathered by participant observation in a 65-bed proprietary nursing home located in a suburb of a large midwestern city. Participant

* Charles I. Stannard, "Old Folks and Dirty Work: The Social Conditions for Patient Abuse in a Nursing Home," *Social Problems* 20: 3 (Winter, 1973): 329–42.

442

observation involves the researcher entering a group or organization, observing interaction patterns, and discussing the meaning
and import of the interactions with group members (Bruyn,
1966; Schwartz and Schwartz, 1955; Zelditch, 1962). The aim
of such research is to develop a systemic or holistic model of
the group under investigation (Becker, 1958; Weiss, 1968). This
leads to an emphasis on the similarities and commonalities in
the patterns of interaction, rather than an emphasis on the differences or variations, as is the case in other modes of research,
especially survey research (Becker, et al., 1961, p. 22).

Initial contact with the nursing home began in the fall of
1967. From September to December, I made a dozen visits to
the home; more intensive contact began in June 1968, and lasted
until February 1969. During this period, my identity was that
of a sociologist writing a book on nursing homes. Later, in the
summer of 1969, I worked as a janitor in the home for six weeks.

Personnel Problems: Marginality, Turnover, and Absenteeism

The greatest problem the nursing home faced was securing
and maintaining an adequate staff. The people who worked
there reflected the unattractiveness of this type of work and the
low wages the home paid, problems that appear common to
nursing homes (U.S. Department of Labor, 1969; Kansas State
Department of Health, 1964, p. 82). Most of the people who
worked in the nursing home occupied marginal positions in the
labor market. Most nonsupervisory employees were from the
urban lower class. Of these, the bulk were black women who
were divorced or widowed. Whites working in the home were
often migrants from the rural South. With the exception of a
few middle-class high school girls who worked as aides during
the summer, the employees had little in the way of education,
training, or skills.

Even the supervisory personnel often lacked training or ac-
creditation. Of the five Registered Nurses (RN) employed at the
home, two were no longer licensed, though this did not prevent
them from performing the same duties as the licensed nurses.

443

Only one Licensed Practical Nurse (LPN) had received formal training for that position; the others became LPNs by passing a special waiver examination created to increase the number of LPNs in the state.

Some of the people who worked in the home had "spoiled identities" (Goffman, 1963). These included former mental patients, several men who had criminal records (one was on probation while working at the home), a former alcoholic, several men who appeared to be homosexuals, several people whose bizarre behavior seemed to indicate mental illness, and several men who appeared to be drifters in need of temporary employment.

Nonsupervisory personnel did not develop strong commitments to their jobs or to the home. This is suggested by the turnover and absenteeism among employees. The nursing home had a very difficult time maintaining a numerically adequate staff. During 1968, 225 people worked at the home. Since 45 people constituted a full complement of employees, the turnover was extremely high, 500 percent.

A record was also kept of the total number of bi-monthly pay periods a person worked at the home during 1968. These were tallied for those people who were working there in December 1968, which gives some measure of the degree to which people were likely to stay on at the home and provides an indication of the amount of continuity and experience among the staff. The distribution was found to be distinctly bimodal: an employee either worked at the home a relatively short time—two months or less—or he worked the entire year. Thus, of the 45 people employed in the final pay period of 1968, 56 percent worked two months or less and the bulk of these people (15 out of 24) worked a month or less at the home. At the other extreme, a third of the employees worked the entire year.

The tendency to remain employed at the home was not evenly distributed among the employees. Those in supervisory positions were much more likely to stay on than those in non-supervisory positions. Eight of the 15 who worked the entire year were RNs or LPNs. The nine supervisory people working at the end of 1968 averaged 21.6 pay periods of employment, while the other employees (aides, orderlies, janitors, kitchen help) averaged only 7.8 pay periods.

Absenteeism was also a chronic problem. In order to estimate the amount of absenteeism in the home, a sample of three months—April, May, and October—was chosen randomly. For each day of these months, a count was taken of the number of absences as noted on the official payroll sheets. A record was also kept of the particular shift on which an absence occurred (day, evening, and night), and whether the person was directly engaged in patient care (RN, LPN, aide, orderly) or supporting patient care (janitor, cook, dishwasher, laundryman). This distinction is important because absences among those in the

Table 1
The Number of Absences by Shift Worked
For April, May, and October

Shift	7-3		3-11		11-7		Support*	
Number of Absences	Days	Percent	Days	Percent	Days	Percent	Days	Percent
None	13	14%	19	20%	79	86%	28	30%
One	22	24	31	34	13	14	31	34
Two	18	20	18	20	——	——	21	23
Three or more	39	42	24	26	——	——	12	13
Total	92	100	92	100	92	100	92	100

* Includes all employees not engaged in patient care: cooks, janitors, dishwashers, laundrymen.

support group created different problems for those in charge of the home. The data on absenteeism are presented in Table 1.

Like turnover, absenteeism was extremely common among the employees. On the day shift someone was absent 86 percent of the time; on the evening shift an absence occurred 80 percent of the time; 14 percent of the time someone was absent on the night shift; and 70 percent of the time someone working in the support group was absent.

Furthermore, on many days there were multiple absences. On the day shift two people were absent 20 percent of the time; three or more people were absent 42 percent of the time. At one time during the period sampled, more than one-third of the people scheduled to work did not show up.

The other shifts, with the exception of the night shift, fared only slightly better. On the evening shift two or more people were absent 46 percent of the time; three or more people were absent 26 percent of the time. One evening during the period sampled, two-thirds of those scheduled to work on this shift did not show up. Among those working in support activities, two or more people were absent 36 percent of the time. Absences among these employees were more of a problem because many of the tasks of this group could not be neglected or shared if the patients were to be cared for. The meals had to be cooked, the dishes cleaned and stacked, meals set up, and the linen and laundry cleaned. This made an absence on this shift doubly troublesome because it meant that someone, usually an aide, had to be taken from her job and assigned to one of these tasks, thereby, creating a shortage among those caring for patients.

Personnel Problems and the Role of the Nurse

The problems of maintaining a sufficient staff to run the home, while affecting everyone in the home, had their greatest impact on the RNs who ran the home on a daily basis. The vulnerability of the nurses to the effects of the personnel problems lay in the centrality and visibility of the nurse's role.

The prime responsibility for the day-to-day provision of patient care and the operation of the home rested with the nurses. They held themselves responsible for the type of care administered and were held responsible for this by all the people who interacted within the home. The owner, the patients' doctors and relatives, the other employees, and the patients, all looked to the nurses for information, direction, decisions, help, and guidance in the daily affairs of the home.

The central problem for the nurses was that, though they were charged with the responsibility for the type of care the patients received, in actuality they provided little of this care themselves. Rather, they were, like their counterparts in general hospitals, administrators (Mauksch, 1966; Corwin & Taves, 1963) who organized, coordinated, and directed the activities of the aides. With the exception of giving injections or other specialized medical procedures such as subcutaneous feedings and examining sick patients, the aides took care of the patients' needs. The bulk of the nurses' time was taken up with administrative duties, which included, when the owner was not present in the home,[1] ordering supplies, hiring employees, and dealing with people seeking admission to the home for themselves or a relative.

This meant that in order for the nurses to fulfill the mandate of their position (Hughes, 1958), they had to rely heavily on the performances of the other employees in the home. If these people did not perform well, the nurses were held accountable by the other status groups, especially the relatives. The problem for the nurses was that the unreliability of the other employees and the patients themselves[2] continually called into question their ability to fulfill this mandate to provide good care for the patients.

The plight of the nurses was manifested in bitter cynicism and adamant custodialism. They were extremely cynical, doubting the intentions, sincerity, and capabilities of all the other people who interacted with them in the home and continually imputing illegitimate motives to these people's actions. The nurses were most suspicious of the other employees, regarding them as unreliable, untrustworthy, dishonest, and immoral. Thus, they were skeptical when an employee called in sick or offered mitigating circumstances as an excuse for an absence. One time an aide called in and told the nurses that she would not be coming to work because a relative had died. She was especially suspect because it was Monday morning. A nurse commented that the aide was probably hung over from the weekend, and also said that this particular relative had "died" before. Because theft was a recurrent problem, the nurses warned new employees to keep their money and wallets on their persons at all times when in the home. Patients' relatives were also told to remove any of the patients' valuables from the home or to put them in the owner's office in the basement so they would not be stolen. The nurses were also doubtful of the ability and willingness of the employees to work, and felt that many of the people who worked there were lazy, stupid, or just did not want

447

to learn how to do their jobs well. Finally, they doubted the moral probity of the employees and saw them living immoral lives, replete with illicit sex and excessive drinking. As one nurse said of the aides: "They have the morals of an alley cat."

The employee problems affected the nurses' relations with other status groups in the home by creating conflicts with them. Because of these conflicts, the nurses saw these people as ignorant of their difficulties in running the home and unsympathetic to their plight. What is important to note about the complaints the nurses had with these people is that these complaints were directly related to their difficulties in running the home, which, in turn, stemmed in large measure from the problems with the employees.

The nurses were irritated by doctors who were reluctant or unwilling to prescribe tranquilizing drugs for fear of "snowing the patients under," which made it harder for the nurses to control the patients and prevent them from disrupting the daily routines of the home or from escaping or injuring themselves. In dealing with these doctors, the nurses would try, often unsuccessfully, to persuade them of the importance or necessity of tranquilizers for problem patients. The relatives created similar problems for the nurses by refusing to let them restrain the patients, thereby increasing the potential for an accident or escape, both of which reflected badly on the nurses. Complaints about the care given by the home were taken to indicate ill will on the part of the relatives. The Health Department was always finding what the nurses regarded as trivial faults in the home—burned out light bulbs, dirt in closets, inadequate charts—but overlooked the real problems the help created. The nurses viewed the owner as unsympathetic and unconcerned with the home. He demonstrated this to them by his low involvement in the affairs of the home, his hiring and wage policies, his occasional attempts to fire employees the nurses regarded as reliable and competent, and by his allowing his mother-in-law to meddle in the affairs of the home, always an upsetting experience. Finally, the patients, by their constant rule-breaking and their complaints to their relatives, also frustrated and irritated the nurses.

A custodial ideology dominated the home. The nurses emphasized the hopeless conditions of the patients, their enfeebled mental states, and the necessity of controlling them with drugs and cloth restraints. Care, thus, was defined minimally in terms of tending to the bodily needs of the patients and keeping them and the home clean and orderly—"pediatrics senior-grade" in the words of one nurse. The personnel problems even made achieving these minimal goals uncertain (cf. Stannard, 1971; chap. 3).

The Social Conditions for Patient Abuse

Most people who worked in the nursing home regarded patient abuse as wrong and evil. The nurses felt especially strongly about this. They claimed that such activities happened infrequently in the home and that when they discovered an instance of abuse, they fired the person responsible for it right on the spot. The head nurse claimed that she had come across such behavior only a few times during her three year tenure at the home, and each time she did, the person perpetrating it was fired immediately. During the research, this happened only once, when a LPN observed an aide kicking a patient and fired her. Because of its purported infrequency, the nurses did not regard patient abuse as a problem.

The aides felt the same way as the nurses, that in view of their deteriorated physical and mental conditions, the patients should be humored and helped, not hurt. Yet patient abuse did occur in the home.[3] This happened when a patient assaulted an aide or was perceived as deliberately making her job more difficult than it had to be. Kicking, biting, punching, or spitting at an aide, were, in the aides' minds, inexcusable and punishable behavior. Likewise, a patient who defecated on the floor or in a waste basket when, according to the aide, she was perfectly able to use the toilet, was liable to receive abusive treatment. The fact that the patient violated institutionalized expectations of proper patient behavior temporarily neutralized or suspended (Sykes and Matza, 1957; Matza, 1966) the norm prohibiting abuse of patients. In so doing, it momentarily freed the aide from the restraining power of the norm and allowed her to use illicit force in dealing with the patient.

449

Why were the nurses unaware that aides and orderlies occasionally abused patients? There are several reasons for this. First, the way work was organized left the aides physically isolated with patients. Second, the nurses' hostility toward and suspicion of the other employees reduced the amount of interaction and communication between these two groups. Three, the character of the patients and personnel of the home provided the nurses with ready "accounts"[4] for allegations of abuse. These accounts worked by denying the claim of abuse and imputing malice or ignorance to the person making the claim.

Work in the home was organized so that aides, for the most part, had a set group of patients for whom they alone provided care. The aides received very little direct supervision from the nurses, who were occupied with administrative duties at the nurses' station. As a result, much of what went on between the aide and the patient was not observable to the other aides or to the nurses. The patient's room, the toilets, the tub rooms, were areas where important interaction occurred between aides and patients that were also "private" or could be made so by closing the door (Schwartz, 1968) to suit the aide's or patient's needs. This isolation reduced the chances that the aide would be detected acting improperly with a patient.

Of course, this isolation of aide-patient interaction could be effective only to the extent that the patients did not verbalize their mistreatment to other aides, nurses, relatives, or doctors. Thus, this factor was important especially with those patients who were unable or unwilling to communicate with people about their experiences in the home.

However, this isolation did not prevent abuse from being observed occasionally. Once in a while an aide observed another aide abusing a patient. In some instances the aide was sympathetic to the other aide, feeling that her actions were justified by the patient's actions. In those instances where the aide felt that the other aide acted improperly with a patient, she either did nothing at all or told the other aides about it. When the latter happened, the aides spoke about the personal attributes ("meanness") or objective conditions (widowed and living alone, too old for this type of work) of the aide which they regarded as responsible for the aide's actions.

450

The aides rarely reported such actions to the nurses. One reason was the solidarity and cohesiveness that obtained among the small group of regular and steady employees, who did not want to harm another aide and be responsible for someone losing a job. Among the less well integrated employees, it can be that their lack of integration into the core group of aides left them uncertain about how they were to act and vulnerable to sanctions from the more experienced aides, primarily in the form of lack of cooperation and information about their jobs, and thus unlikely to report abuse to the nurses.

Equally important in restricting information about abuse were the hostility and suspicion that separated the nurses from the other employees, especially the aides. The nurses publicly communicated their dislike, distrust, and low opinion of the lower-level employees, particularly the aides, to these people as they griped about their unreliability, inferiority, immorality, and low intelligence at the nurses' station and other places where the nurses gathered. They literally treated these employees as "nonpersons," derogating their characters openly and in their presence, thus minimizing communication and interaction between them and other employees.

Finally, sometimes patients, their relatives, or an employee complained to the nurses about mistreatment. The usual response of the nurses to such claims was to deny the occurrence of abuse. They did this by making a counter-claim about the person making the complaint, denied the legitimacy and validity of the contentions, and accounted for them by referring to discrediting attributes of the person making the allegation. Thus, the nurses argued that the patients who made such complaints were troublemakers or crazy and did not have to be taken seriously. Similarly, they felt that relatives who took up a patient's case were ignorant of the situation in the home, dupes of a crazy patient, or crazy themselves, and did not have to be taken seriously. When an employee made such an allegation, the nurses and owner imputed ulterior motives to him and in so doing debunked his claim; or they received it skeptically and did nothing.

The various accounts that the nurses offered to deny such claims of maltreatment were based on their definitions of reality in the home. They formed a common "vocabulary of motives"

(Mills, 1941) that stemmed from the basic characteristics of the work force and patients in the home. From the nurses' perspective, both the employees and patients had in common the fact that they were likely to have discrediting attributes or characteristics which made them untrustworthy and unreliable, characteristics which were responsible for their being in the nursing home in the first place. Furthermore, both groups manifested these attributes daily and in so doing made life miserable for the nurses. The employees did not come to work; when they did, they did not perform well; many had elements in their pasts such as criminal arrests, a history of drunkenness, illegitimate children, etc., that were shocking and stigmatizing in terms of the nurses' conventional standards. The patients were unreliable by definition, since one of the reasons for their incarceration was the fact that they could not care for themselves in the outside world (Goffman, 1961, p. 76) and exhibited their incapacities and incompetence daily by their helplessness and frequently bizarre behavior.

Accounting for Abuse: An Example

The interplay of these factors can be seen in the two radically different interpretations of an event that arose during the research. The nurses and owner interpreted the event one way; the aides and other employees another way. The event that precipitated these rival interpretations was the scalding of a patient one evening. Two weeks after the scalding, the patient died in the intensive care unit of a local general hospital. His demise was directly attributable to the scalding in the nursing home.

According to the nurse who was working the evening of the scalding, it was the result of a complicated series of events that began on the day shift. On that day, the man who worked in the laundry did not come to work. Because of this, the nurses on the day shift had to assign an aide to work in the laundry, which was located in the basement of the home. One of the duties of the person doing the laundry was to bring the clean linen and laundry to the floors where the aides and orderlies worked. For one reason or another the person who did the

452

laundry that day neglected to do this for the evening shift, so that shift was short of linen, towels, clothes, and diapers for the incontinent patients.

That night the evening shift was also short of help; there were four people to do the work of nine. The shortage was so great that even the RN on that shift was putting patients to bed. Early in the evening an orderly went to put a patient, Mr. Jones, to bed. The patient had soiled himself and his bed. According to the nurse, the orderly had the "good sense" to clean him and change his linen, something not every employee could be relied on to do. He undressed the patient and put him in a bath tub. After washing him, the orderly went to get a towel and clean linen, but there were none in the linen closet. The janitor who worked on the day shift happened to be on the floor at the time, so the orderly asked him to watch the patient while he went to the basement for some clean towels and linen. Instead of watching the patient, the janitor took some trash cans out to the garbage bin behind the home. He and the orderly returned to the floor at about the same time and found Mr. Jones sitting in a tub of hot water with the faucet on. Both of them panicked when they saw this. They picked the patient up, wrapped him in a clean sheet, and put him to bed. They did not tell the nurse what had happened.

About an hour after the patient was scalded, the evening nurse came to the second floor and "just happened" to look in on Mr. Jones. There, lying in bed, was Mr. Jones with the skin and tissue on his legs and lower trunk "coming off in hunks." After recovering from the horror of her gruesome discovery, the nurse called an ambulance, and he was taken to a local hospital.

No one knew for sure what had happened while the patient was alone in the tub. The nurses and the owner theorized that Mr. Jones, in his mental confusion, was attracted by the shininess of the faucet and reached out for it, accidentally turning on the hot water. Because of the pain and his confusion, he was unable to turn off the water. Thus he sat there while the tub filled with hot water until the orderly and janitor found him.

Some time after the patient died and an inquest was held which cleared the staff of any criminal charges, another version of the events of that evening surfaced. According to this version, the orderly put the patient into the tub of hot water in order to punish the patient for cursing him.[5] The shortage of help that night gave the orderly the chance to use this form of punishment on Mr. Jones, a form he had learned while he was working in a mental hospital. This version was relayed to me by the janitor who was on the floor at the time. He said that he, another janitor who came to the floor, and the orderly got together and fabricated the other story to protect the people who owned the home and those that worked there. In the interim between the scalding and his telling me this, the orderly and other janitor had quit working at the home.

Shortly after hearing this, I left town for several days. On returning I told the charge nurse what I had heard. During this interval, the janitor who told me this was fired, along with two aides. He and the aides were drinking in the home one evening and created a disturbance for which they were fired. According to the nurse who was on duty at the time, they were all a "bunch of wiseass kids." The janitor and one of the aides then purportedly went to Philadelphia together.

My version of the causes of the scalding upset the charge nurse, who said that she had heard something similar from the aides but did not pay any attention to it. She was puzzled when the scalding occurred because, as she said: "There have been thousands of baths in that tub and nothing ever happened before." It was this uneasiness that prompted her and the evening nurse to question the people who were on the floor that evening several times. To her, my tale only provided more confirmation of the poorly developed moral sense of the "colored." She said: "They only tell you what they think you want to hear."[6] She decided to tell the owner what I told her and let him decide what to do.

The next day I saw the owner of the nursing home. The nurse had told him the new version of the events of that evening. He told me that the janitor had already told him his story just before he left for Philadelphia. The owner said that he told the janitor that he should tell his story to the police and not to him.

In the owner's mind, the scalding was the result of a chance and tragic conjunction of events in the home: the absence of the laundryman on the day shift, which eventuated in a shortage of linen, towels, and clothes on the second floor that evening; the patient soiling himself; the shortage of employees to watch over the patient while the orderly went to the basement; the *"non compos mentis"* status of the patient, which led to his reaching for the faucet and turning on the hot water, his inability to turn off the water, and the debilitated condition of his skin. These were the causes of the patient's death, not the deliberate actions of an employee.

He responded to the janitor's claim that the death was not an accident by arguing that the janitor made up the story to blackmail him, and said that the janitor's girlfriend, the aide he went to Philadelphia with, put him up to this. She was angered at the owner because he was making her move out of the room she rented in his home and was working through the janitor to get back at him. Such behavior was not unusual from the people who worked at the home and, in fact, one might expect the type of people who worked there to try to make private capital out of such a tragedy. He said that just that week a former employee had made a threat on his life. Not believing the janitor's story and not feeling personally responsible for reopening the investigation (this was the janitor's duty), he was content to "let sleeping dogs lie." Though challenged, the official version managed to maintain its integrity because it did not contradict the nurses' and owner's version of normal events in the home.

The janitor's version made sense to the aides and other employees because it was consonant with their perceptions of reality in the home. Patients did assault aides and orderlies verbally and physically. Sometimes when this happened an aide or orderly retaliated with force. To them, the scalding was an example of this type of interplay between aide and patient, more extreme than most, but still one of a class of events with which they were familiar. What made this event unusual was the extremity of the orderly's response against a patient who, in the words of one aide, "didn't know any better" and, therefore, was not responsible for his actions. The aide said that the orderly should have known that this patient was crazy. If he did, he would have known that crazy patients are not punished for cursing aides.

The events surrounding the scalding of Mr. Jones highlight

the effects that the hostility, cynicism, and distrust of the nurses and owner had on relations and activities in the home. The nurses and owner were reluctant to take seriously allegations of abuse in the home. They rebutted such assertions by referring to discrediting elements in the character of the person making the complaints. In essence, they adopted the principle that "seeing is believing" with regard to abuse, while their low frequency of interaction with aides or patients made such observation unlikely.

On the side of the lower-level employees, there was the tendency to look the other way when another employee abused a patient. Their involvement in their roles was so minimal that they not only seldom reported abuse to the nurses, they seldom even sanctioned the person doing it, even if they thought it was unjustified.

The end result of these corresponding attitudes of suspicion and resentment was that some of the abuse that could have been detected and punished in the home went undetected and unpunished at the supervisory level. These attitudes acted as an information screen (Caplow, 1964) that prevented the nurses from seeing that abuse was a recurrent response of the aides to their problems with patients.

Discussion

Here I would like to extrapolate from the single case study and suggest that similar processes with regard to abusive behavior may be present in a variety of similar institutions. The literature on nursing homes (Henry, 1963, chap. 10; Coe, 1965; Bennett and Nehemow, 1965; Glaser and Strauss, 1968, chap. 4), on the social structure of hospital wards dealing with the elderly (Coser, 1963), and on state mental hospitals (Rowland, 1938; Belknap, 1956; Dunham and Weinberg, 1960; Salisbury, 1962; Strauss et al., 1964, chap. 5) suggests that the social organization of these different institutions is not very different from that found in our nursing home. All of these institutions deal with clients of low social worth who are relatively powerless, whose prognosis for recovery is pessimistic, and whose credibility is tarnished. The disruptive effects of employee turn-over, absenteeism, and poor role performance are common in these institutions (Belknap, 1956; Kahne, 1968; Coser, 1963), treatment is defined in custodial (cf. Smith, 1965) rather than therapeutic terms, and hostility and mutual antipathy character-ize the relationships between the professional and supervisory staff and those individuals who deal directly with the inmates of these institutions.

The people who work in these institutions, including the professionals, tend to occupy marginal positions in the labor market. The occupants of the lowest positions, the aides and orderlies, who have the greatest contact with inmates share a latent culture (Becker and Geer, 1960) due to their lower social-class origins, which regards the use of force and aggression as a legitimate means of resolving conflicts (Blumenthal et al., 1971). Because of their social class and low levels of education, these people do not entertain sophisticated and complex notions about human motivation and mental illness. Their interpreta-tion of patients' actions are likely to be based on lay rather than medical ideologies (Strauss et al., 1964, pp. 95–96). This in-creases their likelihood of using already established and familiar means of handling difficulties with patients, namely force.

Conflicts between staff and patients are likely because these organizations cannot rely on rewards or the internalization by the patients of their goals or norms to generate a commitment to their rules (Etzioni, 1961). As a result, those people who work most closely with patients find control of the patients to be their greatest problem and abuse to be one way of coping with it.

The professionals and semiprofessionals who work in these institutions are the less successful members of their professions. Work in custodial mental hospitals and nursing homes does not bring professional recognition and is regarded as a step down by their professions in general. Once in these institutions, they find themselves with patients they cannot help, confronted by staff problems which make it difficult or impossible to achieve the goals expounded by their professions. The lofty goals of help and service learned during their professional training give way to more realistic goals of custody and order maintenance.[7] Rather

457

than taking active leadership in caring for patients, they withdraw from this aspect of their role, become cynical, and concentrate their attention and energy on activities which reduce their contact with patients and lower-level employees. Patient care becomes the almost exclusive province of the lower-level employees to whom the professionals delegate a great deal of discretionary power. This insulates the lay perspectives of the lower-level employees from the more sophisticated and potentially ameliorative ideas of the professionals.

In such a context, the supervisory and professional staff will seldom see abusive behavior on the part of the other employees. Furthermore, they will probably develop a culture of accounts to deal with reputed cases of abuse which will enable them to deny the routine nature of abuse. In fact, these organizations may necessitate such a culture of accounts.[8] The professionals who stay on in such organizations will be those who have been successfully socialized to this culture. Those who do not accept the definitions and premises of such a culture are forced to leave the organization because of the dissonance created by the discrepancy between their self-images as professionals and the acknowledgment of what is really going on in the organization. The end result of these processes is the continuance of abuse.

Notes

1. The owner of the nursing home was seldom at the home for more than a few hours each day. Some days he would not even come to the home. One time he did not come to the home for several weeks. During this period the nurses could not reach him directly because he moved to a neighboring town, had an unlisted phone installed, and did not give the nurses the phone number. The only way they could reach him was to call his mother, who would relay the message to him.

2. The patients in the home generally were quite infirm. Many were bedridden, incontinent, and suffering mental impairments.

3. Abuse refers to behavior which would lead to negative sanctions if it were observed by a nurse. This definition is similar to the definition of deviance of Black and Reiss, Jr. (1970:63). Pulling a patient's hair, slapping, hitting, kicking, pinching, or violently shaking a patient, throwing water or food on a patient, tightening restraining belts so that they cause a patient

458

pain, and terrorizing a patient by gesture or word are examples of abusive behavior. During the research, I occasionally witnessed aides abusing patients in one or another of these manners. Most of the data on abuse comes from discussions with aides about the way they and their fellow workers dealt with the patients.

4. "An account is a linguistic device employed whenever an action is subject to valuative enquiry. Such devices are a crucial element in the social order since they prevent conflicts from arising by verbally bridging the gap between action and expectation. Moreover, accounts are "situated" according to the statuses of the interactants, and are standardized within cultures so that certain accounts are terminologically stabilized and routinely expected when an activity falls outside the domain of expectations." (Scott & Lyman, 1968:46).

5. This patient never spoke to people except in anger or fear, when he would utter a barely intelligible curse, usually "son of a bitch." The only person to visit him was his wife, who rarely came to the home.

6. The nurses were all white and strongly prejudiced against blacks. Their racism was part of the culture of accounts they developed; but it should be noted that they were hostile to and cynical about white employees as well.

7. Powelson and Bendix (1951) find this is the case for psychiatrists who work in prisons. The situation also seems analogous to that of lawyers. Carlin (1966) found that the less successful lawyers often found themselves in situations where the corruption of their professional ethics and goals was possible and reasonable.

DYING:
THE CAREER
OF THE
NURSING-HOME PATIENT*
Elizabeth Gustafson

Introduction

In this study, the "career timetables" format developed by Julius Roth in *Timetables: Structuring the Passage of Time in Hospital Treatment and Other Careers* (1963) is applied to the experience of elderly persons in convalescent hospitals and nursing homes. One theoretical objective of the paper is to demonstrate that analytical sets appropriate for the study of young and middle-aged Americans can be useful in the study of the aged. Another is to study the concept of careers in a different setting. The analysis of the degree to which careers of nursing-home patients fit Roth's paradigm throws light on their social and psychological problems. The conclusions indicate that nursing-home staffs should develop ways of helping their patients to live fully and die gracefully.

This paper presents an hypothesis about life in the nursing home which may be amenable to partial empirical substantiation. It is based on an informed but informal study of events in one nursing home where the author was employed for one year. Visits in other nursing homes and familiarity with the literature suggests that the hypothesis has merit. Fortunately, there is no chance that a systematic bias was built into the observations

* Elizabeth Gustafson, "Dying: The Career of the Nursing-Home Patient," *Journal of Health and Social Behavior* 13 (1972): 226–35.

because all experience in the nursing home preceded exposure to Roth's theory.

The development and uses of a career timetable are the subject of Roth's book. Roth claims that "when many people go through the same series of events, we speak of this as a career and of the sequence and timing of events as their career timetable" (1963, p. 93). Roth uses the institutionalized TB patient as his model. According to his definition, a career is

> a series of related stages or phases of a given sphere of activity that a group of people goes through in a progressive fashion (that is, one step follows another) in a given direction or on the way to a more or less definite and recognizable end-point or goal. (1963, p. 94)

Roth found that people involved in a career try to define when certain salient things will happen to them. By pooling their observations in an unsystematic way, career participants develop time norms against which to measure their individual progress. The benchmarks on this timetable are the significant events that occur in the average career.

When the career is "part of a service or authority relationship," each of the two groups establishes a timetable for the same set of events. The norms of the two groups are bound to be somewhat different because their criteria for progress and their idea of proper timing are different (Roth, 1963, p. 107). Bargaining occurs when the career participant tries to bring the judgment of the authority figure into line with his own more optimistic view of his status on the timetable.

Roth's paradigm consists of these three aspects. The career is a series of commonly defined stages on the way to a recognizable end point. The timetable consists of benchmarks which identify these stages. Bargaining between the career participants and figures in authority occurs when their respective opinions as to the patient's position on the timetable are not compatible.

The Career

A majority of patients in a nursing home for old people are, more or less actively, dying. Except in cases where the patient is

461

severely incapacitated intellectually, patient, relatives, and staff almost always know that, generally speaking, this is a "terminal case." So there exists what Glaser and Strauss (1965) call "an open awareness context." This is true whether the patient is suffering from a rapidly progressive disease of which he will soon die or from the general deterioration of old age, in which case he may linger indefinitely. He may not know which is his situation, and he may deny the fact that his days are numbered, but he does know that he has come to stay until he dies.

The nursing home is the last resource for old people and their families (if they have any), who have tried to maintain their social independence as long as possible (Kahana, 1971; Jacobs, 1969). Admission to a nursing home is widely considered the ultimate failure in one's social career. Roth himself perceives the nursing-home patient as a "career failure" existing in a "chronic side-track" (1963, p. 105). He claims that life in such a cul-de-sac is not a career because it moves in no direction. It is marked only by a "failure timetable," which serves the most limited function: "to split long blocks of time into smaller, more manageable units" (Roth, 1963, p. 12).

Our interpretation of the picture, however, is that the simple facts of advanced debility and chronological age prevent the nursing-home patient from fitting into the "side-tracked" category. It may be that the TB or mental patient or the prisoner with a life sentence at age 30 also has nothing to look forward to but death, but it is still so far away that he and his peers do not associate it with their present existence. For the aged patient, the passage of days of itself brings him noticeably closer to the end of the road. Admission to the nursing home immediately launches him into a new, regressive career ending in death.

Although in common parlance the term "career" signifies a forward or upward progress of some sort, Roth's definition (see p. 41) clearly can include the regressive experience of the nursing home patient. Group definition of timetable benchmarks and of the end-point of the career are the crucial factors, not the positive or negative nature of the goal. (Erving Goffman, whose book *Asylums* is the source of many of Roth's concepts, also defines career as "any social strand of any person's course through life . . . Such a career can no more be a success than a failure" (1961, p. 127). There is universal acknowledgment that death is the end of the nursing-home career and there is a generally accepted timetable which will be described in this paper.

The fact that the nursing-home patient's career is regressive instead of progressive constitutes the important difference between this career and the career of TB patients and others. In the case of the TB patient, minimizing treatment time constitutes

Figure 1.

Schematic View of TB and Nursing Home Patient Careers

TB Hospital	H E A L	Timetable of events[a]	Recovery
		Bargaining	
Nursing Home	T H	Timetable of events[a]	
		Bargaining[b]	Death

[a] The time which elapses between any two benchmarks is fairly regular in the TB treatment career and is often very irregular in the nursing home career.

[b] The discontinuation of bargaining by the nursing home patient is discussed later in the paper.

success. For the nursing-home patient, success is the maximum delay of passage from one stage to the next. This contrast is pictured in Figure 1.

In the TB patient's career, passage of significant events and bargaining efforts move in the same direction, towards recovery. In the nursing-home patient's career, events progress in one direction (towards death) and bargaining efforts pull in the other direction, back towards health. This tension makes life very difficult, but it may be essential to the maintenance of any kind of life at all. This idea is considered in more detail later.

Before we go on with the discussion, it will be useful to elaborate briefly on the nature of death. Death includes both physical termination and a final social separation. The ordinary person does not conceptualize these aspects separately. Therefore the scheme in Figure 1 represents well enough the view of dying held by the ordinary patient and staff member: it is one

463

continuous and irreversible process of physical deterioration and social loss. A more careful scrutiny suggests a breakdown of the total career into social dying—progressive separation—and biological or psychological death, both of which imply total psychic separation from the environment. (See Fig. 2.)

This scheme makes it clear that during most of his career, the patient is really fighting social death, the increasing degrees of separation. In the ideal scheme, only the onset of the terminal phase signifies the appropriate end of social life and of efforts to maintain it.

Figure 2

Components of Death

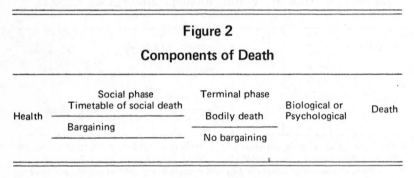

The Career Participants

It will be clear at once that not all patients in a nursing home are involved in the establishment of the timetable and bargaining efforts. Some patients are out of touch with reality before they are admitted. Others are too depressed or severely ill at admission to take part in bargaining behavior. Some patients once active in these matters have become senile, psychotic, or very ill. A very few may have been able to give up bargaining behavior consciously (more on this later) but it seems unlikely that there are any mentally competent patients who *never* take part in this activity simply because they "don't fear death" (cf. Kastenbaum, 1967). Patients may welcome a prospective end to physical fatigue and pain but the bargaining behavior we will discuss is a response to social death. Moreover, it seems probable that ambivalent feelings are common in this matter. Even if one is not afraid, surely one might be glad to delay the event as long as possible. Schneidman claims that "psyde (death)-postponing is the habitual, indeed the unthinking, orientation of most humans towards cessation . . . the psyde-postponer is one who . . . wishes it would not occur for as long as possible" (1963, p. 218). The disinclination of the patient to give up this lifelong stance we feel is reinforced by the fact that life in the nursing home puts pressure on him to give it up prematurely.

The Timetable

A person moves through his career as a nursing-home patient according to a timetable informally defined by the patients and their caretakers. The timetable may be said to consist of four overlapping categories of benchmarks on a regression scale. Physical deterioration is measured by degees of social activity, mobility, and functional control. Mental deterioration is measured by declining mental control. (See Fig. 3.)

This informal timetable of overlapping scales stands in marked contrast to the formalized system of classification and status-identifying privileges that Roth reports from TB hospitals (1963, p. 101). The fact that these reference points are not formally defined means that the discrepancy between functional and status positions, which confuses the scene at the TB hospital (Roth, 1963, p. 19), is hard to perceive in the nursing home.

An additional difference between this and the TB treatment scheme is that there is no standard duration for each stage of the nursing home career (cf. Roth, 1963, p. 22) and there is no guarantee that every patient will move in an orderly way through this regressive scheme. Improved health and relapses occur frequently and cause constant shifts in the patient's time perspective.

One reason why the benchmarks on these scales are so general is that considerably limited communication in the nursing-home situation makes it difficult to construct a more elaborate scheme. The top medical staff, of course, has a different and more detailed set of norms by which to judge a patient's position. The patient has little access to these reliable medical clues, however. Strauss and Glaser point out that, for medical personnel, "the highest professional reward is in the patient's recovery and return to his normal personal and social life" (1965, p. 178).

Figure 3.
Timetable Scales in Nursing-Home Career

Physical deterioration scales			Mental deterioration scale
Social Activity	Mobility	Functional Control	Mental Control
1. Passes to "outside"	1. Walks	1. Continent	1. Occasional forgetfulness
2. Responsibility for own affairs; social contacts			
3. Meaningful hobby or job	3. Hobbles		
4. Physical recreation			4. Occasional incoherence
5. Spectator recreation	5. Wheelchair	5. Incontinent	5. Considerable disorientation
6. Minimal activity	6. Bed		
7. Lassitude[b]	7. Extreme weakness[b]		7. Totally *non compos mentis*[a]
8. Coma	8. Transfer to gen'l hospital		

[a] Persons who have regressed to this point are too far out of touch to take any part in the definition and accomplishment of their careers. Their progress is of interest only to the medical staff and other people.

[b] These symptoms often signify the onset of the "terminal phase." (See Fig. 2.)

In order to uphold staff morale, in most general hospitals in "wards that contain dying patients there is some typical ratio of both certain and uncertain death" (Glaser and Strauss, 1965, p. 179). The nursing home cannot provide this balance and as a result is the most demoralizing (and least prestigious) setting for medical personnel to work in. Doctors feel justified in giving first priority to patients elsewhere who show some promise of recovery, and therefore they visit nursing-home patients only rarely and briefly as a rule. Often, his own unresolved anxieties about death prevent the doctor from participating in an honest discussion with the patient of his condition (Kubler-Ross, 1969; Strauss and Glaser, 1965; Quint, 1967).

The staff of a nursing home consists mainly of minimally trained nurses' aides, who rarely know anything useful to the patient and even more rarely give up the cheerful, noncommittal and evasive line used with aged and dying patients. Friends and relatives are usually in the same self-protective situation as the nurses' aides. The chief nurse is the staff member most often in a knowledgeable position and may occasionally provide a useful clue for the patient.

Communication among patients also tends to be minimal. There are a number of explanations for the striking lack of interaction among patients. Although public opinion lumps all old persons into one social class, they are not of course a homogeneous group. Even within one nursing home, especially if it serves both welfare and private patients, the variety of experiential backgrounds is likely to be great. Therefore patients may simply find that they have very little in common, very little to talk about, with one another. The disengagement theory of Cumming and Henry (1961) offers another explanation for the lack of communication. However, in this situation as in the outside world, disengagement may not be voluntary. Although no staff member or relative will directly discourage the patient from making new friends in the nursing home, he is often not expected or encouraged to do so. As we have mentioned earlier, admission to the home is usually treated as the end of one's useful social career. A clear correlation between degree and duration of institutionalization and lack of communication has been found in several studies (Rosenfelt and Slater, 1964; Coe, 1965; Kahana, 1971; and others).

Erving Goffman describes withdrawal behavior as characteristic of the newcomer to the mental hospital ward. The function of withdrawal is to deny the new identity of self with inmates (1961, p. 146). Admission to a nursing home often follows rapidly upon the occurrence of a paralyzing stroke, amputation, or similar trauma to both body and psyche. Thus, withdrawal may understandably be pronounced. Moreover, the nursing-home patient may remain in this stage longer than the mental patient because there is no progressive career for him to enter.

Another possible explanation for isolationist behavior is that many patients are already bearing such a "grief load," including grief over their own imminent deaths (Wiesner, 1968; Birren, 1964; Feifel, 1959), that they are not willing to take the emotional risk of establishing a friendship with yet another person who may well die soon.

In most cases, a combination of all of these factors is probably involved in the low level of communication among nursing-home patients. The most interesting hypothesis from the point of view of this study is that the patients are intuitively conniving to minimize the exchange of information about timetable norms so that they can more easily delude themselves that they are holding out against death better than they really are.

Just as the incomplete exchange of information about timetable norms may have a function in a regressive career, perhaps the obviously limited dependability of the reference points also has some use. The scales are approximate at best and in any case are not really a reliable indicator of the approach of death, which could unexpectedly overtake the patient at any time. However, there is a utility in this kind of timetable for a regressive career. When things look bad, one can find fault with the benchmarks. When things look good, one ignores the fact that death does not always "follow the rules" implied by the timetable. Objectively speaking, the norms are not reliable, but psychologically speaking, they are comforting. Working out one's position on a career timetable is in itself a lively, hopeful, social activity.

At the end of the regression, the reality is harder to avoid.

Confinement to bed accompanied by extreme lassitude or coma are pretty sure signs. And transfer to a general hospital, except for repair of fractures or routine treatments, suggests that the end is near. (For this reason, routine trips to the general hospital can be very traumatic for the patient who has not been helped to understand the reason for the trip.) There is an obvious utility in this scheme. Early in his career, norms are vague and the patient is kept busy evaluating his status and bargaining for a sense of social viability. At the end of the career, perhaps within a week or two of death, the signs are much more dependable and the imminence of death cannot be avoided. At this point the patient enters the terminal phase (see Fig. 2) and is encouraged by unavoidable signs to "let go" all social ties and bargaining effort, to resign himself to death.

Bargaining

Bargaining is as important an aspect of life in a nursing home as it is in the TB hospital, but it has a subtly different meaning. Goffman has commented that the concept of career is two-sided: it refers both to such internal matters as one's "image of self and self-identity" and also to one's public status and official position (Goffman, 1961, p. 127). The TB patient bargains for a change in his official position: he wants those in authority to do something to change his status. Patients in nursing homes are not assigned to any official position. Therefore the nursing home patient bargains for moral and social support for his self-image: he wants both authorities and peers to do and say things assuring him that he is maintaining a "lively" status, that he is important to other people, and that his social death will not precede his physical death. Thus the objectives of bargaining in the nursing home are harder to define but easier, if tact outweighs strict honesty, to confer.

Patterns of bargaining in the nursing home are similar to those in the sanatorium, but of course they work in reverse. While the TB patient increases his bargaining activity as he moves towards the end of his hospital career (Roth, 1963, p. 40), the nursing-home patient starts out actively bargaining and often gives up this effort towards the end of his career. In both cases, the change in bargaining intensity is related to a changing time perspective. Both TB and nursing-home patients commonly start their careers with the idea that it won't take long—to get cured, or to die (Roth, 1963, p. 104). In almost all cases, the patient soon learns that the goal is much further away than he thought at first. This realization discourages the TB patient from bargaining hard until the chances for success seem greatest: at the end of his progressive career. But the realization is a kind of reprieve for the nursing-home patient and encourages him to fight for the maintenance of his social life. When the end does come into sight, it is not worth the effort to bargain any more.

For patients suffering primarily from impairment of intelligence, all socially coherent bargaining will take place before they move into level seven of the mental control scale. (See Fig. 3.) Patients located at an earlier point on this scale may be aware of the timetable and make efforts to control their status on it. They try hard to control their intellectual processes—by moving and talking with deliberation, by cooperating with staff in matters of rest, diet, drugs, and activities, and by conserving their energies to make special efforts for the doctor and family when they visit. They are well satisfied when they succeed in persuading everyone that they are doing very well, even if they "crash" afterwards.

Bargaining on the physical deterioration scales is easy but so unsophisticated that the patient may have trouble fooling even himself. Patients attach great importance to such signs of time-table status as personal social contacts, participation in recreation activities, ability to walk and to control bladder and bowels. The patient avoids admitting that his rating according to some indicators may be determined less by his own vigor than by the enthusiasm of staff and relatives to help him. (See Roth, 1963, p. 50.) Passes to visit away from nursing home, participation in social activities, provision with "nonessential" physical aids and therapies, and retraining in bladder control are all areas in which the contribution of other people is important. (The exception to this rule is seen in cases where the patient stubbornly gets into bed and refuses to do things that he could and should do. This can be interpreted as a perverse kind of disease-defying

470

behavior in which the patient says, "I will not allow this disease to limit my activities: I will limit them right now of my own free will!" This is as effective a way as any of handling the time-table.)

When there is no escaping a clear symptom of debility, the patient may prefer to interpret it as a minor temporary ailment: the stroke patient denies the permanent paralysis of his arm and hand by saying he "sprained his wrist last week." Another avoidance technique is finding fault with the nursing home. Petty complaints about the staff arise from a deep underlying grievance: the staff resists bargaining efforts. The patient with means transfers from one institution to another in a hopeless and unconscious search for a place with a different kind of timetable on which he will rate higher.

Patients in the nursing home use another bargaining trick found in the TB hospital (Roth, 1963, pp. 36–39): they choose inappropriate models for themselves. In a common example, the patient classifies himself with persons of similar socioeconomic background when this gives him confidence about his timetable status, instead of with other patients suffering from the same type of disease. The usual presence of both physically and mentally ill patients in the same facility is well used. The physically ill patient chooses to compare himself (to obvious advantage) with senile or other confused patients. On the other hand, the mentally ill patient often categorizes himself with the physically ill group, for the obvious reason that he is in reassuringly better physical health than they. By using this device, he not only puts death far away but avoids facing the probability of his own de-cline into incoherence and social incompetence, which is as in-acceptable to many as physical death.

In the nursing home, as in the TB hospital, patients some-times use extraneous criteria to improve their bargaining posi-tion. Provision with glasses, hearing aids, dentistry, occupational and physical therapy, and other aids and services which staff may consider nonessential are often highly valued by patients mainly as status symbols indicating that they have social value and possibly a long future. The old lady never reads but indig-nantly fights for new glasses: by getting them for her the staff shows that they consider her to have a future. Private possessions assume great importance as signs of viable social life for some patients; this accounts for the compulsive hoarding of "junk" such as Bingo prizes, greeting cards, holiday decorations, and items made in craft programs.

Like TB patients (Roth, 1963, p. 38), nursing home patients introduce moral criteria sometimes: "I have led an honest, hard-working life and therefore should be spared longer than that no-good Charlie." (People who use this approach often have doubts about the actual uprightness of their lives which they constantly beg friends and staff to allay.)

Conclusions

The unreliable nature of the career timetable of the nursing-home patient and the type of unrealistic bargaining that it provokes are basic factors underlying the social scene in the nursing home. There are always some patients who are pitifully hopeful about their bargaining position until they die. A larger number drop out of the bargaining scene, especially towards the end of the career, as Figure 1 indicates. Some of these have become too ill to maintain bargaining behavior. For others, it becomes impossible to avoid the fact that one is "serving an indeterminate sentence on death row." This has been called a perfect hell, and it is indeed for many aged persons. The stress of this situation contributes to the depression-apathy-passivity syndrome in many and may play a causative role in some kinds of senility and psychosis. Some patients whose personalities survive this test soon come to prefer death itself to this torture and attempt suicide or try to will themselves to death (Glaser and Strauss, 1965; among others). An emotionally exhausted patient often gives up bargaining attitudes for a period, only to return to them when his emotional strength has returned and it becomes clear that his will to die is not yet going to be effective.

It is our hypothesis that this most unsatisfactory bargaining situation is partially caused by the fact that the career of the nursing-home patient is perceived by patient and staff alike to follow an undifferentiated regressive trend as represented by the diagram in Figure 1. The most difficult thing about the nursing-

472

home career as so defined is that there is no one but God—or death—to bargain with. In most careers, including TB treatment, the authority figure has only incomplete control over the passage of events; for example, the response of an individual case to treatment. In the case of the nursing-home patient, however, medical authorities influence appearances but exert *no* real control over events. The timetable norms are irrelevant to the actual approach of death, which could "jump the gun" and occur at any time. The patient really bargains for more time directly with his disease, or death, or God.

Dealing with an opponent who is not human is terribly frustrating, for we do not know his norms. The fact that people keep on bargaining in this situation when almost all other social activity is discontinued suggests that this is a primary form of social behavior. Gregory Rochlin goes so far as to suggest that the process (career?) of becoming civilized is a lifetime bargaining process that starts when the child (at around three years of age) perceives that he has limitations, including mortality. His life from this point on is dedicated to resolving (by bargaining tactics?) the conflicts with others and within himself that constitute limitations on his potential (Rochlin, 1967, pp. 62–63). Insofar as these limitations are symbols of, or perhaps in a philosophical sense even derive from, his mortality, the whole process of becoming civilized and mature involves a constant bargaining with death. Conflict with others over his needs and desires is a constant in the life of the individual virtually from birth. Skills in bargaining for his various career interests are among the first a child learns and are so basic to social existence that he uses them even when they are ineffectual, just to assure himself that he is still socially alive.

Is it necessary that this desparate and ineffectual bargaining be the main source of social life for the nursing-home patient? The popular concept of the dying career as a simple case of physical deterioration allows no hope to patient or staff, even when the patient's life stretches out over months or years. The staff attempts halfheartedly to keep up the patient's false hopes and to maintain his comfort. The patient, finding the staff unresponsive to the real meaning of his bargaining, becomes frantic and eventually lapses into despair (or senility or psychosis).

The differentiated view of death as including a social phase and a terminal phase before the final separation caused by psychological or biological death (Fig. 2) puts things into a different perspective. In this light it becomes clear that during the social stage, which includes most of the career, the patient is putting up a justifiable fight against the tendency of society (as represented by relatives, staff, visitors, and peers) to force him into premature social death. This kind of bargaining will and should continue in the best of institutions. But it will become effective and wholesome when the staff members and visitors respond by doing all they can to facilitate the preservation of the patient's maximum status according to the timetable scales. The staff member with this positive goal will find it easier to acknowledge (sometimes directly to the patient) that death is the inevitable end of the career. The patient who feels he has been valued and respected during this phase will find it easier to approach the end of his life willingly.

Only when the patient moves into the terminal phase should he feel he is bargaining directly with God for more time. Staff personnel can be trained to deal honestly with the patient in this phase and to help him move beyond the bargaining process in a positive way before he dies. A number of experts have discussed—and some have practiced—ways in which medical staff and relatives can be helped to accept the patient's death and become a source of strength to him. (See especially Kubler-Ross (1969); Quint (1967); Glaser and Strauss (1965); and Weisman and Kastenbaum (1968).) The abandonment of bargaining signifies that the patient is ready to give up both social and biological life, willing to accept death graciously. It is important to note the fine psychological line between this patient and the suicidal patient who wants to be spared the torture of bargaining with death. The suicide's intention is to take the initiative into his own hands, to take the control of time and place and manner of death, at least, away from his Opponent (Schneidman, 1970, p. 40). The accepting patient lays down his arms, literally lays down his life, and takes up death in a positive and willing frame of mind. Only persons who can do this will "die happy," will die "in a state of grace." It should become the common goal of staff and patients that each dying career should end in this positive way.

Summary

This analysis of the nursing-home patient's experience supports and extends Julius Roth's examination of human experience in terms of career timetables. The last phase of life, when it takes place in an institution, can be considered a career as appropriately as any other phase of life.[1] Nursing-home patients and their overseers establish timetables by which to measure the status of individuals in the dying career. The vague and unreliable nature of the benchmarks, which would make the timetable of a progressive career close to useless, serves a function in this case where success consists of moving, or appearing to move, from one stage to the next as slowly as possible.

Medical staff, friends, and relatives, and often patients themselves think of the patient career as an unbroken decline towards death. Instinct and will-to-live cause the patient to fight against the premature social death forced upon him in this situation. The increasing tension makes this a hellish existence for the patient. The social instinct to bargain for one's career interests is so strong, however, that patients often maintain this behavior, despite the pain it causes, after most other social behavior has been given up. Thus bargaining alone sustains social life.

It is suggested that a differentiated view of the dying career as consisting of a social stage and a terminal stage would be useful to nursing-home staff and others concerned with the aged patient. A staff with this view would endeavor to extend the patent's social life for as long as possible, thus introducing vitality and honesty into the inevitable conflict between patient and staff interests during this phase; and to support the patient during the transition (the terminal phase) to an accepting and acceptable death.

Notes

1. The effects of different environments (for example, community, open institution, total insituation) and of relative duration on the career of the dying patient would make a useful study. Other studies are needed to elucidate the ways in which such variables as sex, education, wealth, fulfillment of life expectations, mental health, and family relations influence the bargaining behavior of aged dying patients.

7

Death and Dying

INTRODUCTION TO PART VII

Death, and the dying process itself, is being looked upon more and more as the "terminal phase" of the life cycle. In doing so, gerontologists have sought to understand the psychological aspects of dying as well as society's attempts to "organize" death. Approaches have ranged from concentration on what could be learned through the simple observation of behaviors in the terminal phase to the employment of knowledge about other life phases for understanding "death and dying." The papers in this part reflect the broad range of approaches.

Are there psychological consequences of impending death for aged individuals? Lieberman and Coplan, in the first paper, show that indeed psychological qualities associated with impending death could be detected up to a year prior to death. Individuals who died within a year of testing showed poorer cognitive performance, more fear of and preoccupation with death under certain life conditions, and other related differences on a series of measures reflecting emotional life, when compared with individuals who survived at least three years after testing. Most provocatively, these authors postulate a psychological process which may monitor impending death.

In a more sociological vein, Marshall, in the second paper, argues that the social setting is an important factor in the preparation for impending death. Glen Brae is viewed as a retirement village in which residents have an opportunity to deal with their own deaths, to talk about death and dying and to observe death "in a kind of role-modeling process." Community involvement and collective socialization to death are viewed as facilitating factors in the preparation for death.

Mortality is a fact of life in every human society. Since mortality tends to disrupt the ongoing life of society's groups, all societies must develop some forms of containing its impact. The third paper, by Robert Blauner, moves further into the jurisdiction of sociology and deals with the impact of death upon the wider social structure. Blauner discusses specifically the mortuary institutions, which address the special problems of disposal of the dead and the rituals of transition from life to death, generational continuities, and the status of the aged as this relates to the society's views of death.

In the final paper in this part, Richard Kalish explores the inevitable decisions involved in the dying process of the aged individual: who lives and who dies, where death occurs, how and when the death comes about, who is to be with the dying patient, and how he or she is to learn of the imminent death. Kalish suggests that personal encounters with the aged and the dying are highly upsetting and commonly avoided by many. As a result, there is often a reluctance to examine decisions regarding the dying process, and such decisions are ignored or postponed, to the detriment of the dying individual.

DISTANCE FROM
DEATH AS A VARIABLE
IN THE
STUDY OF AGING*[1]

Morton A. Lieberman
and Annie Siranne Coplan

The simple fact that older people know their time is running short and acknowledge their own death as a current psychological reality[2] suggests that studies of death and dying can contribute to an understanding of the psychology of aging. Several important theoretical formulations of the psychology of aging (Butler, 1963; Cummings & Henry, 1961; Erickson, 1950) view the psychological sequela associated with the increasing certainty of impending death as central in the psychology of the elderly and imply that the awareness of finitude is an organizing or focal concern for the aged. Yet, the rapidly accelerating accumulation of empirical work on death and dying—studies of attitudes and fears, issues on social context, practical treatment on the management of the dying, etc.—does not substantially increase the understanding of the psychology of aging, particularly when juxtaposed to the potent suggestions in the theoretical postulations. The present study was designed to explore the psychological importance of impending death in the very aged as evidenced by inner psychological changes in elderly persons approaching natural death. The research strategy was based on the assumption that the imminence of death provided an opportunity to discover the maximum impact of death on the aged.

* Morton Lieberman and Annie Siranne Coplan, "Distance from Death as a Variable in the Study of Aging," *Developmental Psychology* 2 (1969): 71–84. Copyright © 1969 by the American Psychological Association. Reprinted by permission.

481

The idea that psychological changes might occur systematically evolved from two previous studies of older people (Lieberman, 1965, 1966) in which systematic changes in cognitive functioning were associated with the approach of death. In the first study, cognitive changes noted in aged subjects who died 6-9 months after termination of the study were not found in subjects who survived for at least 2 years after termination of the study. In the second study, differences in several psychological realms were found for matched pairs of death-near (DN) and death-far (DF) aged subjects. The subjects in both studies were ambulatory, physically intact individuals living in social contexts which did not necessarily imply that they were dying. Taken together, the two studies suggested a hypothesis of a total system decline in those near to death. These studies, however, uncovered few systematic data reflecting affective changes in those approaching death. In order to bridge this gap, the present study compared subjects who died within a year of testing (DN) to subjects who survived at least 3 years after testing (DF) on 23 variables reflecting emotional life.

Method

Subjects[3]

Eighty subjects 65-91 years of age were studied. At the time they were selected for study, all subjects were ambulatory, free of major incapacitating illnesses, and showed no gross signs of altered brain function (defined by poor performance on the Mental Status Questionnaire, more than four errors, and the Face-Hand test, more than two errors, eyes open). The sample, all urban, Jewish, lower middle class (small shopkeepers, skilled tradesmen), included men and women from four socioenvironmental contexts: (a) subjects accepted and waiting to enter homes for the aged ($n = 16$); (b) recent entrants (less than 2 months residence) into homes for the aged ($n = 28$); (c) subjects who had lived 3-5 years in these institutions ($n = 26$); and (d) community living subjects matched for age, sex, and functional health status to those awaiting entrance into homes for the aged ($n = 10$). The subjects were studied over 3 years, being seen at least once each year for 12–15 hours of testing and interviewing. Forty died within 12 months ($\bar{x}$ = 8.6) after the last testing session. The 40 were paired with 40 subjects who survived an average of 3 years beyond the last testing session. Matching was based on a hierarchical sequence of six criteria: living arrangements (for those not in the institution, living arrangements included living alone or with children), type of institutional setting, sex, age, birthplace (United States, Western Europe, Eastern Europe), marital status, and educational level. Table 1 shows the sample characteristics of the two groups.

Measures

Twenty-three variables that reflected the subjects' emotional lives were chosen from the Adaptation and Survival Under Stress project. The measures tapped five affective realms: (*a*) emotional states (anxiety, mood tone, etc.), (*b*) orientation to emotional life, (*c*) body imagery, (*d*) self-concept, and (*e*) time perception. Measures of cognitive functioning (Realm I) were included to provide a basis for comparison with findings from the two earlier studies on psychological factors associated with impending death.

Table 2 presents the variables, tests, and a brief description of each measure, as well as the interrater reliability, when appropriate, and stability coefficient.

Results

All the statistical analyses in this study are reported between members of matched pairs. In addition to the variability across socioenvironmental contexts, this method of analysis was suggested to counteract the extreme intraindividual variation reported for similar populations (Lieberman, 1962) as well as the high interindividual variation reported for most psychological measures of aged populations.

A nonparametric test, equivalent to matched pairs *t* tests,[4] was used—Wilcoxon matched-pair signed-ranks test (Siegel, 1956). Table 3 shows group means and *Z* for the 27 variables (Variable 21 has eight subsections, Variable 22, five).

Twelve of the 37 analyses were significant at $p \geqslant .10$. These differences occurred in three of the six realms—Realm I, cognitive functioning; Realm III, orientation to emotional life; and Realm V, self-image. Realm I, showed differences for the mental status (1), the word learning (2) (DNs performed more poorly), and clock time (5) (DNs performed more adequately); Realm III showed differences for affective complexity (13) and

Table 1

Sample Characteristics

Characteristic	DN	DF
Sex—% females	75%	73%
Age		
M	79.8	78.6
Range	63-91	65-87
Birthplace		
United States	12	8
Eastern Europe	23	26
Western Europe	5	6
Marital status		
Married	5	2
Widowed	31	31
Single	3	3
Divorced	1	4
Education (mean yr.)	7.2	5.9

Note: DN = death near; DF = death far.

introspective stance (14); the DNs were less affectively complex and less introspective than the DFs; Realm V showed a number of differences on the self-sort (21), hostile-aggressive (DE), rebellious-mistrustful (FG), docile-dependent (JK), warm (LM), and responsible-hypernormal (NO). In addition mechanisms of self-maintenance (22) differences were found on utilization of current examples and distortion. The self-image results showed the DN group as less assertive, aggressive, and more docile, dependent and intimacy oriented than their paired counterparts. They used less evidence from current life but relied less on distortion to maintain self-image.

Table 2

Measures

Variable	Description
Realm I: Cognitive functioning	
Impairment 1. Mental status	10 questions, orientation in time and space error score (Kahn, Pollach, & Goldfarb, 1961), $St = .91$.
2. Learning-retention	Paired-word association learning tests (Inglis, 1959); 3 pairs of unrelated words; scored number of trials to criteria, $St = .39$.
Complexity 3. Visual organization	Designs 1, 3, & 8; 9 Bender-Gestalt (Bender, 1938) designs; Pascal and Suttell Scoring System (Pascal & Suttell, 1951). $R = $ (rho) 97; 2 raters, $St = .66$.
4. Perceptual adequacy	Murray TAT Cards 1, 2, 6BM, 7BM, 10, & 17BM; instructional set—demonstration procedure; scoring, Dana System (Dana, 1955); $R = (po)$ (rho) $= 85$, (pr) (rho) $= .72$ St, total score $(po + pr) = .60$.
5. Time judgment	Method of time reproduction of 30- and 60-sec. intervals; $St = .68$.
Realm II: Emotional states	
6. Expansiveness-restriction	Bender-Gestalt designs; eclosed area summed, increasing size associated with expansiveness, $St = .73$.
7. Anxiety	Cattell 16PF (Form C) anxiety factor, $St = .46$.
Mood 8. Life satisfaction	Ratings of interviews (Neugarten & Havighurst, & Tobin, 1961) on five 5-point scales—zest vs. apathy, resolution-fortitude, congruence between desire and achieve goals, positive self-concept, and mood tone, $R = .84$, $St = .69$.
9. Anomie	Srole Anomies scales (Srole, 1956). Degree of agreement or disagreement to 5 items about general world views, $St = .61$.

Table 2 (Cont'd)

Measures

Variable	Description
Realm II: Emotional states (cont'd)	
10. Acceptance of life	Factor analysis (principal component, Varimax solution) of 21 affect measures revealed 4 factors. The 21 measures included projective tasks (SCT, TAT, & Reitman); structural tasks, size of Bender-Gestalt Test and time estimate; self-report tasks; Cattell 16 PF; Srole Anomie scale; and the Osgood Semantic Differential; and interview items for judgments of mood in the earliest memory, life satisfaction, mood tone, and depression. Acceptance of Life (fourth factor) included (a) quantity of positive affect to Park Bench TAT Card, (b) acceptance of death in completion of SCT stem "To me, death is . . .," and (c) positive attitude toward past life in completion of SCT stem "My past life . . ."
11. Loss	5-point ordinal scale of Ss' earliest memory (Tobin, 1968). Scale from nonloss themes (1), loss defended themes (2), interpersonal loss themes (3), mutilization themes (4), death themes (5). $R = 3$ judges, 57% exact agreement, agreement of 2 or 3 judges on remaining 43%, ST = .46.
Realm III: Orientation to emotional life	
12. Emotional reactivity	See factor analysis, Variable 9 (third factor), Cattell Factor I and number of positive emotions seen in Reitman Stick Figure Test (Reitman & Robertson, 1950).
13. Affective complexity	Interview schedule on 8 affects: depression, happiness, guilt, pride, etc. 8 emotions, Guttman scaled for difficulty of talking and describing. $R = 100\%$ interjudge agreement, $St = .39$.
14. Introspective stance	Adaptation of Gendlin (Gendlin, 1964) rating system, 1–7, for degree of introspection, $R = 49\%$ one step agreement, $St = .57$.
15. Introversion-extraversion	Cattell, 16PF, Form C, $St = .50$.

Table 2 (Cont'd)

Measures

Variable	Description
Realm IV: Health and body orientation	
Functional health status 16. Health evaluation	Self-report on the ability to get about, walk stairs, etc. (Shanas, 1961), St = .59.
Body orientation 17. Body preoccupation scale	20 sentence-completion items, degree of preoccupation based upon number of body references to items not calling for such responses. R = 97% exact agreement, St = .46.
18. Body image scale	Negative or positive qualities associated with 3 sentence-completion items referring to body. R = 92% exact agreement, St = .56.
19. Negative body image	12 line drawings portraying the human form (Reitman & Robertson, 1950), scored for absence or presence of negative body images. R = 99% exact agreement, St = .24.
Realm V: Self-image	
20. Self-esteem	Semantic differential (Osgood, Suci, & Tannenbaum, 1957). 5 self-evaluative dimensions, St = .25.

21. Contents of self-image
    Octant AP power-success
    Octant BC narcissistic-exploitative
    Octant DE hostility
    Octant FG unconventional
    Octant HI weakness
    Octant JK conformity-trust
    Octant LM collabor.-pure love
    Octant NO tenderness-generous
	48 self-descriptive statements based upon 8 octant category system of Leary (Leary, 1957). Instructional set, pick as few or as many of the 48 cards that describe his present self-image, St = .83.

22. Mechanisms of self-maintenance	Self-image interview. S provides specific, concrete, recent example of each of the statements he chose from the self-sort. Scored (Rosner, 1968) in terms of adequacy of examples (a) current, (b) past, (c) conviction, (d) wished for, (e) distortion categories. R = 79% exact agreement; St = .10, .69, .32, .32, .10, respectively.

Table 2 (Cont'd)

Measures

Variable	Description
Realm VI: Time	
23. Futurity	Interview questions, meaning of time, planning ahead, meaning of future; 4-point rating system; R = 88% exact agreement, 2 raters, St = .62.
24. Extensionality	Sentence-completion test—3 items: "I look forward . . ." "An hour is . . ." and "Time is . . ." 3-point rating scale. R = 93% exact agreement, St = .44.
25. Past 26. Present 27. Future	Past, present, future things, events or situations on the 5 Murray TAT cards. R = (rho) 65, St = .60.

For a number of psychological areas the expected association with impending death did not obtain. In Realm II, for example, no differences were found in anxiety or mood tone, whether measured by self report or projective data; neither were differences found on self-report of health, body image, or on projective indexes of body (Realm IV).

Implications. In a homogeneous group of very aged, differences in three psychological realms—cognitive functioning, orientation to emotional life, and self-image—were found between matched pairs, one of whom was a year from death, the other, at least 3 years. These findings supported those of a previous study where impending death was associated with cognitive decline. In addition, the present findings suggested that nearness to death was related to some affective psychological reactions. The finding that those closer to death avoided the introspective stance is highlighted by the magnitude and consistency of the findings in Realm III. Those approaching death may have been unwilling or unable to look inward because at some level of consciousness they recognized their impending death; that is, those approaching death may have avoided intro-spection because they feared what they would see. Unfortunately, these findings did not clarify what such a monitoring process might be, nor did they reveal the character of the inner life of such individuals.[5] (Analysis 2 was aimed at uncovering this in-formation.)

Finally, there appeared to be a consistent direction in the self-image of the DNs. Two major bipolar dimensions—assertive-ness-dependency and love-hate (Leary, 1957)—accounted for the eight categories of self-report. In the language of Bakan (1966), those close to death demonstrated a self-image oriented toward communion whereas those further from death empha-sized more agentic aspects. Although Bakan's concepts of agency and communion represent a higher level of abstraction than the self-image data provided here, his application of them in rela-tionship to Freud's concept of death instinct offers a framework for explaining the present self-image data and is consistent with the subsequent analysis of death symbols (Analysis 3).

Analysis II: A Direct Inquiry into Thoughts and Feelings about Death

Analysis of attitudes and feelings toward death. To test whether those close to death had different feelings and attitudes toward death, a series of scales were developed using responses to interview items and several items from a Sentence Comple-tion Test. Direct inquiries about death, and about time in rela-tionship to death, were used. The interviews for both groups of subjects were collated for all direct statements related to death, and the material for each subject was typed on a card without identifying information. The raw data, then, consisted of 80 paragraphs compiling all statements each subject had made about death. A number of attempts, blinded for group (DN or DF), were made to order these data. Many of the scales yielded distributions that could not discriminate among subjects. On a scale for assessing the degree of denial, for example, only 3 of the 80 subjects showed evidence of denial so measured. Two scales that could be reliably rated, Degree of Preoccupation with

Table 3

Analysis I: Comparison of Matched Pairs

Variable	Sample means DN	DF	Z	Variable	Sample means DN	DF	Z
Realm I				21. Self-image characteristics			
1. Mental status (E)[a]	2.1	1.4	1.41*	a. Power success (Octant AP)	8.9	9.6	.08
2. Learning-retention (E)[a]	14.9	13.8	1.75**	b. Narcissistic-exploitative (Octant BC)	13.4	13.5	.12
3. Visual organization (E)[a]	32.8	30.3	1.08	c. Hostile aggressive (Octant DE)	9.8	12.5	2.30**
4. Perceptual adequacy	24.0	23.6	.12	d. Rebellious-mistrustful (Octant FG)	11.1	13.7	2.03**
5. Time judgment	23.7	22.0	1.23*	e. Weakness (Octant HI)	14.1	13.8	.22
Realm II				f. Docile-dependent (Octant JK)	11.8	9.9	2.03**
6. Expansiveness-restriction	5.4	5.6	.89	g. Warm (Octant LM)	16.1	14.3	1.85*
7. Anxiety	25.7	27.3	.58	h. Responsible-hypernormal (Octant NO)	15.3	13.2	2.16**
8. Life satisfaction	16.9	18.0	.60				
9. Anomie	12.4	12.6	.17	22. Self-image styles			
10. Acceptance of life	9.7	9.5	.19	a. Current	39.0	44.4	1.33*
11. Loss	3.2	2.8	.51	b. Past	5.7	4.9	.28
Realm III				c. Conviction	49.2	42.9	1.01
12. Emotional reactivity	4.9	5.3	.57	d. Wished	1.2	1.0	.44
13. Affective complexity	2.0	3.5	2.95***	e. Distorted	4.6	6.9	1.65**
14. Introspective stance	2.0	2.7	3.00****	**Realm VI**			
15. Introversion-extroversion	21.2	21.3	.66	23. Futurity	5.7	5.9	.01
Realm IV				24. Extensionality	6.6	6.9	.59
16. Health evaluation	3.5	3.3	.37	25. Past	4.1	4.0	.57
17. Body preoccupation	4.0	3.9	.09	26. Present	0.8	0.8	.22
18. Body image	1.6	1.4	.48	27. Future	0.8	0.7	.06
19. Negative body image	1.3	1.0	1.11				
Realm V							
20. Self-esteem	23.1	24.1	.78				

Note: All tests of significance were one-tailed on variables having clear positive-negative directions where the death group was hypothesized to be on the lower or less adequate direction; two-tailed tests were used for Variable 21 where such an assumption could not be made; DN = death near; DF = death far.

[a] Higher scores indicate more errors; in all other cases, higher scores indicate score of variable named.

* $p > .10.$ ** $p > .05.$ *** $p > .0001.$

Own Death (Scale 1) and Fear of Death (Scale 2), were developed to discriminate individual differences (interrater reliability, Scale 1, 67 percent exact agreement; Scale 2, 100 percent exact agreement for $n = .10$).

Scales

1. Degree of Preoccupation with Own Death. The following is the 3-point scale used to assess the felt imminence of one's own death: (*a*) death seen as just around the corner; often expressed in concrete imagery of rapid progressive decay, (*b*) acute awareness of age and finitude and relatively stringent limits on time; death seen as occurring in the intermediate future; and (*c*) relative nonpreoccupation. Although not psychologically avoiding death as a personal issue, subjectively experienced time was taken up with some activities and hopes. Death was seen in a lengthier time context than for the previous two scale points.

Subject 486 (DN group) illustrated the low end of this scale (1), while Subject 448, also in this group, illustrated a rating of 3.

> [Subject 486] I'll go to sleep [bitter], I ain't so strong; weakest part is not being well. Death is nothing, just going to sleep. One hour is just another hour gone. Time means nothing. Everyone tries to plan, but it is impossible. No future. Does not think about things.
> [Subject 448] I would like to be strong and healthy—death is unavoidable. One hour is a blessed thing. I look forward to living a long life with my wife. The thing I like about myself is that I am all together in one piece. Time is to foresee things ahead. Don't plan. Next year I would like to live and tell of good events of the past year. The future is to look ahead for better things to come. Thinks more about the future. The past is gone.

2. Fear of Death. The following 4-point scale, ranging from few or primitive means of coping with fear to integrative mechanisms, was used to reduce fear (frequently expressed through a developed "personal philosophy"): (*a*) an unambivalent wish to be dead with no evidence of fear, (*b*) unmitigated fear, usually associated with no existing, (*c*) a feeling of personal helplessness

491

in the face of death's inevitability often accompanied by reliance on something outside of self for coping, and (*d*) processes indicative of relative adequacy to cope with fear of dying and death, such as placing one's own death in an interpersonal context with emphasis on separation rather than death; viewing death as the interruption of ongoing life processes with some emphasis on loss, but with the losing of life rather than death being paramount; focusing on the processes or the means or the mechanism of death so that not death, but the way of going was feared.

Raters were instructed to rate the dominant message on a scale rather than all the messages, and to rate in terms of the lowest point of the scale.

Subject 410 (DF group) illustrated a low (1) rating on Scale 2:

> [Subject 410] I'll be sick and die. I don't think they'll throw me out of here. There's nothing to hope for, I'm a nothing. I'll get worse and that's all. I can't fool myself. Hope means to die and not to suffer. My body isn't perfect. The weakest part of me, probably I have many weak spots. I'm dissatisfied with myself. There are times when I just don't like to live. Death would be a relief, my dear. I can't walk, I can't see, I can't hear. Right now I like to think about summer. I look forward to it without pain and suffering. Time does not mean much. People die every day like flies here. Next year I would like to die. Future means death and pleasure from the family.

In contrast, Subject 457 (also from the DF group) was rated 4 on the scale:

> [Subject 457] I'm better than many people. I prepare myself always, I even have the stone next to my wife. I told the children that if I possibly . . . the best thing is just to go. Each day goes by. Death is like a shot, when she died it was just like a shot. Time is gone. I plan ahead. Next year I'd like to go someplace, I still would like to go to Europe, but I don't know if I can go. The future is the best thing if I have a companion. The future is to get a companion, go out together and not to lose one's mind.

Subject 457 has developed some mechanisms for binding fear of death.

492

Subject 308, who was given a 3 rating, illustrated a contrast in coping:

[Subject 308] Knows he is almost through. Nothing more to worry about. Only thing is that they'll bury me. I fear I will die. Sometimes I feel disappointed because I feel young and I am not. Each day goes away and another comes. Dead is something I never was yet, I won't think about it until I die. No point otherwise. My mind is floating, nothing sure to me. Time here is worthless. Time is gone. I'd like to be a free man if I live. The future is for children.

Table 4

Death Attitude Scales

No. matched pairs where	Scale	
	Preoccupation with death	Fear of death
DN $>$ DF	16	18
DF $>$ DN	7	7
DN $=$ DF	17	15
Sample means		
DN	2.22	1.73
DF	2.60	2.18

Note: DN = death near; DF = death far.

Unlike the previous illustration, Subject 308 has not developed any consistent attitudes toward his own death.

The Wilcoxon matched-pairs signed-ranks test (one-tailed) was used to compare those near to death with their matched pairs. Table 4 shows the comparisons of matched pairs and sample means. The DNs were significantly more preoccupied with death ($z = 2.05$, $p = .02$) and had a greater fear of death ($z = 1.49$, $p = .07$) than their matched pairs.[6] Inspection of the distribution for the death attitude scales showed low preoccupation and low fear for approximately 40 percent of the DNs, suggesting either that the sensitivity of these scales was poor, or that the phenomenon tapped by these measures applied only to a subsample of the DNs. Further analysis was required to determine the significance of the large number of DN individuals who did not respond as anticipated on these two scales. The tendency toward low introspection noted in the first analysis suggested that many of these individuals may have been unable to discuss their thoughts about death and dying directly. This possibility implied the need for an instrument that was less amenable to such conscious control (Analysis 3).

Analysis 3: Death Symbols

Responses were analyzed to a series of Thematic Apperception Test (TAT) cards (The old Age TAT Cards 1, 2, 4, 5, 7: Lieberman & Lakin, 1963) which depicted old people in a number of interpersonal situations. The cards related to issues of separation-rejection, intimacy, and dependency which it was thought might stimulate the subjects' thinking about death. Several schemes were explored for indexing attitudes, feelings, and thoughts about death—ratings of depressive content, analysis of "unusual" responses, categorization of the hero's motivational states, and coding of symbolic representations of death. All indexes except the symbol analysis were abandoned because of infrequent occurrence, low reliability, or internal inconsistency.

Four types of symbols were analyzed: (*a*) direct references to death and dying—such as struggling to save life as in drowning, (*b*) issues of rebirth, (*c*) inscrutable events or mysterious trips, and (*d*) death figures or the spectre of death, such as a figure with hands folded or face covered (interrater reliability, $N = 20$, absence or presence of death symbols by the subject, 85 percent agreement).

Case 436 (DN group) illustrated an individual who expressed several of these symbols in his responses to the Old Age TAT.

> [Card 1: Packing scene] [Long pause] Well, he's opening up this box. Now let me adjust my spectacles so I can see better. He opened up that box and this lady . . . well, all I can see is that he opened up the box and he was looking for something. What it was I don't know. This lady is also taking a glance into the box. They lifted up some objects but I don't see the type of objects they lifted up. I just can't tell what it is so that I can decipher it for you. It's

very invisible thing. Very undecipherable to me. I see some other people—about three of them—in the back there. I don't know who they are. They have no significance to me. And now I've told you my opinion of this picture.

[Card 2: Entering scene] This one is walking up the stairway of a threshhold. There are one to five steps he's going to climb. All I can see is that he's carrying a satchel. Seems to me that he has a baby or something in front of him [pointed to white in front of man's face]. Or maybe it's a dolly instead of a baby. Anyway he's interested in looking at this strange thing. To me it's undecipherable. It's very faded and obscure. But I can see that this man is observing the object in the way of his task. [pause] By the way, I

Table 5

Death Symbols

Group	Absent	Present	Total
Near to death	6	34	40
Controls	31	9	40

Note: x^2 = 32.2, df = 1, p = .001.

can see that this man seems to be old. Yes, he's really an old man. That's all that I can tell you about this picture.

[Card 5: Roommate scene] those two men are having a conversation. This fellow [1] is trying to convert him [r]. The old man on the right says, "I'm trying to change your opinion." Then he goes on to say, "You say you're going to live longer than Winston Churchill, but you're not." By the way, did you know I'm still waiting for the Messiah. Christian Messiah that is, has come but we Jews have been waiting for the real Messiah for 5,000 years. I prophesy his coming.

The 80 subjects were rated for the presence or absence of one or more of the death symbols for each TAT response. The results of this blind analysis are shown in Table 5.

This analysis pointed to a process of "recognition" or monitoring that occurred in the DNs but yielded no information which helped to specify the emotional meaning of this monitoring process to the individual. The findings presented so far suggested that there were systematic psychological characteristics associated with imminent death and that those close to death were registering it at some level of consciousness. The final analysis pursued the question of emotional reactivity toward death in the DNs.

Analysis 4: Effects of Stress on Reactions to Death

Previous studies (Alekamdrowica, 1961; Fried, 1963; Friedsam, 1961; Lieberman, 1961; Lieberman & Lakin, 1963; Lieberman, Prock, & Tobin, 1968; Miller & Lieberman, 1965) have indicated that instability in the sociopsychological environment of the aged has profound, primarily negative, effects on the aged over several psychological dimensions (e.g., self-image, anxiety, life satisfaction) of importance to the current study. The subjects were divided into two groups on the basis of socioenvironmental setting. Twenty-two pairs of subjects were waiting to enter homes (unstable condition). Eighteen pairs of subjects had lived in an institution 3–5 years or were living in the community (stable condition). Analysis 4 compared the matched pairs now divided into two groups—those in circumstances defined as crisis situations and those in noncrisis situations to determine whether the psychological effects and experiences of closeness to death differed depending on whether the subject was in a crisis or a noncrisis situation. Based on the previous studies, crisis was defined as a situation involving separation from personal and familial relationships, an overwhelming task of self-redefinition, and a series of major coping tasks and complex adjustments. The material presented in the first three analyses was reanalyzed on the basis of group differences. In these analyses, matched pairs were used as the unit of analysis. Matching was particularly important here because of known differences between stable and unstable groups irrespective of distance from death.

The data on the six psychological realms presented in Analysis 1 (Table 3) were reanalyzed. Differences between matched pairs were used as scores for a T-test analysis which compared those in the stable and unstable environments. The results of this analysis yielded four variables that were significant at $p \geqslant .10$, not above the chance level for the number of analyses. Thus no statistical significances were obtained which discriminated the DNs in a stable environment from DNs in an unstable environment for the six realms.

The two groups of diers were compared (Tables 6 and 7) on the death attitude scales by means of the Wilcoxon matched-pairs signed-ranks tests. The results indicated that on both Scales 1 and 2 the subjects in the unstable environment had significantly more fear ($T = 15, p = .05$) and preoccupation ($T = 34, p = .05$) than their matched controls.

Table 6

Comparisons on Death Preoccupation Scales:
Stable and Unstable Conditions

Condition	DN means	Matched pairs		
		Dead more preoccupied	Dead less preoccupied	Dead equal to matched pair
Unstable	1.1	10	2	10
Stable	2.4	6	5	7

Note: DN = death near.

The DN subjects in the stable condition did not differ from their controls. It is recalled that in the initial analysis of these scales (Table 4), although statistical significance was obtained between the DN and DF subjects, approximately 40 percent of DN subjects did not show preoccupation or fear; Analysis 4 indicated that of the DNs it was the group in unstable conditions which was responsible for the significant difference from the DF group in Scales 1 and 2.

The TAT death symbols data could not be used to compare the two groups since 34 of the 40 diers showed death symbols, and the different symbol types did not discriminate between the two groups. A measure which could directly assess emotional reactions to death was needed to support the hypothesis of varying reactivity to impending death.

An anxiety measure was developed based on discrepancies in performance on the Murray and Old Age TATs. The Dana

(1959) system for scoring adequacy of performance on the Murray series of TAT cards was adapted to the Old Age TAT. This measure was applied to the two sets of TAT cards for the 80 subjects. A lower (comparative) performance on the Old Age TAT was taken to indicate anxiety associated with death and dying (by inference, because 34 of the 40 DNs did symbolize death on the Old Age TAT).

The DN subjects in a stable environment were compared to DNs in an unstable environment, using the TAT discrepancy

Table 7

Comparisons on Fear Scales:
Stable and Unstable Conditions

Condition	M	Matched pairs		
		Dead higher fear	Dead lower fear	Dead equal to matched pair
Unstable	1.4	12	4	6
Stable	2.2	6	3	9

scores. The statistical comparison was based on the number of times each matched pair of subjects scored more or less on the Old Age TAT than the Murray TAT as shown in Table 8. An analysis of the frequency yielded on a chi-square (omitting three tied cases) significant at $p = .01$ ($x^2 = 9.33$, $df = 1$). In the unstable group, 67 percent showed poorer performance on the Old Age TAT than on the Murray TAT, while in the stable group, only 23 percent showed a similar pattern.

The discrepancies scores for the DN unstable group indicated that these individuals reacted with apprehension or anxiety when faced with the Old Age TAT which they interpreted as symbolic of death and dying. In contrast, DNs in the stable environment produced an equal number of death symbols, but did not react with apprehension as indicated by their discrepancies scores on the TAT comparisons. In fact, in comparison to their DF controls, this group did better on the Old Age TAT than their general level of cognitive performance would predict

(Analysis 1, cognitive realm). Thus, while those close to death and under crisis reacted with anxiety to stimuli associated with death, those close to death but not in crisis reacted to the same death stimuli with highly integrated responses.

Discussion

The findings supported previous work (Lieberman, 1965) suggesting a time line based on distance from death as more

Table 8

Matched Pair Comparisons on TAT Discrepeancy Scores

Test	Diers in unstable condition	Diers in stable condition
Murray > Old Age	10	5
Old Age > Murray	3	16
Old Age = Murray	2	1

useful than chronological age for organizing psychological phenomena in the aged, particularly changes in psychological functioning. The present study also found additional, noncognitive factors associated with distance from death. The earlier study demonstrated that the cognitive changes observed were idiographic—changes from the individual's own base line. The present study, particularly in the symbolic responses to the Old Age TAT, suggested further that such changes had a signal function. The subjects were registering a process[7] within themselves and projecting it onto a TAT stimulus.

How may this process be understood? In the previous study acute illness crises were not pathonogmic to approaching death. Individuals who had recovered from illnesses did not show the same pattern of decline as diers. It seems equally unlikely that the signaling process was set off by self-detected changes related to decrements of aging—social and personal losses, physical incapacities, and the many onslaughts undermining self-image. All subjects (mean age = 83) had suffered multiple losses associated

with aging. Although all were ambulatory at the start of the study—
the overwhelming majority evidenced degenerative (though stabilized) illness patterns such as diabetes or some degree of arteriosclerosis. Those close to and far from death showed similar
departures from their physical status at age 50 or 60.

The findings also eliminated environmental setting as a factor that might have generated the symbolizing process occurring
in those close to death, since no differences between community and institutional subjects were apparent in the psychological
qualities associated with impending death. If environment influenced symbol production, institutionalized subjects would be
expected to differ, inasmuch as the old age home, itself, is sometimes taken as a death symbol and, in fact, possesses the institutional apparatus for dying. The symbolizing process appeared to
be unrelated to anxiety, since only subjects in the unstable environment evidenced anxiety as a response to the Old Age TAT.
Conscious attitudes about death were also unrelated to the symbolizing process.

What was observed is suggestive of a psychosomatic relationship—in this case a body process manifested in a mental expression. This signaling appeared to be relatively, if not absolutely,
specific to the individual; decrements of old age, acute illness,
or residence do not explain the phenomenon. It may be that the
failure of integrative functions in different individuals reaches a
point where it becomes unique or idiographic and that when
this threshold is crossed the symbolic expression or monitoring
of the final disintegration process, death, begins to occur.

The findings also suggested that in investigating death and
dying as a psychological isssue in the aged it is important to
differentiate subjects with respect to socioenvironmental conditions as well as distance from death. DN subjects in a stable
environment showed no evidence that they perceived it as a
debilitating event. They exhibited no storminess, no reactivity,
no disruptiveness; it was as if they were dealing with a developmental task that they were coping with adequately. (Munnichs,
1966, expressed similar observations.) This picture of equanimity is consistent even with the low introspective stance of this
group if it is assumed that they were not avoiding unpleasant
affect, but had resolved issues concerning self, including the

death issue. This view is supported by interviewers' ratings—individuals in this group were perceived by the interviewers as "comfortable, but shallow and uninteresting people."

DN subjects who were in unstable environments, on the other hand, experienced disruption and anxiety about death. Many lacked an articulate personal philosophy to deal with death. Environmental change is known to constitute a severe crisis for elderly people; previous patterns of relationships, meanings of significant others, and the self-image are challenged and tested by disruption of the environment. Individuals in this crisis state may have been anxious over impending death, not because their approaching death was of such great concern to them, but because life again had impinged on them, forcing them to make new adjustments and face anew previously solved problems (including, perhaps, a previous resolution of the death issue). If death were the essential threat, rather than the life yet to reorganize, more signs of avoidance, denial, or similar psychological mechanisms would be expected in response to death stimuli.

The variety of methods and populations used across age groups makes it difficult to say whether the aged give more attention to the death issue than nonaged populations. The direction of the findings would support a view that death is perhaps a more overt issue for the aged. Clearly, death played a part in the psychology of the subjects. Their willingness to talk openly about death suggests that they viewed it as a legitimate topic of discussion. Further, many subjects had worked out the meaning of death for themselves and most have developed a personal viewpoint toward their own death. That death is a topic of conversational interchange among the aged does not indicate that it is a critical psychological focal point toward which the last decade of life is oriented.

It seems appropriate, in the light of these findings, to question the salience of death as an ubiquitous issue over the final two decades of life. The view of death as an overriding issue to be grappled with, or as an organizing spectre during these years, while not contradicted, is not supported by the data. It is not that death has no meaning for the very aged, but rather that its meaning as a primary issue is limited to specific, restricted conditions. Death becomes a meaningful issue for the very aged

501

when distance from death is relatively brief, that is, a year or two prior to death. Perhaps the discrepancies between theories and empirical studies on the meaning of death in the psychology of the aged are partly explained by this finding. If death becomes a focal psychological issue only in relation to particular crisis points, then studies which employed general samples of aged would yield large variances. If for such a homogeneous sample as used here, death was a more critical psychological issue for those whose death was imminent, clearly it would be difficult to substantiate a general theory about the importance or centrality of death and dying for a more diverse population spanning a 25-year age range.

It seems likely, although unsupported by evidence, that the death issue is crucial much earlier in life, perhaps in late middle age. At any rate, the psychological teleology advanced in theories of aging perhaps does not fit the empirical findings parsimoniously, more because it is an invention of the young than because the studies of death and the aged have been inadequate.

Notes

1. This investigation was supported wholly by Public Health Service Research Grant No. HD-00364 from the National Institute of Child Health and Human Development and by Research Career Development Award 5-K3-HD-20,342.

2. Only 3 out of 80 subjects in the present study showed any sign of avoidance or denial when direct questions about death were rated for blatant refusals to think or talk about death and for metaphorical and euphemistic references to or an unambivalent belief in an afterlife.

3. Subjects were drawn from a pool of 182 subjects participating in a research program, Adaptation and Survival Under Stress in the Aged, University of Chicago, Ill.

4. The relatively low intercorrelations among the measures within each realm suggested that the degree of independence between variables was sufficient for such an approach. Realm I, average $r = .34$ $(.18-.51)$; Realm II, average $r = .15$ $(-.06-.40)$; Realm III, average $r = .09$ $(-.01-.48)$; Realm IV, average $r = -.06$ $(-.18-.09)$; Realm V (interdependency of data, i.e., single source makes r's impractical to compute); Realm VI, average $r = .04$ $(-.22-.28)$.

502

5. The literature on changes associated with proximity to death in both aged and nonaged persons has frequently discussed depression and/or withdrawal as the dominant psychological characteristic. This relationship was not borne out by these data. A number of the measures of emotional state used in this study as well as less direct indexes such as body preoccupation and time perspective, could be seen as tapping aspects of depression. No differences were obtained on any of these indexes.

6. Although based on the same set of data, two scales were sufficiently independent $(r = .43,$ DN; $r = .40,$ DF) for separate analysis.

7. The data do not permit a definite statement about the level of consciousness-unconsciousness of the monitoring process. For most subjects it is likely that the sense of imminent death was not within immediate awareness, but there are no data about the ease with which that awareness could be recalled under appropriate interview intervention. The absence of observed defense processes, for example, denial or avoidance, however, makes it unlikely that the sense of impending death was at one time in awareness, but had been made less available by defensive maneuvers.

SOCIALIZATION
FOR IMPENDING DEATH
IN A
RETIREMENT VILLAGE*[1]
Victor W. Marshall

Legitimation of Death

In their most general terms, the arguments which follow stem
from the perspective of Berger and Luckmann (Berger, 1969;
Berger and Luckmann, 1967) concerning the symbolic ordering
of biography. As these authors put it (1967, p. 100): "The symbolic universe provides order for the subjective apprehension of
biographical experience . . . the individual passing from one biological phase to another can view himself as repeating a sequence
that is given in the 'nature of things,' or in his own 'nature.'
That is, he can assure himself that he is living 'correctly' . . .
As the individual looks back upon his past life, his biography is
intelligible to him in these terms." In short, the individual is
able to view his own identity as nonproblematical if it can be
incorporated within shared, taken-for-granted reality and viewed
as a typical life in a typical situation. Moreover, the individual
is fundamentally motivated to seek an incorporation of his
biography into taken-for-granted social reality: to do otherwise
would subject him to the anomy or meaninglessness of a non-
validated (by others) reality (Berger and Luckmann, 1967, pp.
64, 102; Berger, 1969, pp. 23-24; McHugh, 1968, pp. 50-53).[2]

* Victor W. Marshall, "Socialization for Impending Death in a Retirement Village,"
American Journal of Sociology 80 (1975): 1124-44. Reprinted by permission of
the University of Chicago Press. © The University of Chicago.

The individual, then, seeks to *legitimate* his biography in terms of socially shared reality or, in Berger and Luckmann's words, the "symbolic universe," which constitutes the taken-for-granted reality of the individual and his fellowmen. Death postulates a key problem for the legitimation of biography (Berger and Luckman, 1967, p. 101):

> A strategic legitimating function of symbolic universes for individual biography is the "location" of death. The experience of the death of others and, subsequently, the anticipation of one's own death posit the marginal situation par excellence for the individual. Needless to elaborate, death also posits the most terrifying threat to the taken-for-granted realities of everyday life. The integration of death within the paramount reality of social existence is, therefore, of the greatest importance for any institutional order. This legitimation of death is, consequently, one of the most important fruits of symbolic universes.

Any symbolic universe may be employed in legitimating death, a process which may be seen as two-faceted, for both the death of others and the impending death of the individual must be made understandable (Berger and Luckmann, 1967, p. 101): "All legitimations of death must carry out the same essential task—they must enable the individual to go on living in society after the death of significant others and to anticipate his own death with, at the very least, terror sufficiently mitigated so as not to paralyze the continued performance of the routines of everyday life."

In 1969–70 I studied a retirement village, Glen Brae, through participant observation and intensive interviewing techniques. This setting can be viewed, at a micro level, as a small society in reference to Berger and Luckmann's discussion of the need for legitimation of death if life in society is to carry on. Moreover, this is a society in which death is prevalent and where the members, because they are in their later years, experience most poignantly the need for legitimating death. Glen Brae will be described shortly. I turn first to evidence that in such a society death does appear to be successfully legitimated for most participants.

505

Successful Legitimation of Death

The legitimation of death is a fairly successful accomplishment at Glen Brae. For whatever reasons, most residents of the retirement community are able to accept that death—whether that of others, their own, or both—is legitimate. I do not mean that death is viewed in isolation as a positive event (although this might be the case for some) but, rather, that it is viewed as appropriate, given contextual factors and the logical alternative—continued life. Perhaps the greatest evidence of such legitimation lies in the ease with which residents could formulate thoughts about death and dying—including their own—to me as an investigator. Certain specific indicators provide additional evidence.

The residents in the study were asked if they would like to live to be 100 years old. Of 79 respondents, none answered with an unconditional yes. Conditional yes answers were given by 19 residents,[3] while 60 gave unconditional no answers. Conditional replies indicate that the individual entertains certain formulable reasons why continued life to that age *could* be appropriate but no certainty that these reasons will obtain. Negative replies indicate that the subject can formulate no adequate or legitimate reasons why life extending to age 100 would be appropriate or more appropriate than death; they do not indicate whether continued life within that parameter is viewed as legitimate. This indicator, then, gives a very conservative measure of the legitimation of death.

Additional evidence that death is legitimated in the Glen Brae community by most residents comes from responses to three attitudinal questions.[4] The fact that these have been asked of a representative national sample by John Riley (1970; see Riley and Foner [1968, pp. 332-37] for additional discussion of findings) allows for comparison. Just over half of Riley's respondents were under age 41, but the insignificant effects of age on the responses given can be seen by comparing the overall results with those for persons age 61+ (Table 1). It is clear from this table that the great majority of Glen Brae residents have legitimated death, at least in a general way, and, further, that the extent to which they have done so exceeds that found in the overall population. This is not, as far as can be ascertained, attributable to the higher educational level of the Glen Brae population. Riley found college-educated people over 61 less likely to agree that death always comes too soon (29 percent vs. 59 percent for those with less education), but the proportion of the college-educated group agreeing with the statement is still more than twice that for the Glen Brae residents. At Glen Brae a higher level of education is associated with a decreasing proportion of residents agreeing that death always comes too soon,

Table 1

Comparison of Riley's Sample for Selected Indicators

	Percentage Agreeing with Statement		
	Glen Brae	Riley, Age 61+	Total Riley
Would you agree or disagree with the following statements?			
Death is sometimes a blessing	98	91	89
Death is not tragic for the person who dies, only for the survivors . .	91*	85	82
Death always comes too soon	12†	51	53
Total *N*	79	249	1,428

* Excludes 11 "don't know" and 6 uncodable responses; includes 16 responses indicating that death is tragic for neither the person who dies nor the survivors (based on probing apparently not done in the Riley study).
† Excludes one "don't know" response.

but the trend does not reach significance. Level of education makes no discernible difference in the responses to the question concerning the tragic aspect of death. We are left, then, with some indication that death is highly legitimated in this community—and with the task of seeking an explanation for this fact.

It is important to recognize that legitimation of death is not a defeat—or not necessarily so—for many residents. It can signify a genuine feeling of appropriateness, as indicated by the remarks of an 81-year-old widow when asked how old she would like to live to be: "Heavens! I've lived my life. I'd be delighted to have it end. The sooner the better. I nearly went with a heart attack. It would have been more convenient to go when my daughter was in —— rather than in ——. I feel I've lived my life, and I don't want to be a care to anybody. That's why I'm glad to be here [in Glen Brae]. No, I don't want to mourn when I go. I've had a good life. It's time."

Others see little point in living longer, and death does not seem to enter into their considerations. As another resident put her response to the question "Would you like to live to be 100?": "No point, I have no one dependent on me. And I've looked after my few descendants I have. And I haven't any great problem to resolve." This woman is 88 and feels "it's time people shuffled off by 90."

Another says of her husband that he died well: "I mean he had never done anything to regret. Nothing to complete. Nothing to make right."

A woman who would like to live until "the day after tomorrow" says that, although she is "disgustingly healthy," "you get tired of the routine." These examples suggest people for whom the legitimation of biography is highly important for the legitimation of death. Death itself is not a big problem for them, except perhaps in not coming soon enough. This can be seen more clearly in the following analysis.

For a subset of the Glen Brae residents surveyed, good evidence that they have legitimated their own deaths comes from cross-tabulating their responses to two questions. These are a fixed-choice question asking the individual to estimate how old he thinks he will live to be and a direct question, "How old would you like to live to be?" The first question, involving the selection of a statement representing the respondent's estimate of how old he will live to be, produced codable data for 50 respondents. The question on how old people would like to live to be produced many "don't know" responses but codable responses for 32 residents. Answers were transformed into years the respondent desired to add to his present age, and then the categories were collapsed. The categories are somewhat different from those for the life-estimate question, because of the language employed by the residents. The difference in coding in fact enhances the utility of the data for purposes of comparison. Regrettably, the low usable response on both questions leaves us with a cross-tabulation containing only 24 cases (Table 2).

Of those 24, only 4 expressed a desire to live longer than was anticipated. Kendall's rank-order correlation test shows a significant correlation of the ranking, indicating that the number of years individuals desire to live adjusts to the number they anticipate living.[5] But the more important finding lies in the display itself. At least 10 respondents indicated a desire to live less long than they anticipated living. The remaining 10 individuals wished either to die at a time when they expected to or to live beyond that time.

Table 2

Desired Life Expectancy in Relation to Anticipated Life Expectancy

	Anticipated Remaining Years of Life		
	10+	5-10	Less than 5 years
Respondent would like to live an additional			
10+ years.	3	1	0
5-9 years.	3	1	3
0-4 years.	1	6	6

Note: Kendall's tau *B* = .404, significant beyond .003. The selectivity on the question asking the individual to specify the number of years he would like to live suggests caution in the interpretation of this table.

These data provide striking evidence that, for a sizable proportion of the residents, death is legitimated as more reasonable than continued living.[6] For many, the evidence goes beyond mere acquiescence to or acceptance of impending death and indicates a positive desire for death rather than continued living beyond a specific age. This and the attitudinal indicators concerning the lack of tragedy and the blessings of death, together with the fact that no respondents expressed an unqualified desire to live to be 100, provide strong evidence that death is legitimated for many residents of Glen Brae.

The remaining sections of this paper seek to establish the importance, in providing acceptance of death, of the social organization for death and dying which is fostered at Glen Brae.

509

This analysis is focused at the level of the community. A complementary analysis at the level of the individual in interaction with others appears elsewhere (Marshall 1972b). My point in this paper is that the particular features of an age-segregated environment, rather than age segregation itself, significantly affect the degree of successful legitimation.

The Research Site

The data used in this analysis stem primarily from extensive field research supplemented by interviewing in the retirement village of Glen Brae (for other reports, see Marshall [1972a, 1972b, 1973a, 1973b]). This retirement community is a rambling, modern, 300-apartment structure housing about 400 residents in a campuslike setting in a suburban environment near the eastern seaboard of the United States. Residents purchase their apartments on a "life-care" principle which includes their right to receive care in an attached nursing-care facility should this become necessary. More than two-thirds of the residents were born in the state where they now live or in a neighboring one. Their age ranges from 64 to 96, the average age being 80. As in most similar communities, they are educationally privileged, with less than one-fifth having no more than a high school education. By major breadwinner, 58 percent of the sample (which is representative) are from business and 38 percent from professional families. Their religious adherence is mixed but almost exclusively Protestant. Fully 78 percent are female; 28 percent are married, 46 percent widowed, and 27 percent single (77 percent of the males but only 15 percent of the females are married; all other males are widowed, while about one-third of the females were never married).

As it has been noted that retirement communities tend to have a natural history and a life cycle of their own (Rosow, 1966; Carp, 1972), it is important to note that at the time these data were gathered the community was moving from its fifth to its sixth year. The "sea of mud" phase (Rosow, 1966) which began the life of the community was over. My description of the development and functioning of institutions within the

510

community for socialization for impending death is thus based not only on extensive interviewing (an average of three hours per respondent) and observational data gathering but also on a reconstruction from interview material and documents available to me.

Much of orderly social behavior depends on common definitions and assumptions about the location of events in time (Moore, 1963, p. 8; Lyman and Scott, 1970, pp. 194-99). I am speaking of time not as a boundary condition but as a sequence of activities. Moore (1963) speaks of the "timing" of organizational life, referring to the synchronization, sequencing, and frequency of activities. Lyman and Scott (1970, p. 195; see also Calkins, 1970; Gustafson, 1972) speak of the pace and sequence of temporal orderings. At Glen Brae time is structured so as to be both full and involving the residents. In large measure, Glen Brae residents structure their own time. The lives they lead are worked out by themselves instead of being structured for them by the administration.

The daily routine of living at Glen Brae is broken up by mealtime, but meals are not highly structured. Individuals dine at tables of their choice and at times of their choosing during extensive dining hours. They may also dine in their own kitchen-equipped apartments or in a snack bar. In the dining room, meals are served by waitresses; this, coupled with the freedom to choose one's table partners, leads to broad-ranging and extensive informal interaction. A hostess will introduce newcomers or isolates who might wish to share a table with another resident. Varying table sizes and freedom to choose one's companions encourage the residents to treat dining as a social occasion.[7] As meals are paid for in the rental package, it is also a simple and inexpensive matter to arrange a small gathering in an apartment for a drink or two before dinner. In proximity to the dining room are the residents' library and a lounge, which provide additional social opportunities.

Dining arrangements are paradigmatic of the informal social organization of Glen Brae. Recreational pursuits are similarly flexible. Throughout the day one will see residents busy at lawn bowls or shuffleboard, swimming, engaged in bridge games in the many lounges, or tending their small flower gardens outside their apartments. The sameness of daily life is broken on a regular basis by activities which, though routinized, are scheduled at a different pace. These include concerts, movies, and lectures. These activites, which provide a range of social opportunities, are planned by the residents themselves, through their own "house government," the Forum.

The Forum itself provides another opportunity for residents to initiate their own form of social organization in the community. It meets annually and at other times according to need, and its many committees are active throughout the year.

Not the least important of the Forum-initiated activities is a "corridor-chairman" system. For each corridor in the village the Forum appoints one individual to act as "den mother." This person checks the health status of each resident on his or her corridor each day and can mobilize formal and informal community support when· needed. Attempts are made to incorporate isolates. Particular watchfulness is exercised in situations of potential crisis, such as the death of a spouse or friend; thus, the corridor-chairman system is able. to act as a kind of informal "widow-to-widow" crisis intervention system (Silverman and Englander, 1973). In a general way the system serves to define the atmosphere of the community as one of mutual support.

A resident newspaper, the *Glen Call,* is published quarterly, providing a calendar of upcoming events, a commentary on past events, and an opportunity for the community's poets, gossips, and social critics to develop a sense of community. An article in the *Glen Call* illustrates the informal character of social activities at Glen Brae: "July and August are somnolent months at Glen Brae, a marking-time period for those who spend summer here, a time for friendly games of cards, swimming and bowling for those who are athletically inclined, a time to get better acquainted with one another."

In back issues of the *Glen Call,* the origins of many regular and irregularly scheduled activities can be seen. These were not initiated by the administration to carry out an activities policy; rather, they arose over the five years during which the community of Glen Brae residents developed a reasonably full routine of activities. The Forum was itself initiated by interested residents, and many of the activities listed above are under its sponsorship. There is generally "something doing" for Glen Brae residents. Time, as a sequence of activities, is full, the pace is swift, the time between activities and events of note short. However, it is important to note that the individual resident can adapt himself freely to the temporal routines. The resident who wishes to fill his time can do so; the resident who does not wish to be active need not take part in the social activities.

Glen Brae as a Place to Die

A move to Glen Brae is the last move for most of its residents, making it a place where people go to die, althoug this fact might be obscured by the emphasis on living. An early issue of the *Glen Call* quotes the medical director: "Our philosophy at Glen Brae is that this is a place to come to and live; not to die. It is one of keeping residents healthy, active, virile and mentally alert."

But people do die at Glen Brae, and they go there knowing they will die there. Moreover, the move to the retirement village serves to heighten the resident's awareness of his finitude. The move is fundamentally a calculation involving the life estimate, both on the part of the resident and on the part of the management, and both parties realize this. Also, for both parties, this realization is heightened by financial factors.

Glen Brae is financed by the death of its residents, a fact which sets up an ironic conflict of interest, at least on a theoretical level.[8] An insurance company holds a mortgage on the multi-million-dollar physical plant. This is being amortized through the initial fees, or "founders' gifts," which residents pay to guarantee a lifetime lease. Monthly rates are calculated for the sole purpose of meeting operating expenses. An initial 25-year mortgage was negotiated on the basis of estimated turnover of apartments; however, this estimate was overly "optimistic," as the residents did not die as quickly or frequently as anticipated. The mortgage has been rewritten on a 30-year basis. Thus, the administrators of Glen Brae can and do speak with pride of their ability to keep people alive longer than might be expected in less advantageous surroundings; but their pride must be somewhat tempered by the consequent financial difficulties.

I have no data on the basis for the initial actuarial estimates, but I suspect that the planners' "optimism" was due to a failure to take account of social class (see Mayer and Hauser, 1953) and health selection factors (Gove, 1973). The estimates for the revised 30-year mortgage take account of the fact that "the occupants would probably exercise selction similar to that of purchasers of annuities. That is to say, an individual or couple in ill health would probably not pay the relatively large sum required as a founder's gift since there would be no refund in the event of their early death" (from administration records).

The chief administrator of Glen Brae attributes the unexpected longevity of its residents to two factors: freedom from worries and the availability and utilization of excellent medical care facilities, reasons that are seconded by many residents. One of them articulates well the residents' understanding of this problem: "I've heard you get such beautiful care here you haven't a chance of dying. Here's the administration wanting you to die because they want to sell apartments, and the medical staff wanting you to live."

In any case, heightened longevity can cause problems for the residents as well as for the administration, especially with the steep rise in monthly rates which has characterized the history of the community.[9] Payment of the founder's gift commits the resident to further investment of his resources in the form of the monthly rental fee. But the amount of further investment is uncertain, as it depends on relative stability or predictability of the fee and on actual life expectancy, the latter of which can be only subjectively estimated. If the Glen Brae resident greatly underestimates his life expectancy,[10] he may literally exhaust his financial resources. One resident vividly captured the dilemma as she spoke of trying to manage her limited resources: "I just got my bank statement, and it isn't too high. I'll have to be careful from now on. If you knew how long you had [to live] you could figure it out to the cent. But you can't."

It is clear from many interviews with residents that even those with extensive personal financial resources are keenly aware of this dilemma, because they see it affecting other, less

514

fortunate members of their community. Another resident claimed: "I think with the rapid increase in rates here that there are people in great anguish that they will not die until they've spent everything they've got—you see, if you could just make it come out even it would be very nice."

The large financial investment involved in a move to Glen Brae emphasizes subjective life expectancy and is closely related to awareness of finitude. As one resident declared, "They come here to die, you know, to spend their last days." He claims, "It's a form of insurance to come here—based on life expectancy."

Community Organization for Death and Dying

The administration has not made plans for the management of dying and death as a community event. But by the time Glen Brae had been in existence for a year, the residents had begun to organize as a community of the dying. This was expressed in a 1966 editorial in the *Glen Call* by the president of the Forum, which I cite in full:

> Most of us have been residents in Glen Brae for more than a year. We realize its present and ever increasing beauty. Friendships are being formed. Life is taking on new and important meaning. It is a rewarding way of life.
>
> And new responsibilities are ours too. Fifteen deaths have occurred to date, which was the predicted actuarial estimate.[11] The rate will increase as we grow older. With 100 new residents arriving next year[12] it is forecast that we can expect a death amongst us as frequently as one every two weeks. This is a sober thought.
>
> Our responsibility, therefore, involves a point of view, a determination. Either Glen Brae will turn into a place shrouded in a funeral parlor atmosphere of tears and perpetual sadness, or it will play its intended role—the best place to be when crises occur. It is suggested that each of us look toward the future and be prepared, that we respect the faith of others, the wishes of the survivor, and above all else that we reduce to a minimum the prolongation of sorrow, the discussion of pain, loss, tragedy. It is up to us, not management, to make Glen Brae the haven we desire.

This early statement characterizes the present treatment of death at Glen Brae, that treatment being informal and resident-initiated social organization for death and dying. Deaths at Glen Brae are marked only by a discreet notice placed on the bulletin board and a name-only obituary listing in the *Glen Call.*

Funerals are held elsewhere, and survivors make every effort to prevent their grief from casting shadows on their fellow residents. A resident whose husband is still alive says, "This angers me here—that there is so little external appearance of grieving. This angered me ever since I came; that people would lose a spouse, and in most cases go along doing interesting things."

But I would judge that the majority of residents approve of the low-key management of death and grief. In the words of one, "Here we are in the midst of death, so to speak, because you see notices often. I think death is very philosophically treated here." Another resident maintains that when a spouse dies the widow takes it "very well. [Other] people rally round—make dates for lunch with them. It's wonderful how widows don't have to move."

May (1967, p. 58) has written of the effects of death on the human community:

> The awareness of death also has another value, and this is that it is the ultimate source of human humility. The fact that you and I at some time will die puts us, in the last analysis, in the same boat with every other man, free or enslaved, male or female, child or adult. The facing of death is the strongest motive, and indeed requirement, for learning to be fellow men ... in the long run, we are all in the same boat. This is what Theseus meant in Sophocles' play *Oedipus at Colonus* when he said: "I know that I am only a man, and I have no more to hope for in the end than you have."

The fact that all at Glen Brae are approaching death seems indeed to be a humanizing factor. Most residents would agree with May as he continues: "[Death] places us all in need of mercy and forgiveness by the others, and makes us all participate in the human drama in which no man can stand above another."

The "common-fate" approach of Glen Brae residents to their impending death was perhaps helpful in their reaction to a

516

less-than-subtle reminder of their finitude from the administration: a questionnaire given to all residents rather blatantly soliciting information as to funeral arrangements. It represents an effort to effect efficient disposition of a body upon the death of a resident in keeping with his own wishes. Detailed questions are asked concerning preference for cremation, open or closed casket, obituaries, and other pertinent matters. As far as I could tell, the questionnaire is received with humor by most residents (although some have still not completed it). For example, the following poem appeared shortly thereafter in the *Glen Call:*

Ode to Immortality

(In answer to a questionnaire about our demise. To be sung to first verse of "Yankee Doodle.")

They asked you all to make your will.
We hope you're well provided,
So, favorite son, and daughter, too,
Will not think you're one-sided.

Have you kept out your favorite dress?
Please don't let it get spattered,
And if you think you'll live too long,
Be sure it won't be tattered.

Will men be wearing double breast,
Or will they be that formal?
Or, do you think a business suit
Will make them look more normal?

Lead righteous lives, dear girls and boys
And don't commit outrageous sin,
So when you reach the pearly gates,
St. Pete will say, "Come in, come in."

At Glen Brae, as anywhere else, dying is a social event in that people die in the context of others who define their dying in ways amenable to a sociological role analysis (Glaser & Strauss, 1965, 1968, 1971). Glaser and Strauss (1968, p. 6) use the term "dying trajectory" to refer to an individual's socially defined course of dying. As socially perceived, the dimensions of dying

517

"depend on whether the perceiver initially *defines* someone as dying and on his expectations of how that dying will proceed. Dying trajectories themselves, then, are perceived courses of dying rather than their actual courses."

In this respect we may note with Sudnow (1967, p. 62) that "the characterizations 'he is dead' and 'he is dying' . . . are the products of assessment procedures, i.e., constitute the outcomes of investigative inquiries of more or less detail, undertaken by persons more or less practically involved in the consequences that discovery of those outcomes foreseeably have."

The definition of a resident as dying has interactional consequences. At some point, the dying of a resident at Glen Brae will lead to his removal to the extended-care facility, which is somewhat separated from the residential section. However, because the extended-care facility handles many short-term emergencies, a move there is not necessarily clearly indicative to other residents of impending death. The administration has the authority to move a seriously ill resident to the extended-care facility and lease his apartment to someone else. This action usually signals impending death; sometimes it simply represents a prognosis of continued severe disability requiring extensive nursing care. The administration claims that sometimes this procedure leads the person himself to get upset and "see himself as dying."

Because I did not conduct research in the extended-care facility itself, I have not gathered data as to the definitional properties of the very last phase of dying. I feel, however, that the provision for removing the seriously ill from the residential section of Glen Brae serves the function, for other residents, of effectively removing the vivid presence of death (Friedman, 1966). This is not to say that the residents are not aware that they live in the midst of death. It would be impossible for them not to be aware of that, given the fact that many among them die. But their awareness of the hard, cold fact of death, as opposed to their strong awareness of finitude, is probably somewhat buffered by this geographical segregation of the terminally ill.

In summary, Glen Brae is a place where people go to live out the last days of their lives in a relatively problem-free environment. The cost of freedom from housekeeping and medical serivce worries is heightened awareness both of the dying of other members of the community and of one's own finitude. Yet the residents of Glen Brae have developed a system of mutual support and a normative pattern of behavior with regard to death. In the next section, I explore the effects of this social organization of death and dying on the anticipation of death and dying.

Plans for Death and Dying

Living in the community of the dying provides Glen Brae residents with role models with which to anticipate their own dying. Experience with the death of kin performs a similar function. There thus exists, for many residents, a conception of the appropriate course of dying. As one subject put it: "I think the thing that is feared is dying, not death. You see you want to die nobly, and you're afraid you won't be able to." Another, describing what she would like to accomplish in her future, said: "I haven't any idea. I hope to live comfortably and not be too much of a care to my children. And to die 'gracefully.' I aim to die without yelling, 'Hey, I'm going.' "

Persons highly aware of finitude live in anticipation of the most important status passage they have ever anticipated—that from life to death.[13] Living in a congregate residential facility for the aging and dying quite naturally encourages an appreciation of this fact:

> The older you get and the more you are in a place like this, and the more you see, you begin to wonder what's going to happen to you, what's in store. . . . You are aware that people are dying all the time—or that they won't last much longer. Since I've been here there have been seven people whom I knew more or less well who have gone.

> Until I was 87 [the previous year] I never thought about how old I was. Now that I am here and am with a lot of older people I know how old I am. I was busy—I just didn't think about it. I was well until I got here. Then I had accidents, was in the infirmary. Then I began to think.

519

When people begin to think about their impending deaths, they frequently talk with others about it; this proves beneficial in assisting them to come to terms with it. Glen Brae is, in a sense, organized to provide such assistance by encouraging a high level of social interaction which allows death to be dealt with informally. The community also, however, provides models which enable the individual to anticipate with greater clarity what his own death might be like, and thus to structure his own planning for death.

Glen Brae residents see slow and painful deaths but also quick and painless ones. One resident told me that, on learning she had a heart condition, she felt great relief, for now she could anticipate not only that she would not live too much longer (and suffer decline of mental or physical health) but also that her death would probably be the relatively painless, and frequently unexpected, death from a heart attack. Other respondents echoed the same preference for a quick and easy death:

> I hope . . . when the end comes it'll be snappy. You know, I know one person here who carries a cyanide pill with him. . . . I think he dreads a terrible siege.

> I hope that when that time comes it will come fast. I've given the doctors instructions that way.

> I don't know what I hope to accomplish. I hope for a quick death when it comes.

> I'd just like to go to sleep and never wake up. Kind of cowardly, but I haven't anyone to say goodbye to.

> Everybody wishes they'd have a sudden heart attack. No one wants a lingering incapacity.

These quotations reflect a concern not with the legitimation of death—we have seen that most residents have legitimated their impending deaths—but with the appropriate style of dying.

520

Living in a community of the dying, these people "know" what is a good and what is a bad style of dying. Being ready to die, they want their dying to be of no trouble to themselves or to anyone else. As one widow said, "I hope I don't struggle or make a scene."

This concern has been translated by many into direct requests that heroic measures not be taken to sustain their lives. A series of meetings have been held with the medical staff to discuss a variety of issues concerning health care. A recent issue of the *Glen Call* reported:

> The problem of care in a terminal illness came up in every one of the 13 meetings. . . . No heroic measures, urged several residents, and the doctors assured us they would honor our wishes. "With or without your signature on the blanks obtainable in the clinic [for stating such wishes], we will treat each resident as we ourselves want to be treated. Only oxygen, nutrition and pain relief; no heroic measures." In this way the doctors set at rest many of our worries and fears.

Death thus becomes something that is to a certain extent planned for (Miller, Galanter, & Pribram 1960, pp. 141–42), and in more aspects than noted above. Approximately 90 percent of the Glen Brae residents feel that it is better to plan for death than to ignore it; a similar proportion have already made plans for their own deaths. (Riley & Foner [1968, pp. 336–37] report a similar proportion of old people feeling it is best to plan, but fewer who do.) The administration of Glen Brae requires them to do so, as we saw in the discussion of the questionnaire requesting a report of such plans. Actual plans range from spiritual ones, which, however, are infrequently mentioned at Glen Brae, to concrete details for funerals and interment:

> I'm getting a stone up in the cemetery with my name on it. All but the date.

> [My wife] and I bought a plot and a stone five or six years ago. The stone's up now.

521

I had the man from the funeral home yesterday—after Mrs. ——— [another resident] died. It gets us all scared. She's probably been dead 24 hours. They found her in her bed.

———————

I joined that organization that is trying to have simple cheap observances. I've arranged to give my eyes to the cause of science. I think all of us have done something like that. I'm just changing my will.

Of the few who have not made specific plans for their impending deaths, some know that this is being attended to by their children. One widow thus turned to spiritual preparation: "[Making plans for death] is up to my family. You know, you teach your children, 'Now I lay me down to sleep. I pray the Lord my soul to keep. And if I die before I wake, I pray the Lord my soul to take.' Now that is becoming to be my prayer."

Planning at Glen Brae for death and dying takes place in an expectational milieu where impending death has been legitimated and where it is accepted that the act of dying is not supposed to be prolonged or to cause great disruption in the lives of others. The details of the ritual markings of residents' deaths have, for the most part, already been planned by themselves. While the great majority of Glen Brae residents feel that others close to them will be affected by their deaths, only about 15 percent feel that the lives of others will be seriously disrupted. In general, there seems to be an effort to minimize any hardship for others that would be caused by their deaths (just as others are relieved of the care of their parents when the parents move to a retirement community). Like the majority of Glen Brae residents, one respondent, for example, would prefer to have family members present at her death—"someone to hang on to." However, she continued, "on the other hand, there again, if I thought that my going would be terribly hard on my husband and son, then I'd want to spare them that. I'd rather die alone."

Routinization of Death

We have seen that Glen Brae is a community setting in which the residents are remarkably successful in legitimating their impending deaths. The success of Glen Brae in this regard is partially due, I have tried to show, to the low-keyed but resourceful approach taken by the residents themselves as they organize aspects of their lives so as to deal with death and dying.

The low-keyed approach, as I have demonstrated, was working out well in the early years of the community, and it continues as a deliberate practice. Thus, when a resident dies, the surviving spouse carries on: "Most of the time, outside of going to the funerals, they pick up and go on in very remarkable fashion. And they do it purposefully—for the other residents. It's very obvious."

This is not to say that conversational resources are not available when needed: "There are several people who have come here rather soon after they have lost a mate. They will speak about that, and interestingly enough when that happens you are almost under a compulsion to explain that you have lost one also." The loss of spouses is discussed, but "in a little way, not in a great way. I think most of the people here are quite reserved. Generally speaking, it's a happy attitude here." As a result, death can continue to be taken for granted by the residents: "I think it's an accepted thing. They talk about it the same as a game of bridge. I've been surprised with this group. They don't resent [death], do they? . . . It's an accepted fact. You see that when people read a notice of a death on the bulletin board. It might just as well have been about anything else."

This comment testifies to the degree of success of socialization for death within the Glen Brae community. Death is not built up into a great philosophical problem for the residents. That they will die is taken for granted by them; why they die is legitimated conversationally. Glen Brae residents learn not to make a great fuss about their dying. Thrown together with a large number of others facing the same fate, they have developed a community of tacit understanding which legitimates their impending deaths. In this sense they are like the residents of Moosehaven described by Kleemeier (1954): "As there is sickness in Moosehaven, so there is death. It comes often as an old friend. There is a comfortable matter-of-factness about the way Moosehaven people face death. There is no false sense of values which denies the inevitability of death. Nor is there morbid preoccupation with it."

At Glen Brae, I, too, could learn a great deal about dying that could be applicable to myself, despite my own long life expectancy. I learned that under favorable conditions I would be able to anticipate my own death with equanimity.

Conclusion

Speaking of death as a community event, a resident of Glen Brae said, "It's a very 'understanding' community. Everybody is in the same conditions of their lives." But that is not enough to provide socialization for impending death. To comprehend the way "understanding" becomes operative in dealing with impending death, we have to look at the way the community organizes itself to deal with death. Given the absence, in this analysis, of a wider spectrum of community settings for the aged, I can offer no definitive list of community organization variables which enhance socialization for death. However, some suggestions can be made.

A major adjustment that faces the aging individual is, I have argued, adjustment to his impending death. This is thought of as a process of legitimation, by which the aging individual comes to accept death, including his own impending death, as appropriate and nonproblematical within a shared system of meanings. To legitimate impending death in this manner allows the individual to go on living with others while facing his death with equanimity. The legitimation of death, like any process of legitimation, is best accomplished in a conversational process, for any reality is maintained primarily through conversation (Berger & Kellner, 1964).

One is also better able to face his impending death if he can observe, in a kind of role-modeling process (Hochschild, 1973, p. 80), that the deaths of his fellows occur within a taken-for-granted framework where they are considered appropriate. The rendering of death as appropriate must be a community event in which the individual can himself participate. If community involvement in the social organization for death and dying is to be developed, there must be an underlying substratum of community involvement and social interaction. Simply put, if individuals

are to deal with their own deaths in their
have opportunities to interact, to talk a
and to deal with it in a process of realii
schild (1973, p. 79) characterized anoth
aged and dying in this manner. Describin;
income apartment project for the aged, sh
a fact of life . . . and there was no taboo aga
Although each individual faced death ess
was a collective concern with, as they put   ˛ ⸤Ɐᵤ̥y and
facing up, a concern the young could not share with them in
quite the same way. The deaths of fellow residents meant a great
deal to the community and they reveal a great deal about it."

Hochschild's valuable analysis demonstrates that persons of
lower-class backgrounds and low educational level can, given the
appropriate community setting, successfully socialize each other
for impending death. Her study thus lends indirect support to
my stress on organizational factors rather than factors of selection as the important determinants of successful legitimation.[14]

Merrill Court, like Glen Brae, is a community where residents maintain an active formal and informal social life with
one another. Residents maintain watchfulness over their fellow
community members for sickness and death (Hochschild, 1973,
p. 53). Such mutual concern probably cannot be legislated by
the administration of any congregate facility for the aging, but
it can arise when a degree of independence and social interaction is fostered as a foundation. We have seen, for instance, that
such prosaic administration policies as those concerning dining
arrangements can contribute to building such a foundation.

Two additional features of Glen Brae have reinforced both
the awareness of residents that they are in fact a community of
the dying and their community response to this awareness.
These are the financial dilemma caused by the founder's gift-
rental system and the fact that residents do have options when
planning the material concomitants of their deaths, such as funeral and burial. Both features involve residents in concerns
about finitude and death. Both ask residents to assume some
control over their final years. I noted earlier, in quoting Rollo
May, that facing death is the strongest motive for learning to be
a fellowman. Paradoxically, then, the financial dilemma in a

nances the process of socialization for death, just as enng that one's departure from this world will cause no bother or others leads to a personal feeling that one's house is in order.

The vivid presence of death probably does not in itself make for an understanding community wherein death can be legitimated. Legitimation of death will probably occur only when community characteristics are favorable. I believe that an administration, although it cannot legitimate death, can provide conditions conducive to community involvement which in turn can provide the interactional substrata for community socialization for death. This paper cannot substantiate that argument, for to do so would require comparative data from a variety of congregate residential facilities, data which I do not have. My paper thus represents a case study in an area rich in research opportunities.

Beyond giving some suggestions as to the organizational factors which enhance socialization for death, I have, however, attempted to document the important fact which seems not often to be accepted by those who work with or study the aged and dying: that impending death can be and often is accepted as a matter-of-fact aspect of individual human lives. Legitimation of death does not mean resignation. It means acceptance of one's impending death as appropriate. Impending death can be seen as an appropriate end to one's biography and, like any portion of biography, the end will most likely be seen as appropriate when consensus is developed between an individual and his community.

Notes

1. This research was supported by the Canada Council and Princeton University. I am grateful for the perceptive criticism of an anonymous referee for the *AJS*, which led to extensive revision of this paper.

2. Anomy as employed here should not be confused with alienation. The distinction is underscored by Berger (1969, pp. 86-87) and by Berger and Pullberg (1965): "Alienation is the process by which man forgets that the world he lives in has been produced by himself." Anomy occurs when events cannot be subsumed under the socially shared reality (Berger and Luckmann, 1967, p. 102). This usage reflects but one (the meaningless) dimension of anom*ie* as discussed by McHugh (1968, p. 53).

3. Includes one "don't know." None of the 27 Glen Brae residents in a pilot study gave an unconditional yes.

4. The third of these questions, which asked for agreement or disagreement with the statement "Death always comes too soon," was followed by a probe for reasons why death might not come too soon. Similarly, the question asking if the individual would like to live to be 100 was followed by the question "Why not?" Elsewhere (Marshall 1972a, 1972b) I present a typology of such legitimations and show that the type is related to the individual's age, personal estimate of life expectancy, sex, marital status, friendship ties, perceived health, and length of time in the community. The principal legitimation types hold that death is preferable to continued life because of declines in physical and mental health, fear of becoming a burden, and loss of the ability to remain active. Religious legitimations are notably absent at Glen Brae, whereas limited data from a Catholic home for the aged suggest that they are the most prevalent type there. The association of duration of residence with changes in the prevalence of particular legitimations, together with the existence of the different types in two different settings, provides evidence that not only the existence but also the type of legitimation is influenced by community life. This inference is explored in Marshall (1972b).

5. This direction of causation is inferred.

6. If ability to produce a codable response to the two indicators is viewed as indicative of an active concern with impending death, the cautious interpretation here would be that most of those for whom impending death is of great concern have legitimated their impending deaths.

7. Compare the table excitement in Thomas Mann's *The Magic Mountain.* In contrast, Gustafson (1972) found in a nursing home that "although no staff member or relative will directly discourage the patient from making new friends . . . , he is often not expected or encouraged to do so. . . . Admission to the home is usually treated as the end of one's useful social career.

8. I investigate this further in Marshall (1973b).

9. This is complicated by the additional gamble on the part of the administration that the resident has enough money to continue paying his monthly rental fee. Applicants are screened for financial status. Unfortunately, the administration did not accurately estimate the steep rise in operating expenses (see Marshall 1973b).

10. Because most in fact do, I investigate in Marshall (1973a) the manner in which estimates of life expectancy are formed.

11. It was in fact less than the estimate.

12. Refers to an expansion of Glen Brae.

13. I am not attempting here to put forth a formal theory of dying as a status passage. A characterization of the formal properties of dying itself as a status passage has been given by Glaser and Strauss (1971, pp. 8-9), who describe these properties thus: "Dying is almost always unscheduled; the sequence of steps is not institutionally prescribed; and the actions of the various participants are only partly regulated. . . . Dying (though not necessarily death itself when it comes) is usually defined as undesirable and is usually involuntary. Among the other relevant but highly variable properties are: the degree to which the signs are disguised; the clarity of the signs; . . . the amount of control which the participants . . . have" (see also Gustafson, 1972).

14. An anonymous *AJS* reader of an earlier draft of this paper rightly pointed out that I present no direct evidence that the residents of Glen Brae do not arrive there already having legitimated their impending deaths. Elsewhere (Marshall 1972b) I address this issue theoretically and give evidence that legitimation of death becomes a concern for most residents after they have arrived at Glen Brae, for it is only when the realization develops that their time is running short that legitimating death becomes a relevant concern (see also Marshall 1973a).

DEATH
AND
SOCIAL STRUCTURE*
Robert Blauner

Death is a biological and existential fact of life that affects every human society. Since mortality tends to disrupt the ongoing life of social groups and relationships, all societies must develop some forms of containing its impact. Mortuary institutions are addressed to the specific problems of the disposal of the dead and the rituals of transition from life to death. In addition, fertility practices, family and kinship systems, and religion take their shape partly in response to the pressure of mortality and serve to limit death's disorienting possibilities. In this paper I shall be concerned with the social arrangements by which the impact of mortality is contained, and with the ways in which these arrangements are related to the demographic characteristics of a society. In particular, I hope to throw some light on the social and cultural consequences of modern society's organization of death. Because of the abstractness of these questions and the inadequacy of the empirical data on which I draw, many of my statements should be read as speculative hypotheses rather than as established facts.

Mortality and its impact are not constants. In general, the demographic structure of preindustrial societies results in an exposure to death that appears enormous by the standards of

* Robert Blauner, "Death and Social Structure," *Psychiatry* 29 (1966): 378-94. Reprinted by special permission of The William Alanson White Psychiatric Foundation, Inc. © by The Foundation.

modern Western life. Malinowski, writing of the Trobriand Islanders and other natives of Eastern New Guinea, states that "death . . . causes a great and permanent disturbance in the equilibrium of tribal life."[1] The great impact of mortality and the vividness of death as a theme in life emerge clearly from Goody's account of the LoDagaa of West Africa.[2] Jules Henry's study of the Kaingang "Jungle People" of the Brazil highlands depicts a tribe whose members are in daily contact with death and greatly obsessed with it.[3] Kingsley Davis speculates that many characteristics of Indian life, such as the high birth rate, the stress on kinship and joint households, and the religious emphasis, may be attributed to the nearness to death that follows from the conditions of that subcontinent.[4] The relatively small scale of communities in most preindustrial societies compounds death's impact. Its regular occurrence—especially through the not infrequent catastrophes of war, famine, and epidemics—involves more serious losses to a society of small scale, a point that has been made forcibly by Krzywicki:

> Let us take, for instance, one of the average Australian tribes (usually numbering 300–600 members). The simultaneous loss of 10 persons is there an event which quantitatively considered, would have the same significance as the simultaneous death of from 630,000 to 850,000 inhabitants in the present Polish state. And such catastrophes, diminishing an Australian tribe by some 10 persons, might, of course, occur not infrequently. An unfortunate war-expedition, a victorious night attack by an enemy, a sudden flood, or any of a host of other events might easily cause the death of such a number of tribesmen: in addition, there were famines, such as that which forced the Birria, for instance, to devour all their children, or the epidemics which probably occurred from time to time even in primitive communities. And, what is most important, conditions of primitive life sometimes created such situations that there was a simultaneous loss of about a dozen or a score of persons of the same sex and approximately the same age. Then such a misfortune affecting a community assumed the dimensions of a tribal disaster.[5]

This is not to suggest that a continuous encounter with mortality is equally prevalent in all preindustrial societies. Variations

530

among primitive and peasant societies are as impressive as common patterns; I simply want to make the point that *many* non-modern societies must organize themselves around death's recurrent presence. Modern societies, on the other hand, have largely succeeded in containing mortality and its social disruptiveness. Yet the impact of mortality on a society is not a simple matter of such demographic considerations as death rates and the size of the group. Also central is the manner in which a society is organized, the way it manages the death crisis, and how its death practices and mortuary institutions are linked to the social structure.

Life Expectancy, Engagement, and the Social Relevance of the Dead

Death disrupts the dynamic equilibrium of social life because a number of its actual or potential consequences create problems for a society. One of these potential consequences is a social vacuum. A member of society and its constituent groups and relationships is lost; and some kind of gap in institutional functioning results. The extent of this vacuum depends on how deeply engaged the deceased has been in the life of the society and its groups. The system is more disrupted by the death of a leader than by that of a common man; families and work groups are typically more affected by the loss of those in middle years than by the death of children or old people. Thus a key determinant of the impact of mortality is the age and social situation of those who die, since death will be more disruptive when it frequently strikes those who are most relevant for the functional activities and the moral outlook of the social order.

In modern Western societies, mortality statistics are more and more made up of the very old. The causes are obvious: the virtual elimination of infant and child mortality and the increasing control over the diseases of youth and middle life. Almost one million American males died in 1960. Eight percent were younger than 15 years. Fifty-five percent were 65 or older (29 percent were past 75), and another 18 percent were between 55 and 64. The middle years, between 15 and 54, claimed the

531

remaining 19 percent of the deaths.[6] As death in modern society becomes increasingly a phenomenon of the old, who are
usually retired from work and finished with their parental responsibilities, mortality in modern society rarely interrupts the
business of life. Death is uncommon during the highly engaged
middle years, and the elderly are more and more segregated into
communities and institutions for their age group.

Although accurate vital statistics for contemporary preindustrial societies are rare, the available data indicate that the
primary concentration of death is at the opposite end of the life
span, in the years of infancy and childhood. For example, among
the Sakai of the Malay Peninsula, approximately 50 percent of
the babies born die before the age of three; among the Kurnai
tribe of Australia 40 to 50 percent die before the age of 10.[7]
Fifty-nine percent of the 1956 male deaths in Nigeria among
the "indigenous" blacks were children who had not reached
their fifth birthday. Thirty-five percent of an Indian male cohort born in the 1940's died before the age of 10.[8] The same
concentration of mortality in the early years was apparently
also true of historical preindustrial societies.

Aside from this high infant and child mortality, there is no
common pattern in the age composition of death in preindustrial societies. In some, there appears to be a secondary concentration in old age, suggesting that when mortality in the early
years is very high, the majority of those who survive may be
hardy enough to withstand the perils of middle life and reach
old age. This seems to be the situation with the Tikopia, according to the limited demographic data. Thirty-six percent of the
deaths in one period studied were those of people over 58, almost equaling the proportion who died in the first seven years.[9]

In other societies and historical periods, conditions are such
that mortality remains heavy in the middle years; and few people reach the end of a normal life span. Thus calculations of age
at death taken from gravestones erected during the early Roman
empire (this method is notoriously unreliable, but the figures
are suggestive) typically find that 30 to 40 percent of the deceased were in their twenties and thirties; the proportion who
died past the age of 50 was only about 20 percent.[10] The life
table of the primitive Cocos also illustrates this pattern. Only

16 percent of the deaths are in the old-age group (past 55 years), since mortality continues high for that minority of the population which survives childhood.[11] The contrast in death frequency during the middle years is suggested by the data shown in Table 1 on mortality rates for specific age periods for four countries.

The demographic pattern where mortality is high in the middle years probably results in the most disruption of ongoing life. Procedures for the reallocation of the socially necessary

Table 1

Number of Deaths During Specified Year of Age
Per 1,000 Males Alive at Beginning of Age Period*

Country	Age				
	20-25	25-30	30-35	35-40	40-45
Congo, 1950-52	54	49	68	82	96
Mexico, 1940	46	53	62	71	84
U.S.A., 1959	9	9	10	14	23
Canada, 1950-52	2	2	2	2	3

* From United Nations, *Demographic Yearbook,* 13th ed. (New York: Department of Economic and Social Affairs, 1961), p. 360. Decimals have been rounded off to the nearest integer.

roles, rights, and responsibilities of the deceased must be institutionalized. This is most essential when the roles and responsibilities are deemed important and when there is a tight integration of the society's groups and institutions. Such is the situation among the LoDagaa of West Africa, where many men die who are young and middle-aged. Since the kinship structure is highly elaborated, these deaths implicate the whole community, particularly the kinship group of the bereaved spouses. The future rights to these now unattached women, still sexually active and capable of childbearing, emerge as an issue that must be worked

out in the funeral ceremonies through a transfer to new husbands.[12] In contrast, in modern Western societies, the death of
a husband typically involves only the fragmented conjugal family; from the point of view of the social order as a whole, it
makes little difference whether a widow replaces her deceased
husband, because of the loose integration of the nuclear family
into wider kinship, economic, and political spheres.

Another way of containing the impact of mortality is to
reduce the real or ideal importance of those who die. Primitive
societies, hard hit by infant and child mortality, characteristically do not recognize infants and children as people; until a certain age they are considered as still belonging to the spirit world
from which they came, and therefore their death is often not
accorded ritual recognition—no funeral is held.[13] Aries has noted
that French children were neither valued nor recognized in
terms of their individuality during the long period of high infant mortality:

> No one thought of keeping a picture of a child if that
> child had . . . died in infancy . . . it was thought that the
> little thing which had disappeared so soon in life was not
> worthy of rememberance. . . . Nobody thought, as we or-
> dinarily think today, that every child already contained a
> man's personality. Too many of them died.[14]

One of the consequences of the devaluation of the old in modern society is the minimization of the disruption and moral
shock death ordinarily brings about.

But when people die who are engaged in the vital functions
of society—socializing the young, producing sustenance, and
maintaining ceremonies and rituals—their importance cannot be
easily reduced. Dying before they have done their full complement of work and before they have seen their children off toward
adulthood and their own parenthood, they die with *unfinished
business.* I suggest that the almost universal belief in ghosts in
preindustrial societies[15] can be understood as an effect of this
demographic pattern on systems of interpersonal interaction,
and not simply as a function of naive, magical, and other "unsophisticated" world views. Ghosts are reifications of this unfinished business, and belief in their existence may permit some

continuation of relationships broken off before their natural terminus. Perhaps the primitive Manus have constructed the most elaborate belief system which illustrates this point:

> Each man worships a spirit who is called the Sir-Ghost, usually the spirit of his father, though sometimes it may be the son, or brother, or one who stood in the mother's brother-sister's relationship. The concrete manifestation of this Sir-Ghost is the dead person's skull which is placed in a bowl above the inside of the front entry of the house. Any male can speak to his Sir-Ghost and receive communications from him. The Sir-Ghost acts as a ward, protecting his son from accidents, supervising his morals, and hopefully bringing him wealth. The relationship between the Sir-Ghost and his ward is a close parallel to that between father and son. With some changed emphases, it continues the relationship that existed in life and was broken by death. Since Manus die early, the tenure of a Sir-Ghost is typically only one generation. When the ward, the son, dies, this is seen as proof of the ghost's ineffectiveness, and the son's son casts him out, installing his own newly deceased father as Sir-Ghost. The sample spirit, however, is not a Sir-Ghost to other families, but only a regular ghost and as such thought to be malicious.[16]

More common in primitive societies is an ambivalent attitude toward the ghost. Fear exists because of the belief that the dead man, frustrated in his exclusion from a life in which he was recently involved, wants back in, and, failing this, may attempt to restore his former personal ties by taking others along with him on his journey to the spirit world. The elaborate, ritually appropriate funeral is believed to keep the spirit of the dead away from the haunts of the living,[17] and the feasts and gifts given for the dead are attempts to appease them through partial inclusion in their life. It would appear that the dead who were most engaged in the life of society have the strongest motives for restoring their ties; and the most feared ghosts tend to be those whose business has been the least completed. Ghosts of the murdered, the suicide, and others who have met a violent end are especially feared because they have generally died young with considerable strength and energy remaining. Ghosts of women dying in childbirth and of the unmarried and childless are considered particularly malignant because these souls have been robbed of life's major purpose; at the funeral the unmarried are often given mock marriages to other dead souls. Ghosts of dead husbands or wives are dangerous to their spouses, especially when the latter have remarried.[18] The spirit of the grandparent who has seen his children grow up and procreate is, on the other hand, the least feared; among the LoDagaa only the grandparent's death is conceded to be a natural rather than a magical or malignant event, and in many societies there is only a perfunctory funeral for grandparents, since their spirits are not considered to be in conflict with the living.[19]

The relative absence of ghosts in modern society is not simply a result of the routing of superstition by science and rational thought, but also reflects the disengaged social situation of the majority of the deceased. In a society where the young and middle-aged have largely liberated themselves from the authority of and emotional dependence upon old people by the time of the latters' death, there is little social-psychological need for a vivid community of the dead. Whereas in high-mortality societies, the person who dies often literally abandons children, spouses, and other relatives to whom he is owing affection and care, the deceased in advanced societies has typically completed his obligations to the living; he does not owe anything. Rather, the death is more likely to remind survivors of the social and psychological debts they have incurred toward him—debts that they may have been intending to pay in the coins of attention, affection, care, appreciation, or achievement. In modern societies, the living use the funeral and sometimes a memorial to attempt to "make up for" some of these debts that can no longer be paid in terms of the ordinary give and take of social life.

The disengagement of the aged in modern societies enhances the continuous functioning of social institutions and is a corollary of social structure and mortality patterns. Disengagement, the transition period between the end of institutional functioning and death, permits the changeover of personnel in a planned and careful manner, without the inevitably disruptive crises of disorganization and succession that would occur if people worked to the end and died on the job. The unsettling character of the Kennedy assassination for our nation suggests the chaos that would exist if a bureaucratic social structure were combined with high mortality in the middle years.[20]

For the older person, disengagement may bring on great psychological stress if his ties to work and family are severed more abruptly and completely than he desires. Yet it may also have positive consequences. As Robert Butler has described, isolation and unoccupied time during the later years permit reviewing one's past life.[21] There is at least the potential (not always realized) to better integrate the manifold achievements and disappointments of a lifetime, and doing so, to die better. Under favorable circumstances, disengagement can permit a person to complete his unfinished business before death: to right old wrongs, to reconcile longstanding hostile relations with relatives or former friends; to take the trip, write the play, or paint the picture that he was always planning. Of course, often the finances and health of the aged do not permit such a course, and it is also possible that the general status of the aged in a secular, youth-and-life oriented society is a basic obstacle to a firm sense of identity and self-worth during the terminal years.

Bureaucratization of Modern Death Control

Since there is no death without a body—except in mystery thrillers—the corpse is another consequence of mortality that contributes to its disruptiveness, tending to produce fear, generalized anxiety, and disgust.[22] Since families and work groups must eventually return to some kind of normal life, the time they are exposed to corpses must be limited. Some form of disposal (earth or sea burial, cremation, exposure to the elements) is the core of mortuary institutions everywhere. A disaster that brings about massive and unregulated exposure to the dead, such as that experienced by the survivors of Hiroshima and also at various times by survivors of great plagues, famines, and death-camps, appears to produce a profound identification with the dead and a consequent depressive state.[23]

The disruptive impact of a death is greater to the extent that its consequences spill over onto the larger social territory and affect large numbers of people. This depends not only on the frequency and massiveness of mortality, but also on the physical and social settings of death. These vary in different societies, as does also the specialization of responsibility for the care of the dying and the preparation of the body for disposal. In premodern societies, many deaths take place amid the hubbub of life, in the central social territory of the tribe, clan, or other familial group. In modern societies, where the majority of deaths are now predictably in the older age brackets, disengagement from family and economic function has permitted the segregation of death settings from the more workaday social territory. Probably in small towns and rural communities, more people die at home than do so in urban areas. But the proportion of people who die at home, on the job, and in public places must have declined consistently over the past generations with the growing importance of specialized dying institutions—hospitals, old people's homes, and nursing homes.[24]

Modern societies control death through bureaucratization, our characteristic form of social structure. Max Weber has described how bureaucratization in the West proceeded by removing social functions from the family and the household and implanting them in specialized institutions autonomous of kinship considerations. Early manufacturing and entrepreneurship took place in or close to the home; modern industry and corporate bureaucracies are based on the separation of the workplace from the household.[25] Similarly, only a few generations ago most people in the United States either died at home, or were brought into the home if they had died elsewhere. It was the responsibility of the family to lay out the corpse—that is, to prepare the body for the funeral.[26] Today, of course, the hospital cares for the terminally ill and manages the crisis of dying; the mortuary industry (whose establishments are usually called "homes" in deference to past tradition) prepares the body for burial and makes many of the funeral arrangements. A study in Philadelphia found that about 90 percent of funerals started out from the funeral parlor, rather than from the home, as was customary in the past.[27] This separation of the handling of illness and death from the family minimizes the average person's exposure to death and death's disruption of the social process. When the dying are segregated among specialists for whom

538

contact with death has become routine and even somewhat impersonal, neither their presence while alive nor as corpses interferes greatly with the mainstream of life.

Another principle of bureaucracy is the ordering of regularly occurring as well as extraordinary events into predictable and routinized procedures. In addition to treating the ill and isolating them from the rest of society, the modern hospital as an organization is committed to the routinization of the handling of death. Its distinctive competence is to contain through isolation, and reduce through orderly procedures, the disturbance and disruption that are associated with the death crisis. The decline in the authority of religion as well as shifts in the functions of the family underlies this fact. With the growth of the secular and rational outlook, hegemony in the affairs of death has been transferred from the church to science and its representatives, the medical profession and the rationally organized hospital.

Death in the modern hospital has been the subject of two recent sociological studies: Sudnow has focused on the handling of death and the dead in a county hospital catering to charity patients; and Glaser and Strauss have concentrated on the dying situation in a number of hospitals of varying status.[28] The county hospital well illustrates various trends in modern death. Three quarters of its patients are over 60 years old. Of the 250 deaths Sudnow observed, only a handful involved people younger than 40.[29] This hospital is a setting for the concentration of death. There are 1,000 deaths a year; thus approximately 3 die daily, of the 330 patients typically in residence. But death is even more concentrated in the four wards of the critically ill; here roughly 75 percent of all mortality occurs, and 1 in 25 persons will die each day.[30]

Hospitals are organized to hide the facts of dying and death from patients as well as visitors. Sudnow quotes a major text in hospital administration:

> The hospital morgue is best located on the ground floor and placed in an area inaccessible to the general public. It is important that the unit have a suitable exit leading onto a private loading platform which is concealed from hospital patients and the public.[31]

Personnel in the high-mortality wards use a number of techniques to render death invisible. To protect relatives, bodies are not to be removed during visiting hours. To protect other inmates, the patient is moved to a private room when the end is foreseen. But some deaths are unexpected and may be noticed by roommates before the hospital staff is aware of them. These are considered troublesome because elaborate procedures are required to remove the corpse without offending the living.

The rationalization of death in the hospital takes place through standard procedures of covering the corpse, removing the body, identifying the deceased, informing relatives, and completing the death certificate and autopsy permit. Within the value hierarchy of the hospital, handling the corpse is "dirty work"; and when possible attendants will leave a body to be processed by the next work shift. As with so many of the unpleasant jobs in our society, hospital morgue attendants and orderlies are often Negroes. Personnel become routinized to death and are easily able to pass from mention of the daily toll to other topics; new staff members stop counting after the first half-dozen deaths witnessed.[32]

Standard operating procedures have even routinized the most charismatic and personal of relations, that between the priest and the dying patient. It is not that the church neglects charity patients. The chaplain at the county hospital daily goes through a file of the critically ill for the names of all known Catholic patients, then enters their rooms and administers extreme unction. After completing his round on each ward, he stamps the index card of the patient with a rubber stamp which reads: "Last Rites Administered. Date —— Clergyman ——." Each day he consults the files to see if new patients have been admitted or put on the critical list. As Sudnow notes, this rubber stamp prevents him from performing the rites twice on the same patient.[33] This example highlights the trend toward the depersonalization of modern death, and is certainly the antithesis of the historic Catholic notion of "the good death."

In the hospitals studied by Glaser and Strauss, depersonalization is less advanced. Fewer of the dying are comatose; and as paying patients with higher social status they are in a better position to negotiate certain aspects of their terminal situation.

Yet nurses and doctors view death as an inconvenience, and manage interaction so as to minimize emotional reactions and fuss. They attempt to avoid announcing unexpected deaths because relatives break down too emotionally; they prefer to let the family members know that the patient has taken "a turn for the worse," so that they will be able to modulate their response in keeping with the hospital's need for order.[34] And drugs are sometimes administered to a dying patient to minimize the disruptiveness of his passing—even when there is no reason for this in terms of treatment or the reduction of pain.

The dying patient in the hospital is subject to the kinds of alienation experienced by persons in other situations in bureaucratic organizations. Because doctors avoid the terminally ill, and nurses and relatives are rarely able to talk about death, he suffers psychic isolation.[35] He experiences a sense of meaninglessness because he is typically kept unaware of the course of his disease and his impending fate, and is not in a position to understand the medical and other routines carried out in his behalf.[36] He is powerless in that the medical staff and the hospital organization tend to program his death in keeping with their organizational and professional needs; control over one's death seems to be even more difficult to achieve than control over one's life in our society.[37] Thus the modern hospital, devoted to the preservation of life and the reduction of pain, tends to become a "mass reduction" system, undermining the subjecthood of its dying patients.

The rationalization of modern death control cannot be fully achieved, however, because of an inevitable tension between death—as an event, a crisis, an experience laden with great emotionality—and bureaucracy, which must deal with routines rather than events and is committed to the smoothing out of affect and emotion. Although there was almost no interaction between dying patients and the staff in the county hospital studied by Sudnow, many nurses in the other hospitals became personally involved with their patients and experienced grief when they died. Despite these limits to the general trend, our society has gone far in containing the disruptive possibilities of mortality through its bureaucratized death control.

The Decline of the Funeral in Modern Society

Death creates a further problem because of the contradiction between society's need to push the dead away, and its need "to keep the dead alive."[38] The social distance between the living and the dead must be increased after death, so that the group first, and the most affected grievers later, can reestablish their normal activity without a paralyzing attachment to the corpse. Yet the deceased cannot simply be buried as a dead body: The prospect of total exclusion from the social world would be too anxiety-laden for the living, aware of their own eventual fate. The need to keep the dead alive directs societies to construct rituals that celebrate and insure a transition to a new social status, that of spirit, a being now believed to participate in a different realm.[39] Thus, a funeral that combines this status transformation with the act of physical disposal is universal to all societies, and has justly been considered one of the crucial *rites de passage.*[40]

Because the funeral has been typically employed to handle death's manifold disruptions, its character, importance, and frequency may be viewed as indicators of the place of mortality in society. The contrasting impact of death in primitive and modern societies, and the diversity in their modes of control, are suggested by the striking difference in the centrality of mortuary ceremonies in the collective life. Because death is so disruptive in simple societies, much "work" must be done to restore the social system's functioning. Funerals are not "mere rituals," but significant adaptive structures, as can be seen by considering the tasks that make up the funeral work among the LoDagaa of West Africa. The dead body must be buried with the appropriate ritual so as to give the dead man a new status that separates him from the living; he must be given the material goods and symbolic invocations that will help guarantee his safe journey to the final destination and at the same time protect the survivors against his potentially dangerous intervention in their affairs (such as appearing in dreams, "walking," or attempting to drag others with him); his qualities, lifework, and accomplishments must be summed up and given appropriate recognition, his property, roles, rights, and privileges must be distributed so that social and economic life can continue; and, finally the social units—family, clan, and community as a whole—whose very existence and functioning his death has threatened, must have a chance to vigorously reaffirm their identity and solidarity through participation in ritual ceremony.[41]

Such complicated readjustments take time; and therefore the death of a mature person in many primitive societies is followed by not one, but a series of funerals (usually two or three) that may take place over a period ranging from a few months to two years, and in which the entire society, rather than just relatives and friends, participates.[42] The duration of the funeral and the fine elaboration of its ceremonies suggest the great destructive possibilities of death in these societies. Mortuary institutions loom large in the daily life of the community; and the frequent occurrence of funerals may be no small element in maintaining societal continuity under the precarious conditions of high mortality.[43]

In Western antiquity and the middle ages, funerals were important events in the life of city-states and rural communities.[44] Though not so central as in high-mortality and sacred primitive cultures (reductions in mortality rates and secularism both antedate the industrial revolution in the West), they were still frequent and meaningful ceremonies in the life of small-town, agrarian America several generations ago. But in the modern context they have become relatively unimportant events for the life of the larger society. Formal mortuary observances are completed in a short time. Because of the segregation and disengagement of the aged and the gap between generations, much of the social distance to which funerals generally contribute has already been created before death. The deceased rarely have important roles or rights that the society must be concerned about allocating; and the transfer of property has become the responsibility of individuals, in cooperation with legal functionaries. With the weakening of beliefs in the existence and malignancy of ghosts, the absence of "realistic" concern about the dead man's trials in his initiation to spirithood, and the lowered intensity of conventional beliefs in an afterlife, there is less demand for both magical precautions and religious ritual. In a society where disbelief or doubt is more common than a firm

543

acceptance of the reality of a life after death,[45] the funeral's classic function of status transformation becomes attenuated.

The recent attacks on modern funeral practices by social critics focus on alleged commercial exploitation by the mortuary industry and the vulgar ostentatiousness of its service. But at bottom this criticism reflects this crisis in the function of the funeral as a social institution. On the one hand, the religious and ritual meanings of the ceremony have lost significance for many people. But the crisis is not only due to the erosion of the sacred spirit by rational, scientific world views.[46] The social substructure of the funeral is weakened when those who die tend to be irrelevant for the ongoing social life of the community, and when the disruptive potentials of death are already controlled by compartmentalization into isolated spheres where bureaucratic routinization is the rule. Thus participation and interest in funerals are restricted to family members and friends rather than involving the larger community, unless an important leader has died.[47] Since only individuals and families are affected, adaptation and bereavement have become their private responsibility, and there is little need for a transition period to permit society as a whole to adjust to the fact of a single death. Karl Marx was proved wrong about "the withering away of the state," but with the near disappearance of death as a public event in modern society, the withering away of the funeral may become a reality.

In modern societies, the bereaved person suffers from a paucity of ritualistic conventions in the mourning period. He experiences grief less frequently, but more intensely, since his emotional involvements are not diffused over an entire community, but are usually concentrated on one or a few people.[48] Since mourning and a sense of loss are not widely shared, as in premodern communities, the individualization and deritualization of bereavement make for serious problems in adjustment. There are many who never fully recover and "get back to normal," in contrast to the frequently observed capacity of the bereaved in primitive societies to smile, laugh, and go about their ordinary pursuits the moment the official mourning period is ended.[49] The lack of conventionalized stages in the mourning process results in an ambiguity as to when the bereaved person

544

has grieved enough and thus can legitimately and guiltlessly feel free for new attachments and interests.[50] Thus at the same time that death becomes less disruptive to the society, its prospects and consequences become more serious for the bereaved individual.

Some Consequences of Modern Death Control

I shall now consider some larger consequences that appear to follow from the demographic, organizational, and cultural trends in modern society that have diminished the presence of death in public life and have reduced most persons' experience of mortality to a minimum through the middle years.[51]

The Place of the Dead in Modern Society

With the diminished visibility of death, the perceived reality and the effective status and power of the dead have also declined in modern societies. A central factor here is the rise of science: Eissler suggests that "the intensity of service to the dead and the proneness for scientific discovery are in reverse proportion."[52] But the weakening of religious imagery is not the sole cause; there is again a functional sociological basis. When those who die are not important to the life of society, the dead as a collective category will not be of major significance in the concerns of the living.

Compare the situation in high-mortality primitive and peasant societies. The living have not liberated themselves emotionally from many of the recently deceased and therefore need to maintain symbolic interpersonal relations with them. This can take place only when the life of the spirits and their world is conceived in well-structured form, and so, as Goode has phrased it, "practically every primitive religious system imputes both power and interest to the dead."[53]

Their spheres of influence in preindustrial societies are many: Spirits watch over and guide economic activities, and may determine the fate of trading exchanges, hunting and fishing

545

expeditions, and harvests. Their most important realm of authority is probably that of social control: They are concerned with the general morality of society and the specific actions of individuals (usually kin or clansmen) under their jurisdiction. It is generally believed that the dead have the power to bring about both economic and personal misfortunes (including illness and death) to serve their own interests, to express their general capriciousness, or to specifically punish the sins and errors of the living. The fact that a man as spirit often receives more deference from, and exerts greater power over, people than while living may explain the apparent absence of the fear of death that has been observed in some primitive and ancestor-worship societies.[54]

In modern societies the influence of the dead is indirect and is rarely experienced in personified form. Every cultural heritage is in the main the contribution of dead generations to the present society,[55] and the living are confronted with problems that come from the sins of the past (for example, our heritage of Negro slavery). There are people who extend their control over others after death through wills, trust funds, and other arrangements. Certain exceptional figures such as John Kennedy and Malcolm X become legendary or almost sainted and retain influence as national symbols or role models. But, for the most part, the dead have little status or power in modern society, and the living tend to be liberated from their direct, personified influence.[56] We do not attribute to the dead the range of material and ideal interests that adheres to their symbolic existence in other societies, such as property and possessions, the desire to recreate networks of close personal relationships, the concern for tradition, and the morality of the society. Our concept of the inner life of spirits is most shadowy. In primitive societies a full range of attitudes and feelings is imputed to them, whereas a scientific culture has emptied out specific mental and emotional contents from its vague image of spirit life.[57]

Generational Continuity and the Status of the Aged

The decline in the authority of the dead, and the widening social distance between them and the living, are both conditions and consequences of the youthful orientation, receptivity to innovation, and dynamic social change that characterize modern society. In most preindustrial societies, symbolic contacts with the spirits and ghosts of the dead were frequent, intimate, and often long-lasting. Such communion in modern society is associated with spiritualism and other deviant belief-systems; "normal" relations with the dead seem to have come under increasing discipline and control. Except for observing Catholics perhaps, contact is limited to very specific spatial boundaries, primarily cemeteries, and is restricted to a brief time period following a death and possibly a periodic memorial.[58] Otherwise the dead and their concerns are simply not relevant to the living in a society that feels liberated from the authority of the past and orients its energies toward immediate preoccupations and future possibilities.

Perhaps it is the irrelevance of the dead that is the clue to the status of old people in modern industrial societies. In a low-mortality society, most deaths occur in old age, and since the aged predominate among those who die, the association between old age and death is intensified.[59] Industrial societies value people in terms of their present functions and their future prospects; the aged have not only become disengaged from significant family, economic, and community responsibilities in the present, but their future status (politely never referred to in our humane culture) is among the company of the powerless, anonymous, and virtually ignored dead.[60] In societies where the dead continue to play an influential role in the community of the living, there is no period of the life span that marks the end of a person's connection to society; and the aged before death begin to receive some of the awe and authority that is conferred on the spirit world.

The social costs of these developments fall most heavily on our old people, but they also affect the integrity of the larger culture and the interests of the young and middle-aged. The traditional values that the dead and older generations represent lose significance, and the result is a fragmentation of each generation from a sense of belonging to and identity with a lineal stream of kinship and community. In modern societies where mobility and social change have eliminated the age-old sense of closeness to "roots," this alienation from the past—expressed in the distance between living and dead generations—may be an important source of tenuous personal identities.

These tendencies help to produce another contradiction. The very society that has so greatly controlled death has made it more difficult to die with dignity. The irrelevance of the dead, as well as other social and cultural trends, brings about a crisis in our sense of what is an appropriate death. Most societies, including our own past, have a notion of the ideal conditions under which the good man leaves the life of this world: For some primitives it is the influential grandfather; for classical antiquity, the hero's death in battle; in the Middle Ages, the Catholic idea of "holy dying." There is a clear relationship between the notion of appropriate death and the basic value emphases of the society, whether familial, warlike, or religious. I suggest that American culture is faced with a crisis of death because the changed demographic and structural conditions do not fit the traditional concepts of appropriate death, and no new ideal has arisen to take their place. Our nineteenth-century ideal was that of the patriarch, dying in his own home in ripe old age but in the full possession of his faculties, surrounded by family, heirs, and material symbols of a life of hard work and acquisition. Death was additionally appropriate because of the power of religious belief, which did not regard the event as a final ending. Today people characteristically die at an age when their physical, social, and mental powers are at an ebb, or even absent, typically in the hospital, and often separated from family and other meaningful surroundings. Thus "dying alone" is not only a symbolic theme of existential philosophers; it more and more epitomizes the inappropriateness of how people die under modern conditions.

I have said little about another modern prototype of mortality, mass violence. Despite its statistical infrequency in "normal times," violent death cannot be dismissed as an unimportant theme, since it looms so large in our recent past and in our anxieties about the future. The major forms, prosaic and bizarre, in which violent death occurs, or has occurred, in the present period are:

1. Automobile and airplane accidents;
2. The concentration camp; and
3. Nuclear disaster.

All these expressions of modern violence result in a most inappropriate way of dying. In a brilliant treatment of the preponderance of death by violence in modern literature, Frederick Hoffman points out its inherent ambiguities. The fact that many people die at once, in most of these situations, makes it impossible to mitigate the effects on the survivors through ceremonies of respect. While these deaths are caused by human agents, the impersonality of the assailant, and the distance between him and his victim, make it impossible to assign responsibility to understandable causes. Because of the suddenness of impact, the death that is died cannot be fitted into the life that has been lived. And finally, society experiences a crisis of meaning when the threat of death pervades the atmosphere, yet cannot be incorporated into a religious or philosophical context.[61]

A Final Theoretical Note: Death and Social Institutions

Mortality implies that population is in a constant (though usually a gradual) state of turnover. Society's groups are fractured by the deaths of their members and must therefore maintain their identities through symbols that are external to, and that outlast, individual persons. The social roles through which the functions of major societal institutions are carried out cannot be limited to particular individuals and their unique interpretations of the needs of social action; they must partake of general and transferable prescriptions and expectations. The order and stability required by a social system are threatened by the eventual deaths of members of small units such as families, as well as political, religious, and economic leaders. There is, therefore, a need for more permanent institutions embedding "impersonal" social roles, universal norms, and transcendent values.

The frequent presence of death in high-mortality societies is important in shaping their characterisitc institutional structure.

To the extent that death imperils the continuity of a society, its major institutions will be occupied with providing that sense of identity and integrity made precarious by its severity. In societies with high death rates the kinship system and religion tend to be the major social institutions.

Kinship systems organized around the clan or the extended family are well suited to high-mortality societies because they provide a relative permanence and stability lacking in the smaller nuclear group. Both the totem of the clan and the extended family's ties to the past and the future are institutionalized representations of continuity. Thus the differential impact of mortality on social structure explains the apparent paradox that the smaller the scale of a community the larger in general is its ideal family unit.[62] The very size of these kinship units provides a protection against the disintegrating potential of mortality making possible within the family the varied resources in relational ties, age-statuses, and cultural experience that guarantee the socialization of all its young, even if their natural parents should die before they have become adults.

In primitive and peasant societies, the centrality of magic and religion is related to the dominant presence of death. If the extended family provides for the society's physical survival, magic and countermagic are weapons used by individuals to protect themselves from death's uncontrolled and erratic occurrence. And religion makes possible the moral survival of the society and the individual in an environment fraught with fear, anxiety, and uncertainty. As Malinowski and others have shown, religion owes its persistence and power (if not necessarily its origin) to its unique capacity to solve the societal and personal problems that death calls forth.[63] Its rituals and beliefs impart to the funeral ceremonies those qualities of the sacred and the serious that help the stricken group reestablish and reintegrate itself through the collective reaffirmation of shared cultural assumptions. In all known societies, it serves to reassure the individual against possible anxieties concerning destruction, nonbeing, and finitude by providing beliefs that make death meaningful, afterlife plausible, and the miseries and injustices of earthly existence endurable.

In complex modern societies there is a proliferation and

differentiation of social institutions that have become autonomous in relationship to kinship and religion, as Durkheim pointed out.[64] In a sense these institutions take on a permanence and autonomy that makes them effectively independent of the individuals who carry out the roles within them. The economic corporation is the prototype of a modern institution. Sociologically it is a bureaucracy and therefore relatively unconnected to family and kinship; constitutionally it has been graced with the legal fiction of immortality. Thus the major agencies that organize productive work (as well as other activities) are relatively invulnerable to the depletion of their personnel by death, for their offices and functions are impersonal and transferable from one role-incumbent to another. The situation is very different in traditional societies. There family ties and kinship groups tend to be the basis of economic, religious, and other activities; social institutions interpenetrate one another around the kinship core. Deaths that strike the family therefore reverberate through the entire social structure. This type of social integration (which Durkheim termed "mechanical solidarity") makes premodern societies additionally vulnerable to death's disruptive potential—regardless of its quantitative frequency and age distribution.

On the broadest level, the relationship between death and society is a dialectic one. Mortality threatens the continuity of society and in so doing contributes to the strengthening of social structure and the development of culture. Death weakens the social group and calls forth personal anxieties; in response, members of a society cling closer together. Specific deaths disrupt the functioning of the social system and thereby encourage responses in the group that restore social equilibrium and become customary practices that strengthen the social fabric. Death's sword in time cuts down each individual; but with respect to the social order it is double-edged. The very sharpness of its disintegrating potential demands adaptations that can bring higher levels of cohesion and continuity. In the developmental course of an individual life, death always conquers; but, as I have attempted to demonstrate throughout this essay, the social system seems to have greatly contained mortality in the broad span of societal and historical development.

Notes

1. Bronislaw Malinowski, *Argonauts of the Western Pacific* (London: Routledge & Kegan Paul, Ltd., 1922), p. 490; cited in Lucien Levy-Bruhl, *The "Soul" of the Primitive* (London: George Allen & Unwin, 1928) p. 226.

2. Jack Goody, *Death, Property and the Ancestors* (Stanford: Stanford University Press, 1962). This is the most thorough investigation in the literature of the relations between the mortuary institutions of a society and its social structure; I am indebted to Goody for many ideas and insights.

3. Jules Henry, *Jungle People* (Richmond, Va.: William Byrd Press, 1941).

4. Kingsley Davis, *The Population of India and Pakistan* (Princeton, N.J.: Princeton University Press, 1951), p. 64.

5. Ludwik Krzywicki, *Primitive Society and Its Vital Statistics* (London: Macmillan & Co., Ltd., 1934), p. 292. The very scale of modern societies is thus an important element of their control of mortality; unlike the situation in a remote village of India or the jungle highlands of Brazil, it would require the ultimate in catastrophic mortality, all-out nuclear war, for death to threaten societal survival.

6. United Nations, *Demographic Yearbook, 1961,* 13th ed. (New York: Department of Economic and Social Affairs, 1961), see Table 15. A very similar age distribution results when a cohort of 100,000 born in 1929 is tabulated in terms of the proportions who die in each age period. See Louis I. Dublin and Alfred J. Lotka, *Length of Life* (New York: Ronald Press, 1936), p. 12. The outlook for the future is suggested by a more recent life-table for females in Canada. Of 100,000 babies born in the late 1950s, only 15 percent will die before age sixty. Seventy percent will be 70 years old or more at death; 42 percent will die past 80. See United Nations, *Demographic Yearbook,* pp. 622-76.

7. See Krzywicki, *Primitive Society,* pp. 148, 271. A more recent demographic study of the Cocos-Keeling Islands in the Malay Peninsula found that 59 percent die before age 5. See T. E. Smith, "The Cocos-Keeling Islands: A Demographic Laboratory," *Population Studies* 14 (1960): 94-130. Among 89 deaths recorded in 1952-1953 among the Tikopia, 39 percent were of infants and children below age 8. See W. D. Borrie, Raymond Firth, and James Spillius, "The Population of Tikopia, 1929 and 1952," *Population Studies* 10 (1957): 229-53. The Rungus Dusun, "a primitive, pagan agricultural" village community in North Borneo, lose 20 percent of their females in the first year of life, and another 50 percent die between the first birthday and motherhood. See P. J. Koblenzer and N. H. Carrier, "The Fertility, Mortality and Nuptiality of the Rungus Dusun," *Population Studies* 13 (1960): 266-77.

8. See United Nations, *Demographic Yearbook,* pp. 622-76.

9. See Borrie, Firth, and Spillius, *op. cit.*, p. 238.

10. Calculated from tables in J. C. Russell, "Late Ancient and Medieval Population," *Transactions of the American Philosophical Society* 48, pt. 3: 25-29.

11. See Smith, "Cocos-Keeling Islands." In Nigeria during 1956, only 13 percent of male deaths recorded were of men older than 55 years. Twenty-eight percent occurred among males between 5 and 54. Similarly, in Algeria during the same year, 30 percent of all male deaths among the Moslem population took people during the middle years of life (between 15 and 49). Only 13 percent were old men past 60. See United Nations, *Demographic Yearbook,* Table 15.

12. See Goody, *Death, Property, Ancestors,* pp. 30, 73 ff. In some high-mortality societies, such as traditional India, remarriage is not prescribed for the affected widows. Perhaps this difference may be related to the much greater population density of India as compared to West Africa.

13. Robert Hertz, "The Collective Representation of Death," in Hertz, *Death and the Right Hand,* trans. Rodney and Claudia Needham (Aberdeen: Cohen and West, 1960), pp. 84-86. See also Goody, *op. cit.,* pp. 208 ff.

14. Phillipe Aries, *Centuries of Childhood: A Social History of Family Life,* trans. Robert Baldick (New York: Alfred A. Knopf, Inc., 1962), pp. 38 ff.

15. After studying 71 tribes from the human area files, Leo Simmons generalizes that the belief in ghosts is "about as universal in primitive societies as any trait could be." See Simmons, *The Role of the Aged in Primitive Society* (New Haven: Yale University Press, 1945), pp. 223 ff. Another student of death customs reports that "The fear of a malignant ghost governs much of the activity of primitive tribes." See Norman L. Egger, "Contrasting Attitudes Toward Death Among Veterans With and Without Battle Experience and Non-Veterans" (Master's thesis, Department of Psychology, University of California, Berkeley, 1948), p. 33.

16. Adapted from William Goode, *Religion Among the Primitives* (New York: Free Press, 1951), pp. 64 ff., 194 ff. The former Sir-Ghost, neglected after his forced retirement, is thought to wander on the sea between the villages, endangering sea voyages. Eventually he becomes a seaslug. A similar phenomenon is reported with respect to the shades of ancient Rome; a deceased husband began as a shade with a distinct personality, but was degraded to the rank of the undifferentiated shades that haunt the world of the dead after time passed and the widow remarried. Thus the unfinished buisness had been completed by someone else. See James H. Leuba, *The Belief in God and Immortality* (Boston: Sherman, French, 1916), pp. 95-96.

17. The most complete materials on ambivalence toward ghosts are found in James G. Frazer, *The Fear of the Dead in Primitive Religion,* 3 vols. (London: Macmillan & Co., Ltd., 1933, 1934, and 1936). Volume II is devoted to various methods of keeping dead spirits away.

The connection between the ambivalent attitude toward the ghost and the neomort's uncompleted working out of his obligations on earth is clear in Henry's description of the Kaingang: "The ghost-soul loves and pities the living whom it has deserted, but the latter fear and abhor the ghost-soul. The ghost-soul longs for those it has left behind, but they remain cold to its longings. 'One pities one's children, and therefore goes with them (that is, takes them when one dies). One loves (literally, lives in) one's children, and dies and goes with one's children, and one (the child) dies.' The dead pity those they have left alone with no one to care for them. They have left behind parts of themselves, for their children are those 'in whom they live.' But to the pity, love and longing of the ghost-soul, the children return a cry of 'Mother, leave me and go!' as she lies on the funeral pyre. The Kaingang oscillate between a feeling of attachment for the dead and a desire never to see them again." See Henry, *Jungle People,* p, 67.

Eissler suggests that an envy of the living who continue on is one of the universal pains of dying. Such an attitude would be understandably stronger for those who die in middle life. See Kurt R. Eissler, *The Psychiatrist and the Dying Patient* (New York: International Universities Press, Inc., 1955), pp. 149–50.

18. See Frazer, *Fear of the Dead,* III, 103–260.

19. See Goody, *Death, Property, Ancestors,* pp. 208–9; Levy-Bruhl, *"Soul" of the Primitive,* p. 219; and Hertz, *Death and the Right Hand,* p. 84.

20. See Elaine Cumming and William E. Henry, *Growing Old* (New York: Basic Books, 1961) for a theoretical discussion and empirical data on the disengagement of the old in American society. In a more recent statement, Cumming notes that disengagement "frees the old to die without disrupting vital affairs," and that "the depth and breadth of a man's engagement can be measured by the degree of potential disruption that would follow his sudden death." See "New Thoughts on the Theory of Disengagement," in *New Thoughts on Old Age,* ed. Robert Kastenbaum (New York: Springer, 1964), pp. 4, 11.

21. Robert N. Butler, "The Life Review: An Interpretation of Reminiscence in the Aged," *Psychiatry* 26 (1963): 65–76; see p. 67.

22. Many early anthropologists, including Malinowski, attributed human funerary customs to an alleged instinctive aversion to the corpse. Although there is no evidence for such an instinct, aversion to the corpse remains a widespread, if not universal, human reaction. See the extended discussion of the early theories in Goody, *Death, Property, Ancestors,* pp. 20–30; and for some exceptions to the general rule, Robert W. Habenstein,

"The Social Organization of Death," *International Encyclopedia of the Social Sciences,* (forthcoming).

23. Robert J. Lifton, "Psychological Effects of the Atomic Bomb in Hiroshima: The Theme of Death," *Daedalus* 92 (1963): 462-97. Among other things, the dead body is too stark a reminder of man's mortal condition. Although man is the one species that knows he will eventually die, most people in most societies cannot live too successfully when constantly reminded of this truth. On the other hand, the exposure to the corpse has positive consequences for psychic functioning, as it contributes to the acceptance of the reality of a death on the part of the survivors. A study of deaths in military action during World War II found that the bereaved kin had particulrly great difficulty in believing in and accepting the reality of their loss because they did not see the body and witness its disposal. T. D. Eliot, "Of the Shadow of Death," *Annals of the American Academy of Political and Social Science* 229 (1943): 87-99.

24. Statistics on the settings of death are not readily available. Robert Fulton reports that 53 percent of all deaths in the United States take place in hospitals, but he does not give any source for this figure. See Fulton, *Death and Identity* (New York: Wiley, 1965), pp. 81-82. Two recent English studies are also suggestive. In the case of the deaths of 72 working-class husbands, primarily in the middle years, 46 died in the hospital; 22 at home; and 4 at work or in the street. See Peter Marris, *Widows and Their Families* (London: Routledge & Kegan Paul, 1958), p. 146. Of 359 Britishers who had experienced a recent bereavement, 50 percent report that the death took place in a hospital; 44 percent at home; and 6 percent elsewhere. See Geoffrey Gorer, *Death, Grief, and Mourning* (London: The Cresset Press, Ltd., 1965), p. 149.

25. Max Weber, *Essays in Sociology,* trans. and ed. H. H. Gerth and C. Wright Mills (New York: Oxford University Press, 1953), pp. 196-98. See also ———, *General Economic History,* trans. Frank H. Knight (New York: Free Press, 1950).

26. Leroy Bowman reports that aversion to the corpse made this preparation an unpleasant task. Although sometimes farmed out to experienced relatives or neighbors, the task was still considered the family's responsibility. See Bowman, *The American Funeral: A Study in Guilt, Extravagance and Sublimity* (Washington, D.C.: Public Affairs Press, 1959), p. 71.

27. William K. Kephart, "Status after Death," *The American Sociological Review* 15 (1950): 635-43.

28. David N. Sudnow, "Passing On: The Social Organization of Dying in the County Hospital" (Doctoral thesis, University of California, Berkely, 1965). Sudnow also includes comparative materials from a more well-to-do Jewish-sponsored hospital where he did additional field work; but most of

his statements are based on the county institution. Barney G. Glaser and Anselm L. Strauss, *Awareness of Dying* (Chicago: Aldine, 1965).

29. See Sudnow, *op. cit.,* pp. 107, 109. This is even fewer than would be expected by the age-composition of mortality, because children's and teaching hospitals in the city were likely to care for many terminally ill children and younger adults.

30. Ibid., pp. 49, 50.

31. J. K. Owen, *Modern Concepts of Hospital Administration* (Philadelphia: W. B. Saunders, 1962), p. 304; cited in Sudnow, *op. cit.,* p. 80. Such practice attests to the accuracy of Edgar Morin's rather melodramatic statement: "Man hides his death as he hides his sex, as he hides his excrements." See E. Morin, *L'Homme et La Mort dans L'Histoire* (Paris: Correa, 1951), p. 331.

32. See Sudnow, *op. cit.,* pp. 20-40, 49-50.

33. See Sudnow, "Passing On," p. 114.

34. See Glaser and Strauss, *Awareness of Dying,* pp. 142-43, 151-52.

35. On the doctor's attitudes toward death and the dying, see August M. Kasper, "The Doctor and Death," in *The Meaning of Death,* ed. Herman Feifel (New York: McGraw-Hill Book Company, Inc., 1959), pp. 259-70. Many writers have commented on the tendency of relatives to avoid the subject of death with the terminally ill; see, for example, Herman Feifel's "Attitudes toward Death in Some Normal and Mentally Ill Populations," *Meaning of Death,* pp. 114-32.

36. The most favorable situation for reducing isolation and meaninglessness would seem to be "where personnel and patient both are aware that he is dying, and where they act on this awareness relatively openly." This atmosphere, which Glaser and Strauss term an "open awareness context," did not typically predominate in the hospitals they studied. More common were one of three other awareness contexts they distinguished: "The situation where the patient does not recognize his impending death even though everyone else does" (closed awareness); "The situation where the patient suspects what the others know and therefore attempts to confirm or invalidate his suspicion" (suspected awareness); and "The situation where each party defines the patient as dying, but each pretends that the other has not done so" (mutual pretense awareness). See Glaser and Strauss, *Awareness of Dying,* p. 11.

37. See Ibid., p. 129. Some patients, however, put up a struggle to control the pace and style of their dying; and some prefer to leave the hospital and end their days at home for this reason (see Glaser and Strauss, *op. cit.,* pp. 95, 181-83). For a classic and moving account of a cancer victim who struggled to achieve control over the conditions of his death, see Lael T. Wertenbaker, *Death of a Man* (New York: Random House, 1957).

For discussions of isolation, meaninglessness, and powerlessness as dimensions of alienation, see Melvin Seeman, "On the Meaning of Alienation," *The American Sociological Review* 24 (1959): 783-91; and Robert Blauner, *Alienation and Freedom: The Factory Worker and His Industry* (Chicago: University of Chicago Press, 1964).

38. Franz Borkenau, "The Concept of Death," *The Twentieth Century* 157 (1955): 313-29, reprinted in Fulton, *Death and Identity,* pp. 42-56.

39. The need to redefine the status of the departed is intensified because of tendencies to act toward him as if he were alive. There is a status discongruity inherent in the often abrupt change from a more or less responsive person to an inactive, nonresponding one. This confusion makes it difficult for the living to shift their mode of interaction toward the neomort. Glaser and Strauss report that relatives in the hospital often speak to the newly deceased and caress him as if he were alive; they act as if he knows what they are saying and doing. Nurses who had become emotionally involved with the patient sometimes back away from post-mortem care because of a "mystic illusion" that the deceased is still sentient. See Glaser and Strauss, *Awareness of Dying,* pp. 113-14. We are all familiar with the expression of "doing the right thing" *for the deceased,* probably the most common conscious motivation underlying the bereaved's funeral preparations. This whole situation is sensitively depicted in Jules Romains's novel, *The Death of a Nobody* (New York: Alfred A. Knopf, 1944).

40. Arnold Van Gennep, *The Rites of Passage* (London: Routledge & Kegan Paul, 1960 [first published in 1909]). See also, W. L. Warner, *The Living and the Dead* (New Haven: Yale University Press, 1959), especially chapter 9; and Habenstein, "Social Organization," for a discussion of funerals as "dramas of disposal."

41. See Goody, *Death, Property, Ancestors,* for the specific material on the LoDagaa. For the general theoretical treatment, see Hertz, *Death and the Right Hand,* and also Emile Durkheim, *The Elementary Forms of the Religious Life* (New York: Free Press, 1947), especially p. 447.

42. Hertz, *op. cit.,* took the multiple funerals of primitive societies as the strategic starting point for his analysis of mortality and social structure. See Goody, *op. cit.,* for a discussion of Hertz (pp. 26-27), and the entire book for an investigation of multiple funerals among the LoDagaa.

43. I have been unable to locate precise statistics on the comparative frequency of funerals. The following data are suggestive. In a year and a half, Goody attended 30 among the LoDagaa, a people numbering some 4,000 (see *op. cit.*). Of the Barra people, a Roman Catholic peasant folk culture in the Scottish Outer Hebrides, it is reported that "most men and women participate in some ten to fifteen funerals in their neighborhood every year." See D. Mandelbaum, "Social Uses of Funeral Rites," in *The Meaning of Death,* p. 206.

Considering the life expectancy in our society today, it is probable that only a minority of people would attend one funeral or more per year. Probably most people during the first 40 (or even 50) years of life attend only one or two funerals a decade. In old age, the deaths of the spouse, collateral relations, and friends become more common; thus funeral attendance in modern societies tends to become more age-specific. For a discussion of the loss of intimates in later years, see J. Moreno, "The Social Atom and Death," in *The Sociometry Reader,* ed. J. Moreno (New York: Free Press, 1960), pp. 62-66.

44. For a discussion of funerals among the Romans and early Christians, see Alfred C. Rush, *Death and Burial in Christian Antiquity* (Washington, D.C.: Catholic University of America Press, 1941), especially pt. 3, pp. 187-273. On funerals in the medieval and preindustrial West, see Bertram S. Puckle, *Funeral Customs* (London: T. Werner Laurie, Ltd., 1926).

45. See Eissler, *Psychiatrist,* p. 144: "The religious dogma is, with relatively rare exceptions, not an essential help to the psychiatrist since the belief in the immortality of the soul, although deeply rooted in man's unconscious, is only rarely encountered nowadays as a well-integrated idea from which the ego could draw strength." On the basis of a sociological survey, Gorer confirms the psychiatrist's judgment: ". . . how small a role dogmatic Christian beliefs play . . ." (see Gorer, *Death, Grief, Mourning,* p. 39). Forty-nine percent of his sample affirmed a belief in an afterlife; 25 percent disbelieved; 26 percent were uncertain or would not answer (Ibid., p. 166).

46. The problem of sacred institutions in an essentially secular society has been well analyzed by Robert Fulton. See Fulton and Gilbert Geis, "Death and Social Values," pp. 67-75, and Fulton, "The Sacred and the Secular," pp. 89-105, in *Death and Identity.*

47. LeRoy Bowman interprets the decline of the American funeral primarily in terms of urbanization. When communities were made up of closely knit, geographically isolated groups of families, the death of an individual was a deprivation of the customary social give and take, a distinctly felt diminution of the total community. It made sense for the community as a whole to participate in a funeral. But in cities, individual families are in a much more limited relationship to other families; and the population loses its unity of social and religious ideals. For ethical and religious reasons, Bowman is unwilling to accept "a bitter deduction from this line of thought . . . that the death of one person is not so important as once it would have been, at least to the community in which he has lived." But that is the logical implication of his perceptive sociological analysis. See Bowman, *American Funeral,* pp. 9, 113-15, 126-28.

48. Edmund Volkart, "Bereavement and Mental Health," in *Explorations in Social Psychiatry,* ed. Alexander H. Leighton, John A. Clausen, and Robert N. Wilson (New York: Basic Books, 1957), pp. 281-307.

Volkart suggests that bereavement is a greater crisis in modern American society than in similar cultures because our family system develops selves in which people relate to others as persons rather than in terms of roles (see pp. 293-95).

49. In a study of bereavement reactions in England, Geoffrey Gorer found that 30 of a group of 80 persons who had lost a close relative were mourning in a style he characterized as *unlimited.* He attributes the inability to get over one's grief "to the absence of any ritual, either individual or social, lay or religious, to guide them and the people they come in contact with." The study also attests to the virtual disappearance of traditional mourning conventions. See Gorer, *Death, Grief, Mourning,* pp. 78-83.

50. See Marris, *Widows,* pp. 39-40.

51. Irwin W. Goffman suggests that "a decline in the significance of death has occurred in our recent history." See "Suicide Motives and Categorization of the Living and the Dead in the United States" (Syracuse, N.Y.: Mental Health Research Unit, February, 1966), p. 140.

52. See Eissler, *op. cit.,* p. 44.

53. See Goode, *Religion,* p. 185. Perhaps the fullest treatment is by Frazer; see *Fear of the Dead,* especially Vol. I.

54. See Simmons, *Aged,* pp. 223-24. See also, Effie Bendann, *Death Customs* (New York: Alfred A. Knopf, 1930), p. 180. However, there are primitive societies, such as the Hopi, that attribute little power and authority to dead spirits; in some cultures, the period of the dead man's influence is relatively limited; and in other cases only a minority of ghosts are reported to be the object of deference and awe. The general point holds despite these reservations.

55. See Warner, *The Living and the Dead,* pp. 4-5.

56. The novel *Death of a Nobody,* by Romains, is a sensitive treatment of how its protagonist, Jacques Godard, affects people after his death; his influence is extremely short-lived; and his memory in the minds of the living vanishes after a brief period. Goffman suggests that "parents are much less likely today to tell stories of the dead, of their qualities, hardships, accomplishments and adventures than was true a hundred years ago." See "Suicide Motives," p. 30.

57. In an interesting treatment of the problem from a different theoretical framework, Goffman (Ibid.) has concluded that the sense of contrast between what is living and what is dead in modern society has become attenuated, in large part because of the decline in exposure to death. He has assembled evidence on social differences within our society: For example, women, lower-class people, and Catholics tend to have closer and more frequent contact with death or images of the dead than men, middle-class persons, and Protestants.

The question of what is the representative American imagery of after-life existence would be a fruitful one for research. Clear and well-developed imageries are probably typical only among Catholics, fundamentalists, and certain ethnic groups. The dominant attitude (if there is one) is likely quite nebulous. For some, the dead may be remembered as an "absent presence," never to be seen again; for others as "a loved one with whom I expect (or hope) to be reunited in some form someday." Yet the background of afterlife existence is only vaguely sketched, and expectation and belief probably alternate with hope, doubt, and fear in a striking ambiguity about the prospect and context of reunion.

58. In primitive societies, ghosts and spirits of the dead range over the entire social territory or occupy central areas of the group's social space. In ancestor-worship civilizations such as Rome and China, spirits dwell in shrines that are located in the homes or family burial plots. In these preindustrial societies symbolic contact with the dead may be a daily occurrence.

Likewise, in the Middle Ages, cemeteries were not on the periphery of the societal terrain but were central institutions in the community; regularly visited, they were even the sites for feasts and other celebrations, since it was believed that the dead were gladdened by sounds of merry-making. (See Puckle, *Funeral Customs,* p. 145–46.) The most trenchant analysis of the cemetery as a spatial territory marking the social boundaries between the "sacred dead and the secular world of the profane living" in a small modern community is found in Warner, *The Living and the Dead,* chapter 9. Yet Warner also notes that people tend to disregard cemeteries as a "collective representation" in rapidly changing and growing communities, in contrast to the situation in small, stable communities. Goffman ("Suicide Motives," p. 29) notes that "increasingly the remains of the dead are to be found in huge distant cemeteries that are not passed or frequented as part of everyday routines . . . [or] in cities in which our very mobile population *used* to live."

59. Feifel has suggested that American society's rejection of (and even revulsion to) the old may be because they remind us unconsciously of death. See "Attitudes toward Death," p. 122.

60. According to Kastenbaum, the tendency of psychiatrists to eschew psychotherapy with the aged and to treat them, if at all, with supportive (rather than more prestigious depth) techniques may be a reflection of our society's future orientation, that results in an implicit devaluing of old people because of their limited time prospects. See Kastenbaum, "The Reluctant Therapist," in *New Thoughts of Old Age,* pp. 139–45. The research of Butler, a psychiatrist who presents evidence for significant personality change in old age despite the common contrary assumption, would seem to support Kastenbaum's view. (See Butler, "Life Review.")

Sudnow contributes additional evidence of the devaluation of old people. Ambulance drivers bringing critical or "dead-on-arrival" cases the the county hospital's emergency entrance blow their horns more furiously and act more frantic when the patient is young than when he is old. A certain proportion of "dead-on-arrival" cases can be saved through mouth-to-mouth resuscitation, heart massages, or other unusual efforts. These measures were attempted with children and young people but not with the old; one intern admitted being repulsed by the idea of such close contact with them. See Sudnow, "Passing On," pp. 160-63.

61. Frederick J. Hoffman, *The Mortal No: Death and the Modern Imagination* (Princeton, N.J.: Princeton University Press, 1964), see especially Part 2. In a second paper on Hiroshima, Robert J. Lifton also notes the tendency for the threat of mass death to undermine the meaning systems of society, and the absence of a clear sense of appropriate death in modern cultures. See "On Death and Death Symbolism: The Hiroshima Disaster," *Psychiatry* 27 (1964): 191-210. Gorer has argued that our culture's repression of death as a natural event is the cause of the obsessive focus on fantasies of violence that are so prominent in the mass media. See Geoffrey Gorer, "The Pornography of Death," in *Identity and Anxiety,* ed. Maurice Stein and Arthur Vidich (New York: Free Press, 1960), pp. 402-7; also reprinted in Gorer's *Death, Grief, Mourning.*

The inappropriateness inherent in the automobile accident, in which a man dies outside a communal and religious setting, is poignantly captured in the verse and chorus of the country and western song, "Wreck on the Highway," popularized by Roy Acuff:

"Who did you say it was, brother?/Who was it fell by the way?/When whiskey and blood run together,/Did you hear anyone pray?"

Chorus: "I didn't hear nobody pray, dear brother/I didn't hear nobody pray./I heard the crash on the highway,/But I didn't hear nobody pray."

62. The important distinction between ideal family structures and actual patterns of size of household, kinship composition, and authority relations has been stressed recently by William Goode, *World Revolution and Family Patterns* (New York: Free Press, 1963); and by Marion Levy, "Aspects of the Analysis of Family Structure," in A. J. Coale and Marion Levy, *Aspects of the Analysis of Family Structure* (Princeton, N.J.: Princeton University Press, 1965), pp. 1-63.

63. Bronislaw Malinowski, *Magic, Science and Religion* (Garden City, N.Y.: Doubleday Anchor, 1955), see pp. 47-53.

64. Emile Durkheim, *Division of Labor* (New York: Free Press, 1949).

THE AGED
AND THE
DYING PROCESS:
THE INEVITABLE DECISIONS*[1]
Richard A. Kalish

The dying process, like any other stage in human development, is influenced by numerous decisions. Although we often perceive the events that surround dying as automatic, inevitable, or beyond our control, in actuality they are constantly affected by cultural traditions and human decision makers.

The decisions "who," "where," "when," and "how" are part of the dying process of each individual. This paper will explore and speculate upon the decisions and decision makers involved in the dying process of the aged individual, although we recognize that comparable problems are faced when dying occurs at any age. We will deal with such decisions as who lives and who dies, where death occurs, how and when death comes about, who is to be with the dying patient, and how he is to learn of his imminent dying. Omitted for now will be such vital and relevant matters as war, fallout, air and water pollution control, socialized medicine, crime and accident prevention, and food and drug inspection, although each demands decisions which bear an obvious relationship to the dying process.

An important thread running through numerous behavioral science discussions of dying is the degree to which death and the dying are avoided (e.g., Wahl, 1959). Although the professional behavioral scientist studying these topics is no longer

* Richard A. Kalish, "The Aged and the Dying Process: The Inevitable Decisions," *Journal of Social Issues* 21 (1965): 87–96.

venturing into quite the taboo area reported by Feifel (1963), he is still likely to be accused of investigating a "morbid" topic. Even the geriatrician or gerontologist, while acknowledged to be making a pertinent contribution, seems to elicit wistful smiles and "I don't think I could take work like that" statements from his professional confreres.

Those who work with geriatric patients also find their own feelings make their work more difficult. A competent physician spends a sleepless week trying to decide how to inform a cheerful, alert octogenarian that her illness is terminal. A geriatric hospital nurse quickly explains that she *never* upsets a patient by telling him of the death of a close friend and ward-mate (thus leaving him to contemplate the significance of the empty bed). A young internist abruptly and affectlessly informs an elderly woman that she will be dead of cancer within three months (it took her six months, but the doctor had achieved his real goal, which was to propel her death away from his consciousness). A nursing-home aide tells her friend that "Right after work, I go home, take a stiff shot, and forget about that depressing place until I show up in the morning." A Veterans Administration social worker encourages the son of a dying World War I veteran to avoid letting his father learn of his condition, and thus both the son and the social worker can suppress the coming death encounter—at least for a while.

Probably one of the most interesting and most telling examples of how the dying are avoided was cited in Bowers, et al. (1964). One of the authors, Lawrence LeShan, computed the length of time it took hospital nurses to respond to call lights for terminal cases and compared it to the time for nonterminal cases; the nurses, although not the observer, were startled to learn how much they delayed answering the ring of the dying.

In essence, the number and proportion of the post-65-year-olds are increasing, as are the facilities and the professional, financial, and political interest. At the same time, the personal encounter with the aged and the dying still seems highly upsetting and is most commonly avoided. Within this framework, we can better understand that the increasing need to examine our decisions regarding the dying process has outdistanced our willingness to do so. As a result, many decisions involving the dying

563

process are ignored, avoided, postponed, or not seen as occurrences which involve decisions in the first place.

The Decisions and the Decision Makers

In a large West Coast city, it has been reported to the author, a carefully selected panel of physicians and nonphysicians must decide which of numerous applicants will be entitled to the use of highly limited medical facilities necessary to extend their lives by several years. At present, those rejected can expect to live only a very brief time. Rarely do we see, except for juries and the military, a more obvious (and probably anguishing) demand for making decisions regarding who lives and who dies. Most decisions involving the dying process are less dramatic, and most decision makers are less aware of their role in the decision-making process. Nonetheless, society is constantly involved in decisions regarding the "who," the "where," the "when," and the "how" of dying.

Who Lives and Who Dies?

Determining who dies is certainly one of the most vital decisions made concerning the dying process. Such factors as age, race, sex, finances, and—perhaps—personality seem to affect decisions and decision makers.

Age. Research has indicated that the lives of younger people are considered to be worth much more time and expense than the lives of the elderly (Kastenbaum, 1964a), and have more social value (Glaser and Strauss, 1964). Research and treatment of children and adolscents elicit more sympathy and attract more workers than research and treatment of the aged, and psychotherapy for the aged holds little interest for many, perhaps most, therapists (Kastenbaum, 1964b). The reasons for this are many, varied, and consistent with the value systems most widely maintained in our society. Although geriatrics and gerontology have received a recent impetus in this country, this author feels they still lag behind study and care of other age groupings. Thus,

564

probably without being fully aware of what they are doing, physicians, nurses, psychologists, social workers, and those responsible for the policies of funding organizations have helped decide who shall live and who shall die.

Race. Differential treatment of Negroes by physicians, teachers, lawyers, policemen, realtors, and employers, to name just a few, has contributed to the higher rate of Negro mortality at all ages. In some instances—those that often make the headlines—the Negro has been the victim of a direct attempt upon his life, or of overt exclusion from adequate medical care or legal protection. But more frequently, and probably more destructive, the Negro is selected to die sooner because of subtler causes, such as having to spend a higher proportion of his income on housing, leaving less for food and medical care, or for being forced to live in less advantageous sections of the community, regardless of income. In addition, of course, are his lesser job opportunities and more limited access to the type of information and education that provides the sort of knowledge and understanding that extends life.

Sex. Women, as is well known, live longer than men. Whatever constitutional bases might determine this differential life expectancy, we may speculate that certain implicit cultural norms are also involved. To give but one example: our cultural traditions allow women to seek medical care, but encourage a moderate to high degree of spartanism for men. Thus, the male may die sooner, partly as the result of his decision to adhere to the standard male role.

Finances. The indigent can receive competent medical care, which they pay for largely with time; the wealthy can receive competent medical care, which they can pay for readily with money. For the great majority of the elderly, however, medical care takes a high proportion of their financial assets. With Medicare, the economic advantages of the wealthy are considerably reduced, but many differences still exist, such as the opportunity to make long-term use of good nursing-home facilities.

Personality. Personality not only affects the ability of an individual to seek and profit from medical and related help, but affects the responses an individual elicits from others. In a geriatric facility, for example, we observe the pleasant and cooperative

565

patient receiving better care and treatment on the ward than the irritable and belligerent patient. The patient who growls at the physician may get a more superficial examination than the one who cooperates; the good-natured aged woman is wheeled to the sunny spot on the porch and is taken to activities, while her grumpy, complaining ward-mate is left in bed longer, is spoken to less frequently, and is less likely to receive extra attention.

Thus, as the result of age, race, sex, finances, and personality, decisions are made which affect who lives and who dies. These decisions are made by medical personnel, hospital ward personnel, other patients, relatives—just about everyone, including the elderly patients themselves. Such decisions are based upon tacit assumptions and cultural values that need illumination and thorough dialogue.

Deciding Where the Death Occurs

Traditionally, people died in their homes. Only a few decades ago, the hospital was considered the "place where people went to die," and was avoided by many, including the dying, for that very reason. Now, perhaps ironically, that the hospital is seen as being primarily for short-term care, people enter more readily— and die there more often. However, many terminal patients prefer to die at home. The administrator of one large hospital, which averages some 600 deaths annually, has suggested that the dying process could and should occur at home more frequently than it now does. At this hospital, the next-of-kin are often asked if they wish to take the patient home, where he can die in familiar surroundings, rather than in the impersonal hospital where the ebb and flow of events is controlled by routine and by strangers.[2]

But how does the family feel? Both professional literature (e.g., Kalish, in press) and personal experience remind us constantly of the degree to which the dying person is avoided in our society. One highly emotional forty-ish housewife exclaimed that she would never be able to live in her house again if her aged father were to die there. Another woman of similar age and duties agreed with her 79-year-old father's complaint that "no one is allowed to die at home any more—and what's worse, they won't even leave the poor body around long enough for a wake. No, they ship it off to a funeral home right away." In between is a variety of expressed attitudes. (These quotations were extracted from interviews the author recently conducted with adult children of geriatric hospital patients; analysis of these data is still in process.[3]

Sometimes the decision to hospitalize is made because adequate care is lacking at home, or because the fight for life can be made more effectively in a medical facility. Often, however, the decision is made by default since the participants, the patient, his family, and the physician, are never actively aware that the possible alternative decision to die at home is a reasonable one. Some may feel the sacrifice of a few days of life is a not unreasonable exchange for the opportunity to die at home. Although, for the most part, the next-of-kin interviewees felt that their parent did not care where he died, only 2 of the 37 felt the elderly person would prefer the hospital, while 8 stated that home was preferable.[4] A large proportion of dying geriatric patients are not sufficiently lucid, of course, to know where they are when they die. Nonetheless, whatever is known about their wishes may be respected.

The elderly themselves, however, frequently wish to be removed from their home when they become unable to take care of themselves or cannot afford to hire others who can care for them. Unlike other places and other times, the elderly are so much concerned lest they become a "burden" on others that they often decide to place themselves in nursing homes or similar facilities. They thus divest themselves of the right to be cared for by their children, a right that the contemporary Japanese or traditional American or European would take as his due.

When asked how they themselves felt about growing old, our sample of adult children most frequently mentioned their fear of "being a burden." In a geriatric facility, the "burdensome" quality of daily (and often abrasive) contact with children is substantially eliminated. It absolves guilt of the parent and multiplies the guilt of the children, according to clinicians in the geriatrics field.

The fear of becoming a burden is not the only pressure upon the elderly to decide to live, and thus die, in nursing homes. Some prefer to be where medical care is more readily available; others prefer the impersonal care; sometimes an aged parent believes that his effect upon the people with whom he lives is destructive. A number of elderly persons also prefer to avoid the role reversal in which the once-dominant parent must regress to the status of helpless infant, nurtured by the children he once nurtured himself; a geriatric facility enables him to maintain the original parent-child relationship intact as long as possible.

Thus, the elderly person may prefer to die at home, with his possessions surrounding him, and with familiar faces near. Nonetheless, a barrage of medical, psychological, and financial pressures often produces the decision to die in a hospital or geriatric facility.

Numerous researchable problems emerge in considering where the dying process occurs. We could attempt to learn where the elderly patient prefers to die, and what relationship this bears to his feelings at previous developmental stages. We could also investigate how different types of geriatric patients are affected by various living (and dying) arrangements. The possibility that separation from family through placement in a nursing home leads to premature death is one contemplated study. We recognize the impact of separation upon infants and children; perhaps the aged person, often highly dependent also, would have similar reactions to this type of separation. It would also be valuable to learn who actually makes the decision, on what . basis, and with what implications for the psychological functioning of all those concerned.

When Does the Patient Die?

How long is existence to be extended? Some physicians believe it is their responsibility to maintain existence as long as possible, while others interpret their role more flexibly. This decision becomes more difficult as the definition of "living" becomes more complex. Shneidman (1963) has discussed this problem at some length, but for present purposes we need to keep in mind that the cessation of the heart beat is technically the end of life only because we continue to accept this traditional definition. Could the future define the end of life as the end of self-awareness? If it seems axiomatic that life continues as long as the heart beats, what will define "life" when an artificial or transplanted heart becomes an actuality? We might keep a beating heart encased indefinitely within an otherwise lifeless body. When does life cease? Who is to decide?

A hospital administrator has suggested that a panel be established to decide when life has, for practical purposes, ended, and the heart may be allowed to stop beating. When one physician berated him for "playing God," his rejoinder was that the physician was "playing God" by sustaining existence beyond the time that God apparently had decided it should cease. Although it is clearly murder to remove an intravenous tube from a dying patient, the act of not inserting it in the first place is a totally different matter. The battle lines on this issue are just being drawn, and its resolution is far in the future.

If it is "playing God" to make a decision affecting the length of life, then physicians and next-of-kin are both forced into this controversial role. Whether or not to operate on an elderly person is a decision which often must be made. Any surgery, of course, entails risk, and an operation on the elderly entails more than the normal amount. The decision must be made as to whether the possible reduction of suffering or extension of life is worth the risk of death on the operating table. Someone must make the decision—usually the physician and the patient jointly or, if the patient is not sufficiently lucid, the next-of-kin. And the need for such a decision immediately creates other decisions. Who determines whether a patient is sufficiently lucid to make decisions involving his own life and death? The aged, even those who frequently seem disoriented, often have days or hours when they appear alert. Does the physician obtain permission for a dangerous operation during a lucid period? Does he bypass the patient altogether?

The answer seems to depend upon the individual physician and his interaction with both patient and family. In actual practice, the physician may decide whom to ask and when to ask, often based, consciously or unconsciously, on his perceptions of how to receive the response he wishes. Obviously, he will

569

consider professional ethics, legal restrictions, the possibility of incurring family wrath, or a malpractice lawsuit. When indigents without families are involved, the decision may be influenced by the sort of operation or treatment needed for instruction for the interne and resident staff. In the case of clearly senile patients, decisions regarding the dying process are made by the physician, often in conjunction with the family. Sometimes the family members appreciate having a part in the decision-making process; at other times, they resent the physician for forcing them into taking a share of responsibility, even though the medical man must be the final decision maker. It is he who must decide which relative is the proper one to represent the patient, and when the interests of the patient conflict with the decisions suggested by the family. In more than one case, the physician has had to evaluate the financial investment the family has in the patient's death.

Provocative ethical and legal problems emerge from this discussion, although somewhat tangential to the immediate topic. At what point do "you" cease to be "yours?" That is, when do you cease to have responsibility for what happens to your body or your thinking? Lack of responsibility for "you" ceases before death, if evidence can be given that "you" are not capable of taking responsibility. Thus, "you" may be medicated, sedated, tranquilized, operated upon, fed, bathed, and dressed without the prerogative of being an agent in the decision-making process.

The "How" Decisions

To an appreciable extent, we are unable to control how we die, any more than we can control when we die. However, the modern world certainly makes more effective decisions regarding the "how" and "when" of the dying process than ever before. Ignoring for this presentation such death-decisions as suicide or homicide, we need to consider the condition of the patient as he goes through the dying process.

Most people would probably accept the premise that the physician should reduce the suffering of a dying person as much as possible. But the reduction of discomfort often requires

570

sedation, sometimes to the point that the patient leads an almost vegetative, albeit comfortable, existence. Is this preferable to having pain, but remaining alert and able to communicate? Who makes this decision? Sometimes the decision of when to die depends directly upon the decision how to die. A patient may need to decide whether to live a substantial number of years in pain, or a lesser number of comfortable years. Additional decisions include who will be with the patient as he dies and how the patient is informed of his terminal condition.

Who Is with the Patient As He Dies?

Do elderly patients want their families with them as they die? Generalizing from our sample of 37, their adult children believe so. Do the family members want to be there? The answer is again, generally, in the positive, although frequently with the qualification that "father can recognize me," or "if there is any point in it." The range of responses is great, however, from: "I don't want to be within twenty miles at that point," (from a very emotional housewife) to "I'd sit with him day and night in case he could talk to me for a few minutes before he dies," (from the daughter of a man whose stroke a year earlier left him almost completely paralyzed).

But decisions regarding who can stay with the dying are not always left to the patient or to the individual family members. An adult may make the decision that the patient's grandchildren might wish to do so; a physician might decide that the terminal illness is contagious and the patient should be isolated; a hysterical son might be kept from his mother's side "for his own good" or for hers.

Informing the Terminal Geriatric Patient

The patient's "right to know" has generated more questions than answers, and each question requires a decision. One school of thought insists that the patient be apprised, as objectively as possible, of his condition. Another school believes that the

571

patient should be protected against such knowledge, which will rob him of hope and perhaps hasten his death. Intermediate positions call for discussing the possible seriousness, but purposely remaining unduly optimistic; answering only direct questions; being vaguely encouraging without giving specific information; telling the patient things will get worse before they get better, which often deflects further questioning; and so forth. The decisions must be made, not only what to tell the patient, but who is to do the telling: The physician? The next-of-kin? A social worker or psychologist? Or a chance hint inadvertently supplied by a visitor or nurse?

Informing the terminally ill person of his condition is not a popular task. Ward personnel usually avoid it at all costs, sometimes being obviously and ridiculously optimistic in their patient contact to do so. Family members and physicians are likely to pass the buck back and forth to each other, until the patient senses the situation and grasps for himself what is happening without being told. In many instances the patient understands his condition long before the attending doctor or relative has even decided whether or not to present the information. On other occasions, the patient becomes terminal and dies without ever attaining sufficient lucidity to understand the significance of what is happening to him.

Dr. Avery Weisman, a consultant psychiatrist on a research project for the aged, believes that few dying patients need to be told they are nearing death, but that many more would like to discuss their prognosis than doctors and nurses generally realize. "Most patients already sense the diagnosis long before they are told," (Weisman and Hackett, 1962), and misleading or patronizing answers to serious questions will only alienate the physician and the patient. Although the doctor should convey only that information which the patient is emotionally and intellectually able to absorb, he should respond so that the patient finds his words understandable and according to the meaning the patient intended. Questions such as "Will I ever leave here?" or "Will I die soon?" may be circumvented or rephrased, but the meaning the patient is communicating should never be distorted. In no instance should the patient be told a falsehood or given an inappropriately optimistic outlook. Most dying patients,

572

Dr. Weisman feels, are afraid of losing their last enduring relationships. "Focus upon the time that is left and concentrate upon the patient's residue of autonomy, control, choice, and responsibility."[5] This author would agree and believes that emphasis should be upon the participation of the patient and upon his ability to choose, rather than upon a specific estimate of the remaining time, which is rarely a crucial issue and which, perhaps fortunately, cannot be predicted as accurately as other aspects of a fatal illness.

A Concluding Note

In a sense we each make daily decisions affecting the dying processes of ourselves and others. The food we decide to eat, the speed at which we drive our car, the ballot we cast, the charity donation we make, all these influence dying, although we may be only sporadically aware of it. We also tend to be unaware of some of the basic assumptions we have regarding dying. For example, care offered in the hospital is better for the dying person than care offered elsewhere. Dying usually means pain and discomfort. The death of a child is "worse" than the death of an elderly person. Existence should be extended as long as possible. Living, except for isolated cases, is better than dying. Women are constitutionally predisposed to live longer than men. These are but a few of the underlying premises we maintain, often without evaluation, that affect our decisions as we manipulate the process of dying.

Notes

1. The author would like to offer his thanks to Dr. Robert Kastenbaum and Mrs. Isabel Banay of Cushing Hospital, Framingham, Massachusetts, and to Dr. Avery Weisman, Massachusetts General Hospital, Boston, for their contributions to the ideas presented in this paper.

2. Personal communication.

3. Research supported by USPHS Mental Health Project, MHO-1520 at Cushing Hospital, Framingham, Mass.

4. The author feels that respondents, who were responsible for the hospitalization in the first place, would tend to underestimate their parents' desires to return home to die.

5. Personal communication from Dr. Avery Weisman, consultant to MHO-1520 project.

REFERENCES

Not all of the references are listed here. Some are incorporated in the text
of the articles in which they occur. Certain others are listed as notes
and appear at the ends of the articles in which they are cited.

PART I
THEORETICAL APPROACHES TO SOCIAL AGING

Introduction to Part I.

Cavan, R. S.; Burgess, E. W.; Havighurst, R.; and Goldhammer, H. 1949.
Personal adjustment in old age. Chicago: Science Research Associates.

Cottrell, L. S., Jr. 1942. The adjustment of the individual to his age and
sex roles. *American Sociological Review* 7:617-20.

Cumming, E., and Henry, W. H. 1961. *Growing old: the process of disengagement.* New York: Basic Books.

Kastenbaum, R. 1965. Theories of human aging: the search for a conceptual framework. *Journal of Social Issues* 21:13-36.

Maddox, G. 1963. Activity and morale: a longitudinal study of selected
elderly subjects. *Social Forces* 42:195-204.

Philibert, M. A. J. 1965. The emergence of social gerontology. *Journal of
Social Issues* 21:4-12.

An Exploration of the Activity Theory of Aging: Activity Types and Life Satisfaction Among In-Movers to a Retirement Community.
Bruce W. Lemon, Vern L. Bengtson, James A. Peterson

Bengtson, V. 1969. Adult socialization and personality differentiation:
The social psychology of aging. In *Contemporary gerontology: Issues
and concepts,* ed. J. Birren. Los Angeles: Gerontology Ctr., USC.

Bengtson, V.; Chiriboga, D.; and Keller, A. W. 1969. Occupational differences in retirement: Patterns of life-outlook and role activity among
Chicago teachers and steelworkers. In *Adjustment to retirement: A
cross-national study,* ed. R. J. Havighurst et al. Netherlands: Van
Gorkum.

REFERENCES

Burgess, E. W. 1954. Social relations, activities, and personal adjustment. *American Journal of Sociology* 59:352-60.

Cavan, R. 1962. Self and role in adjustment during old age. In *Human behavior and social processes,* ed. A. Rose. Boston: Houghton-Mifflin.

Cumming, E. M., and Henry, W. 1961. *Growing old.* New York: Basic Books.

Cutler, N. 1972a. Aging and political affiliation: A cohort of generational analysis. Paper presented at the meeting of the American Political Science Association, Chicago.

———. 1972b. Aging and generations in politics: The conflict of explanations and inference. In *Public opinion and political attitudes: A reader,* ed. A. R. Wilcox. New York: John Wiley.

Goodman, L. A., and Kruskal, W. H. 1954. Measurement of association for cross classifications. *Journal of the American Statistical Association* 49:732-64.

Hamovitch, M.; Peterson, J.; and Larson, A. 1969. Housing needs and satisfactions of the elderly. *Gerontologist* 9:30-32.

Havighurst, R. J., and Albrecht, R. 1953. *Older people.* New York: Longmans, Green.

Havighurst, R. J.; Neugarten, B. L.; Munnichs, J. M. A.; and Thomae, H., eds. 1969. *Adjustment to retirement: A cross-national study.* Netherlands: Van Gorkum.

Kerlinger, F. 1964. *Foundations of behavioral research.* New York: Holt, Rinehart & Winston.

Kinch, J. W. 1963. A formalized theory of self-concept. *American Journal of Sociology* 68:481-86.

Kutner, B.; Fanshel, D.; Togo, A.; and Langner, S. W. 1956. *Five hundred over sixty.* New York: Russell Sage Foundation.

Kuypers, J. A.; and Bengtson, V. L. 1973. Competence and social breakdown: A social-psychological model of aging. *Human Development.*

Lebo, D. 1953. Some factors said to make for happiness in old age. *Journal of Clinical Psychology* 9:384-90.

Lowenthal, M. F., and Haven, C. 1968. Interaction and adaptation: Intimacy as a critical variable. *American Sociological Review* 33:20-30.

Maddox, G. 1963. Activity and morale: A longitudinal study of selected elderly subjects. *Social Forces* 42:195-204.

———. 1964. Disengagement theory: A critical evaluation. *Gerontologist* 4:80-82.

———. 1965. Fact and artifact: Evidence bearing on disengagement theory from the Duke longitudinal study. *Human Development* 8:117-30.

———. 1969. Themes and issues in sociological theories of human aging. *Proceedings 1,* 8th International Congress of Gerontology, Washington.

McCall, G. J., and Simmons, J. L. 1966. *Identities and interactions.* New York: Free Press.

576

Neugarten, B., and Havighurst, R. J. 1969. Disengagement reconsidered in a cross-national context. Ch. 9 in *Adjustment to retirement: A cross-national study*, ed. Havighurst et al. Netherlands: Van Gorkum.

Neugarten, B.; Havighurst, R.; and Tobin, S. S. 1961. The measurement of life satisfaction. *Journal of Gerontology* 16:134-43.

———. 1968. Personality and patterns of aging. In *Middle age and aging: A reader in social psychology*, ed. B. Neugarten. Chicago: University of Chicago Press.

Peterson, J.; Hadwen, T.; and Larson, A. 1968. *A time for work, a time for leisure: A study of retirement in-movers*. Los Angeles: Gerontology Ctr., USC.

Phillips, B. S. 1957. A role theory approach to adjustment in old age. *American Sociological Review* 22:212-17.

Reichard, S.; Livson, F.; and Peterson, P. G. 1962. *Aging and personality*. New York: John Wiley.

Riley, M. W. 1971. Social gerontology and the age stratification of society. *Gerontologist* 11:79-87.

Riley, M. W., and Foner, A. 1968. *Aging and society, vol. 1, An inventory of research findings*. New York: Russell Sage Foundation.

Rose. A. 1964. A current issue in social gerontology. *Gerontologist* 4:45-50.

Rose, A. ed. 1962. *Human behavior and social processes*. Boston: Houghton-Mifflin.

Rosow, I. 1967. *Social integration of the aged*. New York: Free Press.

Shibutani, T. 1961. *Society and personality*. Englewood Cliffs, N.J.: Prentice-Hall.

Somers, R. H. 1962. A new asymetric measure of association for ordinal variables. *American Sociological Review* 27:82-94.

Tallmer, M., and Kutner, B. 1970. Disengagement and morale. *Gerontologist* 10:317-20.

Tobin, S. S., and Neugarten, B. L., 1961. Life satisfaction and social interaction in the aging. *Journal of Gerontology* 16:344-46.

Youmans, E. G. 1969. Some perspectives on disengagement theory. *Gerontologist* 9:254-58.

Zetterberg, H. 1965. *On theory and verification in sociology*. New York: Bedminister Press.

Social Gerontology and the Age Stratification of Society.
Matilda White Riley

Back, K. W. 1969. The ambiguity of retirement. In *Behavior and adaptation in late life.*, eds. E. W. Busse and E. Pfeiffer. Boston: Little, Brown.

577

Benedict, R. 1938. Continuities and discontinuities in cultural conditioning. *Psychiatry* 1:161-67. (Reprinted in *Personality in nature, society and culture,* ed. C. Kluckhohn; H. A. Murray; and D. Schneider. 1953.) New York: Knopf.

Bernstein, M. C. 1969. Aging and the law. In *Aging and society,* vol. 2, *Aging and the professions,* ed. M. W. Riley; J. W. Riley, Jr.; and M. E. Johnson. New York: Russell Sage Foundation.

Brim, O. G., Jr. 1968. Adult socialization. In *Socialization and society,* ed. J. A. Clausen. Boston: Little, Brown.

Brim, O. G., Jr., and Wheeler, S. 1966. *Socialization after childhood: Two essays.* New York: Wiley.

Burgess, E. W., ed. 1960. *Aging in Western societies.* Chicago: University of Chicago Press.

Cicetti, F. 1970. Campuses revisited: New trend at Seton Hall. *Newark Evening News,* Sept. 30, 1970.

Clausen, J. A. 1971. The life course of individuals. In *Aging and society.* vol. 3, *A sociology of age stratification,* ed. M. W. Riley; M. E. Johnson; and A. Foner. New York: Russell Sage Foundation.

Donahue, W.; Orbach, H. L.; and Pollak, O. 1960. Retirement: The emerging social pattern. In *Handbook of social gerontology,* ed. C. Tibbitts. Chicago: University of Chicago Press.

Eisenstadt, S. N. 1956. *From generation to generation; age groups and social structure.* Glencoe, Ill.: Free Press.

Foner, A. 1969. The middle years: Prelude to retirement? PhD dissertation, New York University.

Glick, P. C., and Parke, R., Jr. 1965. New approaches in studying the life cycle of the family. *Demography* 2:187-202.

Havighurst, R. J.; Munnichs, J. M. A.; Neugarten, B. L.; and Thomae, H., eds. 1969. *Adjustment to retirement: A cross-national study.* Assen. The Netherlands: Koninklijke van Gorcum.

Hess, B. 1971. Friendship. In *Aging and society,* vol. 3, *A sociology of age stratification,* ed. M. W. Riley; M. E. Johnson; and A. Foner. New York: Russell Sage Foundation.

Kalish, R. A. 1969. The old and the new as generation gap allies. *Gerontologist* 9:83-89.

Lazarsfeld, P. F., and Merton, R. K. 1954. Friendship as social process: A substantive and methodological analysis. In *Freedom and control in modern society,* ed. M. Berger; T. Abel; and C. H. Page. New York: Van Nostrand.

McConnell, J. W. 1960. Aging and the economy. In *Handbook of social gerontology,* ed. C. Tibbitts. Chicago: University of Chicago Press.

Madge, J. 1969. Aging and the fields of architecture and planning. In *Aging and society*, vol. 2, *Aging and the professions*, ed. M. W. Riley; J. W. Riley, Jr., and M. E. Johnson. New York: Russell Sage Foundation.

Mannheim, K. 1952. The problem of generations. In *Essays on the sociology of knowledge*, ed. and trans. P. Kecskemeti. London: Routledge & Kegan Paul (1928).

Manpower Report of the President, Mar., 1970. Washington: Government Printing Office.

Merton, R. K. 1957. *Social theory and social structure*, rev. ed. Glencoe, Ill.: Free Press.

National Center for Health Statistics. Age and menopause, United States 1960-1962. *Vital and health statistics, 1966*, PHS Pub. No. 1000-Series 11, No. 19, Washington: Government Printing Office.

Parsons, T., and Platt, G. M. 1971. Higher education and changing socialization. In *Aging and society*, vol. 3, *A sociology of age stratification*, ed. M. W. Riley; M. E. Johnson; and A. Foner. New York: Russell Sage Foundation.

Reich, C. Reflections: The greening of America. *New Yorker*, 26 September, 1970, p. 42 ff.

Riley, M. W.; Foner, A.; and Associates. 1968. *Aging and society*. vol. I, *An inventory of research findings*. New York: Russell Sage Foundation.

Riley, M. W.; Foner, A.; Hess, B; and Toby, M. L. 1969. Socialization for the middle and later years. In *Handbook of socialization theory and research*, ed. D. A. Goslin. Chicago: Rand McNally.

Riley, M. W.; Riley, J. W., Jr.; and Johnson, M. E. 1969. *Aging and society*, vol. 2, *Aging and the professions*. New York: Russell Sage Foundation.

Riley, M. W.; Johnson, M. E.; and Foner, A. 1971. *Aging and society*, vol. 3, *A sociology of age stratification*. New York: Russell Sage Foundation.

Rossi, A. S. Equality between the sexes: An immodest proposal. *Daedalus*, Spring 1964, 607-52.

Ryder, N. B. 1965. The cohort as a concept in the study of social change. *American Sociological Review* 30:843-61.

Shanas, E. 1968. *Old people in three industrial societies*. New York: Atherton Press.

———. 1969. Living arrangements and housing of old people. In *Behavior and adaptation in late life*, ed. E. W. Busse and E. Pfeiffer. Boston: Little, Brown.

Shanas, E., and Associates. 1966. Family help patterns and social class in three countries. Paper presented at the meetings of the American Sociological Assn., Miami.

REFERENCES

Simmons, L. W. 1960. Aging in preindustrial societies. In *Handbook of social gerontology,* ed. C. Tibbitts. Chicago: University of Chicago Press.

Smelser, N. J. 1968. Sociological history: The industrial revolution and the British working-class family. In *Essays in sociological explanation,* ed. N. J. Smelser. Englewood Cliffs, N.J.: Prentice-Hall.

Spengler, J. J. 1969. The aged and public policy. In *Behavior and adaptation in late life,* ed. E. W. Busse and E. Pfeiffer. Boston: Little, Brown.

Starr, B. C. 1971. The community. In *Aging and society.* vol. 3, *A sociology of age stratification,* ed. M. W. Riley; M. E. Johnson; and A. Foner. New York: Russell Sage Foundation.

Streib, G. F. 1965. Intergenerational relations: Perspectives of the two generations on the older parent. *Journal of Marriage and the Family* 27:469-76.

Streib, G. F., and Thompson, W. E. 1960. The older person in a family context. In *Handbook of social gerontology,* ed. C. Tibbitts. Chicago: University of Chicago Press

Susser, M. 1969. Aging and the field of public health. In *Aging and society,* vol. 2, *Aging and the professions,* ed. M. W. Riley; J. W. Riley, Jr.; and M. E. Johnson. New York: Russell Sage Foundation.

Tanner, J. M. 1962. *Growth at adolescence,* 2d ed. Oxford: Blackwell, Davis Co.

PART II
METHODOLOGICAL ISSUES IN SOCIAL GERONTOLOGY

Introduction to Part II.

Atchley, Robert. 1972. *Social forces in later life.* Belmont, California: Wadsworth.

Birren, James. 1959. *Handbook of aging and the individual.* Chicago: University of Chicago Press.

Aging Regions of the United States: 1970.
Cary S. Kart and Barbara B. Manard

Caplow, T., Bahr, H., Kart, C., Manard, B., and van Gils, D. 1974. *The elderly and old age institutions.* University of Virginia, Center for Program Effectiveness Studies.

Chevan, A., and O'Rourke, J. F. 1972. Aging regions of the United States. *Journal of Gerontology* 27(1):119-26.

Rummel, R. J. 1970. *Applied factor analysis.* Evanston: Northwestern University Press.

United States Bureau of the Census. 1970. *Detailed characteristics of the population, Parts 1-51.* Washington: Government Printing Office.

———. 1973a. *Subject report: Mobility among the states, 1970.* Washington: Government Printing Office.

———. 1973b. *Subject report: Housing of senior citizens, 1970.* Washington: Government Printing Office.

The Measurement of Life Satisfaction.

Bernice L. Neugarten, Robert J. Havighurst, Sheldon S. Tobin

Cavan, Ruth S.; Burgess, E. W.; Havighurst, R. J.; and Goldhamer, H. 1949. *Personal adjustment in old age.* Chicago: Science Research Associates.

Cumming, Elaine; Dean, Lois R.; and Newell, D. S. 1958. What is "morale"? A case history of a validity problem. *Hum. Organization* 17(2):3-8.

Cumming, Elaine, and Henry, W. E. *Growing old.* New York; Basic Books.

Havighurst, R. J. 1957. The social competence of middle-aged people. *Genet. Psychol. Monogr.* 56:297-375.

Havighurst, R. J., and Albrecht, Ruth. 1953. *Older people.* New York: Longmans, Green.

Kuhlen, R. G. 1948. Age trends in adjustment during the adult years as reflected in happiness ratings. *Amer. J. Psychol.* 3:307 (Abstract).

Kutner, B.; Fanshel, D.; Togo, Alice M.; and Langner, T. S. 1956. *Five hundred over sixty.* New York: Russell Sage Foundation.

Lebo, D. 1953. Some factors said to make for happiness in old age. *J. clin. Psychol.* 9:385-90.

Morrison, D., and Kristjanson, G. A. 1958. *Personal adjustment among older persons.* Agricultural Experiment Station Technical Bulletin no. 21. Brookings: South Dakota State College.

Pollak, O. 1948. *Social adjustment in old age.* New York: Social Science Research Council.

Rose, A. M. 1955. Factors associated with life satisfaction of middle-class, middle-aged persons. *Marriage & Family Living* 17:15-19.

Rosow, I. Adjustment of the normal aged: concept and measurement. Paper given at the International Research Seminar on the Social and Psychological Aspects of Aging, Berkeley, August 1960; to be published in R. H. Williams, J. E. Birren, Wilma Donahue, and C. Tibbitts (eds.), *Psychological and social processes of aging: An international seminar.*

REFERENCES

The 4% Fallacy: A Methodological and Empirical Critique of Extended Care Facility Population Statistics.
Robert Kastenbaum and Sandra E. Candy

Riley, M. W., and Foner, A. 1968. *Aging and society, vol. 1, An inventory of research findings.* New York: Russell Sage Foundation.
Markson, E. W., and Hand, J. 1970. Referral for death: Low status of the aged and referral for psychiatric hsopitalization. *Aging and human development* 1:261-72.
Kastenbaum, R., and Aisenberg, R. B. 1972. *The psychology of death.* New York: Springer.

PART III
BIOLOGICAL AND PSYCHOLOGICAL ASPECTS OF AGING

Some Biological Aspects of Aging.
Cary S. Kart

Atchley, R. 1972. *Social forces and later life.* Belmont, Calif.: Wadsworth.
Blumenthal, H. T. 1968. Some biomedical aspects of aging. *Gerontologist* 8:3-5.
Comfort, A. 1964. *The process of aging.* New York: New American Library.
Curtis, H. 1966. *Biological mechanisms of aging.* Springfield, Ill.: Charles C. Thomas.
Leaf, A. 1973. Getting old. *Scientific American* 229:45-52.
Rockstein, M. 1974. *Theoretical aspects of aging.* New York: Academic Press.
Sobel, H. 1966. When does human aging start? *Gerontologist* 6:17-22.
Strehler, B. 1962. *Time, cells, and aging.* New York: Academic Press.
Wilson, D. L. 1974. The programmed theory of aging. In *Theoretical aspects of aging,* ed. M. Rockstein, pp. 11-22. New York: Academic Press.

Psychological Aspects of Aging: Intellectual Functioning.
James E. Birren

Babcock, H., and Levy, L. 1940. *Test and manual of directions, the revised examination for the measurement of efficiency of mental function.* Chicago: C. H. Stoelting Co.
Birren, J. E. 1964 (a). Neural basis of personal adjustment in aging. In *Age with a future,* ed. P. F. Hansen. Copenhagen: Munksgaard.

————. 1964 (b). *The psychology of aging.* Englewood Cliffs, N.J.: Prentice-Hall.

Birren, J. E.; Botwinick, J.; Weiss, A. D.; and Morrison, D. F. 1963. Interrelations of mental and perceptual tests given to healthy elderly men. In *Human Aging*, ed. J. E. Birren; R. N. Butler; S. W. Greenhouse; L. Sokoloff; and M. R. Yarrow. Public Health Service Pub. No. 986. Washington, D.C.

Botwinick, J., and Birren, J. E. 1951. The measurement of intellectual decline in the senile psychoses. *J. consult. Psychol.* 15:145-50.

Copple, G. E. 1948. *Senescent decline on the Wechsler-Bellevue Intelligence Scale.* Doctoral dissertation, Univ. of Pittsburgh.

Fox, C., and Birren, J. E. 1950. Intellectual deterioration in the aged: Agreement between the Wechsler-Bellevue and the Babcock-Levy. *J. consult. Psychol.* 14:305-10.

Personality and Patterns of Aging.
Robert J. Havighurst

Cumming, E., and Henry, W. E. 1961. *Growing old.* New York: Basic Books.

Havighurst, R. J.; Neugarten, B. L.; and Tobin, S. S. 1964. Disengagement, personality and life satisfaction in later years. In *Age with a future.* Copenhagen: Munksgaard.

Neugarten, B. L. 1965. Personality and patterns of aging. *Gawein* 13: 249-56.

Reichard, S.; Livson, F.; and Peterson, P. G. 1962. *Aging and personality.* New York: Wiley.

PART IV
WORK, RETIREMENT, AND LEISURE

Retirees of the 1970s.
Lola M. Irelan and Kathleen Bond

Barfield, Richard, and Morgan, James. 1969. *Early retirement: The decision and the experience.* Ann Arbor: Survey Research Center, Institute for Social Research. University of Michigan.

Bixby, Lenore E. 1970. Income of people aged 65 and older: Overview from 1968 survey of the aged. *Social Security Bulletin* (April).

Cain, Leonard D., Jr. 1967. Aged status and generational phenomena: The new old people in contemporary America. *Gerontologist* 7:83-92.

Easterlin, Richard A. 1973. Does money buy happiness? *The Public Interest* (Winter), pp. 3-10.

Edwards, John N., and Klemmack, David L. 1973. Correlates of life satisfaction: A reexamination. *Journal of Gerontology* 28:497-502.

Gurin, Gerald; Veroff, Joseph; and Feld, Sheila. 1960. *Americans view their mental health: A nationwide interview study.* New York: Basic Books.

Hill, Reuben, et al. 1970. *Family development in three generations.* Cambridge: Schenkman Publishing Co.

Irelan, Lola, and Bell, Bruce. 1972. Understanding subjectively defined retirement: A pilot analysis. *Gerontologist* (Winter), pp. 354-56.

Jaffe, A. J. 1972. The retirement dilemma. *Industrial Gerontology* 14 (Summer).

Kerckhoff, Alan C. 1964. Husband-wife expectation and reactions to retirement. *Journal of Gerontology* 19:510-16.

Kutner, Bernard, et al. 1956. *Five hundred over 60: A community survey on aging.* New York: Russell Sage Foundation.

Lauriat, Patience, and Rabin, William. 1970. Men who claim benefits before age 65: Findings from the Survey of New Beneficiaries, 1968. *Social Security Bulletin* (November).

Morgan, James, et al. 1962. *Income and welfare in the United States.* New York: McGraw-Hill.

Motley, Dena K. 1972. Health in the years before retirement. Retirement History Study Report no. 2. *Social Security Bulletin* (December).

Murray, Janet. 1971. Living arrangements of people aged 65 and older: Findings from the 1968 Survey of the Aged. *Social Security Bulletin* (October).

———. 1973. Family structure in the preretirement years. Retirement History Study Report no. 4. *Social Security Bulletin* (October).

Reno, Virginia. 1971. Why men stop working at or before age 65. *Preliminary Findings from the Survey of New Beneficiaries.* Report No. 3 U.S. Department of Health, Education, and Welfare, Social Security Administration, Office of Research and Statistics.

Riley, M. W., and Foner, Anne. 1968. *Aging and society,* vol. 1. *An inventory of research findings.* New York: Russell Sage Foundation.

Schwab, Karen. 1974. Early withdrawal from the labor force. *Social Security Bulletin* (forthcoming).

Shanas, Ethel. 1961. *Family relationships of older people.* Health Information Foundation Research Series 20. New York: Health Information Foundation.

Sherman, Sally R. 1973. Assets on the threshold of retirement. Retirement History Study Report No. 3. *Social Security Bulletin* (August).

584

Simmons, Leo W. 1960. Aging in pre-industrial societies. In *Handbook of Social Gerontology*, ed. Clark Tibbitts. Chicago: University of Chicago Press.

Streib, Gordon F., and Schneider, Clement J., Jr. 1971. *Retirement in American society: Impact and process.* Ithaca: Cornell University Press.

Sussman, Marvin, and Burchinal, Lee. 1962. Kin family network: Unheralded structure in current conceptualizations of family functioning. *Marriage and Family Living* 24:231-40.

Sussman, Marvin, and Slater, Sherwood B. 1963. Re-appraisal of urban kin networks: Empirical evidence. Paper read at annual meeting of the American Sociological Association, Los Angeles.

U.S. Bureau of the Census. 1970a. *Employment Status and Work Experience* PC(2)-6A, 1970 Census.

———. 1970b. *Persons by Family Characteristics* PC(2)-4B, 1970 Census.

———. 1973. Some Demographic Aspects of Aging in the United States. *Current Population Reports, Special Studies,* Series P-23, No. 43.

U.S. Department of Labor. 1970. *The pre-retirement years: A longitudinal study of the labor market experience of men.* Vol. 1. Manpower Research Monograph no. 15.

The Effects of Aging on Activities and Attitudes.
Erdman B. Palmore

Blalock, H. M. 1961. *Causal inferences in nonexperimental research.* Chapel Hill: Univ. N. C. Press.

Burke, C. J. 1963. Measurement scales and statistical models. In *Theories in Contemporary Psychology,* ed. M. H. Marx. New York: Macmillan.

Cavan, R. S.; Burgess, E. W.; Havighurst, R. J.; and Goldhamer, H. 1949. *Personal adjustment in old age.* Chicago: Science Research Associates.

Cameron, P. 1968. Masculinity-feminity in the aged. *J. Geront.* 10:63-65.

Cumming, E., and Henry, W. E. 1961. *Growing old.* New York: Basic Books.

Goldfarb, N. 1960. *Longitudinal statistical analysis.* Glencoe, Ill.: Free Press.

Havighurst, R. J. 1951. Validity of the Chicago Attitude Inventory as a measure of personal adjustment in old age. *J. abnorm. (soc.) Psychol.* 46:24-29.

———. 1957. The social competence of middle-aged people. *Genet. Psychol. Monogr.* 56:297-375.

———. 1961. Successful aging. *Gerontologist* 1:4-7.

Havighurst, R. J., and Albrecht, R. 1953. *Older people.* New York: Longmans, Green.

REFERENCES

Jeffers, F. C., and Nichols, C. R. 1961. The relationship of activities and attitudes to physical well-being in older people. *J. Geront.* 16:67-70.

Kleemeier, R. W. 1964. Leisure and disengagement in retirement. *Gerontologist* 4:180-84.

Kutner, B. 1956. *Five hundred over sixty.* New York: Russell Sage Foundation.

Labovitz, S. 1967. Some observations on measurement and statistics. *Soc. Forces* 46:151-60.

Maddox, G. 1962. A longitudinal, multidisciplinary study of human aging. *Proc. Social Statistics Section,* Amer. Stat. Ass., pp. 280-85.

———. 1963. Activity and morale: A longitudinal study of selected elderly subjects. *Soc. Forces* 42:195-204.

———. 1965. Fact and artifact: evidence bearing on disengagement theory from the Duke Geriatrics Project. *Hum. Develop.* 8:117-30.

———. 1966. Persistence of life style among the elderly. *Proc. 7th Internat. Congr. Geront.,* Wien. Med. Akad., Wien.

Moberg, D. O. 1965. Religiosity in old age. *Gerontologist* 5:78-87.

Neugarten, B. L. 1964. A developmental view of adult personality. In *Relations of Development and Aging,* ed. J. F. Birren. Springfield, Ill.: Charles C. Thomas.

Retirement and Leisure Participation: Continuity or Crisis?
Robert C. Atchley

Atchley, R. C. Retired women: A study of self and role. PhD. dissertation, American University, Washington, D.C., 1967.

———. 1969. Respondents vs. refusers in an interview study of retired women: An analysis of selected characteristics. *Journal of Gerontology* 24:42-47.

———. 1970. Recreation and Leisure. In *Understanding American society: The dynamics of social institutions.* Belmont, Calif.: Wadsworth.

Back, K. W., and Guptill, C. S. 1966. Retirement and self-ratings. In *Social aspects of aging,* ed. I. H. Simpson; K. W. Back; and J. C. McKinney. Durham: Duke University Press.

Cottrell, F. 1970. Technological change and labor in the railroad industry. Lexington, Mass.: D. C. Heath.

Cottrell, F., and Atchley, R. C. 1969. *Women in retirement: A preliminary report.* Oxford, Ohio: Scripps Foundation.

Havighurst, R. J. 1963. Successful aging. In *Processes of aging,* vol. 1, ed. R. H. Williams; C. Tibbitts; and W. Donahue. New York: Atherton.

Miller, S. J. 1965. The social dilemma of the aging leisure participant. In *Older people and their social world,* ed. A. M. Rose and W. A. Peterson. Philadelphia: F. A. Davis.

586

Riley, M. W., and Foner A. 1968. *Aging and society.* New York: Russell Sage Foundation.

Simpson, I. H.; Back, K. W.; and McKinney, J. C. 1966. Continuity of work and retirement activities. In *Social aspects of aging.* Durham: Duke University Press.

PART V
LIVING ENVIRONMENTS

The Impact of Environment on Old People.
Frances M. Carp

Bottenberg, R. A., and Ward, J. H., Jr. *Applied multiple linear regression.* 6570th Personnel Research Laboratory, Aerospace Medical Division, Air Force Systems Command, Lackland Air Force Base, Texas. An unclassified technical documentary report, March 1963.

Carp, F. 1966. *A future for the aged: The residents of Victoria Plaza.* Austin: Univ. of Texas Press.

The Appeal of Age Segregated Housing to the Elderly Poor.
Linda Winiecke

Briggs, John C. 1968. Ecology as gerontology. *Gerontologist* 8(2):78-79.

Brody, Elaine M., and Gummer, Burton. 1967. Aged applicants and non-applicants to a voluntary home: an exploratory comparison. *Gerontologist* 7(4):234-43.

Bultena, Gordon, and Wood, Vivian. 1969. The American retirement community: bane or blessing? *Journal of Gerontology* 24(2):209-17.

Cantor, Marjorie; Rosenthal, Karen; and Mayer, Mary. 1970. *The elderly in the rental market of New York City.* New York: New York City Office for the Aging.

Carp, Frances M. 1966. *A future for the aged.* Austin: University of Texas Press.

———. 1967. The impact of environment on old people. *Gerontologist* 7(2):106-08, 135.

Hollingshead, August, and Redlich, Fredrick C. 1958. *Social class and mental illness.* New York: John Wiley.

Hoyt, G. C. 1954. The life of the retired in a trailer park. *American Journal of Sociology* 59:361-70.

Messer, Mark. 1967. The possibility of an age concentrated environment becoming a normative system. *Gerontologist* 7(4):247-51.

REFERENCES

Nash, George, and Nash, Patricia. 1968. *The style of life in urban high-rise, low rent buildings for the independent elderly.* Philadelphia Geriatric Center and Columbia University Bureau of Applied Social Research.

Rosenberg, George S. 1970. *The worker grows old.* San Francisco: Jossey-Bass.

Rosow, Irving. 1961. Retirement housing and social integration. *Gerontologist* 1(2):85-91.

———. 1967. *Social integration of the aged.* New York: Free Press.

Rossi, Peter. 1955. *Why families move.* New York: Free Press.

Sacramento Housing Authority Annual Report 1969-1970. Prepared by the Sacramento Housing Authority, 1971.

Schooler, Kermit K. 1970. The relationship between social interaction and morale of the elderly as a function of environmental characteristics. *Gerontologist* 10(1):25-29.

Teitelbaum, Margaret. *Year of the crane.* Sacramento Housing Authority Annual Report 1970-1971. Sacramento Housing Authority, 1972.

U.S. Bureau of the Census. Census of Housing: 1970, Block Statistics, Final Report HC(3)-20, Sacramento, California Urbanized Area. U.S. Government Printing Office, Washington, D.C. 1971a.

———. Current Population Reports, Series P-23, No. 37, Social and Economic Characteristics of the Population in Metropolitan and Non-Metropolitan Areas: 1970 and 1960. U.S. Government Printing Office, Washington, D.C., 1971b.

An Ethnographic Study of a Retirement Setting.
Jerry Jacobs

Cumming, E., and Williams, H. H. 1961. *Growing old: The process of disengagement.* New York: Basic Books.

Hochschild, A. R. 1973. *The unexpected community.* Englewood Cliffs, N.J.: Prentice-Hall.

Jacobs, J. 1974. *Fun City: An ethnographic study of a retirement community.* New York: Holt, Rinehart, & Winston.

Kuhlen, R. G. 1968. Developmental changes in motivation during the adult years. In *Middle age and aging,* ed. B. L. Neugarten. Chicago: University of Chicago Press.

Rose, A. M. 1964. A current theoretical issue in social gerontology. *Gerontologist* 4:46-50.

PART VI
INSTITUTIONALIZATION

Differences in Proprietary Institutions Caring for Affluent and Nonaffluent Elderly.
Jordan I. Kosberg

Anderson, N. N.; Holmberg, R. H.; Schneider, R. E.; and Stone, L. B. 1969. *Policy issues regarding nursing homes: Findings from a Minnesota survey.* Minneapolis: Inst. for Interdisciplinary Studies, American Rehabilitation Foundation.

Cook County Dept. of Public Aid. *The assistance to the aged, blind, and disabled.* Chicago. 1966.

Gilbert, D. C., and Levinson, D. J. 1957. "Custodialism" and "humanisms" in mental hospital structure and in staff ideology. In *The patient and the mental hospital,* ed. M. Greenblatt; D. J. Levinson; and R. H. Williams. Glencoe, Ill.: Free Press.

Gold, J. B. K. A study of kinship ties and the institutionalized aged. Unpublished MA thesis, Sociology Dept., Univ. of Illinois, 1971.

Greenwald, S. R., and Linn, M. W. 1971. Intercorrelations of data on nursing homes. *Gerontologist* 11:337–40.

Hefferin, E. A. 1968. Rehabilitation in nursing-home situations: A survey of the literature. *Journal of the American Geriatrics Society* 16: 296-313.

Hollingshead, A. B., and Redlich, F. C. 1958. *Social class and mental illness: A community study.* New York: Wiley.

Katz, D. The waiting places. *Illinois State Register,* Springfield, 24 February 1970.

Kosberg, J. I. The relationship between organizational characteristics and treatment resources in nursing homes. Unpublished PhD dissertation, Sch. of Social Service Admin., Univ. of Chicago, 1971.

———. Opinions and expectations of nursing home administrators. Paper presented at the 25th Annual Meeting of Gerontological Society, San Juan, December 1972.

Kosberg, J. I., and Tobin, S. S. 1972. Variability among nursing homes. *Gerontologist* 12:214-19.

Markson, E. 1971. A hiding place to die. *Transaction* 9 (November-December):48-54.

National Council on Aging. 1970. *The golden years—a tarnished myth.* New York: NCA.

Penchansky, R., and Taubenhaus, L. J. 1965. Institutional factors affecting the quality of care in nursing homes. *Geriatrics* 20:591-98.

REFERENCES

Special Committee on Aging, U.S. Senate. 1971. *The multiple hazards of age and race: The situation of aged blacks in the U.S.* Washington: U.S. Government Printing Office.

Townsend, P. 1964. *The last refuge.* London: Routledge & Kegan Paul.

Weeks, H. A., and Benjamin, J. D. 1968. *The urban aged: Race and medical care.* Bureau of Public Health Economics, Research Series no. 14. Ann Arbor: Univ. of Michigan Press.

Why Nursing Homes Do What They Do.
Leonard E. Gottesman and Norman C. Bourestom

Barney, J. 1974. Community presence as a key to quality of life in nursing homes. *American Journal of Public Health* 3:265-68.

Bourestom, N. C., and Gottesman, L. E. 1973. Design and methodology of a study of aged patients and nursing home services. Paper presented at meeting of American Public Health Assn., Atlantic City.

Glaser, B., and Strauss, H. 1968. *Time for dying.* Glencoe, Ill.: Free Press.

Gottesman, L. E. 1974. Nursing home performance as related to resident traits, ownership, size, and source of payment. *American Journal of Public Health* 3:269-76.

Old Folks and Dirty Work: The Social Conditions for Patient Abuse in a Nursing Home.
Charles I. Stannard

Becker, Howard S. 1958. Problems of inference and proof in participant observation. *American Sociological Review* 23 (December):652-60.

Becker, Howard S. and Geer, Blanche. 1960. Latent culture: A note on the theory of latent social roles. *Administrative Science Quarterly* 5 (September):304-13.

Becker, Howard S.; Geer, Blanche; Hughes, Everett C.; and Strauss, Anselm L. 1961. *Boys in white.* Chicago: University of Chicago Press.

Belknap, Ivan. 1956. *Human problems of a state mental hospital.* New York: McGraw-Hill.

Bennett, Ruth, and Nehemow, Lucille. 1965. Institutional totality and criteria of adjustment in residences for the aged. *Journal of Social Issues* 21 (October):44-78.

Black, Donald J., and Reiss, Albert J., Jr. 1970. Police control of juveniles. *American Sociological Review* 35 (February):63-77.

Blumenthal, Monica D.; Kahn, Robert L.; Andrews, Frank M.; and Head, Kendra B. 1971. *Justifying violence.* Ann Arbor, Michigan: Institute for Social Research, University of Michigan.

590

Caplow, Theodore. 1964. *Principles of organization.* New York: Harcourt, Brace and World.

Carlin, Jerome E. 1966. *Lawyer's ethics.* New York: Russell Sage Foundation.

Coe, Rodney M. 1965. Self-conception and institutionalization. In *Older People and Their Social World,* ed. Arnold M. Rose and Warren A. Peterson, pp. 225–43. Philadelphia: F. A. Davis.

Corwin, Ronald G., and Taves, Marvin J. 1963. Nursing and other health professionals. In *Handbook of Medical Sociology,* ed. Howard E. Freeman, Sol Levine, Leo G. Reeder, pp. 187–212. Englewood Cliffs, N.J.: Prentice-Hall.

Coser, Lewis L. 1969. Visibility of evil. *Journal of Social Issues* 25:101-9.

Coser, Rose Laub. 1963. Alienation and social structure. In *The Hospital in Modern Society,* ed. Eliot Freidson, pp. 213-65. New York: Free Press.

Dunham, H. Warren, and Weinberg, S. Kierson. 1960. *The culture of the state mental hospital.* Detroit: Wayne State University Press.

Etzioni, Amitai. 1961. *Complex organizations.* New York: Free Press.

Glaser, Barney G. and Strauss, Anselm L. 1968. *Time for dying.* Chicago: Aldine.

Goffman, Erving. 1961. On the characteristics of total institutions: Staff-inmate relations. In *The Prison,* ed. Donald R. Cressey, pp. 68-106. New York: Holt, Rinehart and Winston.

———. 1963. *Stigma.* Englewood Cliffs, N.J.: Prentice-Hall.

Henry, Jules. 1963. *Culture against man.* New York: Random House.

Hughes, Everett Cherrington. 1958. *Men and their work.* New York: Free Press.

Kahne, Merton J. 1968. Suicide in mental hospitals: A study of the effects of personnel and patient turnover. *Journal of Health and Social Behavior* 9 (September):255–66.

Kansas State Department of Health. 1964. *Kansas long-term care study.* Topeka, Kansas.

Matza, David. 1966. *Delinquency and drift.* New York: Wiley.

Mauksch, Hans O. 1966. The organizational context of nursing practices. In *The Nursing Profession,* ed. Fred Davis, pp. 109-37., New York: Wiley.

Merton, Robert K. 1957. *Social theory and social structure.* New York: Free Press.

Mills, C. Wright. 1941. Situated actions and vocabularies of motives. *American Sociological Review* 5 (December):904-13.

Moore, Wilbert E., and Tumin, Melvin M. 1966. Some social functions of ignorance. *American Sociological Review* 14 (December):787-95.

REFERENCES

Powelson, Harvey, and Bendix, Reinhard. 1951. Psychiatry in prison. *Psychiatry* 14 (February):73-86.

Rowland, Howard. 1938. Interaction processes in the state mental hospital. *Psychiatry* 1 (August):323-37.

Salisbury, Richard F. 1962. *Structure of custodial care.* University of California Publications in Culture and Society, vol. 8. Berkeley: University of California Press.

Schwartz, Barry. 1968. The social psychology of privacy. *American Journal of Sociology* 73 (May):741-52.

Schwartz, Morris, and Schwartz, Charlotte Green. 1955. Problems of participant observation. *American Journal of Sociology* 60 (January): 343-53.

Scott, Marvin B. and Lyman, Stanford M. 1968. Accounts. *American Sociological Review* 33 (February):46-52.

Smith, Dorothy E. 1965. The logic of custodial organization. *Psychiatry* 28 (November):311-23.

Stannard, Charles I. 1971. Old folks and dirty work: The social organization of a nursing home. Unpublished Doctoral Dissertation, Northwestern University.

Strauss, Anselm L.; Schatzman, Leonard; Bucher, Rue; Ehrlich, Danuta; and Sabshin, Melvin. 1964. *Psychiatric ideologies and institutions.* New York: Free Press.

Sykes, Gresham M., and Matza, David. 1957. Techniques of neutralization: A theory of delinquency. *American Sociological Review* 22 (December):664-70.

U.S. Department of Labor, Bureau of Statistics. 1969. *Industry wage survey: Nursing homes and related facilities, October 1967 and April 1968.* Washington, D.C.: Government Printing Office.

Weiss, Robert J. 1968. Issues in holistic research. In *Institutions and the person,* ed. Howard S. Becker, Blanche Geer, David Riesman, and Robert J. Weiss, pp. 342-50. Chicago: Aldine.

Zelditch, Morris, Jr. 1962. Some methodological problems of field studies. *American Journal of Sociology* 67 (March):566-76.

Dying: The Career of the Nursing-Home Patient.
Elizabeth Gustafson

Birren, James. 1964. *The psychology of aging.* Englewood Cliffs, N.J.: Prentice-Hall.

Brim; Freeman; Levine; and Scotch (eds.). 1970. *The dying patient.* New York: Russell Sage Foundation.

Coe, Rodney. 1965. Self-conception and institutionalization. In *Older people and their social world*, ed. Arnold Rose and Warren Peterson, pp. 225–43. Philadelphia: Davis Company.

Cumming, E., and Henry, W. 1961. *Growing old*. New York: Basic Books.

Duff and Hollingshead. 1968. *Sickness and society*. New York: Harper & Row.

Feifel, H. 1959. *The meaning of death*. New York: McGraw-Hill.

Glaser, Barney G., and Strauss, Anselm L. 1965. *Awareness of dying*. Chicago: Aldine.

———. 1968. *Time for dying*. Chicago: Aldine.

Goffman, Erving. 1961. *Asylums*. New York: Doubleday, Anchor Books.

Jacobs, Ruth. 1969. Adjustment to a home for the aged. *Gerontologist* 9 (Winter):268–75.

Kahana, Eva. 1961. Emerging issues in institutional services for the aging. *Gerontologist* 11 (Spring):51–58.

Kastenbaum, Robert (ed.). 1964a. *New thoughts on old age*. New York: Springer.

———. 1964b. The interpersonal context of death in a geriatric institution. Paper presented at Seventeenth Annual Scientific Meeting, Gerontological Society: Minneapolis.

———. 1967. The mental life of dying patients. *Gerontologist* 7 (June): 97–100.

Kübler-Ross, Elisabeth. 1969. *On death and dying*. London: Macmillan.

Quint, Jeanne. 1967. *The nurse and the dying patient*. New York: Macmillan.

Rochlin, Gregory. 1967. How young children view death and themselves. In *Explaining death to children*, ed. Earl Grollman, pp. 51–87. Boston: Beacon Press.

Rosenfelt, R.; Kastenbaum, R.; and Slater, P. 1964. Patterns of short-range time orientation in geriatric patients. In *New thoughts on old age*, ed. Robert Kastenbaum, pp. 291–99. New York: Springer.

Roth, Julius. 1963. *Timetables: Structuring the passage of time in hospital treatment and other careers*. Indianapolis: Bobbs-Merrill.

Roth, Julius, and Eddy, Elizabeth. 1967. *Rehabilitation for the unwanted*. New York: Atherton Press.

Schneidman, Edwin. 1963. Orientations towards death. In *Study of lives*, ed. Robert White, pp. 200–27. New York: Atherton Press.

———. 1970. The enemy. *Psychology Today* (August):37ff.

Weisman, A. D., and Hackett, T. 1961. Predeliction to death. *Psychosomatic Medicine* 23, (May–June):232–56.

Weisman, A.D., and Kastenbaum, R. 1968. The psychological autopsy. Community Mental Health Monograph no. 4.

Wodinsky, Abraham. 1964. Psychiatric consultation with nurses on a leuke-
mia service. *Mental Hygiene* 48 (April):282-87.

PART VII
DEATH AND DYING

Distance from Death as a Variable in the Study of Aging.
Morton A. Lieberman and Annie Siranne Coplan

Alekamdrowica, D. R. 1961. Fire and its aftermath on a geriatric ward.
Bulletin Menninger Clinic 25:23-32.

Bakan, D. 1966. *The duality of human existence.* Chicago: Rand McNally.

Bender, L. 1938. A visual motor gestalt test and its clinical use. *American
Orthopsychiatric Association Research,* no. 3.

Butler, R. N. 1963. The life review: An interpretation of reminiscence in
the aged. *Psychiatry* 26:65-76.

Cumming, E., and Henry, W. E. 1961. *Growing old.* New York: Basic
Books.

Dana, R. H. 1955. Clinical diagnosis and objective TAT scoring. *Journal of
Abnormal and Social Psychology* 50:19-25.

———. 1959. Proposal for objective scoring system of the TAT. *Perception and Motor Skill* 9:27-43.

Erikson, E. 1950. *Childhood and society.* New York: Norton.

Fried, M. 1963. Grieving for a lost home. In *The urban condition,* ed. L. J.
Duhl. New York: Basic Books.

Friedsam, H. J. 1961. Reactions of older persons to disaster-caused losses:
An hypothesis of relative deprivation. *Gerontologist* 1:34-37.

Gendlin, E. 1964. A theory of personality change. In *Personality change,*
ed. P. Worchel and D. Bryne. New York: Wiley.

Inglis, J. 1959. A paired-associate learning test for use with elderly psychiatric patients. *Journal of Mental Science* 103:44-443.

Kahn, R. L.; Pollack, M.; and Goldfarb, A. I. 1961. Factors related to individual differences in mental status of institutionalized aged. In *Psychopathology of aging,* ed. P. H. Hock and J. Zubin. New York:
Grune & Stratton.

Leary, T. 1957. *Interpersonal diagnosis of personality.* New York: Ronald
Press.

Lieberman, M. A. 1961. The relationship of mortality rates to entering a
home for the aged. *Geriatrics* 16:515-19.

———. Intra-individual variability and age Paper presented at the meeting
of the American Psychological Associa.ion Washington, D.C. August
1962.

——. 1965. Psychological correlates of impending death: Some preliminary observations. *Journal of Gerontology* 20:182-90.

——. 1966. Observation on death and dying. *Gerontologist* 6:70-73.

Lieberman, M. A., and Lakin, M. 1963. On becoming an aged institutionalized individual. In *Social and psychological processes of aging*, ed· W. Donahue, C. Tibbitts, and R. Williams. New York: Atherton.

Lieberman, M. A.; Prock, V. N.; and Tobin, S. S. 1968. Psychological effects of institutionalization. *Journal of Gerontology* 23:343-53.

Miller, D., and Lieberman, M. A. 1965. The relationship of affect state and adaptive capacity to reactions to stress. *Journal of Gerontology* 20: 492-97.

Munnichs, J. M. 1966. Old age and finitude: A contribution to psychogerontology. *Bibliotheca Vita Humana*, no. 4.

Neugarten, B.; Havighurst, R.; and Tobin, S. 1961. The measurement of life satisfaction, *Journal of Gerontology* 16:134-43.

Osgood, C.; Suci, G.; and Tannenbaum, P. H. 1957. *The measurement of meaning.* Urbana: University of Illinois Press.

Pascal, G. R., and Suttell, B. J. 1951. *The Bender-Gestalt Test: Quantification and validity for adults.* New York: Grune & Stratton.

Reitman, F., and Robertson, J. P. 1950. Reitman's Pin Man Test: A means of disclosing impaired conceptual thinking. *Journal of Nervous and Mental Diseases* 112:498-510.

Rosner, A. Stress and the maintenance of self concept in the aged. Unpublished doctoral dissertation, University of Chicago, 1968.

Shanas, E. 1961. Family relationships of older people. *Health Information Foundation Research*, Series 20.

Siegel, S. 1956. *Non-parametric statistics for the behavioral sciences.* New York: McGraw-Hill.

Srole, L. 1956. Social integration and certain corollaries: An exploratory study. *American Sociological Review* 21:709-16.

Tobin, S. S. 1968. Effects of stress on earliest memory. *Archives of General Psychiatry* 19:435-44.

Socialization for Impending Death in a Retirement Village.
Victor W. Marshall

Berger, Peter. 1969. *The sacred canopy.* Garden City, N.Y.: Doubleday Anchor.

Berger, Peter, and Kellner, H. 1964. Marriage and the construction of reality. *Diogene* 46(2):3-32.

Berger, Peter, and Luckmann, Thomas. 1967. *The social construction of reality.* Garden City, N.Y.: Doubleday Anchor.

REFERENCES

Berger, Peter, and Pullberg, Stanley. 1965. Reification and the sociological critique of consciousness. *History and Theory* 4(2):196-211.

Calkins, Kathy. 1970. Time: Perspectives, markings, and styles of usage *Social Problems* 17 (Spring):487-501.

Carp, Frances. 1972. Mobility among members of an established retirement community. *Gerontologist* 12 (Spring):48-56.

Friedman, E. 1966. Friendship choice and clique formation in a home for the aged. PhD dissertation, Yale University.

Glaser, Barney, and Strauss, Anselm. 1965. *Awareness of dying.* Chicago: Aldine.

————. 1968. *Time for dying.* Chicago: Aldine.

————. 1971. *Status passage.* Chicago: Aldine-Atherton.

Goffman, Erving. 1961. On the characteristics of total institutions. In *Asylums,* ed. Erving Goffman, pp. 1-124. Garden City, N.Y.: Doubleday Anchor.

Gove, Walter R. 1973. Sex, marital status, and mortality. *American Journal of Sociology* 79(1):45-67.

Gustafson, Elizabeth. 1972. Dying: The career of the nursing home patient. *Journal of Health and Social Behavior* 13 (September):226-35.

Hochschild, Arlie. 1973. *The unexpected community.* Englewood Cliffs, N.J.: Prentice-Hall.

Kleemeier, Robert. 1954. Moosehaven: Congregate living in a community of the retired. *American Journal of Sociology* 59(4):347-51.

Lyman, Stanford, and Scott, Marvin. 1970. On the time track. In *A sociology of the absurd,* ed. S. Lyman and M. Scott, pp. 189-212. New York: Appleton-Century-Crofts.

McHugh, Peter. 1968. *Defining the situation.* Indianapolis: Bobbs-Merrill.

Marshall, Victor. 1972a. Continued living and dying as problematical aspects of old age: An empirical study. Paper presented at the Ninth International Congress of Gerontology, Kiev, USSR.

- ——. 1972b. *Continued living and dying as problematical aspects of old age.* PhD dissertation, Princeton University.

————. 1973a. Awareness of finitude and developmental theory in gerontology: Some speculations. Paper prepared for the Berkeley Conference on Death and Dying, July, 1973.

————. 1973b. Game-analyzable dilemmas in a retirement village: A case study. *International Journal of Aging and Human Development* 4(4): 285-91.

May, Rollo. 1967. *Existential psychotherapy.* Toronto: CBC Publications.

Mayer, Albert, and Hauser, Philip. 1953. Class differentials in expectation of life at birth. In *Class, status, and power,* ed. R. Bendix and S. M. Lipset, pp. 281-84. Glencoe, Ill.: Free Press.

596

Miller, George; Galanter, Eugene; and Pribram, Karl. 1960. *Plans and the structure of behavior.* New York: Holt, Rinehart & Winston.

Moore, Wilbert E. 1963. *Man, time, and society.* New York: Wiley.

Riley, John. 1970. What people think about death. In *The dying patient,* ed. O. Brim, Jr., H. Freeman, S. Levine, and N. Scotch, pp. 30-41. New York: Sage.

Riley, Matilda, and Foner, Anne. 1968. *Aging and society,* vol. 1: *An inventory of research findings.* New York: Sage.

Riley, Matilda; Foner, Anne; Hess, Beth; and Toby, Marcia. 1969. Socialization for the middle and later years. In *Handbook of socialization theory and research,* ed. David Goslin, pp. 951-82. Chicago: Rand McNally.

Rosow, Irving. 1966. Discussion following Maurice B. Hamovitch's paper. In *The retirement process,* ed. F. Carp, pp. 127-35. Public Health Service Publication no. 1778. Washington, D.C.: Government Printing Office.

Silverman, Phyllis, and Englander, Sue. 1973. The widow's view of her dependent children. Paper prepared for the Berkeley Conference on Death and Dying, March 1973.

Sudnow, David. 1967. *Passing on: The social organization of dying.* Englewood Cliffs, N.J.: Prentice-Hall.

The Aged and the Dying Process: The Inevitable Decisions.
Richard A. Kalish

Bowers, M.; Jackson, Edgar N.; Knight, J. A.; and LeShan, Lawrence. 1964. *Counseling the dying.* New York: Thomas Nelson.

Feifel, Herman. 1963. Death. In *Taboo topics,* ed. N. L. Farberow. New York: Atherton Press, pp. 8-21.

Glaser, Barney G., and Strauss, Anselm L. 1964. The dying patient and his social loss. *American Journal of Nursing* 64 (June):119-21.

Kalish, Richard A. Social distance and the dying. Community Mental Health Journal, in press.

Kastenbaum, Robert. 1964a. The interpersonal context of death in a geriatric institution. Paper presented at the 17th annual meeting, Gerontological Society, Minneapolis.

———. 1964b. The reluctant therapist. In *New Thoughts on Old Age,* ed. R. Kastenbaum. New York: Springer, pp. 139-148.

Schneidman, Edwin S. 1963. Orientations toward death: A vital aspect of the study of lives. In *The study of lives,* ed. R.W. White. New York: Atherton Press, pp. 201-227.

REFERENCES

Wahl, Charles W. 1959. The fear of death. In *The meaning of death,* ed. H. Feifel. New York: McGraw-Hill, pp. 16–29.

Weisman, Avery, and Hackett, Thomas P. 1962. The dying patient. *Forest Hospital Publications,* Des Plaines, Illinois. 1:16–21.